POPULAR MUSIC STUDIES

A SELECT INTERNATIONAL BIBLIOGRAPHY

Compiled and Edited by

John Shepherd, David Horn, Dave Laing, Paul Oliver, Philip Tagg, Peter Wicke
and Jennifer Wilson

MANSELL
London and Washington

First published 1997 by
Mansell Publishing Limited, *A Cassell imprint*
Wellington House, 125 Strand, London WC2R 0BB, England
PO Box 605 Herndon, VA 20172, USA

© John Shepherd, David Horn, Dave Laing, Paul Oliver, Philip Tagg, Peter Wicke, Jennifer Wilson 1997

British Library Cataloguing in Publication Data

A catalogue record for this book is available from the British Library

0-7201-2344-5

Library of Congress Cataloging-in-Publication Data

Popular music studies : a select international bibliography / compiled
    and edited by John Shepherd . . . [et al.].
        p.   cm.
    Includes indexes.
    Added title page title: Encyclopedia of popular music of the world.
    ISBN 0-7201-2344-5
1. Popular music—History and criticism—Bibliography. I. Shepherd, John, 1947–   .
II. Title: Encyclopedia of popular music of the world
ML128.P63P67   1997
016.78163–dc21   97-7515
                                                           CIP
                                                           MN

Typeset, printed and bound in Great Britain by
Page Bros (Norwich) Ltd

CONTENTS

CONTENTS

CONTENTS

PREFACE

While individual studies of popular music can be traced back to the nineteenth century, the study of popular music as a continuous intellectual tradition with an identifiable community of scholars began only in the late-1970s. In much the same way that former generations brought up on jazz demonstrated that jazz and, subsequently, blues were genres worthy of serious study, so another generation of young scholars raised on the culture of the 1960s began to create institutional spaces for the serious study of all genres of popular music.

A remarkable feature of this generation was its international character. Along with the anticipated Americans and British were Swedes, Italians, Dutch, East Germans, Bulgarians, Cubans, Canadians and Australians. Under the leadership of Philip Tagg, a British scholar working in the Department of Musicology at the University of Gothenburg in Sweden, the International Association for the Study of Popular Music (IASPM) was established in 1981. Its expansion was dramatic. By the mid-1980s it had around 800 members from over 30 countries.

This Bibliography, along with the projected encyclopedia of which it forms a part, is an expression of this development. As early as the mid-1980s, as members of IASPM's Executive Committee, Paul Oliver and David Horn proposed a major reference work which would cover the popular musics of the world (not just the Anglo-American world) in more than just a biographical fashion. From this, the *Encyclopedia of Popular Music of the World* (EPMOW) was born.

By this time, Philip Tagg had become convinced of the need for a comprehensive bibliography in the area, and had begun to develop DOPMUS (Documentation of Popular Music). He generously made his files from this project available to the Encyclopedia. Under the auspices of the Centre for American and Commonwealth Arts and Studies at the University of Exeter, and its Director Mick Gidley, work commenced on a bibliography.

In 1991, Philip began a two-year term as the Encyclopedia's executive editor and moved to the University of Liverpool to join David Horn, Director of the University's Institute of Popular Music, where the project was initially head-quartered. Work on developing the Encyclopedia's headword list and list of contributors continued until the mid-1990s, when the project moved its head-quarters to Carleton University (Ottawa). Dave Laing and Peter Wicke joined David Horn, Paul Oliver and John Shepherd on the Editorial Board, and Jennifer Wilson was appointed the Encyclopedia's editorial and administrative assistant.

At this time, the decision was taken to precede the publication of the Encyclopedia with the compilation of a select international bibliography of popular music studies.

This decision was taken for three reasons. First, the project had access to Philip Tagg's work on DOPMUS and, through IASPM and a developing list of Encyclopedia contributors, to a broadly-based team of international scholars.

Secondly, there does not exist a bibliography of the study of popular music on a world basis, organized according to principles of academic research. Most bibliographies are genre-based, that is, focused on broad western traditions such as blues, jazz or rock. Alternatively, information on popular music studies can be found in bibliographies of publications on different geo-cultural areas of the world. These bibliographies are not, however, concerned specifically with popular music studies. Further, most reference works concerned with popular music are biased heavily in favor of biographical material. In contrast, this Bibliography is dedicated to predominantly non-biographical scholarship on popular music, and only half of the Encyclopedia's entries will be dedicated to biographical material.

Thirdly, the Bibliography serves to announce the Encyclopedia and the unique scope of its coverage. It reflects the way in which non-biographical material in the Encyclopedia will be organized conceptually in terms of genres, the industry, social and cultural contexts, musical practises and locations. The Bibliography also gives an indication of the broad range of international contributors who will be writing entries for the Encyclopedia.

The Bibliography is intended primarily for popular music scholars and those in related and cognate disciplines, students in university and college courses that have popular music content or where a knowledge of popular music is useful, and professionals working in information services.

Developing the Encyclopedia and, indeed, the Bibliography has not been an easy task. Because so much reference material in popular music studies is based on biography and biased toward the Anglo-American world, there was no existing suitable model for developing a basic structure for the Encyclopedia and, by extension, the Bibliography. Furthermore, research in popular music studies is to be found in unimaginably disparate places, and scholars publishing research of relevance to popular music studies are to be found in almost every discipline throughout the world. In short, there is no satisfactory or systematic way in which to identify scholars and their work.

It is these difficulties that confirm the need for the Encyclopedia and the Bibliography. However, the difficulties also call for a word of caution. While every effort has been made to ensure that the Bibliography is representative of the current state of popular music studies, it would be foolhardy to make claims for comprehensiveness.

The Bibliography will be followed by the publication of the Encyclopedia, which is expected to comprise six volumes and approximately three million words. While most entries in the Encyclopedia will conclude with a list of references, the Encyclopedia will not contain its own bibliography. Rather, the intention is to follow the publication of the Encyclopedia with a second edition of this Bibliography.

An important purpose of publishing this Bibliography—beyond those of providing an important resource for popular music scholarship, and of announcing the Encyclopedia—is thus to encourage scholars who know of work not represented here to contact the editorial team so that omissions may be included in the second edition.

In this way, the Bibliography will further one of the intentions behind the founding of IASPM some fifteen years ago: the creation of means through which popular music scholars can become aware of and share each other's work, and through which they can maintain networks of communication which sustain popular music scholarship.

Ottawa, Canada
October 1996

ACKNOWLEDGMENTS

The Editorial Board's first debt of gratitude is to Philip Tagg, who over a two-year period developed a detailed taxonomy of popular music, its practise, and its study. This taxonomy served as a basic model for developing the structure of the Encyclopedia, as well as its major sections and headword list. The taxonomy's influence is thus very much felt in the structure and content of the Bibliography. We are also grateful to Philip for making available his work on DOPMUS (Documentation of Popular Music), a bibliographical project he began while teaching popular music in the Department of Musicology at the University of Gothenburg, Sweden.

A special word of thanks is due to Alyn Shipton, whose vision and dedication in the formative period of the project were vital to the development and long-term viability of an ambitious publishing venture.

Thanks are due also to the University of Liverpool, Carleton University (Ottawa), the University of Exeter, and the University of Gothenburg (Sweden), all of which have made significant financial contributions, as well as contributions in kind, in support of this project.

A number of individuals have made important contributions to the development of the Encyclopedia and the Bibliography. We are especially grateful to Carole Pegg, who at Exeter conducted an important initial study on the feasibility of developing an encyclopedia on world popular music, and to Jean-Pierre Sévigny at Carleton for his extensive work on the Encyclopedia's headword list and list of contributors. We are grateful also to Mick Gidley, Alison Pringle and Ben Gidley for their work on the Bibliography at the University of Exeter, to Dai Griffiths at Oxford Brookes University, and to Joy Gugelar and Alan Stanbridge at Carleton for specialized forms of editorial assistance, to Marion Leonard for helping Sara Cohen with her contributions to the Bibliography, and to Tony Mitchell, Karl Neuenfeldt, Anthea Parker, Graeme Smith, John Whiteoak and Gemma Reeve for assisting Bruce Johnson with his.

The work involved in compiling and editing a bibliography such as this is considerable. The Editorial Board wishes to place on record its sincere appreciation for the work undertaken at Carleton University by the editorial team: Jennifer Wilson, Jennifer Rae-Brown, Emily Wilson, Emma Phillips and Graham Faulkner. Thanks are due also to Rick Bardawill, the new media projects manager of Carleton University's Centre for Art and Technology (School for Studies in Art and Culture), for his unending willingness to troubleshoot computer hardware and software problems, and to Natasha Gay at the University of Liverpool's Institute of Popular Music for her excellent secretarial assistance.

ACKNOWLEDGMENTS

The Board also wishes to thank Janet Joyce and Veronica Higgs at Cassell for their unwavering support and great good humor during the intense months leading up to the Bibliography's publication, and Lysa Schwartz at Milex Data and Graham Roberts at Page Bros. for their technical advice and support.

Finally, the Board wishes to extend its heartfelt thanks to Jennifer Wilson, the Encyclopedia's editorial and administrative assistant, who led the editorial team at Carleton. It is safe to say that, without the commitment she demonstrated through many long hours of exacting and tedious work, her professionalism in planning and leading the work of her colleagues, and her ability to anticipate and solve problems, this project would have taken much longer than it did.

Compilers, Editors and Contributors

Compilers and Editors

John Shepherd (Director, School for Studies in Art and Culture, Carleton University, Ottawa, Canada)

David Horn (Director, Institute of Popular Music, University of Liverpool)

Dave Laing (Music Research Group, University of Westminster, London)

Paul Oliver (American and Commonwealth Arts and Studies (AmCAS), University of Exeter)

Philip Tagg (Institute of Popular Music, University of Liverpool)

Peter Wicke (Director, Centre for Popular Music Research, The Humboldt University, Berlin)

Jennifer Wilson (Carleton University, Ottawa, Canada)

Contributors
National affiliations refer to country of residence

Roberto Agostini (Italy)
Lara Allen (UK)
Michael Ancliffe (UK)
Gary Atkinson (UK)
John Baily (UK)
Christopher Ballantine (South Africa)
Rafael J. de M. Bastos (Brazil)
Clive Behagg (UK)
Edward Berlin (USA)
Michael Brocken (UK)
Adam Brown (UK)
David Buckley (Germany)
George Carney (USA)
Norm Cohen (USA)
Sara Cohen (UK)
Evgeny Dukov (Russia)
Wayne Eagles (Canada)
David Evans (USA)
Franco Fabbri (Italy)
Jon Fitzgerald (Australia)
Reebee Garofalo (USA)
Juan-Pablo González (Chile)

Dai Griffiths (UK)
Bob Hall (UK)
Charles Hamm (USA)
Antoine Hennion (France)
Trevor Herbert (UK)
David Horn (UK)
Harald Huber (Austria)
Bruce Johnson (Australia)
Steve Jones (USA)
Elaine Keillor (Canada)
William Kelly (UK)
Hroar Klempe (Norway)
Christian Lahusen (Germany)
Dave Laing (UK)
James Leary (USA)
Marion Leonard (UK)
Claire Levy (Bulgaria)
George Lewis (USA)
Elizabeth Lucas (Brazil)
William Mahar (USA)
Peter Manuel (USA)
Richard March (USA)

CONTRIBUTORS

Portia Maultsby (USA)
Morten Michelsen (Denmark)
Richard Middleton (UK)
Tony Mitchell (Australia)
Torû Mitsui (Japan)
Lutgard Mutsaers (The Netherlands)
Paul Oliver (UK)
Deborah Pacini Hernandez (USA)
Dave Penny (UK)
Burton Peretti (USA)
Robert Pruter (USA)
Motti Regev (Israel)
Neil Rosenberg (Canada)
Dave Russell (UK)
Howard Rye (UK)
T.M. Scruggs (USA)
Barry Shank (USA)
John Shepherd (Canada)

Alyn Shipton (UK)
Dick Spottswood (USA)
Alan Stanbridge (Canada)
Rosemary Statelova (Bulgaria)
Martin Stokes (Northern Ireland)
Will Straw (Canada)
John Street (UK)
Philip Tagg (UK)
Garry Tamlyn (Australia)
Paul Théberge (Canada)
Sarah Thornton (UK)
Janet Topp Fargion (UK)
Peter Wade (UK)
Don Wallace (Canada)
Robert Walser (USA)
Peter Wicke (Germany)
Mel Wilhoit (USA)
Ralph Willett (UK)

INTRODUCTION

Popular Music Studies: A Select International Bibliography is the first bibliography of scholarly work on popular music that attempts to be representative of the field of popular music studies as a whole. As such, the Bibliography is concerned with the study of popular music on a world basis, rather than with publications dedicated solely to specific genres such as blues, jazz or rock, which is what has characterized most popular music bibliographies thus far. In this way, the Bibliography attempts, as far as possible, to rectify the Anglo-American bias of most other reference works in the field of popular music studies.

The Bibliography is also distinct from most other popular music reference works in concerning itself largely with non-biographical material. In this, it emphasizes a distinctive feature of the larger project of which it forms a part, the *Encyclopedia of Popular Music of the World*. This Encyclopedia, whose publication will follow that of this Bibliography, will be only 50 percent biographical, with critical biographical entries containing bibliographical references. Biographies constitute the area that is covered most by existing encyclopedias and bibliographies. As it is easier to find biographical material in popular music studies than it is to find publications on other popular music subjects, most items in the Bibliography are of a non-biographical character.

In covering publications other than biographical, the Bibliography is divided into seven major sections: General Works, Genres, The Industry, Social and Cultural Contexts, Musical Practises, Locations, Theory and Method. Each section is further divided into a number of subjects. In the case of General Works, Genres, The Industry, Social and Cultural Contexts, and Theory and Method, these subjects are listed alphabetically within each section. In the case of Musical Practises and Locations, other principles of ordering have been used, which are intended to make it easier to find items within the Bibliography. In some instances, a hierarchy of ordering has been used (as with sub-genres within genres). The ordering of sections and subjects is set out in the Table of Contents.

Individual entries are numbered sequentially throughout the Bibliography. This numbering forms the basis of both author and subject indexes. Reference to authors and subjects within these indexes is by entry number rather than by page number. The relevance of each entry to subjects other than the one or ones in which it has been placed can be determined through the subject index. Readers are encouraged to use the subject index to identify items of relevance to subjects other than those in which items have been entered. This notwithstanding, there are instances in which items have been entered in more than one subject for ease of finding.

All items listed in the Bibliography are of a scholarly or serious character and will be of use to researchers, teachers, and students. The Bibliography is made up overwhelmingly of books and articles in refereed or well-established and respected journals. Dissertations and liner notes are not listed. Magazine and newspaper articles are listed only when they are of particular importance. Complete issues of journals and magazines are included when they are dedicated to, or felt to be of special relevance to, the subject in which they are listed.

The criteria for the inclusion of items have been the same whether they are in English or another language: (a) they must be representative of areas customarily covered by the language of the item in question, or (b) they must, in some way, be distinctive in an international context. In this way, the Bibliography attempts to reflect the existing geographic and linguistic distribution of scholarly popular music research, as well as the existence of international phenomena and genres.

GENERAL WORKS

GENERAL BIBLIOGRAPHIES

1 Gray, Michael. 1983. *Bibliography of Discographies. Vol. 3, Popular Music.* New York and London: Bowker.

2 Hirsch, Jean-François and Maynadié, Robert. 1971. Dossier pop music: bibliographie, revues, filmographie, discographie pop de base. *Musique en jeu* 2: 102–10.

3 Horn, David and Mitsui, Torû, et al. 1982–. Booklist. *Popular Music* 2–.

4 Iwaschkin, Roman. 1986. *Popular Music: A Reference Guide.* New York: Garland.

5 Philip Tagg, ed. 1989. *DOPMUS: Documentation of Popular Music Studies.* Göteborg: IASPM.

6 Taylor, Paul. 1985. *Popular Music Since 1955: A Critical Guide to the Literature.* London: Mansell.

GENERAL REFERENCE WORKS

7 American Society of Composers, Authors and Publishers. 1981. *ASCAP Biographical Dictionary*, 4th edition. New York and London: Bowker.

8 Clarke, Donald. 1989. *The Penguin Encyclopedia of Popular Music.* London: Penguin.

9 Dachs, David. 1972. *Encyclopedia of Pop/ Rock.* New York: Scholastic Book Services.

10 *Enciclopedia del rock italiano.* 1993. Milano: Arcana.

11 Gammond, Peter and Clayton, Peter. 1960. *A Guide to Popular Music.* London: Phoenix House.

12 Hardy, Phil and Laing, Dave. 1990. *The Faber Companion to 20th Century Popular Music.* London: Viking.

13 Havlice, Patricia Pate, comp. 1975. *Popular Song Index.* Metuchen, NJ: Scarecrow Press.

14 Havlice, Patricia Pate, comp. 1978–89. *Popular Song Index: Supplements 1–3.* Metuchen, NJ: Scarecrow Press.

15 *Il dizionario della canzone italiana.* 1991. 2 vols. Milano: Armando Curcio Editore.

16 Kinkle, Roger D. 1974. *The Complete Encyclopedia of Popular Music and Jazz, 1900–1950.* New Rochelle, NY: Arlington House.

16a Larkin, Colin, ed. 1995. *The Guinness Encyclopedia of Popular Music.* 6 vols, 2nd enlarged ed. Enfield: Guinness Publishing.

17 Lax, Roger and Smith, Peter. 1984. *The Great Song Thesaurus.* New York and London: Oxford University Press.

18 Pollock, Bruce, ed. 1988–91. *Popular Music.* 15 vols. Detroit, MI: Gale Research.

19 Shapiro, Nat, ed. 1964–73. *Popular Music: An Annotated Index of American Popular Songs.* 6 vols. New York: Adrian Press.

20 Shapiro, Nat and Pollock, Ned, eds. 1985. *Popular Music, 1920–1979: A Revised Cumulation.* 3 vols. Detroit, MI: Gale Research.

21 Tyler, Don. 1985. *Hit Parade: An Encyclopedia of the Top Songs of the Jazz, Depression, Swing and Sing Eras.* New York: Quill.

22 Wetzel, Lutz G. and Klonus, Herbert, eds. 1983. *Handbuch der populären Musik.* Bad Honnef: Bock und Herchen.

23 Wicke, Peter and Ziegenrücker, Wieland. 1985. *Rock, Pop, Jazz, Folk: Handbuch der Populären Musik.* Leipzig: Deutscher Verlag für Musik.

GENRES

AFRICAN–AMERICAN MUSIC

General Works

24 De Lerma, Dominique-René, ed. 1970. *Black Music in Our Culture: Curricular Ideas on the Subjects, Materials and Problems*. Kent, OH: Kent State University Press.

25 De Lerma, Dominique-René, ed. 1973. *Reflections on Afro-American Music*. Kent, OH: Kent State University Press.

26 Haydon, Geoffrey, and Marks, Denis, eds. 1985. *Repercussions: A Celebration of Afro-American Music*. London: Century.

27 Hurston, Zora Neale. 1935. *Mules and Men*. Philadelphia: J.B. Lippincott.

28 Jackson, Irene V., ed. 1985. *More than Drumming: Essays on African and Afro-Latin American Music and Musicians*. Westport, CT: Greenwood Press.

29 Wright, Josephine and Floyd, Samuel A., eds. 1992. *New Perspectives on Music: Essays in Honor of Eileen Southern*. Warren, MI: Harmonie Press.

Reference

30 Berry, Lemuel. 1978. *Biographical Dictionary of Black Musicians and Music Educators*. Guthrie, OK: Educational Book Publishers.

31 De Lerma, Dominique-René. 1970. *Black Music Now: A Source Book on 20th Century Black American Music*. Kent, OH: Kent State University Press.

32 De Lerma, Dominique-René. 1981. *Bibliography of Black Music, Vol. 1: Reference Materials*. Westport and London: Greenwood Press.

33 De Lerma, Dominique-René. 1981. *Bibliography of Black Music, Vol. 2: Afro-American Idioms*. Westport and London: Greenwood Press.

34 De Lerma, Dominique-René. 1982. *Bibliography of Black Music, Vol. 3: Geographical Studies*. Westport and London: Greenwood Press.

35 De Lerma, Dominique-René. 1984. *Bibliography of Black Music, Vol. 4: Theory, Education and Related Studies*. Westport and London: Greenwood Press.

36 Ferris, William R., comp. 1971. *Mississippi Black Folklore: A Research Bibliography and Discography*. Hattiesburg, MS: University and College Press of Mississippi.

37 Floyd, Samuel A. 1974. Black Music in the Driscoll Collection. *The Black Perspective in Music* 2(2): 158–73.

38 Floyd, Samuel A. and Reisser, Marsha. 1983. *Black Music in the United States: An Annotated Bibliography of Selected Reference and Research Materials*. Millwood, NY: Kraus.

39 Floyd, Samuel A. and Reisser, Marsha. 1987. *Black Music Biography: An Annotated Bibliography*. White Plains, NY: Kraus.

40 Maultsby, Portia K. 1996. Music. In *The Encyclopedia of African-American Culture and History, Vol. 4*, ed. Jack Salzman, David Lionel Smith and Cornel West. New York: Macmillan Library Reference USA. 1888–1907.

41 Oliver, Paul and Harrison, Max. 1986. *The New Grove Book of Gospel, Blues and Jazz, with Spirituals and Ragtime*. New York: Norton.

42 Sampson, Henry. 1980. *Blacks in Blackface: A Source Book of Early Black*

Music Shows. Metuchen, NJ: Scarecrow Press.

43 Southern, Eileen. 1973. Afro-American Musical Materials. *The Black Perspective in Music* 1(1): 24–32.

44 Southern, Eileen. 1981. *Biographical Dictionary of Afro-American and African Musicians*. Westport, CT: Greenwood Press.

45 Szwed, John F. and Abrahams, Roger D. 1978. *Afro-American Folk-Culture: An Annotated Bibliography of Materials from North, Central and South America*. Philadelphia: Institute for the Study of Human Issues.

46 Tudor, Dean and Tudor, Nancy. 1979. *Black Music*. Littleton, CO: Libraries Unlimited, Inc.

47 Vann, Kimberly R. 1990. *Black Music in Ebony: An Annotated Guide to the Articles on Music in Ebony Magazine, 1945–1985*. Chicago: Center for Black Music Research.

48 Williams, Brett. 1983. *John Henry: A Bio-Bibliography*. Westport and London: Greenwood Press.

History

49 Berry, Jason. 1988. African Cultural Memory in New Orleans Music. *Black Music Research Journal* 8(1): 3–12.

50 Bogle, Donald. 1980. *Brown Sugar: Eighty Years of America's Black Female Superstars*. New York: Harmony Books.

51 Brooks, Tilford. 1984. *America's Black Musical Heritage*. Englewood Cliffs, NJ: Prentice-Hall.

52 Courlander, Harold. 1992. (1963) *Negro Folk Music, U.S.A.* New York: Dover.

53 Cuney-Hare, Maud. 1936. *Negro Musicians and Their Music*. Washington, DC: Associated Publishers.

54 Dennison, Tim. 1963. *The American Negro and His Amazing Music*. New York: Vantage Press.

55 Dett, Nathaniel. 1918. The Emancipation of Negro Music. *Southern Workman* 47: 176–86.

56 Dugan, James and Hammond, John. 1974. (1938) From Spirituals to Swing. *The Black Perspective in Music* 2(2): 191–206.

57 Ekwueme, Lazarus. 1974. African-Music Retentions in the New World. *The Black Perspective in Music* 2(2): 128–44.

58 Ellison, Mary. 1989. *Lyrical Protest: Black Music's Struggle Against Discrimination*. New York: Praeger.

59 Emery, Lynne Fauley. 1988. *Black Dance in the United States: From 1619 to Today*, 2nd revised edition. Manchester, NH: Ayer.

60 Epstein, Dena J. 1973. African Music in British and French America. *Musical Quarterly* 59(1): 61–91.

61 Epstein, Dena J. 1977. *Sinful Tunes and Spirituals: Black Folk Music to the Civil War*. Urbana, IL: University of Illinois Press.

62 Fernett, Gene. 1970. *Swing Out: The Great Negro Dance Bands*. Midland, MI: Pendell.

63 Fletcher, Tom. 1984. (1954) *100 Years of the Negro in Show Business*. New York: Da Capo Press. First published New York: Burdge & Co. Ltd., 1954.

64 Floyd, Samuel A. 1990. *Black Music in the Harlem Renaissance*. Westport and London: Greenwood Press.

65 Floyd, Samuel A. 1995. *The Power of Black Music: Interpreting Its History from Africa to the United States*. New York: Oxford University Press.

66 Fox, Ted. 1983. *Showtime at the Apollo Theatre*. New York: Holt.

67 Garofalo, Reebee. 1990. Crossing Over: 1939–1989. In *Split Image: African Americans in the Mass Media*, ed. Jannette L. Dates and William Barlow. Washington, DC: Howard University Press. 57–121.

68 George, Nelson. 1988. *The Death of Rhythm and Blues*. New York: Pantheon.

69 Handy, D. Antoinette. 1981. *Black Women in American Bands and Orchestras*. Metuchen and London: Scarecrow Press.

70 Hazzard-Gordon, Katrina. 1990. *Jookin': The Rise of Social Dance Formation in African-American Culture*. Philadelphia: Temple University Press.

71 Hündgen, Gerald. 1989. *Chasin' a Dream: Die Musik des schwarzen Amerika von Soul bis Hip Hop*. Köln: Kiepenheuer & Witsch.

72 Jerde, Curtis D. 1990. Black Music in New Orleans: A Historical Overview. *Black Music Research Journal* 10(1): 18–24.

73 Jones, Hettie. 1974. *Big Star Fallin' Mama: Five Women in Black Music*. New York: Viking.

74 Jones, LeRoi (Imamu Amiri Baraka). 1967. *Black Music*. New York: William Morrow.

75 Jones, LeRoi (Imamu Amiri Baraka). 1980. (1963) *Blues People: Negro Music in White America*. Westport, CT: Greenwood Press. First published New York: Harper and Row, 1963.

76 Kebede, Ashenafi. 1982. *Roots of Black Music: The Vocal, Instrumental and Dance Heritage of Africa and Black America*. Englewood Cliffs, NJ: Prentice-Hall.

77 Keck, George R. and Martin, Sherril V., eds. 1988. *Feel the Spirit: Essays in Nineteenth-Century Afro-American Music*. New York: Greenwood Press.

78 Kofsky, Frank. 1970. *Black Nationalism and the Revolution in Music*. New York: Pathfinder Press.

79 Krehbiel, Henry Edward. 1962. *Afro-American Folk-Songs: A Study in Racial and National Music*. New York: Ungar.

80 Leonard, Susan M. 1988. An Introduction to Black Participation in the Early Recording Era, 1890–1920. In *Annual Review of Jazz Studies 4*, ed. Dan Morgenstern, Charles Nanry and David A. Cayer. New Brunswick, NJ: Transaction. 31–44.

81 Levine, Lawrence. 1977. *Black Culture and Black Consciousness: Afro-American Folk Thought from Slavery to Freedom*. Oxford and New York: Oxford University Press.

82 Levy, Claire. 1996. Afro-amerikanskata muzika i savremennite pop stilove. In *Muzikata i uchilishteto: vchera, dnes, utre*, ed. Maria Popova. Sofia: CIUU. 24–36.

83 Locke, Alain LeRoy. 1988. (1936) *The Negro and His Music: Negro Art, Past and Present*. Salem, MA: Ayer. First published Washington: Associates in Negro Folk Education, 1936.

84 Long, Richard A. 1986. Black Music Biography: A Research Prospectus. *Black Music Research Journal* 6: 49–56.

85 Lotz, Rainer E. 1990. The Black Troubadours: Black Entertainers in Europe, 1896–1915. *Black Music Research Journal* 10(2): 253–73.

86 Martin, Denis-Constant. 1991. Filiation or Innovation: Some Hypotheses to Overcome the Dilemma of Afro-American Music's Origins. *Black Music Research Journal* 11(1): 19–33.

87 Maultsby, Portia K. and Burnim, Mellonee. 1987. From Backwoods to City Streets: The Afro-American Musical Journey. In *Expressively Black*, ed. Geneva Gay and Willie L. Barber. New York: Praeger. 109–36.

88 Morgan, Thomas L. and Barlow, William. 1992. *From Cakewalks to Concert Halls: An Illustrated History of African American*

Popular Music from 1895–1930.
Washington, DC: Elliott & Clark.

89 Murray, Albert. 1989. *Stomping the Blues.*
New York: Da Capo Press.

90 Oliver, Paul. 1984. *Songsters and Saints:
Vocal Traditions on Race Records.*
Cambridge: Cambridge University Press.

91 Olmstead, Frederick Law. 1976. (1856)
Negro Jodling: The Carolina Yell. *The
Black Perspective in Music* 4(2): 140–41.

92 Petrie, Gavin, ed. 1974. *Black Music.*
London: Hamlyn.

93 Pomerance, Alan. 1988. *Repeal of the Blues:
How Black Entertainers Influenced Civil
Rights.* Secaucus, NJ: Citadel Press.

94 Ramsey, Frederic. 1960. *Been Here and
Gone.* New Brunswick, NJ: Rutgers
University Press.

95 Roberts, John Storm. 1974. (1972) *Black
Music of Two Worlds.* New York: William
Morrow. First published New York/
London: Praeger/Allen Lane, 1972.

96 Shaw, Arnold. 1986. *Black Popular Music
in America: From the Spirituals, Minstrels
and Ragtime to Soul, Disco and Hip-Hop.*
New York: Schirmer.

97 Southern, Eileen, ed. 1983. (1971)
Readings in Black American Music. New
York: W.W. Norton.

98 Southern, Eileen. 1983. (1971) *The Music
of Black Americans: A History.* New York:
W.W. Norton.

99 Spencer, Jon Michael. 1992. *Sacred Music
of the Secular City: From Blues to Rap.*
Durham, NC: Duke University Press.

100 Trotter, James M. 1968. *Music and Some
Highly Musical People: With Sketches of the
Lives of Remarkable Musicians of the
Coloured Race.* New York: Johnson.

101 Vincent, Ted. 1989. The Social Context
of Black Swan Records. *Living Blues*: 34–
40.

102 Wells, Alan. 1987. Black Artists in
American Popular Music, 1955–1985.
Phylon 48(4) (Winter): 309–16.

103 Westcott, William. 1977. Ideas of Afro-
American Musical Acculturation in the
USA: 1900 to the Present. *Journal of the
Steward Anthropological Society* 8.

104 Woll, Allen. 1989. *Black Musical Theatre:
From Coontown to Dreamgirls.* Baton
Rouge, LA: Louisiana State University
Press.

Analysis and Interpretation

105 Ames, Russell. 1950. Protest and Irony in
Negro Folksong. *Science & Society* 14.

106 Balmir, Guy-Claude. 1982. *Du chant au
poème: essai de littérature sur le chant et la
poésie populaires des noirs américains.* Paris:
Payot.

107 Brown, Ernest D. 1990. Something from
Nothing and More from Something: The
Making and Playing of Music Instru-
ments in African-American Cultures.
Selected Reports in Ethnomusicology 8:
275–91.

108 Carby, Hazel V. 1992. In Body and
Spirit: Representing Black Women
Musicians. *Black Music Research Journal*
11(2): 177–92.

109 Chernoff, John M. 1985. The Artistic
Challenge of African Music: Thoughts on
the Absence of Drum Orchestras in Black
American Music. *Black Music Research
Journal* 5: 1–20.

110 Cronbach, Lee. 1981. Two Pieces on
Tonal Stratification in Black American
Music: Structural Polytonality in
Contemporary Afro-American Popular
Music. *Black Music Research Journal*: 15–
33.

111 Doucet, Vincent. 1989. *Musique et rites afro-américains*. Paris: L'Harmattan.

112 Floyd, Samuel A. 1991. Ring Shout! Literary Studies, Historical Studies and Black Music Inquiry. *Black Music Research Journal* 11(2): 265–78.

113 Floyd, Samuel A. 1993. Troping the Blues: From Spirituals to the Concert Hall. *Black Music Research Journal* 13(1): 31–51.

114 Gilroy, Paul. 1993. 'Jewels Brought from Bondage': Black Music and the Politics of Authenticity. In *The Black Atlantic: Modernity and Double Consciousness*. London: Verso. 72–110.

115 Heckman, Don. 1970. Black Music and White America. In *Black Americans*, ed. John F. Szwed. Washington, DC: Voice of America Forum Lectures. 171–84.

116 Jones, Bessie and Hawes, Bessie Lomax. 1972. *Step It Down: Games, Plays, Songs and Stories from the Afro-American Heritage*. New York: Harper & Row.

117 Jost, Ekkehard. 1981. *Jazzmusiker: Materialien zur Soziologie der afro-amerikanischen Musik*. Berlin: Ullstein.

118 Lomax, Alan. 1970. The Homogeneity of African-American Musical Style. In *Afro-American Anthropology: Contemporary Perspectives*, ed. Norman E. Whitten and John F. Szwed. New York: Free Press. 180–202.

119 Maultsby, Portia K. 1990. Africanisms in African-American Music. In *Africanisms in American Culture*, ed. Joseph E. Holloway. Bloomington, IN: Indiana University Press. 185–210.

120 Metfessel, Milton. 1981. (1926) *Phonophotography in Folk Music: American Negro Songs in New Notation*. Durham, NC: University of North Carolina Press.

121 Monson, Ingrid. 1990. Forced Migration, Asymmetrical Power Relations and African-American Music: Reformulation of Cultural Meaning and Form. *The World of Music* 32(3): 22–45.

122 Murphy, Paula. 1987. Films for the Black Music Researcher. *Black Music Research Journal* 7: 45–66.

123 Nketia, J.H. Kwabena. 1973. The Study of African and Afro-American Music. *The Black Perspective in Music* 1(1): 7–15.

124 Oderigo, Nestor R. Ortiz. 1956. Negro Rhythm in the Americas. *African Music* 1(3): 68–70.

125 Odum, Howard and Johnson, Guy B. 1976. *The Negro and His Songs: A Study of Typical Negro Songs in the South*. Westport, CT: Negro Universities Press.

126 Odum, Howard and Johnson, Guy B. 1969. (1926) *Negro Workaday Songs*. Chapel Hill, NC: University of North Carolina Press.

127 Ransby, Barbara and Matthews, Tracye. 1993. Black Popular Culture and the Transcendence of Patriarchal Illusions. *Race and Class* 35(1): 57–68.

128 Scarborough, Dorothy. 1963. (1925) *On the Trail of Negro Folk-Songs*. Hatboro, PA: Folklore Associates. First published Cambridge: Harvard University Press, 1925.

129 Shepp, Archie. 1983. Music and Black Identity. In *Laulu ottaa kantaa – aineistoa 1970-luvun lauliliikkeestä*. Helsinki: Työväenenmusiikki-institutti. 173–80.

130 Sidran, Ben. 1983. (1971) *Black Talk*. New York: Da Capo Press. First published New York: Riverrun Press, 1971.

131 Small, Christopher. 1987. *Music of the Common Tongue*. New York: Riverrun Press.

132 Standifer, James. 1980. Musical Behaviours of Black People in American Society. *Black Music Research Journal* 1: 51–62.

133 Szwed, John F. 1968. Negro Music: Urban Renewal. In *American Folklore*, ed. Tristram P. Coffin. Washington, DC: Voice of America Forum Lectures. 305–16.

134 Szwed, John F. 1970. Afro-American Musical Adaptation. In *Afro-American Anthropology: Contemporary Perspectives*, ed. Norman E. Whitten and John F. Szwed. New York: Free Press. 219–30.

135 Tagg, Philip. 1989. Open Letter: 'Black Music,' 'Afro-American Music' and 'European Music'. *Popular Music* 8(3): 285–98.

136 Thomas, W.H. 1965. (1926) Some Current Folksongs of the Negro and Their Economic Interpretation. In *Rainbow in the Morning*, ed. J. Frank Dobie. Hatboro, PA: Folklore Associates. 3–13. First published Austin: Texas Folklore Associates, 1926.

137 Tucker, Bruce. 1984. Prejudice Lives: Toward a Philosophy of Black Music Biography. *Black Music Research Journal* 4: 1–21.

138 Walton, Ortiz. 1980. (1972) *Music: Black, White & Blue. A Sociological Survey of the Use and Misuse of Afro-American Music*. New York: Morrow Quill Paperback.

139 Waterman, Richard. 1963. On Flogging a Dead Horse: Lessons Learnt from the Africanisms Controversy. *Ethnomusicology* 7(2): 83–88.

140 White, Newman I. 1965. *American Negro Folk-Songs*. Hatboro, PA: Folklore Associates.

141 Wilson, Olly. 1974. The Significance of the Relationship Between Afro-American Music and West African Music. *The Black Perspective in Music* 1(3): 3–22.

142 Work, John Wesley. 1969. (1915) *Folk Song of the American Negro*. New York: Negro Universities Press. First published Nashville: Fiske University Press, 1915.

143 Zook, Kristal Bent. 1992. Reconstructions of Nationalist Thought in Black Music and Culture. In *Rockin' the Boat: Mass Music and Mass Movements*, ed. Reebee Garofalo. Boston, MA: South End Press. 255–66.

Styles

Gospel

144 Allen, Ray. 1988. African-American Sacred Quartet Singing in New York City. *New York Folklore* 14(3–4): 7–22.

145 Allgood, B. Dexter. 1990. Black Gospel Music in New York City. *The Black Perspective in Music* 18(1,2): 101–15.

146 Bontemps, Arna. 1967. Rock, Church! Rock! In *International Library of Negro Life and History: The Negro in Music and Art*, ed. Lindsay Patterson. New York: Publisher's Company. 74–81.

147 Boyer, Horace Clarence. 1974. An Analysis of His Contributions: Thomas A. Dorsey, Father of Gospel Music. *Black World* 23: 20–28.

148 Boyer, Horace Clarence. 1979. Contemporary Gospel. *The Black Perspective in Music* 7(1): 1–58.

149 Boyer, Horace Clarence. 1983. Charles Albert Tindley: Progenitor of Black-American Gospel Music. *The Black Perspective in Music* 11(2): 103–32.

150 Boyer, Horace Clarence. 1984–85. The 'Old Meter Hymn' and Other Types of Gospel Songs. *Views on Black American Music* 2: 41–46.

151 Boyer, Horace Clarence. 1988. Tracking the Tradition: New Orleans Sacred Music. *Black Music Research Journal* 8(1): 135–47.

152 Boyer, Horace Clarence. 1995. *How Sweet the Sound: The Golden Age of Gospel*. Washington, DC: Elliott & Clark Publishing.

153 Broughton, Viv. 1985. *Black Gospel: An Illustrated History of the Gospel Sound.* Poole: Blandford Press.

154 Burnim, Mellonee. 1980. Gospel Music Research. *Black Music Research: Journal* 1980: 63–70.

155 Burnim, Mellonee. 1985. Culture Bearer and Tradition Bearer: An Ethnomusicologist's Research on Gospel Music. *Ethnomusicology* 29(3): 432–47.

156 Burnim, Mellonee. 1988. Functional Dimensions of Gospel Music Performance. *Western Journal of Black Studies* 12(2): 112–21.

157 Burnim, Mellonee. 1989. The Performance of Black Gospel Music as Transformation. *Concilium: International Review of Theology* 2 (March/April): 52–61.

158 Crawford, David. 1977. Gospel Songs in Court: From Rural Music to Urban Industry in the 1950s. *Journal of Popular Culture* 11(3): 551–67.

159 Cullaz, Maurice. 1990. *Gospel.* Paris: Jazz Hot.

160 Dargan, William Thomas and Bullock, Kathy White. 1989. Willie Mae Ford Smith of St. Louis: A Shaping Influence upon Black Gospel Singing Style. *Black Music Research Journal* 9(2): 249–70.

161 Davis, Gerald L. 1985. *I Got the Word in Me and I Can Sing It, You Know: A Study of the Performed African-American Sermon.* Philadelphia: University of Pennsylvania Press.

162 Djedje, Jacqueline Cogdell. 1978. *American Black Spiritual and Gospel Songs from Southeast Georgia: A Comparative Study.* Los Angeles: University of California Center for Afro-American Studies.

163 Djedje, Jacqueline Cogdell. 1986. Change and Differentiation: The Adoption of Black American Gospel Music in the Catholic Church. *Ethnomusicology* 30(2): 223–52.

164 Djedje, Jacqueline Cogdell. 1989. Gospel Music in the Los Angeles Black Community. *Black Music Research Journal* 9(1): 35–79.

165 Djedje, Jacqueline Cogdell. 1993. Los Angeles Composers of African American Gospel Music: The First Generations. *American Music* 11(4) (Winter): 412–57.

166 Dodge, Timothy. 1994. From Spirituals to Gospel Rap: Gospel Music Periodicals. *Serials Review* 20(4): 67–78.

167 Dorsey, Thomas A. 1973. Gospel Music. In *Reflections on Afro-American Music.* Kent, OH: Kent State University Press. 189–95.

168 Evans, David. 1976. The Roots of Afro-American Gospel Music. *Jazzforschung/Jazz Research* 8: 119–35.

169 Godrich, John and Dixon, Robert M.W., comps.1982. (1962) *Blues & Gospel Records, 1902–1943.* Chigwell: Storyville Publications.

170 Harris, Michael W. 1992. *The Rise of Gospel Blues: The Music of Thomas Andrew Dorsey in the Urban Church.* New York and Oxford: Oxford University Press.

171 Hayes, Cedric. 1973. *A Discography of Gospel Records, 1937–1971.* Copenhagen: Knudsen.

172 Heilbut, Anthony. 1992. (1975) *The Gospel Sound: Good News and Bad Times.* New York: Limelight Editions. First published Garden City: Anchor Press/Doubleday, 1975.

173 Jackson, Irene V. 1979. *Afro-American Religious Music: A Bibliography and a Catalogue of Gospel Music.* Westport, CT: Greenwood Press.

174 Jackson, Irene V. 1990. Developments in Black Gospel Performance and

Scholarship. *Black Music Research Journal* 10(1): 36–42.

175 Jones, Ralph H. 1982. *Charles Albert Tindley: Prince of Preachers*. Nashville, TN: Abingdon Press.

176 Landes, John L. 1987. WLAC, The Hossman and Their Influence on Black Gospel. *Black Music Research Journal* 7: 67–82.

177 Lornell, Kip. 1988. *'Happy in the Service of the Lord': Afro-American Gospel Quartets in Memphis*. Champaign, IL: University of Illinois Press.

178 Lornell, Kip, comp. 1989. *Virginia's Blues, Country and Gospel Records, 1902–1943: An Annotated Discography*. Lexington, KY: University Press of Kentucky.

179 Mahoney, Dan. 1966. *The Columbia 13/14000-D Series: A Numerical Listing*. Stanhope, NJ: Allen.

180 Oliver, Paul, Max Harrison and William Bolcom. 1986. *The New Grove Book of Gospel, Blues and Jazz, with Spirituals and Ragtime*. London: Macmillan.

181 Reagon, Bernice Johnson. 1981. *In Search of Charles Albert Tindley*. Washington, DC: Smithsonian Institution, National Museum of American History, Program in Black American Culture.

182 Reagon, Bernice Johnson, ed. 1992. *We'll Understand It Better By and By: Pioneering African American Gospel Composers*. Washington and London: Smithsonian Institution Press.

183 Ricks, George R. 1977. *Some Aspects of the Religious Music of the United States Negro: An Ethnomusicological Study with Special Emphasis on the Gospel Tradition*. New York: Arno Press.

184 Spencer, Jon Michael. 1992. *Black Hymnody: A Hymnological History of the African-American Church*. Knoxville, TN: University of Tennessee Press.

185 Tallmadge, William H. 1961. Dr Watts and Mahalia Jackson: The Development, Decline and Survival of a Folk Style in America. *Ethnomusicology* 5(2): 95–100.

186 Tallmadge, William H. 1968. The Responsorial and Antiphonal Practice in Gospel Singing. *Ethnomusicology* 12(2): 219–38.

187 van Rijn, Guido. 1990. *Roosevelt's Blues: African-American Blues and Gospel Artists on President Franklin D. Roosevelt*. Oxford, MS: University of Mississippi Press.

188 Warrick, Mancel. 1977. *The Progress of Gospel Music: From Spirituals to Contemporary Gospel*. New York: Vantage Press.

189 Williams-Jones, Pearl. 1975. Afro-American Gospel Music: A Crystallization of the Black Aesthetic. *Ethnomusicology* 19(3) (September): 373–85.

Popular Religious Music

190 Burnim, Mellonee. 1992. Conflict and Controversy in Black Religious Music. In *Proceedings of the Symposium 'African-American Religion: Research Problems and Resources for the 1990s'*. New York: Schomberg Center for Research in Black Culture, The New York Public Library. 82–97.

191 Maultsby, Portia K. 1975. Music of Northern Independent Black Churches During the Ante-Bellum Period. *Ethnomusicology* 19(3): 401–20.

192 Maultsby, Portia K. 1981. *Afro-American Religious Music: A Study in Musical Diversity*. Springfield, OH: The Hymn Society of America, Wittenberg University, Paper No. XXXV.

193 Maultsby, Portia K. 1983. The Use and Performance of Hymnody, Spirituals and Gospels in the Black Church, revised version. *The Hymnology Annual: An International Forum on the Hymn and Worship* II: 11–26. (First published in *The*

Western Journal of Black Studies **VII** (Fall) (1983).)

194 Reagon, Bernice Johnson. 1987. Let the Church Sing 'Freedom'. *Black Music Research Journal* 7: 105–18.

195 Ricks, George R. 1977. *Some Aspects of the Religious Music of the United States Negro: An Ethnomusicological Study with Special Emphasis on the Gospel Tradition*. New York: Arno Press.

Spirituals and Slave Songs

196 Abrahams, Roger D. 1992. *Singing the Master: The Emergence of African American Culture in the Plantation South*. New York: Pantheon Books.

197 Allen, William Francis, Charles Pickard Ware and Lucy McKim Garrison, eds. 1992. (1867) *Slave Songs of the United States*. Baltimore, MD: Clearfield Co. First published New York: A. Simpson and Company, 1867.

198 Botkin, B.A. 1945. *Lay My Burden Down: A Folk History of Slavery*. Chicago: University of Chicago Press.

199 Cone, James H. 1980. *The Spiritual and the Blues: An Interpretation*. New York: Seabury.

200 Dixon, Christa K. 1976. *Negro Spirituals from Bible to Folk Song*. Philadelphia: Fortress Press.

201 Djedje, Jacqueline Cogdell. 1978. *American Black Spiritual and Gospel Songs from Southeast Georgia: A Comparative Study*. Los Angeles: University of California Center for Afro-American Studies.

202 Eaklor, Vicki L. 1988. *American Antislavery Songs: A Collection and Analysis*. Westport, CT: Greenwood Press.

203 Engel, Carl. 1926. Negro Spirituals. *Musical Quarterly* 12: 299–314.

204 Epstein, Dena J. 1977. *Sinful Tunes and Spirituals: Black Folk Music to the Civil War*. Urbana, IL: University of Illinois Press.

205 Epstein, Dena J. 1983. A White Origin for the Black Spiritual? An Invalid Theory and How It Grew. *American Music* 1(2): 53–59.

206 Fisher, Miles Mark. 1990. (1953) *Negro Slave Songs in the United States*. New York: Citadel Press Book.

207 Forten, Charlotte. 1961. *The Journal of Charlotte Forten: A Free Negro*, ed. Ray Allen Billington. New York: Collier Books.

208 Gilroy, Paul. 1993. 'Jewels Brought from Bondage': Black Music and the Politics of Authenticity. In *The Black Atlantic: Modernity and Double Consciousness*. London: Verso. 72–110.

209 Johnson, James Weldon and Johnson, J. Rosamund. 1977. (1944) *The Books of American Negro Spirituals*. New York: Da Capo Paperback. First published New York: Viking, 1944.

210 Keck, George R., and Martin, Sherril V., eds. 1988. *Feel the Spirit: Essays in Nineteenth-Century Afro-American Music*. New York: Greenwood Press.

211 Kemble, Frances Anne. 1961. (1863) *Journal of a Residence on a Georgian Plantation*, ed. John A. Scott. New York: Knopf. First published London: Longman, Green, 1863.

212 Kennedy, R. Emmett. 1925. *Mellows: A Chronicle of Unknown Singers*. New York: Albert & Charles Boni.

213 Kennedy, R. Emmett. 1931. *More Mellows*. New York: Dodd, Mead & Co.

214 Krehbiel, Henry Edward. 1914. *Afro-American Folksongs: A Study in Racial and National Music*. New York: Schirmer.

215 Lehmann, Theo. 1965. *Negro Spirituals: Geschiche und Theologie*. Berlin: Eckhart.

216 Levine, Lawrence. 1971. Slave Songs and Slave Consciousness. In *Anonymous Americans*, ed. Tamara Hareven. Englewood Cliffs, NJ: Prentice-Hall. 99–130.

217 Levine, Lawrence. 1977. *Black Culture and Black Consciousness: Afro-American Folk Thought from Slavery to Freedom*. Oxford and New York: Oxford University Press.

218 Lovell, John. 1986. (1972) *Black Song: The Forge and the Flame. The Story of How the Afro-American Spiritual Was Hammered Out*. New York: Paragon House. First published New York: Macmillan, 1972.

219 Maultsby, Portia K. 1976. Black Spirituals: An Analysis of Textual Forms and Structures. *The Black Perspective in Music* 4(1): 54–69.

220 McDonagh, Gary, ed. 1992. *The Florida Negro: A Federal Writers' Project Legacy*. Jackson, MI: University Press of Mississippi.

221 Olmstead, Frederick Law. 1959. (1856) *A Journey in the Seaboard Slave States*. New York: Putnam.

222 Parrish, Lydia, ed. 1942. *Slave Songs of the Georgian Sea Islands*. New York: Farrar, Strauss.

223 Silveri, Louis. 1988. The Singing Tours of the Fisk Jubilee Singers: 1871–1874. In *Feel the Spirit: Essays in Nineteenth-Century Afro-American Music*, ed. George R. Keck and Sherril V. Martin. New York: Greenwood Press. 105–16.

224 Taylor, John E. 1975. Somethin' on My Mind: A Cultural and Historical Interpretation of a Spiritual Text. *Ethnomusicology* 19(3): 387–400.

225 Thurman, Howard. 1947. *The Negro Spiritual Speaks of Life and Death: Being the Ingersoll Lecture on the Immortality of Man*. New York: Harper & Row.

226 Thurman, Howard. 1969. *Deep River: Reflections on the Religious Insight of Certain of the Negro Spirituals*. Port Washington, WI: Kennikat.

Work Songs

227 Abrahams, Roger D. 1992. *Singing the Master: The Emergence of African American Culture in the Plantation South*. New York: Pantheon Books.

228 Jackson, Bruce. 1974. *Wake Up Dead Man: Afro-American Worksongs from Texas Prisons*. Cambridge, MA: Harvard University Press.

229 Joyner, Charles. 1984. *Down by the Riverside: A South Carolina Slave Community*. Urbana, IL: University of Illinois Press.

230 McDonagh, Gary, ed. 1992. *The Florida Negro: A Federal Writers' Project Legacy*. Jackson, MI: University Press of Mississippi.

231 Odum, Howard and Johnson, Guy B. 1969. (1926) *Negro Workaday Songs*. Chapel Hill, NC: University of North Carolina Press.

AFRO–CUBAN MUSIC

232 Boggs, Vernon. 1991. Musical Transculturation: From Afro-Cuban to Afro-Cubanism. *Popular Music & Society* 15(4): 71–83.

233 Boggs, Vernon. 1992. *Salsiology: Afro-Cuban Music and the Evolution of Salsa in New York City*. New York: Excelsior Music Publishing Company.

234 Leon, Argeliers. 1991. Of the Axe and the Hinge: Nationalism, Afro-Cubanism and Music in Pre-Revolutionary Cuba. In *Essays on Cuban Music: North American and Cuban Perspectives*, ed. Peter Manuel.

Lanham, MD: University Press of America. 267–82.

AMBIENT MUSIC

235 Tamm, Eric. 1989. *Brian Eno: His Music and the Vertical Color of Sound*. Boston and London: Faber & Faber.

236 Toop, David. 1995. *Ocean of Sound*. London: Serpent's Tail.

ARABESK

237 Belge, Murat. 1990. Toplumsal Degisme ve Arabesk. *Birikim* 17.

238 Egribel, Ertan. 1984. *Nicin Arabesk degil?* Ankara: Surec.

239 Gungor, Nazife. 1990. *Arabesk: Sosyo-kulturel Acidan Arabesk Muzigi*. Ankara: Bilgi.

240 Ozbek, Meral. 1991. *Populer Kultur ve Orhan Gencebay Arabeski*. Istanbul: Iletisim.

241 Stokes, Martin. 1989. Music, Fate and State: Turkey's Arabesk Debate. *Middle East Report and Information Project* 160: 27–30.

242 Stokes, Martin. 1992. *The Arabesk Debate: Music and Musicians in Modern Turkey*. Oxford: Oxford University Press.

243 Stokes, Martin. 1992. Islam, the Turkish State and Arabesk. *Popular Music* 11(2): 213–28.

244 Stokes, Martin. 1994. 'Local Arabesk' and the Turkish-Syrian Border. In *The Anthropology of Borders*, ed. Hastings Donnan and Thomas Wilson. New York: Academic Press. 31–52.

245 Stokes, Martin. 1994. Turkish Arabesk and the City: Urban Popular Music as Spatial Practice. In *Islam, Globalization and Postmodernity*, ed. Akbar Ahmed and Hastings Donnan. London: Routledge. 21–37.

246 Stokes, Martin. 1995. Islam and the State in Turkey's Arabesk Debate. In *Popular Music Perspectives III*, ed. Peter Wicke. Berlin: Zyankrise. 320–25.

BACHATA

247 Pacini Hernandez, Deborah. 1990. Cantando la cama vacia: Love, Sexuality and Gender Relationships in Dominican 'Bachata'. *Popular Music* 9(3): 351–67.

248 Pacini Hernandez, Deborah. 1992. Bachata: From the Margins to the Mainstream. *Popular Music* 11(3): 359–64.

249 Pacini Hernandez, Deborah. 1995. *Bachata: A Social History of a Dominican Popular Music*. Philadelphia: Temple University Press.

BALLADS

250 Belden, H.M. 1973. (1940) *Ballads and Songs, Collected by the Missouri Folklore Society*. Columbia, MO: University of Missouri Press.

251 Buchanan, David. 1972. *The Ballad and the Folk*. London: Routledge and Kegan Paul.

252 Coffin, Tristram P. 1963. *The British Traditional Ballad in North America*. Philadelphia: American Folklore Society.

253 Dugaw, Dianne. 1989. *Warrior Women and Popular Balladry, 1650–1850*. Cambridge: Cambridge University Press.

254 Dugaw, Dianne. 1995. *The Anglo-American Ballad: A Folklore Casebook*. New York: Garland.

255 Elkins, Charles. 1980. The Voice of the Poor: The Broadside as a Medium of Popular Culture and Dissent in Victorian

England. *Journal of Popular Culture* 14(2): 262–74.

256 Entwistle, William J. 1951. (1939) *European Balladry*. Oxford: Oxford University Press.

257 Faolain, Turlough. 1983. *Blood on the Harp: Irish Rebel History in Ballad*. Troy, NY: Whitston Publishing Co.

258 Gerould, Gordon Hall. 1932. *The Ballad of Tradition*. Oxford: Clarendon Press.

259 Hall, James W. 1968. Concepts of Liberty in American Broadside Ballads, 1850–1870: A Study of the Mind of American Mass Culture. *Journal of Popular Culture* 2(2): 252–77.

260 Healy, James, ed. 1968. *The Second Book of Irish Ballads*. Cork: Mercier Press.

261 Henderson, W., ed. 1937. *Victorian Street Ballads: A Selection of Popular Ballads Sold in the Street in the Nineteenth Century*. London: Country Life.

262 Hodgart, M.J. 1962. *The Ballads*. New York: W.W. Norton.

263 James, Barbara and Mossman, Walter. 1983. *Glasbruch 1848: Flugblattlieder und Dokumente einer zerbrochenen Revolution*. Darmstadt: Luchterhand.

264 Laws, G. Malcolm, Jr. 1957. *American Balladry from British Broadsides: A Guide for Students and Collectors of Traditional Song*. Philadelphia: American Folklore Society.

265 Laws, G. Malcolm, Jr. 1968. Stories Told in Song: The Ballads of America. In *American Folklore*, ed. Tristram P. Coffin. Washington, DC: Voice of America Forum Lectures. 93–104.

266 Laws, G. Malcolm, Jr. 1974. (1964) *Native American Balladry: A Descriptive Study and a Biographical Syllabus*. Austin, TX: University of Texas Press. First published Philadelphia: American Folklore Society, 1964.

267 Leach, MacEdward. 1955. *The Ballad Book*. New York: A.S. Barnes.

268 Leach, MacEdward and Coffin, Tristram P. 1961. *The Critics and the Ballad: Readings Selected and Edited*. Carbondale, IL: Southern Illinois University Press.

269 Leach, MacEdward and Coffin, Tristram P., eds. 1973. (1961) *The Critics and the Ballad: Readings*. Carbondale, IL: Southern Illinois University Press.

270 Lomax, John A. 1947. *Adventures of a Ballad Hunter*. New York: Macmillan.

271 Muir, Willa. 1965. *Living with Ballads*. London: Hogarth Press.

272 Palmer, Roy. 1978. *Strike the Bell*. Cambridge: Cambridge University Press.

273 Palmer, Roy. 1979. *A Ballad History of England from 1588 to the Present Day*. London: Batsford.

274 Paredes, Américo. 1958. *'With a Pistol in His Hand': A Border Ballad and Its Hero*. Austin, TX: University of Texas Press.

275 Pinto, V. de Sola and Rodway, A.E. 1957. *The Common Muse: An Anthology of British Ballad Poetry, XIV–XXth Centuries*. London: Chatto and Windus.

276 Pound, Louise. 1922. *American Ballads and Songs*. New York: Scribner's & Sons.

277 Shephard, Leslie. 1962. *The Broadside Ballad: The Development of the Street Ballad from Traditional Songs to Popular Newspaper*. London: Herbert Jenkins.

278 Shields, Hugh, ed. 1985. *Ballad Research: The Stranger in Ballad Narrative and Other Topics*. Dublin: Folk Music Society of Ireland.

279 Simpson, Claude M. 1966. *The British Broadside Ballad and Its Music*. New Brunswick, NJ: Rutgers University Press.

280 Thomas, Jean. 1964. (1939) *Ballad Making in the Mountains of Kentucky.* New York: Oak Publications.

281 Wimberly, Lowry C. 1959. (1928) *Folklore in the English and Scottish Ballads.* New York: Frederick Ungar Publishing Co.

282 Wood, Olive Burt. 1958. *American Murder Ballads and Their Stories.* New York: Oxford University Press.

BARBERSHOP

283 Abbott, Lynn. 1992. 'Play That Barbershop Chord': A Case for the African-American Origin of Barbershop Harmony. *American Music* 10(3): 289–325.

284 Johnson, James Weldon. 1929. The Origin of the 'Barber Chord'. *The Mentor* 17(1): 53–65.

285 Martin, D. 1955. Three Eras of Barbershop Harmony. *The Harmonizer* 15(2): 20–35.

286 Martin, D. 1965. The Evolution of Barbershop Harmony. *Music Journal Annual* 1965: 40–53.

287 Spaeth, Sigmund. 1940. *Barbershop Ballads and How To Sing Them.* New York: Prentice-Hall.

BHANGRA

288 Banerji, Sabita. 1987. Bhangra, Ghazals and Beyond. *Folkroots* 51 (September): 30–33.

289 Banerji, Sabita. 1988. Ghazals to Bhangra in Great Britain. *Popular Music* 7(2): 207–14.

290 Banerji, Sabita and Baumann, Gerd. 1990. Bhangra 1984–8: Fusion and Professionalisation in a Genre of South Asian Dance Music. In *Black Music in Britain: Essays on the Afro-Asian Contribution to Popular Music,* ed. Paul Oliver. Milton Keynes: Open University Press. 137–52.

291 Baumann, Gerd. 1990. The Reinvention of Bhangra: Social Change and Aesthetic Shifts in a Punjabi Music in Britain. *The World of Music* 32(2): 81–95.

BLUES

General Works

292 Albold, Volker. 1987. *Blues heute: Musik zwischen Licht und Schatten.* Berlin: Lied der Zeit.

293 Charters, Samuel B. 1978. (1975) *The Legacy of the Blues: A Glimpse into the Art and the Lives of Twelve Great Bluesmen. An Informal Study.* New York: Plenum. First published London: Calder and Boyars, 1975.

294 Cohn, Lawrence, ed. 1993. *Nothing But the Blues: The Music and the Musicians.* New York: Abbeville Press.

295 Cook, Bruce. 1973. *Listen to the Blues.* New York: Charles Scribner's Sons.

296 Finn, Julio. 1986. *The Bluesman: The Musical Heritage of Black Men & Women in the Americas.* London: Quartet.

297 Guralnick, Peter. 1971. *Feel Like Going Home: Portraits in Blues and Rock & Roll.* New York: Outerbridge & Dienstfrey.

298 Guralnick, Peter. 1982. *The Listener's Guide to the Blues.* Poole: Blandford Press.

299 Leadbitter, Mike, ed. 1971. *Nothing But the Blues: An Illustrated Documentary.* London: Hanover Books.

300 Murray, Albert. 1989. *Stomping the Blues.* New York: Da Capo Press.

301 Oliver, Paul. 1965. *Conversation with the Blues.* London: Cassell.

302 Oliver, Paul. 1985. *Blues Off the Record: Thirty Years of Blues Commentary*. Tunbridge Wells: Baton Press.

303 Oliver, Paul, Max Harrison and William Bolcom. 1986. *The New Grove Book of Gospel, Blues and Jazz, with Spirituals and Ragtime*. London: Macmillan.

304 Ramsey, Frederic. 1960. *Been Here and Gone*. New Brunswick, NJ: Rutgers University Press.

Reference

305 Arnaudon, Jean-Claude. 1977. *Dictionnaire du Blues*. Paris: Filipacchi.

306 Bogaert, Karel. 1972. *Blues Lexicon: Blues, Cajun, Boogie Woogie & Gospel*. Antwerp: Standaard Uitgeverij.

307 Cowley, John. 1996. *The New Blackwell Guide to Recorded Blues*. Oxford: Blackwell.

308 Harris, Sheldon. 1981. (1979) *Blues Who's Who: A Biographical Dictionary of Blues Singers*. New York: Da Capo Press. First published New Rochelle: Arlington House, 1979.

309 Hart, Mary L., Brenda M. Eagles and Lisa N. Howorth, 1989. *The Blues: A Bibliographical Guide*. New York: Garland.

310 Herzhaft, Gérard. 1990. *Encyclopédie du blues*. Paris: Laffont.

311 Moll, Dieter. 1989. *Das Buch vom Blues*. Königswinter: Heel.

312 Taft, Michael. 1984. *Blues Lyric Poetry: A Concordance*. New York and London: Garland.

Discographies

313 Fancourt, Leslie, comp. 1983. *Chess Blues Discography*. Faversham: Leslie Fancourt.

314 Fancourt, Leslie. 1989. *British Blues on Record (1957–1970)*. Faversham: Privately printed.

315 Godrich, John and Dixon, Robert M.W., comps. 1982. (1962) *Blues & Gospel Records, 1902–1943*. Chigwell: Storyville Publications.

316 Leadbitter, Mike and Slaven, Neil. 1987. *Blues Records, 1943–70: A Selective Discography*. London: Record Information Services.

317 Lornell, Kip, comp. 1989. *Virginia's Blues, Country and Gospel Records, 1902–1943: An Annotated Discography*. Lexington, KY: University Press of Kentucky.

318 Mahoney, Dan. 1966. *The Columbia 13/14000-D Series: A Numerical Listing*. Stanhope, NJ: Allen.

319 Ruppli, Michel. 1983. *The Chess Labels: A Discography*. Westport and London: Greenwood Press.

320 Vreede, Max E. 1971. *Paramount 12000 13000*. Chigwell: Storyville Publications.

History

321 Barlow, William. 1989. *'Looking Up at Down': The Emergence of Blues Culture*. Philadelphia: Temple University Press.

322 Broonzy, William. 1964. (1955) *Big Bill Blues: William Broonzy's Story as Told to Yannick Bruynoghe*. New York: Oak Publications. First published London: Cassell, 1955.

323 Charters, Samuel B. 1981. *The Roots of the Blues*. London: Quartet.

324 Charters, Samuel B. 1991. *The Blues Makers*. New York: Da Capo Press. First published in 2 vols. as *The Bluesmen and Sweet as Showers of Rain*. New York: Oak, 1967–77.

325 Cowley, John. 1981. Really 'Walking Blues': Son House, Muddy Waters,

Robert Johnson and the Development of the Traditional Blues. *Popular Music* 1: 57–71.

326 Dixon, Robert M.W. and Godrich, John. 1970. *Recording the Blues*. London: November Books.

327 Evans, David. 1972. Africa and the Blues. *Living Blues* 10: 27–29.

328 Ferris, William R. 1974. Blues Roots and Development. *The Black Perspective in Music* 2(2): 112–27.

329 Groom, Bob. 1971. *The Blues Revival*. London: November Books.

330 Handy, W.C. 1970. (1941) *Father of the Blues: An Autobiography*. New York: Collier. First published New York: Macmillan, 1941.

331 Haralambos, Michael. 1994. (1974) *Right On: From Blues to Soul in Black America*. Ormskirk: Causeway. First published London: Eddison Press, 1974.

332 Jones, LeRoi (Imamu Amiri Baraka). 1980. (1963) *Blues People: Negro Music in White America*. Westport, CT: Greenwood Press. First published New York: Harper and Row, 1963.

333 Levine, Lawrence. 1977. *Black Culture and Black Consciousness: Afro-American Folk Thought from Slavery to Freedom*. Oxford and New York: Oxford University Press.

334 Lomax, Alan. 1993. *The Land Where Blues Began*. New York: Pantheon.

335 Oakley, Giles. 1983. *The Devil's Music: A History of the Blues*. London: Ariel/BBC.

336 Oliver, Paul. 1969. *The Story of the Blues*. London: Barrie and Jenkins.

337 Oliver, Paul. 1970. *Savannah Syncopators: African Retentions in the Blues*. London: Studio Vista.

338 Oliver, Paul. 1984. *Songsters and Saints: Vocal Traditions on Race Records*. Cambridge: Cambridge University Press.

339 Oliver, Paul. 1991. That Certain Feeling: Blues and Jazz in 1890? *Popular Music* 10(1): 11–19.

340 Russell, Tony. 1970. *Blacks, Whites and Blues*. London: Studio Vista.

341 Shaw, Arnold. 1978. *Honkers and Shouters: The Golden Years of Rhythm and Blues*. New York: Macmillan.

342 Southern, Eileen. 1971. (1933) *The Music of Black Americans: A History*. New York: W.W. Norton.

343 Springer, Robert. 1995. *Le blues authentique*. Lewiston, NY: Edwin Mellen Press.

Regional Studies

344 Bastin, Bruce. 1971. *Crying for the Carolines*. London: Studio Vista.

345 Bastin, Bruce. 1986. *Red River Blues: The Blues Tradition in the Southwest*. Urbana, IL: University of Illinois Press.

346 Beyer, Jimmy. 1980. *Baton Rouge Blues: A Guide to the Baton Rouge Bluesmen and Their Music*. Baton Rouge, LA: Arts and Humanities Council of Greater Baton Rouge.

347 Broven, John. 1962. Louisiana Blues. *Jazz Journal* 16: 10–12.

348 Broven, John. 1978. (1974) *Rhythm and Blues in New Orleans*. Bexhill-on-Sea: Blues Unlimited.

349 Brunning, Bob. 1986. *The Blues: The British Connection*. Poole: Blandford Press.

350 Evans, David. 1987. (1982) *Big Road Blues: Tradition and Creativity in the Folk Blues*. New York: Da Capo Press.

351 Ferris, William R. 1979. *Blues from the Delta*. Garden City, NY: Doubleday.

352 Governar, Alan. 1985. *Living Texas Blues*. Dallas, TX: Dallas Museum of Art.

353 Governar, Alan. 1985. *Meeting the Blues*. Dallas, TX: Taylor Publishing Company.

354 Hannusch, Jeff. 1985. *I Hear You Knockin': The Sound of New Orleans Rhythm and Blues*. Ville Platte, LA: Swallow.

355 Leadbitter, Mike. 1968. *Crowley, Louisiana Blues: The Story of J.D. Miller and His Blues Artists*. Bexhill-on-Sea: Blues Unlimited.

356 Lee, George W. 1969. (1934) *Beale Street: Where the Blues Began*. College Park, MD: McGrath. First published New York: Vail-Ballou, 1934.

357 Lornell, Kip, comp. 1989. *Virginia's Blues, Country and Gospel Records, 1902–1943: An Annotated Discography*. Lexington, KY: University Press of Kentucky.

358 McKee, Margaret and Chisenhall, Fred. 1981. *Beale Black and Blue: Life and Music on Black America's Main Street*. Baton Rouge, LA: Louisiana State University Press.

359 Mitchell, George. 1983. *Blow My Blues Away*. New York: Da Capo Press.

360 Olsson, Bengt. 1970. *Memphis Blues and Jug Bands*. London: Studio Vista.

361 Palmer, Robert. 1981. *Deep Blues*. New York: Viking.

362 Pearson, Barry. 1990. *Virginia Piedmont Blues: The Lives and Art of Two Virginia Bluesmen*. Philadelphia: University of Pennsylvania Press.

363 Rowe, Mike. 1973. *Chicago Breakdown*. London: Eddison Press.

364 Sacre, Robert, ed. 1987. *The Voice of the Delta: Charley Patton and the Mississippi Blues Traditions, Influences and Comparisons*. De Liege: Presses Universitaires.

365 Tracy, Steven C. 1993. *Going to Cincinnati: A History of the Blues in the Queen City*. Urbana, IL: University of Illinois Press.

Analysis and Interpretation

366 Baker, Houston A., Jr. 1984. *Blues, Ideology and Afro-American Literature: A Vernacular Theory*. Chicago: University of Chicago Press.

367 Barnie, John. 1978. Oral Formulas in the Country Blues. *Southern Folklore Quarterly* 42(1): 39–52.

368 Boyd, Joe. 1964. South Side Blues: Blues Lyrics, Chicago-Style. In *ABC TV Hootenanny*. New York: SMP Publishing. 22–23.

369 Brown, Sterling A. 1952. The Blues. *Phylon* 13: 318–27.

370 Chambers, Iain. 1979. It's More Than A Song To Sing: Music, Cultural Analysis and the Blues. *Anglistica* 22(1): 18–31.

371 Charters, Samuel B. 1970. (1963) *The Poetry of the Blues*. New York: Avon. First published New York: Oak Publications, 1963.

372 Cone, James H. 1980. *The Spiritual and the Blues: An Interpretation*. New York: Seabury.

373 Dauer, Alfons M. 1983. *Blues aus 100 Jahren: 43 Beispiele zur Typologie der vokalen Bluesformen*. Frankfurt am Main: Fischer.

374 Ellison, Mary. 1989. *Extensions of the Blues*. London and New York: J. Calder/Riverrun Press.

375 Evans, David. 1974. Techniques of Blues Composition Among Black Folksingers.

Journal of the American Folklore Society 87(345): 240–49.

376 Evans, David. 1978. Structure and Meaning in the Folk Blues. In *The Study of American Folklore*, ed. Jan Harold Brunvald. New York: W.W. Norton. 421–47.

377 Ferris, William R. 1970. The Blues Aesthetic. *Blues World* 43 (Summer).

378 Ferris, William R. 1970. Racial Repertoires Among Blues Performers. *Ethnomusicology* 14(3): 439–49.

379 Garon, Paul. 1979. *Blues and the Poetic Spirit*. New York: Da Capo Press.

380 Haralambos, Michael. 1970. Soul Music and Blues: Their Meaning and Relevance in Northern United States Ghettos. In *Afro-American Anthropology: Contemporary Perspectives*, ed. Norman E. Whitten and John F. Szwed. New York: Free Press. 367–84.

381 Hatch, David and Millward, Stephen. 1987. *From Blues to Rock: An Analytical History of Pop Music*. Manchester: Manchester University Press.

382 Jahn, Janheinz. 1990. Residual African Elements in the Blues. In *Mother Wit from the Laughing Barrel*, ed. Alan Dundes. Jackson, MS: University Press of Mississippi. 95–103.

383 Johnson, Guy B. 1990. Double Meanings in the Popular Negro Blues. In *Mother Wit from the Laughing Barrel*, ed. Alan Dundes. Jackson, MS: University Press of Mississippi. 258–66.

384 Keren, Zvi. 1980. Variants of the Blues Progression. *Israel Studies in Musicology* 2: 157–69.

385 Lacava, Jacques D. 1992. The Theatricality of the Blues. *Black Music Research Journal* 12(1): 127–39.

386 Lehmann, Theo. 1967. *Blues and Trouble*. Berlin: Henschel.

387 Lomax, Alan. 1934. 'Sinful' Songs of the Southern Negro. *Southwest Review* 19(2): 105–31.

388 Lutz, Tom. 1992. Curing the Blues: W.E.B. Du Bois, Fashionable Diseases and Degraded Music. *Black Music Research Journal* 11(2): 137–56.

389 McCarthy, S. Margaret W. 1976. The Afro-American Sermon and the Blues: Some Parallels. *The Black Perspective in Music* 4(3): 269–77.

390 Miani, Guido. 1992. Gesti melodici del blues. In *Dal blues al liscio: Studi sull'esperinza musicale comune*, ed. Gino Stefani. Verona: Ianua. 11–48.

391 Middleton, Richard. 1972. *Pop Music and the Blues: A Study of the Relationship and Its Significance*. London: Gollancz.

392 Oliver, Paul. 1976. Blue-Eyed Blues: The Impact of Blues on European Popular Culture. In *Approaches to Popular Culture*, ed. C.W.E. Bigsby. London: Edward Arnold.

393 Oliver, Paul. 1982. Blues and the Binary Principle. In *Popular Music Perspectives, 1*, ed. David Horn and Philip Tagg. Göteborg and Exeter: IASPM. 163–73.

394 Oliver, Paul. 1989. (1968) *Screening the Blues: Aspects of the Blues Tradition*. New York: Da Capo Press. First published London: Cassell, 1968.

395 Oliver, Paul. 1990. *Blues Fell This Morning: The Meaning of the Blues*, revised edition. Cambridge: Cambridge University Press. First published London: Cassell, 1960.

396 Prévos, André J.M. 1992. Four Decades of French Blues Research in Chicago: From the Fifties into the Nineties. *Black Music Research Journal* 12(1): 97–112.

397 Smith, Steven G. 1992. Blues and Our Mind-Body Problem. *Popular Music* 11(1): 41–52.

398 Spencer, Jon Michael. 1992. *Sacred Music of the Secular City: From Blues to Rap.* Durham, NC: Duke University Press.

399 Spencer, Jon Michael. 1993. *Blues and Evil.* Knoxville, TN: University of Tennessee Press.

400 Springer, Robert. 1976. The Regulatory Function of the Blues. *The Black Perspective in Music* 4(3): 278–88.

401 Straats, Gregory R. 1979. Sexual Imagery in Blues Music: A Basis for Black Stereotypes. *Journal of Jazz Studies* 5(2): 40–60.

402 Titon, Jeff Todd. 1979. *Early Downhome Blues: A Musical and Cultural Analysis.* Urbana, Chicago and London: University of Illinois Press.

Styles

Barrelhouse and Boogie

403 Blumenfeld, Aaron. 1989. *The Art of Blues and Barrelhouse Piano Improvisation.* San Leandro, CA: P/F Publishing.

404 Borneman, Ernest. 1957. Boogie-Woogie. In *Just Jazz,* ed. Sinclair Traill and Gerald Lascelles. London: Peter Davies. 13–40.

405 Hall, Bob and Noblett, Richard. 1975. A Handful of Keys, Part 4. *Blues Unlimited* 115 (September/October): 20–22.

406 Hall, Bob and Noblett, Richard. 1975. A Handful of Keys, Part 5. *Blues Unlimited* 116 (November/December): 20–21.

407 Hall, Bob and Noblett, Richard. 1976. A Handful of Keys, Part 6. *Blues Unlimited* 117 (January/February): 22–23.

408 Jones, LeRoi (Imamu Amiri Baraka). 1973. Blues & Boogie-Woogie. In *The New Music Lovers' Handbook,* ed. Elie Siegmeister. Irvington-on-Hudson, NY: Harvey House. 469–74.

409 Kriss, Eric. 1974. *Barrelhouse and Boogie Piano.* New York: Oak Publications.

410 Lippmann, Horst, ed. 1993. *Das Barrelhouse-Buch.* Frankfurt: Societäts-Verlag.

411 Logan, Wendell. 1984. The Ostinato Idea in Black Improvised Music. *The Black Perspective in Music* 12(2): 193–215.

412 Newberger, Eli H. 1976. Archetypes and Antecedents of Piano Blues and Boogie-Woogie Style. *Journal of Jazz Studies* 4(1): 84–109.

413 Russell, William. 1959. Three Boogie-Woogie Blues Pianists. In *The Art of Jazz,* ed. Martin Williams. London: Oxford University Press.

414 Russell, William. 1977. (1939) Boogie-Woogie. In *Jazzmen,* ed. Frederic Ramsey and Charles E. Smith. New York: Harcourt, Brace. 183–205.

415 Sylvester, Peter J. 1986. *A Left Hand Like God: A Study of Boogie-Woogie.* London: Quartet.

416 zur Heide, Karl. 1970. *Deep South Piano.* London: Studio Vista.

Classic Blues

417 Bradford, Perry. 1965. *Born with the Blues: The True Story of the Pioneering Blues Singers and Musicians in the Early Days of Jazz.* New York: Oak Publications.

418 Harrison, Daphne Duval. 1988. *Black Pearls: Blues Queens of the 1920s.* New Brunswick, NJ: Rutgers University Press.

419 Stewart-Baxter, Derrick. 1970. *Ma Rainey and the Classic Blues Singers.* London: Studio Vista.

Country Blues

420 Barnie, John. 1978. Formulaic Lines and Stanzas in the Country Blues. *Ethnomusicology* 22(3): 457–74.

421 Charters, Samuel B. 1975. (1959) *The Country Blues*. New York: Da Capo Press. First published London: Michael Joseph, 1959.

422 Leadbitter, Mike. 1968. *Delta Country Blues*. Bexhill-on-Sea: Blues Unlimited.

423 Oster, Harry. 1969. *Living Country Blues*. Detroit, MI: Folklore Associates.

424 Otto, Solomon and Burns, Augustus M. Tough Times: Downhome Blues Recordings as Folk History. *Southern Quarterly* 21(3).

425 Smith, Chris. 1986. Country Blues and Blues Country. *Keskidee: A Journal of Black Musical Traditions* 1: 41–45.

Urban Blues

426 Bas-Rabérin, Philippe. 1973. *Le blues moderne, 1945–1973*. Paris: A. Michel.

427 Keil, Charles. 1966. *Urban Blues*. Chicago: Chicago University Press.

428 Spencer, Jon Michael. 1992. The Diminishing Rural Residue of Folklore in City and Urban Blues, Chicago, 1915–1950. *Black Music Research Journal* 12(1): 25–41.

BOLERO

429 Castillo, Rafael. 1991. *Fenomenología del bolero*. Caracas: Monte Avila Editores.

430 Orovio, Helio. 1995. *El bolero latino*. La Habana: Editorial Letras Cubanas.

431 Pineda, Adela. 1990. La evolución del bolero urbano en Agustín Lara. *Heterofonía* 102–103 (January-December): 4–23.

432 Sinay, Sergio. 1994. *Inolvidable: El libro del bolero y del amor*. Buenos Aires: Espasa Hoy.

BOSSA NOVA

433 Béhague, Gerard. 1973. Bossa & Bossas: Recent Changes in Brazilian Urban Popular Music. *Ethnomusicology* 27(2): 209–33.

434 Campos, Augusto de. 1974. *Balanço da Bossa e outras bossas*, revised edition. Sao Paulo: Editora Perspectiva. First published Sao Paulo: Perspectiva, 1968.

435 Castro, Ruy. 1990. *Chega de Saudade: A História e as Histórias da Bossa Nova*. Sao Paulo: Companhia das Letras.

436 Chediak, Almir, ed. 1991. *Songbook: Bossa Nova*. 5 vols, revised edition. Rio de Janeiro: Lumiar Editora. First published Rio de Janeiro: Lumiar Editora, n.d.

437 Delfino, Jean-Paul. 1988. *Brasil Bossa Nova*. Aix-en-Provence: Edisud.

438 Reily, Suzel-Ana. 1996. Tom Jobim and the Bossa Nova Era. *Popular Music* 15(1): 1–16.

BURLESQUE

439 Allen, Robert C. 1991. *Horrible Prettiness: Burlesque and American Culture*. Chapel Hill, NC: University of North Carolina Press.

440 Corrio, Ann. 1968. *Burlesque*. New York: Grosset and Dunlap.

441 Heywood, Charles. 1966. Negro Minstrelsy and Shakespearean Burlesque. In *Folklore and Society: Essays in Honor of Benjamin A. Botkin*, ed. Bruce Jackson. Hatboro, PA: Folklore Associates. 77–92.

442 Rella, Ettore. 1940. *A History of Burlesque*. San Francisco: Works Projects Administration.

443 Sobel, Bernard. 1931. *Burleycue: An Underground History of Burlesque Days*. New York: Farrer & Rinehart.

444 Sobel, Bernard. 1956. *A Pictorial History of Burlesque*. New York: Bonanza Books.

445 White, Richard Grant. 1869–70. The Age of Burlesque. *The Galaxy* 8: 256–66.

446 Zeidman, Irving. 1967. *The American Burlesque Show*. New York: Hawthorne Books.

CABARET

447 Hippen, Reinhard. 1986. *Das Kabarett-Chanson: Typen, Themen, Temperamente*. Zürich: Rendo.

448 Rösler, Walter. 1980. *Das Chanson im deutschen Kabarett, 1901–1933*. Berlin: Henschel.

449 Tichwinskaya, L. 1995. *Kabare y teatr miniatjur v Rossya 1908–1917*. Moskva: Kultura.

CAJUN

450 Ancelet, Barry Jean. 1984. *The Makers of Cajun Music/Musiciens cadiens et créoles*. Austin, TX: University of Texas Press.

451 Ancelet, Barry Jean. 1988. Zydeco/Zarico: Beans, Blues and Beyond. *Black Music Research Journal* 8(1).

452 Borders, Florence E. 1988. Researching Creole and Cajun Music in New Orleans. *Black Music Research Journal* 8(1): 15–31.

453 Bourque, Darrell. 1989. Plainsongs of the Marais Bouleur. *Journal of Popular Culture* 23(1): 47–64.

454 Broven, John. 1983. *South to Louisiana: The Music of the Cajun Bayous*. Gretna, LA: Pelican Publishing Company.

455 Daigle, Pierre V. 1972. *Tears, Love and Laughter: The Story of the Acadians*. Church Point, LA: Acadian Publishing Enterprise.

456 Doucet, Sharon Arms. 1989. Cajun Music: Songs and Psyche. *Journal of Popular Culture* 23(1): 89–100.

457 Gould, Philip. 1992. *Cajun Music and Zydeco*. Baton Rouge, LA: Louisiana State Press.

458 Kershaw, Doug. 1971. *Lou'siana Man*. New York: Collier Books.

459 Leadbitter, Mike and Shuler, Eddie. 1969. *From the Bayou: The Story of Goldband Records*. Bexhill-on-Sea: Blues Unlimited.

460 Marcel-Dubois, Claudie. 1978. Reflexions sur l'Heritage Musical Français en Louisiane. *Selected Reports in Ethnomusicology* 3(1): 25–75.

461 Savoy, Ann Allen, ed. 1984. *Cajun Music: A Reflection of a People*. Eunice, LA: Bluebird Press.

462 Spitzer, Nicholas R. 1989. Zydeco. In *Encyclopedia of Southern Culture, Vol. 3*, ed. Charles Reagan Wilson and William R. Ferris. New York: Doubleday Anchor. 346–50.

463 Strachwitz, Chris and Welding, Pete, eds. 1970. The World of Cajun Music. In *The American Folk Music Occasional, No. 2*. New York: Oak Publications. 8–29.

CALYPSO

464 Allen, Rose-Mary. 1988. Una panorámica del Calypso en Curazao. *Montalbán* 20: 205–28.

465 Austin, R.L. 1968. Understanding Calypso Content: A Critique and an Alternative Explanation. *Caribbean Quarterly* 22(2 & 3).

466 Brown, Lloyd W. 1971. The Mask That Grins: The Calypso Tradition in the West Indies. *Journal of Popular Culture* 4(3): 683–89.

467 Campbell, Susan. 1989. Carnival, Calypso and Class Struggle in Nineteenth Century Trinidad. *History Workshop* 26: 1–27.

468 Crowley, Daniel J. 1959. Toward a Definition of 'Calypso' (Part I). *Ethnomusicology* 3(2): 57–66.

469 Crowley, Daniel J. 1959. Toward a Definition of 'Calypso' (Part II). *Ethnomusicology* 3(3): 117–25.

470 Devenish, Michael. 1985. Kaiso! *Musical Traditions* 4: 15–19.

471 Elder, J.D. 1968. The Male/Female Conflict in Calypso. *Caribbean Quarterly* 14: 23–41.

472 Hill, Donald. 1993. *Calypso Calaloo: Early Carnival Music in Trinidad.* Gainesville, FL: University Press of Florida.

473 Hill, Errol. 1967. On the Origin of the Term Calypso. *Ethnomusicology* 11(3): 395ff.

474 Liverpool, Hollis. 1987. *Calypsonians to Remember.* Trinidad: Juba Publications.

475 Mahabir, Cynthia. 1996. Wit and Popular Music: The Calypso and the Blues. *Popular Music* 15(1): 55–81.

476 Noblett, Richard. 1985. Golden Age of Calypso. *Musical Traditions* 4: 9–14.

477 Patton, John H. 1994. Calypso as Rhetorical Performance: Trinidad Carnival, 1993. *Latin American Music Review* 15(1): 55–74.

478 Quevedo, Raymond. 1983. *Attila's Kaiso: A Short History of Trinidad Calypso,* ed. Errol Hill. St. Augustine: University of the West Indies.

479 Rohlehr, Gordon. 1990. *Calypso and Society in Pre-Independence Trinidad.* Port of Spain.

480 Schwarz, Alice. 1995. Calypso und Calypsonians. Kontextualisierungs- und Intentionalitätsveränderungen durch den Einfluß der Massenmedien. *PopScriptum* 3: 101–48.

481 Warner, Keith. 1982. *The Trinidad Calypso: A Study of the Calypso as Oral Literature.* London: Arrow.

482 Warner, Keith. 1985. *Kaiso! The Trinidad Calypso: A Study of the Calypso as Oral Literature.* Washington, DC: Three Continents Press.

CANZONE

483 Banfi, Emanuele and Winkler, Daniele. 1996. Riflessi dell' 'italiano in movimento' in un *corpus* di canzoni italiane di area alto-atesina. In *Analisi e canzoni,* ed. Rossana Dalmonte. Trento: Università di Trento. 125–44.

484 Borgna, Gianni. 1991. *Storia della canzone italiana.* Milano: Mondadori.

485 Fabbri, Franco. 1989. The System of Canzone in Italy Today. In *World Music, Politics and Social Change,* ed. Simon Frith. Manchester: Manchester University Press. 122–42.

486 Saffioti, Tito. 1978. *Enciclopedia della canzone popolare e della nuova canzone politica.* Milano: Longanesi.

CHANSONS

487 Baudot, Alain. 1980. *La chanson québécoise, documentation sélective.* Toronto: Glendon College, York University.

488 *Béranger, Servat, Vigneault . . . chansons politiques d'aujourd'hui.* 1976. Paris: Syros.

489 Brécy, Robert. 1991. *Autour de la Muse rouge: groupe de poètes et chansonniers révolutionnaires 1901–1939.* Paris: C. Pirot.

490 Brunschwig, Chantal, Louis-Jean Calvet and Jean-Claude Klein. 1981. *Cent ans de chanson française*. Paris: Editions du Seuil.

491 Charpentreau, Jacques and Vernillat, France. 1968. *Dictionnaire de la chanson française*. Paris: Larousse.

492 *Colloque de recherche sur la chanson française, novembre 1983, Sainte-Baume*. 1984. Montréal: Triptyque.

493 Cormier, Normand, et al. 1975. *La chanson au Québec 1965–1975*. Bibliographies québécoises, no. 3. Montréal: Gouvernement du Québec, Ministère des Affaires Culturelles.

494 Coulonges, Georges. 1969. *La chanson en son temps: de Béranger au juke box*. Paris: Editeurs français réunis.

495 Fléouter, Claude. 1988. *Un siècle de chansons*. Paris: PUF.

496 Gagné, Marc and Poulin, Monique. 1985. *Chantons la chanson*. Québec: Les presses de l'Université Laval.

497 Gauthier, Marie-Véronique. 1992. *Chanson, sociabilité et grivoiserie au XIXe siècle*. Paris: Aubier.

498 Giroux, Robert, ed. 1993. *En avant la chanson*. Montréal: Triptyque.

499 Giroux, Robert and La Rochelle, Réal. 1987. *La Chanson dans tous ses états*. Montréal: Triptyque.

500 Kernel, Brigitte, ed. 1987. *Chanter made in France*. Paris: M. de Maule.

501 Klein, Jean-Claude. 1990. *Florilège de la chanson française*. Paris: Bordas.

502 Klein, Jean-Claude. 1991. *La Chanson à l'affiche: Histoire de la chanson française du café-concert à nos jours*. Paris: Du May.

503 Laforte, Conrad. 1995. *La chanson de tradition orale: Une découverte des écrivains du XIXe siècle, en France et au Québec*. Montréal: Triptyque.

504 Lamothe, Maurice. 1994. *La chanson populaire ontaroise 1970–1990: ses produits, sa pratique*. Montréal/Ottawa: Triptyque/Le Nordir, Université d'Ottawa.

505 Neef, Wilhelm. 1972. *Das Chanson*. Leipzig: Koehler u. Amelang.

506 Poupart, René. 1988. *Aspects de la chanson poétique: Des lectures de Georges Brassens, Guy Béart, Claude Nougaro, Jacques Brel et François Béranger*. Paris: Didier-Erudition.

507 Rieger, Dietmar, ed. 1990. *La Chanson en France (Das Chanson in Frankreich)*. Marburg: Hitzeroth.

508 Rioux, Lucien. 1994. *Cinquante ans de chansons françaises*, nouvelle édition augmentée. Paris: Archipel.

509 Rösler, Walter. 1980. *Das Chanson im deutschen Kabarett 1901–1933*. Berlin: Henschel.

510 Roy, Bruno. 1977. *Panorama de la chanson au Québec*. Ottawa: Leméac.

511 Saka, Pierre. 1988. *La chanson française à travers ses succès*. Paris: Larousse.

512 Saka, Pierre. 1989. *Histoire de la chanson française*. Paris: Nathan.

513 Salachas, Gilbert and Bottet, Béatrice. 1989. *Le guide de la chanson*. Paris: Syros-Alternatives.

514 Schmidt, Felix. 1987. *Das Chanson. Herkunft, Entwicklung, Interpretation*. Frankfurt am Main: Fischer.

515 Schulz-Köhn, Dietrich. 1969. *Vive la chanson. Kunst zwischen Show und Poesie*. Gütersloh: Bertelsmann.

516 Sevran, Pascal. 1988. *Le dictionnaire de la chanson française*. Paris: M. Lafon.

517 Vassal, Jacques. 1980. *La Chanson bretonne*. Paris: Albin Michel.

518 Vernillat, France and Charpentreau, Jacques, eds. 1968. *Dictionnaire de la chanson française*. Paris: Larousse.

519 Vernillat, France and Charpentreau, Jacques. 1983. (1977) *La Chanson française*, 3e édition. Paris: PUF.

CHILDREN'S MUSIC

520 Foley, Martha. 1941. Mother Goose – The Inside Story! Nursery Rhymes Haven't Always Been So Innocent. *New York Herald Tribune Magazine* 17.

521 Griese, Christof. 1994. Jazzimprovisation für Kinder oder Wie der Horizontdiatonisch erweitert werden kann. In *Populäre Musik und Pädagogik – Grundlagen und Praxismaterialien*, ed. Jürgen Terhag. Oldershausen: Institut für Didaktik der populären Musik. 100–106.

522 Jones, Bessie and Hawes, Bessie Lomax. 1972. *Step It Down: Games, Plays, Songs and Stories from the Afro-American Heritage*. New York: Harper & Row.

523 Opie, Iona and Opie, Peter. 1985. *The Singing Game*. Oxford: Oxford University Press.

524 Petersham, Maud and Petersham, Mishka. 1945. *The Rooster Crows: A Book of American Rhymes and Jingles*. New York: Macmillan.

525 Reimers, Lennart. 1979. Den svenska barnvisan. In *Skriftfest: 19 uppsatser tillägnade Martin Tegen – 60 år*. Stockholm: Institutionen för musikvetnskap. 150–60.

526 Reimers, Lennart. 1983. *Alice Tegnérs barnvisor*. Göteborg: Skrifter från Musikvetenskapliga institutionen, 8.

527 Reimers, Lennart. 1985. Vom Musikalisch-Kindlichen: Fünf Versuche zur kurzen Musik. In *Analytica: Studies in the Description and Analysis of Music*. Stockholm: Kungliga Musikaliska Akademien. 47–56.

528 Roe, Keith and Felitzen, Cecilia von. 1990. Children and Music: An Exploratory Study. In *Popular Music Research*, ed. Keith Roe and Ulla Karlsson. Göteborg: NORDICOM-Sweden, No. 1–2. 53–70.

529 Schecter, John. 1983. Corona y Baile: Music in the Child's Wake of Ecuador and Hispanic South America, Past and Present. *Latin American Music Review* 4(1): 1–80.

530 Schmidt, Jochen. 1994. Techno mit Kindern?! In *Populäre Musik und Pädagogik – Grundlagen und Praxismaterialien*, ed. Jürgen Terhag. Oldershausen: Institut für Didaktik der populären Musik. 107–16.

531 Steffen-Wittek, Marianne. 1994. Zu Gast beim Vampir! Musik zwischen Kinderzimmer, Spielplatz und Fernseher. In *Populäre Musik und Pädagogik – Grundlagen und Praxismaterialien*, ed. Jürgen Terhag. Oldershausen: Institut für Didaktik der populären Musik. 63–80.

532 Wedel-Wolff, Annegret. 1982. *Geschichte der Sammlung und Erforschung des deutschsprachigen Volkskinderliedes und Volkskinderreimes im 19. Jahrhundert*. Göppingen: Kümmerle.

533 Wolford, Leah Jackson. 1976. *The Play-Party in Indiana*. New York: Arno Press.

CLASSICAL MUSIC

534 Brown, Robert L. 1976. Classical Influences on Jazz. *Journal of Jazz Studies* 3: 19–35.

535 Cuker, A. 1993. *Y rok, y synfonya*. Moskva: Kompositor.

536 Duxbury, Janell R. 1992. *Rockin' the Classics and Classicizin' the Rock: A Selectively Annotated Discography*. Westport, CT: Greenwood Press.

537 Gerzon, Michael. 1987. The Electronic Music Tradition: Influences from

Classical on Popular Music. *Re Records Quarterly* 2(1): 17–21.

538 Jaffa, Max. 1991. *A Life on the Fiddle.* London: Hodder & Stoughton.

539 Lipperini, L. 1990. *Mozart in Rock.* Firenze: Sansoni.

540 Pleasants, Henry. 1962. *Death of a Music? The Decline of the European Tradition and the Rise of Jazz.* London: Jazz Book Club/ Gollancz.

541 Pleasants, Henry. 1969. *Serious Music and All That Jazz: An Adventure in Music Criticism.* London: Gollancz.

542 Prato, Paolo. 1985. Musical Kitsch: Close Encounters Between Pops and Classics. In *Popular Music Perspectives, 2,* ed. David Horn. Göteborg and Exeter: IASPM. 375–86.

543 Wicke, Peter. 1981. Strawinsky und der Jazz. *Musik und Gesellschaft* XXXII(6): 343–49.

COLLEGE SONGS

544 *Carmina Collegensia: A Complete Collection of the Songs of the American Colleges, with Selections from the Student Songs of the English and German Universities.* 1876. Boston, MA: O. Ditson.

545 Guth, William. 1916. *College Hymns and Songs.* New York: The Century Company.

546 Hagen, John. 1931. *Western College Songs: Music Songs of the Universities and Colleges of the Far West.* San Francisco: Sherman.

547 O'Brien, Robert. 1991. *School Songs of America's Colleges and Universities: A Directory.* New York: Greenwood Press.

548 Stevens, Charles. 1871. *College Song Book: A Collection of American College Songs.* New York: S.T. Gordon & Son.

CONTEMPORARY CHRISTIAN MUSIC

549 Baker, Paul. 1985. *Contemporary Christian Music: Where It Came From, What It Is, Where It's Going,* revised edition. Westchester, IL: Crossway Books. First published Waco: Word Books, 1979.

550 Baker, Paul. 1991. *Paul Baker's Topical Index of Contemporary Christian Music.* Cincinnati: Standard Publishing.

551 Best, Harold. 1993. The World of Christian Popular Music. In *Music Through the Eyes of Faith.* San Francisco: HarperCollins. Chapter 8.

552 Crouch, Andre. 1974. *Through It All.* Waco, TX: Word Books.

553 Cusic, Don. 1990. *The Sound of Light: A History of Gospel Music.* Bowling Green, OH: Bowling Green University Popular Press.

554 Darden, Bob. 1994. Contemporary Christian Music. *Billboard* 106(18): 35–47.

555 Hefner, April. 1996. Don't Know Much About History. *Contemporary Christian Music* 18(10): 38–42.

556 Howard, Jay R. and Streck, John M. 1996. The Splintered Art World of Contemporary Christian Music. *Popular Music* 15(1): 37–54.

557 Hustad, Donald. 1993. Worship/Music Revolution in the Late 20th Century. In *Jubilate: Church Music in Worship and Renewal,* revised edition. Carol Stream, IL: Hope Publishing Company. Chapter 11. First published Carol Stream: Hope Publishing Company, 1981.

558 Miller, Steve. 1993. *The Contemporary Christian Music Debate.* Wheaton, IL: Tyndale House Publisher.

GENRES

559 Petrie, Phil. 1996. The History of Gospel Music. *Contemporary Christian Music* 18(8): 46–49.

560 Price, Deborah. 1995. Contemporary Christian: It's Not Just for Sundays Anymore. *Billboard* 107(17): 33–38.

561 Price, Milburn. 1993. The Impact of Popular Culture on Congregational Song. *The Hymn: A Journal of Congregational Song* 44(1): 11–19.

562 Rabey, Steve. 1991. Maranatha! Music Comes of Age. *Christianity Today* 35(5): 44–47.

563 *Rejoice: The Gospel Music Magazine.* 1987–94. Jackson, MS: Center for Study of Southern Culture, University of Mississippi.

564 Styll, John, ed. 1991. *The Best of CCM Interviews.* Nashville, TN: Star Song.

565 Webber, Robert, ed. 1993/4. *The Complete Book of Christian Worship*, Vol. III, IV (Books 1, 2). Nashville, TN: Star Song Publishing Group.

CORRIDOS

566 Herrera-Sobek, María. 1992. *The Mexican Corrido: A Feminist Analysis.* Bloomington, IN: Indiana University Press.

567 Leal, Luis. 1987. México y Aztlán: El corrido. *Aztlán: International Journal of Chicano Studies Research* 18(2): 15–26.

568 Limón, José. 1983. The Rise, Fall and 'Revival' of the Mexican-American Corrido: A Review Essay. *Studies in Latin American Popular Culture* 2: 202–207.

569 McNeil, B. 1946. Corridos of the Mexican Border. In *Mexican Border Ballads and Other Lore*, ed. Mody C. Boatwright. Austin, TX: Texas Folklore Society.

570 Mendoza, Vicente. 1974. *El corrido mexicano.* Mexico: Fondo de Cultura Económica.

COUNTRY

General Works

571 Gaillard, Frye. 1978. *Watermelon Wine: The Spirit of Country Music.* New York: St. Martin's Press.

572 Kingsbury, Paul, and Axelrod, Alan, eds. 1988. *Country: The Music and the Musicians.* New York: Abbeville Press.

573 Malone, Bill C. and McCulloch, Judith. 1975. *Stars of Country Music: Uncle Dave Macon to Johnny Rodriguez.* Urbana, IL: University of Illinois Press.

574 Mason, Michael, ed. 1985. *The Country Music Book.* New York: Scribners.

575 Morthland, John. 1984. *The Best of Country Music.* New York: Doubleday.

576 Nash, Alanna. 1988. *Behind Closed Doors: Talking with the Legends of Country Music.* New York: Alfred A. Knopf.

577 Oermann, Robert K. 1983. *The Listener's Guide to Country Music.* Poole: Blandford Press.

578 Tosches, Nick. 1977. *Country: The Biggest Music in America.* New York: Stein and Day.

579 Tosches, Nick. 1985. *Country: Living Legends and Dying Metaphors in America's Biggest Music.* New York: Scribners.

Reference

580 Butterfield, Arthur. 1985. *Encyclopedia of Country Music.* London: Multimedia.

581 Dellar, Fred and Lackett, Alan. 1987. *The Illustrated Encyclopedia of Country Music*, revised edition. London: Salamander Books. First published New York: Harmony Books, 1977.

26

582 Dellar, Fred and Wootton, Richard. 1984. *The Country Music Book of Lists.* London: Thames & Hudson.

583 Jeier, Thomas. 1987. *Lexikon der Country Music.* München: Heyne.

584 Lornell, Kip, comp. 1989. *Virginia's Blues, Country and Gospel Records, 1902–1943: An Annotated Discography.* Lexington, KY: University Press of Kentucky.

585 Moore, Thurston, ed. 1960. *Country Music Who's Who.* Cincinnati: Cardinal Enterprises.

586 Osborne, Jerry. 1976. *Fifty-Five Years of Recorded Country/Western Music.* Phoenix, AZ: O'Sullivan Woodside.

587 Rasaf, Henry. 1985. (1982) *The Folk, Country and Bluegrass Musician's Catalogue.* London: Pluto Press. First published New York: Seaview, 1982.

588 Rose, Michel. 1986. *Encyclopédie de la country et du rockabilly.* Paris: Grancher.

589 Shestack, Melvin. 1993. (1974) *The New Country Music Encyclopedia.* New York: Simon & Schuster. First published New York: Crowell, 1974.

590 Smyth, Willie, comp. 1984. *Country Music Recorded Prior to 1943: A Discography of LP Reissues.* Los Angeles: John Edwards Memorial Foundation.

591 Stambler, Irwin and Landon, Grelun. 1983. (1969) *Encyclopedia of Folk, Country and Western Music.* New York: St. Martin's Press. First published London: St. James Press, 1969.

History

592 Brown, Charles T. 1986. *Music U.S.A.: America's Country & Western Tradition.* Englewood Cliffs, NJ: Prentice-Hall.

593 Bufwack, Mary A. and Oermann, Robert K. 1993. *Finding Her Voice: The Saga of Women in Country Music.* New York: Crown.

594 Carr, Patrick. 1980. *The Illustrated History of Country Music.* Garden City, NY: Doubleday/Dolphin.

595 Cohen, John. 1967. (1963) The Folk Music Interchange: Negro and White. In *The American Folk Scene: Dimensions of the Folk Song Revival,* ed. David De Turk and A. Poulin. New York: Dell Publishing. 59–66.

596 Coltman, Bob. 1976–77. Across the Chasm: How the Depression Changed Country Music. *Old Time Music* 23 (Winter): 6–12.

597 Cornfield, Robert. 1976. *Just Country: Country People, Stories, Music.* New York: McGraw-Hill.

598 Dew, Joan. 1977. *Singers and Sweethearts: The Women of Country Music.* Garden City, NY: Doubleday.

599 Green, Douglas B. 1976. *Country Roots: The Origins of Country Music.* New York: Hawthorne Books.

600 Malone, Bill C. 1985. (1968) *Country Music USA: A Fifty Year History,* revised edition. Austin and London: University of Texas Press.

601 Malone, Bill C. 1993. *Singing Cowboys and Musical Mountaineers: Southern Culture and the Roots of Country Music.* Athens, GA: University of Georgia Press.

602 Morton, David and Wolfe, Charles K. 1991. *De Ford Bailey: A Black Star in Early Country Music.* Knoxville, TN: University of Tennessee Press.

603 Price, Stephen D. 1974. *Take Me Home: The Rise of Country and Western Music.* New York: Praeger.

604 Shelton, Robert. 1966. *The Country Music Story: A Picture History of Country and Western Music.* New Rochelle, NY: Arlington House.

GENRES

605 Simone, Mariano de. 1985. *Country Music: musica popolare e società nella storia degli Stati Uniti d'American dell tradizione inglese a Nashville*. Rome: Datanews.

606 Stockwell, Richard P. 1983. The Evolution of Country Radio Format. *Journal of Popular Culture* 16(4): 144–51.

607 Webber, Malcolm. 1941. *Medicine Show*. Caldwell, ID: Caxton Printers.

608 Willett, Ralph. 1985. Country Music: How a Popular Form Became 'Real Popular'. In *Popular Music Perspectives, 2*, ed. David Horn. Göteborg and Exeter: IASPM. 367–74.

609 Wolfe, Charles K. 1973. Nashville and Country Music, 1925–1930: Notes on Early Nashville Media and Its Response to Old-Time Music. *Journal of Country Music* 4: 2–16.

Regional Studies

610 Crump, George D. 1985. *Write It Down: A History of Country Music in Hampton Roads*. Norfolk, VA: Donning.

611 Endres, Clifford. 1987. *Austin City Limits: The Story Behind Television's Most Popular Country Music Program*. Austin, TX: University of Texas Press.

612 Escott, Colin. 1986. *The Sun Country Years: Country Music in Memphis, 1950–1959*. Bremen: Bear Family Records.

613 Reid, Jan. 1974. *The Improbable Rise of Redneck Rock*. Austin, TX: Heidelburg Publications.

614 Tribe, Ivan M. 1984. *Mountaineer Jamboree: Country Music in West Virginia*. Lexington, KY: University Press of Kentucky.

615 Watson, Eric. 1982. (1975) *Country Music in Australia, Vol. 1*. Australia: Angus & Robertson Publishers.

616 Watson, Eric. 1983. *Country Music in Australia, Vol. 2*. Australia: Cornstalk Publishing.

617 Watson, Eric. 1987. Country Music: The Voice of Rural Australia. In *Missing in Action: Australian Popular Music*, ed. Marcus Breen. Melbourne: Verbal Graphics Pty. 47–77.

618 Wolfe, Charles K. 1977. *Tennessee Strings: The Story of Country Music in Tennessee*. Knoxville, TN: University of Tennessee Press.

619 Wolfe, Charles K. 1982. *Kentucky Country: Folk and Country Music of Kentucky*. Lexington, KY: University Press of Kentucky.

Grand Ole Opry

620 Flippo, Chet. 1981. Hank Williams Hits the Opry: 1949. *Journal of Country Music* VIII(3): 5–17.

621 Hagan, Chet. 1989. *Grand Ole' Opry*. New York: Henry Holt & Co.

622 Hurst, Jack. 1975. *Nashville's Grand Ole Opry*. New York: Abrams.

623 Keillor, Garrison. 1974. Onward and Upward with the Arts at the Opry. *The New Yorker* 50(11) (6 May): 46–70.

624 Morton, David and Wolfe, Charles K. 1991. *De Ford Bailey: A Black Star in Early Country Music*. Knoxville, TN: University of Tennessee Press.

625 Peterson, Richard A. and DiMaggio, Paul. 1974. The Early Opry: Its Hillbilly Image in Fact and Fancy. *Journal of Country Music* 4 (Summer): 38–51.

626 Tassin, Myron. 1975. *Fifty Years at the Grand Ole Opry*. Gretna, LA: Pelican Publishing.

627 Wolfe, Charles K. 1975. *The Grand Ole Opry: The Early Years, 1925–35*. London: Old Time Music, Booklet 1.

Analysis and Interpretation

628 Cobb, James C. 1982. From Muskogee to Luckenbach: Country Music and the Southernization of America. *Journal of Popular Culture* 16(3): 81–90.

629 DiMaggio, Paul, et al. 1972. Country Music: Ballad of the Silent Majority. In *The Sounds of Social Change: Studies in Popular Culture*, ed. R. Serge Denisoff and Richard A. Peterson. Chicago: Rand McNally & Co. 38–55.

630 Emblidge, David. 1976. Down Home with the Band: Country-Western Music and Rock. *Ethnomusicology* 20(3): 541–52.

631 Fenster, Mark. 1988. Country Music Video. *Popular Music* 7(3): 285–302.

632 Fox, Aaron A. 1992. The Jukebox of History: Narratives of Loss and Desire in the Discourse of Country Music. *Popular Music* 11(1): 53–72.

633 Gritzner, Charles F. 1978. Country Music: A Reflection of Popular Culture. *Journal of Popular Culture* 11(4): 857–64.

634 Kingsbury, Paul. 1992. Women in Country: A Special Report. *Journal of Country Music* 15(1): 12–35.

635 Lewis, George H. 1991. Duellin' Values: Tension, Conflict and Contradiction in Country Music. *Journal of Popular Culture* 24(3): 103–18.

636 Lund, Jens. 1972. Fundamentalism, Racism and Political Reaction in Country Music. In *The Sounds of Social Change: Studies in Popular Culture*, ed. R. Serge Denisoff and Richard A. Peterson. Chicago: Rand McNally & Co. 79–91.

637 Peterson, Richard A. 1975. *Single-Industry Firm to Conglomerate Synergistics: Alternative Strategies for Selling Insurance and Country Music*. Los Angeles: John Edwards Memorial Foundation. Originally published in *Growing Metropolis: Aspects of Development in Nashville*, ed. J. Blumenstein and B. Walter. Nashville: Vanderbilt University Press, 1975: 341–57.

638 Peterson, Richard A. and McLaurin, Melton A., eds. 1992. *You Wrote My Life: Lyrical Themes in Country Music (Cultural Perspectives on the American South, Vol. 6)*. Philadelphia: Gordon and Breach.

639 Saucier, Karen A. 1986. Healers and Heartbreakers: Images of Women and Men in Country Music. *Journal of Popular Culture* 20(3): 147–66.

640 Wacholtz, Larry E. 1986. *Inside Country Music*. New York: Billboard Publications.

641 Whidden, Lynn. 1985. How Can You Dance to Beethoven? Native People and Country Music. *Canadian University Music Review* 1984/5: 87–103.

642 Wilgus, D.K. 1970. Country-Western Music and the Urban Hillbilly. *Journal of American Folklore* 83(328): 157–79.

643 Wilson, Pamela. 1995. Mountains of Contradiction: Gender, Class and Region in the Star Image of Dolly Parton. *South Atlantic Quarterly* 94(1) (Winter): 109–34.

Styles

Bluegrass

644 Adler, Thomas A. 1974. Manual Formulaic Composition: Innovation in Bluegrass Banjo Styles. *Journal of Country Music* 5: 55–64.

645 Adler, Thomas A. 1982. The Uses of Humor by Bluegrass Musicians. *Mid-America Folklore* 10(2) (Fall-Winter): 17–26.

646 Adler, Thomas A. 1985. Dueling Banjos: Overt and Covert Competition in Amateur Bluegrass Performance. *JEMF Quarterly* 21: 9–16.

647 Adler, Thomas A. 1988. Bluegrass Music and Meal-Fried Potatoes: Food, Festival,

Community. In *'We Gather Together':
Food and Festival in American Life,* ed.
Theodore C. Humphrey and Lin T.
Humphrey. Ann Arbor, MI: UMI
Research Press. 195–204.

648 Artis, Bob. 1975. *Bluegrass.* New York:
Hawthorne Books.

649 Bartenstein, Fred. 1973. The Audience
for Bluegrass: *Muleskinner News* Reader
Survey. *Journal of Country Music* 4: 74–
105.

650 Bealle, John. 1993. Self Involvement in
Musical Performance: Stage Talk and
Interpretive Control at a Bluegrass
Festival. *Ethnomusicology* 37: 63–86.

651 Cantwell, Robert. 1984. *Bluegrass
Breakdown: The Making of the Old
Southern Sound.* Urbana, IL: University of
Illinois Press.

652 Carney, George O. 1974. Bluegrass
Grows All Around: The Spatial
Dimensions of a Country Music Style.
Journal of Geography 73: 34–55.

653 Clarkson, Atelia and Montell, W.
Lynwood. 1975. Letters to a Bluegrass
DJ: Social Documents of Southern White
Migrants in Southeastern Michigan,
1964–1974. *Southern Folklore Quarterly*
39: 219–32.

654 Ellis, Bill. 1994. Reinventing the Anglo-
American Ballad: Dave Evan's
Performance Style. *Southern Folklore* 51:
219–40.

655 Fenster, Mark. 1995. Alison Krauss and
the Contemporary-Traditional Conflict in
Modern Bluegrass. In *All That Glitters:
Country Music in America,* ed. George H.
Lewis. Bowling Green, OH: Bowling
Green University Popular Press. 317–28.

656 Fenster, Mark. 1995. Commercial (and/
or?) Folk: The Bluegrass Industry and
Bluegrass Traditions. *South Atlantic
Quarterly* 94(1) (Winter): 81–108.

657 Hale, Antony. 1983. Grassroots Bluegrass
in Memphis: The Lucy Opry. *Tennessee
Folklore Society Bulletin* 49: 51–64.

658 Hambly, Scott. 1980. San Francisco Bay
Area Bluegrass and Bluegrass Musicians:
A Study in Regional Characteristics.
JEMF Quarterly 16 (Fall): 110–20.

659 Helt, Richard C. 1977. A German
Bluegrass Festival: The 'Country-Boom'
and Some Notes on the History of
American Popular Music in West
Germany. *Journal of Popular Culture*
10(4): 821–32.

660 Hill, Fred. 1980. *Grass Roots: Illustrated
History of Bluegrass and Mountain Music.*
Rutland, VT: Academy Books.

661 Kisliuk, Michelle. 1988. 'A Special Kind
of Courtesy': Action at a Bluegrass
Festival Jam Session. *The Drama Review*
32(2) (Fall): 141–55.

662 Koon, William. 1974. Newgrass,
Oldgrass and Bluegrass. *JEMF Quarterly*
10 (Spring): 15–18.

663 Lightfoot, William E. 1983. Playing
Outside: Spectrum. *Appalachian Journal*
10: 194–98.

664 Malone, Bill C. 1985. From Bluegrass to
Newgrass. *Journal of Country Music* 10:
2–19.

665 Marshall, Howard Wight. 1974. *Keep on
the Sunny Side of Life: Pattern and Religious
Expression in Bluegrass Gospel Music.* Los
Angeles: John Edwards Memorial
Foundation. (First published in *New
York Folklore Quarterly* 30(1) (1974): 3–
43.)

666 Nusbaum, Philip. 1993. Bluegrass and
the Folk Revival: Structural Similarities
and Experienced Differences. In
*Transforming Tradition: Folk Music
Revivals Examined,* ed. Neil V. Rosenberg.
Urbana, IL: University of Illinois Press.
203–19.

667 Price, Stephen D. 1975. *Old as the Hills: The Story of Bluegrass Music*. New York: Viking.

668 Rasaf, Henry. 1985. (1982) *The Folk, Country and Bluegrass Musician's Catalogue*. London: Pluto Press. First published New York: Seaview, 1982.

669 Rosenberg, Neil V. 1967. *From Sound to Style: The Emergence of Bluegrass*. Los Angeles: John Edwards Memorial Foundation. (First published in *Journal of American Folklore* 80(316) (1967): 143–50.)

670 Rosenberg, Neil V. 1974. *Bill Monroe and His Blue Grass Boys: An Illustrated Discography*. Nashville, TN: Country Music Foundation.

671 Rosenberg, Neil V. 1983. Image and Stereotype: Bluegrass Sound Tracks. *American Music* 1 (Fall): 1–22.

672 Rosenberg, Neil V. 1985. *Bluegrass: A History*. Urbana, IL: University of Illinois Press.

673 Rosenberg, Neil V. 1991. Bluegrass Scholarship: A Survey. *Bluegrass Unlimited* (September): 39–40.

674 Rosenberg, Neil V. 1992. From the Sound Recordings Review Editor: Bluegrass Today. *Journal of American Folklore* 105: 459–70.

675 Rosenberg, Neil V. 1993. Starvation, Serendipity and the Ambivalence of Bluegrass Revivalism. In *Transforming Tradition: Folk Music Revivals Examined*, ed. Neil V. Rosenberg. Urbana, IL: University of Illinois Press. 194–202.

676 Rumble, John. 1975. Cultural Dimensions of the Bluegrass Boom, 1970–1975. *Journal of Country Music* 6(3) (Fall): 109–21.

677 Scruggs, Earl. 1984. *The Big Book of Bluegrass*. New York: Morrow.

678 Smith, Mayne. 1965. An Introduction to Bluegrass. *Journal of American Folklore* 78: 245–56.

679 Tunnell, Kenneth D. 1992. 99 Years Is Almost for Life: Punishment for Violent Crime in Bluegrass Music. *Journal of Popular Culture* 26(3): 165–83.

680 Wright, John. 1993. *Traveling the High Way Home: Ralph Stanley and the World of Traditional Bluegrass Music*. Urbana, IL: University of Illinois Press.

Countrypolitan

681 Corbin, Everett J. 1980. *Storm Over Nashville: A Case Against Modern Country Music*. Nashville, TN: Ashlar Press.

682 Grissim, John. 1970. *Country Music: White Man's Blues*. New York: Coronet Communications.

683 Hemphill, Paul. 1971. *The Nashville Sound: Bright Lights and Country Music*. New York: Simon & Schuster.

Hillbilly

684 Abbott, Lynn and Seroff, Doug. 1993. America's Blue Yodel. *Musical Traditions* 11: 2–11.

685 *Commercially Disseminated Folk Music: Sources and Resources (A Symposium)*. 1971. Los Angeles: John Edwards Memorial Foundation. (First published in *Western Folklore* 30(3) (1971): 171–246.)

686 *Gennett Records of Old Time Tunes: A Catalog Reprint*. 1975. Los Angeles: John Edwards Memorial Foundation.

687 Ginell, Cary, comp. 1989. *The Decca Hillbilly Discography, 1927–1945*. New York: Greenwood Press.

688 Green, Archie. 1965. *Hillbilly Music: Source and Symbol*. Los Angeles: John Edwards Memorial Foundation.

689 Greenway, John and Wilgus, D.K., eds. 1965. *Journal of American Folklore (Hillbilly Issue)* 78(309) (July-September).

690 Jones, Louis M. 'Grandpa' and Wolfe, Charles K. 1984. *Everybody's Grandpa: Fifty Years Behind the Mike.* Knoxville, TN: University of Tennessee Press.

691 Kahn, E. 1966. (1965) *Hillbilly Music: Source and Resource.* Los Angeles: John Edwards Memorial Foundation. (First published in *Journal of American Folklore* 78 (1965): 256–66.)

692 Kearns, William. 1974. From Black to White: A Hillbilly Version of Gussie Davis's 'The Fatal Wedding'. *The Black Perspective in Music* 1(3): 29–36.

693 McCulloch, Judith. 1967. (1966) *Some Child Ballads on Hillbilly Records.* Los Angeles: John Edwards Memorial Foundation. First published in *Folklore and Society: Essays in Honor of Benjamin A. Botkin,* ed. Bruce Jackson. Hatboro: Folklore Associates, 1966: 107–29.

694 McCulloch, Judith. 1968. (1967) *Hillbilly Records and Tune Transcriptions.* Los Angeles: John Edwards Memorial Foundation. (First published in *Western Folklore* 26 (1967): 225–44.)

695 Russell, Tony. 1970. *Blacks, Whites and Blues.* London: Studio Vista.

696 Smith, Graeme. 1994. Australian Country Music and the Hillbilly Yodel. *Popular Music* 13(3): 297–311.

697 Wilgus, D.K. 1968. The Hillbilly Movement. In *American Folklore,* ed. Tristram P. Coffin. Washington, DC: Voice of America Forum Lectures. 295–304.

698 Wilgus, D.K. 1970. *Country-Western Music and the Urban Hillbilly.* Los Angeles: John Edwards Memorial Foundation. (First published in *Journal of American Folklore* (April-June 1970): 157–79.)

699 Wolfe, Charles K. 1993. The White Man's Blues, 1922–40. *Journal of Country Music* 15(3): 38–44.

Honky Tonk

700 Blaser, Kent. 1985. 'Pictures from Life's Other Side': Hank Williams, Country Music and Popular Culture in America. *South Atlantic Quarterly* 84(1) (Winter): 12–26.

701 Claypool, Bob. 1980. *Saturday Night at Gilley's.* New York: Grove Press.

702 Cohen, Scott. 1975. Webb. *Country Music* 3(5): 34–37.

703 Fenster, Mark. 1990. Buck Owens, Country Music and the Struggle for Discursive Control. *Popular Music* 9(3) (October): 275–90.

704 Fox, Aaron A. 1993. Split Subjectivity in Country Music and Honky-Tonk Discourse. In *All That Glitters: Country Music in America,* ed. George H. Lewis. Bowling Green, OH: Bowling Green State University Press. 131–39.

705 Haggard, Merle and Russell, Peggy. 1981. *Merle Haggard: Sing Me Back Home.* New York: Simon & Schuster.

706 Jensen, Joli. 1993. Honky-Tonking: Mass Mediated Culture Made Personal. In *All That Glitters: Country Music in America,* ed. George H. Lewis. Bowling Green, OH: Bowling Green State University Press. 118–30.

707 Leppert, Richard and Lipsitz, George. 1990. 'Everybody's Lonesome for Somebody': Age, the Body and Experience in the Music of Hank Williams. *Popular Music* 9(3) (October): 259–74.

708 Malone, Bill C. 1982. Honky Tonk: The Music of the Southern Working Class. In *Folk Music and Modern Sound,* ed. William R. Ferris and Mary L. Hart. Jackson, MS: University Press of Mississippi. 119–28.

709 Neuenfeldt, Karl. 1993. Alienation and Single Musicians on the Honky-Tonk Circuit. In *All That Glitters: Country Music in America*, ed. George H. Lewis. Bowling Green, OH: Bowling Green State University Press. 140–48.

710 Oermann, Robert K. 1994. Honky-Tonk Angels: Kitty Wells and Patsy Cline. In *Country: The Music and the Musicians*, ed. Paul Kingsbury. New York: Abbeville Press. 212–33.

711 Otto, John S. and Burns, Augustus M. 1989. Roadhouses. In *Encyclopedia of Southern Culture, Vol. 3*, ed. Charles Reagan Wilson and William R. Ferris. New York: Doubleday Anchor. 681–83.

712 Pugh, Ronnie. 1978. Ernest Tubb's Performing Career: Broadcast, Stage and Screen. *Journal of Country Music* 7(3): 67–93.

713 Rodgers, Jimmie N. 1983. *The Country Music Message: All About Lovin' and Livin'*. Englewood Cliffs, NJ: Prentice-Hall.

714 Rodgers, Jimmie N. 1989. *The Country Music Message, Revisited*. Fayetteville, AR: University of Arkansas Press.

715 Tosches, Nick. 1994. Honky Tonkin': Ernest Tubb, Hank Williams and the Bartender's Muse. In *Country: The Music and the Musicians*, ed. Paul Kingsbury. New York: Abbeville Press. 152–75.

716 Wolfe, Charles K. 1986. Honky-Tonk Starts Here: The Jim Back Dallas Studio. *Journal of Country Music* XI(1): 25–30.

New Country

717 Gill, Andy. 1986. Kicking the Horseshit Out of Nashville. *New Musical Express* 6 (September): 28–29.

718 Guterman, Jimmy. 1987. What Happened to the New Country Rock. *Journal of Country Music* XI(3): 6–11.

719 The Old Sound of New Country (Special JCM Report). 1986. *Journal of Country Music* XI(1): 2–24.

720 Vaughan, Andrew. 1990. (1989) *Who's Who in New Country Music*. New York: St. Martin's Press. First published London: Omnibus, 1989.

Progressive Country (Outlaw)

721 Bane, Michael. 1978. *The Outlaws: Revolution in Country Music*. New York: Country Music Magazine Press, Doubleday.

722 Cooper, Daniel. 1992. Johnny Paycheck: Up From Low Places. *Journal of Country Music* 15(1): 36–47.

723 Corbin, Everett J. 1980. *Storm Over Nashville: A Case Against Modern Country Music*. Nashville, TN: Ashlar Press.

724 Grissim, John. 1970. *Country Music: White Man's Blues*. New York: Coronet Communications.

725 Guralnick, Peter. 1982. *Lost Highway: Journeys and Arrivals of American Musicians*. New York: Vintage.

726 Tucker, Stephen R. 1984. Progressive Country Music, 1972–76: Its Impact and Creative Highlights. *Southwestern Quarterly* 2(3): 93–110.

Western Swing

727 Carney, George O. 1982. The Southwest in American Country Music: Regional Innovators and Stylistic Contributions. In *Southwest Cultural Heritage Festival 1981*, ed. W. David Baird. Stillwater, OK: Oklahoma State University Press. 13–27.

728 Ginell, Cary. 1995. *Milton Brown and the Founding of Western Swing*. Champaign, IL: University of Illinois Press.

729 Green, Doug B. 1994. Tumbling Tumbleweeds: Gene Autry, Bob Wills and the Dream of the West. In *Country: The Music and the Musicians*, ed. Paul

Kingsbury. New York: Abbeville Press. 79–103.

730 Logsdon, Guy. 1976. Western Swing. In *What's Going On! Publications of the Texas Folklore Society, No. 40*, ed. Francis Edward Abernathy. Austin, TX: Encino Press.

731 Malone, Bill C. 1985. (1968) The Cowboy Image and the Growth of Western Music. In *Country Music, U.S.A.* Austin, TX: University of Texas Press. 137–75.

732 Russell, Tony. 1970. Out West. In *Blacks, Whites and Blues*. London: Studio Vista. 78–92.

733 Shelton, Robert. 1966. Way Out West: Singing Cowboys and Western Swing. In *The Country Music Story*. Indianapolis, IN: Bobbs-Merrill. 145–77.

734 Spitzer, Nicholas R. 1975. Bob Wills Is Still the King: Romantic Regionalism and Convergent Culture in Central Texas. *John Edwards Memorial Foundation Quarterly* 12(4): 191–97.

735 Stricklin, Al and McConal, Jon. 1976. *My Years with Bob Wills*. San Antonio, TX: Naylor Press.

736 Townsend, Charles. 1976. *San Antonio Rose: The Life and Music of Bob Wills*. Urbana, IL: University of Illinois Press.

737 Zolten, Jerry. 1974. Western Swingtime Music: A Cool Breeze in the American Desert. *Sing Out!* 23(2): 2–5.

COWBOY SONGS

738 Allen, Jules Verne. 1933. *Cowboy Lore*. San Antonio, TX: Naylor Company.

739 Clark, Kenneth S., ed. 1932. *The Cowboy Sings*. New York: Paull-Pioneer Music Company.

740 Clifford, John. 1955. Range Ballads. *Kansas Historical Quarterly* 21(8): 588–95.

741 Dobie, J. Frank. 1959. When Work's All Done This Fall. *Western Folklore* 18: 323–25.

742 Dunne, Michael. 1993. Romantic Narcissism in 'Outlaw' Cowboy Music. In *All That Glitters: Country Music in America*, ed. George H. Lewis. Bowling Green, OH: Bowling Green State University Press. 226–38.

743 Fenster, Mark. 1989. Preparing the Audience, Informing the Performers: John A. Lomax and *Cowboy Songs and Other Frontier Ballads. American Music* 7 (Fall): 260–77.

744 Fife, Austin and Fife, Alta. 1969. *Cowboy and Western Songs*. New York: Clarkson N. Potter.

745 Fife, Austin and Fife, Alta. 1989. *Heaven on Horseback: Revivalist Songs and Verse in the Cowboy Idiom*. Logan, UT: Utah State University Press.

746 Gaines, Newton. 1928. Some Characteristics of Cowboy Songs. *Publications of the Texas Folk-Lore Society* 7: 145–54.

747 Horstman, Dorothy. 1975. *Sing Your Heart Out, Country Boy*. New York: E.P. Dutton.

748 Hull, Myra E. 1939. Cowboy Ballads. *Kansas Historical Quarterly* 8(1): 35–60.

749 Larkin, Margaret. 1931. *Singing Cowboys: A Book of Western Songs*. New York: Alfred A. Knopf.

750 Lee, Katie. 1985. *Ten Thousand Goddam Cattle: A History of the American Cowboy in Song, Story and Verse*. Jerome, AZ: Katydid.

751 Lingenfelter, Richard E., Richard A. Dwyer and David Cohen. 1968. *Songs of*

the American West. Berkeley and Los Angeles: University of California Press.

752 Lomax, John A. 1911. Cowboy Songs of the Mexican Border. *Sewanee Review* 19(1): 1–18.

753 Lomax, John A. 1919. *Songs of the Cattle Trail and Cow Camp*. New York: Macmillan.

754 Lomax, John A. 1967. *Cow Camps & Cattle Herds*. Austin, TX: Encino Press.

755 Lomax, John A. and Lomax, Alan. 1938. (1910) *Cowboy Songs and Other Frontier Ballads*. New York: Macmillan. First published New York: Sturgis and Walton, 1910.

756 Moore, Chauncey O. and Moore, Ethel. 1964. *Ballads and Folksongs of the Southwest*. Norman, OK: University of Oklahoma Press.

757 Ohrlin, Glenn. 1973. *The Hell-Bound Train: A Cowboy Songbook*. Urbana, IL: University of Illinois Press.

758 Owens, William A. 1983. *Tell Me a Story, Sing Me a Song: A Texas Chronicle*. Austin, TX: University of Texas Press.

759 Silber, Irwin and Robinson, Earl. 1967. *Songs of the Great American West*. New York: Macmillan.

760 Sires, Ina. 1928. *Songs of the Open Range*. Boston, MA: C.C. Birchard and Company.

761 Thorp, N. Howard. 1966. (1908) *Songs of the Cowboys*. New York: Clarkson N. Potter. First published Estancia: New Print Shop, 1908.

762 Tinsley, Jim Bob. 1981. *He Was Singin' This Song: A Collection of Forty-Eight Traditional Songs of the American Cowboy*. Orlando, FL: University Presses of Florida.

763 White, John and Shakley, George, comps. 1929. *The Lonesome Cowboy Songs of the Plains and Hills*. New York: George T. Worth and Company.

764 White, John I. 1967. A Montana Cowboy Poet. *Journal of American Folklore* 80: 113–29.

765 White, John I. 1968. 'Great Grandma' and 'A Ballad in Search of Its Author'. Los Angeles: John Edwards Memorial Foundation. (First published in *Western American Literature* 2 (1967): 58–62; 3 (1968): 27–32.)

766 White, John I. 1975. *Git Along, Little Dogies: Songs and Songmakers of the American West*. Urbana, IL: University of Illinois Press.

COWBOYS (SINGING COWBOYS)

767 Autry, Gene and Herskowitz, Mickey. 1978. *Back in the Saddle Again*. Garden City, NY: Doubleday.

768 Bond, Johnny. 1976. *Reflections: The Autobiography of Johnny Bond*. Los Angeles: John Edwards Memorial Foundation.

769 Bovee, Bob. 1989. Way Out West: Cowboy Songs and Singers. *Old-Time Herald* 2 (August-October): 6–9, 43.

770 Collins, William, Douglas B. Green and Frederich LaBour. 1992. *Riders in the Sky*. Salt Lake City, UT: Gibbs Smith.

771 Green, Douglas B. 1978. The Singing Cowboy: An American Dream. *Journal of Country Music* 7(2): 4–61.

772 Griffus, Ken. 1986. *Hear My Song: The Story of the Celebrated Sons of the Pioneers*. Camarillo, CA: Norken.

773 Hurst, Richard Maurice. 1979. *Republic Studios: Between Poverty Row and the Majors*. Metuchen, NJ: Scarecrow Press.

774 Koon, William and Collins, Carol. 1973. Jules Verne Allen, the Original Singing

Cowboy. *Old Time Music* 10 (Autumn): 17–19.

775 Malone, Bill C. 1993. *Singing Cowboys and Musical Mountaineers: Southern Culture and the Roots of Country Music.* Athens, GA: University of Georgia Press.

776 Malone, Bill C. and McCulloch, Judith, eds. 1975. *Stars of Country Music: Uncle Dave Macon to Johnny Rodriguez.* Urbana, IL: University of Illinois Press.

777 Oermann, Robert K. and Bufwack, Mary A. 1981. Patsy Montana and the Development of the Cowgirl Image. *Journal of Country Music* 7(3): 18–33.

778 Ratcliffe, Sam D. 1984. The American Cowboy: A Note on the Development of a Musical Image. *John Edwards Memorial Foundation Quarterly* 20 (Spring-Summer): 2–7.

779 Rogers, Roy, Dale Evans and Carlton Stowers. 1979. *Happy Trails.* Waco, TX: Word Books.

780 Rothel, David. 1978. *The Singing Cowboys.* South Brunswick, NJ: A.S. Barnes.

781 Russell, William. 1977. *Tumbleweed: Best of the Singing Cowboys.* Fairfax, VA: Western Revue.

782 Savage, William W., Jr. 1983. *Singing Cowboys and All That Jazz: A Short History of Popular Music in Oklahoma.* Norman, OK: University of Oklahoma Press.

783 Smith, William R. 1972. Hell Among the Yearlings. *Old Time Music* 5 (Summer): 16–19.

784 Tinsley, Jim Bob. 1981. *He Was Singin' This Song.* Orlando, FL: University Press of Florida.

785 White, John I. 1970. Carl T. Sprague: The Original 'Singing Cowboy'. *John Edwards Memorial Foundation Quarterly* 6(1): 32–34.

DOOWOP

786 Allan, Tony and Treadwell, Faye. 1993. *Save the Last Dance for Me: The Musical Legacy of the Drifters, 1953–1993.* Ann Arbor, MI: Popular Culture, Ink.

787 Baptista, Todd R. 1996. *Group Harmony: Behind the Rhythm and the Blues.* New Bedford, MA: TRB Enterprises.

788 Gottlieb, Martin. 1993. The Durability of Doo-Wop. *New York Times* (17 January).

789 Gribin, Anthony and Schiff, Matthew M. 1992. *Doo-Wop: The Forgotten Third of Rock 'n' Roll.* Iola, WI: Krause Publications.

790 Groia, Phil. 1983. *They All Sang on the Corner: A Second Look at New York City's Rhythm and Blues Vocal Groups.* West Hempstead, NY: Phillie Dee Enterprises.

791 Keyes, Johnny. 1987. *Du-Wop.* Chicago: Vesti Press.

792 McCutcheon, Lynn Ellis. 1971. *Rhythm and Blues.* Arlington, VA: R.W. Beatty, Ltd.

793 Pruter, Robert. 1996. *Doowop: The Chicago Scene.* Urbana, IL: University of Illinois Press.

794 Toop, David. 1991. *Rap Attack 2: Africa Rap to Global Hip Hop.* London: Serpent's Tail.

795 Warner, Jay. 1992. *The Billboard Book of American Singing Groups: A History, 1940–1990.* New York: Billboard Books.

ENVIRONMENTAL MUSIC

796 Jones, Andrew. 1995. *Plunderphonics, Pataphysics and Pop Mechanics: An Introduction to Musique Actuelle.* Wembley: SAF.

797 Schafer, R. Murray. 1973. The Music of the Environment. *Cultures* 1.

798 Schafer, R. Murray. 1974. *The New Soundscape*. Wien: Universal Edition.

799 Schafer, R. Murray. 1977. *The Tuning of the World*. Bancroft: Arcana Editions.

FADO

300 Barreto, Mascarenhas. n.d. *Fado: Origens Liricas e Motivaçao Poética*. Lisbon: Aster.

301 Pinto de Carvalho, José. 1982. *Historia do Fado*. Lisbon: Publicaçoes Dom Quixote.

FILM AND TELEVISION MUSIC

Film Music (General)

302 Altman, Rick. 1985. The Evolution of Sound Today. In *Film Sound: Theory and Practice*, ed. Elisabeth Weis and John Belton. New York: Columbia University Press. 44–53.

303 Atkins, Irene Kahn. 1983. *Source Music in Motion Pictures*. Rutherford, NJ: Fairleigh Dickinson University Press.

304 Bazelon, Irwin. 1975. *Knowing the Score: Notes on Film Music*. New York: Arco.

305 Bertolina, Gian Carlo. 1986. Appunti sulla musica per film italiana dopo il 1970. *Musica/Realtà* 20: 19–29.

306 Blanchard, Gérard. 1984. *Images de la musique de cinéma*. Paris: Edilig.

307 Boer, Laurent. 1987. La Nuit Américaine de Truffaut/Delerue 'Providence': Alain Resnais/Miklos Rózsa. *Vibrations* 4: 179–202.

308 Boiles, Charles. 1975. La signification dans la musique de film. *Musique en Jeu* 19: 69–85.

809 Brown, Royal S. 1994. *Overtones and Undertones: Reading Film Music*. Berkeley, CA: University of California Press.

810 Carlin, Dan. 1990. *Music in Film and Video Production*. London: Focal Press.

811 Cooper, Lindsay. 1984. Composing for Films, ed. Mandy Merck. *Screen* 25(3) (May-June): 40–54.

812 Darby, William. 1991. *American Film Music: Major Composers, Techniques, Trends, 1915–1990*. Jefferson, NC: McFarland.

813 Dolan, Robert E. 1967. *Music in the Modern Media: Techniques in Tape, Disc and Film Recording, Motion Picture and Television Scoring and Electronic Music*. New York: Schirmer.

814 Elsas, Diana, ed. 1977. *Factfile: Film Music*. American Film Institute.

815 Evans, Mark. 1975. *Soundtrack: The Music of the Movies*. New York: Hopkinson and Blake.

816 Fano, Michel. 1987. Musique et film: filmusique. *Vibrations* 4: 23–27.

817 Flinn, Caryl. 1992. *Strains of Utopia: Gender, Nostalgia and Hollywood Film Music*. Princeton, NJ: Princeton University Press.

818 Fresnais, Gilles. 1980. *Son, musique et cinéma*. Chicoutimi: Gaëtan Morin.

819 Frith, Simon. 1984. Mood Music: An Inquiry into Narrative Film Music. *Screen* 25(3) (May-June): 78–87.

820 Gorbman, Claudia. 1987. *Unheard Melodies: Narrative Film Music*. Bloomington and London: Indiana University Press/BFI Publishing.

821 Green, Stanley. 1981. *Encyclopedia of the Musical Film*. New York and Oxford: Oxford University Press.

822 Hacquard, Georges. 1959. *La musique et le cinéma*. Paris: PUF.

823 Hagen, Earle. 1971. *Scoring for Films*. New York: Criterion Books.

GENRES

824 Harris, Steve. 1988. *Film, Television and Stage Music on Phonograph Records: A Discography*. Kent, OH: McFarland.

825 Huckvale, David. 1990. 'Twins of Evil': An Investigation into the Aesthetics of Film Music. *Popular Music* 9(1): 1–36.

826 Huntley, John. 1972. (1947) *British Film Music*. New York: Arno Press.

827 Jelinek, H. 1968. Musik in Film und Fernsehen. *Österreichisches Musikzeitschrift* 23: 122–35.

828 Jost, François. 1987. Approche narratologique des fonctions de la musique de film. *Vibrations* 4: 42–57.

829 Julien, Jean-Rémy, ed. 1987. Bibliographie (musiques des films). *Vibrations* 4: 218–28.

830 Julien, Jean-Rémy. 1987. Défense et illustration des fonctions de la musique de film. *Vibrations* 4: 28–41.

831 Karlin, Fred and Wright, Rayburn. 1990. *On the Track: A Guide to Contemporary Film Scoring*. New York: Schirmer Books.

832 Klein, Jean-Claude and Calvet, Louis-Jean. 1987. Chanson et cinéma. *Vibrations* 4: 98–109.

833 Lacombe, Alain and Rocle, Claude. 1979. *La musique du film*. Paris: Editions van de Velde.

834 Lacombe, Alain. 1983. *Des compositeurs pour l'image*. Neuilly-sur-Seine: Musique et promotion.

835 Lacombe, Alain. 1984. *La chanson dans le cinéma français*. Paris: Pierson.

836 La Motte-Haber, Helga de and Emons, Hans. 1980. *Filmmusik: eine systematische Beschreibung*. Munich and Vienna: Hanser.

837 Larson, Randall D. 1985. *Musique fantastique: A Survey of Film Music in the Fantastic Cinema*. Metuchen and London: Scarecrow Press.

838 Levy, Louis. 1948. *Music for the Movies*. London: Sampson Low.

839 Limbacher, James L., ed. 1974. *Film Music: From Violins to Video*. Metuchen, NJ: Scarecrow Press.

840 Limbacher, James L. 1981. *Keeping Score: Film Music, 1952–1972*. Metuchen, NJ: Scarecrow Press.

841 Limbacher, James L. 1981. *Keeping Score: Film Music, 1972–1979*. Metuchen, NJ: Scarecrow Press.

842 Limbacher, James L. and Wright, Stephen H. 1991. *Keeping Score: Film and Television Music, 1980–1988*. Metuchen, NJ: Scarecrow Press.

843 Lönstrup, Ansa. 1986. *Musik, film og filmopplevelse: En tværestetisk studie over 'Medlöberen'*. Århus: Århus Universitetsforlag.

844 Lustig, Milton. 1974. *Music Editing for Motion Pictures*. New York: Hastings House.

845 Mancini, Henry and Lees, Gene. 1989. *Did They Mention the Music?* New York: Contemporary Books.

846 Manvell, Roger, et al. 1975. *The Technique of Film Music*. London and New York: Focal Press.

847 Marks, Martin. 1982. Film Music: The Material, Literature and Present State of Research. *Journal of the University Film and Video Association* 34(1): 3–40.

848 McCarty, Clifford. 1972. *Film Composers in America: A Checklist of Their Work*. New York: Da Capo Press.

849 Meeker, David, ed. 1977. *Jazz in the Movies: A Guide to Jazz Musicians, 1917–1977*. London: Talisman.

850 Miceli, Sergio. 1982. *La musica nel film: Arte e artigianato*. Firenze: Discanto Edizioni.

851 Minganti, Franco. 1991. L'universo sonoro dell' 'hard-boiled'. *Cinema e Cinema* 18(60): 65–76.

852 Murphy, Paula. 1987. Films for the Black Music Researcher. *Black Music Research Journal* 7: 45–66.

853 Nisbett, Robert F. 1995. Pare Lorentz, Luis Gruenberg and *The Fight for Life*: The Making of a Film Score. *Musical Quarterly* 79(2): 231–55.

854 Palmer, Christopher. 1992. *The Composer in Hollywood*. London: Marion Boyars.

855 Parish, James Robert and Pitts, Michael R. 1991. *Hollywood Songsters: A Biographical Dictionary*. London and New York: Garland.

856 Philippot, Michel. 1987. Musique à ne pas voir. *Vibrations* 4: 58–64.

857 Pitts, Michael R. 1978. *Hollywood on Record: The Film Stars' Discography*. Metuchen, NJ: Scarecrow Press.

858 Porcille, François. 1969. *Présence de la musique à l'écran*. Paris: Éditions du Cerf.

859 Prendergast, Roy M. 1977. *Film Music, a Neglected Art: The History and Techniques of a New Art Form from Silent Films to the Present Day*. New York: W.W. Norton.

860 Risbourg, Isabelle. 1987. Les musiciens de jazz noirs et leur représentation dans le cinéma hollywoodien. *Vibrations* 4: 125–44.

861 Roland-Manuel, Claude. 1987. Rhythme cinématographique et musical. *Vibrations* 4: 11–22.

862 Rondolino, Gianni. 1991. *Cinema e musica. Breve storia della musica cinematografica*. Torino: Libraria UTET.

863 Sabaneev, Leonid. 1935. *Music for the Films*. London: Pitman.

864 Schneider, Norbert Jürgen. 1988. Pensieri sull musica elettronica per il cinema negli anni 80. In *Trento Cinema – Incontri internazionali con la musica per il cinema 1988*. Trento: Provincia Autonoma di Trento – Servizio Attività Culturali. 28–29.

865 Simeon, Ennio. 1988. Musicologia e musica per film. In *Trento Cinema – Incontri internazionali con la musica per il cinema 1988*. Trento: Provincia Autonoma di Trento – Servizio Attività Culturali. 314–16.

866 Skinner, Frank. 1950. *Underscore: A Combination Method-Text-Treatise on Scoring Music for Film or TV*. New York: Criterion Music.

867 Steven, Peter, ed. 1985. *Jump Cut: Hollywood, Politics and Counter Cinema*. Toronto: Between the Lines.

868 No entry.

869 Tagg, Philip, ed. 1980. *Film Music, Mood Music and Popular Music Research. Interviews, Conversations, Entretiens*. Göteborg: Musicology Department, University of Gothenburg.

870 Tagg, Philip. 1991. Muzak, sigle televisive, temi conduttori e musiche da film. *Cinema e Cinema* 18(60): 77–86.

871 Thomas, Tony. 1973. *Music for the Movies*. South Brunswick, NJ: Barnes.

872 Tiomkin, Dimitri. 1974. Composing for Films. In *Film Music: From Violins to Video*, ed. James L. Limbacher. Metuchen, NJ: Scarecrow Press. 55–61.

873 *Trento Cinema – Incontri internazionali con la musica per il cinema 1988*. 1988. Trento: Provincia Autonoma di Trento – Servizio Attività Culturali.

874 Warner, Alan. 1984. *Who Sang What (On the Screen)*. London: Angus & Robertson.

875 Westcott, Steven D. 1985. *A Comprehensive Bibliography of Music for Film and Television.* Detroit, MI: Information Coordinators.

876 Winqvist, Sven G. 1980. *Musik i svenska ljudfilmer 1929–1939.* Stockholm: STIM.

Cartoon Film Music

877 Alarcon, Isabelle. 1987. Figuralisme et écriture musicale dans le dessin animé. *Vibrations* 4: 110–24.

878 Newsom, Jon. 1980. A Sound Idea: Music for Animated Films. *Quarterly Journal of the Library of Congress* 37: 279–309.

Film Musical

879 Altman, Rick, ed. 1981. *Genre: The Musical.* London: Routledge.

880 Altman, Rick. 1987. (1986) *The American Film Musical,* ed. Tania Modleski. Bloomington, IN: Indiana University Press.

881 Aylesworth, Thomas G. 1984. *History of the Movie Musical.* Greenwich and London: Bison/Hamlyn.

882 Babington, Bruce and Evans, Peter William. 1985. *Blue Skies and Silver Linings: Aspects of the Hollywood Musical.* Manchester and Dover: Manchester University Press.

883 Burt, Rob. 1986. *Rock and Roll: The Movies.* New York: Sterling.

884 Burton, Jack. 1953. *The Blue Book of Hollywood Musicals: Songs from the Sound Tracks and the Stars Who Sang Them Since the Birth of the Talkies a Quarter-Century Ago.* Watkins Glen, NY: Century House.

885 Delamater, Jerome. 1981. *Dance in the Hollywood Musical.* Ann Arbor, MI: UMI Research Press.

886 Druxman, Michael B. 1980. *The Musical: From Broadway to Hollywood.* South Brunswick, NJ: Barnes.

887 Feuer, Jane. 1978. The Theme of Popular vs. Elite Art in the Hollywood Musical. *Journal of Popular Culture* 12(3): 491–99.

888 Feuer, Jane. 1982. *The Hollywood Musical.* London: British Film Institute/Macmillan.

889 Fordin, Hugh. 1975. *The World of Entertainment: Hollywood's Greatest Musicals.* New York: Doubleday.

890 Green, Stanley. 1981. *Encyclopedia of the Musical Film.* New York: Oxford University Press.

891 Hansch, Michael. 1980. *Vom Singen im Regen. Filmmusical gestern und heute.* Berlin: Henschel.

892 Hirschorn, Clive. 1981. *The Hollywood Musical.* London: Octopus.

893 Kobal, John. 1983. *Gotta Sing, Gotta Dance: A History of Movie Musicals.* London: Hamlyn.

894 Kreuger, Miles. 1975. *The Movie Musical from Vitaphone to 42nd Street.* New York.

895 Lynch, Richard Chigley, ed. 1989. *Movie Musicals on Record: A Directory of Recordings of Motion Picture Musicals, 1927–1987.* Westport and London: Greenwood Press.

896 McVay, J. Douglas. 1967. *The Musical Film.* London: Zwemmer.

897 Parish, James Robert and Pitts, Michael R. 1991. *Hollywood Songsters: A Biographical Dictionary.* London and New York: Garland.

898 Rickard, Sue. 1996. Movies in Disguise: Negotiating Courtship and Patriarchy Through the Dances of Fred Astaire and Ginger Rogers. In *Approaches to the American Musical,* ed. Robert Lawson-

Peebles. Exeter: University of Exeter Press. 72–88.

899 Sennett, Ted. 1981. *Hollywood Musicals.* New York: Abrams.

900 Springer, John. 1991. *They Sang! They Danced! They Romanced!: Hollywood Musicals from the Advent of Sound Until Today.* New York: Carol Publishing.

901 Thomas, Tony. 1985. *That's Dance! A Glorious Celebration of Dance in the Hollywood Musical.* Harmondsworth: Penguin.

902 Toll, Robert C. 1982. *The Entertainment Machine: American Show Business in the Twentieth Century.* New York and London: Oxford University Press.

903 Vallance, Tom. 1970. *The American Musical.* London: Zwemmer.

904 Wildbihler, Hubert and Völkleien, Sonja. 1986. *The Musical: An International Annotated Bibliography.* Munich and London: K.G. Saur.

905 Willett, Ralph. 1996. From Gold Diggers to Bar Girls: A Selective History of the American Movie Musical. In *Approaches to the American Musical,* ed. Robert Lawson-Peebles. Exeter: University of Exeter Press. 44–54.

906 Woll, Allen. 1976. *Songs from Hollywood Musical Comedies, 1927 to the Present: A Dictionary.* New York: Garland.

907 Woll, Allen. 1983. *The Hollywood Musical Goes to War.* Chicago: Nelson-Hall.

Indian Film Music

908 Arnold, Alison E. 1988. Popular Film Song in India: A Case of Mass Market Musical Eclecticism. *Popular Music* 7(2): 177–89.

909 Arnold, Alison E. 1992. Aspects of Production and Consumption in the Popular Hindi Film Song Industry. *Asian Music* 24(1): 122–36.

910 Arora, V.N. 1986. Popular Songs in Hindi Films. *Journal of Popular Culture* 20(2): 143–66.

911 Coppola, Carlo. 1977. Politics, Social Criticism and Indian Film Songs: The Case of Sahir Ludhianvi. *Journal of Popular Culture* 10(4): 896–901.

912 Marcus, Scott. 1992. Recycling Indian Film-Songs: Popular Music as a Source of Melodies for North Indian Folk Musicians. *Asian Music* 24(1): 101–10.

913 Oliver, Paul. 1988. Movie Mahal: Indian Cinema on ITV Channel 4. *Popular Music* 7(2): 215–16.

914 Skillman, Teri. 1986. The Bombay Hindi Film Song Genre: A Historical Survey. *Yearbook for Traditional Music* 18: 133–44.

Rock and Pop on Film

915 Betrock, Alan. 1986. *The I Was A Teenage Juvenile Delinquent Rock 'n' Roll Beach Party Movie Book: A Complete Guide to the Teen Exploitation Film, 1954–1969.* New York: St. Martin's Press.

916 Dellar, Fred. 1981. *NME Guide to Rock Cinema.* London: Hamlyn.

917 Denisoff, R. Serge and Romanowski, William D. 1991. *Risky Business: Rock in Film.* New Brunswick, NJ: Transaction.

918 Doherty, Thomas. 1988. *Teenagers and Teenpics: The Juvenilization of American Movies in the 1950s.* Winchester, MA: Unwin Hyman Books.

919 Ehrenstein, David. 1982. *Rock on Film.* New York: Delilah Books.

920 Jelot-Blanc, Jean-Jacques. 1978. *Le cinéma musical: du rock au disco 1953–1967.* Paris: Editions PAC.

921 Jelot-Blanc, Jean-Jacques. 1979. *Le cinéma musical: du rock au disco 1958–1979.* Paris: Editions PAC.

922 Jenkinson, Philip. 1974. *Celluloid Rock: Twenty Years of Movie Rock*. London: Lorrimer.

923 Lacombe, Alain. 1985. *L'écran du rock: 30 ans de cinéma et de rock-music*. Paris: Llernminier.

924 McGee, Mark Thomas. 1990. *The Rock and Roll Movie Encyclopedia of the 1950s*. Jefferson, NC: McFarland.

925 Romanowski, William D. and Denisoff, R. Serge. 1987. Money for Nothin' and the Charts for Free: Rock and the Movies. *Journal of Popular Culture* 21(3): 63–78.

926 Romney, Jonathan and Wooton, Adrian, eds. 1993. *Celluloid Jukebox: Popular Music and the Movies Since the 50s*. London: British Film Institute.

927 Sandahl, Linda. 1987. *Encyclopedia of Rock Music on Film: A Viewer's Guide to Three Decades of Musical, Concerts, Documentaries and Soundtracks, 1955–1986*. Poole: Blandford Press.

928 Schulz, Berndt. 1988. *Rocker, Punks und Teenies: vom Rebellenfilm der 50er Jahre zum Popcorn-Kino*. Bergisch Gladbach: Bastei Lübbe.

Silent Film Music

929 Anderson, Gillian B. 1988. *Music for Silent Films, 1894–1929*. Washington, DC: Library of Congress.

930 Berg, Charles Merrell. 1976. *An Investigation of the Motives for and Realization of Music Accompanying the American Silent Film, 1896–1927*. Chicago: Arno Press.

931 Beynon, George W. 1921. *The Musical Presentation of Motion Pictures*. New York: Schirmer.

932 Hofmann, Charles. 1970. *Sounds for Silents*. New York: Arno Press.

933 Hunsberger, D. 1982. Orchestral Accompaniment for Silent Films. *Image* 25(1): 7ff.

934 Lang, Edith and West, George. 1986. (1920) Musical Accompaniment of Moving Pictures. In *The History of the Cinema, 1895–1940*, ed. Kurt London. Alexandria, VA: Chadwyck-Healey. 161–75.

935 Pauli, Hansjörg. 1981. *Filmmusik: Stummfilm*. Stuttgart: Klett-Cotta.

936 Rapée, Ernö, ed. 1974. (1924) *Encyclopedia of Music for Films*. New York: Arno Press. First published New York: Schirmer, 1924.

937 Serra, Jean-Dominique. 1987. Musique et horreur dans le cinéma muet. *Vibrations* 4: 79–97.

938 Waldekranz, Rune. 1979. Stumfilmens musik. In *Skriftfest: 19 uppsatser tillägnade Martin Tegen – 60 år*. Stockholm: Institutionen för musikvetnskap. 179–99.

939 Winkler, Max. 1974. (1951) The Origins of Film Music. In *Film Music: From Violins to Video*, ed. James L. Limbacher. Metuchen, NJ: Scarecrow Press. 15–24.

Television Music

940 Bastian, Hans Günther. 1986. *Musik im Fernsehen: Funktion und Wirking bei Kindern und Jugendlichen*. Wilhelmshaven: F. Noetzel.

941 Caps, John. 1980. TV Music: Music Makes All the Difference. In *Motion Picture Music*, ed. Luc van de Ven. Mechelen: Soundtrack. 64–68.

942 Gelfand, Steve. 1993. *Television Theme Recordings: An Illustrated Discography, 1951–1991*. Ann Arbor, MI: Popular Culture Ink.

943 Harris, Steve. 1988. *Film, Television and Stage Music on Phonograph Records: A Discography*. Jefferson, NC: McFarland.

944 Lynch, Richard Chigley. 1990. *TV and Studio Cast Musicals on Record.* New York: Greenwood Press.

945 Westcott, Steven D. 1985. *A Comprehensive Bibliography of Music for Film and Television.* Detroit, MI: Information Coordinators.

Theme and Title Music

946 Preston, Mike. 1995. *Tele-tunes.* Morecambe: Mike Preston.

947 Ransom, Phil. 1980. *By Any Other Name: A Guide to the Popular Names and Nicknames of Classical Music and to Theme Music in Films, Radio, Television and Broadcast Adverts.* Newcastle: Northern Regional Library Systems.

948 Tagg, Philip. 1979. *Kojak: 50 Seconds of Television Music. Towards the Analysis of Affect in Popular Music.* Göteborg: Skrifter från Göteborgs universitet, Musikvetenskapliga institution, 2.

949 Tagg, Philip. 1981. The Analysis of Title Music as a Method of Decoding Implicit Ideologies in the Mass Media. In *Mass Communications & Culture,* 5, ed. Gunnar Andrén and Hans Strand. Stockholm: Akademi Litteratur. 90–105.

FLAMENCO

950 Dumas, Danielle. 1973. *Chants Flamencos: Coplas Flamencas.* Paris: Aubier-Montaigne.

951 Greci, Juan. 1973. *La Guitarra Flamenca.* Madrid: Union Musical Española.

952 Hecht, Paul. 1968. *The Wind Cried: America's Discovery of the World of Flamenco.* New York: Dial Press.

953 Leblon, Bernard. 1990. *Musiques tsiganes et flamenco.* Paris: L'Harmattan.

954 Manuel, Peter. 1989. Andalusian, Gypsy and Class Identity in the Contemporary Flamenco Complex. *Ethnomusicology* 33(1): 47–65.

955 Pohren, D.E. 1962. *The Art of Flamenco.* Jerez de la Frontier: Jerez Industrial.

956 Schreiner, Claus. 1985. *Flamenco gitano-andaluz.* Frankfurt am Main: Fischer.

957 Schreiner, Claus, et al., eds. 1990. (1985) *Flamenco: Gypsy Dance and Music from Andalusia.* Portland, OR: Amadeus Press.

958 Thompson, Barbara. 1985. Flamenco: A Tradition in Evolution. *The World of Music* 27(3): 67–78.

959 Vollhardt, Anja. 1988. *Flamenco: Kunst zwischen gestern und morgen, mit Fotos von Elke Stolzenberg.* Weingarten: Kunstverlag.

960 Washabaugh, William. 1994. The Flamenco Body. *Popular Music* 13(1): 75–90.

961 Washabaugh, William. 1996. *Flamenco: Passion, Politics and Popular Culture.* Oxford and Washington: Berg.

FUNK

962 Brown, M.P. 1994. Funk Music as Genre: Black Aesthetics, Apocalyptic Thinking and Urban Protest in Post-1965 African-American Pop. *Cultural Studies* 8(3): 484–508.

963 Corbett, John. 1994. *Extended Play: Sounding Off from John Cage to Dr Funkenstein.* Champaign, IL: University of Illinois Press.

964 Ertl, Franz. 1992. *Rap – Funk – Soul: Ein Nachschlagewerk.* Köln: Herbst.

965 Vincent, Rickey. 1996. *Funk: The Music, the People and the Rhythm of The One.* New York: St. Martin's Griffith.

966 Yúdice, George. 1994. The Funkification of Rio. In *Microphone Fiends: Youth Music*

and Youth Culture, ed. Andrew Ross and
Tricia Rose. London: Routledge.

GIRL GROUPS

967 Betrock, Alan. 1982. *Girl Groups: The
Story of a Sound*. New York: Delilah.

968 Bradby, Barbara. 1990. Do-Talk and
Don't-Talk: The Division of the Subject
in Girl-Group Music. In *On Record: Rock,
Pop and the Written Word*, ed. Simon Frith
and Andrew Goodwin. London:
Routledge. 341–68.

969 Greig, Charlotte. 1989. *Will You Still
Love Me Tomorrow? Girl Groups From the
50s On*. London: Virago.

970 Marcus, Greil. 1970. The Girl Groups. In
*The Rolling Stone Illustrated History of
Rock and Roll*, ed. Jim Miller. New York:
Rolling Stone Press. 160–61.

GOSPEL HYMNS/GOSPEL SONGS

971 Benson, Louis. 1962. (1915) The Offset:
The 'Gospel Hymn'. In *The English
Hymn*. Richmond, KY: John Knox Press.

972 Bruce, Dickson D. 1974. *And They All
Sang Hallelujah: Plainfolk Camp-Meeting
Religion, 1800–1845*. Knoxville, TN:
University of Tennessee Press.

973 Cockrell, Dale. 1987. Of Gospel Hymns,
Minstrel Shows and Jubilee Singers:
Toward Some Black South African
Musics. *American Music* 5(4): 417–32.

974 Cusic, Don. 1990. *The Sound of Light: A
History of Gospel Music*. Bowling Green,
OH: Bowling Green University Popular
Press.

975 Downey, James C. 1965. Revivalism, the
Gospel Songs and Social Reform.
Ethnomusicology 9(2): 115–25.

976 Gentry, Theodore. 1993. The Origins of
Evangelical Pianism. *American Music*
11(1): 90–111.

977 Hall, J.H. 1971. (1914) *Biography of
Gospel Song and Hymn Writers*. New
York: AMS Press.

978 Hustad, Donald. 1993. (1981) *Jubilate:
Church Music in Worship and Renewal*,
Chapters 9, 10. Carol Stream, IL: Hope
Publishing Company.

979 Muranyi, R.A. 1970. The First
Appearance of the Gospel Hymns in
Hungary. *Studia Musicologica Academiae
Scientiarum Hungaricae* 12: 311–17.

980 Peterson, John. 1976. *The Miracle Goes
On*. Grand Rapids, MI: Zondervan
Publishing House.

981 Riedel, Johannes. 1975. *Soul Music, Black
and White: The Influence of Black Music on
the Churches*. Minneapolis, MN:
Augsburg.

982 Rodeheaver, Homer. 1936. *Twenty Years
with Billy Sunday*. Nashville, TN:
Cokesbury Press.

983 Sankey, Ira. 1906. *My Life and the Story of
the Gospel Hymns*. New York and
Philadelphia: Harper and Brothers.

984 Shea, George. 1968. *Then Sings My Soul*.
Old Tappan, NJ: Fleming H. Revell.

985 Shorney, George, Jr. 1978. The History of
Hope Publishing Company. In
*Dictionary-Handbook to Hymns for the
Living Church*, ed. Donald Hustad. Carol
Stream, IL: Hope Publishing Company.
1–21.

986 Sizer, Sandra. 1978. *Gospel Hymns and
Social Religion: The Rhetoric of Nineteenth-
Century Revivalism*. Philadelphia: Temple
University Press.

987 Stebbins, George. 1971. (1924)
Reminiscences and Gospel Hymn Stories.
New York: AMS Press. First published
New York: Doran, 1924.

988 Weisberger, Bernard A. 1966. (1958)
*They Gathered at the River: The Story of the
Great Revivalists and Their Impact upon*

Religion in America. Chicago: Quadrangle Books. First published Boston: Little, Brown, 1958.

989 Whittle, Daniel. 1877. *Memoirs of Philip P. Bliss*. New York: A.S. Barnes.

990 Wilhoit, Mel. 1991. Sing Me a Sankey: Ira D. Sankey and Congregational Song. *The Hymn: A Journal of Congregational Song* 42(1): 13–19.

991 Wilhoit, Mel. 1995. Alexander the Great: Or, Just Plain Charlie. *The Hymn: A Journal of Congregational Song* 46(2): 20–28.

GOSPEL MUSIC (SOUTHERN WHITE)

992 Anderson, Robert and North, Gail. 1979. *Gospel Music Encyclopedia*. New York: Sterling Publishing Co.

992a Baxter, J.R. and Polk, Videt. 1971. *Gospel Song Writers Biography*. Dallas, TX: Stamps-Baxter Music and Printing Company.

993 Becker, Paula. 1971. *Let the Song Go On: Fifty Years of Gospel Singing with the Speer Family*. Nashville, TN: Impact Books.

994 Blackwell, Lois. 1978. *The Wings of the Dove: The Story of Gospel Music in America*. Norfolk, VA: The Donning Company.

995 Blackwood, James. 1975. *The James Blackwood Story*. Monroeville, PA: Whitaker House.

996 Burt, Jesse and Allen, Duane. 1971. *The History of Gospel Music*. Nashville, TN: K & S Press, Inc.

997 Gaither, Gloria. 1977. *Because He Lives*. Old Tappan, NJ: Fleming H. Revell.

998 Gentry, Linnell. 1969. *A History and Encyclopedia of Country, Western and Gospel Music*. Nashville, TN: Clairmont Corporation.

999 Oldham, Doug. 1973. *I Don't Live There Anymore*. Nashville, TN: Impact Books.

1000 Wicks, Sammie Ann. 1988. A Belated Salute to the 'Old Way' of 'Snaking' the Voice on Its (ca) 345th Birthday. *Popular Music* 8(1): 59–96.

1001 Wolfe, Charles K. 1992. Presley and the Gospel Tradition. In *The Elvis Reader: Texts and Sources on the King of Rock 'n' Roll*, ed. Kevin Quain. New York: St. Martin's Press.

GYPSY MUSIC

1002 Garfias, Robert. 1984. Dance Among the Urban Gypsies of Romania. *Yearbook for Traditional Music* 16: 84–96.

1003 Kovalcsik, Katalin. 1984. Popular Dance Music Elements in the Folk Music of Gypsies in Hungary. *Popular Music* 4: 45–66.

1004 Leblon, Bernard. 1990. *Musiques tsiganes et flamenco*. Paris: L'Harmattan.

1005 Sarosi, Bálint. 1971. *Gypsy Music*. Budapest: Corinna Press.

1006 Sarosi, Bálint. 1971. Gypsy Musicians and Hungarian Peasant Music. In *1970 Yearbook of the International Folk Music Council*, ed. Alexander L. Ringer. Urbana, IL: University of Illinois Press. 8–27.

1007 Tzerbakova, T. 1984. *Cyganskoye muzykalnoye ispolnitelstvo y tvordzestvo v Rossya*. Moskva: Muzyka.

HIGHLIFE

1008 Collins, John. 1976. Ghanaian Highlife. *African Arts* 10(3): 62–68.

1009 Collins, John. 1989. The Early History of West African Highlife Music. *Popular Music* 8(3): 221–30.

1010 Collins, John. 1995. *Highlife Time.* Accra: Anansesem Publications.

1011 Coplan, David. 1978. Go to My Town, Cape Coast! The Social History of Ghanaian Highlife. In *Eight Urban Musical Cultures: Tradition and Change*, ed. Bruno Nettl. Urbana and London: University of Illinois Press. 96–114.

1012 King, Bruce. 1966. Introducing the High-Life. *Jazz Monthly* 12(5): 3.

1013 Oppong, Christine, ed. 1983. *Female and Male in West Africa.* London: George Allen and Unwin.

1014 Sprigge, Robert. 1961. The Ghanaian Highlife: Notation and Sources. *Music in Ghana* 2: 70–94.

HIP HOP, RAP AND NEW URBAN BLACK POP

1015 Adler, Bill and Beckman, Janette. 1991. *Rap! Portraits and Lyrics of a Generation of Black Rockers.* London: Omnibus.

1016 Adler, Jerry. 1990. The Rap Attitude. *Newsweek* (19 March): 56–59.

1017 Baker, Houston A., Jr. 1991. Hybridity, the Rap Race and Pedagogy for the 1990s. In *Technoculture*, ed. Constance Penley and Andrew Ross. Minneapolis, MN: University of Minnesota Press. 197–210.

1018 Baker, Houston A., Jr. 1993. *Black Studies: Rap and the Academy.* Chicago: University of Chicago Press.

1019 Beckman, Janette and Adler, Bill. 1991. *Rap: Portraits and Lyrics of a Generation of Black Rockers.* New York: St. Martin's Press.

1020 Berry, Venise T. 1990. Rap Music, Self Concept and Low-Income Black Adolescents. *Popular Music & Society* 14(3) (Fall): 89–109.

1021 Berry, Venise T. 1994. Feminine or Masculine: The Conflicting Nature of Female Images in Rap Music. In *Cecilia Reclaimed: Feminist Perspectives on Gender and Music*, ed. Susan C. Cook and Judy S. Tsou. Urbana, IL: University of Illinois Press. 183–201.

1022 Berry, Venise T. 1994. Parents Just Don't Understand: Redeeming the Rap Music Experience. In *Adolescents and Their Music*, ed. Jonathan Epstein. New York: Garland .

1023 Berry, Venise T. and Horold, Looney. 1996. Rap Music, Black Men and the Police. In *African-Americans and Mass Communication: Contemporary Issues*. Thousand Oaks, CA: Sage.

1024 Blair, Elizabeth M. 1993. Commercialization of the Rap Music Subculture. *Journal of Popular Culture* 27(3): 21–34.

1025 No entry.

1026 Branzaglia, Carlo, Pierfrancesco Pacoda and Alba Solaro. 1992. *Posse italiane: Centri sociali, underground musicale e cultura giovanile degli anni '90 in Italia.* Firenze: Tosca.

1027 Brennan, Tim. 1994. Off the Gangsta Tip: A Rap Appreciation, or Forgetting About Los Angeles. *Critical Inquiry* 20: 663–93.

1028 Considine, J.D. 1992. Fear of a Rap Planet. *Musician* (1 February): 34–43, 92.

1029 Cornyetz, Nia. 1994. Fetishized Blackness: Hip Hop and Racial Desire in Contemporary Japan. *Social Text* 41: 113–39.

1030 Costello, Mark and Wallace, David Foster. 1990. *Signifying Rappers: Rap and Race in the Urban Present.* New York: Ecco Press.

1031 Craddock-Willis, Andre. 1991. Rap Music and the Black Musical Tradition:

A Critical Assessment. *Radical America* 23(4): 29–38.

1032 Crenshaw, Kim. 1991. Beyond Racism and Misogyny: Black Feminism and the 2 Live Crew. *Boston Review* 16(6) (December): 6–33.

1033 Cross, Brian. 1993. *It's Not About a Salary . . .: Rap, Race and Resistance in Los Angeles*. London and New York: Verso.

1034 Dery, Mark. 1988. Rap. *Keyboard* (November): 32–56.

1034a Desse & SBG. 1993. *Freestyle: Interview*. Paris: F. Massot & F. Millet.

1035 Dimitriadis, Greg. 1996. Hip Hop: From Live Performance to Mediated Narrative. *Popular Music* 15(2): 179–94.

1036 Dixon, Wheeler Winston. 1989. Urban Black American Music in the Late 1980s: The 'Word' as Cultural Signifier. *The Midwest Quarterly* 30 (Winter): 229–41.

1037 Dyson, Michael Eric. 1991. Performance, Protest, and Prophecy in the Culture of Hip-Hop. *Black Sacred Music* 5(1): 12–24.

1038 Dyson, Michael Eric. 1996. *Between God and Gansta Rap: Bearing Witness to Black Culture*. New York and Oxford: Oxford University Press.

1039 Ebron, Paula. 1991. Rapping Between Men: Performing Gender. *Radical America* 23(4): 23–27.

1040 Ertl, Franz. 1992. *Rap – Funk – Soul: Ein Nachschlagewerk*. Köln: Herbst.

1041 Eure, Joseph D. and Spady, James G., eds. 1991. *Nation Conscious Rap: The Hip Hop Vision*. New York and Philadelphia: PC International Press.

1042 Fernando, S.H., Jr. 1994. *The New Beats: Exploring the Music, Culture and Attitudes of Hip-Hop*. New York: Doubleday.

1043 Fornäs, Johan. 1994. Listen to Your Voice: Authenticity and Reflexivity in Rock, Rap and Techno Music. *New Formations* 24: 155–73.

1044 Gaunt, Kyra D. 1995. The Veneration of James Brown and George Clinton in Hip-Hop Music: Is It Live? Or Is It Re-Memory? In *Popular Music: Style and Identity*, ed. Will Straw, et al. Montréal: The Centre for Research on Canadian Cultural Industries and Institutions. 117–22.

1045 George, Nelson. 1985. *Fresh: Hip Hop Don't Stop*. New York: Pantheon Books.

1046 George, Nelson, ed. 1990. *Stop the Violence: Overcoming Self-Destruction*. New York: Pantheon Books.

1047 George, Nelson. 1992. *Buppies, B-Boys, Baps and Bohos: Notes on Post-Soul Black Culture*. New York: HarperCollins.

1048 Gilroy, Paul. 1993. 'Jewels Brought from Bondage': Black Music and the Politics of Authenticity. In *The Black Atlantic: Modernity and Double Consciousness*. London: Verso. 72–110.

1049 Gilroy, Paul. 1994. 'After the Love Has Gone': Bio-Politics and Etho-Poetics in the Black Public Sphere. *Public Culture* (7)1: 49–76.

1049a Grandmaster Blast. 1984. *All You Need to Know About Rappin'*. Chicago: Contemporary Books.

1050 Guevara, Nancy. 1987. Women Writin' Rappin' Breakin'. In *The Year Left, Vol. 2: An American Socialist Yearbook*, ed. Mike Davis. London: Verso. 160–75.

1051 Hager, Steven. 1984. *Hip Hop: The Illustrated History of Break Dancing, Rap Music and Graffiti*. New York: St. Martin's Press.

1052 Halberstam, Judith. 1989. Starting from Scratch: Female Rappers and Feminist Discourse. *Revisions* 2(2) (Winter): 1–4.

1053 Irving, Katrina. 1993. 'I Want Your Hands On Me': Building Equivalences Through Rap Music. *Popular Music* 12(2) (May): 105–21.

1054 Jacob, Günther. 1993. *Agit-Pop: Schwarze Musik und weiße Hörer. Texte zu Rassismus und Nationalismus – Hip Hop und Raggamuffin.* Berlin and Amsterdam: Edition ID-Archiv.

1055 Kandel, Minouche. 1990. Racist Censorship and Sexist Rap. *Reconstruction* 1(2): 21–25.

1056 Kitwano, Bakari. 1994. *The Rap on Gangsta Rap.* Chicago: Third World Press.

1057 Kopytko, Tanya. 1986. Breakdance as an Identity Marker in New Zealand. *Yearbook for Traditional Music* 18: 20–26.

1058 Lapassade, Georges and Rouselot, Philippe. 1990. *Le Rap ou la fureur de dire.* Paris: Lois Talmart.

1059 Light, Alan. 1992. About a Salary or Reality? Rap's Recurrent Conflict. In *Present Tense: Rock & Roll and Culture,* ed. Anthony DeCurtis. Durham, NC: Duke University Press. 219–34.

1060 Liperi, Felice. 1994. L'Italia s'è desta. Tecno-splatter e posse in rivolta. In *Ragazzi senza tempo: Immagini, musica, conflitti delle cultura giovanili,* ed. Massimo Canevacci. Genoa: Costa & Nolan. 163–205.

1061 Lipsitz, George. 1994. Diasporic Noise: History, Hip Hop and the Post-Colonial Politics of Sound. In *Dangerous Crossroads: Popular Music, Postmodernism and the Poetics of Place.* London: Verso. 23–48.

1062 Lusane, Clarence. 1993. Rap, Race and Politics. *Race and Class* 35(1): 41–56.

1063 Maxwell, Ian. 1994. True to the Music: Authenticity, Articulation and Authorship in Sydney Hip Hop Culture. *Social Semiotics* 4(12): 117–37.

1064 Maxwell, William. 1991. Sampling Authenticity: Rap Music, Postmodernism and the Ideology of Black Crime. *Studies in Popular Culture* 14(1): 1–16.

1065 McCoy, Judy. 1992. *Rap Music in the 1980s: A Reference Guide.* Metuchen, NJ: Scarecrow Press.

1066 Mitchell, Tony. 1995. Questions of Style: Notes on Italian Hip Hop. *Popular Music* 14(3): 333–48.

1067 Mitchell, Tony. 1996. *Popular Music and Local Identity: Rock, Pop and Rap in Europe and Oceania.* Leicester: University of Leicester Press.

1068 Musiques rock, reggae, raï, rap. 1991. *Les Cahiers de l'IFOREP* 64.

1069 Nelson, Angela Spence. 1991. Theology in the Hip-Hop of Public Enemy and Kool Moe Dee. *Black Sacred Music* 5(1): 51–59.

1070 Nelson, Angela Spence. 1992. The Persistence of Ethnicity in African American Popular Music: A Theology of Rap Music. *Explorations in Ethnic Studies* 15(1) (1 January): 47–57.

1071 Nelson, Havelock and Gonzales, Michael A. 1991. *Bring the Noise: A Guide to Rap Music and Hip-Hop Culture.* New York: Harmony Books.

1072 Noys, Benjamin. 1995. Into the 'Jungle'. *Popular Music* 14(3): 321–32.

1073 Perkins, William Eric. 1991. Nation of Islam Ideology in the Rap of Public Enemy. *Black Sacred Music* 5(1): 41–50.

1074 Perkins, William Eric. 1996. *Droppin' Science: Critical Essays on Rap Music and Hip Hop Culture.* Philadelphia: Temple University Press.

1075 Peterson-Lewis, Sonja. 1991. A Feminist Analysis of the Defenses of Obscene Rap Lyrics. *Black Sacred Music* 5(1): 68–79.

1076 Ransby, Barbara and Matthews, Tracye. 1993. Black Popular Culture and the Transcendence of Patriarchal Illusions. *Race and Class* 35(1): 57–68.

1077 Roberts, Robin. 1996. (1991) Music Videos, Performance and Resistance: Feminist Rappers. In *Gangsta: Merchandising the Rhymes of Violence*. New York: St. Martin's Press. (First published in *Journal of Popular Culture* 25 (Fall) (1991): 141–52.)

1078 Rose, Tricia. 1989. Orality and Technology: Rap Music and Afro-American Cultural Resistance. *Popular Music & Society* 13(4) (Winter): 35–44.

1079 Rose, Tricia. 1990. 'Fear of a Black Planet': Rap Music and Black Cultural Politics in the 1990's. *Journal of Negro Education* 60(3): 276–90.

1080 Rose, Tricia. 1991. Never Trust a Big Butt and a Smile. *Camera Obscura* (May): 108–31.

1081 Rose, Tricia. 1994. *Black Noise: Rap Music and Black Culture in Contemporary America*. Hanover and London: Wesleyan University Press.

1082 Ross, Andrew and Rose, Tricia, eds. 1994. *Microphone Fiends: Youth Music and Youth Culture*. New York and London: Routledge.

1083 Royster, Philip M. 1991. The Rapper as Shaman for a Band of Dancers of the Spirit: 'U Can't Touch This'. *Black Sacred Music* 5(1) 60–67.

1084 No entry.

1085 Sexton, Adam, ed. 1995. *Rap on Rap: Straight-Up Talk on Hip-Hop Culture*. New York: Dell Publishing.

1086 Shusterman, Richard. 1991. The Fine Art of Rap. *New Literary History* 22(3): 613–32.

1087 Skeggs, Beverley. 1993. Two Minute Brother: Contestation Through Gender, 'Race' and Sexuality. *Innovation* 6(3): 299–322.

1088 Slovenz, Madeline. 1988. 'Rock the House': The Aesthetic Dimension of Rap Music in New York City. *New York Folklore* 14(3–4): 151–64.

1089 Small, Michael. 1992. *Break It Down: The Story from the New Leaders of Rap*. New York: Citadel Press.

1090 Spencer, Jon Michael. 1991. Introduction. *Black Sacred Music* 5(1): 1–11.

1091 Spencer, Jon Michael, ed. 1991. The Emergency of Black and the Emergence of Rap. *Black Sacred Music* 5(1)(special issue).

1092 Stanley, Lawrence A., ed. 1992. *Rap: The Lyrics*. New York: Penguin.

1093 Stephens, Gregory. 1992. Interracial Dialogue in Rap Music: Call-and-Response in a Multicultural Style. *New Formations* 16: 62–79.

1094 Stephens, Ronald J. 1991. What the Rap Is About: A History and Criticism of Contemporary Rap Music and Culture. *Word* I (Spring): 21–44.

1095 Swedenburg, Ted. 1992. Homies in the Hood: Rap's Commodification of Insubordination. *New Formations* 18: 53–66.

1096 Tate, Greg. 1992. *Flyboy in the Buttermilk: Essays on Contemporary America*. New York: Simon & Schuster.

1097 Toop, David. 1991. (1984) *Rap Attack 2: African Rap to Global Hip Hop*. London: Serpent's Tail.

1098 Torp, Lisbet. 1986. Hip Hop Dances: Their Adoption and Function Among Boys in Denmark, 1983–1984. *Yearbook for Traditional Music* 18: 29–86.

1099 Walser, Robert. 1995. Rhythm, Rhyme and Rhetoric in the Music of Public Enemy. *Ethnomusicology* 39(2): 193–217.

1100 Wark, McKenzie. 1992. Ornament and Crime: The Hip Hop Avant Garde of the Late 1980s. *Perfect Beat* 1(1): 48–62.

1101 Wheeler, Elizabeth A. 1991. 'Most of My Heroes Don't Appear on No Stamps': The Dialogics of Rap Music. *Black Music Research Journal* 11(2): 193–216.

1102 Zanger, Mark. 1992. The Intelligent Forty-Year-Old's Guide to Rap, Part II. *Boston Review* (February): 5–8.

HOOTENANNY AND SINGALONG

1103 Brand, Oscar. 1962. *The Ballad Mongers*. New York: Funk and Wagnalls.

1104 Denisoff, R. Serge. 1971. *Great Day Coming: Folk Music and the American Left*. Urbana, IL: University of Illinois Press.

1105 Dunaway, David King. 1982. *How Can I Keep from Singing: Pete Seeger*. New York: McGraw-Hill.

1106 Guthrie, Woody. 1961. *American Folksong; Woody Guthrie*, ed. Moses Asch. New York: Oak Publications.

1107 Guthrie, Woody. 1943. *Bound for Glory*. New York: E.P. Dutton.

1108 Ives, Burl. 1948. *Wayfaring Stranger*. New York: McGraw-Hill.

1109 Lawless, Ray McKinley. 1965. (1960) *Folksingers and Folksongs in America: A Handbook of Biography*. Westport, CT: Greenwood Press. First published New York: Duell, Sloan & Pearce, 1960.

1110 Seeger, Pete. 1967. How 'Hootenanny' Came To Be. *Sing Out!* 5: 32–33.

1111 Seeger, Pete. 1992. (1972) *The Incompleat Folksinger*. Lincoln, NE: University of Nebraska Press.

1112 Seeger, Pete. 1993. *Where Have All the Flowers Gone: A Singer's Stories, Songs, Seeds, Robberies*. Bethlehem, PA: Sing Out.

IRISH–AMERICAN MUSIC

1113 Gronow, Pekka, ed. 1979. *The Columbia 33000-F Irish Series: A Numerical Listing*. Los Angeles: John Edwards Memorial Foundation.

1114 McCullough, L.E. 1974. An Historical Sketch of Traditional Irish Music in the United States. *Folklore Forum* 7: 177ff.

1115 McCullough, L.E. 1980. The Role of Language, Music and Dance in the Revival of Irish Culture in Chicago. *Ethnicity* 7: 436ff.

1116 O'Connor, Nuala. 1991. *Bringing It All Back Home: The Influence of Irish Music*. London: BBC Books.

1117 O'Neill, Francis. 1910. *Irish Folk Music: A Fascinating Hobby*. Chicago: Regan Printing House.

1118 O'Neill, Francis. 1973. (1913) *Irish Minstrels & Musicians*. Darby, PA: Norwood Editions. First published Chicago: Regan Printing, 1913.

1119 Wright, Robert. 1975. *Irish Emigrant Ballads and Songs*. Bowling Green, OH: Bowling Green University Popular Press.

JAIPONGAN

1120 Bass, Colin. 1994. Jaipongan: Worse Than the Twist! In *World Music: The Rough Guide*, ed. Simon Broughton, et al. London: Rough Guides. 428–30.

1121 Manuel, Peter and Baier, Randall. 1986. Jaipongan: Indigenous Popular Music of West Java. *Asian Music* 18(1) (Fall/Winter): 91–110.

JAZZ

General Works and Collected Criticism

1122 Balliett, Whitney. 1962. *Dinosaurs in the Morning: 41 Pieces on Jazz*. Philadelphia: Lippincott.

1123 Balliett, Whitney. 1966. *Such Sweet Thunder: 49 Pieces on Jazz*. Indianapolis, IN: Bobbs-Merrill.

1124 Balliett, Whitney. 1971. *Ecstasy at the Onion: 31 Pieces on Jazz*. New York: Bobbs-Merrill.

1125 Balliett, Whitney. 1976. *New York Notes: A Journal of Jazz, 1972–75*. Boston, MA: Houghton Mifflin.

1126 Balliett, Whitney. 1978. *The Sound of Surprise: 46 Pieces on Jazz*. New York: Da Capo Press. First published New York: Dutton, 1959.

1127 Balliett, Whitney. 1981. *Night Creature: A Journal of Jazz, 1975–1980*. New York and Oxford: Oxford University Press.

1128 Berendt, Joachim-Ernst, ed. 1978. (1975) *The Story of Jazz: From New Orleans to Rock Jazz*. London: Barrie & Jenkins.

1129 Blesh, Rudi. 1971. *Combo: USA; Eight Lives in Jazz*. New York: Chilton.

1130 Bohländer, Carlo. 1954. *Das Wesen der Jazzmusik*. Frankfurt am Main: Grahl & Niclas.

1131 Crouch, Stanley. 1995. *The All-American Skin Game, or, The Decoy of Race: The Long and the Short of It, 1990–1994*. New York: Pantheon Books.

1132 Dankworth, Avril. 1968. *Jazz: An Introduction to Its Musical Basis*. London: Oxford University Press.

1133 Deffaa, Chip. 1990. *Voices of the Jazz Age: Profiles of Eight Vintage Jazzmen*. Urbana, IL: University of Illinois Press.

1134 Feather, Leonard. 1975. *From Satchmo to Miles*. London: Quartet.

1135 Feather, Leonard. 1977. *Inside Jazz*. New York: Da Capo Press.

1136 Feather, Leonard. 1977. *The Pleasure of Jazz: Leading Jazz Performers on Their Lives, Their Music, Their Contemporaries*. New York: Dell Publishing.

1137 Fox, Charles. 1972. *The Jazz Scene*. London: Hamlyn.

1138 Francis, André. 1991. *Jazz: l'histoire, les musiciens, les styles, les disques*. Paris: Seuil.

1139 Giddins, Gary. 1981. *Riding on a Blue Note: Jazz and American Pop*. New York and Oxford: Oxford University Press.

1140 Gleason, Ralph J. 1961. *Jam Session: An Anthology of Jazz*. London: Jazz Book Club.

1141 Goldman, Albert. 1971. Jazz: The Art That Came in from the Cold. In *Freakshow: The Rocksoulbluesjazzsickjewblackhumorsexpoppsych Gig and Other Scenes from the Counter-Culture*. New York: Athenaeum. 265–325.

1142 Green, Benny. 1962. *The Reluctant Art: Five Studies in the Growth of Jazz*. London: MacGibbon & Kee.

1143 Grime, Kitty. 1983. *Jazz Voices*. London: Quartet.

1144 Grossman, William J. and Farrell, Jack W. 1976. (1956) *The Heart of Jazz*. New York: Da Capo Press. First published New York: New York University Press, 1956.

1145 Harrison, Max. 1991. *A Jazz Retrospect*. London: Quartet. First published London: Crescendo, 1976.

1146 Hentoff, Nat. 1978. (1961) *The Jazz Life*. New York: Da Capo Press. First published New York: Dial, 1961.

1147 Hodes, Art and Hansen, Chadwick, eds. 1977. *Selections from the Gutter: Jazz Portraits from the 'Jazz Record'*. Berkeley, CA: University of California Press.

1148 James, Burnett. 1990. (1961) *Essays on Jazz*. New York: Da Capo Press.

1149 Jones, LeRoi (Imamu Amiri Baraka). 1980. *Black Music*. Westport, CT: Greenwood Press. First published New York: William Morrow, 1967.

1150 Keepnews, Orrin. 1989. *The View from Within: Jazz Writings, 1948–1987*. New York and Oxford: Oxford University Press.

1151 Kernfeld, Barry. 1995. *What to Listen for in Jazz*. New Haven and London: Yale University Press.

1152 Levy, Joseph. 1983. *The Jazz Experience: A Guide to Appreciation*. Englewood Cliffs, NJ: Prentice-Hall.

1153 Lyons, Len. 1983. *The Great Jazz Pianists Speaking of Their Lives and Music*. New York: Quill.

1154 Oliver, Paul, Max Harrison and William Bolcom. 1986. *The New Grove Gospel, Blues and Jazz, with Spirituals and Ragtime*. London: Macmillan.

1155 Ramsey, Frederic and Smith, Charles E., eds. 1977. (1939) *Jazzmen*. New York: Harcourt, Brace.

1156 Rockwell, John. 1983. *All American Music: Composition in the Late Twentieth Century*. New York: Alfred A. Knopf.

1157 Santoro, Gene. 1994. *Dancing in Your Head: Jazz, Blues, Rock and Beyond*. New York and Oxford: Oxford University Press.

1158 Schaeffner, André. 1988. *Le Jazz*. Paris: J.M. Place.

1159 Shapiro, Nat and Hentoff, Nat, eds. 1979. (1957) *The Jazz Makers: Essays on the Greats of Jazz*. New York: Da Capo Press. First published New York: Rinehart, 1957.

1160 Taylor, Arthur. 1993. *Notes and Tones: Musician-to-Musician Interviews*. New York: Da Capo Press. First published New York: Perigree Books, 1982.

1161 Toledano, Ralph de, ed. 1966. (1962) *Frontiers of Jazz*. London: Jazz Book Club. First published New York: Ungar, 1962.

1162 Vian, Boris. 1981. *Autres écrits sur le jazz*. Paris: Christian Bourgois.

1163 Vian, Boris. 1988. *Round About Close to Midnight*. London: Quartet.

1164 Williams, Martin. 1985. *Jazz Heritage*. New York and Oxford: Oxford University Press.

1165 Williams, Martin. 1989. *Jazz in Its Time*. New York and Oxford: Oxford University Press.

1166 Williams, Martin. 1991. *Jazz Changes*. New York and Oxford: Oxford University Press.

1167 Zwerin, Mike. 1983. *Close Enough for Jazz*. London: Quartet.

Reference

General Works

1168 Arnaud, Gérald and Chesnel, Jacques. 1989. *Les Grands Createurs de Jazz.* Paris: Bordas.

1169 Baresel, Alfred. 1929. *Das neue Jazzbuch,* revised edition. Leipzig: J.H. Zimmermann.

1170 Bennett, Bill. 1981. Jazz. In *Handbook of American Popular Culture, Vol. 3,* ed. M. Thomas Inge. Westport, CT: Greenwood Press. 91–111.

1171 Berendt, Joachim-Ernst. 1978. (1977) *Ein Fenster aus Jazz. Essays, Portraits, Reflexionen,* revised edition. Frankfurt am Main: Fischer.

1172 Berendt, Joachim-Ernst. 1982. *The Jazz Book: From Ragtime to Fusion and Beyond,* revised edition. Westport, CT: Lawrence Hill. First published Frankfurt am Main: Fischer Bücherei, 1953; Westport: Lawrence Hill, 1975.

1173 Berindei, Mihai. 1976. *Dictionar de Jazz.* Bucaresti: Editura stiintifica si enciclopedica.

1174 Bohländer, Carlo, Karl Heinz Holler and Christian Pfarr, eds. 1989. *Reclams Jazzführer.* Stuttgart: Philipp Reclam Jun.

1175 Carles, Philippe, Andre Clergeat and Jean-Louis Comolli, eds. 1988. *Dictionnaire du Jazz.* Paris: Robert Laffont.

1176 Carr, Ian, Digby Fairweather and Brian Priestley. 1987. *Jazz: The Essential Companion.* London: Grafton Books.

1177 Carr, Ian, Digby Fairweather and Brian Priestley. 1995. *Jazz: The Rough Guide.* London: Rough Guides.

1178 Case, Brian, Stan Britt and Chrissie Murray. 1987. *The Illustrated Encyclopedia of Jazz,* revised edition. London: Salamander Books. First published London: Salamander Books, 1978.

1179 Chilton, John. 1989. *Who's Who of Jazz: Storyville to Swing Street,* 5th edition. London: Papermac (Macmillan London Ltd.). First published London: Bloomsbury Book Shop, 1970.

1180 Claghorn, Charles. 1982. *Biographical Dictionary of Jazz.* Englewood Cliffs, NJ: Prentice-Hall.

1181 Clarke, Donald, ed. 1989. *The Penguin Encyclopedia of Popular Music.* London: Penguin.

1182 Clayton, Peter and Gammond, Peter. 1986. *Jazz A-Z.* London: Guinness.

1183 Clayton, Peter and Gammond, Peter. 1989. *The Guinness Jazz Companion.* London: Guinness.

1184 *Die Enzyklopädie des Jazz: Die Geschichte des Jazz im Spiegel der wichtigsten Aufnahmen.* 1993. Bern, München and Wien: Scherz Verlag.

1185 Durant, J.B. 1984. *A Student's Guide to American Jazz and Popular Music: Outlines, Recordings and Historical Commentary.* Scottsdale, AZ: The author.

1186 Feather, Leonard. 1957. *The Book of Jazz: A Guide to the Entire Field.* London: Arthur Barker.

1187 Feather, Leonard, ed. 1966. *The Encyclopedia of Jazz in the Sixties.* New York: Horizon Press.

1188 Feather, Leonard, ed. 1982. *The Encyclopedia of Jazz,* revised edition. New York: Da Capo Press. First published New York: Horizon Press, 1955, 1960.

1189 Feather, Leonard and Gitler, Ira, eds. 1976. *The Encyclopedia of Jazz in the Seventies.* New York: Horizon Press.

1190 Fordham, John. 1993. *Jazz: The Essential Companion for Every Jazz Fan*. London: Elm Tree Press.

1191 Gourse, Leslie. 1995. *Madame Jazz: Contemporary Women Instrumentalists*. New York: Oxford University Press.

1192 Gridley, Mark C. 1992. *Concise Guide to Jazz*. Englewood Cliffs, NJ: Prentice-Hall.

1193 Jörgensen, John and Wiedemann, Erik. 1966. *Mosaik Jazzlexicon*. Hamburg: Mosaik.

1194 Kernfeld, Barry, ed. 1988. *The New Grove Dictionary of Jazz*. London: Macmillan.

1195 Kinkle, Roger D. 1974. *The Complete Encyclopedia of Popular Music and Jazz, 1900–1950*. 4 vols. New Rochelle, NY: Arlington House.

1196 Kunzler, Martin. 1988. *Jazz-Lexikon, 1: Von AABA-Form bis Kyle*. Reinbek bei Hamburg: Rowohlt.

1197 Kunzler, Martin. 1988. *Jazz-Lexikon, 2: Von La Barbera bis Zwingenberger*. Reinbek bei Hamburg: Rowohlt.

1198 Kynaston, Trent P. 1978. *Jazz Improvisation*. Englewood Cliffs, NJ: Prentice-Hall.

1199 Larkin, Colin, ed. 1992. *The Guinness Who's Who of Jazz*. Enfield: Guinness Publishing.

1200 Leonard, Neil. 1972. Jazz and the Other Arts. In *American Music: From Storyville to Woodstock*, ed. Charles Nanry. New Brunswick, NJ: Transaction. 152–67.

1201 McCalla, James. 1982. *Jazz: A Listener's Guide*. Englewood Cliffs, NJ: Prentice-Hall.

1202 McRae, Barry. 1988. *The Jazz Handbook*. London: Longman.

1203 Meeker, David, ed. 1977. *Jazz in the Movies: A Guide to Jazz Musicians, 1917–1977*. London: Talisman.

1204 Newton, Francis. 1959. *The Jazz Scene*. London: MacGibbon & Kee.

1205 Noglik, Bert. 1984. *Jazzwerkstatt International*. Reinbek bei Hamburg: Rowohlt.

1206 Oderigo, Nestor R. Ortiz. 1959. *Diccionario del Jazz*. Buenos Aires: Ricordi Americana.

1207 Panassié, Hugues. 1946. *La Veritable Musique de Jazz*. Paris: Laffont.

1208 Panassié, Hugues and Gautier, Madeleine. 1956. (1954) *Dictionary of Jazz*. London: Cassell. First published Paris: Laffont, 1954.

1209 Panassié, Hugues and Gautier, Madeleine. 1971. *Dictionnaire du jazz*. Paris: Editions Albin Michel.

1210 Postgate, John. 1973. *A Plain Man's Guide to Jazz*. London: Hanover Books.

1211 Sidran, Ben. 1983. (1971) *Black Talk*. New York: Da Capo Press.

1212 Ulanov, Barry. 1960. *A Handbook of Jazz*. London: Jazz Book Club. First published New York: Viking, 1957.

1213 Wagner, Jean. 1989. *Le guide du jazz*. Paris: Syro-Alternatives.

1214 Wölfer, Jürgen. 1979. *Handbuch des Jazz*. München: Heyne.

1215 Wölfer, Jürgen. 1993. *Lexikon des Jazz*. Bergisch-Gladbach: Heyne.

Bibliographies

1216 Allen, Daniel, comp. 1981. *Bibliography of Discographies, Vol. 2: Jazz*. New York: R.R. Bowker.

1217 Carl Gregor, Duke of Mecklenburg, comp. 1969. *International Jazz*

Bibliography: Jazz Books from 1919–1968. Strasbourg: P.H. Heitz.

1218 Carl Gregor, Duke of Mecklenburg and Ruecker, Norbert, comps. 1983. *International Bibliography of Jazz Books, Vol. I: 1921–1949.* Baden-Baden: Koerner.

1219 Carl Gregor, Duke of Mecklenburg and Ruecker, Norbert, comps. 1988. *International Bibliography of Jazz Books, Vol. II: 1950–1959.* Baden-Baden: Koerner.

1220 Carner, Gary, comp. 1990. *Jazz Performers: An Annotated Bibliography of Biographical Materials.* Westport, CT: Greenwood Press.

1221 Cooper, David Edwin, comp. 1975. *International Bibliography of Discographies: Classical Music and Jazz & Blues, 1962–1972. A Reference Book for Record Collectors, Dealers and Libraries.* Littleton, CO: Libraries Unlimited.

1222 Gray, John, comp. 1991. *Fire Music: A Bibliography of the New Jazz, 1959–1990.* Westport, CT: Greenwood Press.

1223 Hefele, Bernhard, comp. 1981. *Jazz-Bibliography: International Literature on Jazz, Blues, Spirituals, Gospel and Ragtime Music with a Selected List of Works on the Social and Cultural Background from the Beginning to the Present.* München: K.G. Saur.

1224 Kennington, Donald and Read, Danny L. 1980. *The Literature of Jazz: A Critical Guide,* revised edition. Chicago: American Library Association. First published London: Library Association, 1970.

1225 Markewich, Reese, comp. 1974. *New Expanded Bibliography of Jazz Compositions Based on the Chord Progressions of Standard Tunes.* Riverdale, NY: The author.

1226 Meadows, Eddie S. 1981. *Jazz References and Research Materials: A Bibliography.* New York: Garland.

1227 Meadows, Eddie S. 1995. *Jazz Research and Performance Materials: A Select Annotated Bibliography,* 2nd edition. New York: Garland. First published New York: Garland, 1981.

1228 Merriam, Alan P, comp. 1974. *A Bibliography of Jazz,* revised edition. New York: Da Capo Press. First published Philadelphia: American Folklore Society, 1954.

1229 Moon, Pete, comp. 1969. *A Bibliography of Jazz Discographies Published Since 1960,* ed. Barry Witherden. London: British Institute of Jazz Studies.

1230 Reisner, Robert George, ed. 1954. *The Literature of Jazz: A Preliminary Bibliography.* New York: New York Public Library.

Discographies and Record Guides

1231 Bruyninckx, Walter, comp. 1978. *60 Years of Recorded Jazz.* Mechelen: Bruyninckx.

1232 Cook, Richard and Morton, Brian. 1994. *The Penguin Guide to Jazz on CD, LP and Cassette,* revised edition. London: Penguin. First published London: Penguin, 1992.

1233 Cuscuna, Michael and Ruppli, Michel, eds. 1988. *The Blue Note Label: A Discography.* Westport, CT: Greenwood Press.

1234 Fordham, John. 1991. *Jazz on CD: The Essential Guide.* London: Kyle Cathie.

1235 Harrison, Max, Charles Fox and Eric Thacker. 1984. *The Essential Jazz Records, Vol. 1: Ragtime to Swing.* London: Mansell.

1236 Harrison, Max, et al. 1978. *Modern Jazz: The Essential Records.* London: Aquarius Books.

1237 Kernfeld, Barry, ed. 1991. *The Blackwell Guide to Recorded Jazz*. Oxford and Cambridge: Blackwell.

1238 Kernfeld, Barry and Rye, Howard. 1994. Comprehensive Discographies of Jazz, Blues and Gospel. *Notes* 51(2): 501–47.

1239 Kernfeld, Barry and Rye, Howard. 1994. Comprehensive Discographies of Jazz, Blues and Gospel, Part Two. *Notes* 51(3): 865–91.

1240 Leder, Jan, comp. 1985. *Women in Jazz: A Discography of Instrumentalists, 1913–1968*. Westport, CT: Greenwood Press.

1241 Litchfield, Jack. 1982. *The Canadian Jazz Discography*. Toronto: University of Toronto Press.

1242 Lyons, Len. 1980. *The 101 Best Jazz Albums: A History of Jazz on Records*. New York: Morrow.

1243 McCalla, James. 1982. *Jazz: A Listener's Guide*. Englewood Cliffs, NJ: Prentice-Hall.

1244 McCarthy, Albert, Paul Oliver and Max Harrison. 1968. *Jazz on Record: A Critical Guide to the First 50 Years, 1917–1967*. London: Hanover Books.

1245 Nicolausson, Harry. 1983. *Swedish Jazz Discography*. Stockholm: Swedish Music Information Centre.

1246 Patrick, James. 1972. The Uses of Jazz Discography. *Notes* 29: 17–23.

1247 Patrick, James. 1973. Discography as a Tool for Music Research and Vice Versa. *Journal of Jazz Studies* 1(1): 65–81.

1248 Priestley, Brian. 1988. In *Jazz on Record: A History*. London: Elm Tree Books.

1249 Raben, Erik, comp. 1969. *A Discography of Free Jazz: Albert Ayler, Don Cherry, Ornette Coleman, Pharoah Sanders, Archie Shepp, Cecil Taylor*. Copenhagen: Karl Emil Knudsen.

1250 Raben, Erik, comp. 1984. *Jazz Records, 1942–1980: A Discography*. 8 vols. Copenhagen: JazzMedia Aps.

1251 Ruppli, Michel. 1980. *The Prestige Label: A Discography*. Westport, CT: Greenwood Press.

1252 Ruppli, Michel. 1980. *The Savoy Label: A Discography*. Westport, CT: Greenwood Press.

1253 Ruppli, Michel. 1986. *The Clef/Verve Labels: A Discography*. New York and London: Greenwood Press.

1254 Rust, Brian, comp. 1978. *Jazz Records, 1897–1942*. 2 vols., 4th revised edition. New Rochelle, NY: Arlington House.

1255 Schleman, Hilton R. 1978. (1936) *Rhythm on Record: A Complete Survey and Register of All the Principal Recorded Dance Music, 1906–1936*. Westport, CT: Greenwood Press. First published London: Melody Maker, 1936.

1256 Stratemann, Klaus. 1981. *Negro Bands on Film: An Exploratory Filmo-Discography*. Lubbecke: Uhle & Kleimann.

1257 Swenson, John, ed. 1985. *The Rolling Stone Jazz Record Guide*. New York: Random House.

Iconographies

1258 Berendt, Joachim-Ernst. 1979. *Jazz: A Photo History*. London: Deutsch.

1259 Driggs, Franklin S. and Lewine, Harris. 1982. *Black Beauty, White Heat: A Pictorial History of Classic Jazz, 1920–1950*. New York: William Morrow.

1260 Keepnews, Orrin and Grauer, Bill, Jr., eds. 1981. *A Pictorial History of Jazz: People and Places from New Orleans to Modern Jazz*, revised edition. New York:

Bonanza Books. First published New York: Hamlyn, 1955.

1261 Klaasse, Piet. 1985. (1982) *Jam Session: Portraits of Jazz and Blues Musicians Drawn on the Scene*. Newton Abbot: David & Charles. First published Königstein: Athenaeum, 1982.

1262 Longstreet, Stephen. 1986. *Storyville to Harlem: Fifty Years in the Jazz Scene*. New Brunswick, NJ: Rutgers University Press.

1263 Marsh, Graham and Callingham, Glyn, eds. 1992. *California Cool: West Coast Jazz of the 50s and 60s*. San Francisco: Chronicle Books.

1264 Marsh, Graham and Callingham, Glyn, eds. 1992. *New York Hot: East Coast Jazz of the 50s and 60s*. San Francisco: Chronicle Books.

1265 Marsh, Graham, Felix Cromey and Glyn Callingham, eds. 1991. *Blue Note: The Album Cover Art*. San Francisco: Chronicle Books.

1266 Smith, Bill. 1985. *Imagine the Sound No. 5, The Book: Photographs and Writings by Bill Smith*. Toronto: Nightwood.

1267 Stewart, Chuck. 1986. *Chuck Stewart's Jazz Files: Photographs*. New York: Graphic Society.

1268 Wilmer, Valerie. 1976. *The Face of Black Music: Photographs by Valerie Wilmer*. New York: Da Capo Press.

History

1269 Alkyer, Frank, ed. 1995. *Down Beat: 60 Years of Jazz*. Milwaukee, WI: Hal Leonard Corporation.

1270 Bartsch, Ernst. 1956. *Neger, Jazz und tiefer Süden*. Leipzig: F.A. Brockhaus.

1271 Berendt, Joachim-Ernst, ed. 1978. (1975) *The Story of Jazz: From New Orleans to Rock Jazz*. London: Barrie & Jenkins.

1272 Berry, Jason. 1986. *Up from the Cradle of Jazz: New Orleans Music Since World War II*. Athens, GA: University of Georgia Press.

1273 Billard, François. 1989. *La vie quotidienne des jazzmen americains jusqu'aux années cinquante*. Paris: Vachette.

1274 Blesh, Rudi. 1980. (1946) *Shining Trumpets: A History of Jazz*. New York: Da Capo Press. First published New York: Knopf, 1946.

1275 Bushell, Garvin and Tucker, Mark, eds. 1988. *Jazz from the Beginning*. Ann Arbor, MI: University of Michigan Press.

1276 Chilton, John. 1979. *Jazz*. London: Hodder & Stoughton.

1277 Collier, James L. 1981. *The Making of Jazz: A Comprehensive History*. London: Papermac.

1278 Collier, James L. 1981. *The Reception of Jazz in America: A New View*. New York: Institute for Studies in American Music.

1279 Colyer, Ken. 1968. *New Orleans and Back*. Delph, Yorks: Brooks and Pratt.

1280 Condon, Eddie. 1974. (1948) *We Called It Music: A New Generation of Jazz*. London: Hale.

1281 Dahl, Linda. 1984. *Stormy Weather: The Music and Lives of a Century of Jazzwomen*. New York: Pantheon Books.

1282 Dahl, Linda. 1992. Equal Time: A Historical Overview of Women in Jazz. In *America's Musical Pulse: Popular Music in Twentieth-Century Society*, ed. Kenneth Bindas. Westport, CT: Praeger. 205–12.

1283 Dance, Stanley. 1961. *Jazz Era: The 'Forties*. London: MacGibbon & Kee.

1284 Dauer, Alfons M. 1961. *Jazz: Die magische Musik*. Bremen: Schünemann.

1285 Dauer, Alfons M. 1977. (1958) *Der Jazz: Seine Ursprünge und Seine Entwicklung*, 3rd edition. Kassell: E. Röth.

1286 Dauer, Alfons M. 1985. *Tradition afrikanischer Blasorchester und Entstehung des Jazz*. Graz: Akademische Druck- und Verlagsanstalt.

1287 DeVeaux, Scott. 1989. The Emergence of the Jazz Concert, 1935–1945. *American Music* 7(1): 6–29.

1288 Erenberg, Lewis. 1989. Things to Come: Swing Bands, Bebop and the Rise of a Postwar Jazz Scene. In *Recasting America: Culture and Politics in the Age of Cold War*, ed. Larry May. Chicago and London: University of Chicago Press. 221–45.

1289 Erenberg, Lewis. 1993. News from the Great Wide World: Duke Ellington, Count Basie and Black Popular Music, 1927–1943. *Prospects* 18: 483–506.

1290 Fiehrer, Thomas. 1991. From Quadrille to Stomp: The Creole Origins of Jazz. *Popular Music* 10(1): 21–38.

1291 Finkelstein, Sidney. 1975. *Jazz: A People's Music*. New York: Da Capo Press. First published New York: Citadel Press, 1948.

1292 Fox, Charles. 1969. *Jazz in Perspective*. London: BBC Publications.

1293 Francis, André. 1991. *Jazz: l'histoire, les musiciens, les styles, les disques*. Paris: Seuil.

1294 Gabbard, Krin. 1996. *Jammin' at the Margins: Jazz and the American Cinema*. Chicago and London: University of Chicago Press.

1295 Gridley, Mark C. 1987. *Jazz Styles: History & Analysis*, 3rd edition. Englewood Cliffs, NJ: Prentice-Hall. First published Englewood Cliffs: Prentice-Hall, 1978, 1985.

1296 Gumplowicz, Philippe. 1991. *Le Roman du jazz: première époque, 1893–1930*. Paris: Fayard.

1297 Hamm, Charles. 1983. The Golden Age of Jazz. In *Music in the New World*. New York: W.W. Norton. 498–547.

1298 Hennessey, Thomas J. 1994. *From Jazz to Swing: African-American Musicians and Their Music, 1890–1935*. Detroit, MI: Wayne State University Press.

1299 Hentoff, Nat. 1975. *The Jazz Life*. New York: Da Capo Press. First published London: P. Davies, 1962.

1300 Hentoff, Nat and McCarthy, Albert, eds. 1974. (1959) *Jazz: New Perspectives on the History of Jazz by Twelve of the World's Foremost Jazz Critics and Scholars*. New York: Da Capo Press. First published New York: Rinehart, 1959.

1301 Hodeir, André. 1975. *Jazz: Its Evolution and Essence*. New York: Da Capo Press. First published Paris: Portulan, 1954; New York: Grove Press, 1956.

1302 Jost, Ekkehard. 1982. *Sozialgeschichte des Jazz in den USA*. Frankfurt am Main: Fischer.

1303 Kaufman, Frederick and Guckin, John P. 1979. (1964) *The African Roots of Jazz*. Sherman Oaks, CA: Alfred Publishing Co.

1304 Knauer, Wolfram. 1990. Betrachtungen zur Entwicklung des Jazz zwischen Bebop und Free Jazz. In *Darmstädter Jazzforum 89: Beiträge zur Jazzforschung*, ed. Ekkehard Jost. Hofheim: Wolke. 85–99.

1305 Leonard, Neil. 1964. (1962) *Jazz and the White Americans: The Acceptance of a New Art Form*. London: Jazz Book Club.

1306 Levine, Lawrence. 1993. Jazz and American Culture. In *The Unpredictable Past: Explorations in American Cultural*

History. New York and Oxford: Oxford University Press. 172–88.

1307 Litweiler, John. 1984. *The Freedom Principle: Jazz After 1958*. New York: Da Capo Press. First published New York: William Morrow, 1984.

1308 Lodetti, A. 1990. *Alle radici del jazz: Le origini, la teoria, gli stili e il divenire storico della musica afro-americana*. Milano: Arcana.

1309 Malson, Lucien. 1976. *Histoire du jazz et des musiques afro-américaines*. Paris: UGE.

1310 Mäusli, Theo, ed. 1994. *Jazz und Sozialgeschichte*. Zürich: Chronos.

1311 Megill, Donald D. and Demory, Richard S. 1993. *Introduction to Jazz History*, 3rd edition. Englewood Cliffs, NJ: Prentice-Hall. First published Englewood Cliffs: Prentice-Hall, 1984, 1989.

1312 Mellers, Wilfrid. 1987. *Music in a New Found Land: Themes and Developments in the History of American Music*, revised edition. London: Faber & Faber. First published New York: Alfred A. Knopf, 1965.

1313 Merriam, Alan P. and Garner, Fradley H. 1968. Jazz: The Word. *Ethnomusicology* 12(3): 373–96.

1314 Middleton, Richard. 1979. *The Rise of Jazz*. Milton Keynes: Open University Press.

1315 Moody, Bill. 1993. *The Jazz Exiles: American Musicians Abroad*. Reno, NV: University of Nevada Press.

1316 Morris, Ronald L. 1980. *Wait Until Dark: Jazz and the Underworld, 1880–1940*. Bowling Green, OH: Bowling Green University Popular Press.

1317 Murray, Albert. 1989. *Stomping the Blues*. New York: Da Capo Press.

1318 Ogren, Kathy J. 1989. *The Jazz Revolution: Twenties America and the Meaning of Jazz*. New York and Oxford: Oxford University Press.

1319 Ogren, Kathy J. 1992. Debating with Beethoven: Understanding the Fear of Early Jazz. In *America's Musical Pulse: Popular Music in Twentieth-Century Society*, ed. Kenneth Bindas. Westport, CT: Praeger. 249–55.

1320 Oliver, Paul. 1991. That Certain Feeling: Blues and Jazz in 1890? *Popular Music* 10(1): 11–19.

1321 Ovtschinikov, E. 1994. *Istoria dzaza*. Moskva: Muzyka.

1322 Patrick, James. 1976. Musical Sources for the History of Jazz. *The Black Perspective in Music* 4(1): 46–53.

1323 Paul, Eliot. 1957. *That Crazy Music: The Story of North American Jazz*. London: Frederick Muller.

1324 No entry.

1325 Peretti, Burton W. 1992. *The Creation of Jazz: Music, Race and Culture in Urban America*. Urbana, IL: University of Illinois Press.

1326 Perrin, Michel. 1984. *Le jazz a cent ans*. Paris: France-Empire.

1327 Placksin, Sally. 1985. *Jazzwomen: 1900 to the Present. Their Words, Lives and Music*. London: Pluto Press.

1328 Pöhlert, Werner. 1989. *Jazz – 100 Jahre: Die Geschichte des authentischen Jazz vom Blues der schwarzen Sklaven bis zum Free Jazz der 60er Jahre*. Schwetzingen: Schimper.

1329 Porter, Lewis, Michael Ullman and Edward Hazell. 1993. *Jazz: From Its Origins to the Present*. Englewood Cliffs, NJ: Prentice-Hall.

1330 Priestley, Brian. 1988. *Jazz on Record: A History*. London: Elm Tree Books.

1331 Rimler, Walter. 1984. *Not Fade Away: A Comparison of the Jazz Age with the Rock Era*. Ann Arbor, MI: Pierian Press.

1332 Sandner, Wolfgang. 1982. *Jazz: Zur Geschichte und stilistischen Entwicklung afro-amerikanischer Musik*. Laaber: Laaber-Verlag.

1333 Schuller, Gunther. 1968. *Early Jazz: Its Roots and Musical Development*. New York and Oxford: Oxford University Press.

1334 Shapiro, Nat and Hentoff, Nat, eds. 1966. (1955) *Hear Me Talkin' To Ya: The Story of Jazz by the Men Who Made It*. New York: Dover. First published New York: Rinehart, 1955.

1335 Smith, Hugh L. 1960. George W. Cable and Two Sources of Jazz. *African Music* 2(3): 59–62.

1336 Stearns, Marshall. 1970. *The Story of Jazz*. New York: Oxford University Press.

1337 Stokes, W. Royal. 1991. *The Jazz Scene: An Informal History from New Orleans to 1990*. New York and Oxford: Oxford University Press.

1338 Tirro, Frank. 1993. (1977) *Jazz: A History*, 2nd edition. New York: W.W. Norton. First published New York: W.W. Norton, 1977.

1339 Travis, Dempsey J. 1983. *An Autobiography of Black Jazz*. Chicago: Urban Research Institute.

1340 Ulanov, Barry. 1958. *A History of Jazz in America*. London: Hutchinson.

1341 Viera, Joe. 1993. *Jazz: Musik unserer Zeit*. Schaftlach: Oreos.

1342 Williams, Martin. 1980. *Jazz Masters in Transition, 1957–69*. New York: Da Capo Press. First published New York: Macmillan, 1970.

1343 Williams, Martin. 1993. *The Jazz Tradition*, 2nd revised edition. New York and Oxford: Oxford University Press. First published Oxford: Oxford University Press, 1970, 1983.

Regional Studies

1344 Bataschev, Aleksej. 1973. *Sovjetskij dschaz*. Moskva: Muzyka.

1345 Bausch, Armando. 1985. *Jazz in Europa*. Trier: Editions Phi.

1346 Bender, Otto. 1993. *Swing unterm Hakenkreuz in Hamburg 1933–1943*. Hamburg: Christians.

1347 Bissett, Andrew. 1979. *Black Roots, White Flowers: A History of Jazz in Australia*. Sydney: Golden Press.

1348 Boulton, David. 1960. (1958) *Jazz in Britain*. London: Jazz Book Club.

1349 Boyd, Herb. 1983. *Detroit Jazz Who's Who*. Detroit, MI: Jazz Research Institute.

1350 Carr, Ian. 1973. *Music Outside: Contemporary Jazz in Britain*. London: Latimer.

1351 Charters, Samuel B. and Kunstadt, Leonard. 1981. (1962) *Jazz: A History of the New York Scene*. New York: Da Capo Press. First published New York: Doubleday, 1962.

1352 Chevigny, Paul. 1991. *Gigs: Jazz and the Cabaret Laws in New York City*. London: Routledge.

1353 Chilton, John. 1996. *Who's Who of British Jazz*. London: Cassell.

1354 Danzi, Michael. 1985. *American Musicians in Germany, 1924–1939: Memoirs of the Jazz Entertainment and Music World of Berlin During the Weimar Republic and the Nazi Era*. Frankfurt am Main: Rücker.

1355 Davis, Urula Broschke. 1986. *Paris Without Regret.* Iowa City, IA: University of Iowa Press.

1356 Ecklund, K.O. 1995. *Jazz West 2: The A-Z Guide to West Coast Jazz Music.* San Rafael, CA: Donna Ewald.

1357 Gioia, Ted. 1992. *West Coast Jazz: Modern Jazz in California, 1945–1960.* New York and Oxford: Oxford University Press.

1358 Godbolt, Jim. 1976. *All This and 10%.* London: Hale.

1359 Godbolt, Jim. 1984. *A History of Jazz in Britain, 1919–50.* London: Quartet.

1360 Gordon, Robert. 1986. *Jazz West Coast: The Los Angeles Jazz Scene of the 1950s.* London: Quartet.

1361 Graef, Jack de. 1980. *De Swingperiode (1935–1947): Jazz in Belgie.* Antwerp: Dageraad.

1362 Ita, Chief Bassey. 1984. *Jazz in Nigeria: An Outline Cultural History.* Calibar: Radical House.

1363 Knauer, Wolfram. 1993. *Jazz in Europa.* Hofheim: Wolke.

1364 Konttinen, Matti. 1982. *Finnish Jazz.* Helsinki: Finnish Music Information Centre.

1365 Konttinen, Matti. 1987. The Jazz Invasion. *Finnish Music Quarterly* 3–4: 21–25.

1366 Kotek, Josef. 1975. *Kronika èeské synkopy: Pù stoleti èeského jazzu a moderni populárni hudby v obrazech a svedìctvi souèasnikù, 1903–1938.* Praha: Supraphon.

1367 Lange, Horst H. 1966. *Jazz in Deutschland: Die deutsche Jazz-Chronik 1900–1960.* Berlin: Colloquium.

1368 Malecz, Attila. 1981. *A jazz Magyarországon.* Budapest: Tömegkommunikácios Kutatóközpont.

1369 Oliver, Paul. 1975. Jazz Is Where You Find It: The European Experience of Jazz. In *Superculture: American Popular Culture and Europe*, ed. C.W.E. Bigsby. London: Elek. 140–51.

1370 Polster, Bernd, ed. 1989. *'Swing Heil': Jazz im Nationalsozialismus.* Berlin: Transit Buchverlag.

1371 Smith, Gregory E. 1991. In Quest of a New Perspective on Improvised Jazz: A View from the Balkans. *The World of Music* 33(3): 29–52.

1372 Starr, S. Frederick. 1983. *Red and Hot: The Fate of Jazz in the Soviet Union, 1917–1980.* New York and Oxford: Oxford University Press.

1373 Tercinet, Alain. 1986. *West Coast Jazz.* Roquevaire: Parenthèses.

1374 Traynor, Frank and Clarke, Bruce. 1987. Jazz in Discussion (Interviews). In *Missing in Action: Australian Popular Music*, ed. Marcus Breen. Melbourne: Verbal Graphics Pty. 98–112.

1375 Zwerin, Mike. 1985. *Tristesse de St. Louis: Swing Under the Nazis.* London and New York: Quartet.

Chicago

1376 Kennedy, Rick. 1994. *Jelly Roll, Bix and Hoagy: Gennett Studios and the Birth of Recorded Jazz.* Bloomington, IN: Indiana University Press.

1377 Kenney, William Howland. 1993. *Chicago Jazz: A Cultural History, 1904–1930.* New York: Oxford University Press.

1378 Kriss, Eric. 1974. *Barrelhouse and Boogie Piano.* New York: Oak Publications.

1379 Lax, John. 1974. Chicago's Black Jazz Musicians in the Twenties: Portrait of an

Era. *Journal of Jazz Studies* 1(2): 107–27.

1380 Ostendorf, Berndt. 1982. *Black Literature in White America*. Brighton: Harvester Press.

1381 Vincent, Ted. 1992. The Community that Gave Jazz to Chicago. *Black Music Research Journal* 12(1): 42–55.

Kansas City

1382 Hester, Mary Lee. 1980. *Going to Kansas City*. Sherman, TX: Early Bird Press.

1383 Pearson, Nathan W. 1987. *Goin' to Kansas City*. Urbana, IL: University of Illinois Press.

1384 Pearson, Nathan W. 1989. Political and Musical Forces that Influenced the Development of Kansas City Jazz. *Black Music Research Journal* 9(2): 181–92.

1385 Russell, Ross. 1981. (1971) *Jazz Style in Kansas City and the Southwest*. Berkeley, CA: University of California Press.

New Orleans

1386 Barker, Danny and Buerkle, Jack V., eds. 1973. *Bourbon Street Black: The New Orleans Black Jazzman*. New York: Oxford University Press.

1387 Brown, Sterling A. 1944. Farewell to Basin Street. *The Record Changer* (December): 7–9, 51.

1388 Burns, Mick. 1994. Tuba Fats: Keeping the Swing on the Streets. *New Orleans Music* 5(2): 14–15.

1389 Burns, Mick. 1996. Milton Batiste Talks about Brass Bands. *New Orleans Music* 6(3): 6–11.

1390 Carew, Roy. 1954. The New Orleans Legend: Reflections on the Early Days of Jazz in the Crescent City. *Jazz Music* 5(6): 3–10; 23–24.

1391 Carter, William. 1991. *Preservation Hall: Music from the Heart*. Oxford and New York: Bayou Press/W.W. Norton.

1392 Charters, Samuel B. 1983. *Jazz: New Orleans, 1885–1963. An Index to the Negro Musicians of New Orleans*, revised edition. New York: Da Capo Press. First published Belleville: Walter C. Allen, 1958.

1393 Chilton, John. 1980. *A Jazz Nursery: The Story of the Jenkins' Orphanage Bands of Charleston, South Carolina*. London: Bloomsbury Book Shop.

1394 Foster, Pops and Stoppard, Tom. 1971. *Pops Foster: The Autobiography of a New Orleans Jazzman*. Berkeley, Los Angeles and London: University of California Press.

1395 Marquis, Donald M. 1978. *In Search of Buddy Bolden: First Man of Jazz*. Baton Rouge and London: Louisiana State University Press.

1396 Martinez, Raymond J. 1971. *Portraits of New Orleans Jazz: Its People and Places*. New Orleans: Hope Publications.

1397 Miller, Paul Eduard. 1947. Fifty Years of New Orleans Jazz. In *Esquire's Jazz Book*, ed. Paul Eduard Miller. London: Peter Davies. 99–111.

1398 Rose, Al. 1967. *New Orleans Jazz: A Family Album*. Baton Rouge, LA: Louisiana State University Press.

1399 Rose, Al and Souchon, Edmond. 1984. *New Orleans Jazz: A Family Album*, revised edition. Baton Rouge and London: Louisiana State University Press. First published Baton Rouge and London: Louisiana State University Press, 1967.

1400 Russell, Bill. 1994. *New Orleans Style*, ed. Barry Martyn and Mike Hazeldine. New Orleans: Jazzology Press.

1401 Russell, William and Smith, Stephen W. 1977. (1939) New Orleans Music. In

Jazzmen, ed. Frederic Ramsey and Charles E. Smith. New York: Harcourt, Brace. 7–37.

1402 Schafer, William J. 1978. Further Thoughts on Jazz Historiography: That Robert Charles Song. *Journal of Jazz Studies* 5(1): 19–27.

1403 Schafer, William J. and Allen, Richard B. 1977. *Brass Bands and New Orleans Jazz.* Baton Rouge, LA: Louisiana State University Press.

1404 Turner, Frederick. 1982. *Remembering Song: Encounters with the New Orleans Jazz Tradition.* New York: Viking.

1405 Williams, Martin. 1979. *Jazz Masters of New Orleans.* New York: Da Capo Press.

1406 zur Heide, Karl. 1994. Who Was the Leader of Charles Bolden's Orchestra? *New Orleans Music* 5(2): 6–10.

Analysis and Interpretation

1407 Asriel, Andre. 1985. *Jazz: Analysen und Aspekte.* Berlin: Lied der Zeit.

1408 Bailey, Derek. 1993. *Improvisation: Its Nature and Practice in Music,* revised edition. New York: Da Capo Press. First published Ashbourne: Moorland Publishing/Incus Records, 1980.

1409 Baker, David, ed. 1990. *New Perspectives on Jazz.* Washington, DC: Smithsonian Institution Press.

1410 Baraka, Amiri. 1991. The 'Blues Aesthetic' and the 'Black Aesthetic': Aesthetics as the Continuing Political History of a Culture. *Black Music Research Journal* 11(2): 101–109.

1411 Baraka, Amiri and Baraka, Amina. 1987. *The Music: Reflections on Jazz and Blues.* New York: William Morrow.

1412 Becker, Howard. 1972. The Professional Jazz Musician and His Audience. In *The Sounds of Social Change: Studies in Popular Culture,* ed. R. Serge Denisoff

and Richard A. Peterson. Chicago: Rand McNally & Co. 248–60. (First published in *American Journal of Sociology* 57 (1951): 136–44.)

1413 Berger, Morroe. 1972. Jazz: Resistance to the Diffusion of a Culture Pattern. In *American Music: From Storyville to Woodstock,* ed. Charles Nanry. New Brunswick, NJ: Transaction.

1414 Berliner, Paul F. 1994. *Thinking in Jazz: The Infinite Art of Improvisation.* Chicago and London: University of Chicago Press.

1415 Bohländer, Carlo. 1979. *Jazz – Geschichte und Rhythmus.* Mainz: Schott.

1416 Bohländer, Carlo. 1986. *Die Anatomie des Swing.* Frankfurt am Main: Schmitt.

1417 Borneman, Ernest. 1946. *A Critic Looks at Jazz.* London: Jazz Music Books.

1418 Brown, Charles T. 1989. *The Jazz Experience.* Dubuque, IA: William C. Brown.

1419 Brown, Robert L. 1976. Classical Influences on Jazz. *Journal of Jazz Studies* 3(2): 19–35.

1420 Buckner, Reginald T. and Weiland, Steven, eds. 1991. *Jazz in Mind: Essays on the History and Meanings of Jazz.* Detroit, MI: Wayne State University Press.

1421 Budds, Michael J. 1990. *Jazz in the Sixties: The Expansion of Musical Resources and Techniques,* revised edition. Iowa City, IA: University of Iowa Press. First published Iowa City: University of Iowa Press, 1978.

1422 Burbat, Wolfgang. 1988. *Die Harmonik des Jazz.* Kassel: dtv/Bärenreiter.

1423 Byrnside, Ronald, et al. 1975. The Performer as Creator: Jazz Improvisation. In *Contemporary Music and Music Cultures.* Englewood Cliffs, NJ: Prentice-Hall. 223–51.

1424 Cayer, David A. 1974. Black and Blue and Black Again: Three Stages of Racial Imagery in Jazz Lyrics. *Journal of Jazz Studies* 1(2): 38–71.

1425 Coker, Jerry. 1964. *Improvizing Jazz.* Englewood Cliffs, NJ: Prentice-Hall.

1426 Coker, Jerry. 1978. *Listening to Jazz.* Englewood Cliffs, NJ: Prentice-Hall.

1427 Collier, Graham. 1973. *Inside Jazz.* London: Quartet.

1428 Corbett, John. 1994. *Extended Play: Sounding Off from John Cage to Dr. Funkenstein.* Durham and London: Duke University Press.

1429 Dean, Roger Thornton. 1992. *New Structures in Jazz and Improvised Music Since 1960.* Buckingham: Open University Press.

1430 DeVeaux, Scott. 1991. Constructing the Jazz Tradition: Jazz Historiography. *Black American Literature Forum* 25(3): 525–60.

1431 Dollase, Rainer. 1978. *Das Jazzpublikum: Zur Sozialpsychologie einer kulturellen Minderheit.* Mainz: Schott.

1432 Durant, Alan. 1989. Improvisation in the Political Economy of Music. In *Music and the Politics of Culture,* ed. Christopher Norris. London: Lawrence & Wishart. 252–82.

1433 Frith, Simon. 1988. Playing with Real Feeling: Making Sense of Jazz in Britain. *New Formations* 4: 7–24.

1434 Gabbard, Krin, ed. 1995. *Jazz Among the Discourses.* Durham and London: Duke University Press.

1435 Gabbard, Krin, ed. 1995. *Representing Jazz.* Durham and London: Duke University Press.

1436 Gennari, John. 1991. Jazz Criticism: Its Development and Ideologies. *Black American Literature Forum* 25(3): 449–523.

1437 Gioia, Ted. 1988. *The Imperfect Art: Reflections on Jazz and Modern Culture.* New York and Oxford: Oxford University Press.

1438 Hartman, Charles O. 1991. *Jazz Text: Voice and Improvisation in Poetry, Jazz, and Song.* Princeton, NJ: Princeton University Press.

1439 Heble, Ajay. 1988. The Poetics of Jazz: From Symbolic to Semiotic. *Textual Practice.* 2(1): 51–68.

1440 Hentoff, Nat. 1972. Paying Dues: Changes in the Jazz Life. In *American Music: From Storyville to Woodstock,* ed. Charles Nanry. New Brunswick, NJ: Transaction. 99–114.

1441 Hobsbawm, Eric John. 1989. (1959) *The Jazz Scene.* London: Weidenfeld and Nicolson. Originally published under pseudonym of Francis Newton.

1442 Hodeir, André. 1972. (1954) *Hommes et problèmes du Jazz.* New York: Grove Press.

1443 Hodeir, André. 1972. *The Worlds of Jazz.* New York: Grove Press.

1444 Hodeir, André. 1990. (1961) *Toward Jazz.* New York: Da Capo Press.

1445 Holbrook, Morris B. 1979. The Spatial Representation of Responses Toward Jazz: Applications of Consumer Esthetics to Mapping the Market for Music. *Journal of Jazz Studies* 5(2): 3–22.

1446 Hughes, Philip S. 1974. Jazz Appreciation and the Sociology of Jazz. *Journal of Jazz Studies* 1(2): 79–96.

1447 Johnson, Bruce. 1993. Hear Me Talkin' to Ya: Problems of Jazz Discourse. *Popular Music* 12(1): 1–12.

1448 Jones, LeRoi (Imamu Amiri Baraka). 1963. *Blues People: Negro Music in White America*. New York: William Morrow.

1449 Kenney, William Howland, III. 1992. The African-American Contribution to Jazz. In *America's Musical Pulse: Popular Music in Twentieth-Century Society*, ed. Kenneth Bindas. Westport, CT: Praeger. 167–73.

1450 Kjellberg, Erik. 1985. Rena Rama and Lisa's Piano: An Essay in Jazz Analysis. In *Analytica: Studies in the Description and Analysis of Music*. Stockholm: Kungliga Musikaliska Akademien. 323–36.

1451 Knauer, Wolfram. 1991. *Jazz und Komposition*. Hofheim: Wolke.

1452 Köhler, Peter and Schacht, Konrad. 1983. *Die Jazzmusiker: zur Soziologie einer kreativen Randgruppe*. Freiburg: Peter Weininger, Roter Punkt Verlag.

1453 Leonard, Neil. 1987. *Jazz: Myth and Religion*. New York and Oxford: Oxford University Press.

1454 Lewis, Alan. 1987. The Social Interpretation of Modern Jazz. In *Lost in Music: Culture, Style and the Musical Event*, ed. Avron Levine White. London: Routledge. 33–55.

1455 Malson, Lucien. 1983. *Des musiques de jazz*. Paris: Editions Parenthèses.

1455a Meltzer, David, ed. 1993. *Reading Jazz*. San Francisco: Mercury House.

1456 Monson, Ingrid. 1994. Doubleness and Jazz Improvisation: Irony, Parody and Ethnomusicology. *Critical Inquiry* 20(2): 283–313.

1457 Nanry, Charles. 1972. Jazz and All That Sociology. In *American Music: From Storyville to Woodstock*, ed. Charles Nanry. New Brunswick, NJ: Transaction. 168–86.

1458 Nanry, Charles. 1979. *The Jazz Text*. New York: Van Nostrand.

1459 Newberger, Eli H. 1976. The Transition from Ragtime to Improvised Piano Style. *Journal of Jazz Studies* 3(2): 3–18.

1460 Ostransky, Leroy. 1960. *The Anatomy of Jazz*. Westport, CT: Greenwood Press.

1461 Ostransky, Leroy. 1971. *Jazz City: The Impact of Our Cities in the Development of Jazz*. Englewood Cliffs, NJ: Prentice-Hall.

1462 Panassié, Hugues. (1945). Notes on the Ensemble Playing of the New Orleans Clarinettists. In *American Jazz, No. 1*, ed. James Asman and Bill Kinnell. Newark and Nottingham: Jazz Appreciation Society. 1–3.

1463 Peterson, Richard A. 1972. Market and Moralist Censors of a Black Art Form: Jazz. In *The Sounds of Social Change: Studies in Popular Culture*, ed. R. Serge Denisoff and Richard A. Peterson. Chicago: Rand McNally & Co. 236–47.

1464 Phillips, Alan. 1965. *Jazz Improvisation and Harmony: Elementary to Advanced Principles*. London: Robbins Music.

1465 Pleasants, Henry. 1962. *Death of a Music? The Decline of the European Tradition and the Rise of Jazz*. London: Jazz Book Club/Gollancz.

1466 Pleasants, Henry. 1969. *Serious Music and All that Jazz: An Adventure in Music Criticism*. London: Gollancz.

1467 Porter, Lewis. 1985. John Coltrane's *A Love Supreme*: Jazz Improvisation as Composition. *Journal of the American Musicological Society* 38(3): 593–621.

1468 Porter, Lewis. 1988. Some Problems in Jazz Research. *Black Music Research Journal* 8(2): 195–206.

1469 Radano, Ronald M. 1993. *New Musical Figurations: Anthony Braxton's Cultural*

Critique. Chicago and London: University of Chicago Press.

1470 Ramsey, Doug. 1989. *Jazz Matters: Reflections on the Music and Some of Its Makers.* Fayetteville, AR: University of Arkansas Press.

1471 Reed, Harry A. 1979. The Black Bar in the Making of a Jazz Musician: Bird, Mingus and Stan Hope. *Journal of Jazz Studies* 5(2): 76–90.

1472 Risbourg, Isabelle. 1987. Les musiciens de jazz noirs et leur représentation dans le cinéma hollywoodien. *Vibrations* 4: 125–44.

1473 Russo, William. 1974. (1963) *Jazz Composition and Orchestration.* Chicago and London: University of Chicago Press.

1474 Sargeant, Winthrop. 1964. (1959) *Jazz.* London: McGraw-Hill. First published London: Jazz Book Club, 1959.

1475 Sargeant, Winthrop. 1975. *Jazz: Hot and Hybrid,* revised edition. New York: Da Capo Press. First published New York: Arrow, 1938.

1476 Sinclair, John and Levin, Robert. 1971. *Music and Politics.* New York: World.

1477 Stebbins, Robert A. 1972. A Theory of the Jazz Community. In *American Music: From Storyville to Woodstock,* ed. Charles Nanry. New Brunswick, NJ: Transaction. 115–34.

1478 Tanner, Paul O.W. 1976. *A Study of Jazz.* Dubuque, IA: Brown.

1479 Tomlinson, Gary. 1992. Cultural Dialogics and Jazz: A White Historian Signifies. In *Disciplining Music: Musicology and Its Canons,* ed. Katherine Bergeron and Philip V. Bohlman. Chicago and London: University of Chicago Press. 64–94. (First published in *Black Music Research Journal* 11(2) (1991): 229–64.)

1480 Van der Merwe, Peter. 1989. *Origins of the Popular Style: The Antecedents of Twentieth-Century Popular Music.* Oxford: Clarendon Press.

1481 Williams, Martin, ed. 1979. *The Art of Jazz: Essays on the Nature and Development of Jazz.* New York: Da Capo Press. First published New York: Oxford University Press, 1959.

Instruments

1482 Breithaupt, Robert B. 1995. The Drum Set: A History. In *Encyclopedia of Percussion,* ed. John H. Beck. New York: Garland. 173–85.

1483 Britt, Stan. 1984. *The Jazz Guitarists.* Poole: Blandford Press.

1484 McCarthy, Albert. 1967. (1945) *The Trumpet in Jazz.* London: Dent.

1485 Mongan, Norman. 1983. *The History of the Guitar in Jazz.* New York: Oak Publications.

1486 Newberger, Eli H. 1977. The Development of New Orleans and Stride Piano Styles. *Journal of Jazz Studies* 4(2): 43–71.

1487 Summerfield, Maurice J. 1978. *The Jazz Guitar: Its Evolution and Its Players.* Gateshead: Ashley Mark.

1488 Taylor, Billy. 1983. *Jazz Piano: A Jazz History.* Dubuque, IA: W.C. Brown & Co.

1489 Unterbrink, Mary. 1983. *Jazz Women at the Keyboard.* Jefferson, NC: McFarland.

1490 Wildman, Joan M. 1979. The Function of the Left Hand in the Evolution of Jazz Piano. *Journal of Jazz Studies* 5(2): 23–39.

Styles

Bebop and Modern

1491 Balliett, Whitney. 1986. *American Musicians: Fifty-Six Portraits in Jazz*. New York: Oxford University Press.

1492 Davis, Miles and Troupe, Quincy. 1989. *Miles: The Autobiography*. New York: Simon & Schuster.

1493 Enstice, Wayne and Rubin, Paul. 1992. *Jazz Spoken Here: Conversations with Twenty-Two Musicians*. Baton Rouge, LA: Louisiana State University Press.

1494 Feather, Leonard. 1949. *Inside Bebop*. New York: J.J. Robbins.

1495 Feather, Leonard. 1972. *From Satchmo to Miles*. London: Quartet. First published New York: Stein and Day, 1972.

1496 Feather, Leonard. 1990. *The Passion for Jazz*. New York: Da Capo Press. First published New York: Horizon Press, 1980.

1497 Giddins, Gary. 1981. *Riding on a Blue Note: Jazz and American Pop*. New York: Oxford University Press.

1498 Gillespie, Dizzy. 1980. *Dizzy: To Be Or Not To Bop*, ed. Al Fraser. London: W.H. Allen.

1499 Gitler, Ira. 1966. *Jazz Masters of the Forties*. New York: Macmillan.

1500 Gitler, Ira. 1985. *Swing to Bop: An Oral History of the Transition in Jazz in the 1940s*. Oxford and New York: Oxford University Press.

1501 Hellhund, Herbert. 1985. *Cool Jazz: Grundzüge seiner Entstehen und Entwicklung*. Mainz: Schott.

1502 Hess, Jacques B. 1989. *Bebop*. Paris: Editions de l'Instant.

1503 Hobart, Mike. 1981. The Political Economy of Bop. *Media, Culture and Society* 3(3): 261–80.

1504 Jost, Ekkehard. 1987. *Europas Jazz, 1960–80*. Frankfurt am Main: Fischer.

1505 Malson, Lucien. 1961. *Histoire du Jazz Moderne*. Paris: La Table Ronde.

1506 Morgan, Alun. 1977. *Modern Jazz: A Survey of Developments Since 1939*. Westport, CT: Greenwood Press.

1507 Nicholson, Stuart. 1990. *Jazz: The Modern Resurgence*. London: Simon & Schuster.

1508 Noglik, Bert and Heinz-Jürgen, Lindner. 1978. *Jazz im Gespräch*. Berlin: Neue Musik.

1509 Owens, Thomas. 1974. Applying the Melograph to 'Parker's Mood'. *Selected Reports in Ethnomusicology* 2(1): 167–75.

1510 Owens, Thomas. 1995. *Bebop: The Music and Its Players*. New York: Oxford University Press.

1511 Porter, Roy. 1991. *There and Back*, ed. David Keller. Wheatley: Bayou Press.

1512 Rivelli, Pauline. 1963. *Jazz Conversations*. New York: Jazz Press.

1513 Rivelli, Pauline and Levin, Robert, eds. 1979. (1970) *Giants of Black Music*. New York: Da Capo Press.

1514 Rosenthal, David H. 1987. Jazz in the Ghetto, 1950–70. *Popular Music* 7(1): 51–56.

1515 Rosenthal, David H. 1992. *Hard Bop: Jazz and Black Music, 1955–1965*. New York: Oxford University Press.

1516 Rusch, Robert D. 1984. *Jazztalk: The Cadence Interviews*. Secaucus, NJ: Lyle Stuart.

1517 Spellman, A.B. 1985. (1966) *Four Lives in the Bebop Business*. New York:

Limelight Editions. First published New York: Pantheon, 1966.

1518 Taylor, Arthur. 1993. *Notes and Tones: Musician-to-Musician Interviews.* New York: Da Capo Press. First published New York: Perigee Books, 1982.

1519 Tercinet, Alain. 1986. *West Coast Jazz.* Roquevaire: Parenthèses.

1520 Thomas, J.C. 1975. *Chasin' the Trane: The Music and Mystique of John Coltrane.* New York: Doubleday & Company.

1521 Waite, Brian. 1986. *Modern Jazz Piano: A Study in Harmony and Improvisation.* Tunbridge Wells: Spellmount.

1522 Wang, Richard. 1973. Jazz Circa 1945: A Convergence of Styles. *Musical Quarterly* 59(4): 531–46.

1523 Weinstein, Norman C. 1992. *A Night in Tunisia: Imaginings of Africa in Jazz.* Metuchen, NJ: Scarecrow Press.

1524 Werther, Iron. 1989. *Bebop: Die Geschichte einer musikalischen Revolution und ihrer Interpretation.* Frankfurt am Main: Fischer Taschenbuch.

1525 Wilson, John S. and Steuart, John. 1966. *Jazz: The Transition Years, 1940–1960.* New York: Appleton-Century-Crofts.

Contemporary

1526 Baraka, Amiri and Baraka, Amina. 1987. *The Music: Reflections on Jazz and Blues.* New York: William Morrow.

1527 Brinkmann, Rolf, ed. 1978. *Avantgarde, Jazz, Pop.* Mainz: Schott.

1528 Corbett, John. 1994. *Extended Play: Sounding Off from John Cage to Dr. Funkenstein.* Durham and London: Duke University Press.

1529 Crouch, Stanley. 1995. *The All-American Skin Game, or, The Decoy of Race: The Long and the Short of It, 1990–1994.* New York: Pantheon Books.

1530 Davis, Francis. 1986. *In the Moment: Jazz in the 1980s.* New York and Oxford: Oxford University Press.

1531 Davis, Francis. 1990. *Outcats: Jazz Composers, Instrumentalists and Singers.* New York and Oxford: Oxford University Press.

1532 Giddins, Gary. 1986. *Rhythm-a-ning: Jazz Tradition and Innovation in the '80s,* revised edition. New York and Oxford: Oxford University Press. First published Oxford: Oxford University Press, 1985.

1533 Nicholson, Stuart. 1990. *Jazz: The Modern Resurgence.* London: Simon & Schuster.

1534 Rockwell, John. 1983. *All American Music: Composition in the Late Twentieth Century.* New York: Alfred A. Knopf.

1535 Santoro, Gene. 1994. *Dancing in Your Head: Jazz, Blues, Rock and Beyond.* New York and Oxford: Oxford University Press.

1536 Schaefer, John. 1990. *New Sounds: The Virgin Guide to New Music.* London: Virgin.

1537 Solothurnmann, Jürg. 1990. Pluralismus und Neues Denken: Zur kulturellen Situation des Jazz und der improvisierten Musik. In *Darmstädter Jazzforum 89: Beiträge zur Jazzforschung,* ed. Ekkehard Jost. Hofheim: Wolke. 28–48.

1538 Szadkowski, Dita von. 1983. *Auf schwarz-weißen Flügeln: Jazz-Musik, europäische Perspektiven.* Gießen: Focus Verlag.

Early Jazz

1539 Bechet, Sidney. 1978. *Treat It Gentle: An Autobiography.* New York: Da Capo Press. First published New York: Twayne Publishers, 1960.

1540 Berlin, Edward E. 1977. Ragtime and Improvised Jazz: Another View. *Journal of Jazz Studies* 4(2): 4–10.

541 Daniels, Douglas Henry. 1986. Big Top Blues: Jazz-Minstrel Bands and the Young Family Traditions. *Jazz Research* 18: 133–53.

542 Fiehrer, Thomas. 1991. From Quadrille to Stomp: The Creole Origins of Jazz. *Popular Music* 10(1): 21–38.

543 Lange, Horst H. 1978. *The Fabulous Five.* Chigwell: Storyville Publications.

544 Lange, Horst H. 1991. *Als der Jazz begann, 1916–1923: Von der 'Original Dixieland Jazz Band' zu King Olivers 'Creole Jazz Band'.* Berlin: Colloquium.

545 Lomax, Alan. 1993. *Mister Jelly Roll: The Fortunes of Jelly Roll Morton, New Orleans Creole and 'Inventor of Jazz'.* New York: Pantheon Books. First published New York: Duell, Sloan and Pearce, 1949.

546 Lyttelton, Humphrey. 1981. *The Best of Jazz: Basin Street to Harlem.* London: Robson.

547 Milhaud, Darius. 1924. The Jazz Band and Negro Music. *Living Age* CCCXXIII: 169–73.

548 Ogren, Kathy J. 1990. *The Jazz Revolution: Twenties America and the Meaning of Jazz.* New York and Oxford: Oxford University Press.

549 Panassié, Hugues. 1973. (1960) *The Real Jazz.* Westport, CT: Negro Universities Press. First published New York: Barnes, 1960.

550 Panassié, Hugues. 1976. *Hot Jazz: A Guide to Swing Music.* Westport, CT: Negro Universities Press.

551 Schuller, Gunther. 1986. (1968) *Early Jazz: Its Roots and Musical Development.* New York: Oxford University Press.

552 Vincent, Ted. 1995. *Keep Cool: The Black Activists Who Built the Jazz Age.* London and New Haven: Pluto Press.

1553 Wang, Richard. 1988. Researching the New Orleans-Chicago Jazz Connection: Tools and Methods. *Black Music Research Journal* 8(1): 101–12.

1554 Whiteman, Paul. 1974. (1926) *Jazz.* New York: Arno Press.

Free Jazz and Improvised Music

1555 Bailey, Derek. 1993. *Improvisation: Its Nature and Practice in Music,* revised edition. New York: Da Capo Press. First published Ashbourne: Moorland Publishing/Incus Records, 1980.

1556 Bartlett, Andrew W. 1995. Cecil Taylor, Identity Energy and the Avant-Garde African American Body. *Perspectives of New Music* 33(1&2): 274–93.

1557 Baskerville, J.D. 1994. Free Jazz: A Reflection of Black Power Ideology. *Journal of Black Studies* 24(4): 484–97.

1558 Carles, Philippe and Comolli, Jean-Louis. 1971. *Free Jazz/Black Power.* Paris: Éditions Champ Libre.

1559 Childs, Barry and Hobbs, Christopher, eds. 1982/83. Forum: Improvisation. *Perspectives of New Music* 21(1&2): 26–111.

1560 Corbett, John. 1994. *Extended Play: Sounding Off from John Cage to Dr. Funkenstein.* Durham and London: Duke University Press.

1561 Corbett, John. 1995. Ephemera Underscored: Writing Around Free Improvisation. In *Jazz Among the Discourses,* ed. Krin Gabbard. Durham and London: Duke University Press. 217–40.

1562 Dean, Roger Thornton. 1989. *Creative Improvisation.* Milton Keynes: Open University Press.

1563 Dean, Roger Thornton. 1992. *New Structures in Jazz and Improvised Music Since 1960.* Buckingham: Open University Press.

1564 Durant, Alan. 1989. Improvisation in the Political Economy of Music. In *Music and the Politics of Culture*, ed. Christopher Norris. London: Lawrence & Wishart. 252–82.

1565 Feigin, Leo. 1986. (1985) *Russian Jazz: New Identity*. London and New York: Quartet.

1566 Gridley, Mark C. 1987. Free Jazz. In *Jazz Styles: History & Analysis*, 3rd edition. Englewood Cliffs, NJ: Prentice-Hall. 226–42. First published Englewood Cliffs: Prentice-Hall, 1978, 1985.

1567 Hersch, C. 1996. Let Freedom Ring: Free Jazz and African-American Politics. *Cultural Critique* 32: 97–123.

1568 Jones, LeRoi (Imamu Amiri Baraka). 1980. *Black Music*. Westport, CT: Greenwood Press. First published New York: William Morrow, 1967.

1569 Jost, Ekkehard. 1981. *Free Jazz*. New York: Da Capo Press. First published Graz: Universal Edition, 1974.

1570 Jost, Ekkehard. 1987. *Europas Jazz, 1960–1980*. Frankfurt am Main: Fischer Taschenbuch.

1571 Jost, Ekkehard. 1991. Free Jazz. In *The Blackwell Guide to Recorded Jazz*, ed. Barry Kernfeld. Oxford and Cambridge: Blackwell. 385–418.

1572 Kofsky, Frank. 1982. Black Nationalism in Jazz: The Forerunners Resist Establishment Repression, 1958–1963. *Journal of Ethnic Studies* 10(2): 1–27.

1573 Kofsky, Frank. 1983. (1970) *Black Nationalism and the Revolution in Music*. New York: Pathfinder Press.

1574 Lemery, Denys. 1971. Musique contemporaine, pop-music et free-jazz, convergences et divergences. *Musique en jeu* 2: 80–87.

1575 Litweiler, John. 1984. *The Freedom Principle: Jazz After 1958*. New York: Da Capo Press.

1576 Lock, Graham. 1988. *Forces in Motion: Anthony Braxton and the Meta-Reality of Creative Music. Interviews and Tour Notes, England 1985*. London: Quartet.

1577 McRae, Barry. 1967. *The Jazz Cataclysm*. London: Dent.

1578 Megill, Donald D. and Demory, Richard S. 1993. Free Jazz, 1960-. In *Introduction to Jazz History*, 3rd edition. Englewood Cliffs, NJ: Prentice-Hall. 223–53. First published Englewood Cliffs: Prentice-Hall, 1984, 1989.

1579 Miller, Lloyd and Skipper, James K. 1972. Sounds of Black Protest in Avant-Garde Jazz. In *The Sounds of Social Change: Studies in Popular Culture*, ed. R. Serge Denisoff and Richard A. Peterson. Chicago: Rand McNally & Co. 26–37.

1580 Noglik, Bert. 1991. *Klangspuren: Wege improvisierter Musik*. Frankfurt am Main: Fischer.

1581 Porter, Lewis and Ullman, Michael. 1993. The Avant-Garde Since Coltrane. In *Jazz: From Its Origins to the Present*. Englewood Cliffs, NJ: Prentice-Hall.

1582 Radano, Ronald M. 1985. The Jazz Avant-Garde and the Jazz Community: Action and Reaction. *Annual Review of Jazz Studies* 3: 71–79.

1583 Radano, Ronald M. 1993. *New Musical Figurations: Anthony Braxton's Cultural Critique*. Chicago and London: University of Chicago Press.

1584 Sinclair, John and Levin, Robert. 1971. *Music and Politics*. New York: World.

1585 Spellman, A.B. 1985. *Black Music: Four Lives*. New York: Limelight Editions. First published New York: Pantheon Books, 1966.

1586 Such, David G. 1993. *Avant-Garde Jazz Musicians: Performing 'Out There'*. Iowa City, IA: University of Iowa Press.

1587 Thomas, Lorenzo. 1995. Ascension: Music and the Black Arts Movement. In *Jazz Among the Discourses*, ed. Krin Gabbard. Durham and London: Duke University Press. 256–74.

1588 Wilmer, Valerie. 1987. *As Serious As Your Life: The Story of the New Jazz*, revised edition. London: Pluto Press. First published London: Allison & Busby, 1977.

Fusion, Jazz-Rock and World Music Influences

1589 Boggs, Vernon. 1992. *Afro-Cuban Music and the Evolution of Salsa in New York City*. Westport, CT: Greenwood Press.

1590 Bourne, Mike. 1989. Fusion: Jazz-Rock-Classical. *Down Beat* (September): 79–80.

1591 Budds, Michael J. 1990. Other Influences. In *Jazz in the Sixties: The Expansion of Musical Resources and Techniques*, revised edition. Iowa City, IA: University of Iowa Press. 85–95. First published Iowa City: University of Iowa Press, 1978.

1592 Coryell, Julie and Friedman, Laura. 1978. *Jazz-Rock Fusion: The People, the Music*. New York: Dell Publishing.

1593 Delfino, Jean-Paul. 1988. *Brasil Bossa Nova*. Aix-en-Provence: Edisud.

1594 Farrell, Gerry. 1988. Reflecting Surfaces: Indian Music in Popular Music and Jazz. *Popular Music* 7(2): 189–206.

1595 Gilbert, Mark. 1991. Fusion. In *The Blackwell Guide to Recorded Jazz*, ed. Barry Kernfeld. Oxford and Cambridge: Blackwell. 419–42.

1596 Gridley, Mark C. 1983. Clarifying Labels: Jazz, Rock, Funk and Jazz-Rock. *Popular Music & Society* 9(2): 27–34.

1597 Gridley, Mark C. 1987. Twenty Years of Jazz, Rock and American Popular Music: The Mid-1960s to the Mid-1980s. In *Jazz Styles: History & Analysis*, 3rd edition. Englewood Cliffs, NJ: Prentice-Hall. 312–43. First published Englewood Cliffs: Prentice-Hall, 1978, 1985.

1598 König, Burghard, ed. 1983. *Tendenzen einer modernen Musik: Jazzrock*. Reinbek bei Hamburg: Rowohlt.

1599 Lippegaus, Karl. 1978. (1975) Rock Jazz. In *The Story of Jazz: From New Orleans to Rock Jazz*, ed. Joachim-Ernst Berendt. London: Barrie & Jenkins. 154–71.

1600 Mayer, John. 1969–70. Indo-Jazz Fusions. *Composer* 34: 5.

1601 Megill, Donald D. and Demory, Richard S. 1993. Jazz/Rock Fusion, 1968-. In *Introduction to Jazz History*, 3rd edition. Englewood Cliffs, NJ: Prentice-Hall. 255–91. First published Englewood Cliffs: Prentice-Hall, 1984, 1989.

1602 Mooney, H.F. 1980. Twilight of the Age of Aquarius? Popular Music in the 1970s. *Popular Music & Society* 7: 182–98.

1603 Palmer, Robert. 1980. Jazz Rock. In *The Rolling Stone Illustrated History of Rock & Roll*, ed. Jim Miller. New York: Random House. 353–56.

1604 Porter, Lewis and Ullman, Michael. 1993. Fusion. In *Jazz: From Its Origins to the Present*. Englewood Cliffs, NJ: Prentice-Hall.

1605 Reynard, Guy. 1990. *Fusion*. Paris: Instant: Jazz Hot.

1606 Roberts, John Storm. 1979. *The Latin Tinge: The Impact of Latin American*

Music on the United States. New York and Oxford: Oxford University Press.

1607 Siders, Harvey. 1989. Chicago: Jazz-Rock Pioneers. *Down Beat* (September): 81–82.

1608 Tomlinson, Gary. 1992. Cultural Dialogics and Jazz: A White Historian Signifies. In *Disciplining Music: Musicology and Its Canons*, ed. Katherine Bergeron and Philip V. Bohlman. Chicago and London: University of Chicago Press. 64–94. (First published in *Black Music Research Journal* 11(2) (1991): 229–64.)

1609 Weinstein, Norman C. 1992. *A Night in Tunisia: Imaginings of Africa in Jazz*. Metuchen, NJ: Scarecrow Press.

1610 Werner, Otto. 1992. *The Latin Influence on Jazz*. Dubuque, IA: Kendall/Hunt.

Swing and Big Bands

1611 Allen, Walter C. 1973. *Hendersonia: The Music of Fletcher Henderson and His Musicians*. Highland Park, NJ: Walter C. Allen.

1612 Barker, Danny. 1988. *A Life in Jazz*, ed. Alyn Shipton. New York: Oxford University Press. First published London: Macmillan, 1986.

1613 Barnet, Charlie and Dance, Stanley. 1984. *Those Swinging Years*. Baton Rouge, LA: Louisiana State University Press.

1614 Basie, Count. 1986. *Good Morning Blues: The Autobiography of Count Basie*, ed. Albert Murray. London: William Heinemann.

1615 Bernhardt, Clyde E.B. 1986. *I Remember: Eighty Years of Black Entertainment, Big Bands and the Blues*, ed. Sheldon Harris, Philadelphia: University of Pennsylvania Press.

1616 Bigard, Barney. 1985. *With Louis and the Duke*, ed. Barry Martyn, London: Macmillan.

1617 Calloway, Cab, and Rollins, Bryant. 1976. *Of Minnie the Moocher and Me*. New York: Thomas Y. Crowell Company.

1618 Cheatham, Doc. 1996. *I Guess I'll Get the Papers and Go Home*, ed. Alyn Shipton. London: Cassell.

1619 Coleman, Bill. 1990. (1981) *Trumpet Story*. London: Macmillan.

1620 Dance, Stanley. 1974. *The World of Swing*. New York: Charles Scribner's Sons.

1621 Dance, Stanley. 1977. *The World of Earl Hines*. New York: Charles Scribner's Sons.

1622 Dance, Stanley. 1980. *The World of Count Basie*. New York: Charles Scribner's Sons.

1623 Deffaa, Chip. 1989. *Swing Legacy*. Metuchen, NJ: Scarecrow Press.

1624 Fernett, Gene. 1966. *A Thousand Golden Horns: The Exciting Age of America's Greatest Dance Bands*. Midland, MI: Pendell Publishing Company.

1625 Fernett, Gene. 1970. *Swing Out: Great Negro Dance Bands*. Midland, MI: Pendell Publishing Company.

1626 Gammond, Peter and Horricks, Raymond, eds. 1981. *Big Bands*. Cambridge: Stephens.

1627 Gitler, Ira. 1985. *Swing to Bop: An Oral History of the Transition in Jazz in the 1940s*. New York: Oxford University Press.

1628 Goodman, Benny and Kolodin, Irving. 1961. (1939) *The Kingdom of Swing*. New York: Frederick Ungar. First published New York: Stackpole, 1939.

1629 Hall, Fred. 1989. *Dialogues in Swing: Intimate Conversations with the Stars of the Big Band Era*. Ventura, CA: Pathfinder.

1630 Hall, Fred. 1991. *More Dialogues in Swing: Intimate Conversations with the Stars of the Big Band Era*. Ventura, CA: Pathfinder.

1631 Horricks, Raymond. 1955. The Search for Orchestral Progression. In *Jazzbook 1955*, ed. Albert McCarthy. London: Cassell. 22–34.

1632 Jones, Quincy. 1959. Starting a Big Band. *Jazz Review* 2(8): 16–17.

1633 Kirk, Andy. 1991. *Twenty Years on Wheels*, ed. Amy Lee. Wheatley: Bayou Press.

1634 Lally, Michael. 1975. *The Swing Era*. Washington, DC: Lucy and Ethel.

1635 McCarthy, Albert. 1971. *The Dance Band Era, 1910–1950*. Philadelphia: Chilton Book Co.

1636 McCarthy, Albert. 1974. *Big Band Jazz*. London/New York: Barrie & Jenkins/ G.P. Putnam's & Sons.

1637 Rollini, Arthur. 1987. *Thirty Years with the Big Bands*. London: Macmillan.

1638 Schickhaus, Wolfgang. 1990. Der 'swingende beat'. Untersuchungen zum Phänomen swing. In *Darmstädter Jazzforum 89: Beiträge zur Jazzforschung*, ed. Ekkehard Jost. Hofheim: Wolke. 190–206.

1639 Schuller, Gunther. 1989. (1968) *The Swing Era: The Development of Jazz, 1930–1945*. New York: Oxford University Press.

1640 Shaw, Artie. 1963. (1952) *The Trouble with Cinderella: An Outline of Identity*. New York: Collier. First published New York: Farrar, Strauss & Young, 1952.

1641 Simon, George T. 1971. *Simon Says: The Sights and Sounds of the Swing Era, 1935–1955*. New Rochelle, NY: Arlington House.

1642 Simon, George T. 1981. *The Big Bands*, revised edition. New York: Schirmer Books. First published New York: Macmillan, 1967, 1971, 1974.

1643 Smith, W.O. 1991. *Sideman: The Long Gig of W.O. Smith. A Memoir*. Nashville, TN: Rutledge Hill Press.

1644 Snow, George and Green, Jonathon. 1976. *Glenn Miller and the Age of Swing*. London: Dempsey & Squires.

1645 Stewart, Rex. 1982. (1972) *Jazz Masters of the Thirties*. New York: Da Capo Press. First published New York/ London: Macmillan/Collier-Macmillan, 1972.

1646 Stewart, Rex. 1991. *Boy Meets Horn*, ed. Claire P. Gordon. Wheatley: Bayou Press.

1647 Stowe, David W. 1994. *Swing Changes: Big-Band Jazz in New Deal America*. Cambridge and London: Harvard University Press.

1648 Treadwell, Bill. 1946. *Big Book of Swing*. New York: Cambridge House.

1649 Walker, Leo. 1978. *The Big Band Almanac*. Pasadena, CA: Ward Ritchie Press.

1650 Wells, Dicky. 1971. *The Night People*, ed. Stanley Dance. Boston, MA: Crescendo.

Third Stream

1651 Balliett, Whitney. 1962. Third Stream. In *Dinosaurs in the Morning: 41 Pieces on Jazz*. Philadelphia: Lippincott.

1652 Blake, Ran. 1992. Third Stream: Vorrang des Ohrs. In *Jazz und Komposition*, ed. Wolfram Knauer. Hofheim: Wolke. 141–48.

1653 Brown, Robert L. 1976. Classical Influences on Jazz. *Journal of Jazz Studies* 3: 19–35.

1654 Budds, Michael J. 1990. Structural Design. In *Jazz in the Sixties: The Expansion of Musical Resources and Techniques,* revised edition. Iowa City, IA: University of Iowa Press. 71–84. First published Iowa City: University of Iowa Press, 1978.

1655 Russo, William. 1958. Jazz and Classical Music. In *The New Yearbook of Jazz*, ed. Leonard Feather. New York: Horizon.

1656 Schuller, Gunther. 1982. Jazz and Classical Music. In *The Encyclopedia of Jazz*, ed. Leonard Feather, revised edition. New York: Da Capo Press. First published New York: Horizon, 1960.

1657 Schuller, Gunther. 1986. Jazz and the Third Stream. In *Musings: The Musical Worlds of Gunther Schuller*. New York and Oxford: Oxford University Press. 1–150.

1658 Schuller, Gunther. 1990. The Influence of Jazz on the History and Development of Concert Music. In *New Perspectives on Jazz*, ed. David Baker. Washington, DC: Smithsonian Institution Press. 9–23.

1659 Williams, Martin. 1980. Third Stream Problems. In *Jazz Masters in Transition, 1957–69*. New York: Da Capo Press. 112–19. First published New York: Macmillan, 1970. (First published in *Evergreen Review* 7(30) (1963): 113–25.)

1660 Williams, Martin. 1985. Third Stream Problems. In *Jazz Heritage*. New York and Oxford: Oxford University Press. 69–79. (First published in *Evergreen Review* 7(30) (1963): 113–25.)

Traditional Revival

1661 Deffaa, Chip. 1993. *Traditionalists and Revivalists in Jazz*. Metuchen, NJ: Scarecrow Press.

1662 Goodey, Brian R. 1968. New Orleans to London: Twenty Years of the New Orleans Jazz Revival in Britain. *Journal of Popular Culture* 2(2): 173–94.

1663 Matthew, Brian. 1960. *Trad Mad*. London: World Distributors.

1664 Stagg, Tom and Crump, Charlie. 1973. *New Orleans – The Revival: A Tape and Discography of Negro Traditional Jazz Recorded in New Orleans or by New Orleans Bands, 1937–1972*. Dublin: Bashall Eaves.

JEWISH MUSIC

1665 Bohlman, Philip V. 1984. Central European Jews in Israel: The Reurbanisation of Musical Life in an Immigrant. *Yearbook for Traditional Music* 16: 67–83.

1666 Cohen, Erik and Shiloah, Amnon. 1983. The Dynamics of Change in Jewish Oriental Music in Israel. *Ethnomusicology* 27(2): 227–52.

1667 Cohen, Erik and Shiloah, Amnon. 1985. Major Trends of Change in Jewish Oriental Ethnic Music in Israel. *Popular Music* 5: 199–223.

1668 Corenthal, Michael G. 1984. *Cohen on the Telephone: A History of Jewish Recorded Humour and Popular Music, 1892–1942*. Milwaukee, WI: Yesterday's Memories.

1669 Heskes, Irene, comp. 1985. *The Resource Book of Jewish Music*. Westport and London: Greenwood Press.

1670 Hirschberg, Jehoash. 1989. *The Role of Music in the Renewed Self-Identity of Karaite Jewish Refugee Communities from*

Cairo. New York: International Council for Traditional Music.

1671 Kanter, Kenneth Aaron. 1982. *The Jews in Tin Pan Alley: The Jewish Contribution to American Popular Music, 1830–1940.* New York: Ktav Publishing House.

1672 Nulman, Nancy. 1975. *Concise Encyclopedia of Jewish Music.* New York: McGraw-Hill.

1673 Sapoznik, Henry. 1988. From Eastern Europe to East Broadway: Yiddish Music in Old World and New. *New York Folklore* 14(3–4): 117–28.

1674 Slobin, Mark. 1982. *Tenement Songs: The Popular Music of Jewish Immigrants.* Urbana, IL: University of Illinois Press.

1675 Villiers, Douglas. 1976. Jewish Influences in 20th Century Pop Music and Entertainment. In *Jerusalem: Portraits of the Jew in the Twentieth Century.* New York: Viking.

JUJU

1676 Alaja-Browne, Afolabi. 1985. *Juju Music: A Study of Its Social History and Style.* Pittsburgh, PA: University of Pittsburgh.

1677 Alaja-Browne, Afolabi. 1989. A Diachronic Study of Change in Juju Music. *Popular Music* 8(3): 231–42.

1678 Alaja-Browne, Afolabi. 1989. The Origin and Development of Juju Music. *The Black Perspective in Music* 17(2): 55–72.

1679 Alaja-Browne, Afolabi. 1991. On Music, Emotions and Mobilization. *Worldbeat* 1: 46–54.

1680 Thomas, T Ajayi. 1992. *History of Juju Music: A History of African Popular Music from Nigeria.* New York: Thomas Organization.

1681 Waterman, Christopher A. 1990. *Juju: A Social History and Ethnography of African Music.* Chicago: University of Chicago Press.

KLEZMER

1682 Broughton, Simon. 1992. Klezmerized. *Folk Roots* 109 (July): 25–29.

1683 Feldman, Walter. 1994. Bulgareasa/Bulgarish/Bulgar: The Transformation of a Klezmer Dance Genre. *Ethnomusicology* 38(1): 1–35.

1684 Fragiacomo, Mario. 1994. Vecchio e nuovo 'Klezmer', il jazz ebraico. *Musica Jazz* 7: 52–53.

1685 Slobin, Mark. 1984. Klezmer Music: An American Ethnic Genre. *Yearbook for Traditional Music* 16: 34–41.

KRONCONG

1686 Becker, Judith. 1981. (1975) Kroncong, Indonesian Popular Music. *Asian Music* 7(1): 14–19.

1687 Heins, Ernst. 1975. Two Cases of Urban Folk Music in Jakarta: Kroncong and Tanjidor. *Asian Music* 7(1): 20–32.

1688 No entry.

LABOR SONGS

1689 Alloy, Evelyn. 1976. *Working Women's Music: The Songs and Struggle of Women in the Cotton Mills, Textile Plants and Needle Trade.* Somerville, MA: Free Press.

1690 Behagg, Clive. 1996. The Song of the Workplace: Singing, Dancing and the Control of Work in the Nineteenth and Early Twentieth Centuries. *Social History Society Bulletin* 21 (Spring): 9–10.

1691 Brazier, Richard. 1972. The Industrial Workers of the World's 'Little Red Songbook'. In *The Sounds of Social Change: Studies in Popular Culture*, ed. R. Serge Denisoff and Richard A. Peterson. Chicago: Rand McNally & Co. 60–71.

1692 Colls, Robert. 1977. *The Collier's Rant: Songs and Culture in the Industrial Village*. London: Croom Helm.

1693 Dallas, Karl. 1974. *One Hundred Songs of Toil: 450 Years of Workers Songs*. London: Wolfe Publications.

1694 De Caux, Len. 1978. *The Living Spirit of the Wobblies*. New York: International Publishers.

1695 Edelstein, T.J. 1980. They Sang the 'Song of the Shirt': The Visual Iconology of the Seamstress. *Victorian Studies* 23(2) (Winter): 183–210.

1696 Foner, Philip Sheldon. 1975. *American Labour Songs of the Nineteenth Century*. Urbana and London: University of Illinois Press.

1697 Fowke, Edith and Glazer, Joe. 1973. (1960) *Songs of Work and Protest*, revised edition. New York: Dover Publications. First published Chicago: Roosevelt University Press, 1960.

1698 Green, Archie, ed. 1993. *Songs About Work: Essays in Occupational Culture for Richard A. Reuss*. Bloomington, IN: Indiana University Folklore Institute.

1699 Halker, Clark. 1991. *For Democracy, Worker and God: Labor Song-Poems and Labor Protest, 1865–1895*. Urbana and Chicago: University of Illinois Press.

1700 Kurkela, Vesa. 1983. Worker's Music in a Finnish Industrial Town. *Suomen antropologi* 4: 218–23.

1701 MacColl, Ewan, ed. 1954. *The Shuttle and Cage: Industrial Folk Ballads*. London: Workers Music Association for Hargail Music Press.

1702 Man, Henrik de. 1978. (1930) Die Wirkung des Rhythmus im Vollzug industrialisierter Werkarbeit. *Musik und Gesellschaft* 1(2): 41–43.

1703 Marty, Laurent. 1982. *Chanter pour survivre: culture ouvrière, travail et techniques dans le textile, Roubaix, 1850–1914*. Lille: Fédération Léo Lagrange.

1704 Palmer, Roy. 1973. *The Painful Plough: A Portrait of the Agricultural Labourer in the Nineteenth Century from Folk Songs and Ballads and Contemporary Accounts*. Cambridge: Cambridge University Press.

1705 Raven, Jon. 1977. *The Urban and Industrial Folksongs of the Black Country and Birmingham*. Wolverhampton: Broadside.

1706 Raven, Jon. 1978. *Victoria's Inferno: Songs of the Old Mills, Mines, Canals and Railways*. Wolverhampton: Broadside.

1707 Rediker, Marcus. 1987. *Between the Devil and the Deep Blue Sea: Merchant Seamen, Pirates and the Anglo-American Maritime World, 1700–1750*. Cambridge: Cambridge University Press.

1708 Reuss, Richard. 1983. *Songs of American Labor, Industrialization and the Urban Work Experience: A Discography*. Ann Arbor, MI: University of Michigan Press.

1709 Seeger, Pete and Reiser, Bob. 1986. *Carry It On: A History in Song and Pictures of the Working Men and Women of America*. Poole: Blandford Press.

1710 Smith, L.D. 1979. *The Carpet Weaver's Lament: Songs and Ballads of Kidderminster in the Industrial Revolution*. Kidderminster: Kenneth Tomkinson Ltd.

1711 Vicinus, Martha. 1974. *The Industrial Muse: A Study of Nineteenth Century British Working Class Literature*. London: Croom Helm.

1712 Watson, Ian. 1983. *Song and Democratic Culture in Britain: An Approach to Popular Culture in Social Movements.* London: Croom Helm.

MARABI

1713 Coplan, David. 1980. Marabi Culture: Continuity and Transformation in African Music in Johannesburg, 1920-1940. *African Urban Studies* 6: 49–76.

1714 Coplan, David and Rycroft, David. 1981. Marabi: The Emergence of African Working-Class Music in Johannesburg. In *Discourse in Ethnomusicology II: A Tribute to Alan P. Merriam.* Bloomington, IN: Ethnomusicology Publications Group, Indiana University. 43–65.

MERENGUE

1715 Castillo, José del and García, Manuel. 1989. *Antología del merengue.* Santo Domingo: Banco Antillano.

MEXICAN–AMERICAN MUSIC

1716 Bensusan, Ben. 1985. A Consideration of Norteña and Chicano Music. *Studies in Latin American Popular Culture* 4: 158–69.

1717 Cosgrove, Stuart. 1984. The Zoot Suit and Style Warfare. *History Workshop* 18: 77–90.

1718 Dickey, Dan W. 1989. Música Tejana. In *Encyclopedia of Southern Culture, Vol. 3,* ed. Charles Reagan Wilson and William R. Ferris. New York: Doubleday Anchor. 316–21.

1719 Lipsitz, George. 1990. *Time Passages: Collective Memory and American Popular Culture.* Minneapolis, MN: University of Minnesota Press.

1720 Lipsitz, George. 1992. Chicano Rock: Cruisin' Around the Historical Bloc. In *Rockin' the Boat: Mass Music and Mass Movements,* ed. Reebee Garofalo. Boston, MA: South End Press. 267–80.

1721 Lewis, George H. 1992. La Pistola y El Corazon: Protest and Passion in Mexican-American Popular Music. *Journal of Popular Culture* 26(1): 51–68.

1722 Limon, José. 1983. Texas-Mexican Popular Music and Dancing: Some Notes on History and Symbolic Process. *Latin American Music Review* 4(2): 229–46.

1723 Loza, Steven. 1992. From Veracruz to Los Angeles: The Reinterpretation of the Son Jarocho. *Latin American Music Review* 13(2): 179–94.

1724 Loza, Steven. 1993. *Barrio Rhythm: Mexican-American Music in Los Angeles.* Urbana, IL: University of Illinois Press.

1725 Marre, Jeremy. 1985. Tex-Mex: The Music of the Texas-Mexican Borderlands. In *Beats of the Heart: Popular Music of the World,* ed. Jeremy Marre and Hannah Charlton. London: Pluto Press. 104–21.

1726 Paredes, Américo. 1976. *A Texas-Mexican Cancionero: Folksongs of the Lower Border.* Urbana, IL: University of Illinois Press.

1727 Peña, Manuel. 1980. Ritual Structure in a Chicano Dance. *Latin American Music Review* 1(1): 47–73.

1728 Peña, Manuel. 1985. From Ranchero to Jaitón: Ethnicity and Class in Texas-Mexican Music (Two Styles in the Form of a Pair). *Ethnomusicology* 29(1): 29–55.

1729 Peña, Manuel. 1985. *The Texas-Mexican Conjunto: History of a Working-Class Music.* Austin, TX: University of Texas Press.

1730 Peña, Manuel. 1987. Music for a Changing Community: Three

Generations of a Chicano Family Orquestra. *Latin American Music Review* 8(2): 230–45.

1731 Riedel, Johannes and Martinez, Santos J., eds. 1979. *Dale Kranque: Chicano Music and Art in South Texas.* Minneapolis, MN: University of Minnesota Media Resources.

1732 Tavera-King, Ben. 1984. ¡Ajúa! Música Chicana Takes Off. *Musical Traditions* 3: 4–7.

MILITARY MUSIC

1733 Binns, P.L. 1959. *A Hundred Years of Military Music: The Story of Kneller Hall.* Dorset: Blackmore Press.

1734 Farmer, Henry George. 1912. *The Rise and Development of Military Music.* London: Reeves.

1735 Farmer, Henry George. 1949. Crusading Martial Music. *Music and Letters* 30 (July): 243–49.

1736 Farmer, Henry George. 1950. *Military Music.* London: Max Parrish.

1737 Goldman, Richard F. 1939. *The Band's Music.* London: Pitman.

1738 Mackenzie-Rogan, J. 1926. *Fifty Years of Army Music.* London: Methuen.

1739 Smith, N., and Stoutamire, A. 1979. *Band Music Notes*, 2nd edition. San Diego, CA: Kjos West Publishers.

MINING SONGS

1740 Adams, James T. 1941. *Death in the Dark.* Big Laurel, VA: Adams-Mullin Press.

1741 Green, Archie. 1972. *Only a Miner: Studies in Recorded Coal-Mining Songs.* Urbana, IL: University of Illinois Press.

1742 Harker, Dave. 1980. Songs of Pitmen and Pitwork. In *One for the Money: Politics and Popular Song.* London: Hutchinson. 159–90.

1743 Korson, George. 1927. *Songs and Ballads of the Anthracite Miner.* New York: F.H. Hitchcock.

1744 Korson, George. 1964. *Minstrels of the Mine Patch: Songs and Stories of the Anthracite Industry.* Hatboro, PA: Folklore Associates.

1745 Korson, George. 1965. *Coal Dust on the Fiddle: Songs and Stories of the Bituminous Industry.* Hatboro, PA: Folklore Associates.

1746 Lloyd, A.L., ed. 1952. *Coaldust Ballads.* London: Workers Music Association.

1747 Lloyd, A.L., ed. 1952. *Come All Ye Bold Miners.* London: Lawrence and Wishart.

MINSTRELSY

1748 Austin, William. 1988. (1975) *'Susanna', 'Jeanie', and 'The Old Folks at Home': The Songs of Stephen C. Foster from His Time to Ours.* Urbana, IL: University of Illinois Press.

1749 Berret, Anthony. 1986. *Huckleberry Finn* and the Minstrel Show. *American Studies* 27(2): 37–49.

1750 Blair, John. 1990. Blackface Minstrels in Cross-Cultural Perspective. *American Studies International* 28(2): 52–65.

1751 Bratton, J.S. 1981. English Ethiopians: British Audiences and Black-Face Acts, 1835–1865. *Yearbook of English Studies:* **127–42.**

1752 Briggs, Thomas F. 1992. (1855) *Briggs' Banjo Instructor: Containing the Elementary Principles of Music, Together with Examples and Lessons, Necessary to Facilitate the Acquirement of a Perfect Knowledge of the Instrument.* Bremo

Bluff, VA: Tuckahoe Music. First published Boston: Oliver Ditson, 1855.

1753 Browne, Ray B. 1960. Shakespeare in American Vaudeville and Negro Minstrelsy. *American Quarterly* 12: 374–91.

1754 Buckley, James. 1995. (1860) *Buckley's New Banjo Book: Containing Full and Complete Instructions for Learning to Play the Banjo With, or Without a Teacher.* Bremo Bluff, VA: Tuckahoe Music. First published New York/Boston: Firth, Pond and Co./Oliver Ditson and Co., 1860.

1755 Cockrell, Dale. 1987. Of Gospel Hymns, Minstrel Shows and Jubilee Singers: Toward Some Black South African Musics. *American Music* 5(4): 417–32.

1756 Converse, Frank B. 1993. (1865) *Frank B. Converse's New and Complete Method for the Banjo With or Without a Master.* Bremo Bluff, VA: Tuckahoe Music. First published New York: S.T. Gordon, 1865.

1757 Conway, Cecilia. 1995. *African Banjo Echoes in Appalachia: A Study in Folk Traditions.* Knoxville, TN: University of Tennessee Press.

1758 Costonis, Maureen. 1991. Martha Graham's *American Document:* A Minstrel Show in Modern Dance Dress. *American Music* 9(3): 297–310.

1759 Dennison, Sam. 1982. *Scandalize My Name: Black Imagery in American Popular Music.* New York: Garland.

1760 Duncan, Edmondstoune. 1907. *The Story of Minstrelsy.* London: The Walter Scott Publishing Co.

1761 Ellison, Ralph. 1964. Change the Joke and Slip the Yoke. In *Shadow and Act.* New York: Random House. 45–59.

1762 Engle, Gary D., ed. 1978. *This Grotesque Essence: Plays from the American Minstrel Stage.* Baton Rouge, LA: Louisiana State University Press.

1763 Erlmann, Veit. 1991. *African Stars: Studies in Black South African Performance.* Chicago: University of Chicago Press.

1764 Fletcher, Tom. 1984. (1954) *100 Years of the Negro in Show Business.* New York: Da Capo Press. First published New York: Burdge & Co. Ltd., 1954.

1765 Goertzen, Chris. 1991. Mrs. Joe Person's Popular Airs: Early Blackface Minstrels in Oral Tradition. *Ethnomusicology* 35(1): 31–53.

1766 Green, Alan W.C. 1970. 'Jim Crow', 'Zip Coon': The Northern Origins of Negro Minstrelsy. *Massachusetts Review* 11 (Spring): 385–97.

1767 Hamm, Charles. 1979. 'Jim Crow': or, The Music of the Early American Minstrel Show. In *Yesterdays: Popular Song in America.* New York: W.W. Norton. 89–108.

1768 Hamm, Charles. 1995. The Last Minstrel Show? In *Putting Popular Music in Its Place.* Cambridge: Cambridge University Press. 354–66.

1769 Hare, Walter. 1921. *The Minstrel Encyclopedia.* Boston, MA: Baker.

1770 Haverly, Jack. 1969. (1909) *Negro Minstrels: A Complete Guide to Negro Minstrelsy.* Chicago: Literature House. First published Chicago: F.J. Drake & Co., 1909.

1771 Haywood, Charles. 1961. The Negro Minstrelsy. In *A Bibliography of North American Folklore and Folksong, Vol. 1.* New York: Dover Publications. 522–41.

1772 Haywood, Charles. 1966. Negro Minstrelsy and Shakespearean Burlesque. In *Folklore and Society: Essays in Honor of Benjamin A. Botkin,* ed. Bruce Jackson. Hatboro, PA: American Folklore Society. 77–92.

1773 Holmberg, Carl Bryan and Schneider, Gilbert D. 1986. Daniel Decatur Emmett's Stump Sermons: Genuine Afro-American Culture, Language and Rhetoric in the Negro Minstrel Show. *Journal of Popular Culture* 19(4): 27–38.

1774 Keck, George R. and Martin, Sherril V., eds. 1988. *Feel the Spirit: Essays in Nineteenth-Century Afro-American Music.* New York: Greenwood Press.

1775 Krohn, Ernest C. 1971. Nelson Kneass: Minstrel Singer and Composer. *Yearbook for Inter-American Musical Research* 7: 17–41.

1776 Lott, Eric. 1991. 'This Seeming Counterfeit': Racial Politics and Early Blackface Minstrelsy. *American Quarterly* 43(2) (June): 223–54.

1777 Lott, Eric. 1993. *Love and Theft: Blackface Minstrelsy and the American Working Class.* New York and Oxford: Oxford University Press.

1778 Mahar, William J. 1985. Black English in Early Blackface Minstrelsy: A New Interpretation of the Sources for Minstrel Show Dialect. *American Quarterly* 37(2) (Summer): 260–85.

1779 Mahar, William J. 1988. 'Backside Albany' and Early Blackface Minstrelsy: A Contextual Study of America's First Blackface Song. *American Music* 6(1): 1–27.

1780 Mahar, William J. 1991. Ethiopian Skits and Sketches: Contents and Contexts of Blackface Minstrelsy. *Prospects* 16: 241–79.

1781 Moreau, Charles, ed. 1891. *Negro Minstrelsy in New York.* 2 vols. Cambridge, MA: Harvard Theatre Collection.

1782 Nathan, Hans. 1952. The First Negro Minstrel Band and Its Origins. *Southern Folklore Quarterly* 16: 132–44.

1783 Nathan, Hans. 1977. *Dan Emmett and the Rise of Early Negro Minstrelsy.* Norman, OK: University of Oklahoma Press.

1784 Ostendorf, Berndt. 1982. *Black Literature in White America.* Brighton: Harvester Press.

1785 Paskman, Dailey and Spaeth, Sigmund. 1976. (1928) *'Gentlemen, Be Seated': A Parade of the American Minstrels.* New York: Potter. First published Garden City: Doubleday Doran & Co., 1928.

1786 Pickering, Michael. 1986. White Skin, Black Masks: 'Nigger' Minstrelsy in Victorian Britain. In *Music Hall: Performance and Style*, ed. J.S. Bratton. Milton Keynes: Open University Press. 78–91.

1787 Rehin, George S. 1975. Harlequin Jim Crow: Continuity and Convergence in Blackface Clowning. *Journal of Popular Culture* 9: 682–701.

1788 Rehin, George S. 1981. Blackface Street Minstrels in Victorian London and Its Resorts: Popular Culture and Its Racial Connotations as Revealed in Polite Opinion. *Journal of Popular Culture* 15(1): 19–38.

1789 Rehin, George S. 1981. The Darker Image: American Negro Minstrelsy Through the Historian's Lens. *Journal of American Studies* 9(3): 365–73.

1790 Reynolds, Harry. 1928. *Minstrel Memories: The Story of Burnt Cork Minstrelsy in Great Britain from 1836 to 1927.* London: A. Rivers.

1791 Rice, Edward Leroy. 1911. *Monarchs of Minstrelsy: From Daddy Rice to the Present.* New York: Kenny.

1792 Rice, Phil. 1858. *Phil. Rice's Correct Method for the Banjo, With or Without a Master.* Boston, MA: Oliver Ditson.

1793 Roediger, David R. 1991. Class, Coons and Crowds in Antebellum America. In

The Wages of Whiteness: Race and the Making of the American Working Class. London and New York: Verso. 95–114.

1794 Rourke, Constance. 1986. (1931) American Humor: A Study of National Character. Tallahassee, FL: University of Florida Press. First published Garden City: Doubleday, 1931.

1795 Sampson, Henry. 1980. Blacks in Blackface: A Source Book of Early Black Music Shows. Metuchen, NJ: Scarecrow Press.

1796 Saxton, Alexander. 1975. Blackface Minstrelsy and Jacksonian Ideology. American Quarterly 27(1) (March): 3–28.

1797 Saxton, Alexander. 1990. Blackface Minstrelsy. In The Rise and Fall of the White Republic: Class Politics and Mass Culture in Nineteenth-Century America. London and New York: Verso. 165–82.

1798 Simond, Ike. 1974. Old Slack's Reminiscence and Pocket History of the Colored Profession from 1865–1891. Bowling Green, OH: Bowling Green University Popular Press.

1799 Southern, Eileen. 1975. Black Musicians and Early Ethiopian Minstrelsy. The Black Perspective in Music 3(1): 77–83.

1800 Suthern, Orrin Clayton, II. 1971. Minstrelsy and Popular Culture. Journal of Popular Culture 4(3): 658–73.

1801 Toll, Robert C. 1974. Blacking Up: The Minstrel Show in Nineteenth-Century America. New York: Oxford University Press.

1802 Waterhouse, Richard. 1990. From Minstrel Show to Vaudeville: The Australian Popular Stage, 1788–1914. New South Wales: New South Wales Press.

1803 Waterhouse, Richard. 1990. The Minstrel Show and Australian Culture.

Journal of Popular Culture 24(2): 147–66.

1804 Winans, Robert B. 1976. The Folk, the Stage and the Five-String Banjo in the Nineteenth Century. Journal of American Folklore 89: 407–37.

1805 Winans, Robert B. 1984. Early Minstrel-Show Music, 1843–1852. In Musical Theatre in America: Papers and Proceedings of the Conference on Musical Theatre in America, ed. Glenn B. Loney. Westport, CT: Greenwood Press. 71–98.

1806 Wittke, Carl. 1968. (1930) Tambo and Bones: A History of the American Minstrel Stage. New York: Greenwood Press. First published Durham: Duke University Press, 1930.

1807 Zanger, Jules. 1974. The Minstrel Show as Theatre of Misrule. Quarterly Journal of Speech. 60: 33–38.

MOTOWN

1808 Bartlette, Reginald J. 1990. Off the Record: Motown by Master Number, 1959–89, Vol. I. Singles. Ann Arbor, MI: Popular Culture, Ink.

1809 Benjaminson, Peter. 1979. The Story of Motown. New York: Grove Press.

1810 Bianco, David. 1988. Heat Wave: The Motown Fact Book. Ann Arbor, MI: Pierian Press.

1811 Davis, Sharon. 1988. Motown: The History. Enfield: Guinness Publications.

1812 Early, Gerald. 1995. One Nation Under a Groove: Motown and American Culture. Hopewell, NJ: Ecco Press.

1813 Fitzgerald, Jon. 1995. Black or White? Stylistic Analysis of Motown Crossover Hits: 1963–66. In Popular Music: Style and Identity, ed. Will Straw, et al. Montréal: The Centre for Research on

Canadian Cultural Industries and Institutions. 95–98.

1814 Fitzgerald, Jon. 1995. Motown Crossover Hits, 1963–1966 and the Creative Process. *Popular Music* 14(1): 1–11.

1815 Fong-Torres, Ben. 1990. *The Motown Album: The Sound of Young America.* London: Virgin.

1816 Frith, Simon. 1975. You Can Make It If You Try: The Motown Story. In *The Soul Book*, ed. Ian Hoare. London: Methuen. 32–59.

1817 George, Nelson. 1985. *Where Did Our Love Go? The Rise and Fall of the Motown Sound.* New York: St. Martin's Press.

1818 Gordy, Berry. 1994. *To Be Loved: The Music, the Magic, the Memories of Motown.* New York: Warner Books.

1819 Hirshey, Gerri. 1984. *Nowhere to Run: The Story of Soul Music.* New York: Times Books.

1820 Licks, Dr. 1989. *Standing in the Shadows of Motown: The Life and Music of Legendary Bassist James Jamerson.* Wynnewood: Dr. Licks Publishing.

1821 McEwen, Joe and Miller, Jim. 1992. (1976) Motown. In *The Rolling Stone Illustrated History of Rock & Roll*, ed. Anthony DeCurtis and James Henke, revised edition. New York: Straight Arrow. 277–92. First published New York: Random House, 1976.

1822 Mitchell, Elvis. 1990. *The Motown Album: An American Story.* London: Virgin.

1823 Morse, David. 1971. *Motown and the Arrival of Black Music.* New York: Macmillan.

1824 Reeves, Martha and Bego, Mark. 1994. *Dancing in the Street: Confessions of a Motown Diva.* New York: Hyperion.

1825 Robinson, Smokey and Ritz, David. 1989. *Smokey: Inside My Life.* London: Headline.

1826 Ryan, Jack. 1982. *Recollections, the Detroit Years: The Motown Story by the People Who Made It.* Ann Arbor, MI: Jack Ryan.

1827 Shaw, Arnold. 1970. *The World of Soul: Black America's Contribution to the Pop Music Scene.* New York: Cowles.

1828 Singleton, Raynoma, Bryan Brown and Mim Eichler. 1990. *Berry, Me and Motown.* Chicago: Contemporary Books.

1829 Slutsky, Alan. 1993. Motown: The History of a Hit-Making Sound and the Keyboardists Who Made It Happen. *Keyboard* (May): 84–104.

1830 Standing in the Shadows of Motown: The Unsung Session Men of Hitsville's Golden Era. 1983. *Musician* 60: 61–66.

1831 Taraborelli, J. Randy. 1986. *Motown: Hot Wax, City Cool and Solid Gold.* Garden City, NY: Doubleday.

1832 Waller, Don. 1985. *The Motown Story.* New York: Scribner.

1833 Wilson, Mary, Patricia Romanowski and Ahrgus Juilliard. 1986. *Dreamgirl: My Life as a Supreme.* New York: St. Martin's Press.

MUSIC HALL

1834 Aston, Elaine. 1988. Male Impersonation in the Music Hall: The Case of Vesta Tilley. *New Theatre Quarterly* 4: 247–57.

1835 Bailey, Peter. 1982. Custom, Capital and Culture in the Victorian Music Hall. In *Popular Culture and Customs in Nineteenth-Century England*, ed. Robert D. Storch. London and Canberra: Croom Helm. 180–208.

1836 Bailey, Peter, ed. 1986. *Music Hall: The Business of Pleasure*. Milton Keynes: Open University Press.

1837 Bailey, Peter. 1994. Conspiracies of Meaning: Music-Hall and the Knowingness of Popular Culture. *Past and Present* 144: 139–70.

1838 Bratton, J.S., ed. 1986. *Music Hall: Performance and Style*. Milton Keynes: Open University Press.

1839 Bratton, J.S. 1996. Beating the Bounds: Gender Play and Role Reversal in the Edwardian Music Hall. In *The Edwardian Theatre: Essays on Performance and the Stage*, ed. Michael Booth and Joel Kaplan. Cambridge: Cambridge University Press. 86–110.

1840 Busby, Roy. 1976. *British Music Hall: An Illustrated Who's Who from 1850 to the Present Day*. London: Elek.

1841 Cheshire, David F. 1974. *Music Hall in Britain*. Cranbury, NJ: Fairleigh Dickinson University Press.

1842 Davis, Tracy C. 1991. The Moral Sense of the Majorities: Indecency and Vigilance in Late-Victorian Music Halls. *Popular Music* 10(1): 39–52.

1843 Davison, Peter. 1992. (1971). *Songs of the British Music Hall*. New York: Beekman Publishing.

1844 Diamond, Michael. 1990. Political Heroes of the Victorian Music Hall. *History Today* 40 (January): 33–39.

1845 Disher, Maurice. 1938. *Music Hall Parade*. London: B.T. Batsford.

1846 Feschotte, Jacques. 1965. *Histoire du Music-Hall*. Paris: PUF.

1847 Garrett, John M. 1976. *Sixty Years of British Music Hall*. London: Chappell & Co.

1848 Harding, James. 1990. *George Robey and the Music Hall*. London: Hodder and Stoughton.

1849 Harker, Dave. 1981. The Making of the Tyneside Concert Hall. *Popular Music* 1: 27–56.

1850 Helian, Jacques. 1984. *Les grands orchestres de music hall en France: souvenirs et témoignages*. Paris: Filipacchi.

1851 Kift, Dagmar. 1991. *Arbeiterkultur im gesellschaftlichen Konflikt. Die Englische Music Hall im 19. Jahrhundert*. Essen: Klartext Verlag.

1852 Lee, Edward. 1982. *Folksong and Music Hall*. London: Routledge & Kegan Paul.

1853 MacInnes, Colin. 1967. *Sweet Saturday Night: Pop Song, 1840–1920*. London: Macgibbon and Kee.

1854 Mackintosh, Iain and Sell, Michael, eds. 1982. *Curtains!!! or, A New Life for Old Theatres: Being a Complete Gazetteer of All the Surviving Pre-1914 Theatres, Music Halls of Great Britain*. Eastbourne: Offord.

1855 Mander, Raymond and Mitchenson, Joe. 1974. *The British Music Hall*. London: Gentry Books.

1856 Middleton, Richard. 1981. Popular Music of the Lower Classes. In *Music in Britain: The Romantic Age, 1800–1914*, ed. Nicholas Temperley. London: Athlone Press.

1857 Poole, Robert. 1982. *Popular Leisure and the Music Hall in 19th-Century Bolton*. Lancaster: Centre for North-West Regional Studies, University of Lancaster, Occasional Paper No. 12.

1858 Russell, Dave. 1987. *Popular Music in England, 1840–1914: A Social History*. Manchester: Manchester University Press.

1859 Russell, Dave. 1992. 'We Carved Our Way to Glory': The British Soldier in

Music Hall Song and Sketch, c.1880–1914. In *Popular Imperialism and the Military, 1850–1950*, ed. John Mackenzie. Manchester: Manchester University Press. 50–79.

1860 Russell, Dave. 1996. Varieties of Life: The Making of the Edwardian Music Hall. In *The Edwardian Theatre: Essays on Performance and the Stage*, ed. Michael Booth and Joel Kaplan. Cambridge: Cambridge University Press. 61–85.

1861 Rust, Brian. 1979. *British Music Hall on Record*. Harrow: General Gramophone Publications.

1862 Schneider, Ulrich. 1984. *Die Londoner Music Hall und ihre Songs, 1850–1920*. Tübingen: Max Niemeyer.

1863 Senelick, Laurence. 1975. Politics as Entertainment: Victorian Music Hall Songs. *Victorian Studies* 19(2): 149–80.

1864 Senelick, Laurence, David F. Cheshire and Ulrich Schneider, eds. 1981. *British Music Hall, 1840–1923: A Bibliography and Guide to Sources, with a Supplement on European Music-Hall*. Hamden, CT: Archon Books.

1865 Sevran, Pascal. 1978. *Le Music Hall français de Mayol à Julien Clerc*. Paris: Olivier Orban.

1866 Stedman-Jones, Gareth. 1974. Working-Class Culture and Working-Class Politics in London, 1870–1900: Notes on the Remaking of a Working Class. *Journal of Social History* 7(4): 460–508.

1867 Summerfield, Penelope. 1981. The Effingham Arms and the Empire: Deliberate Selection in the Evolution of Music Hall in London. In *Popular Culture and Class Conflict, 1590–1914: Explorations in the History of Labour and Leisure*, ed. Eileen Yeo and Stephen Yeo. Brighton: Harvester Press. 209–40.

1868 Summerfield, Penelope. 1986. Patriotism and Empire: Music Hall Entertainment, 1870–1914. In *Imperialism and Popular Culture*, ed. John Mackenzie. Manchester: Manchester University Press. 17–48.

1869 Traies, Jane. 1986. Jones and the Working Girl: Class Marginality in Music-Hall Song, 1860–1900. In *Music Hall: Performance and Style*, ed. J.S. Bratton. Milton Keynes: Open University Press. 23–48.

1870 Waites, Bernard. 1981. The Music Hall. In *The Historical Development of Popular Culture in Britain, 1*. Milton Keynes: Open University Press. 43–76.

1871 Waters, Chris. 1989. Progressives, Puritans and the Cultural Politics of the Council, 1889–1914. In *Politics and the People of London: The London County Council, 1889–1965*, ed. Andrew Saint. London: Hambledon Press. 49–70.

MUSICA MIZRAKHIT

1872 Halper, Jeff, Edwin Seroussi and Pamela Squires-Kidron. 1989. *Musica Mizrakhit: Ethnicity and Class Culture in Israel*. Cambridge: Cambridge University Press.

1873 Regev, Motti. 1996. Musica Mizrakhit, Israeli Rock and National Culture in Israel. *Popular Music* 15(3): 275–84.

MUSICA SERTANEJA

1874 Reily, Suzel-Ana. 1992. *Música Sertaneja* and Migrant Identity: The Stylistic Development of a Brazilian Genre. *Popular Music* 11(3): 337–58.

MUSICAL THEATER

1875 Alpert, Hollis. 1991. *Broadway: 125 Years of Musical Theatre*. New York: Arcade Publishers.

1876 Banham, Martin, ed. 1992. *The Cambridge Guide to Theatre*. Cambridge: Cambridge University Press.

1877 Baral, Robert. 1962. *Revue: The Great Broadway Period*. New York: Fleet Press.

1878 Bargainnier, Earl F. 1978. W.S. Gilbert and American Musical Theatre. *Journal of Popular Culture* 12(3): 446–58.

1879 Bernstein, Leonard. 1959. American Musical Comedy. In *The Joy of Music*. New York: Simon & Schuster. 152–79.

1880 Bloom, Ken. 1985. *American Song: The Complete Musical Theatre Companion*. New York: Facts on File.

1881 Bloom, Ken. 1991. *Broadway: An Encyclopedic Guide to the History, People and Places of Times Square*. New York: Facts on File.

1882 Bordman, Gerald. 1981. *American Operetta: From H.M.S. Pinafore to Sweeney Todd*. New York: Oxford University Press.

1883 Bordman, Gerald. 1982. *American Musical Comedy: From Adonis to Dreamgirls*. New York: Oxford University Press.

1884 Bordman, Gerald. 1985. *American Musical Revue: From the Passing Show to Sugar Babies*. New York: Oxford University Press.

1885 Bordman, Gerald. 1992. (1978) *American Musical Theatre: A Chronicle*. New York: Oxford University Press.

1886 Bowers, Dwight. 1989. *American Musical Theater: Shows, Songs and Stars*. Washington, DC: Smithsonian Institution Press.

1887 Burton, Jack. 1969. (1952) *The Blue Book of Broadway Musicals*. Watkins Glen, NY: Century House.

1888 Citron, Stephen. 1991. *The Musical: From Inside Out*. London: Hodder and Stoughton.

1889 Ewen, David. 1968. *The Story of America's Musical Theater*. Philadelphia: Chilton Book Co.

1890 Ewen, David. 1970. *New Complete Book of the American Musical Theatre: A Guide to More Than 300 Productions of the American Musical Theatre*. New York: Holt, Rinehart & Winston.

1891 Fields, Armond and Fields, L. Marc. 1993. *From the Bowery to Broadway: Lew Field and the Roots of American Popular Theater*. New York: Oxford University Press.

1892 Gänzl, Kurt. 1986. *The British Musical Theatre*. London: Macmillan.

1893 Gänzl, Kurt. 1990. *The Blackwell Guide to the Musical Theatre on Record*. Oxford: Basil Blackwell.

1894 Gänzl, Kurt. 1994. *The Encyclopedia of the Musical Theatre*. Oxford: Blackwell.

1895 Gänzl, Kurt and Lamb, Andrew. 1988. *Gänzl's Book of the Musical Theatre*. London: Bodley Head.

1896 Gáspár, Margit. 1963. *A mázsák neveletten gyermeke*. Budapest: Zenemukiadó Vállalat.

1897 Gottfried, Martin. 1984. *Broadway Musicals*. New York: Abradale Press.

1898 Green, Stanley. 1976. *Encyclopedia of the Musical Theatre*. New York: Dodd, Mead.

1899 Green, Stanley. 1980. (1960) *The World of Musical Comedy: The Story of the American Musical Stage as Told Through the Careers of Its Foremost Composers and Lyricists*. San Diego, CA: Barnes.

1900 Green, Stanley. 1982. *Broadway Musicals of the 30's*. New York: Da Capo Press.

GENRES

1901 Green, Stanley. 1985. *Broadway Musicals, Show by Show*. Milwaukee, WI: Leonard.

1902 Guernsey, Otis. 1985. *Broadway Song and Story: Playwrights/Lyricists/Composers Discuss Their Hits*. New York: Dodd, Mead.

1903 Hadamowsky, Franz and Otte, Heinz. 1947. *Die Wiener Operette*. Wien: Bellaria.

1904 Harris, Steve. 1988. *Film, Television and Stage Music on Phonograph Records: A Discography*. Jefferson, NC: McFarland.

1905 Hatch, James. 1971. *Black Image on the American Stage: A Bibliography of Plays and Musicals, 1770–1970*. New York: Drama Book Specialists.

1906 Hirsch, Foster. 1989. *Harold Prince and the American Musical Theatre*. Cambridge: Cambridge University Press.

1907 Hischak, Thomas. 1991. *Word Crazy: Broadway Lyricists from Cohan to Sondheim*. New York: Praeger.

1908 Hischak, Thomas. 1993. *Stage It with Music: An Encyclopedic Guide to the American Musical Theatre*. Westport, CT: Greenwood Press.

1909 Hodgins, Gordon W. 1980. *The Broadway Musical: A Complete LP Discography*. Metuchen and London: Scarecrow Press.

1910 Hoover, Cynthia. 1984. Music in Eighteenth-Century American Theater. *American Music* 2(4): 6–18.

1911 Horn, David. 1994. From Catfish Row to Granby Street: Contesting Meaning in *Porgy and Bess*. *Popular Music* 13(2): 165–74.

1912 Johnson, Stephen. 1985. *The Roof Gardens of Broadway Theatres, 1883–1942*. Ann Arbor, MI: UMI Research Press.

1913 Kimball, Robert and Krasker, Tommy. 1988. *Catalog of the American Musical: Musicals of Irving Berlin, George and Ira Gershwin, Cole Porter, Richard Rodgers & Lorenz Hart*. New York: National Institute for Opera and Musical Theater.

1914 Kislan, Richard. 1980. *The Musical: A Look at the American Musical Theatre*. Englewood Cliffs, NJ: Prentice-Hall.

1915 Kreuger, Miles. 1977. *Showboat: The Story of a Classic American Musical*. New York: Oxford University Press.

1916 Kudinova, T. 1982. *Ot vodevil do muzykal*. Moskva: Sovjetskij kompositor.

1917 Lamb, Andrew. 1986. From *Pinafore* to Porter: United States-United Kingdom Interactions in Musical Theatre, 1879–1929. *American Music* 4(1): 34–49.

1918 Laufe, Abe. 1969. *Broadway's Greatest Musicals*. New York: Funk & Wagnalls.

1919 Lawson-Peebles, Robert, ed. 1996. *Approaches to the American Musical*. Exeter: University of Exeter Press.

1920 Lehman, Engel. 1972. *Words with Music*. New York: Macmillan.

1921 Lehman, Engel. 1975. (1967) *The American Musical Theater: A Consideration*. New York: Macmillan.

1922 Lehman, Engel. 1975. *Their Words Are Music: The Great Theatre Lyricists and Their Lyrics*. New York: Crown.

1923 Lehman, Engel. 1977. *The Making of a Musical*. New York: Macmillan.

1924 Lerner, Alan. 1986. *The Musical Theatre: A Celebration*. New York: McGraw-Hill.

1925 Lewine, Richard and Simon, Alfred. 1984. *Songs of the Theater: A Definitive Index to the Songs of the Musical Stage*. New York: H.W. Wilson.

1926 Loney, Glenn B., ed. 1984. *Musical Theatre in America: Papers and*

Proceedings of the Conference on Musical Theatre in America. Westport, CT: Greenwood Press.

1927 Lubbock, Mark. 1962. *The Complete Book of Light Opera*. London: Putnam.

1928 Lynch, Richard Chigley. 1987. *Broadway on Record: A Directory of New York Cast Recordings of Musical Shows, 1931–1986*. New York and London: Greenwood Press.

1929 Lynch, Richard Chigley. 1990. *TV and Studio Cast Musicals on Record*. New York: Greenwood Press.

1930 Marx, Henry. 1986. *Die Broadway Story. Eine Kulturgeschichte des amerikanischen Theaters*. Düsseldorf and Wien: Econ.

1931 Mates, Julian. 1962. *The American Musical Stage Before 1800*. New Brunswick, NJ: Rutgers University Press.

1932 Mates, Julian. 1983. The First Hundred Years of the American Lyric Theater. *American Music* 1(2): 22–38.

1933 Mates, Julian. 1985. *America's Musical Stage: Two Hundred Years of Musical Theatre*. Westport, CT: Greenwood Press.

1934 Mordden, Ethan. 1976. *Better Foot Forward: The History of the American Musical Theatre*. New York: Grossman Publishers.

1935 Mordden, Ethan. 1983. *Broadway Babies: The People Who Made the American Musical*. New York: Oak Publications.

1936 Peterson, Bernard. 1993. *A Century of Musicals in Black and White: An Encyclopedia of Musical Stage Works By, About, or Involving African Americans*. Westport, CT: Greenwood Press.

1937 Porter, Susan. 1992. *With an Air Debonaire: Musical Theatre in America,*

1785–1815. Washington, DC: Smithsonian Institution Press.

1938 Raymond, Jack. 1992. *Show Music on Record: The First 100 Years*. Washington, DC: Smithsonian Institution Press.

1939 Riis, Thomas. 1984. Black Musical Theater, 1870–1930: Research Problems and Resources. *American Music* 2(4): 95–100.

1940 Riis, Thomas. 1989. *Just Before Jazz: Black Musical Theater in New York, 1890–1915*. Washington, DC: Smithsonian Institution Press.

1941 Riis, Thomas. 1992. *More Than Just Minstrel Shows: The Rise of Black Musical Theatre at the Turn of the Century*. Brooklyn, NY: Institute for Studies in American Music.

1942 Root, Deane L. 1981. *American Popular Stage Music, 1860–1880*. Ann Arbor, MI: UMI Research Press.

1943 Rubin, Martin. 1993. *Showstoppers: Busby Berkeley and the Tradition of Spectacle*. New York: Columbia University Press.

1944 Sampson, Henry. 1980. *Blacks in Blackface: A Source Book of Early Black Music Shows*. Metuchen, NJ: Scarecrow Press.

1945 Schlundt, Christena L., et al. 1989. *Dance in the Musical Theatre: Jerome Robbins and His Peers, 1934–1965*. New York: Garland.

1946 Shapiro, Anne. 1984. Action Music in American Pantomime and Melodrama, 1730–1913. *American Music* 2(4): 49–72.

1947 Smith, Cecil and Litton, Glen. 1981. *Musical Comedy in America*. New York: Theatre Arts Books.

1948 Sonderhoff, Joachim. 1986. *Das Musical. Geschichte, Produktion, Erfolge*. Braunschweig: Westermann.

GENRES

1949 Southern, Eileen. 1981. The Origin and Development of Black Musical Theater: A Preliminary Report. *Black Music Research Journal* 1981–82: 1–14.

1950 Swain, Joseph P. 1990. *The Broadway Musical: A Critical and Musical Survey.* New York and London: Oxford University Press.

1951 Szemere, Anna. 1985. Das Petöfi-Theater ein Musical-Theater? *Beiträge zur Musikwissenschaft* 3–4: 295–302.

1952 Tichwinskaya, L. 1995. *Kabare y teatr miniatjur v Rossya 1908–1917.* Moskva: Kultura.

1953 Toll, Robert C. 1982. *The Entertainment Machine: American Show Business in the Twentieth Century.* New York and London: Oxford University Press.

1954 Trauberg, L. 1987. *Dzak Offenbach y drugye.* Moskva: Iskusstvo.

1955 Traubner, Richard. 1983. *Operetta: A Theatrical History.* Garden City, NY: Doubleday.

1956 Tumbusch, Tom. 1972. *Guide to Broadway Musical Theatre.* New York: Richards Rosen Press.

1957 Woll, Allen. 1989. *Black Musical Theatre: From Coontown to Dreamgirls.* Baton Rouge, LA: Louisiana State University Press.

1958 Zadan, Craig. 1986. *Sondheim & Co.* New York: Harper & Row.

1959 Zimmerschied, Dieter. 1988. *Operette. Phänomene und Entwicklung.* Wiesbaden: Breitkopf & Härtel.

MUZAK

1960 Barnes, Stephen H. 1988. *Muzak – The Hidden Messages in Music: A Social Psychology of Culture.* Lewiston, NY: Edwin Mellen Press.

1961 Bücher, Karl. 1978. (1930) Der Rhythmus als ökonomisches Entwicklungsprinzip. In *Musik und Gesellschaft,* ed. Dorothea Kolland. Berlin: Das europäische Buch. 44–46.

1962 Lanza, Joseph. 1995. *Elevator Music.* New York: St. Martin's Press.

1963 MacLeod, Bruce. 1979. Facing the Muzak. *Popular Music & Society* 7(1): 18–31.

1964 Nordström, Gert Z. 1989. Musica durante il lavoro: Un'analisi musico-sociale. *Musica/Realtà* 30: 16–24.

1965 Tagg, Philip. 1989. Musica popolare, innovazione, tecnologia. *Quaderni di Musica/Realtà* 23: 34–43.

1966 Tagg, Philip. 1991. Muzak, sigle televisive, temi conduttori e musiche da film. *Cinema e Cinema* 18(60): 77–86.

NUEVA CANCION

1967 Becerra, Gustavo. 1985. La música culta y la Nueva Canción Chilena. *Literatura Chilena. Creación y Crítica* 9(33–34): 14–21.

1968 Borraza, Fernando. 1972. *Le nueva canción chilena.* Casilla Chile: Editora Nacional Quimantu.

1969 Carrasco-Pirard, Eduardo. 1982. The nueva canción in Latin America. *International Social Science Journal* 34(4): 599–623.

1970 Fairley, Jan. 1984. La nueva canción latinoamericana. *Bulletin of Latin American Research* 3(2): 103–105.

1971 Fairley, Jan. 1985. Annotated Bibliography of Latin-American Popular Music with Particular Reference to Chile and to Nueva Canción. *Popular Music* 5: 305–56.

1972 Fleury, Jean-Jacques. 1985. Castilla y Leon en la nueva canción. *Hispanorama* 41: 81–91.

1973 Fleury, Jean-Jacques. 1985. El indio y el niño en la nueva canción. *Hispanorama – Sonderdruck* (November): 89–94.

1974 Fleury, Jean-Jacques. 1985. La nueva canción en Aragon. *Hispanorama* 41: 75–81.

1974a Lloréns, José-Antonio and Oliart, Patricia. 1985. Perú: la nueva canción. *La del taller* 4: 4–11.

1975 Manns, Patricio. 1987. The Problems of Text in Nueva Canción. *Popular Music* 6(2): 191–95.

1976 Matta, Fernando Reyes. 1988. The 'New Song' and Its Confrontation in Latin America. In *Marxism and the Interpretation of Culture*, ed. Lawrence Grossberg and Cary Nelson. Urbana, IL: University of Illinois Press. 447–60.

1977 Morris, Nancy E. 1984. *Canto porque es necessario cantar: The New Song Movement in Chile, 1973–1983*. Albuquerque, NM: University of Mexico, Latin American Institute.

1978 No entry.

1979 Rehrmann, Norbert, ed. 1985. Bibliographie und Diskographie zur Nueva Canción in Spanien und Lateinamerika (Auswahl). *Hispanorama* 41: 141–43.

1980 Rehrmann, Norbert. 1985. Die Nueva Canción in Spanien: Ein Überblick. *Hispanorama* 41: 63–74.

1981 Rodríguez, Osvaldo. 1984. *Cantores que Reflexionan: Notas para una historia personal de la Nueva Canción Chilena*. Madrid: Ediciones Literatura Americana Reunida.

1982 Tichauer de Alvarez, Eva. 1985. El 'Canto Nuevo': erupción del Chile posterior al '73. *Hispanorama* 41: 95–98.

1983 Tumas-Serna, Jane. 1992. The 'Nueva Canción' Movement and Its Mass-Mediated Performance Context. *Latin American Music Review* 13(2): 139–57.

NUEVA TROVA

1984 Acosta, Leonardo. 1981. *Canciones de la nueva trova*. Cubanas: Editorial Letras Cubanas.

1985 Benmayor, Rina. 1981. 'La nueva trova': New Cuban Song. *Latin American Music Review* 2(1): 11–44.

1986 Díaz Ayala, Cristobal. 1981. *Música cubana del areyto a la nueva trova*, revised edition. San Juan: Editorial Cubanacan.

PARLOR SONGS

1987 Borroff, Edith. 1986. An American Parlor at the Turn of the Century. *American Music* 4(3): 302–308.

1988 Dahlhaus, Carl, ed. 1967. *Studien zur Trivialmusik des 19. Jahrhunderts*. Regensburg: Bosse.

1989 Hewitt, John Hill. 1877. *Shadows on the Wall; Or, Glimpses of the Past*. Baltimore, MD: Turnbull.

1990 Keldany-Mohr, Irmgard. 1977. *'Unterhaltungsmusik' als soziokulturelles Phänomen des 19. Jahrhunderts: Untersuchung über den Einfluß der musikalischen Öffentlichkeit auf die Herausbildung eines neuen Musiktypes*. Regensburg: Bosse.

1991 Nettel, Reginald. 1956. *Seven Centuries of Popular Song: A Social History of Urban Ditties*. London: Phoenix House.

1992 Pearsall, Ronald. 1973. *Victorian Popular Music*. Detroit, MI: Gale Research Company.

1993 Pearsall, Ronald. 1975. *Edwardian Popular Music*. Rutherford, NJ: Fairleigh Dickinson University Press.

1994 Russell, Henry. 1895. *Cheer! Boys, Cheer! Memories of Men and Music.* London: Macqueen.

1995 Scott, Derek B. 1989. *The Singing Bourgeois: Songs of the Victorian Drawing Room and Parlour.* Milton Keynes: Open University Press.

1996 Sims, George R. 1968. *Prepare To Show Them Now: The Ballads of George R. Sims,* ed. Arthur Calder-Marshall. London: Hutchinson.

1997 Spaeth, Sigmund. 1927. *Weep Some More, My Lady.* New York: Doubleday.

1998 Spaeth, Sigmund. 1959. (1927) *Read 'Em and Weep: A Treasury of American Songs.* New York: Arco. First published New York: Doubleday, 1927.

1999 Tawa, Nicholas E. 1980. *Sweet Songs for Gentle Americans: The Parlor Song in America, 1790–1860.* Bowling Green, OH: Bowling Green University Popular Press.

2000 Van der Merwe, Peter. 1989. *Origins of the Popular Style: The Antecedents of Twentieth-Century Popular Music.* Oxford: Clarendon Press.

POLKA

2001 Davis, Susan G. 1978. Utica's Polka Music Tradition. *New York Folklore* 4: 103–24.

2002 *Ethnic Music in America: A Neglected Heritage.* 1982. Washington, DC: Library of Congress, American Folklife Center.

2003 Greene, Victor. 1992. *A Passion for Polka: Ethnic Old Time Music in America, 1880–1960.* Berkeley, CA: University of California Press.

2004 Janda, Robert. 1976. *Entertainment Tonight: An Account of Bands in Manitowoc County since 1910.* Manitowoc, WI: Manitowoc County Historical Society Monograph Series, No. 28.

2005 Keil, Charles. 1984. The Dyna-Tones: A Buffalo Polka Band in Performance, in Rehearsal and on Record. *New York Folklore* 10(34): 117–34.

2006 Keil, Charles and Keil, Angeliki. 1984. In Pursuit of Polka Happiness. *Musical Traditions* 2: 6–11.

2007 Keil, Charles, Angeliki Keil and Dick Blau. 1992. *Polka Happiness.* Philadelphia: Temple University Press.

2008 Leary, James P. 1987. Czech Polka Styles in the United States: From America's Dairyland to the Lone Star State. In *Czech Music from Texas: A Sesquicentennial Symposium,* ed. Clinton Machann. College Station, TX: Komensky Press. 79–95.

2009 Leary, James P. 1990. *Minnesota Polka: Dance Music from Four Traditions.* St. Paul, MN: Minnesota Historical Society Press.

2010 Leary, James P. 1990. The Legacy of Viola Turpeinen. *Finnish Americana* 8: 6–11.

2011 Leary, James P. 1991. *Polka Music, Ethnic Music.* Mount Horeb, WI: Wisconsin Folk Museum Bulletin No. 1.

2012 Leary, James P. 1991. *Yodeling in Dairyland: A History of Swiss Music in Wisconsin.* Mount Horeb, WI: Wisconsin Folk Museum.

2013 Leary, James P. and March, Richard. 1991. Dutchman Bands: Genre, Ethnicity and Pluralism in the Upper Midwest. In *Creative Ethnicity: Symbols and Strategies of Contemporary Ethnic Life,* ed. Stephen Stern and John Allen Cicala. Logan, UT: Utah State University Press.

2014 Leary, James P. and March, Richard. 1996. *Down Home Dairyland: A*

Listener's Guide. Madison, WI: University of Wisconsin-Extension.

2015 Lornell, Kip. 1985 (published 1989). The Early Career of Whoopee John Wilfahrt. *John Edwards Memorial Foundation Quarterly* 21(75–76): 51–53.

2016 Machann, Clinton, ed. 1987. *Czech Music in Texas: A Sesquicentennial Symposium*. College Station, TX: Komensky Press.

2017 March, Richard. 1985 (published 1989). Slovenian Polka Music: Tradition and Transition. *John Edwards Memorial Foundation Quarterly* 21(75–76): 51–53.

2018 March, Richard. 1989. Polkamania. *Wisconsin Trails* 30(4): 41–45.

2019 March, Richard. 1991. Polkas in Wisconsin Music. In *The Illustrated History of Wisconsin Music*, ed. Michael G. Corenthal. Milwaukee, WI: MGC Publications. 385–97.

2020 Nusbaum, Philip. 1989. *Norwegian-American Music from Minnesota*. St. Paul, MN: Minnesota Historical Society Press.

2021 Peña, Manuel. 1985. *The Texas-Mexican Conjunto: History of a Working-Class Music*. Austin, TX: University of Texas Press.

2022 Rippley, LaVern J. 1992. *The Whoopee John Wilfahrt Dance Band: His German-Bohemian Roots*. Northfield, MN: St. Olaf College German Department.

2023 Strachwitz, Chris and Welding, Pete, eds. 1970. Texas Polka Music: Interview with Joe Patek. In *The American Folk Music Occasional, No. 2*. New York: Oak Publications. 73–75.

RAGGA MUFFIN

2024 Bader, Stascha. 1993. *Words Like Fire: Dancehall Reggae and Ragga Muffin*. London: Central Books.

2025 Jacob, Günther. 1993. *Agit-Pop. Schwarze Musik und weiße Hörer. Texte zu Rassismus und Nationalismus – Hip Hop und Raggamuffin*. Berlin and Amsterdam: Edition ID-Archiv.

2026 Wynands, René. 1995. *'Do the Reggay!' Reggae von Pocomania bis Raggamuffin und der Mythos Bob Marley*. München/Mainz: Pieper/Schott.

RAGTIME

2027 Bennighof, James. 1992. Heliotrope Bouquet and the Critical Analysis of American Music. *American Music* 10(4): 391–410.

2028 Berlin, Edward A. 1977. Ragtime and Improvised Jazz: Another View. *Journal of Jazz Studies* 4(2): 4–10.

2029 Berlin, Edward A. 1984. (1980) *Ragtime: A Musical and Cultural History*. Berkeley, CA: University of California Press.

2030 Berlin, Edward A. 1987. *Reflections and Research on Ragtime*. Brooklyn, NY: Institute for Studies in American Music, Brooklyn College.

2031 Berlin, Edward A. 1994. *King of Ragtime: Scott Joplin and His Era*. New York: Oxford University Press.

2032 Blesh, Rudi and Janis, Harriet. 1971. (1950) *They All Played Ragtime*. New York: Oak Publications. First published New York: Knopf, 1950.

2033 Bradford, Perry. 1965. *Born with the Blues: Perry Bradford's Own Story*. New York: Oak Publications.

2034 Charters, A.R. Danbery. 1961. Negro Folk Elements in Classic Ragtime. *Ethnomusicology* 5(3): 174–84.

2035 DeVeaux, Scott. 1992. *The Music of James Scott*, ed. Scott DeVeaux and William Howland Kenney. Washington and London: Smithsonian Institution Press.

2036 Fletcher, Tom. 1984. (1954) *100 Years of the Negro in Show Business*. New York: Da Capo Press. First published New York: Burdge, 1954.

2037 Floyd, Samuel A. and Reisser, Marsha. 1980. Social Dance Music of Black Composers in the Nineteenth Century and the Emergence of Classic Ragtime. *The Black Perspective in Music* 8(2): 161–93.

2038 Gammond, Peter. 1975. *Scott Joplin and the Ragtime Era*. London: Abacus.

2039 Gushee, Lawrence. 1994. The Nineteenth-Century Origins of Jazz. *Black Music Research Journal* 14(1) (Spring): 1–24.

2040 Hamm, Charles. 1996. Alexander and His Band. *American Music* 14(1) (Spring): 65–102.

2041 Harer, Ingeborg. 1989. *Ragtime. Versuch einer Typologie*. Tutzing: Schneider.

2042 Hasse, John Edward, ed. 1985. *Ragtime: Its History, Composers and Music*. New York: Schirmer.

2043 Jasen, David A. 1973. *Recorded Ragtime, 1897–1958*. Hamden, CT: Archon Books.

2044 Jasen, David A. and Tichenor, Trebor Jay. 1989. (1978) *Rags and Ragtime: A Musical History*. New York: Dover Press. First published New York: Seabury, 1978.

2045 Johnson, J. Rosamund. 1976. (1909) Why They Call American Music Ragtime. *The Black Perspective in Music* 4(2): 260–64.

2046 Johnson, James Weldon. 1912. *The Autobiography of an Ex-Colored Man*. Boston, MA: Sherman, French.

2047 Kimball, Robert and Bolcom, William. 1973. *Reminiscing with Sissle and Blake*. New York: Viking.

2048 Marks, Edward B. and Liebling, Abbott J. 1935. *They All Sang from Tony Pastor to Rudy Vallee*. New York: Viking.

2049 Newberger, Eli H. 1976. The Transition from Ragtime to Improvised Piano Style. *Journal of Jazz Studies* 3(2): 3–18.

2050 Oliver, Paul, Max Harrison and William Bolcom. 1986. Ragtime. In *The New Grove Book of Gospel, Blues and Jazz, with Spirituals and Ragtime*. London: Macmillan.

2051 Rabinowitz, Peter J. 1992. Whiting the Wrongs of History: The Resurrection of Scott Joplin. *Black Music Research Journal* 11(2): 157–76.

2052 Reisser, Marsha and Floyd, Samuel A. 1984. The Sources and Resources of Classic Ragtime Music. *Black Music Research Journal* 4: 22–59.

2053 Riis, Thomas. 1989. *Just Before Jazz: Black Musical Theater in New York, 1890–1915*. Washington, DC: Smithsonian Institution Press.

2054 Schafer, William J., et al. 1973. *The Art of Ragtime: Form and Meaning of an Original Black American Art*. Baton Rouge, LA: Louisiana State University Press.

2055 Smith, Willie ('The Lion') and Hoefer, George. 1978. (1964) *Music on My Mind: The Memoirs of an American Pianist*. New York: Da Capo Press. First published New York: Doubleday, 1964.

2056 Tichenor, Trebor Jay. 1989. John Stilwell Stark, Piano Ragtime Publisher: Readings from 'The Intermezzo' and His Personal Ledgers, 1905–1908. *Black Music Research Journal* 9(2): 193–204.

2057 Van Der Merwe, Peter. 1989. *Origins of the Popular Style: The Antecedents of*

Twentieth-Century Popular Music. Oxford: Clarendon Press.

2058 Waldo, Terry. 1984. (1976) *This Is Ragtime.* New York: Da Capo Press. First published New York: Hawthorne, 1976.

2059 Walker, Edward S. and Walker, Steven, eds. 1971. *English Ragtime: A Discography.* Mastin Moor: Walker.

2060 Witmark, Isidore and Goldberg, Isaac. 1976. (1939) *The Story of the House of Witmark: From Ragtime to Swingtime.* New York: Da Capo Press. First published New York: L. Furman, 1939.

RAI

2061 Langlois, Tony. 1996. The Local and Global in North African Popular Music. *Popular Music* 15(3): 259–74.

2062 Prince, Rob. 1989. King of Chebs. *Folk Roots* 77 (November): 15–17.

2063 Sweeney, Philip. 1989. Algerian Rai: The French Connection. In *Rhythms of the World,* ed. Francis Hanly and Tim May. London: BBC Books.

RAILROAD SONGS

2064 Botkin, B.A. and Harlow, Alvin F. 1953. *A Treasury of Railroad Folklore.* New York: Bonanza Books.

2065 Carpenter, Ann Miller. 1972. The Railroad in American Folk Song, 1865–1920. In *Diamond Bessie and the Shepherds,* ed. Wilson M. Hudson. Austin, TX: Encino Press. 103–19.

2066 Chappell, Louis W. 1933. *John Henry: A Folk-Lore Study.* Jena: Frommannsche Verlag.

2067 Cohen, Norm. 1970. *Railroad Folksongs on Record: A Survey.* Los Angeles: John Edwards Memorial Foundation. (First

published in *New York Folklore Quarterly* (June 1970): 91–113.)

2068 Cohen, Norm. 1974. *Robert W. Gordon and the Second Wreck of the 'Old 97'.* Los Angeles: John Edwards Memorial Foundation. (First published in *Journal of American Folklore* 87 (1974): 12–38.)

2069 Cohen, Norm. 1981. *Long Steel Rail: The Railroad in American Folksong.* Urbana, IL: University of Illinois Press.

2070 Donovan, Frank P., Jr. 1940. *The Railroad in Literature.* Boston, MA: Railway and Locomotive Historical Society.

2071 Ferris, William R. 1970. Railroad Chants: Form and Function. *Mississippi Folklore Register* 4(1): 1–14.

2072 Hubbard, Freeman H. 1946. *Railroad Avenue: Great Stories and Legends of American Railroading.* New York: Whittlesey House.

2073 Johnson, Guy B. 1929. *John Henry: Tracking Down a Negro Legend.* Chapel Hill, NC: University of North Carolina Press.

2074 Lyle, Katie Letcher. 1983. *Scalded to Death by Steam: Authentic Stories of Railroad Disasters and the Ballads That Were Written About Them.* Chapel Hill, NC: Algonquin Books.

2075 Manning, Ambrose. 1966. Railroad Work Songs. *Tennessee Folklore Society Bulletin* 32: 41–47.

2076 Milburn, George. 1930. *The Hobo's Hornbook: A Repertory for a Gutter Jongleur.* New York: Ives Washburn.

2077 Sherwin, Sterling and McClintock, Harry K. 1943. *Railroad Songs of Yesterday.* New York: Shapiro-Bernstein.

2078 Smith, John T. 1959. Rails Below the Rio Grande. In *And Horns on the Toads,* ed. Mody C. Boatwright, Wilson M.

Hudson and Allen Maxwell. Dallas, TX: Southern Methodist University Press. 122–35.

2079 *Sounds Like Folk No. 2: The Railways in Song.* 1973. London: English Folksong and Dance Society.

2080 Transportation in American Popular Songs: A Bibliography of Items in the Grosvenor Library. 1945. *Grosvenor Library Bulletin* (June): 27.

2081 Williams, Brett. 1983. *John Henry: A Bio-Bibliography*. Westport, CT: Greenwood Press.

REGGAE

2082 Bader, Stascha. 1993. *Words Like Fire: Dancehall Reggae and Ragga Muffin*. London: Central Books.

2083 Bergman, Billy, et al. 1985. *Reggae and Latin Pop: Hot Sauces*. Poole: Blandford Press.

2084 Cashmore, E. Ellis. 1987. Shades of Black, Shades of White. In *Popular Music & Communication*, ed. James Lull. Newbury Park, CA: Sage. 245–65.

2085 Chambers, Iain. 1977. (1975) A Strategy for Living: Black Music and White Subcultures. In *Resistance Through Rituals: Youth Subcultures in Post-War Britain*, ed. Stuart Hall and Tony Jefferson. London: Hutchinson. 157–66.

2086 Clarke, Sebastian. 1980. *Jah Music: The Evolution of the Popular Jamaican Song*. London: Heinemann Educational Books.

2087 Cushman, Thomas. 1991. Rich Rastas and Communist Rockers: A Comparative Study of the Origin, Diffusion and Defusion of Revolutionary Musical Codes. *Journal of Popular Culture* 25(3): 17–62.

2088 Davis, Stephen. 1977. *Reggae Bloodlines: In Search of the Music and Culture of Jamaica*. Garden City, NY: Anchor Press.

2089 Davis, Stephen and Simon, Peter. 1982. *Reggae International*. London: Thames & Hudson.

2090 Hebdige, Dick. 1977. (1975) Reggae, Rastas, Rudies: Style and the Subversion of Form. In *Resistance Through Rituals: Youth Subcultures in Post-War Britain*, ed. Stuart Hall and Tony Jefferson. London: Hutchinson. 135–53.

2091 Hebdige, Dick. 1987. *Cut 'n' Mix: Culture, Identity and Caribbean Music*. London and New York: Comedia/Methuen.

2092 Hebdige, Dick. 1988. (1979) *Subculture: The Meaning of Style*. London: Routledge.

2093 Johnson, Howard and Pines, Jim. 1982. *Reggae: Deep Roots Music*. London and New York: Proteus.

2094 Johnson, Linton Kwesi. 1980. Some Thoughts on Reggae. In *Race Today Review, 1980*. London: Race Today. 58–65.

2095 Jones, Simon. 1988. *Black Culture, White Youth: The Reggae Tradition from JA to UK*. Basingstoke: Macmillan.

2096 Kallyndyr, Rolston and Dalrymple, Henderson. 1973. *Reggae, a Peoples' Music*. London: Carib-Arawak Publications.

2097 Kunz, Wolfgang. 1986. *Reggae: Kult, Kritik und Kommerz*. Wiesbaden: Breitkopf & Härtel.

2098 Moter, Hermann. 1983. *Reggae Discography*. Pfungstadt: Minotaurus Project.

2099 Mulvaney, Rebekah Michele and Nelson, Carlos I.H. 1990. *Rastafari and Reggae: A Dictionary and Source Book*.

Westport and London: Greenwood Press.

2100 Musiques rock, reggae, raï, rap. 1991. *Les Cahiers de l'IFOREP* 64.

2101 Tröder, Werner. 1993. *Reggae: Vom Mento zum Dance Hall*. Köln: Heel.

2102 Vieth, Udo and Zimmerman, Michael. 1981. *Reggae: Musiker, Rastas und Jamaika*. Frankfurt am Main: Fischer.

2103 Wynands, René. 1995. *'Do the Reggay!' Reggae von Pocomania bis Raggamuffin und der Mythos Bob Marley*. München/ Mainz: Pieper/Schott.

REMBETIKA

2104 Butterworth, Katherine. 1975. *Rembetika: Songs from the Old Greek Underworld*. Athens: Komboloi.

2105 Harrison, John. 1984. Damn Society: An Introduction to Greek Rembetika. *Musical Traditions* 3: 17–21.

2106 Holst, Gail. 1977. *Road to Rembetika: Music from a Greek Subculture. Songs of Love, Sorrow and Hashish*. Athens: Anglo-Hellenic Publishing.

REVUE

2107 Anderson, John Murray. 1954. *Out Without My Rubbers: The Memoirs of John Murray Anderson*. New York: Library Publishers.

2108 Baral, Robert. 1962. *Revue: The Great Broadway Period*. New York: Fleet Press.

2109 Bordman, Gerald. 1985. *American Musical Revue: From the* Passing Show *to* Sugar Babies. New York: Oxford University Press.

2110 Carter, Randolph. 1974. *The World of Flo Ziegfeld*. New York: Praeger.

2111 Farnsworth, Marjorie. 1956. *The Ziegfeld Follies*. New York: Putnam.

2112 Klein, Jean-Claude. 1985. Borrowing, Syncretism, Hybridisation: The Parisian Revue of the 1920's. *Popular Music* 5: 175–88.

2113 Kothes, Franz-Peter. 1977. *Die theatralische Revue in Berlin und Wien 1900–1938. Typen, Inhalte, Funktionen*. Wilhelmshaven: Heinrichshofen.

RHYTHM AND BLUES

2114 Bernhardt, Clyde E.B. and Harris, Sheldon. 1986. *I Remember: Eighty Years of Black Entertainment, Big Bands and the Blues*. Philadelphia: University of Pennsylvania Press.

2115 Berry, Chuck. 1987. *Chuck Berry: The Autobiography*. New York: Harmony Books.

2116 Birchall, Ian. 1969. The Decline and Fall of British Rhythm and Blues. In *The Age of Rock*, ed. Jonathan Eisen. New York: Vintage Books. 94–102.

2117 Broven, John. 1974. *Walking to New Orleans: The Story of New Orleans Rhythm & Blues*. Bexhill-on-Sea: Blues Unlimited.

2118 Broven, John. 1978. (1974) *Rhythm and Blues in New Orleans*. Gretna, LA: Pelican. First published as *Walking to New Orleans: The Story of New Orleans Rhythm & Blues*. Bexhill-on-Sea: Blues Unlimited, 1974.

2119 Dawson, Jim. 1994. *Nervous Man Nervous: Big Jay McNeely and the Rise of the Honking Tenor Sax!* Milford, NH: Big Nickel Publications.

2120 Dawson, Jim. 1995. *The Twist: The Story of the Song and Dance That Changed the World*. Boston, MA: Faber & Faber.

2121 Dawson, Jim and Propes, Steve. 1992. *What Was the First Rock 'n' Roll Record?* Boston, MA: Faber & Faber.

2122 Deffaa, Chip. 1996. *Blue Rhythms: Six Lives in Rhythm and Blues*. Urbana, IL: University of Illinois Press.

2123 Eastman, Ralph. 1989. Central Avenue Blues: The Making of Los Angeles Rhythm and Blues, 1942–1947. *Black Music Research Journal* 9(1): 19–33.

2124 Fancourt, Leslie, comp. 1991. *A Discography of the R 'n' B Artists on the Chess Labels, 1947–1975*. Faversham: Fancourt.

2125 Ferlinger, Robert D. 1976. *A Discography of Rhythm & Blues and Rock & Roll Vocal Groups, 1945–1965*. Pittsburgh, PA: Robert D. Ferlinger.

2126 Gart, Galen. 1989. *ARLD: The American Record Label Directory and Dating Guide, 1940–1959*. Milford, NH: Big Nickel Publications.

2127 Gart, Galen, comp. 1989–1991. *The History of Rhythm and Blues. 6 vols.* Milford, NH: Big Nickel Publications.

2128 Gart, Galen, et al. 1990. *Duke/Peacock Records: An Illustrated History with Discography*. Milford, NH: Big Nickel Publications.

2129 George, Nelson. 1988. *The Death of Rhythm & Blues*. New York: Pantheon.

2130 Gillett, Charlie. 1974. *Making Tracks: Atlantic Records and the Growth of a Multi-Billion-Dollar Industry*. New York: E.P. Dutton and Co.

2131 Gillett, Charlie. 1983. (1970) *The Sound of the City: The Rise of Rock and Roll.* New York: Pantheon. First published New York: Outerbridge and Dienstfrey, 1970.

2132 Gonzalez, Fernando. 1977. *Disco-File: The Discographical Catalogue of American Rock & Roll and Rhythm & Blues Vocal Harmony Groups, 1902–1976*. Flushing, NY: Gonzalez.

2133 Governar, Alan. 1990. *The Early Years of Rhythm and Blues*. Houston, TX: Rice University Press.

2134 Groia, Phil. 1983. *They All Sang on the Corner: A Second Look at New York City's Rhythm and Blues Vocal Groups*. West Hempstead, NY: Phillie Dee Enterprises.

2135 Guralnick, Peter. 1986. *Sweet Soul Music: Rhythm and Blues and the Southern Dream of Freedom*. New York: Harper & Row.

2136 Hannusch, Jeff. 1975. *I Hear You Knocking: The Sound of New Orleans Rhythm & Blues*. Ville Platte, LA: Swallow Publications.

2137 Haslewood, Nigel. 1987. The Jump Bands: An Introduction. *Storyville* 131: 167.

2138 Hildebrand, Lee. 1994. *Stars of Soul and Rhythm & Blues: Top Recording Artists and Showstopping Performers, from Memphis and Motown to Now*. New York: Billboard Books.

2139 Hofstein, Francis. 1991. *Que sais-je? Le Rhythm and Blues*. Paris: Presses Universitaires de France.

2140 Humphrey, Mark. 1993. Bright Lights, Big City: Urban Blues. In *Nothing But the Blues. The Music and the Musicians*, ed. Lawrence Cohn. New York: Abbeville Press.

2141 Jackson, John. 1991. *Big Beat Heat: Alan Freed and the Early Days of Rock and Roll*. New York: Schirmer Books.

2142 Leichter, Albert, comp. 1975. *A Discography of Rhythm & Blues and Rock & Roll, Circa 1946–1964: A Reference Manual*. Staunton, VA: Albert Leichter.

2143 McCutcheon, Lynn Ellis. 1971. *Rhythm & Blues: An Experience and Adventure in*

Its Origin and Development. Arlington, VA: Beatty.

2144 McGowan, James. 1983. *Hear Today! Hear to Stay! A Personal History of Rhythm and Blues.* St. Petersburg, FL: Sixth House Press.

2145 Miller, Doug. 1995. The Moan Within the Tone: African Retentions in Rhythm and Blues Saxophone Style in Afro-American Popular Music. *Popular Music* 14(2): 155–74.

2146 Otis, Johnny. 1973. The History of Rhythm and Blues. In *The Rolling Stone Interviews, 2,* ed. Pete Welding. New York: Warner Books. 295–322.

2147 Otis, Johnny. 1993. *Upside Your Head!: Rhythm and Blues on Central Avenue.* Hanover, NH: Wesleyan University Press.

2148 Palmer, Robert. 1979. *A Tale of Two Cities: Memphis Rock and New Orleans Roll.* Brooklyn, NY: Institute for Studies in American Music.

2149 Pavlow, Big Al. 1983. *The R & B Book: A Disc History of Rhythm & Blues.* Providence, RI: Music House Publishing.

2150 Pearson, Barry. 1993. Jump Steady: The Roots of R&B. In *Nothing But the Blues: The Music and the Musicians,* ed. Lawrence Cohn. New York: Abbeville Press. 313–45.

2151 Redd, Lawrence N. 1974. *Rock Is Rhythm and Blues: The Impact of Mass Media.* East Lansing, MI: Michigan State University Press.

2152 Reilly, April. 1973. The Impact of Technology on Rhythm 'n' Blues. *The Black Perspective in Music* 1(2): 136–46.

2153 Ruppli, Michel. 1985. *The King Labels: A Discography.* Westport, CT: Greenwood Press.

2154 Ruppli, Michel. 1991. *The Aladdin-Imperial Labels: A Discography.* New York: Greenwood Press.

2155 Shaw, Arnold. 1978. *Honkers and Shouters: The Golden Age of Rhythm and Blues.* New York: Macmillan.

2156 Shaw, Arnold. 1980. Researching Rhythm & Blues. *Black Music Research Journal* 1: 71–79.

2157 Tosches, Nick. 1991. (1984) *Unsung Heroes of Rock 'n' Roll: The Birth of Rock in the Wild Years Before Elvis.* New York: Harmony Books.

2158 Warner, Jay. 1992. *The Billboard Book of American Singing Groups: A History, 1940–1990.* New York: Watson-Guptill Publications.

2159 Wexler, Jerry and Ritz, David. 1994. (1993) *Rhythm and the Blues: A Life in American Music.* New York: St. Martin's Press. (First published in New York: Alfred A. Knopf, 1993).

2160 Whitburn, Joel and Grendysa, Peter. 1988. *Joel Whitburn's Top R&B Singles, 1942–1988.* Menomonee Falls, WI: Record Research Inc.

2161 Whitcomb, Ian. 1985. Legends of Rhythm and Blues. In *Repercussions: A Celebration of African-American Music,* ed. Geoffrey Haydon and Denis Marks. London: Century. 54–79.

2162 Zucker, Mark J. 1982. The Saga of Lovin' Dan: A Study of the Iconography of Rhythm & Blues Music of the 1950s. *Journal of Popular Culture* 16(2): 43–51.

ROCK AND POP

General Works

2163 Alessandrini, Marjorie. 1980. *Le Rock au féminin.* Paris: Albin Michel.

2164 Anders, Kenneth. 1994. Trance in Balance: Über die zahlreichen, aber unvermeidlichen Seitänze des Rock 'n' Roll. In *Zwischen Rausch und Ritual*, ed. Konstanze Kriese, et al. Berlin: Zyankrise. 54–69.

2165 Anz, Philipp and Walter, Patrick. 1995. *Techno*. Zürich: Ricco Bilger.

2166 Aprile, Al and Mayer, Luca. 1980. *La musica rock-progressiva Europa*. Milano: Gammalibri.

2167 Arana, Federico. 1988. *Roqueros y Folcloroides*. México: Editorial Joaquín Mortiz.

2168 Baacke, Dieter. 1967. Das Phänomen Beat. *Deutsche Jugend* 12: 552–60.

2169 Baacke, Dieter. 1969. Beat. Ein Versuch. *Merkur* 253: 431–44.

2170 Baacke, Dieter. 1971. Beatkultur – Jugendkultur – Popkultur. *Musica* XXV(2): 124–29.

2171 Bandier, Norbert. 1987. L'espace social du rock. *Économie et Humanisme* 297: 53–64.

2172 Bane, Michael. 1992. *White Boys Singin' the Blues: The Black Roots of White Rock*. New York: Da Capo Press. First published New York and Harmondsworth: Penguin, 1982.

2173 Bangs, Lester and Marcus, Greil, eds. 1987. *Psychotic Reactions and Carburetor Dung: Literature as Rock 'n' Roll, Rock 'n' Roll as Literature*. New York: Alfred A. Knopf.

2174 Barsamian, Jacques and Jouffa, François. 1982. *L'Age d'or de la pop music*. Paris: Ramsay.

2175 Barsamian, Jacques and Jouffa, François. 1985. *L'Age d'or du rock & folk. La pop music américaine des sixties*. Paris: Ramsay.

2176 Barsamian, Jacques and Jouffa, François. 1986. *L'Age d'or de la rock music. Blues, country, rock 'n' roll, soul, San Francisco sound, underground, hippies, festivals*. Paris: Ramsay.

2177 Barsamian, Jacques and Jouffa, François. 1989. *L'Aventure du rock. La préhistoire du rock 1900–1953, l'âge d'or du rock 1954–1989*. Paris: Ramsay.

2178 Bartnik, Norbert and Bordon, Frieda. 1981. *Keep on Rockin'. Rockmusik zwischen Protest und Profit*. Weinheim and Basel: Beltz.

2179 Bayles, Martha. 1994. *Hole in Our Soul: The Loss of Beauty and Meaning in American Popular Music*. New York: The Free Press.

2180 Beadle, Jeremy J. 1993. *Will Pop Eat Itself? Pop Music in the Soundbite Era*. London: Faber & Faber.

2181 Belz, Carl. 1967. Popular Music and the Folk Tradition. *Journal of American Folklore* 80: 130–42.

2182 Belz, Carl. 1972. (1969) *The Story of Rock*, revised edition. New York: Oxford University Press.

2183 Bennett, H. Stith. 1980. *On Becoming a Rock Musician*. Amherst, MA: University of Massachusetts Press.

2184 Bennett, Tony, et al. 1993. *Rock and Popular Music: Politics, Policies, Institutions*. London: Routledge.

2185 Berry, Chuck. 1987. *Chuck Berry: The Autobiography*. New York: Harmony Books.

2186 Berry, Peter E. 1977. '. . . And the Hits Just Keep On Comin''. Syracuse, NY: Syracuse University Press.

2187 Billiet, Frédéric. 1989. *Rock à la clé, la variété rock au collège*. Paris: Magnard.

2188 Binas, Susanne. 1995. Behutsamkeit und Widerstand. Auf der Suche nach neuen Motiven für die Analyse populärer Kultur – und Musikformen. In *Popular*

Music Perspectives III, ed. Peter Wicke. Berlin: Zyankrise. 415–19.

2189 Blankenstein, Alexander. 1990. *Rockin' Through the Years. Rock- und Zeitgeschichte 1965–1990*. Bollschweil: Dr. Grüb Nachf.

2190 Bloemeke, Rüdiger. 1996. *Roll Over Beethoven. Wie der Rock 'n' Roll nach Deutschland kam*. Andrä-Wördern: Hannibal.

2191 Bluestein, Gene. 1994. *Poplore: Folk and Pop in American Culture*. Amherst, MA: University of Massachusetts Press.

2192 Boeckman, Charles. 1972. *And the Beat Goes On: A History of Pop Music in America*. Washington, DC: Luce.

2193 Boris, Siegfried. 1977. *Popmusik. Kunst aus Provokation*. Wiesbaden: Breitkopf & Härtel.

2194 Born, Georgina. 1987. Modern Music Cultures: On Shock, Pop and Synthesis. *New Formations* 2: 51–78.

2195 Braha, Liviu von. 1983. *Phänomene der Rockmusik*. Wilhelmshaven: Heinrichshofen.

2196 Branzaglia, Carlo, Pierfrancesco Pacoda and Alba Solaro. 1992. *Posse italiane: Centri sociali, underground musicale e cultura giovanile degli anni '90 in Italia*. Firenze: Tosca.

2197 Breen, Marcus, ed. 1987. *Missing in Action: Australian Popular Music*. Melbourne: Verbal Graphics Pty.

2198 Brickell, Sean and Rothschild, Rick. 1983. *The Pages of Rock and Roll History*. Norfolk, VA: Donning.

2199 Brödl, Günter. 1985. *Die guten Kräfte. Neue Rockmusik in Österreich*. Wien: Hannibal.

2200 Brown, Charles T. 1992. (1983) *The Art of Rock and Roll*. Englewood Cliffs, NJ: Prentice-Hall.

2201 Burt, Rob. 1986. *Rock and Roll: The Movies*. New York: Sterling.

2202 Burton, T. 1985. Rock Music and Social Change. *Society and Leisure* 8: 665–83.

2203 Buxton, David. 1985. *Le rock: star-système et société de consommation*. Paris: Pensée Sauvage.

2204 Bygrave, Mike. 1978. *Rock*. New York: Watts.

2205 Carducci, Joe. 1990. *Rock and the Pop Narcotic*. Chicago: Redoubt Press.

2206 Carollo, Agostino. 1993. *Il rock in Trentino alto adige: La storia ed il panorama attuale in un'analisi a 360 gradi*. Rovereto: Ritmi Urbani.

2207 Chambers, Iain. 1985. Pop Music, Popular Culture and the Possible. In *Popular Music Perspectives, 2*, ed. David Horn. Göteborg and Exeter: IASPM. 445–50.

2208 Chambers, Iain. 1985. *Urban Rhythms: Pop Music and Popular Culture*. London: Macmillan.

2209 Chambers, Iain. 1987. British Pop: Some Tracks from the Other Side of the Record. In *Popular Music & Communication*, ed. James Lull. Newbury Park, CA: Sage. 231–44.

2210 Chambers, Iain. 1988. Contamination, Coincidence and Collusion: Pop Music, Urban Culture and the Avant-Garde. In *Marxism and the Interpretation of Culture*, ed. Lawrence Grossberg and Cary Nelson. Urbana, IL: University of Illinois Press. 607–15.

2211 Chambers, Iain. 1990. Popular Music and Mass Culture. In *Questioning the Media: A Critical Introduction*, ed. J. Downing, A. Mohammadi and A. Sreberny-Mohammadi. Beverly Hills and London: Sage. 308–17.

GENRES

2212 Charlton, Katherine. 1990. *Rock Music Styles: A History*. Dubuque, IA: C. Brown Publishers.

2213 Chester, Andrew. 1970. For a Rock Aesthetic. *New Left Review* 59: 82–86.

2214 Chester, Andrew. 1970. Second Thoughts on a Rock Aesthetic: The Band. *New Left Review* 62: 75–82.

2215 Christgau, Robert. 1973. *Any Old Way You Choose It: Rock and Other Pop Music, 1967–1973*. Baltimore, MD: Penguin.

2216 Clarke, Paul. 1983. A 'Magic Science': Rock Music as a Recording Art. *Popular Music* 3: 195–213.

2217 Clee, Kenn. 1984–86. *The Directory of American 45 rpm Records*. 3 vols. Philadelphia: Stak-O-Wax.

2218 Coffman, James T. 1972. 'So You Want to Be a Rock & Roll Star!': Role Conflict and the Rock Musician. In *The Sounds of Social Change: Studies in Popular Culture*, ed. R. Serge Denisoff and Richard A. Peterson. Chicago: Rand McNally & Co. 261–73.

2219 Cohen, Sara. 1991. *Rock Culture in Liverpool: Popular Music in the Making*. Oxford: Oxford University Press.

2220 Cohn, Nik. 1969. *Awopbopaloobop-alopbamboom: Pop from the Beginning*. London: Weidenfeld & Nicolson.

2221 Cohn, Nik. 1989. *Ball the Wall*. London: Pan.

2222 Cook, Lez. 1983. Popular Culture and Rock Music. *Screen* 24(3): 44–49.

2223 Crenshaw, Marshall. 1994. *Hollywood Rock: A Guide to Rock 'n' Roll in the Movies*. New York and London: HarperCollins/Plexus.

2224 No entry.

2225 Curtis, Jim. 1987. *Rock Eras: Interpretations of Music and Society, 1954–1984*. Bowling Green, OH: Bowling Green University Popular Press.

2226 Dachs, David. 1964. *Anything Goes: The World of Pop Music*. Indianapolis and London: Bobbs-Merrill.

2227 Dachs, David. 1969. *American Pop*. New York: Scholastic Book Services.

2228 Dallas, Karl. 1987. *Bricks in the Wall*. New York: Shapolsky Publishers.

2229 Daufouy, Phillippe and Sarton, Jean-Pierre. 1972. *Pop Music/Rock*. Paris: Champs Libre.

2230 Davis, Julie, ed. 1977. *Punk*. London: Millington.

2231 DeCurtis, Anthony, ed. 1992. *Present Tense: Rock & Roll and Culture*. Durham, NC: Duke University Press.

2232 DeCurtis, Anthony and Henke, James, eds. 1993. *The Rolling Stone Illustrated History of Rock & Roll: The Definitive History of the Most Important Artists and Their Music*. London: Plexus Publishing.

2233 Dellio, Phil and Woods, Scott. 1993. *I Wanna Be Sedated: Pop Music in the Seventies*. Toronto: Sound and Vision Books.

2234 Denisoff, R. Serge. 1983. *Sing a Song of Social Significance*. Bowling Green, OH: Bowling Green University Popular Press.

2235 Denisoff, R. Serge and Romanowski, William D. 1991. *Risky Business: Rock in Film*. New Brunswick, NJ: Transaction.

2236 Denselow, Robin. 1989. *When the Music's Over*. London: Faber & Faber.

2237 Diettrich, Eva. 1979. *Tendenzen der Pop-Musik. Dargestellt am Beispiel der Beatles*. Tutzing: Schneider.

2238 Dister, Alain. 1992. *L'Age du rock*. Paris: Gallimard.

2239 Dix, Jonathan. 1987. *Stranded in Paradise: New Zealand Rock 'n' Roll, 1955–1988*. Palmerston North: Paradise Publications.

2240 Doney, Malcolm. 1978. *Summer in the City: Rock Music & Way of Life*. Berkhamsted: Lion.

2241 Dorough, Prince. 1992. *Popular Music Culture in America*. New York: Ardsley House.

2242 Doruška, Lubomir. 1978. *Populárna hudba – priemysel, obchod, umenie*. Bratislava: Opus.

2243 Doruška, Lubomir and Doruška, Peter. 1981. *Panorama populárni hudby, 1918–1978*. Praha: Mladá Fronta.

2244 Doukas, James. 1969. *Electric Tibet: The Chronicles and Sociology of the San Francisco Rock Musicians*. North Hollywood, CA: Dominion.

2245 Dufour, Barry. 1979. *Die Story des Pop & Rock*. München and Wien: Schneider.

2246 Duncan, Robert. 1983. *The Noise: Rock 'n' Roll and the Transformation of America*. New Haven, CT: Ticknor & Fields.

2247 Dunson, Josh. 1980. *Freedom in the Air: Song Movements of the Sixties*. Westport, CT: Greenwood Press.

2248 Durant, Alan. 1985. Rock Revolution or Time-No-Changes: Visions of Change and Continuity in Rock Music. *Popular Music* 5: 97–122.

2249 Durgnat, R. 1971. Rock, Rhythm and Dance. *British Journal of Aesthetics* 11: 28–47.

2250 Edwards, John W. 1992. *Rock'n'Roll Through 1969: Discographies of All Performers Who Hit the Charts, Beginning in 1955*. Kent, OH: McFarland.

2251 Ehnert, Günter and Kinsler, Detlef. 1984. (1975) *Rock in Deutschland: Lexikon deutscher Rockgruppen und Interpreten*. Hamburg: Taurus.

2252 Ehrenstein, David. 1982. *Rock on Film*. New York: Delilah Books.

2253 Eisen, Jonathan, ed. 1969. *The Age of Rock: Sounds of the American Cultural Revolution*. New York: Vintage Books.

2254 Eisen, Jonathan, ed. 1970. *The Age of Rock 2: Sights and Sounds of the American Cultural Revolution*. New York: Vintage Books.

2255 Ellis, Royston. 1961. *The Big Beat Scene*. London: Four Square.

2256 Emblidge, David. 1976. Down Home with the Band: Country-Western Music and Rock. *Ethnomusicology* 20(3): 541–52.

2257 Ennis, Philip H. 1992. *The Seventh Stream: The Emergence of Rock 'n' Roll in American Popular Music*. Hanover and London: Wesleyan University Press.

2258 Escott, Colin and Hawkins, Martin. 1992. *Good Rockin' Tonight: Sun Records and the Birth of Rock 'n' Roll*. New York: St. Martin's Press.

2259 Farin, Klaus. 1996. 'Rechtsrock' – eine Bestandsaufnahme. *PopScriptum* 5: 4–13.

2260 Farrell, Gerry. 1988. Reflecting Surfaces: Indian Music in Popular Music and Jazz. *Popular Music* 7(2): 189–206.

2261 Fatela, Joao and Mignon, Patrick. 1979. Le Rock: pour ne pas dire c'est fini. *Esprit*: 5–79.

2262 Faulstich, Werner. 1983. *Vom Rock 'n' Roll bis Bob Dylan*. Gelsenkirchen: Rockpaed.

2263 Faulstich, Werner. 1985. *Rock als 'way of life'. Tübinger Vorlesungen zur*

Rockgeschichte, Teil II, 1964–1971. Gelsenkirchen: Rockpaed.

2264 Faulstich, Werner. 1986. *Zwischen Glitter und Punk. Tübinger Vorlesungen zur Rockgeschichte, Teil III, 1972–1982.* Gelsenkirchen: Rockpaed.

2265 Faulstich, Werner and Schäffner, Gerhard. 1994. *Rockmusik. Die 80er Jahre.* Bardowick: Wissenschaftler-Verlag.

2266 Fawcett, Anthony. 1978. *California Rock, California Sound: The Music of Los Angeles and Southern California.* Los Angeles: Reed Books.

2267 Fernando, S.H., Jr. 1994. *The New Beats: Exploring the Music, Culture and Attitudes of Hip-Hop.* New York: Anchor Books.

2268 Feurich, Hans-Jürgen. 1977. Warengeschichte und Rockmusik. In *Rockmusik,* ed. Wolfgang Sandner. Mainz: Schott. 53–80.

2269 Fiori, Umberto. 1984. Rock Music and Politics in Italy. *Popular Music* 4: 261–77.

2270 Flattery, Paul. 1973. *The Illustrated History of British Pop.* London: Wise.

2271 Flender, Reinhard and Rauhe, Hermann. 1989. *Popmusik. Geschichte, Funktion, Wirkung und Ästhetik.* Darmstadt: Wissenschaftliche Buchgesellschaft.

2272 Fletcher, Colin. 1964. Beat and Gangs on Merseyside. *New Society* 73(20): 11–14.

2273 Fletcher, Peter. 1981. *Roll Over Rock: A Study of Music in Contemporary Culture.* London: Stainer & Bell.

2274 Floh de Cologne, ed. 1980. *Rock gegen Rechts. Beiträge zu einer Bewegung.* Dortmund: Weltkreis.

2275 Fong-Torres, Ben, ed. 1973. *The Rolling Stone Interviews, Vol. 2.* New York: Warner Books.

2276 Fong-Torres, Ben, ed. 1974. *The Rolling Stone Rock 'n' Roll Reader.* Toronto: Bantam.

2277 Fornäs, Johan. 1990. Moving Rock: Youth and Pop in Late Modernity. *Popular Music* 9(3): 291–306.

2278 Frame, Pete, ed. 1974. *The Road to Rock: A Zigzag Book of Interviews.* London: Charisma Books.

2279 Frame, Pete. 1983. (1980) *Rock Family Trees.* London: Omnibus.

2280 Friedlander, Paul. 1996. *Rock and Roll: A Social History.* Boulder, CO: Westview Press.

2281 Frith, Simon. 1978. *The Sociology of Rock.* London: Constable.

2282 Frith, Simon. 1981. The Magic That Can Set You Free: The Ideology of Folk and the Myth of the Rock Community. *Popular Music* 1: 159–68.

2283 Frith, Simon. 1982. The Sociology of Rock: Notes from Britain. In *Popular Music Perspectives, 1,* ed. David Horn and Philip Tagg. Göteborg and Exeter: IASPM. 142–53.

2284 Frith, Simon. 1983. Popular Music, 1950–1980. In *Making Music,* ed. George Martin. New York: Quill. 18–48.

2285 Frith, Simon. 1983. *Sound Effects: Youth, Leisure and the Politics of Rock 'n' Roll.* London: Constable.

2286 Frith, Simon. 1986. Art Versus Technology: The Strange Case of Popular Music. *Media, Culture and Society* 8(3): 263–79.

2287 Frith, Simon. 1988. Art Ideology and Pop Practice. In *Marxism and the Interpretation of Culture,* ed. Lawrence

Grossberg and Cary Nelson. Urbana, IL: University of Illinois Press. 461–76.

2288 Frith, Simon. 1988. *Music for Pleasure: Essays in the Sociology of Pop*. London: Polity.

2289 Frith, Simon. 1989. Europop. *Cultural Studies* 3(2): 166–72.

2290 Frith, Simon. 1989. Video Pop: Picking Up the Pieces. In *Facing the Music*, ed. Simon Frith. New York: Pantheon.

2291 Frith, Simon. 1996. *Performing Rites: On the Value of Popular Music*. Oxford/Cambridge, MA: Oxford University Press/Harvard University Press.

2292 Frith, Simon, and Goodwin, Andrew, eds. 1990. *On Record: Rock, Pop and the Written Word*. London: Routledge.

2293 Frith, Simon and Horne, Howard. 1987. *Art into Pop*. London: Methuen.

2294 Frith, Simon and McRobbie, Angela. 1990. Rock and Sexuality. In *On Record: Rock, Pop and the Written Word*, ed. Simon Frith and Andrew Goodwin. London: Routledge. 371–89.

2295 Fryer, P. 1986. Punk and the New Wave of British Rock: Working Class Heroes and Art School Attitudes. *Popular Music & Society* 10(4): 1–15.

2296 Gaar, Gillian G. 1992. *She's a Rebel: The History of Women in Rock & Roll*. Seattle, WA: Seal.

2297 Gabree, John. 1968. *The World of Rock*. Greenwich, CT: Fawcett.

2298 Garofalo, Reebee. 1987. How Autonomous Is Relative?: Popular Music, the Social Formation and Cultural Struggle. *Popular Music* 6: 77–92.

2299 Garofalo, Reebee, ed. 1992. *Rockin' the Boat: Mass Music and Mass Movements*. Boston, MA: South End Press.

2300 Garofalo, Reebee. 1996. *Rockin' Out: Popular Music in the USA*. Needham Heights, MA: Allyn and Bacon.

2301 Garofalo, Reebee and Chapple, Steve. 1978. From ASCAP to Alan Freed: The Pre-History of Rock 'n' Roll. *Popular Music & Society* 6: 72–80.

2302 Gart, Galen. 1986. *First Pressings: Rock History as Chronicled in Billboard Magazine*. Milford, NH: Big Nickel Publications.

2303 Gelb, Jeff, ed. 1992. *Shock Rock*. New York: Pocket Books.

2304 Gillett, Charlie. 1966. Just Let Me Hear Some of that Rock and Roll Music. *Urban Review* 1(5): 11–14.

2305 Gillett, Charlie. 1983. (1970) *The Sound of the City: The Rise of Rock 'n' Roll*. New York: Pantheon. First published New York: Outerbridge and Dienstfrey, 1970.

2306 Gleason, Ralph J. 1969. *The Jefferson Airplane and the San Francisco Sound*. New York: Ballantine.

2307 Gleason, Ralph J. 1972. A Cultural Revolution. In *The Sounds of Social Change: Studies in Popular Culture*, ed. R. Serge Denisoff and Richard A. Peterson. Chicago: Rand McNally & Co. 137–46.

2308 Goodall, H.L., Jr. 1990. *Living in the Rock 'n' Roll Mystery*. Carbondale, IL: Southern Illinois University Press.

2309 Goodwin, Andrew. 1990. Sample and Hold: Pop Music in the Digital Age of Reproduction. In *On Record: Rock, Pop and the Written Word*, ed. Simon Frith and Andrew Goodwin. London: Routledge. 258–73. (First published in *Critical Quarterly* 30(3) (1988): 34–49.)

2310 Gourdon, Anne-Marie, ed. 1994. *Le Rock: Aspects esthétiques, culturels et sociaux*. Paris: CNRS-Editions.

2311 Graf, Christian. 1994. *Rockmusik Lexikon: Amerika, Band 1, A-K. Band 2, L-Z.* Frankfurt am Main: Fischer.

2312 Graf, Christian. 1994. *Rockmusik Lexikon: Europa, Band 1, A-K. Band 2, L-Z.* Frankfurt am Main: Fischer.

2313 Grossberg, Lawrence. 1983. The Politics of Youth Culture: Some Observations on Rock and Roll in America. *Social Text* 8.

2314 Grossberg, Lawrence. 1984. Another Boring Day in Paradise: Rock and Roll and the Empowerment of Everyday Life. *Popular Music* 4: 225–60.

2315 Grossberg, Lawrence. 1985. If Rock and Roll Communicates, Then Why Is It So Noisy? Pleasure and the Popular. In *Popular Music Perspectives, 2,* ed. David Horn. Göteborg and Exeter: IASPM. 451–63.

2316 Grossberg, Lawrence. 1987. Rock and Roll in Search of an Audience. In *Popular Music & Communication,* ed. James Lull. Newbury Park, CA: Sage. 175–97.

2317 Grossberg, Lawrence. 1989. Rock 'n' Reagan. *Quaderni di Musica/Realtà* 23: 459–77.

2318 Grossberg, Lawrence. 1991. Rock, Territorialization and Power. *Cultural Studies* 5(3): 358–67.

2319 Grossberg, Lawrence. 1992. *We Gotta Get Out of This Place: Popular Conservatism and Postmodern Culture.* New York: Routledge.

2320 Grossman, Lloyd. 1976. *A Social History of Rock Music: From the Greasers to Glitter Rock.* New York: McKay.

2321 Guralnick, Peter. 1978. *Feel Like Going Home: Portraits in Blues and Rock & Roll.* London: Omnibus. First published New York: Sunrise/E.P. Dutton, 1971.

2322 Hall, Douglas Kent. 1970. *Rock: A World Bold as Love.* New York: Cowles.

2323 Hamm, Charles. 1985. Rock 'n' Roll in a Very Strange Society. *Popular Music* 5: 159–74.

2324 Haring, Hermann. 1984. *Rock aus Deutschland/West. Von den Rattles bis NENA. Zwei Jahrzehnte Heimatklang.* Reinbek bei Hamburg: Rowohlt.

2325 Harker, Dave. 1980. *One for the Money: Politics and Popular Song.* London: Hutchinson.

2326 Hatch, David and Millward, Stephen. 1987. *From Blues to Rock: An Analytical History of Pop Music.* Manchester: Manchester University Press.

2327 Hayward, Philip, ed. 1992. *From Pop to Punk to Postmodernism: Popular Music and Australian Culture from the 1960s to the 1990s.* Sydney: Allen and Unwin.

2328 Hebst, Peter, ed. 1981. *The Rolling Stone Interviews, 1967–1980.* London: A. Barker.

2329 Helm, Roland. 1991. *Saar Rock History.* Saarbrücken: Buchverlag Saarbrücker Zeitung.

2330 Henry, Tricia. 1984. Punk and Avant-Garde Art. *Journal of Popular Culture* 17(4): 30–36.

2331 Henry, Tricia. 1989. *Break All Rules! Punk Rock and the Making of Style.* Ann Arbor, MI: UMI.

2332 Herman, Gary. 1992. (1982) *Rock 'n' Roll Babylon,* revised edition. London: Plexus.

2333 Heylin, Clinton, ed. 1992. *The Penguin Book of Rock & Roll Writing.* London: Penguin.

2334 Heylin, Clinton. 1993. *From the Velvets to the Voidoids: A Pre-Punk History for a Post-Punk World.* London: Penguin.

2335 Hibbard, Don and Kaleialoha, Carol. 1983. *The Role of Rock*. Englewood Cliffs, NJ: Prentice-Hall.

2336 Hirsch, Jean-François. 1971. La cause du pop est-elle insaisissable? *Musique en jeu* 2: 66–72.

2337 Hirsch, Jean-François. 1971. La radicalisation pop. *Musique en jeu* 2: 72–74.

2338 Hodek, Johannes and Niermann, Franz. 1984. *Rockmusik – Rockkultur*. Stuttgart: J.B. Metzlersche Verlagsbuchhandlung.

2339 Hoehner, Albert. 1989. *Backstage: Der alltägliche Wahnsinn des Rock 'n' Roll*. Frankfurt am Main: Fischer.

2340 Hoffmann, Raoul. 1981. *Rockstory. Drei Jahrzehnte Rock & Pop Music von Presley bis Punk*. Frankfurt am Main, Berlin and Wien: Ullstein.

2341 Hogg, Brian. 1993. *The History of Scottish Rock and Pop: All That Ever Mattered*. Enfield: Guinness Books.

2342 Hopkins, Jerry. 1970. *The Rock Story*. New York: Signet/New American Library.

2343 Horvath, Ricardo. 1982. *Los rockeros*. Buenos Aires: Centro Editor de América Latina.

2344 Hounsome, Terry. 1990. *Single File: Over One Hundred Thousand British Singles by Thirty Thousand Artists, 1950s to 1980s*. Milford Haven: Hounsome.

2345 Humann, Klaus and Reichert, Carl-Ludwig, eds. 1981. *EuroRock. Länder und Szenen. Ein Überblick*. Reinbek bei Hamburg: Rowohlt.

2346 Jahn, Mike. 1973. *Rock: From Elvis Presley to the Rolling Stones*. New York: Quadrangle.

2347 Jelot-Blanc, Jean-Jacques. 1978. *Le cinéma musical: du rock au disco 1953–1967*. Paris: Editions PAC.

2348 Jelot-Blanc, Jean-Jacques. 1979. *Le cinéma musical: du rock au disco 1958–1979*. Paris: Editions PAC.

2349 Jenkinson, Philip. 1974. *Celluloid Rock: Twenty Years of Movie Rock*. London: Lorrimer.

2350 Jerrentrup, Ansgar. 1981. *Entwicklung der Rockmusik von den Anfängen bis zum Beat*. Regensburg: Gustav Bosse.

2351 Jewell, Derek. 1980. *The Popular Voice: A Musical Record of the 60s & 70s*. London: Deutsch.

2352 Johnson, Derek. 1969. *Beat Music*. Copenhagen/London: Hansen/Chester.

2353 Joyner, David Lee. 1993. *American Popular Music*. Madison, WI: Brown & Benchmark.

2354 Juge, Pascale. 1982. *Rockeuses: les heroïnes de Juke-Box*. Paris: Grancher.

2355 Kaiser, Charles. 1988. *1968 in America: Music, Politics, Chaos. Counterculture and the Shaping of a Generation*. New York: Weidenfeld & Nicolson.

2356 Kaiser, Rolf-Ulrich. 1969. *Das Buch der neuen Popmusik*. Düsseldorf and Wien: Econ.

2357 Kaiser, Rolf-Ulrich. 1972. *Rock-Zeit. Stars, Geschäft und Geschichte der neuen Pop-Musik*. Düsseldorf and Wien: Econ.

2358 Kelly, Michael Bryan. 1991. *The Beatle Myth: The British Invasion of American Popular Music, 1956–1969*. Jefferson and London: McFarland.

2359 Kent, Jeff. 1983. *The Rise & Fall of Rock*. Stoke-onTrent: Witan.

2360 Kershaw, Alan Roy and Hohensee, Michael. 1982. *The Rock Reader. Vol. 1: 1953–1978*. Leura: Afloat Press.

2361 Kersten, Martin. 1996. Jugendkulturen und NS-Vergangenheit. Der schmale Plad zwischen Provokation, Spiel,

Inszenierung und erneuter Faszination vom Punk bis zum Nazi-Rock.. *PopScriptum* 5: 58–89.

2362 Kiefer, Kit. 1991. *They Called It Rock: The Goldmine Oral History of Rock 'n' Roll, 1950–1970.* Iola, WI: Krause Publications.

2363 Kinder, Bob. 1986. *The Best of the First: The Early Days of Rock and Roll.* Chicago: Adams Press.

2364 Kneif, Tibor. 1977. Rockmusik und Bildungsmusik. In *Rockmusik,* ed. Wolfgang Sandner. Mainz: Schott. 131–44.

2365 Kneif, Tibor. 1980. *Sachlexikon Rockmusik: Instrumente, Stile, Techniken, Industrie und Geschichte.* Reinbek bei Hamburg: Rowohlt.

2366 Kneif, Tibor. 1982. *Rock Musik: Ein Handbuch zum kritischen Verständnis.* Reinbek bei Hamburg: Rowohlt.

2367 Kohl, Paul R. 1993. Looking Through a Glass Onion: Rock and Roll as Modern Manifestation of Carnival. *Journal of Popular Culture* 27(1): 143–62.

2368 Kramarz, Volkmar. 1983. *Harmonieanalyse der Rockmusik: Von Folk und Blues zu Rock und New Wave.* Mainz: Schott.

2369 Kramarz, Volkmar. 1985. Rockmusik und Musiktheorie. *Jazzforschung* 17: 99–101.

2370 Kruetzfeldt, Werner. 1985. Über die Beziehungen von Science Fiction und Fantasy zur Pop-Musik. *Jazzforschung* 17: 102–105.

2371 Kuhnke, Klaus, Manfred Miller and Peter Schulze. 1977. *Geschichte der Pop-Musik. Band 1 (Bis 1947).* Bremen: Eres & Archiv für Populäre Musik.

2372 Lacombe, Alain. 1985. *L'écran du rock: 30 ans de cinéma et de rock-music.* Paris: Llernminier.

2373 Laing, Dave. 1969. *The Sound of Our Time.* London: Sheed & Ward.

2374 Laing, Dave. 1985. *One Chord Wonders: Power and Meaning in Punk Rock.* Milton Keynes: Open University Press.

2375 Laing, Dave, et al. 1975. *The Electric Muse: The Story of Folk into Rock.* London: Eyre Methuen.

2376 Landau, Jon. 1972. Rock 1970: It's Too Late to Stop Now. In *American Music: From Storyville to Woodstock,* ed. Charles Nanry. New Brunswick, NJ: Transaction. 238–66.

2377 Lawhead, Stephen. 1987. *Rock of This Age: The Real and Imagined Dangers of Rock Music.* Downers Grove, IL: Intervarsity Press.

2378 Lawhead, Stephen. 1989. *Rock on Trial: Pop Music and Its Role in Our Lives.* Leicester: Intervarsity Press.

2379 Lehtonen, Esko. 1983. *Suomalaisen rockin tietosanakirja.* Tampere: Fanzine Oy.

2380 Leitner, Olaf. 1983. *Rockszene DDR: Aspekte einer Massenkultur im Sozialismus.* Reinbek bei Hamburg: Rowohlt.

2381 Lemery, Denys. 1971. Musique contemporaine, pop-music et free-jazz, convergences et divergences. *Musique en jeu* 2: 80–87.

2382 Lemonnier, Bertrand. 1986. *La révolution pop dans l'Angleterre des années 60.* Paris: Table Ronde.

2383 Leukert, Bernd, ed. 1980. *Thema: Rock gegen Rechts. Musik als politisches Instrument.* Frankfurt am Main: Fischer.

2384 Levy, Claire. 1992. The Influence of British Rock in Bulgaria. *Popular Music* 11(2): 209–12.

2385 Lewis, George H. 1970. The Pop Artist and His Product: Mixed-Up Confusion. *Journal of Popular Culture* 4(2): 327–38.

2386 Lipperini, L. 1990. *Mozart in Rock*. Firenze: Sansoni.

2387 Lipsitz, George. 1994. *Dangerous Crossroads: Popular Music, Postmodernism and the Poetics of Place*. London: Verso.

2388 London, Herbert I. 1984. *Closing the Circle: A Cultural History of the Rock Revolution*. Chicago: Nelson-Hall.

2389 Longerich, Winfried. 1989. *'Da Da Da' – Zur Standortbestimmung der Neuen Deutschen Welle*. Pfaffenweiler: Centaurus.

2390 Lugert, Wulf-Dieter. 1994. Populäre Musik – Eine 'unendliche Geschichte'. In *Populäre Musik und Pädagogik – Grundlagen und Praxismaterialien*, ed. Jürgen Terhag. Oldershausen: Institut für Didaktik der populären Musik. 26–35.

2391 Lull, James. 1992. Listeners' Communicative Uses of Popular Music. In *Popular Music & Communication*, ed. James Lull. Newbury Park, CA: Sage. 140–74.

2392 Lull, James, ed. 1992. (1987) *Popular Music & Communication*. Newbury Park, CA: Sage.

2393 Lydon, Michael. 1973. *Rock Folk: Portraits from the Rock 'n' Roll Pantheon*. New York: Dell Publishing.

2394 Mabey, Richard. 1969. *The Pop Process*. London: Hutchinson Educational.

2395 Madigan, Paul. 1987. Rocking Australia Dead. In *Missing in Action: Australian Popular Music*, ed. Marcus Breen. Melbourne: Verbal Graphics Pty. 113–25.

2396 Makower, Joel. 1989. *Woodstock: The Oral History*. New York/London: Doubleday/Sidgwick & Jackson.

2397 Manoeuvre, Philippe. 1985. *L'Enfant du rock*. Paris: Lattès.

2398 Manuel, Peter. 1988. *Popular Music of the Non-Western World: An Introductory Survey*. New York and Oxford: Oxford University Press.

2399 Marcus, Greil, ed. 1969. *Rock & Roll Will Stand*. Boston, MA: Beacon Press.

2400 Marcus, Greil, ed. 1979. *Stranded: Rock and Roll for a Desert Island*. New York: Knopf.

2401 Marcus, Greil. 1990. *Mystery Train: Images of America in Rock 'n' Roll Music*. London: Omnibus. First published New York: E.P. Dutton, 1975.

2402 Marin, Adolfo. 1984. *La nueva música: del industrial al techno-pop*. Barcelona: Teorema.

2403 Martin, Bernice. 1981. *A Sociology of Contemporary Cultural Change*. Oxford: Blackwell.

2404 Martin, Linda and Segrave, Kerry. 1988. *Anti-Rock: The Opposition to Rock 'n' Roll*. Hamden, CT: Archon Books.

2405 Marvin, Elisabeth West and Hermann, Richard, eds. 1995. *Concert Music, Rock and Jazz Since 1945*. Rochester, NY: University of Rochester Press.

2406 May, Chris and Phillips, Tim. 1974. *British Beat*. London: Sociopack Publications.

2407 McCarthy, David. 1990. *The Golden Age of Rock and Pop*. London: Apple.

2408 McDonnell, Evelyn and Powers, Ann. 1995. *Rock, She Wrote: Women Write About Rock, Pop and Rap*. London: Plexus.

2409 McDonough, Jack. 1985. *San Francisco Rock: The Illustrated History of San Francisco Rock Music*. San Francisco: Chronicle Books.

2410 McGee, Mark Thomas. 1990. *The Rock and Roll Movie Encyclopedia of the 1950s*. Jefferson, NC: McFarland.

2411 Mellers, Wilfrid. 1973. *Twilight of the Gods: The Beatles in Retrospect*. London: Faber & Faber.

2412 Melly, George. 1971. *Revolt into Style: The Pop Arts*. Garden City, NY: Doubleday.

2413 Meltzer, Richard. 1972. *Gulcher: Post-Rock Cultural Pluralism in America*. San Francisco: Straight Arrow Books.

2414 Meltzer, Richard. 1987. (1970) *The Aesthetics of Rock*, revised edition. New York: Da Capo Press.

2415 Mercer, Mick. 1988. *Gothic Rock Black Book*. London: Omnibus.

2416 Mercer, Mick. 1991. *Gothic Rock: All You Ever Wanted to Know*. Birmingham.

2417 Meyer, Thomas. 1995. Aspekte von Rockmusik in der ehemaligen DDR und in der Marktwirtschaft der Bundesrepublik. In *Popular Music Perspectives III*, ed. Peter Wicke. Berlin: Zyankrise. 131–37.

2418 Meyer, Thomas. 1996. 'Rechtsrock' als Messagerock. *PopScriptum* 5: 44–57.

2419 Middleton, Richard. 1972. *Pop Music and the Blues: A Study of the Relationship and Its Significance*. London: Gollancz.

2420 Middleton, Richard. 1983. 'Play It Again, Sam': On the Productivity of Repetition. *Popular Music* 3: 235–71.

2421 Middleton, Richard. 1986. In the Groove, or Blowing Your Mind? The Pleasures of Musical Repetition. In *Popular Culture and Social Relations*, ed. Tony Bennett and Janet Woollacott.

Milton Keynes: Open University Press. 159–76.

2422 Middleton, Richard. 1990. *Studying Popular Music*. Milton Keynes: Open University Press.

2423 Middleton, Richard and Muncie, John. 1981. Pop Culture, Pop Music and Post-War Youth: Countercultures. In *Politics, Ideology and Popular Culture (1)*. Milton Keynes: Open University Press. 63–92.

2424 Mignon, Patrick and Hennion, Antoine, eds. 1991. *Rock: de l'histoire au mythe*. Paris: Anthropos.

2425 Miller, Jim, ed. 1992. *The Rolling Stone Illustrated History of Rock & Roll*. New York: Random House. First published New York: Random House, 1976.

2426 Moll, Dieter. 1985. *Die Geschichte des Rock 'n' Roll*. Hannoversch-Münden: Gauke.

2427 Mooney, H.F. 1974. Just Before Rock: Pop Music 1950–1953, Reconsidered. *Popular Music & Society* 3: 65–108.

2428 Moore, Allan F. 1993. *Rock: The Primary Text*. Buckingham: Open University Press.

2429 Musiques rock, reggae, raï, rap. 1991. *Les Cahiers de l'IFOREP* 64.

2430 Naumann, Michael and Penth, Boris. 1979. *Living in a Rock 'n' Roll Fantasy*. Berlin: Ästhetik und Kommunikation.

2431 Norman, Philip, ed. 1982. *The Road Goes On Forever*. London: Elm Tree.

2432 Ochs, Michael. 1985. *Rock Archives: A Photographic Journey Through the First Two Decades of Rock & Roll*. Poole: Blandford Press.

2433 Oldfield, Paul. 1989. After Subversion: Pop Culture and Power. In *Zoot-Suits and Second-Hand Dresses: An Anthology of Fashion and Music*, ed. Angela

McRobbie. London: Macmillan. 256–66.

2434 Ordovás Blasco, Jesus. 1987. *Historia de la música pop española*. Madrid: Alianza.

2435 Orman, John M. 1984. *The Politics of Rock Music*. Chicago: Nelson-Hall.

2436 Ortner, Lorelies. 1982. *Wortschatz der Pop-/Rockmusik: Das Vokabular der Beiträge über Pop-/Rockmusik*. Düsseldorf: Schwann.

2437 Palmer, Robert. 1979. *A Tale of Two Cities: Memphis Rock and New Orleans Roll*. Brooklyn, NY: Institute for Studies in American Music.

2438 Palmer, Tony. 1976. *All You Need Is Love: The Story of Popular Music*. London: Weidenfeld & Nicolson.

2439 Paraire, Philippe. 1990. *50 ans de musique rock*. Paris: Bordas.

2440 Paraire, Philippe. 1992. (1990) *50 Years of Rock Music*, ed. Sara Newbery and Trevor Pake. Edinburgh: Chambers. First published Paris: Bordas, 1990.

2441 Pascall, Jeremy, et al., ed. 1974. *The Story of Pop*. London: Phoebus/Octopus.

2442 Pattison, Robert. 1987. *The Triumph of Vulgarity: Rock Music in the Mirror of Romanticism*. Oxford and New York: Oxford University Press.

2443 Peck, Richard. 1985. *Rock: Making Musical Choices*. Greenville, SC: Bob Jones University Press.

2444 Peinemann, Steve B. 1980. *Die Wut, die du im Bauch hast: politische Rockmusik*. Reinbek bei Hamburg: Rowohlt.

2445 Peterson, Charles and Azerrad, Michael. 1995. *Screaming Life: The History of Grunge*. San Francisco: HarperCollins.

2446 Peterson, Richard A. 1990. Why 1955? Explaining the Advent of Rock Music. *Popular Music* 9(1): 97–116.

2447 Pichaske, David. 1989. (1979) *A Generation in Motion: Popular Music and Culture in the Sixties*. Granite Falls, MN: Ellis. First published New York: Schirmer, 1979.

2448 Pielke, Robert G. 1986. *Rock Music in American Culture*. Chicago: Nelson-Hall.

2449 Pike, Jeff. 1993. *The Death of Rock 'n' Roll: Untimely Demises, Morbid Preoccupations and Premature Forecasts of Doom in Pop Music*. Boston, MA: Faber & Faber.

2450 Pirot, Christian. 1982. *French Rock*. Paris: Le Vagabond.

2451 Plas, Wim van der. 1985. Can Rock Be Art? In *Popular Music Perspectives, 2*, ed. David Horn. Göteborg and Exeter: IASPM. 397–404.

2452 Plaumann, Klaus. 1978. *The Beat Age*. Frankfurt am Main: Zweitausendundeins.

2453 Pollock, Bruce. 1984. *When the Music Mattered: Rock in the 1960s*. New York: Holt, Rinehart & Winston.

2454 Pollock, Bruce, ed. 1992. *In Their Own Words: Twenty Successful Songwriters Tell How They Write Their Songs*. New York: Collier/Macmillan.

2455 Pollock, Bruce and Wagman, John. 1978. *The Face of Rock & Roll: Images of a Generation*. London: New English Library.

2456 Raemackers, Rémi. 1976. Les lieux propitiatoires du rock. *Musique en jeu* 24: 84–94.

2457 Raisner, Albert. 1973. *L'Aventure Pop*. Paris: Robert Laffont.

2458 Ramet, Pedro and Zamascikov, Sergei. 1990. The Soviet Rock Scene. *Journal of Popular Culture* 24(1): 149–74.

2459 Ramet, Sabrina Petra, ed. 1994. *Rocking the State: Rock Music and Politics in*

Eastern Europe and Russia. Boulder, CO: Westview Press.

2460 Raphael, Amy. 1995. *Never Mind the Bollocks: Women Rewrite Rock.* London: Virago.

2461 Rauhut, Michael. 1993. *Beat in der Grauzone. DDR-Rock 1964 bis 1972 – Politik und Alltag.* Berlin: BasisDruck.

2462 Rauhut, Michael. 1995. Von der Utopie zum Original. Kulturpolitische Koordinaten früher DDR-Rockentwicklung. In *Popular Music Perspectives III*, ed. Peter Wicke. Berlin: Zyankrise. 387–91.

2463 Rauth, R. 1982. Back in the U.S.S.R.: Rock and Roll in the Soviet Union. *Popular Music & Society* 8(3/4): 3–12.

2464 Redd, Lawrence N. 1974. *Rock Is Rhythm and Blues: The Impact of Mass Media.* East Lansing, MI: Michigan State University Press.

2465 Redhead, Steve. 1990. *The End-of-the-Century Party: Youth and Pop Towards 2000.* Manchester: Manchester University Press.

2466 Reid, Jan. 1977. *The Improbable Rise of Redneck Rock.* New York: Da Capo Press. First published Austin: Heidelberg Publishers, 1974.

2467 Reynolds, Simon. 1989. Against Health and Efficiency: Independent Music in the 1980s. In *Zoot-Suits and Second-Hand Dresses: An Anthology of Fashion and Music*, ed. Angela McRobbie. London: Macmillan. 245–55.

2468 Reynolds, Simon. 1990. *Blissed Out: The Raptures of Rock.* London: Serpent's Tail.

2469 Reynolds, Simon and Press, Joy. 1995. *The Sex Revolts: Gender, Rebellion and Rock 'n' Roll.* London: Serpent's Tail.

2470 Rimler, Walter. 1984. *Not Fade Away: A Comparison of the Jazz Age with the Rock Era.* Ann Arbor, MI: Pierian Press.

2471 Rimmer, Dave. 1985. *Like Punk Never Happened.* London: Faber & Faber.

2472 Roberts, John Storm. 1979. *The Latin Tinge: The Impact of Latin American Music on the United States.* New York: Oxford University Press.

2473 Robinson, Richard. 1972. *Pop, Rock and Soul.* New York: Pyramid.

2474 *Rock Record 4: The Directory of Rock Albums and Musicians.* 1991. Dyfed, Wales: Record Researcher Publications.

2475 Rockwell, John. 1985. (1983) *All American Music: Composition in the Late 20th Century.* London: Kahn & Averill. First published New York: Knopf, 1983.

2476 Rogers, Dave. 1982. *Rock 'n' Roll.* London: Routledge & Kegan Paul.

2477 Röhrling (Schiffkowitz), Helmut. 1990. *Wir sind die, vor denen uns unsere Eltern gewarnt haben. Szenen und Personen aus den amerikanischen Sechzigern.* Graz: Nausner & Röhrling.

2478 Romanowski, William D. and Denisoff, R. Serge. 1987. Money for Nothin' and the Charts for Free: Rock and the Movies. *Journal of Popular Culture* 21(3): 63–78.

2479 Ross, Andrew and Rose, Tricia, eds. 1994. *Microphone Fiends: Youth Music and Youth Culture.* London and New York: Routledge.

2480 Roux, Alain. 1973. La musique pop. In *Musique et vie quotidienne*, ed. Paul Beaud and Alfred Willener. Paris: Mame. 109–50.

2481 Rowe, David. 1995. *Popular Cultures: Rock Music, Sport and the Politics of Pleasure.* London: Sage.

2482 Rubin, David S. 1996. *It's Only Rock and Roll: Rock and Roll Currents in Contemporary Art*. Kempen: te Neues Verlag.

2483 Rumley, Gina and Little, Hilary. 1989. *Women and Pop: A Series of Lost Encounters*, ed. Angela McRobbie. London: Macmillan.

2484 Rupprecht, Siegfried P. 1984. *Pop: Von der Musikrevolution zum Jugendkonsum; das große Geschäft mit der Pop-Musik*. Heidelberg: Eggert.

2485 Russo, M. and Warner, D. 1987/88. Rough Music, Futurism and Postpunk Industrial Noise Bands. *Discourse* 10(1): 55–76.

2486 Ryback, Timothy. 1990. *Rock Around the Bloc: A History of Rock Music in Eastern Europe and the Soviet Union*. New York: Oxford University Press.

2487 Sadler, Michael, Dominique Farran and Serge Dutfoy. 1985. *Histoire du rock en bandes dessinées*. Paris: Van de Velde-Edimonde.

2488 Salzinger, Helmut. 1972. *Rock Power oder Wie musikalisch ist die Revolution?* Frankfurt am Main: Fischer.

2489 Sandner, Wolfgang, ed. 1977. *Rockmusik. Aspekte zur Geschichte, Ästhetik, Produktion*. Mainz: Schott.

2490 Savage, Jon. 1989. 'Do You Know How To Pony?': The Messianic Intensity of the Sixties. In *Zoot-Suits and Second-Hand Dresses: An Anthology of Fashion and Music*, ed. Angela McRobbie. London: Macmillan. 121–31.

2491 Savage, Jon. 1989. The Age of Plunder. In *Zoot-Suits and Second-Hand Dresses: An Anthology of Fashion and Music*, ed. Angela McRobbie. London: Macmillan. 169–82.

2492 Schaefer, John. 1990. *New Sounds: The Virgin Guide to New Music*. London: Virgin.

2493 Schafer, William J. 1972. *Rock Music: Where It's Been, What It Means, Where It's Going*. Minneapolis, MN: Augsburg.

2494 Schöler, Franz, ed. 1975. *Let It Rock. Eine Geschichte der Rockmusik von Chuck Berry und Elvis Presley bis zu den Rolling Stones und dem Allman Brothers*. München and Wien: Carl Hanser.

2495 Schulz, Berndt. 1988. *Rocker, Punks und Teenies: Vom Rebellenfilm der 50er Jahre zum Popcorn-Kino*. Bergisch Gladbach: Bastei Lübbe.

2496 Seca, Jean-Marie. 1988. *Vocations rock. L'état acide et l'esprit des minorités rock*. Paris: Méridiens-Klincksieck.

2497 Shank, Barry. 1994. *Dissonant Identities: The Rock 'n' Roll Scene in Austin, Texas*. Hanover, NH: University Press of New England.

2498 Shannon, Bob and Javna, John. 1986. *Behind the Hits: Inside Stories of Classic Pop and Rock and Roll*. New York: Warner.

2499 Shapiro, Harry. 1989. *Waiting for the Man: The Story of Drugs and Popular Music*. London: Quartet.

2500 Shaw, Arnold. 1969. *The Rock Revolution: What's Happening in Today's Music*. New York: Crowell-Collier.

2501 Shaw, Arnold. 1987. (1974) *The Rockin' 50's: The Decade That Transformed the Pop Music Scene*. New York: Da Capo Press. First published New York: Hawthorne, 1974.

2502 Shaw, Greg. 1978. *New Wave on Record: England & Europe, 1975–1978*. Burbank, CA: Bomb.

2503 Shaw, Greg. 1982. *Greg Shaw's BOMP!: Vergessenes, Verschollenes und längst Verdrängtes aus dem legendären kalifornischen Rock 'n' Roll Fanzine*. Reinbek bei Hamburg: Rowohlt.

2504 Shaw, Greg. 1983. *Greg Shaw's BOMP!:*
Die Briten kommen; aus dem Kindergarten
der englischen Rockmusik. Reinbek bei
Hamburg: Rowohlt.

2505 Sinclair, John and Levin, Robert. 1971.
Music and Politics. New York: World.

2506 Skolud, Hubert. 1980. *All We Need Is*
Rock. Die Story der Rockmusik.
Offenburg: Reiff.

2507 Smith, Joe. 1988. *Off the Record: An Oral*
History of Popular Music. New York:
Warner.

2508 Spengler, Peter. 1987. *Rockmusik und*
Jugend: Bedeutung und Funktion einer
Musikkultur für die Identitätsuche im
Jugendalter. Frankfurt am Main: Brandes
and Aspel.

2509 Statelova, Rosemary. 1993. *Obarnatata*
Piramida. Aspekti na populjarnata
muzika. Sofia.

2510 Statelova, Rosemary. 1995. Das
populäre Tagebuch – Der Verlust einer
Funktion. In *Popular Music Perspectives*
III, ed. Peter Wicke. Berlin: Zyankrise.
48–51.

2511 Statelova, Rosemary. 1995. *Prezivjano v*
Bulgaria. Rok, Pop, Folk: 1990–1994.
Sofia.

2512 Steen, Andreas. 1995. Rockmusik in der
VR China. *PopScriptum* 3: 80–100.

2513 Steward, Sue and Garratt, Sheryl. 1984.
Signed, Sealed and Delivered: True Life
Stories of Women in Pop. London: Pluto
Press.

2514 Street, John. 1987. *Rebel Rock: The*
Politics of Popular Music. New York:
Basil Blackwell.

2515 Stuessy, Joe. 1994. *Rock 'n' Roll: Its*
History and Stylistic Development.
Englewood Cliffs, NJ: Prentice-Hall.

2516 Szatmary, David P. 1991. (1987)
Rockin' in Time: A Social History of Rock
and Roll. Englewood Cliffs, NJ: Prentice-
Hall.

2517 Thiessen, Rudi. 1981. *It's Only Rock 'n'*
Roll But I Like It: Zu Kult und Mythos
einer Protestbewegung. Berlin: Medusa.

2518 Thompson, Dave. 1994. *Space Daze:*
The History and Mystery of Electronic
Ambient Space Rock. Los Angeles:
Cleopatra.

2519 Thomson, Elizabeth, ed. 1982. *New*
Women in Rock. London: Omnibus.

2520 Torgue, Henry-Skoff. 1984. *La pop-*
music. Paris: PUF.

2521 Tosches, Nick. 1984. *Unsung Heroes of*
Rock & Roll. New York: Scribners.

2522 Troitzky, Artemy. 1987. *Back in the*
USSR: The True Story of Rock in Russia.
Boston, MA: Faber & Faber.

2523 Troitzky, Artemy. 1994. *Rok v SSSR.*
Moskva: Knigi.

2524 Trondman, Mats. 1990. Rock Taste: On
Rock as Symbolic Capital. A Study of
Young People's Music Taste and Music
Making. In *Popular Music Research*, ed.
Keith Roe and Ulla Karlsson. Göteborg:
NORDICOM-Sweden, No. 1–2. 71–86.

2525 Trow, Mike. 1978. *The Pulse of '64: The*
Mersey Beat. New York: Vantage.

2526 Tschernokoscheva, Elka. 1995. Populäre
Musik und Aneignung des Alltags
Umgang mit Musik als Form der
Lebensbewältigung. In *Popular Music*
Perspectives III, ed. Peter Wicke. Berlin:
Zyankrise. 52–54.

2527 Tucker, Bruce. 1989. 'Tell Tchaikovsky
the News': Postmodernism, Popular
Culture and the Emergence of Rock 'n'
Roll. *Black Music Research Journal* 9(2):
271–95.

2528 Turner, Steve. 1995. *Hungry for Heaven:*
Rock and Roll and the Search for

Redemption. London: Hodder and Stoughton.

2529 Urban, Peter. 1979. *Rollende Worte – die Poesie des Rock. Von der Straßenballade zum Pop-Song.* Frankfurt am Main: Fischer.

2530 Vlček, Josef. 1982. *Rock 2000.* Prague: Jazzova sekce.

2531 Wale, Michael. 1972. *Vox Pop: Profiles of the Pop Process.* London: Harrap.

2532 Walker, John A. 1987. *Cross-Overs: Art into Pop, Pop into Art.* London: Comedia.

2533 Ward, Ed, Geoffrey Stokes and Ken Tucker. 1986. *Rock of Ages: The Rolling Stone History of Rock & Roll.* Englewood Cliffs, NJ: Rolling Stone/Prentice-Hall.

2534 Watts, Michael. 1975. The Call and Response of American Popular Music: The Impact of American Pop Music in Europe. In *Superculture: American Popular Culture and Europe,* ed. C.W.E. Bigsby. London: Elek. 123–39.

2535 Weinstein, Deena. 1983. Rock: Youth and Its Music. *Popular Music & Society* 4: 2–15.

2536 Wenner, Jann, ed. 1971. *The Rolling Stone Interviews, Vol. 1.* New York: Warner Books.

2537 Wenner, Jann, ed. 1987. *Twenty Years of Rolling Stone, 1967–1987.* New York: Friendly Press.

2538 Whitcomb, Ian. 1983. *Rock Odyssey.* Garden City, NY: Doubleday.

2539 Wicke, Peter. 1981. Rock in Opposition. *Musik und Gesellschaft* XXXI(7): 410–17.

2540 Wicke, Peter. 1981. Rockmusik – Aspekte einer Faszination. *Weimarer Beiträge* XXVII(9): 89–127.

2541 Wicke, Peter. 1981. Rockmusik in der DDR. Erfahrungen – Tendenzen – Perspektiven. *Beilage zur Zeitschrift 'Unterhaltungskunst'* 2.

2542 Wicke, Peter. 1981. Rockmusik in der DDR. Stationen einer Entwicklung. *Bulletin* XVII(2–3): 4–9.

2543 Wicke, Peter. 1982. Les avatars du rock. *Connaissance de la RDA* 14: 59–72.

2544 Wicke, Peter. 1982. Rock Music as a Phenomenon of Progressive Mass Culture. In *Popular Music Perspectives, 1,* ed. David Horn and Philip Tagg. Göteborg and Exeter: IASPM. 223–31.

2545 Wicke, Peter. 1983. Rock 'n' Revolution. *Musik und Gesellschaft* XXXIII(9): 538–43.

2546 Wicke, Peter. 1985. Jugend und populäre Musik. *Bulletin* XXI(2): 9–12.

2547 Wicke, Peter. 1985. Rock in Opposition. Neue Tendenzen in der internationalen Rockmusik. *Beilage zur Zeitschrift 'Unterhaltungskunst'* 2.

2548 Wicke, Peter. 1985. Rock 'n' Revolution. Sul significato della rock in una cultura di massa progressista. *Musica/Realtà* 17: 5–11.

2549 Wicke, Peter. 1985. Young People and Popular Music in East Germany: Focus on a Scene. *Communication Research* XII(3): 319–27.

2550 Wicke, Peter. 1986. Theoretische Probleme der Produktion von Rockmusik. *Beilage zur Zeitschrift 'Unterhaltungskunst'* 3.

2551 Wicke, Peter. 1988. (1987) *Anatomie des Rock.* Leipzig: Deutscher Verlag für Musik.

2552 Wicke, Peter. 1990. Populäre Musik und neue Medien – Musikkultur im Umbruch. *Musik und Gesellschaft* XL(10): 480–85.

2553 Wicke, Peter. 1990. (1987) *Rock Music: Culture – Aesthetic – Sociology*. Cambridge: Cambridge University Press. First published Leipzig: Reclam, 1987.

2554 Wicke, Peter. 1992. Jazz, Rock und Popmusik im 20. Jahrhundert. In *Volks- und Popularmusik in Europa*, ed. Doris Stockmann. Laaber: Laaber. 445–78.

2555 Wicke, Peter. 1995. 'Der King vom Prenzlauer Berg'. Vom Mythos des Rock in einer sozialistischen Metropole. In *Berlin – Hauptstadt der DDR 1949–1989: Utopie und Realität*, ed. Bernd Wilzek. Zürich and Baden Baden: Elster-Verlag. 236–47.

2556 Wicke, Peter. 1995. Popmusik – Konsumfetischismus oder kulturelles Widerstandspotential. In *Yesterday. Today. Tomorrow*, ed. M. Heuger and M. Prell. Regensburg: ConBrio Verlagsgesellschaft. 21–35.

2557 Wicke, Peter. 1995. Populäre Musik im sozialen und politischen Wandel. In *Popular Music Perspectives III*, ed. Peter Wicke. Berlin: Zyankrise. 15–22.

2558 Wicke, Peter. 1996. Pop Music in the GDR: Between Conformity and Resistance. In *Changing Identities in East Germany (Studies in GDR Culture and Society 14(15))*, ed. M. Gerber and R. Wood. Lanham, New York and London: University Press of America. 25–37.

2559 Wicke, Peter. 1996. Rock Around Socialism. Jugend und ihre Musik in einer gescheiterten Gesellschaft. In *Jugend und ihre Musik*, ed. Dieter Baacke. München: Juventus. 26–41.

2560 Wicke, Peter and Frevel, Bernd. 1996. 'Wenn die Musik sich ändert zittern die Mauern der Stadt'. Rockmusik als Medium des politischen Diskurses im DDR-Kulturbetrieb. In *Musik und Politik*. Regensburg: Coda. 120–42.

2561 Williams, Paul. 1969. *Outlaw Blues: A Book of Rock Music*. New York: Dutton.

2562 Winders, James. 1983. Reggae, Rastafarians and Revolution: Rock Music in the Third World. *Journal of Popular Culture* 17(1): 61–73.

2563 Wölfer, Jürgen. 1980. *Die Rock- und Popmusik. Eine umfaßende Darstellung ihrer Geschichte und Funktion*. München: Heyne.

2564 Yorke, Ritchie. 1971. *The History of Rock 'n' Roll*. London: Eyre Methuen.

2565 Zimmer, Jochen. 1973. *Popmusik. Zur Theorie und Sozialgeschichte*. Dortmund: Schriftenreihe der Naturfreundejugend.

2566 Zion, Lawrence. 1989. Disposable Icons: Pop Music in Australia. *Popular Music* 8: 165–75.

Reference

General Works

2567 Barnard, Stephen. 1986. *Rock: An Illustrated History*. London: Orbis.

2568 Barnes, Ken. 1973. *Twenty Years of Pop*. London: Kenneth Mason.

2569 Bertoncelli, Ricardo. 1985. *Enciclopedia rock anni '60*. Milano: Arcana.

2570 Betrock, Alan. 1986. *The I Was a Teenage Juvenile Delinquent Rock 'n' Roll Beach Party Movie Book: A Complete Guide to the Teen Exploitation Film, 1954–1969*. New York: St. Martin's Press.

2571 Cross, Colin, Paul Kendall and Mick Farren. 1980. *Encyclopedia of British Beat Groups & Solo Artists of the Sixties*. London: Omnibus.

2572 Dachs, David. 1972. *Encyclopedia of Pop/Rock*. New York: Scholastic Book Services.

2573 *Das große RTL-Lexikon der Popmusik.* 1982. München: Heyne.

2574 Dellar, Fred. 1981. *NME Guide to Rock Cinema.* London: Hamlyn.

2575 DiMartino, Dave. 1994. *Singer-Songwriters: Pop Music's Performer-Composers from A to Zevon.* New York: Billboard Books.

2576 Edenhofer, Julia. 1994. *Rock und Pop von A bis Z.* Bergisch Gladbach: Bastei Lübbe.

2577 Ehnert, Günter and Kinsler, Detlef. 1984. (1975) *Rock in Deutschland: Lexikon deutscher Rockgruppen und Interpreten.* Hamburg: Taurus.

2578 Frame, Pete. 1980. *Rock Family Trees.* London: Omnibus.

2579 Fredericks, Vic. 1958. *Who's Who in Rock 'n' Roll.* New York: Fell.

2580 Gillett, Charlie, ed. 1972. *Rock File.* London: New English Library.

2581 Gillett, Charlie, ed. 1974. *Rock File 2.* St. Alban's: Panther/Granada.

2582 Gillett, Charlie and Frith, Simon, eds. 1975. *Rock File 3.* St. Alban's: Panther/Granada.

2583 Gillett, Charlie and Frith, Simon, eds. 1976. *Rock File 4.* St. Alban's: Panther/Granada.

2584 Gillett, Charlie and Frith, Simon, eds. 1978. *Rock File 5.* St. Alban's: Panther/Granada.

2585 Gillett, Charlie and Frith, Simon, eds. 1996. *The Beat Goes On: The Rock File Reader.* London and East Haven: Pluto Press.

2586 Graf, Christian. 1994. *Rockmusik-Lexikon. Europa.* 2 vols. Frankfurt am Main: Fischer. First published Hamburg: Taurus, 1985.

2587 Graf, Christian and Wohlmacher, Uwe. 1994. *Rockmusik-Lexikon. Übersee: Amerika, Australien, Karibik.* 2 vols. Frankfurt am Main: Fischer. First published Hamburg: Taurus, 1981.

2588 Graves, Barry. 1990. *Rock-Lexikon, Vol. 1: ABBA to Anne Murray; Vol. 2: Gianna Nannini to ZZ Top.* Reinbek bei Hamburg: Rowohlt.

2589 Hardy, Phil and Laing, Dave, eds. 1976. *The Encyclopedia of Rock.* St. Alban's: Granada.

2590 Hardy, Phil and Laing, Dave, eds. 1995. (1990) *The Faber Companion to 20th Century Popular Music,* 2nd edition. London: Faber.

2591 Hausner, Frank. 1992. (1989) *Popographie,* 2nd edition. Altbach: Hausner. First published Altbach: Hausner, 1989.

2592 Helander, Brock. 1982. *The Rock Who's Who: A Biographical and Critical Discography.* New York: Schirmer.

2593 Hendler, Herb. 1983. *Year by Year in the Rock Era.* Westport, CT: Greenwood Press.

2594 Hibbert, Tom. 1983. *Rockspeak! The Dictionary of Rock Terms.* London, New York and Sydney: Omnibus.

2595 Hirsch, Jean-François and Maynadié, Robert. 1971. Dossier pop music: bibliographie, revues, filmographie, discographie pop de base. *Musique en jeu* 2: 102–10.

2596 Kneif, Tibor. 1992. (1978) *Sachlexikon Rockmusik. Instrumente, Stile, Techniken, Industrie und Geschichte,* 3rd edition. Neuausgabe: Bernward Halbscheffel. First published Reinbek bei Hamburg: Rowohlt, 1978.

2597 Laufenberg, Frank and Hake, Ingrid. 1994. *Frank Laufenbergs Rock- und Pop-Lexicon.* Düsseldorf and Wien: Econ.

2598 Leduc, Jean-Marie and Ogouz, Jean-Noël. 1990. *Le Rock de A à Z: dictionnaire illustré*, nouvelle édition augmentée. Paris: Albin Michel.

2599 Logan, Nick and Woffinden, Bob. 1982. (1976) *The Illustrated Encyclopedia of Rock*, 3rd edition. London: Salamander/ Hamlyn. First published London: Salamander/Hamlyn, 1976.

2600 Macken, Bob, et al. 1981. *The Rock Music Source Book*. Garden City, NY: Anchor Press.

2601 Marchbank, Pearce. 1977. *The Illustrated Rock Almanac*. London: Paddington Press.

2602 Matzner, Antonín, Ivan Polednak and Igor Wasserberger, eds. 1989. (1980) *Encyklopedie Jazzu a Moderní Populární Hudby*, 5th edition. Praha: Supraphon.

2603 May, Chris. n.d. *Rock 'n' Roll*. London: Scion/Sociopack Publications.

2604 Nite, Norm N. 1984. (1978) *The Years of Change*. New York: Harper & Row. First published New York: Thomas Y. Cromwell, 1978.

2605 Nite, Norm N. 1985. *Rock On: The Illustrated Encyclopedia of Rock 'n' Roll*. New York: Harper & Row.

2606 Nite, Norm N. 1989. *Rock Almanac: The First Decades of Rock 'n' Roll*. New York: Harper & Row.

2607 *Oor's Eerste Nederlandse Popencyclopedie*. 1994. 9th edition. Amsterdam: Bonaventura.

2608 Pareles, John, ed. 1983. *The Rolling Stone Encyclopedia of Rock*. New York: Rolling Stone Press.

2609 Peellaert, Guy and Schober, Ingeborg. 1973. *Rock Dreams. Bildergeschichte und Rock-Lexikon und Discographie. 20 Jahre Popmusik von A-Z*. München: Schüneman.

2610 Plaumann, Klaus. 1990. *Rock 'n' Roll Music. Eine Bilddokumentation mit einer Rock-Enzyklopädie der 198 Interpreten & ihren Hits*. Frankfurt am Main: Zweitausendeins.

2611 Roxon, Lillian and Naha, Ed. 1980. (1969) *Rock Encyclopedia*. London: Angus & Robertson. First published New York: Grosset & Dunlap, 1969.

2612 Schmidt-Joos, Siegfried and Graves, Barry. 1975. (1973) *Rock-Lexikon*, 2nd edition. Reinbek bei Hamburg: Rowohlt.

2613 Shaw, Arnold. 1982. *Dictionary of American Pop/Rock*. New York: Schirmer Books.

2614 Stambler, Irwin. 1989. (1974) *The Encyclopedia of Pop, Rock and Soul*, revised edition. New York: St. Martin's Press.

2615 Struck, Jürgen. 1985. *Rock Around the Cinema: Spielfilme/Dokumentationen, Video-Clips*. Reinbek: Rowohlt.

2616 Tardos, Péter. 1982. *Rock Lexikon. Második, javitott és bövitett kiadás*. Budapest: Zenemükiadó.

2617 Tobler, John. 1991. *Who's Who in Rock & Roll*. London: Hamlyn.

2618 York, William. 1979. *Who's Who in Rock: An A-Z of Groups, Performers, Session Men and Engineers*. London: Omnibus.

Bibliographies

2619 Hanel, Ed, comp. 1983. *The Essential Guide to Rock Books*. London: Omnibus.

2620 Hoffmann, Frank. 1981. *The Literature of Rock: 1954–1978*. Metuchen, NJ: Scarecrow Press.

2621 Hoffmann, Frank and Cooper, B. Lee. 1986. *The Literature of Rock II: 1979–1983, with Additional Material for the Period 1954–1978*. Metuchen, NJ: Scarecrow Press.

2622 Hoffmann, Frank and Cooper, B. Lee. 1994. *The Literature of Rock III: 1984–1990, with Additional Material for the Period 1954–1983*. Metuchen, NJ: Scarecrow Press.

Discographies

2623 Ferlinger, Robert D. 1976. *A Discography of Rhythm & Blues and Rock & Roll Vocal Groups, 1945–1965*. Pittsburgh, PA: Ferlinger.

2624 Gonzalez, Fernando. 1977. *Disco-File: The Discographical Catalogue of American Rock & Roll and Rhythm & Blues Vocal Harmony Groups, 1902–1976*. Flushing, NY: Gonzalez.

2625 Grosse, Francis and Gueffier, Bernard. 1988. *La discographie du rock français*. Dombasle.

2626 Hounsome, Terry. 1994. *Rock Record 6*. Llandysul, Wales: Terry Hounsome Record Researcher.

2627 Kocandrle, Mirek. 1988. *The History of Rock and Roll: A Selective Discography*. Boston, MA: G.K. Hall.

2628 Leichter, Albert, comp. 1975. *A Discography of Rhythm & Blues and Rock & Roll, Circa 1946–1964: A Reference Manual*. Staunton, VA: The author.

2629 Strong, Martin C. 1994. *The Great Rock Discography*. Edinburgh: Canongate.

Styles

Art-Rock/Out-Rock

2630 Born, Georgina. 1987. Modern Music Culture: On Shock, Pop and Synthesis. *New Formations* 2: 51–78.

2631 Cutler, Chris. 1985. *File under Popular: Theoretical and Critical Writings on Music*. London: November Books.

2632 Gagne, Cole. 1990. *Sonic Transports: New Frontiers in Our Music*. New York: de Falco Books.

2633 Goodwin, Andrew. 1991. Popular Music and Postmodern Theory. *Cultural Studies* 5(2): 174–90.

2634 Jones, Andrew. 1995. *Plunderphonics, Pataphysics & Pop Mechanics: An Introduction to* Musique Actuelle. Wembley: SAF Publishing.

2635 Moore, Allan F. 1993. *Rock: The Primary Text*. Buckingham: Open University Press.

2636 Rockwell, John. 1980. Art Rock. In *The Rolling Stone Illustrated History of Rock and Roll*, ed. Jim Miller. New York: Random House. 347–52.

2637 Rockwell, John. 1983. Art-Rock, Black vs. White & Vanguard Cross-Pollination: Talking Heads. In *All American Music: Composition in the Late Twentieth Century*. New York: Alfred A. Knopf. 234–45.

2638 Schaefer, John. 1990. *New Sounds: The Virgin Guide to New Music*. London: Virgin.

2639 Stratton, Jon. 1989. Beyond Art: Postmodernism and the Case of Popular Music. *Theory, Culture & Society* 6(1): 31–57.

Disco and Dancefloor

2640 Blum, Lucille Hollander. 1966/67. The Discotheque and the Phenomenon of Alone-Togetherness: A Study of the Young Person's Response to the Frug and Comparable Current Dances. *Adolescence* 1(4) (Winter): 351–66.

2641 Fallon, Dennis J. 1980. *The Art of Disco Dancing*. Reston, VA: National Dance Association.

2642 Hanson, Kitty. 1978. *Disco Fever*. New York: A Signet Book.

2643 Hanson, Kitty. 1979. *Disco Fieber*. München: Heyne.

2644 Hughes, Walter. 1994. In the Empire of the Beat: Discipline and Disco. In *Microphone Fiends: Youth Music and Youth Culture*, ed. Andrew Ross and Tricia Rose. London: Routledge.

2645 No entry.

2646 Kopkind, Andrew. 1979. The Dialectic of Disco. *Voice* 12 (February): 1, 11–16.

2647 Kopytko, Tanya. 1986. Breakdance as an Identity Marker in New Zealand. *Yearbook for Traditional Music* 18: 20–26.

2648 Krasnow, Carolyn. 1993. Fear and Loathing in the 70s: Race, Sexuality and Disco. *Stanford Humanities Review* 3(2): 37–45.

2649 Langlois, Tony. 1992. Can You Feel It? DJs and House Music Culture in the UK. *Popular Music* 11(2): 229–38.

2650 Lauren, Jena. 1979. *Disco*. Los Angeles: Price, Stern & Sloan.

2651 Lovisone, Carter. 1979. *The Disco Hustle*. New York: Sterling Publications.

2652 Mooney, H.F. 1980. Disco: A Style for the 1980s? *Popular Music & Society* 7: 84–94.

2653 Radcliffe, Joe. 1980. *This Business of Disco*. New York: Watson-Guptill.

2654 Rose, Cynthia. 1991. *Design After Dark: The Story of Dancefloor Style*. London: Thames & Hudson.

2655 Straw, Will. 1995. The Booth, the Floor and the Wall: Dance Music and the Fear of Falling. In *Popular Music: Style and Identity*, ed. Will Straw, et al. Montréal: The Centre for Research on Canadian Cultural Industries and Institutions. 249–54.

Electronic Rock

2656 Bergman, Billy and Horn, Richard. 1985. *Experimental Pop: Frontiers of the Rock Era*. Poole: Blandford Press.

2657 Bussy, Pascal. 1993. *Kraftwerk: Man, Machine and Music*. London: SAF.

2658 Dockstader, Toll. 1968. Inside-Out: Electronic Rock. *Electronic Music Review* 5: 15–20.

2659 Holmes, Thomas B. 1985. *Electronic and Experimental Music: History, Instruments, Technique, Performers, Recordings*. New York: Charles Scribner's Sons.

2660 Mooney, H.F. 1980. Twilight of the Age of Aquarius? Popular Music in the 1970s. *Popular Music & Society* 7: 182–98.

2661 Moore, Allan F. 1993. *Rock: The Primary Text*. Buckingham: Open University Press.

2662 Schaefer, John. 1990. *New Sounds: The Virgin Guide to New Music*. London: Virgin.

2663 Thompson, Dave. 1994. *Space Daze: The History and Mystery of Electronic Ambient Space Rock*. Los Angeles: Cleopatra.

Folk Rock

2664 Arana, Federico. 1988. *Roqueros y Folcloroides*. México: Editorial Joaquín Mortiz.

2665 Atkinson, Bob. 1974. *Songs of the Open Road: The Poetry of Folk Rock and the Journey of the Hero*. New York: Signet/New American Library.

2666 Barsamian, Jacques and Jouffa, François. 1985. *L'Age d'or du rock & folk. La pop music américaine des sixties*. Paris: Ramsay.

2667 Denisoff, R. Serge. 1981. Folk-Rock: Folk Music, Protest or Commercialism? *Journal of Popular Culture* 3(2): 214–30.

2668 Dunson, Josh. 1967. (1966) Folk Rock: Thunder Without Rain. In *The American Folk Scene: Dimensions of the Folk Song Revival*, ed. David De Turk and A. Poulin. New York: Dell Publishing. 289–97.

2669 Laing, Dave, et al. 1975. *The Electric Muse*. London: Eyre Methuen.

2670 Rogan, Johnny. 1990. (1981) *Timeless Flight: The Definitive Biography of The Byrds*, revised edition. London: Square One. First published London: Scorpion/Dark Star, 1981.

2671 Vassal, Jacques. 1976. *Electric Children: Roots and Branches of Modern Folkrock*. New York: Taplinger. Trans. of *Folksong: une histoire de la musique populaire*.

Glam Rock

2672 Baker, Roger. 1994. *Drag: A History of Female Impersonation in the Performing Arts*. London: Cassell.

2673 Chambers, Iain. 1985. *Urban Rhythms: Pop Music and Popular Culture*. London: Macmillan.

2674 Charlton, Katherine. 1990. *Rock Music Styles: A History*. Dubuque, IA: Wm. C. Brown.

2675 Laing, Dave. 1985. *One Chord Wonders: Power and Meaning in Punk Rock*. Milton Keynes: Open University Press.

2676 Moore, Allan F. 1993. *Rock: The Primary Text*. Buckingham: Open University Press.

2677 Palmer, Tony. 1977. *All You Need Is Love: The Story of Popular Music*. London: Futura.

2678 Thomson, Elizabeth and Gutman, David, eds. 1993. *The Bowie Companion*. London: Macmillan.

2679 Tucker, Ken. 1987. Wham, Glam, Thank You Ma'am. In *Rock of Ages: The*

Rolling Stone History of Rock and Roll, ed. Geoffrey Stokes, Ken Tucker and Ed Ward. New York: Penguin. 487–96.

God Rock

2680 Turner, Steve. 1995. *Hungry for Heaven: Rock and Roll and the Search for Redemption*. London: Hodder and Stoughton.

Heavy Metal

2681 Bashe, Philip. 1985. *Heavy Metal Thunder: The Music, Its History, Its Heroes*. Garden City, NY: Doubleday.

2682 Binas, Susanne. 1992. 'Keep It Heavy, Keep It Hard': Zu einigen Aspekten soziokorporeller Kommunikationsmuster im Prozeß der Geschlechtersozialisation – Heavy-Metal in der 'ehemaligen' DDR. *PopScriptum* I(1): 96–111.

2683 Blanchet, Philippe. 1985. *Heavy Metal Story: la bible du hard rock*. Paris: Calmann-Lévy.

2684 Breen, Marcus. 1991. A Stairway to Heaven or a Highway to Hell? Heavy Metal Rock Music in the 1990s. *Cultural Studies* 5(2): 191–203.

2685 Craig, Steve, ed. 1992. *Men, Masculinity and the Media*. Newbury Park, CA: Sage.

2686 Gaines, Donna. 1991. *Teenage Wasteland: Suburbia's Dead End Kids*. New York: Pantheon.

2687 Gaitandjiev, Gencho. 1988. Za 'hubavoto' i 'loshoto' na muzikata v stil hevi metal. *Smjana* 3: 14–18.

2688 Gross, Robert L. 1990. Heavy Metal Music: A New Subculture in American Society. *Journal of Popular Culture* 24(1): 119–30.

2689 Hale, Mark. 1993. *Headbangers: The Worldwide Megabook of Heavy Metal Bands*. Ann Arbor, MI: Popular Culture, Ink.

2690 Harrell, Jack. 1994. The Poetics of Destruction: Death Metal Rock. *Popular Music & Society* 18(1) (Spring): 91–104.

2691 Harrigan, Brian and Dome, Malcolm. 1981. *Encyclopedia Metallica: The Bible of Heavy Metal.* London: Bobcat.

2692 Herr, Matthias. 1993. *Heavy Metal Lexikon.* Berlin and Hamburg: Herr.

2693 Jasper, Tony and Oliver, Derek. 1991. *The International Encyclopedia of Hard Rock and Heavy Metal.* London: Sidgwick & Jackson.

2694 Obrecht, Jas, ed. 1984. *Masters of Heavy Metal.* New York: Quill.

2695 Picart, Hervé, et al. 1985. *Hard and Heavy: les dieux du rock lourd.* Paris: Grancher.

2696 Straw, Will. 1985. Heavy Metal. *Impulse* (Summer): 38–40.

2697 Straw, Will. 1990. (1984/85) Characterizing Rock Music Culture: The Case of Heavy Metal. In *On Record: Rock, Pop and the Written Word,* ed. Simon Frith and Andrew Goodwin. London: Routledge. 97–110. (First published in *Canadian University Music Review* (1984/85): 104–22.)

2698 Wall Hinds, Mary Jane. 1992. The Devil Sings the Blues: Heavy Metal, Gothic Fiction and 'Postmodern' Discourse. *Journal of Popular Culture* 26(3): 151–64.

2699 Walser, Robert. 1993. Professing Censorship: Academic Attacks on Heavy Metal. *Journal of Popular Music Studies* 5: 68–79.

2700 Walser, Robert. 1993. *Running with the Devil: Power, Gender and Madness in Heavy Metal Music.* Hanover and London: University Press of New England.

2701 Weinstein, Deena. 1991. *Heavy Metal: A Cultural Sociology.* New York: Lexington Books.

New Age

2702 Birosik, Patti Jean. 1989. *The New Age Music Guide: Profiles and Recordings of 500 Top New Age Musicians.* New York: Collier.

2703 Hall, Dennis. 1994. New Age Music: A Voice of Liminality in Postmodern Popular Culture. *Popular Music & Society* 18(2): 13–22.

2704 Lanza, Joseph. 1995. *Elevator Music.* New York: St. Martin's Press.

2705 Schaefer, John. 1990. *New Sounds: The Virgin Guide to New Music.* London: Virgin.

2706 Stroh, Wolfgang Martin. 1994. *Handbuch der New Age Musik.* Regensburg: ConBrio.

2707 Toop, David. 1995. *Ocean of Sound.* London: Serpent's Tail.

Progressive Rock

2708 Aprile, Al and Mayer, Luca. 1982. *La musica rock-progressiva Europa.* Milano: Gammalibri.

2709 Bartnik, Norbert and Bordon, Frieda. 1981. *Keep on Rockin'. Rockmusik zwischen Protest und Profit.* Weinheim and Basel: Beltz.

2710 Chester, Andrew. 1970. Second Thoughts on a Rock Aesthetic: The Band. *New Left Review* 62: 75–82.

2711 Cutler, Chris. 1984. Technology, Politics and Contemporary Music: Necessity and Choice in Musical Forms. *Popular Music* 4: 279–300.

2712 Durant, Alan. 1984. *Conditions of Music.* London: Macmillan.

2713 Floh de Cologne, ed. 1980. *Rock gegen Rechts. Beiträge zu einer Bewegung.* Dortmund: Weltkreis.

2714 Leukert, Bernd, ed. 1980. *Thema: Rock gegen Rechts. Musik als politisches Instrument.* Frankfurt am Main: Fischer.

2715 Macan, Edward. 1996. *Rocking the Classics: English Progressive Rock and the Counterculture.* New York: Oxford University Press.

2716 Pethel, Blair Woodruff. 1988. *Keith Emerson: The Emergence and Growth of Style. A Study of Selected Works.* Ann Arbor, MI: University Microfilms International.

2717 Tamm, Eric. 1989. *Brian Eno: His Music and the Vertical Color of Sound.* Boston and London: Faber & Faber.

2718 Whiteley, Sheila. 1990. Progressive Rock and Psychedelic Coding in the Work of Jimi Hendrix. *Popular Music* 9(1): 37–60.

2719 Whiteley, Sheila. 1992. *The Space Between the Notes: Rock and the Counter-Culture.* London: Routledge.

2720 Wicke, Peter. 1981. Rock in Opposition. *Musik und Gesellschaft* XXXI(7): 410–17.

Psychedelic Rock

2721 Baumeister, Roy. 1984. Acid Rock: A Critical Reappraisal and Psychological Commentary. *Journal of Psychoactive Drugs* 16(4): 339–45.

2722 Colonna, David. 1975. *The San Francisco Sound: A Discography of LP's.* Burbank, CA: Songs & Records International.

2723 Everett, Walter. 1986. Fantastic Remembrance in John Lennon's 'Strawberry Fields Forever' and 'Julia'. *Musical Quarterly* 72(3): 360–91.

2724 Gassen, Timothy. 1991. *Echoes in Time: The Garage and Psychedelic Music Explosion, 1980–1990.* Telford: Borderline.

2725 Joynson, Vernon. 1984. *The Acid Trip: A Complete Guide to Psychedelic Music.* Todmorden: Babylon.

2726 Joynson, Vernon. 1988. *After the Acid Trip: The Flashback. The Ultimate Psychedelic Music Guide.* Telford: Borderline.

2727 Joynson, Vernon. 1994. *Fuzz, Acid and Flowers: A Comprehensive Guide to American Garage, Psychedelic and Hippie Rock (1964–1975).* Telford: Borderline.

2728 Kozak, Roman. 1983. Psychedelic Rock on Comeback Trail. *Billboard* 95: 1, 53.

2729 Sculatti, Gene and Seay, Davin. 1985. *San Francisco Nights: The Psychedelic Music Trip, 1965–1968.* New York: St. Martin's Press.

2730 Stokes, Geoffrey. 1987. Troubles in Pepperland. In *Rock of Ages: The Rolling Stone History of Rock and Roll,* ed. Geoffrey Stokes, Ken Tucker and Ed Ward. New York: Penguin. 403–19.

2731 Walters, David. 1989. *The Children of Nuggets: The Definitive Guide to 'Psychedelic Sixties' Punk Rock on Compilation Albums.* Ann Arbor, MI: Popular Culture, Ink.

2732 Whiteley, Sheila. 1992. *The Space Between the Notes: Rock and the Counter-Culture.* London: Routledge.

Pub Rock

2733 Laing, Dave. 1985. *One Chord Wonders: Power and Meaning in Punk Rock.* Milton Keynes: Open University Press.

2734 Morris, Gina. 1985. *Happy Doin' What We're Doin': The Pub Rock Years, 1972–1975.* San Francisco: Nightbird Press.

2735 Morris, Gina. 1986. *Off-Beat: Pub Rock for the '80s*. San Francisco: Nightbird Press.

Punk and New Wave

2736 Anscombe, Isabelle. 1978. *Not Another Punk Book*. London: Aurum.

2737 Baker, Glenn A. and Coupe, Stuart. 1980. *The New Music*. London: Bay Books.

2738 Bangs, Lester. 1991. *Psychotic Reactions and Carburetor Dung: Literature as Rock 'n' Roll, Rock 'n' Roll as Literature*, ed. Greil Marcus. London: Mandarin.

2739 Barszcz, J. 1982. It's the Same Old Song: Punk, New Wave and the Marketing of Rock. In *American Mass Media*, ed. R. Atwan, B. Orton and W. Vesterman, revised edition. New York: Random House. 282–88.

2740 Belsito, Peter and Davis, Bob. 1983. *Hardcore California: A History of Punk and New Wave*. Berkeley, CA: Last Gasp.

2741 Bianco, David. 1985. *Who's New Wave in Music: An Illustrated Encyclopedia, 1976–1982 (The First Wave)*. Ann Arbor, MI: Pierian Press.

2742 Birch, Ian. 1980. Punk. In *The Rock Primer*, ed. John Collis. Harmondsworth: Penguin. 274–80.

2743 Blair, Dike and Anscomb, Elizabeth. 1978. *Punk: Punk Rock, Style, Stance, People, Stars*. New York: Urizen.

2744 Boston, Virginia. 1978. *Punk Rock*. New York: Penguin.

2745 Burchill, Julie and Parsons, Tony. 1978. *'The Boy Looked at Johnny': The Obituary of Rock and Roll*. London: Pluto Press.

2746 Canova, Gianni and Malagini, Fabio. 1984. *Australia New Wave*. Milano: Gammalibri.

2747 Carter, Angela. 1977. Year of the Punk. *New Society* 14: 834–39.

2748 Cashmore, E. Ellis. 1987. Shades of Black, Shades of White. In *Popular Music & Communication*, ed. James Lull. Newbury Park, CA: Sage. 245–65.

2749 Chantry, Art, ed. 1985. *Instant Litter: Concert Posters from Seattle Punk Culture*. Seattle, WA: Real Comet.

2750 Coon, Caroline. 1977. *1988: The New Wave Punk Rock Explosion*. London: Orbach & Chambers.

2751 Costa, Salvador. 1977. *Punk*. Barcelona: Producciones Editoriales.

2752 Curtis, Deborah. 1995. *Touching from a Distance*. London: Faber.

2753 Davis, Julie. 1977. *Punk*. Ridgewood, NY: Davidson Publishing.

2754 Dewes, Klaus. 1986. *Punk*. München: Heyne.

2755 Döpfner, M.O. and Garms, Thomas. 1984. *Neue deutsche Welle: Kunst oder Mode? Eine sachliche Polemik für und wider die neudeutsche Popmusik*. Frankfurt am Main: Ullstein.

2756 Fitzgerald, f-stop. 1982. *Weird Angle*. San Francisco: Last Gasp.

2757 Frith, Simon and Horne, Howard. 1987. *Art into Pop*. London: Methuen.

2758 George, B. and DeFoe, Martha. 1980. *Volume: International Discography of the New Wave*. New York: One Ten Records.

2759 George, B. and DeFoe, Martha. 1982. *International New Wave Discography: Volume 1982/1983*. London: Omnibus.

2760 Hahn, Bernd and Schindler, Holger, eds. 1983. *Punk. Die zarteste Versuchung seit es Schokolade gibt*. Hamburg: Buntbuch.

2761 Hebdige, Dick. 1988. (1979) *Subculture: The Meaning of Style*. London: Routledge.

2762 Henry, Tricia. 1989. *Break All the Rules: Punk Rock and the Making of a Style*. Ann Arbor, MI: UMI Research Press.

2763 Heylin, Clinton. 1993. *From the Velvets to the Voidoids: A Pre-Punk History for a Post-Punk World*. Harmondsworth: Penguin.

2764 Home, Stewart. 1995. *Cranked Up Really High*. Hove: Codex.

2765 Järisch, Burkhard. 1990. *Flex! U.S. Hardcore Discography*. 4 vols. Böhlingen: Järisch.

2766 Johnson, Garry. 1981. *The Story of Oi*. Manchester: Babylon Books.

2767 Kennedy, David. 1990. Frankenchrist Versus the State: The New Right, Rock Music and the Case of Jello Biafra. *Journal of Popular Culture* 24(1): 131–48.

2768 Kent, Nick. 1994. *The Dark Stuff: Selected Writings on Rock Music, 1972–1993*. Harmondsworth: Penguin.

2769 Laing, Dave. 1985. *One Chord Wonders: Power and Meaning in Punk Rock*. Milton Keynes: Open University Press.

2770 Laing, Dave. 1989. *The Grain of Punk: An Analysis of the Lyrics*, ed. Angela McRobbie, London: Macmillan.

2771 Lau, Thomas. 1992. *Die heiligen Narren: Punk, 1976–1986*. Berlin and New York: De Gruyter.

2772 Lewis, Jon. 1988. Punks in LA: It's Kiss or Kill. *Journal of Popular Culture* 22(2): 87–97.

2773 Lindner, Rolf, ed. 1977. *Punk Rock oder der vermarktete Aufruhr*. Frankfurt am Main: Freie Gesellschaft.

2774 Lydon, John, Keith Zimmerman and Kent Zimmerman. 1994. *Rotten: No Irish, No Blacks, No Dogs*. London: Hodder and Stoughton.

2775 Maleckar, Nez and Mastnak, Tomaz. 1985. *Punk pod Slovenci*. Ljubljana: KRT.

2776 Manley, Frank. 1993. *Smash the State: A Discography of Canadian Punk, 1977–92*. Westmount, Québec: Manley.

2777 Marcus, Greil. 1989. *Lipstick Traces: A Secret History of the Twentieth Century*. London: Secker & Warburg.

2778 Marcus, Greil. 1993. *In the Fascist Bathroom: Writings on Punk, 1977–1992*. London and New York: Viking.

2779 Murray, Charles S. 1991. *Shots from the Hip*, ed. Neil Spencer. Harmondsworth: Penguin.

2780 O'Hara, Craig. 1995. *The Philosophy of Punk: More than Noises*. Edinburgh and San Francisco: AK Press.

2781 Ott, Paul and Hollow, Skai, eds. 1983. *Wir waren Helden für einen Tag: Aus deutschsprachigen Punk-Fanzines*. Reinbek bei Hamburg: Rowohlt.

2782 Palmer, Myles. 1982. *New Wave Explosion: How Punk Became New Wave Became the 80's*. London: Proteus.

2783 Parsons, Tony. 1994. *Dispatches from the Front Line of Popular Culture*. London: Virago.

2784 Penth, Boris and Franzen, Günter. 1982. *Last Exit, Punk: Leben im toten Herz der Städte*. Reinbek bei Hamburg: Rowohlt.

2785 P(erry), Mark. 1978. *The Bible*. [Contains the first 10 'Sniffin' Glue'.] London: Michael Dempsey for Big O Publishing.

2786 Pryor, Laurie and Brennan, Mark. 1994. *The A-Z of Punk*. Rowlands Castle: Castle Communications.

2787 Savage, Jon. 1989. *England's Dreaming: The Sex Pistols and Punk Rock*. London: Faber & Faber.

2788 Savage, Jon. 1996. *Time Travel: From the Sex Pistols to Nirvana. Pop, Media and Sexuality, 1977–96*. London: Chatto & Windus.

2789 Schwarz, David. 1996. Oi Musik, Politik und Gewalt. *PopScriptum* 5: 14–43.

2790 Skai, Hollow. 1981. *Punk*. Hamburg: Sounds.

2791 Stark, Jürgen and Kurzawa, Michael. 1981. *Der große Schwindel? Punk – New Wave – Neue Welle*. Frankfurt am Main: Verlag Freie Gesellschaft.

Queer Song

2792 Baker, Roger. 1994. *Drag: A History of Female Impersonation in the Performing Arts*. London: Cassell.

2793 Gill, John. 1995. *Queer Noises*. London: Cassell.

2794 Hughes, Walter. 1994. In the Empire of the Beat: Discipline and Disco. In *Microphone Fiends: Youth Music and Youth Culture*, ed. Andrew Ross and Tricia Rose. London: Routledge.

2795 Savage, Jon. 1996. *Time Travel: From the Sex Pistols to Nirvana. Pop, Media and Sexuality, 1977–96*. London: Chatto & Windus.

2796 Simpson, Mark. 1994. *Male Impersonators*. London: Cassell.

2797 Smith, Richard. 1995. *Other Voices: Gay Men and Popular Music*. London: Cassell.

2798 Studer, Wayne. 1994. *Rock on the Wild Side: Gay Male Images in Popular Music of the Rock Era*. San Francisco: Leyland Publications.

Rockabilly

2799 Cooper, B. Lee and Haney, Wayne S. 1990. *Rockabilly: A Bibliographic Resource Guide*. Metuchen, NJ: Scarecrow Press.

2800 Escott, Colin and Hawkins, Martin. 1991. *Good Rockin' Tonight: Sun Records and the Birth of Rock and Roll*. New York: St. Martin's Press.

2801 Garbutt, Bob. 1979. *Rockabilly Queens: The Careers and Recordings of Wanda Jackson, Janis Martin and Brenda Lee*. Toronto: Ducktail Press.

2802 Guralnick, Peter. 1981. Rockabilly. In *The Rolling Stone Illustrated History of Rock and Roll*. London: Picador. 61–65.

2803 Hager, Andrew. 1995. *Southern Fried Rock*. New York: Friedman/Fairfax Publishers.

2804 Jandrow, Richard E. 1995. *What It Was Was Rockabilly: A History and Discography, 1927–1994*. Worcester, MA: Boxcar Publishers.

2805 McNutt, Randy. 1987. *Illustrated History of the American Rockabilly Movement*. Fairfield, OH: Hamilton Hobby Press.

2806 McNutt, Randy. 1988. *We Wanna Boogie: An Illustrated History of the American Rockabilly Movement*. Hamilton, OH: HHP Books.

2807 Morrison, Craig. 1996. *Go Cat Go!: Rockabilly Music and Its Makers*. Urbana, IL: University of Illinois Press.

2808 Perkins, Carl and McGee, David. 1996. *Go, Cat, Go! The Life and Times of Carl Perkins, the King of Rockabilly*. New York: Hyperion.

2809 Rose, Michel. 1986. *Encyclopédie de la country et du rockabilly*. Paris: Grancher.

2810 Tosches, Nick. 1991. (1984) *Unsung Heroes of Rock 'n' Roll: The Birth of Rock in the Wild Years Before Elvis*, revised edition. New York: Harmony Press. First published New York: Charles Scribner's Sons, 1984.

Rock 'n' Roll

2811 Belz, Carl. 1972. (1969) *The Story of Rock*, 2nd edition. New York: Oxford University Press.

2812 Betrock, Alan. 1986. *The I Was a Teenage Juvenile Delinquent Rock 'n' Roll Beach Party Movie Book: A Complete Guide to the Teen Exploitation Film, 1954–1969.* New York: St. Martin's Press.

2813 Bradley, Dick. 1992. *Understanding Rock 'n' Roll: Popular Music in Britain, 1955–1964.* Buckingham: Open University Press.

2814 Brown, Charles T. 1992. (1983) *The Art of Rock and Roll.* Englewood Cliffs, NJ: Prentice-Hall.

2815 Byrnside, Ronald. 1975. The Formation of a Musical Style: Early Rock. In *Contemporary Music and Music Cultures*, ed. Charles Hamm, Bruno Nettl and Ronald Byrnside. Englewood Cliffs, NJ: Prentice-Hall. 159–92.

2816 Chambers, Iain. 1985. *Urban Rhythms: Popular Music and Popular Culture.* New York: Macmillan.

2817 Christgau, Robert. 1973. *Any Old Way You Choose It: Rock and Other Pop Music, 1967–1973.* Baltimore, MD: Penguin.

2818 Dawson, Jim and Steve, Propes. 1992. *What Was the First Rock 'n' Roll Record?* Boston, MA: Faber & Faber.

2819 DeCurtis, Anthony and Henke, James, eds. 1993. *The Rolling Stone Illustrated History of Rock & Roll: The Definitive History of the Most Important Artists and Their Music.* London: Plexus Publishing.

2820 Eisen, Jonathan, ed. 1969/70. *The Age of Rock.* 2 vols. New York: Vintage Books.

2821 Ennis, Philip H. 1992. *The Seventh Stream: The Emergence of Rock 'n' Roll in American Popular Music.* Hanover, NH: Wesleyan University Press.

2822 Escott, Colin and Hawkins, Martin. 1992. *Good Rockin' Tonight: Sun Records and the Birth of Rock 'n' Roll.* New York: St. Martin's Press.

2823 Ferlinger, Robert D. 1976. *A Discography of Rhythm & Blues and Rock & Roll Vocal Groups, 1945–1965.* Pittsburgh, CA: Robert D. Ferlinger.

2824 Fong-Torres, Ben, ed. 1974. *The Rolling Stone Rock 'n' Roll Reader.* Toronto: Bantam.

2825 Friedlander, Paul. 1996. *Rock and Roll: A Social History.* Boulder, CO: Westview Press.

2826 Frith, Simon. 1983. *Sound Effects: Youth, Leisure and the Politics of Rock 'n' Roll.* London: Constable.

2827 Gaar, Gillian G. 1992. *She's a Rebel: The History of Women in Rock & Roll.* Seattle, WA: Seal Press.

2828 Garofalo, Reebee. 1996. *Rockin' Out: Popular Music in the USA.* Needham Heights, MA: Allyn and Bacon.

2829 Gillett, Charlie. 1983. (1970) *The Sound of the City: The Rise of Rock and Roll.* New York: Pantheon. First published New York: Outerbridge and Dienstfrey, 1970.

2830 Guralnick, Peter. 1971. *Feel Like Going Home: Portraits in Blues and Rock 'n' Roll.* New York: E.P. Dutton.

2831 Jackson, John. 1991. *Big Beat Heat: Alan Freed and the Early Years of Rock & Roll.* New York: Schirmer Books.

2832 Lydon, Michael. 1968. *Rock Folk: Portraits from the Rock 'n' Roll Pantheon.* New York: Dell Publishing.

2833 Marcus, Greil. 1991. *Mystery Train: Images of America in Rock 'n' Roll Music.* Harmondsworth: Penguin.

2834 Miller, Jim, ed. 1976. *The Rolling Stone Illustrated History of Rock 'n' Roll.* New York: Rolling Stone Press.

2835 Passman, Arnold. 1971. *The Deejays.* New York: Macmillan.

2836 Peterson, Richard A. 1990. Why 1955? Explaining the Advent of Rock Music. *Popular Music* 9(1): 97–116.

2837 Röglin, Claus-D. 1993. *Record Hops – Ducktails and Petticoats: Eine kurze Geschichte des Rock & Roll und seiner grossen Hits.* Oldenburg: Covent-Verlag.

2838 Seay, Davin and Neely, Mary. 1986. *Stairway to Heaven: The Spiritual Roots of Rock 'n' Roll; From the King and Little Richard to Prince and Amy Grant.* New York: Ballantine/Epiphany Press.

2839 Shaw, Arnold. 1978. *Honkers and Shouters: The Golden Years of Rhythm and Blues.* New York: Collier Books.

2840 Shaw, Arnold. 1987. (1974) *The Rockin' '50s: The Decade That Transformed the Pop Music Scene.* New York: Da Capo Press. First published New York: Hawthorne Books, 1974.

2841 Tosches, Nick. 1984. *Unsung Heroes of Rock 'n' Roll.* New York: Charles Scribner's Sons.

2842 Ward, Ed, Geoffrey Stokes and Ken Tucker. 1986. *Rock of Ages (Rolling Stone History of Rock 'n' Roll).* New York: Rolling Stone Press.

2843 Whitcomb, Ian. 1974. *After the Ball: Popular Music from Rag to Rock.* Baltimore, MD: Penguin.

2844 Wicke, Peter. 1990. *Rock Music: Culture, Aesthetics and Sociology.* Cambridge: Cambridge University Press.

Skiffle

2845 Bird, Brian. 1958. *Skiffle.* London: Robert Hale.

2846 Bradley, Dick. 1992. *Understanding Rock 'n' Roll: Popular Music in Britain, 1955–1964.* Milton Keynes: Open University Press.

Surf and Hot Rod Music

2847 Blair, John and McFarland, Stephen J. 1990. *The Illustrated Discography of Hot Rod Music, 1961–1965.* Ann Arbor, MI: Popular Culture, Ink.

2848 Burt, Rob. 1986. *Surf City/Drag City.* Poole: Blandford Press.

2849 Dalley, Robert J. 1988. *Surfin' Guitars: Instrumental Surf Bands of the Sixties.* Surf Publications.

Techno

2850 Berger, Christiane. 1994. *Techno.* Wien: Paul Zsolnay.

2851 Blask, Falko and Fuchs-Gamböck, Michael. 1995. *Techno. Eine Generation in Ekstase.* Bergisch Gladbach: Bastei-Lübbe.

2852 Die Gestalten/Chromapark, ed. 1995. *Localizer 1.0: The Techno House Book.* Berlin: Die-Gestalten-Verlag.

2853 Henkel, Oliva and Wolff, Karsten. 1996. *Berlin Underground. Techno und HipHop zwischen Mythos und Ausverkauf.* Berlin: FAB.

2854 Maaz, Markus. 1994. Sich einfach nur drehen und an nichts denken: Techno als Flowerfahrung. In *Zwischen Rausch und Ritual,* ed. Konstanze Kriese, et al. Berlin: Zyankrise. 30–53.

2855 Pesch, Martin and Weisbeck, Markus. 1995. *Techno Style*. Homebrechtikon and Zürich: Edition Olms.

Urban Folk Revival

2856 Baggelaar, Kristin and Milton, Donald. 1977. (1976) *The Folk Music Encyclopedia*. London: Omnibus. First published New York: Thomas Y. Cromwell, 1976.

2857 Bluestein, Gene. 1994. *Poplore: Folk and Pop in American Culture*. Amherst, MA: University of Massachusetts Press.

2858 Brand, Oscar. 1963. (1962) *The Ballad Mongers: Rise of the Modern Folk Song*. New York: Ungar.

2859 Denisoff, R. Serge. 1971. *A Great Day Coming: Folk Music and the American Left*. Urbana, IL: University of Illinois Press.

2860 Denselow, Robin, et al. 1978. *Folksong*. Reinbek bei Hamburg: Rowohlt.

2861 De Turk, David and Poulin, A., eds. 1967. *The American Folk Scene: Dimensions of the Folk Song Revival*. New York: Dell Publishing.

2862 Gammon, Vic. 1983. Seeger and MacColl Revisited. *English Folk Dance and Song* 45(3): 23ff.

2863 Lawless, Ray McKinley. 1965. (1960) *Folksingers and Folksongs in America: A Handbook of Biography*. Westport, CT: Greenwood Press. First published New York: Duell, Sloan & Pearce, 1960.

2864 Leydi, Roberto. 1972. *Il folk music revival*. Palermo: Flaccovio.

2865 Ling, Jan. 1986. Folk Music Revival in Sweden: The Lilla Edet Fiddle Club. *Yearbook for Traditional Music* 18: 1–8.

2866 MacKinnon, Niall. 1993. *The British Folk Scene: Musical Performance and Social Identity*. Buckingham: Open University Press.

2867 Munro, Ailie. 1984. *The Folk Music Revival in Scotland*. London: Kahn & Averill.

2868 Paulin, Don. 1980. *Das Folk-Music-Lexicon*. Frankfurt am Main: Fischer.

2869 Redhead, Steve and Street, John. 1989. Have I the Right? Legitimacy, Authenticity and Community in Folk's Politics. *Popular Music* 8(2): 177–84.

2870 Sandberg, Larry and Weissman, Dick. 1989. (1976) *The Folk Music Source Book*. New York: Da Capo Press. First published New York: Alfred Knopf, 1976.

2871 Schmidt, Eric von and Rooney, Jim. 1979. *Baby, Let Me Follow You Down: The Illustrated Story of the Cambridge Folk Years*. Garden City, NY: Anchor Books.

2872 Seeger, Pete. 1972. *The Incompleat Folksinger*, ed. Jo Metcalf Schwartz. New York: Simon & Schuster.

2873 Siniveer, Kaarel. 1981. *Folk Lexikon*. Reinbek bei Hamburg: Rowohlt.

2874 Torres, Rodrigo. 1985. La Urbanización de la Canción Folklórica. *Literatura Chilena. Creación y Crítica* 9(33–34): 25–29.

2875 Vassal, Jacques. 1984. (1971) *Folksong: une histoire de la musique populaire aux Etats-Unis*. Paris: Albin Michel.

2876 Watson, Ian. 1983. *Song and Democratic Culture in Britain: An Approach to Popular Culture in Social Movements*. London: Croom Helm.

RUMBA

2877 Acosta, Leonardo. 1991. The Rumba, the Guaguancó and Tio Tem. In *Essays on Cuban Music: North American and Cuban Perspectives*, ed. Peter Manuel. Lanham, MD: University Press of America. 49–74.

2878 Crook, Larry N. 1982. A Musical Analysis of the Cuban Rumba. *Latin American Music Review* 3(1): 93–123.

SALSA

2879 Baron, Robert. 1977. Syncretism and Ideology: Latin New York Salsa Musicians. *Western Folklore* 36: 209–25.

2880 Bergman, Billy, et al. 1985. *Reggae and Latin Pop: Hot Sauces*. Poole: Blandford Press.

2881 Blum, Joseph. 1978. Problems of Salsa Research. *Ethnomusicology* 22(1): 137–49.

2882 Boggs, Vernon, ed. 1992. *Salsiology: Afro-Cuban Music and the Evolution of Salsa in New York*. London: Greenwood Press.

2883 Calvo Ospino, Hernando. 1995. (1992) *¡Salsa! Havana Heat, Bronx Beat*. London: Latin American Bureau.

2884 Duany, Jorge. 1984. Popular Music in Puerto Rico: Toward an Anthropology of Salsa. *Latin American Music Review* 5(2): 186–216.

2885 Figueroa, Rafael. 1993. *Salsa and Related Genres: Bibliographical Guide*. London: Greenwood Press.

2886 Gerard, Charlie and Sheller, Marty. 1988. *Salsa: The Rhythm of Latin Music*. Crown Point, IN: White Cliffs.

2887 Janson-Perez, Brittmarie. 1987. Political Facets of Salsa. *Popular Music* 6(2): 149–60.

2888 Manuel, Peter. 1991. Salsa and the Music Industry: Corporate Control of Grassroots Expression? In *Essays on Cuban Music: North American and Cuban Perspectives*, ed. Peter Manuel. Lanham, MD: University Press of America. 157–80.

2889 Manuel, Peter. 1994. The Soul of the Barrio: 30 Years of Salsa. *NACLA Report on the Americas* 28(2): 22–29.

2890 Padilla, Felix M. 1990. Salsa: Puerto Rican and Latino Music. *Journal of Popular Culture* 24(1): 87–104.

2891 Rondón, César. 1980. *El Libro de la Salsa: Cronica de la Musica del Caribe Urbano*. Caracas: Editorial Arte.

2892 Rondón, César. 1991. *Libro de la salsa: Crónica de la música del Caribe*. Miami, FL: Universal.

2893 Sanabria, Izzy. 1979. Salsa: The Bittersweet Experience. *Latin New York* 2(8): 29–32.

2894 Ulloa Sanmiguel, Alejandro. 1992. *La salsa en Cali*. Cali: Ediciones Universidad del Valle.

SAMBA

2895 Borges, Beatriz. 1982. *Samba-cancao: fratura & paixao; uma analise das letras de Orestes Barbosa, Lupicino Rodrigues, Guilherme de Brito, Nélson Cavaquinho, Cartola, Carlos Cachaca, e um estudio sobré kitsch*. Rio de Janeiro: Editora Codecri.

2896 Browning, Barbara. 1995. *Samba: Resistance in Motion*. Bloomington, IN: Indiana University Press.

2897 Costa, Haraldo. 1984. *Salgueiro: academia de samba*. Rio de Janeiro: Editoria Record.

2898 Crook, Larry N. 1993. Black Consciousness, Samba Reggae and the Re-Africanization of Bahian Carnival Music in Brazil. *The World of Music* 35(2): 70–84.

2899 Garcia, Florencio Oscar. 1992. *Samba – A Bibliography with Introduction: History, People, Lyrics, Recordings*. Albuquerque, NM: FOG Publications.

2900 Guillermoprieto, Alma. 1990. *Samba*. London: Cape.

2901 Menezes Bastos, Rafael José de. 1995. A Origem do Samba como Invenção do Brasil: Sobre o 'Feitio de Oração' de Vadico e Noel Rosa (Por Que as Canções têm Música?). *Cadernos de Estudo – Análise Musical* 8(9): 1–29.

2902 Nascimento, Haydee. 1982. The 'Henrique Preto' Samba. *African Music* 6(2): 120–32.

2903 Raphael, Alison. 1990. From Popular Culture to Microenterprise: The History of Brazilian Samba Schools. *Latin American Music Review* 11(1): 73–83.

2904 Vianna, Hermano. 1995. *O Mistério do Samba*. Rio de Janeiro: Jorge Zahar Editor/Editora da Universidade Federal do Rio.

SCHLAGER

2905 Bardong, Matthias, Herman Demmler and Christian Pfarr. 1992. *Lexikon des deutschen Schlagers*. Ludwigsburg: Edition Louis.

2906 Busse, Burkhard. 1976. *Der deutsche Schlager. Eine Untersuchung zur Produktion, Distribution und Rezeption von Trivialliteratur*. Wiesbaden: Athenaion.

2907 Czerny, Peter and Hofmann, Heinz P. 1968. *Der Schlager: Ein Panorama der leichten Musik*. Berlin: Lied der Zeit.

2908 Haas, Walter. 1957. *Das Schlagerbuch*. München: List.

2909 Helms, Siegmund, ed. 1972. *Schlager in Deutschland*. Wiesbaden: Breitkopf & Härtel.

2910 Kayser, Dietrich. 1976. *Schlager – Das Lied als Ware: Untersuchungen zu einer Kategorie der Illusionsindustrie*. Stuttgart: Metzler.

2911 Kraushaar, Elmar. 1983. *Rote Lippen: Die ganze Welt des deutschen Schlagers*. Reinbek: Rowohlt.

2912 Mezger, Werner. 1975. *Schlager – Versuch einer Gesamtdarstellung unter besonderer Berücksichtigung des Musikmarktes der Bundesrepublik Deutschland*. Tübingen: Tübingen Vereinigung für Volkskunde.

2913 Schmidt-Joos, Siegfried. 1960. *Geschäfte mit Schlagern*. Bremen: Schünemann.

2914 Sönstevold, Gunnar and Blaukopf, Kurt. 1976. Den 'ensamma massans' musik. Bidrag till analysen av schlagermusiken. In *Musik och samhälle*, ed. Olle Berggren. Lund: Cavefors. 91–110.

2915 Sperr, Monika. 1978. *Das große Schlagerbuch. Deutsche Schlager 1800 – heute*. München: Rogner & Bernhard.

2916 Worbs, Hans Christoph. 1963. *Der Schlager. Bestandsaufnahme, Analyse, Dokumentation*. Bremen: Schünemann.

SEGA

2917 Lee, Jacques K. 1990. *Sega: The Mauritian Folk Dance*. London: Nautilus.

SENTIMENTAL BALLAD

2918 Bratton, J.S. 1975. *The Victorian Popular Ballad*. Totowa, NJ: Rowman & Littlefield.

2919 Cipolla, Wilma. 1990. Marketing the American Song in Edwardian London. *American Music* 8(1): 84–94.

2920 Claghorn, Charles. 1937. *The Mocking Bird: The Life and Diary of Its Author, Septimus Winner*. New York: Macmillan.

2921 Forte, Allen. 1995. *The American Popular Ballad of the Golden Era: 1924–1950*. Princeton, NJ: Princeton University Press.

GENRES

2922 Key, Susan. 1995. Sound and Sentimentality: Nostalgia in the Songs of Stephen Foster. *American Music* 13(2): 145–66.

2923 Manheim, James M. 1992. B-Side Sentimentalizer: 'Tennessee Waltz' in the History of Popular Music. *Musical Quarterly* 76(3): 337–54.

2924 Tawa, Nicholas E. 1980. *Sweet Songs for Gentle Americans: The Parlor Song in America, 1790–1860*. Bowling Green, OH: Bowling Green University Popular Press.

SHANTIES

2925 Abrahams, Roger D. 1974. *Deep the Water, Shallow the Shore: Three Essays on Shantying in the West Indies*. Austin and London: University of Texas Press.

2926 Bone, David W. 1932. *Capstan Bars*. New York: Harcourt, Brace.

2927 Carreau, Gerard and Pinchard, Max. 1990. *Les chansons de la mer*. Paris: Éditions Ouvrières.

2928 Colcord, Joanna C. 1938. *Songs of American Sailormen*. London: Putnam.

2929 Doerflinger, William Main. 1951. *Shantymen and Shantyboys*. New York: Macmillan.

2930 Harlow, Frederick Pease. 1962. *Chanteying Aboard American Ships*. Barre, MA: Barre Gazette.

2931 Hugill, Stan. 1961. *Sailortown*. London/New York: Routledge & Kegan Paul/E.P. Dutton & Co.

2932 Hugill, Stan. 1961. *Shanties of the Seven Seas*. London: Routledge & Kegan Paul.

2933 Lloyd, A.L. 1967. *Folk Song in England*. London: Lawrence & Wishart.

2934 Smith, Laura Alexandrine. 1969. (1888) *Music of the Waters*. London: Singing Tree Press, Book Tower. First published London: Kegan Paul, Trench & Co., 1888.

2935 Strobach, Hermann. 1968. *Shanties*. Rostock: Hinstorff.

2936 Terry, Richard R. and Runciman, Sir Walter. 1921. *The Shanty Book, I and II*. London: J. Curwen and Sons.

2937 Wheeler, Mary. 1944. *Steamboatin' Days: Folk Songs of the River Packet Era*. Baton Rouge, LA: Louisiana State University Press.

2938 Williams, Alfred Mason. 1894. American Sea Songs. In *Studies in Folk-Song and Popular Poetry*. Boston, MA: Houghton Mifflin.

SON

2939 Duran, Lucy. 1989. In Pursuit of Son. *Folk Roots* 67: 30–33.

2940 Galan, Natalio. 1983. *Cuba y sus sones*. Valencia: Pre-Textos.

2941 Loza, Steven. 1984. The Origins of the Son. *Aztlán: International Journal of Chicano Studies Research* 15(1): 105–21.

2942 Orozco, Danilo. 1995. *Matamoros y el entorno o lo integrador universal del modo son*. Santiago de Cuba: Editorial Oriente.

2943 Robbins, James. 1990. The Cuban Son as Form, Genre and Symbol. *Latin American Music Review* 11(2): 182–200.

2944 Similä, Jussi. 1983. Suavecito: Verbal Improvisation in Cuban Son Singing. *Suomen antropologi* 4: 244–49.

SOUL

2945 Bowman, Rob. 1995. The Stax Sound: Musicological Analysis. *Popular Music* 14(3): 285–320.

2946 Brackett, David. 1992. James Brown's 'Superbad' and the Double-Voiced Utterance. *Popular Music* 11(3): 309–24.

2947 Cummings, Tony. 1975. *The Sound of Philadelphia*. London: Methuen.

2948 Cummings, Tony, Ian Hoare and Simon Frith, eds. 1975. *The Soul Book*. London: Methuen.

2949 Ertl, Franz. 1992. *Rap – Funk – Soul. Ein Nachschlagewerk*. Köln: Herbst.

2950 Gaar, Gillian G. 1993. *She's a Rebel: The History of Women in Rock and Roll*. London: Blandford Press.

2951 Garland, Phyl, 1969. *The Sound of Soul*. Chicago: Henry Regnery Company.

2952 Garland, Phyl. 1973. Soul Music. In *Reflections on Afro-American Music*. Kent, OH: Kent State University Press. 180–88.

2953 George, Nelson. 1988. *The Death of Rhythm and Blues*. New York: Pantheon.

2954 George, Nelson. 1994. (1992) *Buppies, B-Boys, Baps & Bohos*. New York: HarperPerennial.

2955 Gregory, Hugh. 1991. *Soul Music, A-Z*. London: Blandford Press.

2956 Guralnick, Peter. 1986. *Sweet Soul Music: Rhythm and Blues and the Southern Dream of Freedom*. New York: Harper & Row.

2957 Haralambos, Michael. 1970. Soul Music and Blues: Their Meaning and Relevance in Northern United States Ghettos. In *Afro-American Anthropology: Contemporary Perspectives*, ed. Norman E. Whitten and John F. Szwed. New York: Free Press. 367–84.

2958 Haralambos, Michael. 1979. (1974) *Right On: From Blues to Soul in Black America*. New York: Da Capo Press. First published London: Eddison Press, 1974.

2959 Hildebrand, Lee. 1994. *Stars of Soul and Rhythm & Blues: Top Recording Artists and Showstopping Performers, from Memphis and Motown to Now*. New York: Billboard Books.

2960 Hirshey, Gerri. 1984. *Nowhere to Run: The Story of Soul Music*. New York: Times Books.

2961 Hoare, Ian, ed. 1976. *The Soul Book*. London: Methuen.

2962 Hoskyns, Barney. 1987. *Say It One Time for the Broken-Hearted: The Country Side of Southern Soul*. Glasgow: Fontana/ Collins.

2963 Larkin, Rochelle. 1970. *Soul Music*. New York: Lancer Books.

2964 Larkin, Rochelle. 1972. The Soul Message. In *The Sounds of Social Change: Studies in Popular Culture*, ed. R. Serge Denisoff and Richard A. Peterson. Chicago: Rand McNally & Co. 92–104.

2965 Maultsby, Portia K. 1983. Soul Music: Its Sociological and Political Significance in American Popular Culture. *Journal of Popular Culture* 17(2): 51–60.

2966 Picardie, Justine and Wade, Dorothy. 1993. *Atlantic and the Godfathers of Rock and Roll*. London: Fourth Estate.

2967 Pruter, Robert. 1991. *Chicago Soul*. Urbana, IL: University of Illinois Press.

2968 Pruter, Robert, ed. 1993. *The Blackwell Guide to Soul Recordings*. Oxford: Blackwell Publishers.

2969 Riedel, Johannes. 1975. *Soul Music, Black and White: The Influence of Black Music on the Churches*. Minneapolis, MN: Augsburg.

2970 Shaw, Arnold. 1970. *The World of Soul: Black America's Contribution to the Pop Music Scene*. New York: Cowles Book Co.

2971 Stambler, Irwin. 1989. (1974) *The Encyclopedia of Pop, Rock and Soul*, revised edition. New York: St. Martin's Press.

2972 Stephens, Robert W. 1984. Soul: A Historical Reconstruction of Continuity and Change in Black Popular Music. *The Black Perspective in Music*: 21–44.

2973 Warner, Jay. 1992. *The Billboard Book of American Singing Groups: A History, 1940–1990*. New York: Billboard Books.

SUNG SERMONS

2974 Davis, Gerald L. 1985. *I Got the Word in Me and I Can Sing It, You Know: A Study of the Performed African-American Sermon*. Philadelphia: University of Pennsylvania Press.

2975 Hatch, Gary Layne. 1996. Logic in the Black Folk Sermon: The Sermons of Rev. C.L. Franklin. *Journal of Black Studies* 26(3): 227–44.

2976 McCarthy, S. Margaret W. 1976. The Afro-American Sermon and the Blues: Some Parallels. *The Black Perspective in Music* 4(3): 269–77.

2977 Rosenberg, Bruce A. 1970. *The Art of the American Folk Preacher*. New York: Oxford University Press.

2978 Titon, Jeff Todd, ed. 1989. *C.L. Franklin, Give Me This Mountain: Life History and Selected Sermons*. Urbana, IL: University of Illinois Press.

TANGO

2979 Adolfo Sierra, Luis. 1985. (1966) *Historia de la orquesta típica: evolución instrumental del tango*, revised edition. Buenos Aires: Corregidor. First published Buenos Aires: Orestes S.E.C., 1966.

2980 Åhlén, Carl-Gunnar and Hedström, L. 1984. *Det mesta om tango*. Stockholm: Svenska Dagbladets Förlag.

2981 Åhlén, Carl-Gunnar and Hedström, L. 1987. *Tangon i Europa – en pyrrusseger? Studier kring mottagandet av tangon i Europa och genrens musikaliska omställningsprocess*. Stockholm: Proprius.

2982 Andreu, Jean, et al. 1985. *Le Tango. Hommage à Carlos Gardel*. Toulouse: Université de Toulouse.

2983 Assunçao, Fernando O. 1984. *El tango y sus circunstancias (1880–1920)*. Buenos Aires: Livreria 'El Ateneo' Editorial.

2984 Benavides, Washington. 1965. *Las milongas*. Montevideo: Ediciones de la Banda Oriental.

2985 Cadicamo, Enrique D. 1983. *Bajo el signo de tango*. Buenos Aires: Corregidor.

2986 Canton, Darío. 1968. El mundo de los tangos de Gardel. *Revista Latinoamericana de Sociología* 4: 183–97.

2987 Castro, Donald S. 1984. Popular Culture as a Source for the Historian: The Tango in Its Era of la Guardia Vieja. *Studies in Latin America Popular Culture* 3: 70–85.

2988 Castro, Donald S. 1986. Popular Culture as a Source for Historians: The Tango in Its Epoca de Oro, 1917–1943. *Journal of Popular Culture* 20(3): 45–71.

2989 Chinaro, Andrés. 1965. *El tango y su rebeldía*. Buenos Aires: Continental Service.

2990 Collier, Simon. 1992. The Popular Roots of the Argentinian Tango. *History Workshop* 34: 92–100.

2991 Feldmann-Bürgers, Johannes. 1996. *Tango und Jazz. Kulturelle Wechselbeziehungen?* Münster: Lit Verlag.

2992 Ferrer, Horacio. 1977. *El libro del tango: Crónica y diccionario 1850–1977*. Buenos Aires: Editorial Galerna.

2993 Goyena, Héctor Luis. 1994. El tango en la escena dramática de Buenos Aires durante la décade del veinte. *Latin American Music Review* 15(1): 93–109.

2994 Gronow, Pekka. 1987. The Last Refuge of the Tango. *Finnish Music Quarterly* 3–4: 26–31.

2995 Jakubs, Deborah L. 1983. From Bawdyhouse to Cabaret: The Evolution of the Tango as an Expression of Argentine Popular Culture. *Journal of Popular Culture* 18(1): 133–45.

2996 Janke, Burnett. 1984. *Tango: die Berührung*. Gießen: Focus.

2997 Mafud, Julio. 1966. *Sociología del tango*. Buenos Aires: Editorial Americalee.

2998 Montes, Jorg. 1977. *The History of Tango*. Buenos Aires: Sicamericana.

2999 Pelinski, Ramón. 1982. *Dire le tango*. Montréal: Presses de l'Université de Montréal.

3000 Reichardt, Dieter. 1984. *Tango: Verweigerung und Trauer; Kontexte und Texte*. Frankfurt am Main: Suhrkamp.

3001 Sábato, Ernesto. 1963. *Tango, discusión y clave*. Buenos Aires: Editorial Losada.

3002 Salas, Horacio. 1986. *El Tango*. Buenos Aires: Planeta.

3003 Salmon, Russell O. 1977. The Tango: Its Origins and Meaning. *Journal of Popular Culture* 10(4): 859–66.

3004 Savigliano, Marta E. 1995. *Tango and the Political Economy of Passion*. Boulder, San Francisco and Oxford: Westview Press.

3005 Taylor, Julie. 1976. Tango: Theme of Class and Nation. *Ethnomusicology* 20(2): 273–91.

3006 Taylor, Julie. 1992. Tango. In *Rereading Cultural Anthropology*, ed. George Marcus. Durham, NC: Duke University Press. 377–89.

3007 Vidart, Daniel. 1967. *El tango y su mundo*. Montevideo: Tauro.

3008 Vilariño, Idea. 1981. El tango (1). In *La historia de la literatura argentina. Capitulo 117*. Buenos Aires: Centro Editor de America Latina. 409–32.

3009 Vilariño, Idea. 1981. El tango (2). In *La historia de la literatura argentina. Capitulo 121*. Buenos Aires: Centro Editor de America Latina. 529–52.

TIN PAN ALLEY

3010 Brackett, David. 1994. The Politics and Practice of 'Crossover' in American Popular Music, 1963 to 1965. *Musical Quarterly* 78(4): 774–97.

3011 Burton, Jack. 1951. *The Blue Book of Tin Pan Alley: A Human Interest Encyclopedia of American Popular Music*. Watkins Glen, NY: Century House.

3012 Cohan, George. 1924. *Twenty Years on Broadway*. New York: Harper & Brothers.

3013 Ewen, David. 1962. *Popular American Composers from Revolutionary Times to the Present*. New York: Wilson.

3014 Ewen, David. 1964. *The Life and Death of Tin Pan Alley: The Golden Age of American Popular Music*. New York: Funk and Wagnalls.

3015 Ewen, David. 1977. *All the Years of American Popular Music*. Englewood Cliffs, NJ: Prentice-Hall.

3016 Fuld, James J. 1956. *American Popular Music (Reference Book), 1875–1950*. Philadelphia: Musica Americana.

3017 Furia, Philip. 1991. *The Poets of Tin Pan Alley: A History of America's Greatest*

Lyricists. New York: Oxford University Press.

3018 Goldberg, Isaac. 1930. *Tin Pan Alley: A Chronicle of the American Popular Music Racket*. New York: John Day Company.

3019 Goldberg, Isaac. 1961. *Tin Pan Alley: A Chronicle of American Popular Music*. New York: Ungar.

3020 Green, Abel and Laurie, Joe. 1985. *Showbiz from Vaudeville to Video*. New York: Garland.

3021 Hamm, Charles. 1979. 'After the Ball': or, the Birth of Tin Pan Alley and 'It's Only a Paper Moon': The Golden Years of Tin Pan Alley. In *Yesterdays: American Popular Song*. New York: W.W. Norton. 284–390.

3022 Hamm, Charles. 1979. *Yesterdays: American Popular Song*. New York: W.W. Norton.

3023 Hamm, Charles. 1996. Alexander and His Band. *American Music* 14(1): 65–102.

3024 Harris, Charles. 1926. *After the Ball: Forty Years of Melody*. New York: Frank-Maurice.

3025 Hyland, William. 1995. *The Song Is Ended: Songwriters and American Music, 1900–1950*. New York: Oxford University Press.

3026 Jasen, David A. 1988. *Tin Pan Alley: The Composers, the Songs, the Performers and Their Times. The Golden Age of American Popular Music from 1886 to 1956*. New York: Donald I. Fine.

3027 Johns, Donald. 1993. Funnel Tonality in American Popular Music, ca. 1900–1970. *American Music* 11(4): 458–72.

3028 Kanter, Kenneth Aaron. 1982. *The Jews on Tin Pan Alley: The Jewish Contribution to American Popular Music, 1830–1940*. New York: Ktav Publishing House.

3029 Lissauer, Robert. 1991. *Lissauer's Encyclopedia of Popular Music in America*. New York: Paragon.

3030 Marks, Edward B. 1934. *They All Sang: From Tony Pastor to Rudy Vallee*. New York: Viking.

3031 Meyer, Hazel. 1958. *The Gold in Tin Pan Alley*. Philadelphia: Lippincott.

3032 Middleton, Richard. 1983. 'Play It Again Sam': On the Productivity of Repetition. *Popular Music* 3: 235–71.

3033 Middleton, Richard. 1986. In the Groove, or Blowing Your Mind? The Pleasures of Musical Repetition. In *Popular Culture and Social Relations*, ed. Tony Bennett and Janet Woollacott. Milton Keynes: Open University Press. 159–76.

3034 Pessen, Edward. 1985. The Great Songwriters of Tin Pan Alley's Golden Age: A Social, Occupational and Aesthetic Inquiry. *American Music* 3(2): 180–97.

3035 Pleasants, Henry. 1974. *The Great American Popular Singers*. London: Gollancz.

3036 Scheurer, Timothy E., ed. 1989. *American Popular Music, Vol. 1: The Nineteenth Century and Tin Pan Alley*. Bowling Green, OH: Bowling Green University Popular Press.

3037 Shaw, Arnold. 1987. *The Jazz Age: Popular Music in the 1920s*. New York: Oxford University Press.

3038 Shepherd, John. 1982. *Tin Pan Alley*. London: Routledge & Kegan Paul.

3039 Slobin, Mark. 1982. *Tenement Songs: The Popular Music of the Jewish Immigrants*. Urbana, IL: University of Illinois Press.

3040 Spaeth, Sigmund. 1927. *Weep Some More, My Lady*. New York: Doubleday.

3041 Spaeth, Sigmund. 1934. *The Facts of Life in Popular Song*. New York: Whittlesey House.

3042 Spaeth, Sigmund. 1959. (1927) *Read 'Em and Weep: A Treasury of American Songs*. New York: Arco. First published New York: Doubleday, 1927.

3043 Tawa, Nicholas E. 1990. *The Way to Tin Pan Alley: American Popular Song, 1866–1910*. New York: Schirmer.

3044 Warren, Craig. 1978. *Sweet and Low-Down: America's Popular Song Writers*. Metuchen, NJ: Scarecrow Press.

3045 Whitcomb, Ian. 1973. *After the Ball*. London: Penguin.

3046 White, Mark. 1983. *'You Must Remember This': Popular Songwriters, 1900–1980*. London: Frederick Warne.

3047 Wilder, Alec. 1972. *American Popular Song: The Great Innovators, 1900–1950*. New York: Oxford University Press.

3048 Witmark, Isidore and Goldberg, Isaac. 1939. *From Ragtime to Swingtime: The Story of the House of Witmark*. New York: Furman.

TOPICAL SONGS

3049 Levy, Lester S. 1975. *Give Me Yesterday: American History in Song, 1890–1920*. Norman, OK: University of Oklahoma Press.

3050 Luther, Frank. 1942. *Americans and Their Songs*. New York: Harper & Bros.

3051 Scott, John Anthony. 1966. *The Ballad of America: The History of the United States in Song and Story*. New York: Bantam Pathfinder Editions.

3052 Silber, Irwin. 1967. The Topical Song Revolution at Midpoint. In *The American Folk Scene: Dimensions of the Folk Song Revival*, ed. David De Turk and A.

Poulin. New York: Dell Publishing. 167–72.

TROPICALIA

3053 Favaretto, Celso. 1979. *Tropicália: alegoria alegria*. Sao Paulo: Kairós.

VAUDEVILLE

3054 Barth, Gunther. 1980. *City People: The Rise of Modern City Culture in Nineteenth-Century America*. New York: Oxford University Press.

3055 DiMeglio, John E. 1973. *Vaudeville U.S.A.* Bowling Green, OH: Bowling Green University Popular Press.

3056 Fletcher, Tom. 1984. (1954) *100 Years of the Negro in Show Business*. New York: Da Capo Press. First published New York: Burdge & Co. Ltd., 1954.

3057 Gilbert, Douglas. 1963. (1940) *American Vaudeville: Its Life and Times*. New York: Dover Publications. First published New York: Whittlesey House, 1940.

3058 Green, Abel and Laurie, Joe. 1951. *Show Biz: From Vaude to Video*. New York: Holt.

3059 Kahn, E. 1955. *The Merry Partners: The Age and Stage of Harrigan and Hart*. New York: Random House.

3060 Kudinova, T. 1982. *Ot vodevil do muzykal*. Moskva: Sovjetskij kompositor.

3061 Lahr, John. 1984. *Automatic Vaudeville: Essays on Star Turns*. New York: Knopf.

3062 Laurie, Joe. 1953. *Vaudeville: From the Honky-Tonks to the Palace*. New York: Holt.

3063 Marks, Edward B. 1934. *They All Sang: From Tony Pastor to Rudy Vallee*. New York: Viking.

3064 McLean, A.F., Jr. 1965. *American Vaudeville as Ritual*. Lexington, KY: University of Kentucky Press.

3065 Slide, Anthony. 1981. *The Vaudevillians: A Dictionary of Vaudeville Performers*. Westport, CT: Arlington House.

3066 Slide, Anthony. 1994. *The Encyclopedia of Vaudeville*. Westport, CT: Greenwood Press.

3067 Snyder, Robert. 1989. *The Voice of the City: Vaudeville and Popular Culture in New York*. New York: Oxford University Press.

3068 Stein, Charles W., ed. 1984. *American Vaudeville As Seen By Its Contemporaries*. New York: Alfred A. Knopf.

3069 Toll, Robert C. 1976. *On with the Show: The First Century of Show Business in America*. New York: Oxford University Press.

WAR SONGS

3070 Brophy, John and Partridge, Eric, comps. 1930. *Songs and Slang of the British Soldier, 1914–1918*. London: Eric Partridge.

3071 Heaps, Willard Allison. 1960. *The Singing Sixties: The Spirit of Civil War Days Drawn from the Music of the Times*. Norman, OK: Oklahoma University Press.

3072 Higginson, Thomas Wentworth. 1970. *Army Life in a Black Regiment*, new edition. Boston, MA: Houghton Mifflin. First published Boston: Fields, Osgood, 1870.

3073 McNeil, W.K. 1969. 'We'll Make the Spanish Grunt': Popular Songs About the Sinking of the Maine. *Journal of Popular Culture* 2(4): 537–51.

3074 Moseley, Caroline. 1984. 'When Will Dis Cruel War Be Ober?' Attitudes Towards Blacks in Popular Songs of the Civil War. *American Music* 2(3): 1–26.

3075 Murdoch, Brian. 1990. *Fighting Songs and Warring Words: Popular Lyrics of Two World Wars*. London: Routledge.

3076 Niles, John Jacob, comp. 1927. *Singing Soldiers*. New York: Scribner.

3077 Palmer, Roy, ed. 1977. *The Rambling Soldier*. Harmondsworth: Penguin.

3078 Pring-Mill, Robert. 1987. The Role of Revolutionary Song: A Nicaraguan Assessment. *Popular Music* 6(2): 179–89.

3079 Rothstein, Robert A. 1995. Homeland, Home Town and Battlefield: The Popular Song. In *Culture in Wartime Russia*, ed. Richard Stites. Bloomington, IN: Indiana University Press. 77–107.

3080 Sample, Duane. 1985. The Popular Music of the Spanish-American War: How Popular Was It? In *Popular Music Perspectives, 2*, ed. David Horn. Göteborg and Exeter: IASPM. 360–66.

3081 Spaude-Schulze, Edelgard. 1987. 'Ich sah durchs Land im Weltenbrand.' Anti-Kriegs-Lieder in der Weimarer Republik. In *Ich will aber gerade vom Leben singen . . . Über populäre Musik vom ausgehenden 19. Jahrhundert bis zum Ende der Weimarer Republik*, ed. Sabine Schutte. Reinbek bei Hamburg: Rowohlt. 385–406.

3082 Woll, Allen. 1983. *The Hollywood Musical Goes to War*. Chicago: Nelson-Hall.

WHITE SPIRITUALS

3083 Asbury, Samuel E. and Meyer, Henry E. 1932. Old-Time White Camp Meeting Spirituals. In *Tone the Bell Easy*. Austin, TX: Texas Folklore Society.

3084 Cobb, Buell E. 1978. *The Sacred Harp: A Tradition and Its Music.* Athens, GA: University of Georgia Press.

3085 Green, Archie. 1970. Hear These Beautiful Sacred Selections. In *1970 Yearbook of the International Folk Music Council,* ed. Alexander L. Ringer. Urbana, IL: University of Illinois Press. 28–50.

3086 Horn, Dorothy. 1970. *Sing to Me of Heaven: A Study of Folk and Early American Material in Three Old Harp Books.* Gainesville, FL: University of Florida Press.

3087 Jackson, George Pullen. 1943. *White and Negro Spirituals: Their Life Span and Kinship Tracing 200 Years.* Locust Valley, NY: Augustin.

3088 Jackson, George Pullen. 1965. (1933) *White Spirituals in the Southern Uplands: The Story of the Fasola Folk, Their Songs, Singings and 'Buckwheat' Notes.* New York: Dover Publications. First published Chapel Hill: University of North Carolina Press, 1933.

3089 Patterson, Daniel W. 1979. *The Shaker Spiritual.* Princeton, NJ: Princeton University Press.

3090 Revitt, Paul J. 1964. *The George Pullen Jackson Collection of Southern Hymnody: A Bibliography.* Los Angeles: UCLA.

3091 Stanislaw, Richard J. 1978. *A Checklist of Four-Shape Shape-Note Tunebooks.* Brooklyn, NY: Institute for Studies in American Music.

WORLD MUSIC

3092 Baumann, Max Peter, ed. 1992. *World Music and Musics of the World: Aspects of Documentation, Mass Media and Acculturation.* Wilhelmshaven: Florian Noetzel Verlag.

3093 Blackwood, Alan. 1991. *Music of the World.* New York: Facts on File.

3094 Broughton, Simon, et al. 1994. *World Music: The Rough Guide.* London: Rough Guides.

3095 Erlmann, Veit. 1993. The Politics and Aesthetics of Transnational Musics. *The World of Music* 35(2): 3–15.

3096 Erlmann, Veit. 1995. Ideologie der Differenz: Zur Ästhetik der World Music. *PopScriptum* 3: 6–29.

3097 Fairley, Jan. 1992. European World Music Charts. *Popular Music* 11(2): 241–44.

3098 Frith, Simon. 1989. *World Music, Politics and Social Change.* Manchester: Manchester University Press.

3099 Garofalo, Reebee, ed. 1992. *Rockin' the Boat: Mass Music and Mass Movements.* Boston, MA: South End Press.

3100 Guilbault, Jocelyne. 1993. On Redefining the 'Local' Through World Music. *The World of Music* 35(2): 33–47.

3101 Guilbault, Jocelyne. 1995. A World Music Back Home: The Power of Mediations. In *Popular Music Perspectives III,* ed. Peter Wicke. Berlin: Zyankrise. 147–59.

3102 Guilbault, Jocelyne. 1995. Zur Umdeutung das Lokalen durch die World Music. *PopScriptum* 3: 30–44.

3103 Hanly, Francis and May, Tim. 1989. *Rhythms of the World.* London: BBC Books.

3104 Lipsitz, George. 1994. *Dangerous Crossroads: Popular Music, Postmodernism and the Poetics of Place.* London and New York: Verso.

3105 Manuel, Peter. 1988. *Popular Musics of the Non-Western World: An Introductory Survey.* New York: Oxford University Press.

3106 Marre, Jeremy and Charlton, Hannah. 1985. *Beats of the Heart: Popular Music of the World*. New York: Pantheon.

3107 McAllester, David P. 1971. Some Thought on 'Universals' in World Music. *Ethnomusicology* 15(3): 379–80.

3108 Nettl, Bruno, ed. 1978. *Eight Urban Musical Cultures: Tradition and Change*. Urbana, IL: University of Illinois Press.

3109 Nettl, Bruno. 1978. Some Aspects of the History of World Music in the Twentieth Century: Questions, Problems and Concepts. *Ethnomusicology* 22(2): 123–36.

3110 Nettl, Bruno. 1985. *The Western Impact on World Music: Change, Adaptation and Survival*. New York: Schirmer.

3111 Pacini Hernandez, Deborah. 1993. A View from the South: Spanish Caribbean Perspectives on World Beat. *The World of Music* 35(2): 48–69.

3112 Robinson, Deanna Campbell, Elizabeth B. Buck and Marlene Cuthbert. 1991. *Music at the Margins: Popular Music and Global Cultural Diversity*. Newbury Park, CA: Sage.

3113 Sachs, Curt. 1956. *A Short History of World Music*. London: Dobson.

3114 Sakolsky, Ron and Ho, Fred Wei-Han. 1995. *Sounding Off! Music as Subversion/Resistance/Revolution*. New York: Autonomedia.

3115 Slobin, Mark. 1993. *Subcultural Sounds: Micromusics of the West*. Hanover, NH: Wesleyan University Press.

3116 Sweeney, Philip. 1991. *The Virgin Directory of World Music*. London: Virgin.

3117 Titon, Jeff Todd. 1992. *Worlds of Music. An Introduction to the Music of the World's Peoples*. New York: Schirmer.

3118 Trouillet, Jean von, ed. 1989. *Welt-Beat. Jahrbuch für Globe-HörerInnen*. Lohrbach: Pieper's Medienexperimente.

3119 Wallis, Roger and Malm, Krister. 1984. *Big Sounds from Small Peoples: The Music Industry in Small Countries*. London: Constable.

ZOUK

3120 Guilbault, Jocelyne. 1993. *Zouk: World Music in the West Indies*. Chicago: University of Chicago Press.

3121 Guilbault, Jocelyne. 1994. Créolité and the New Cultural Politics of Difference in Popular Music of the French West Indies. *Black Music Research Journal* 14(2): 161–78.

THE INDUSTRY

ADVERTISING (OF POPULAR MUSIC)

3122 Chantry, Art, ed. 1985. *Instant Litter: Concert Posters from Seattle Punk Culture.* Seattle, WA: Real Comet.

3123 Grushkin, Paul. 1987. *The Art of Rock: Posters from Presley to Punk.* New York: Abbeville Press.

3124 Grushkin, Paul. 1987. *The Rock Poster.* New York: Abbeville Press.

3125 Jones, Steve. 1993. Popular Music, Criticism, Advertising and the Music Industry. *Journal of Popular Music Studies* 5: 79–91.

3126 Tauchnitz, Jürgen. 1990. *Werbung mit Musik.* Heidelberg: Physika.

AWARDS

3127 Fong-Torres, Ben. 1973. The Rockless Grammy Awards: One Hand Washing Another. *Rolling Stone* (23 April): 10–12.

3128 Grenier, Line. 1995. Twelve Years of 'Felix' AWARDs: A Changing Industry and Its Changing Place. In *Popular Music Perspectives*, III. ed. Peter Wicke. Berlin: Zyankrise. 174–89.

3129 O'Neil, Thomas. 1993. *The Grammys for the Record.* New York and London: Penguin.

3130 Sackett, Susan. 1995. *Hollywood Sings!: 60 Years of Academy Awards Nominated Songs.* New York: Billboard Books.

CHARTS

3131 Albert, George and Hoffmann, Frank. 1984. *The Cash Box Black Contemporary Singles Charts, 1960–1984.* Metuchen and London: Scarecrow Press.

3132 Amerika, Nederlandse Top 40, Nationale Hitparade, TROS, Engeland, Elpee, Duitsland. 1979. *De Telegraaf* 1979–10–16.

3133 Anderson, B., et al. 1980. Hit Record Trends, 1940–1977. *Journal of Communication* 32(2): 31–43.

3134 Brackett, David. 1994. The Politics and Practice of 'Crossover' in American Popular Music, 1963 to 1965. *Musical Quarterly* (Winter): 774–97.

3135 Briel, Robert. 1987. *Hitdossier 1958 to 1987.* Haarlem: Becht.

3136 Bronson, Fred. 1992. *The Billboard Book of Number One Hits.* New York: Billboard Publications.

3137 Burns, Gary. 1983. Trends in Lyrics in the Annual Top Twenty Songs in the United States, 1963–1972. *Popular Music & Society* 9(1): 25–39.

3138 Comer, John. 1982. How Can I Use the Top Ten? In *Pop, Rock and Ethnic Music in Schools,* ed. Graham Vulliamy and Edward Lee. London: Cambridge University Press. 7–23.

3139 Coryton, Demitri and Murrells, Joseph, comps. 1989. *Million Sellers of the Sixties.* London: Batsford.

3140 Fairley, Jan. 1992. European World Music Charts. *Popular Music* 11(2): 241–44.

3141 Feilh, John. 1981. *Music Trends: Characteristics of the Billboard Charts, 1955–1977.* Ottawa: Canadian Radio-television and Communications Commission.

3142 Gambaccini, Paul, Tim Rice and Jonathan Rice. 1991. *The Guinness Book of Hit Singles.* London: Guinness Books.

3143 Gambaccini, Paul, et al., eds. 1983. *The Guinness Book of British Hit Albums.* London: Grrr Books.

3144 Garofalo, Reebee. 1994. Culture Versus Commerce: The Marketing of Black Popular Music. *Public Culture* 7(1): 275–87.

3145 George, Nelson. 1984. *Top of the Charts: The Most Complete Listing Ever.* Piscataway, NJ: New Century.

3146 Henson, Brian and Morgan, Colin, comps. 1989. *First Hits: The Book of Sheet Music, 1946–1959.* London: Boxtree.

3147 Hoffmann, Frank and Hoffmann, Lee Ann. 1983. *The Cash Box Singles Charts, 1950–1981.* Metuchen and London: Scarecrow Press.

3148 Jasper, Tony. 1991. *The Top Twenty Book: The Official British Record Charts, 1955–1990.* Poole: Blandford Press.

3149 Laing, Dave. 1969. *The Sound of Our Time.* London: Sheed & Ward.

3150 O'Neil, Thomas. 1993. *The Grammys: For the Record.* New York: Penguin.

3151 Parker, Martin. 1991. Reading the Charts: Making Sense of the Hit Parade. *Popular Music* 10(2): 205–17.

3152 Peterson, Richard A. and Berger, David G. 1975. Cycles in Symbol Production: The Case of Popular Music. *American Sociological Review* 40 (April): 158–73.

3153 Roland, Tom, comp. 1995. *The Billboard Book of Top Country Hits.* New York: Watson-Guptill.

3154 Rust, Godfrey. 1984. Charts, the Inside Story. *Music Week* (29 September; 6 (October): 22–23; 20–21.

3155 Whitburn, Joel. 1987. *The Billboard Book of Top Forty Hits,* 3rd edition. New York: Billboard Publications, Inc.

3156 Whitburn, Joel, comp. 1988. *Top R&B Singles.* Menomonee Falls, WI: Record Research.

3157 Whitburn, Joel, comp. 1990. *Billboard Hot 100 Charts: The Sixties.* Menomonee Falls, WI: Record Research.

3158 Whitburn, Joel, comp. 1990. *Billboard Hot 100 Charts: The Seventies.* Menomonee Falls, WI: Record Research.

3159 Whitburn, Joel. 1991. *The Billboard Book of Top 40 Albums,* revised edition. New York: Billboard Books.

3160 Whitburn, Joel, comp. 1991. *Billboard Hot 100 Charts: The Eighties.* Menomonee Falls, WI: Record Research.

3161 Whitburn, Joel, comp. 1992. *Billboard Pop Charts, 1955–1959.* Menomonee Falls, WI: Record Research.

3162 Whitburn, Joel, comp. 1992. *Bubbling Under the Hot 100, 1959–1985.* Menomonee Falls, WI: Record Research.

3163 Whitburn, Joel, comp. 1992. *Pop Memories, 1890–1954.* Menomonee Falls, WI: Record Research.

3164 Whitburn, Joel, comp. 1993. *Billboard Pop Album Charts, 1965–1969.* Menomonee Falls, WI: Record Research.

3165 Whitburn, Joel, comp. 1994. *Billboard Pop Hits, 1940–1954.* Menomonee Falls, WI: Record Research.

3166 Whitburn, Joel, comp. 1994. *Top Country Singles, 1944–1993.* Menomonee Falls, WI: Record Research.

3167 Whitburn, Joel, comp. 1994. *Top Pop Singles, 1944–1993*. Menomonee Falls, WI: Record Research.

3168 Whitburn, Joel, comp. 1995. *The Billboard Book of Top 40 Albums*, 3rd edition. New York: Watson-Guptill.

3169 Whitburn, Joel, comp. 1995. *Billboard Pop Annual, 1955–1994*. Menomonee Falls, WI: Record Research.

3170 White, Adam and Bronson, Fred, comps. 1995. *The Billboard Book of Rhythm and Blues Hits*. New York: Watson-Guptill.

3171 Wicke, Peter. 1996. Die Charts im Musikgeschäft. *Musik und Unterricht* 40: 9–12.

CHART SHOWS

3172 Blacknell, Steve. 1985. *The Story of Top of the Pops*. London: BBC/Patrick Stephens.

3173 Clark, Dick. 1978. *Rock, Roll and Remember*. New York: Popular Library.

3174 Cubitt, Sean. 1984. Top of the Pops: The Politics of the Living Room. In *Television Mythologies: Stars, Shows and Signs*, ed. Len Masterman. London: Comedia. 46–48.

3175 Shore, Michael and Clark, Dick. 1985. *The History of the American Bandstand: From the Fifties to the Eighties*. New York: Ballantine.

3176 Sieber, Wolfgang. 1982. *Die Hitparade. Studie zu einer Vermittlungsform von Pop-Musik*. Freising: Frisinga.

COMPACT DISK

3177 Blesser, B. 1978. Digitization of Audio. *Journal of the Audio Engineering Society* 26(10) (October): 739–71.

3178 Kagan, S. 1990. The Compact Disc and Its Effect on Contemporary Music. *Popular Music & Society* 14(1): 13–18.

3179 Millard, Andre. 1995. *America on Record: A History of Recorded Sound*. Cambridge: Cambridge University Press.

3180 Pohlmann, Ken C. 1989. *Principles of Digital Audio*. Indianapolis, IN: Sams.

3181 Pohlmann, Ken C. 1992. *The Compact Disc: A Handbook of Theory and Use*, revised edition. Oxford: Oxford University Press. First published Oxford: Oxford University Press, 1989.

COMPUTERS IN MUSIC/MIDI

3182 Ackermann, Philipp. 1991. *Computer und Musik. Eine Einführung in die digitale Klangverarbeitung*. Wien, New York and Berlin: Springer.

3183 Anderton, Craig. 1986. *MIDI for Musicians*. New York: Amsco.

3184 Anderton, Craig. 1988. 20 Great Achievements in 20 Years of Musical Electronics, 1968–1988. *Electronic Musician* 4(7) (July): 28–97.

3185 Bigelow, Steven. 1987. *Making Music with Personal Computers*. La Jolla, CA: Park Row Press.

3186 Chaffin, Jan. 1989. Digital Signal Processing. *Keyboard* 15(8): 32–41, 126.

3187 Chamberlin, Hal. 1980. *Musical Applications of Microprocessors*. Rochelle Park, NJ: Hayden.

3188 di Perna, Alan. 1994. Are We Making Art Yet? Music in the Age of Interactive Entertainment. *Musician* 188 (June): 56–63.

3189 Durant, Alan. 1990. A New Day for Music? Digital Technologies in Contemporary Music-Making. In *Culture, Technology and Creativity in the*

Late Twentieth Century, ed. Philip Hayward. London: John Libbey & Co. 175–96.

3190 Goodwin, Andrew. 1992. (1987) Rationalization and Democratization in the New Technologies of Popular Music. In *Popular Music & Communication*, ed. James Lull, revised edition. Newbury Park, CA: Sage. 75–100.

3191 Hammond, Ray. 1983. *The Musician and the Micro*. Poole: Blandford Press.

3192 Holmes, Thomas B. 1985. *Electronic and Experimental Music: History, Instruments, Technique, Performers, Recordings*. New York: Charles Scribner's Sons.

3193 Huber, David Miles. 1992. *Random Access Audio*. Carmel, IN: Sams Publishing.

3194 Kahn, Douglas. 1990. Track Organology. *October* 55: 67–78.

3195 Kaplan, S. Jerrold. 1989. Developing a Commercial Digital Sound Synthesizer. In *The Music Machine: Selected Readings from 'Computer Music Journal'*, ed. Curtis Roads. Cambridge, MA: MIT. 611–22.

3196 Karlin, Fred and Wright, Rayburn. 1990. Electronic and Contemporary Scoring. In *On the Track: A Guide to Contemporary Film Scoring*. New York: Schirmer. 377–455.

3197 Mackay, Andy. 1981. Computers. In *Electronic Music*. London: Harrow House. 59–62.

3198 Manning, Peter. 1985. *Electronic and Computer Music*. Oxford: Clarendon Press.

3199 Mathews, Max V. 1969. *The Technology of Computer Music*. Cambridge, MA: MIT.

3200 Metlay, Mike. 1996. Is Anybody . . . Out There? Making Music on the Internet.

Music & Computers 2(3) (May/June): 58–65.

3201 Milano, Dominic. 1984. Turmoil in MIDI-Land. *Keyboard* 10(6) (June): 42–63, 106.

3202 Milano, Dominic, ed. 1987. *Mind Over MIDI*. Cupertino, CA: GPI Publications.

3203 Rothstein, Joseph. 1992. *MIDI: A Comprehensive Introduction*. Madison, WI: A-R Editions.

3204 Rumsey, Francis. 1990. *Tapeless Sound Recording*. London: Focal Press.

3205 Scholz, Carter. 1990. Computer Partnerships. *Keyboard* 16(10): 55–63.

3206 Strawn, John, ed. 1987. *Music and Digital Technology: Proceedings of the AES 5th International Conference*. New York: Audio Engineering Society.

3207 Théberge, Paul. 1990. Democracy and Its Discontents: The MIDI Specification. *ONETWOTHREEFOUR* 9: 12–34.

3208 Vail, Mark. 1993. Fairlight CMI. In *Vintage Synthesizers*. San Francisco: GPI Books. 190–95.

3209 Yavelow, Christopher. 1989. Music and Microprocessors: MIDI and the State of the Art. In *The Music Machine: Selected Readings from 'Computer Music Journal'*, ed. Curtis Roads. Cambridge, MA: MIT. 199–234.

CONCERT PROMOTION AND LIVE SHOWS

3210 Bagehot, Richard. 1989. *Music Business Agreements*. London: Waterlow.

3211 Baskerville, David. 1995. (1978) *Music Business Handbook and Career Guide*, 6th revised edition. Thousand Oaks, CA: Sherwood Publishing Company.

3212 Du Noyer, Paul. 1988. I'm with the Band . . .. *Q* (18 March): 40–47.

3213 Graham, Bill and Greenfield, Robert. 1992. *Bill Graham Presents*. New York: Doubleday.

3214 Leighton-Pope, Carl. 1991. Booking Agents. In *The Rock File: Making It in the Music Business*, ed. Norton York. Oxford: Oxford University Press. 194–203.

3215 Moody, James L. 1989. *Concert Lighting: Techniques, Art and Business*. Boston and London: Focal Press.

3216 Nitschke, Dirk. 1994. Des Volkswagen Stimme: Die Instrumentalisierung der Popmusik im Marketing oder Volkswagen presented by Genesis. In *Zwischen Rausch und Ritual*, ed. Konstanze Kriese et al. Berlin: Zyankrise. 125–34.

3217 Spitz, Robert Stephen. 1979. *Barefoot in Babylon: The Creation of the Woodstock Music Festival, 1969*. New York: Viking.

3218 Wale, Michael. 1972. *Voxpop: Profiles of the Pop Process*. London: Harrap.

CONTRACTS

3219 Bagehot, Richard. 1989. *Music Business Agreements*. London: Waterlow.

3220 Cooper, Jay L. 1971. *Record and Music Publishing Forms of Agreement in Current Use*. New York: Law-Arts Books.

COPYRIGHT

3221 Bagehot, Richard. 1989. *Music Business Agreements*. London: Waterlow.

3222 Coon, Wayne O. 1973. *Some Problems with Musical Public-Domain Materials under United States Copyright Law as Illustrated Mainly by the Recent Folk-Song Revival*. Los Angeles: John Edwards Memorial Foundation.

3223 Durant, Alan. 1990. A New Day for Music? Digital Technologies in Contemporary Music-Making. In *Culture, Technology and Creativity in the Late Twentieth Century*, ed. Philip Hayward. London: John Libbey & Co. 175–96.

3224 Ehrlich, Cyril. 1989. *Harmonious Alliance: A History of the Performing Right Society*. Oxford: Oxford University Press.

3225 Fabbri, Franco. 1991. Copyright: The Dark Side of the Music Business. *Worldbeat* 1: 109–14.

3226 Frith, Simon. 1988. Copyright and the Music Business. *Popular Music* 7(1): 57–75.

3227 Frith, Simon, ed. 1993. *Music and Copyright*. Edinburgh: Edinburgh University Press.

3228 Gaines, Jane M. 1992. *Contested Culture: The Image, the Voice and the Law*. London: BFI Publishing.

3229 Groll, Klaus-Michael. 1993. *Noten, Recht und Paragraphen*. Wilhelmshaven: Noetzel.

3230 Hurst, Walter E. 1981. *The Music Industry Book: Protect Yourself Before You Lose Your Rights and Royalties*. Hollywood, CA: Seven Arts.

3231 Jones, Steve. 1992. *Rock Formation: Music, Technology and Mass Communication*. Newbury Park, CA: Sage.

3232 Klaven, Kent J. 1989. *Protecting Your Songs and Yourself: The Songwriters' Legal Guide*. Cincinnati: Writer's Digest Books.

3233 Lowenthal, Daniel K. 1953. *Trends in the Licensing of Popular Song Hits, 1940–1953*. New York: Bureau of Applied Social Research, Columbia University.

THE INDUSTRY

3234 Porter, Vincent. 1991. *Beyond the Berne Convention: Copyright, Broadcasting and the Single European Market.* London: John Libbey & Co.

3235 Ryan, John. 1985. *The Production of Culture in the Music Industry: The ASCAP-BMI Controversy.* Lanham, MD: University Press of America.

3236 Schulze, Erich. 1981. *Urheberrecht in der Musik.* Berlin: De Gruyter.

3237 Sterling, J.A.L. 1992. *Intellectual Property Rights in Sound Recordings, Film and Video: Protection of Phonographic and Cinematographic Recordings and Works in National and International Law.* London: Sweet & Maxwell.

CYLINDERS

3238 Annand, H.H. 1966. *The Complete Catalogue of the United States Everlasting Indestructible Cylinders, 1908–1913.* London: City of London Phonograph and Gramophone Society.

3239 Brady, Erika, ed. 1984. *The Federal Cylinder Project: A Guide to Field Cylinder Collections in Federal Agencies, Vol. 1.* Washington, DC: Library of Congress, American Folklife Center.

3240 Deakins, Duane D. 1956. *Cylinder Records: A Description of the Numbering Systems, Physical Appearance and Other Aspects of Cylinder Records Made by the Major American Companies.* Stockton, CA: Duane D. Deakins.

3241 Frow, George and Sefl, Albert F. 1978. *The Edison Cylinder Phonographs: A Detailed Account of the Entertainment Models Until 1929.* Sevenoaks, Kent: Frow.

3242 Gray, Judith, ed. 1984. *The Federal Cylinder Project: A Guide to Field Cylinder Collections in Federal Agencies, Vol. 2.* Washington, DC: Library of Congress, American Folklife Center.

3243 Koenigsberg, Allen. 1969. *Edison Cylinder Recordings, 1889–1912.* New York: Stellar Productions.

3244 Read, Oliver and Welch, Walter L. 1976. *From Tin Foil to Stereo: The Evolution of the Phonograph,* 2nd edition. Indianapolis/New York: Howard Sams/ Bobbs-Merrill.

DISTRIBUTION AND RETAIL

3245 Busse, Burkhard. 1976. *Der deutsche Schlager. Eine Untersuchung zur Produktion, Distribution und Rezeption von Trivialliteratur.* Wiesbaden: Athenaion.

3246 du Gay, Paul and Negus, Keith. 1994. The Changing Sites of Sound: Music Retailing and the Composition of Consumers. *Media, Culture and Society* 16: 395–413.

3247 Gilroy, Paul. 1993. *Small Acts: Thoughts on the Politics of Black Cultures.* London: Serpent's Tail.

3248 Gray, Herman. 1988. *Producing Jazz: The Experience of an Independent Record Company.* Philadelphia: Temple University Press.

3249 National Association of Record Merchandisers. 1995. *Music Purchasing from Record Clubs and Retail Outlets.* New York: National Association of Record Merchandisers.

3250 Werbin, Stu. 1973. High Noon in Miami Beach: A Visit to the NARM Convention. *Rolling Stone* (25 May): 22–24.

EUROVISION

3251 Björnberg, Alf. 1990. Sounding the Mainstream: An Analysis of the Songs Performed in the Swedish Eurovision Song Contest Semi-Finals, 1959–1983. In *Popular Music Research,* ed. Keith Roe and Ulla Karlsson. Göteborg:

NORDICOM-Sweden, No. 1–2. 121–32.

3252 Borgersen, Terje. 1986. Melodi Grand Prix - Uten lyd og bilde - et pauseinnslag. In *Eurovision Song Contest, 86: 6 upretentsiöse essays.* Trondheim: Nordisk Institutt, Universitetet i Trondheim, AVH. 28–34.

3253 Johnson, Geir. 1986. *Norge i Melodi Grand Prix.* Oslo: Forlaget Atheneum.

GRAMOPHONE

3254 Andrews, Frank. 1986. *The Edison Phonograph: The British Connection.* Rugby: City of London Phonograph and Gramophone Society.

3255 Chew, V.K. 1967. *Talking Machines, 1877–1914.* London: Her Majesty's Stationery Office.

3256 Eisenberg, Evan. 1987. *The Recording Angel: The Experience of Music from Aristotle to Zappa.* New York: Penguin.

3257 Gelatt, Roland. 1977. *The Fabulous Phonograph, 1877–1977.* London: Cassell. First published London: Cassell, 1955.

3258 Harvith, John and Harvith, Susan, eds. 1987. *Edison, Musicians and the Phonograph: A Historical Guide.* Westport and London: Greenwood Press.

3259 Keightley, Keir. 1996. 'Turn It Down!' She Shrieked: Gender, Domestic Space, and High Fidelity, 1948–59. *Popular Music* 15(2): 149–78.

3260 Laing, Dave. 1991. A Voice Without a Face: Popular Music and the Phonograph in the 1890s. *Popular Music* 10(1): 1–9.

3261 Leonard, Neil. 1972. The Impact of Mechanization. In *American Music: From Storyville to Woodstock*, ed. Charles Nanry. New Brunswick, NJ: Transaction. 44–64.

3262 Lowe, Jacques. 1983. *The Incredible Music Machine.* London: Quartet.

3263 Millard, Andre. 1995. *America on Record: A History of Recorded Sound.* Cambridge: Cambridge University Press.

3264 Nketia, J.H. Kwabena. 1956. The Gramophone and Contemporary African Music in the Gold Coast. *Proceedings of the West African Institute of Social and Economic Research* 5: 189–200.

3265 Read, Oliver and Welch, Walter L. 1976. *From Tin Foil to Stereo: The Evolution of the Phonograph,* 2nd edition. Indianapolis/New York: Howard Sams/Bobbs-Merrill.

3266 Schulz-Köhn, Dietrich. 1940. *Die Schallplatte auf dem Weltmarkt.* Berlin: Reher.

HOME TAPING

3267 Davies, Gillian and Hung, Michèle. 1993. *Private Copying of Music and Video.* London: Sweet & Maxwell.

3268 Fabbri, Franco. 1985. La copia privata: problemi e rimedi. In *Musica e sistema dell'informazione in Europa*, ed. Francesco Rampi. Milano: Unicopli. 233–46.

3269 Frith, Simon. 1988. Copyright and the Music Business. *Popular Music* 7(1): 57–75.

3270 Koranteng, Juliana. 1991. Have Blank Tape Sales Reached Their Peak? *Music Business International* (July): 46.

3271 Laing, Dave. 1984. The Tape Levy. *Popular Music* 4: 93–94.

3272 Rignano, Guido. 1985. La copia privata: problemi e rimedi. In *Musica e sistema dell'informazione in Europa*, ed. Francesco Rampi. Milano: Unicopli. 256–60.

3273 Valenza, Pietro. 1985. La copia privata: problemi e rimedi. In *Musica e sistema dell'informazione in Europa*, ed. Francesco Rampi. Milano: Unicopli. 246–50.

INDEPENDENT LABELS

3274 Alsmann, Götz. 1985. *Nichts als Krach: Die unabhängigen Schallplattenfirmen und die Entwicklung der amerikanischen populären Musik*. Drensteinfurt: Huba.

3275 Brown, Mick. 1988. *Richard Branson: The Inside Story*. London: Michael Joseph.

3276 Carducci, Joe. 1990. *Rock and the Pop Narcotic*. Chicago: Redoubt Press.

3277 Escott, Colin and Hawkins, Martin. 1991. *Good Rockin' Tonight: Sun Records and the Birth of Rock 'n Roll*. New York: St. Martin's Press.

3278 George, Nelson. 1988. *The Death of Rhythm & Blues*. London: Omnibus.

3279 Gillett, Charlie. 1974. *Making Tracks: Atlantic Records and the Growth of a Multi-Billion Dollar Industry*. New York: E.P. Dutton.

3280 Goshern, Larry G. 1986. *Indy's Heart of Rock 'n' Roll*. Los Angeles: Metro Publications.

3281 Hamm, Wolfgang. 1985. Crescita e declino dell'indipendenza nel mercato musicale tedesco. In *Musica e sistema dell'informazione in Europa*, ed. Francesco Rampi. Milano: Unicopli. 136–44.

3282 Laing, Dave. 1985. Il settore indipendente dell'industria inglese. In *Musica e sistema dell'informazione in Europa*, ed. Francesco Rampi. Milano: Unicopli. 145–52.

3283 Laing, Dave. 1990. Making Popular Music: The Consumer as Producer. In *Consumption, Identity and Style: Markets, Meaning and the Packaging of Pleasure*, ed. Alan Tomlinson. London: Routledge. 184–94.

3284 Lee, Stephen. 1995. Re-examining the Concept of the 'Independent' Record Company: The Case of Wax Trax! Records. *Popular Music* 14(1): 13–23.

3285 Marshall, George. 1990. *The Two Tone Story*. Glasgow: Zoot Publishing.

3286 Meier, Uta. 1984. *Unabhängige Musikproduktion in Berlin: Zwischen Subkultur und alternativer Öffentlichkeit*. Nijmegen: University of Nijmegen, Department of Mass Communications.

3287 Rose, Tricia. 1994. Contracting Rap: An Interview with Carmen Ashurst-Watson. In *Microphone Fiends: Youth Music and Youth Culture*, ed. Andrew Ross and Tricia Rose. New York and London: Routledge. 122–44.

3288 Schreiber, Norman. 1986. *The Scouting Party Index of Independent Record Labels*. Brooklyn, NY: Scouting Party Press.

JUKEBOX

3289 Bodoh, A.G. 1977. The Jukebox, the Radio and the Record. *Journal of the Audio Engineering Society* 25(10/11): 836–42.

3290 Bowers, Q. David. 1986. *Nickelodeon Theatres and Their Music*. New York: Vestal Press.

3291 Krivine, John. 1977. *Juke Box Saturday Night*. London: New English Library.

3292 McCormick, Moira. 1987. CD Jukeboxes Are Getting Big Play. *Billboard* (21 November): 1, 81.

3293 Pearce, Chris. 1991. *Jukebox Art*. London: H.C. Blossom.

LAWSUITS

3294 Bagehot, Richard. 1989. *Music Business Agreements*. London: Waterlow.

3295 Cloonan, Martin. 1995. 'I Fought the Law': Popular Music and British Obscenity Law. *Popular Music* 14(3): 349–63.

3296 Garfield, Simon. 1986. *Expensive Habits: The Dark Side of the Music Industry*. London: Faber & Faber.

3297 Garfield, Simon. 1986. *Money for Nothing: Greed and Exploitation in the Music Industry*. Boston, MA: Faber & Faber.

3298 Kennedy, David. 1990. Frankenchrist Versus the State: The New Right, Rock Music and the Case of Jello Biafra. *Journal of Popular Culture* 24(1): 131–48.

3299 Lowenthal, Daniel K. 1953. *Trends in the Licensing of Popular Song Hits, 1940–1953*. New York: Bureau of Applied Social Research, Columbia University.

3300 Salewicz, Chris. 1987. See You in Court ... *Q* 1(10): 46–49.

MANAGEMENT

3301 Bagehot, Richard. 1989. *Music Business Agreements*. London: Waterlow.

3302 Bicknell, Ed. 1991. Management. In *The Rock File: Making It in the Music Business*, ed. Norton York. Oxford: Oxford University Press. 183–93.

3303 Dannen, Fredric. 1990. *Hit Men: Power Brokers and Fast Money Inside the Music Business*. New York: Times Books.

3304 George, Nelson. 1988. *The Death of Rhythm & Blues*. London: Omnibus.

3305 Napier-Bell, Simon. 1983. *You Don't Have To Say You Love Me*. London: Nomis.

3306 Rogan, Johnny. 1988. *Starmakers and Svengalis: The History of British Pop Management*. London: Queen Anne Press.

THE MARKET

3307 Breen, Marcus. 1995. The End of the World as We Know It: Popular Music's Cultural Mobility. *Cultural Studies* 9(3) (September): 486–504.

3308 Christianen, Michael. 1995. Cycles in Symbol Production? A New Model to Explain Concentration, Diversity and Innovation in the Music Industry. *Popular Music* 14(1): 55–94.

3309 Frith, Simon. 1981. *Sound Effects*. New York: Pantheon.

3310 Garnham, Nicholas. 1987. Concepts of Culture, Public Policy and Cultural Industries. *Cultural Studies* 1(1): 23–27.

3311 Hesmondhalgh, David. 1996. Flexibility, Post-Fordism and the Music Industries. *Media, Culture and Society* 18(3) (July): 469–88.

3312 Laing, Dave. 1969. *The Sound of Our Time*. London: Sheed & Ward.

3313 Lash, Scott and Urry, John. 1994. *Economies of Signs and Space*. London: Sage.

3314 Miège, Bernard. 1989. *The Capitalisation of Cultural Production*. New York: International General.

3315 Peterson, Richard A. and Berger, David G. 1971. Cycles in Symbol Production: The Case of Popular Music. *American Sociological Review* 40: 158–73.

3316 Rutten, Paul. 1994. Lokale Musik und der internationale Marktplatz. *PopScriptum* 2: 31–45.

3317 Towse, Ruth. 1993. *Singers in the Marketplace: The Economics of the Singing Profession*. Oxford: Clarendon Press.

3318 Zeppenfeld, Werner. 1979. *Tonträger in der Bundesrepublik Deutschland. Anatomie eines medialen Massenmarkts.* Bochum: Studienverlag Brockmeyer.

MARKETING

3319 Barszcz, J. 1982. It's the Same Old Song: Punk, New Wave, and the Marketing of Rock. In *American Mass Media*, ed. R. Atwan, B. Orton and W. Vesterman, 2nd edition. New York: Random House. 282–88.

3320 Hall, Charles W. and Taylor, Frederick J. 1996. *Marketing in the Music Industry.* Needham Heights, MA: Simon & Schuster Custom Publishing.

3321 Negus, Keith. 1992. *Producing Pop: Culture and Conflict in the Popular Music Industry.* London: Edward Arnold.

3322 Negus, Keith. 1993. Plugging and Programming: Pop Radio and Record Promotion in Britain and the United States. *Popular Music* 12(1): 57–68.

3323 Schmitz, Martina. 1987. Record Packaging . . . The Beginning of the Art. *Grammy Pulse* (October): 28–31.

3324 Stokes, Geoffrey. 1976. *Star-Making Machinery: The Odyssey of an Album.* Indianapolis, IN: Bobbs-Merrill.

MUSIC BUSINESS

3325 Bagehot, Richard. 1989. *Music Business Agreements.* London: Waterlow.

3326 Banks, Jack. 1996. *Monopoly Television: MTV's Quest to Control the Music.* Boulder, CO: Westview Press.

3327 Berland, Jody. 1991. Free Trade and Canadian Music: Level Playing Field or Scorched Earth? *Cultural Studies* 5(3): 317–25.

3328 BIPE. 1985. *L'Économie du domaine musical.* Paris: La Documentation française.

3329 Blake, Andrew. 1992. *The Music Business.* London: Batsford.

3330 Borzillo, Carrie. 1993. Many Sides of Muzak Elevate Seattle Co to New Status. *Billboard* (20 February): 1, 79.

3331 Brolinson, Per-Erik and Larsen, Holger. 1981. *Rock . . . Aspekter på industri, elektronik och sound.* Stockholm: Esselte Studium.

3332 Burnett, Robert. 1996. *The Global Jukebox: The International Music Industry.* London: Routledge.

3333 Cable, Michael. 1977. *The Pop Industry Inside Out.* London: W.H. Allen.

3334 Chapple, Steve and Garofalo, Reebee. 1977. *Rock 'n' Roll Is Here to Pay: The History and Politics of the Music Industry.* Chicago: Nelson-Hall.

3335 Christianen, Michael. 1995. Cycles in Symbol Production? A New Model to Explain Concentration, Diversity and Innovation in the Music Industry. *Popular Music* 14(1): 55–94.

3336 Clark, Dick. 1978. *Rock, Roll and Remember.* New York: Popular Library.

3337 Cohen, Sara. 1991. Popular Music and Urban Regeneration: The Music Industries of Merseyside. *Cultural Studies* 13: 332–46.

3338 Collier, James L. 1976. *Making Music for Money.* New York: Watts.

3339 Constantin, Philippe. 1971. Pop et profit: le changement dans la continuité. *Musique en jeu* 2: 95–101.

3340 Csida, Joseph. 1978. *American Entertainment: A Unique History of Popular Show Business.* New York: Watson-Guptill.

3341 Dannen, Fredric. 1990. *Hit Men: Power Brokers and Fast Money Inside the Music Business*. New York: Times Books.

3342 Davis, Norena Ann. 1987. *How the Music Business Works*. Brighton: Harvester Press.

3343 Dearing, James. 1982. *Making Money Making Music: No Matter Where You Live*. Cincinnati: Writer's Digest Books.

3344 de Coster, Michel. 1976. *Le Disque, art ou affaires? Analyse sociologique d'une industrie*. Grenoble: Presses universitaires de Grenoble.

3345 Eliot, Marc. 1990. *Rockonomics: The Money Behind the Music*. London: Omnibus.

3346 Elliot, Dave. 1981. The Rock Music Industry. In *Science, Technology and Popular Culture, 1*. Milton Keynes: Open University Press. 5–51.

3347 Fabbri, Franco. 1985. Sviluppo tecnologico e strutture produttive nell'industria musicale. In *Musica e sistema dell'informazione in Europa*, ed. Francesco Rampi. Milano: Unicopli. 51–60.

3348 Feurich, Hans-Jürgen. 1977. Warengeschichte und Rockmusik. In *Rockmusik*, ed. Wolfgang Sandner. Mainz: Schott. 53–80.

3349 Fink, Michael. 1989. *Inside the Music Business: Music in Contemporary Life*. New York: Schirmer Books.

3350 Fisher, Clive. 1987. *Music Industry Organisations: A Specially Commissioned Report*. London: Longman.

3351 Fox, Ted. 1986. *In the Groove*. New York: St. Martin's Press.

3352 Frith, Simon. 1983. *Sound Effects: Youth, Leisure and the Politics of Rock 'n' Roll*. London: Constable.

3353 Frith, Simon. 1991. Anglo-America and Its Discontents. *Cultural Studies* 5(3): 263–69.

3354 Frith, Simon. 1992. (1987) The Industrialisation of Popular Music. In *Popular Music & Communication*, ed. James Lull, revised edition. Newbury Park, CA: Sage. 49–74. First published London: Sage, 1987.

3355 Gammond, Peter and Horricks, Raymond. 1980. *The Music Goes Round and Round: A Cool Look at the Record Industry*. London: Quartet.

3356 Garfield, Simon. 1986. *Expensive Habits: The Dark Side of the Music Industry*. London: Faber & Faber.

3357 Garofalo, Reebee. 1991. The Internationalization of the US Music Industry and Its Impact on Canada. *Cultural Studies* 5(3): 326–31.

3358 Garofalo, Reebee. 1993. Whose World, What Beat: The Transnational Music Industry, Identity and Cultural Imperialism. *The World of Music* 35(2): 16–32.

3359 Glanvill, Rick. 1989. World Music Mining: The International Trade in New Music. In *Rhythms of the World*, ed. Francis Hanly and Tim May. London: BBC Books. 58–67.

3360 Goldberg, Isaac. 1961. (1930) *Tin Pan Alley: A Chronicle of American Popular Music*. New York: Ungar.

3361 Hammond, Ray. 1983. *Working in the Music Business*. Poole: Blandford Press.

3362 Harker, Dave. 1980. *One for the Money: Politics and Popular Song*. London: Hutchinson.

3363 Hirsch, Paul M. 1970. *The Structure of the Music Industry*. Ann Arbor, MI: Survey Research Center, University of Michigan.

3364 Huntley, Leston. 1965. *The Language of the Music Business*. Nashville, TN: Da Capo Press.

3365 Hurst, Walter E. 1981. *The Music Industry Book: Protect Yourself Before You Lose Your Rights and Royalties*. Hollywood, CA: Seven Arts.

3366 Jones, Steve. 1993. Popular Music, Criticism, Advertising and the Music Industry. *Journal of Popular Music Studies* 5: 79–91.

3367 Jones, Steve. 1994. Populäre Musik, Musikkritik, Werbung und die Musikindustrie. *PopScriptum* 2: 46–61.

3368 Karshner, Roger. 1971. *The Music Machine*. Los Angeles: Nash Publishing.

3369 Kimura, Atsuko. 1991. Japanese Corporations and Popular Music. *Popular Music* 10(3): 317–27.

3370 Kuhnke, Klaus and Miller, Manfred. 1980. Der Kampf ums große Geld. *Anschläge* 2(6): 39–53.

3371 Kurkela, Vesa. 1993. Deregulation of Popular Music in the European Post-Communist Countries: Business Identity and Cultural Collage. *The World of Music* 35(3): 80–196.

3372 Laing, Dave. 1969. *The Sound of Our Time*. London: Sheed & Ward.

3373 Laing, Dave. 1986. The Music Industry and the 'Cultural Imperialism' Thesis. *Media, Culture and Society* 8(3): 331–42.

3374 Laing, Dave. 1992. 'Sadeness', Scorpions and Single Markets: National and Transnational Trends in European Popular Music. *Popular Music* 11(2): 127–40.

3375 Lange, André. 1987. *Stratégies de la musique*. Brussels: Mardaga.

3376 Langman, D. 1993. Australian Women's Contemporary Music Inc.: The Case for Feminist Intervention into the Music Industry. *Perfect Beat* 1(2): 90–94.

3377 Lazarsfeld, Paul F. and Stanton, F.N., eds. 1941. *Radio Research 1941*. New York: Duell, Sloan & Pearce.

3378 Lyng, Robert. 1995. *Die Praxis im Musikbusiness*. Hamburg: PPV Presse Project.

3379 Mabey, Richard. 1968. *Behind the Scene*. London: Penguin.

3380 Malm, Krister and Wallis, Roger. 1984. Transculturation and the Rise of National Pop and Rock in Small Countries. In *Tvärspel: 31 artiklar om musik. Festskrift till Jan Ling*. Göteborg: Skrifter från Musikvetenskapliga institutionen, 9. 79–90.

3381 Malm, Krister and Wallis, Roger. 1992. *Media Policy and Music Activity*. London: Routledge.

3382 Manuel, Peter. 1991. The Cassette Industry and Popular Music in North India. *Popular Music* 10(2): 189–204.

3383 Manuel, Peter. 1991. Salsa and the Music Industry: Corporate Control of Grassroots Expression? In *Essays on Cuban Music: North American and Cuban Perspectives*, ed. Peter Manuel. Lanham, MD: University Press of America. 157–80.

3384 Manuel, Peter. 1993. *Cassette Culture: Popular Music and Technology in North India*. London and Chicago: University of Chicago Press.

3385 McDougald, D., Jr. 1941. The Popular Music Industry. In *Radio Research 1941*, ed. Paul F. Lazarsfeld and F.N. Stanton. New York: Duell, Sloan & Pearce.

3386 Moser, Rolf and Scheuermann, Andreas. 1993. *Handbuch der Musikwirtschaft*. Starnberg: Keller.

3387 Negus, Keith. 1992. *Producing Pop: Culture and Conflict in the Popular Music Industry.* London: Arnold.

3388 Newman, Mark. 1988. *Entrepreneurs of Profit and Pride: From Black Appeal to Radio Soul.* New York: Praeger.

3389 Passman, Donald S. 1991. *All You Need to Know About the Music Business.* New York: Prentice-Hall.

3390 Peterson, Richard A. 1975. *Single-Industry Firm to Conglomerate Synergistics: Alternative Strategies for Selling Insurance and Country Music.* Los Angeles: John Edwards Memorial Foundation.

3391 Peterson, Richard A. and Berger, David G. 1971. Entrepreneurship in Organizations: Evidence from the Popular Music Industry. *Administrative Science Quarterly* 16: 97–106.

3392 Peterson, Richard A. and Berger, David G. 1990. (1975) Cycles in Symbol Production: The Case of Popular Music. In *On Record: Rock, Pop and the Written Word,* ed. Simon Frith and Andrew Goodwin. London: Routledge. 140–59. (First published in *American Sociological Review* 40 (1975): 158–73.)

3393 Rampi, Francesco, ed. 1985. *Musica e sistema dell'informazione in Europa.* Milano: Unicopli.

3394 Rapaport, Diane Sward. 1992. *How to Make and Sell Your Own Recording: A Guide for the Nineties.* Englewood Cliffs, NJ: Prentice-Hall.

3395 Robinson, Deanna Campbell, Elizabeth B. Buck and Marlene Cuthbert, eds.1991. *Music at the Margins: Popular Music and Global Cultural Diversity.* Newbury Park, CA: Sage.

3396 Rupprecht, Siegfried P. 1984. *Pop: Von der Musikrevolution zum Jugendkonsum; das große Geschäft mit der Pop-Musik.* Heidelberg: Eggert.

3397 Rutten, Paul. 1991. Local Popular Music in the National and International Markets. *Cultural Studies* 5(3): 294–305.

3398 Ryan, John. 1985. *The Production of Culture in the Music Industry: The ASCAP-BMI Controversy.* Lanham, MD: University Press of America.

3399 Ryan, John and Peterson, Richard A. 1982. The Product Image: The Fate of Creativity in Country Music Songwriting. In *Mass Media Organisations: Creativity and Constraint,* ed. James S. Ettama and D. Charles Whitney. Beverly Hills, CA: Sage. 11–32.

3400 Sanjek, Russell. 1983. *From Print to Plastic.* Brooklyn, NY: Institute for Studies in American Music.

3401 Sanjek, Russell. 1988. *American Popular Music and Its Business: The First Four Hundred Years. Vol. 1 The Beginning to 1790; Vol. 2 From 1790 to 1900; Vol. 3 From 1900 to 1980.* New York: Oxford University Press.

3402 Sanjek, Russell, and Sanjek, David. 1991. *The American Popular Music Business in the 20th Century.* New York: Oxford University Press.

3403 Schmidt-Joos, Siegfried. 1960. *Geschäfte mit Schlagern.* Bremen: Schünemann.

3404 Schulze, Ralf. 1996. *Die Musikwirtschaft. Marktstrukturen und Wettbewerbsstrategien der Deutschen Musikindustrie.* Hamburg: Kammerer & Unverzagt.

3405 Schulz-Köhn, Dietrich. 1940. *Die Schallplatte auf dem Weltmarkt.* Berlin: Reher.

3406 Seltzer, George. 1989. *Music Matters: The Performer and the American Federation of Musicians.* Metuchen, NJ: Scarecrow Press.

3407 Shemeil, Sidney and Krasilovsky, William. 1990. (1966) *This Business of Music: A Practical Guide to the Music*

Industry for Publishers, Writers, Record Companies, Producers, Artists and Agents, 6th edition. New York: Billboard Books. First published New York: Billboard Books, 1966.

3408 Smith, Joe. 1988. *Off the Record: An Oral History of Popular Music*. New York: Warner Books.

3409 Steinel, Roland. 1992. *Zur Lage und Problematik der Musikwirtschaft*. München: Edition Roland/Intermedia.

3410 Stokes, Geoffrey. 1976. *Star-Making Machinery: The Odyssey of an Album*. Indianapolis, IN: Bobbs-Merrill.

3411 Toll, Robert C. 1982. *The Entertainment Machine: American Show Business in the Twentieth Century*. New York and London: Oxford University Press.

3412 Tunstall, Jeremy. 1977. *The Media Are American*. London: Constable.

3413 Vogel, Harold L. 1996. *Entertainment Industry Economics: A Guide for Financial Analysts*. Cambridge and New York: Cambridge University Press.

3414 Wale, Michael. 1972. *Voxpop: Profiles of the Pop Process*. London: Harrap.

3414a Wallis, Roger. 1995. The Global Cultural Industries: Common Trends and System Defects. In *Popular Music Perspectives III*, ed. Peter Wicke. Berlin: Zyankrise. 23–37.

3415 Wallis, Roger and Malm, Krister. 1984. *Big Sounds from Small Peoples: The Music Industry in Small Countries*. London: Constable.

3416 Wallis, Roger and Malm, Krister. 1987. The International Music Industry and Transnational Communication. In *Popular Music & Communication*, ed. James Lull. Newbury Park, CA: Sage. 112–39.

3417 Wallis, Roger and Malm, Krister. 1990. The Implications of Structural Changes in the Music Industry for Media Policy and Music Activity: A Research Framework. In *Popular Music Research*, ed. Keith Roe and Ulla Karlsson. Göteborg: NORDICOM-Sweden, No. 1–2. 11–20.

3418 Wallis, Roger and Malm, Krister. 1990. (1984) Patterns of Change. In *On Record: Rock, Pop and the Written Word*. ed. Simon Frith and Andrew Goodwin. London: Routledge. 160–80.

3419 No entry.

3420 Wicke, Peter. 1988. Musikindustrie in den USA - Eine Analyse. *Beilage zur Zeitschrift 'Unterhaltungskunst'* 12.

3421 Wicke, Peter. 1991. *Bigger than Life: Musik und Musikindustrie in den USA - Porträt einer Musikszene*. Leipzig: Reclam.

3422 Wolfe, Arnold S. 1985. Reward Systems in Popular Music. *ONE-TWO-THREE-FOUR* 1(2): 35–54.

3423 York, Norton, ed. 1991. *The Rock File: Making It in the Music Business*. Oxford: Oxford University Press.

3424 Zeppenfeld, Werner. 1979. *Tonträger in der Bundesrepublik Deutschland. Anatomie eines medialen Massenmarkts*. Bochum: Studienverlag Brockmeyer.

MUSIC TELEVISION

3425 Banks, Jack. 1996. *Monopoly Television: MTV's Quest to Control the Music*. Boulder, CO: Westview Press.

3426 Cosgrove, Stuart. 1987. TV Pop in Crisis. *New Musical Express* (7 March): 13–17.

3427 Denisoff, R. Serge. 1988. *Inside MTV*. New Brunswick, NJ: Transaction.

3428 Fiske, John. 1986. MTV: Post Structural Post Modern. *Journal of Communication Inquiry* 10(1): 74–79.

3429 Fiske, John. 1987. British Cultural Studies and Television. In *Channels of Discourse: TV and Contemporary Criticism*, ed. Robert C. Allen. Chapel Hill and London: University of North Carolina Press. 254–90.

3430 Frith, Simon. 1989. Europop. *Cultural Studies* 3(2): 166–72.

3431 Goodwin, Andrew. 1993. *Dancing in the Distraction Factory: Music Television and Popular Culture*. London: Routledge.

3432 Grossberg, Lawrence. 1988. You (Still) Have to Fight for Your Right to Party: Music Television as Billboards of Post-Modern Difference. *Popular Music* 7(3): 315–32.

3433 Hartman, John K. 1989. MTV: Second Time Around. *ONE-TWO-THREE-FOUR* 6: 33–39.

3434 Hill, John. 1991. Television and Pop: The Case of the 1950s. In *Popular Television in Britain: Studies in Cultural History*, ed. John Corner. London: BFI Publishing. 54–79.

3435 Kaplan, E. Ann. 1985. A Post-Modern Play of the Signifier? Advertising, Pastiche and Schizophrenia in Music TV. In *Television in Transition*, ed. Phillip Drummond and Richard Paterson. London: British Film Institute. 135–45.

3436 Kaplan, E. Ann. 1986. History, the Historical Spectator and Gender Address in Music Television. *Journal of Communication Inquiry* 10(1): 3–14.

3437 Kaplan, E. Ann. 1987. *Rocking Around the Clock: Music Television, Postmodernism and Consumer Culture*. New York and London: Methuen.

3438 Lorch, Sue. 1988. Metaphor, Metaphysics and MTV. *Journal of Popular Culture* 22(3): 143–56.

3439 Mitchell, Tony. 1993. Treaty Now! Indigenous Music and Music Television in Australia. *Media, Culture and Society* 15: 299–308.

3440 Wallis, Roger and Malm, Krister. 1988. Push-Pull for the Video Clip: A Systems Approach to the Relationship Between the Phonogram/Videogram Industry and Music Television. *Popular Music* 7(3): 267–84.

PAYOLA

3441 Dannen, Fredric. 1990. *Hit Men: Power Brokers and Fast Money Inside the Music Business*. New York: Times Books.

3442 Morthland, John. 1980. Payola. In *The Rolling Stone Illustrated History of Rock and Roll*, ed. Jim Miller. San Francisco: Rolling Stone Books.

3443 Segrave, Kerry. 1994. *Payola in the Music Industry: A History, 1880–1991*. Jefferson and London: McFarland.

PIRACY AND BOOTLEGS

3444 Alloway, Nicholas, ed. 1984. *50 Years of the International Federation of the Phonographic Industry (IFPI)*. London: IFPI.

3445 Coover, James. 1985. *Music Publishing, Copyright and Piracy in Victorian England*. London and New York: Mansell.

3446 Davies, Gillian. 1986. *Piracy of Phonograms*. London: ESC Publishing.

3447 Heylin, Clinton. 1994. *The Great White Wonders: A History of Bootlegs*. London and New York: Viking.

3448 Knoedelseder, William. 1993. *Stiffed: A True Story of MCA, the Music Business and the Mafia*. New York: HarperCollins.

3449 Oswald, John. 1987. Plunderphonics, or Audio Piracy as a Compositional

Prerogative. *Re Records Quarterly* 2(1): 24–29.

3450 Picardie, Justine and Wade, Dorothy. 1993. *Atlantic and the Godfathers of Rock and Roll*. London: Fourth Estate.

3451 Steinmetz, Helmut. 1982. Copyright, Neighbouring Rights and Piracy in Austria. In *The Phonogram in Cultural Communication*. ed. Kurt Blaukopf. Wien: Springer-Verlag. 141–51.

PRODUCTION

3452 Busse, Burkhard. 1976. *Der deutsche Schlager. Eine Untersuchung zur Produktion, Distribution und Rezeption von Trivialliteratur*. Wiesbaden: Athenaion.

3453 Clarke, Paul. 1983. A 'Magic Science': Rock Music as a Recording Art. *Popular Music* 3: 195–213.

3454 Cunningham, Mark, ed. 1996. *A History of Record Production*. London: Castle/ Penguin.

3455 Cutler, Chris. 1985. The Studio as Instrument (2): Whose Future of Music? *Re Records Quarterly* 1(2): 28–30.

3456 Dowd, Tom. 1994. Atlantic Records: Tom Dowd's 50 Year Multitrack Revolution. *Pro Sound News Europe* (January): 20–22.

3457 Fikentscher, Kai. 1991. Supremely Clubbed, Devastatingly Dubbed: Some Observations on the Nature of Mixes on 12-inch Dance Singles. *Tracking: Popular Music Studies* 4(1): 9–15.

3458 Gaisberg, Fred. 1972. (1942) *The Music Goes Round*, revised edition. New York: Arno Press.

3459 Gillett, Charlie. 1980. The Producer as Artist. In *The Phonograph and Our Musical Life*, ed. H. Wiley Hitchcock. Brooklyn, NY: Institute for Studies in American Music/CUNY. 51–56.

3460 Goodwin, Andrew. 1992. Rationalization and Democratization in the New Technologies of Popular Music. In *Popular Music & Communication*, ed. James Lull, 2nd edition. Newbury Park, CA: Sage. 75–100.

3461 Hennion, Antoine. 1981. *Les Professionnels du disque*. Paris: A.-M. Métailié.

3462 Jones, Steve. 1992. *Rock Formation: Music, Technology & Mass Communication*. Newbury Park, CA: Sage.

3463 Lortat-Jacob, Bernard. 1984. Music and Complex Societies: Control and Management of Musical Production. *Yearbook for Traditional Music* 16: 19–33.

3464 Martin, George, ed. 1983. *Making Music*. New York: Quill.

3465 Moore, Steve. 1985. The Recording Studio as a Musical Instrument. *Re Records Quarterly* 1(1): 32–33.

3466 Muirhead, Bert. 1984. *The Record Producers File*. Poole: Blandford Press.

3467 Negus, Keith. 1994. Zwischen Unternehmen und Verbraucher. *PopScriptum* 2: 62–81.

3468 Porcello, Thomas. 1991. The Ethics of Digital Audio Sampling: Engineers' Discourse. *Popular Music* 10(1): 69–84.

3469 Struthers, S. 1987. Technology in the Art of Recording. In *Lost in Music: Culture, Style and the Musical Event*, ed. Avron Levine White. London: Routledge. 241–58.

3470 Tankel, Jonathan David. 1990. The Practice of Recording Music: Remixing as Recoding. *Journal of Communication* 40(3): 34–46.

3471 Tennstedt, Florian. 1979. *Rockmusik und Gruppenprozesse.* München: Wilhelm Fink.

3472 Théberge, Paul. 1989. The 'Sound' of Music: Technological Rationalization and the Production of Popular Music. *New Formations* 8: 99–111.

3473 Tobler, John and Grundy, Stuart. 1982. *The Record Producers.* London: BBC Books.

3474 Vignolle, Jean-Pierre. 1980. Mixing Genres and Reaching the Public: The Production of Popular Music. *Social Science Information* 19(1): 79–105.

3475 Wadhams, Wayne. 1987. *Dictionary of Music Production and Engineering Terminology.* New York: Schirmer.

3476 Welding, Pete. 1987. Control: The Performer/Producer Relationship. *Grammy Pulse* (October): 18–20.

3477 Wicke, Peter. 1986. Theoretische Probleme der Produktion von Rockmusik. *Beilage zur Zeitschrift 'Unterhaltungskunst'* 3.

3478 Wicke, Peter. 1990. Populäre Musik und neue Medien - Musikkultur im Umbruch. *Musik und Gesellschaft* XL(10): 480–85.

PUBLISHING AND PUBLISHERS

3479 Bennett, Roy C. 1983. *The Songwriter's Guide to Writing and Selling Hit Songs.* Englewood Cliffs, NJ: Prentice-Hall.

3480 Cooper, Jay L. 1971. *Record and Music Publishing Forms of Agreement in Current Use.* New York: Law-Arts Books.

3481 Coover, James. 1985. *Music Publishing, Copyright and Piracy in Victorian England.* London and New York: Mansell.

3482 Ehrlich, Cyril. 1989. *Harmonious Alliance: A History of the Performing Right Society.* Oxford: Oxford University Press.

3483 Feist, Leonard. 1980. *An Introduction to Popular Music Publishing in the USA.* New York: National Music Publishers Association.

3484 Fisher, William Arms. 1933. *One Hundred and Fifty Years of Music Publishing in the United States, 1783–1933.* Boston, MA: Ditson.

3485 Jasen, David A. 1988. *Tin Pan Alley: The Composers, the Songs, the Performers and Their Times.* New York/London: Donald A. Fine/Omnibus.

3486 National Music Publishers Association. 1996. *World Music Publishing Revenues.* New York: National Music Publishers Association.

3487 Peacock, Alan and Weir, Ronald. 1975. *The Composer in the Market Place.* London: Faber Music.

3488 Prato, Paolo. 1987. L'editoria della popular music in Italia. *Musica/Realtà* 26: 75–86.

3489 Ryan, John. 1985. *The Production of Culture in the Music Industry: The ASCAP-BMI Controversy.* Lanham, MD: University Press of America.

3490 Tichenor, Trebor Jay. 1989. John Stilwell Stark, Piano Ragtime Publisher: Readings from 'The Intermezzo' and His Personal Ledgers, 1905–1908. *Black Music Research Journal* 9(2): 193–204.

RADIO

3491 Alm, Arí. 1992. Radiomafia: The New Business Approach. In *Broadcasting Research Review, 1992,* ed. Heikki Kasari. Helsinki: Yleisradio. 8–19.

3492 Alm, Arí. 1992. Radion musiikkiviestinän muuttuvat merkitykset. In *Toosa Soi. Musiiki radion kilpailuvälineenä,* ed. Kimmo Salminen and Arí Alm. Helsinki: YLE Tutkimus ja kehitysosasto. 29–47.

3493 Banning, William Peck. 1946. *Commercial Broadcasting Pioneer: The WEAF Experiment, 1922–1925.* Cambridge, MA: Harvard University Press.

3494 Barnard, Stephen. 1989. *On the Radio: Music Radio in Britain.* Milton Keynes: Open University Press.

3495 Barnes, Ken. 1989. Top 40 Radio: A Fragment of the Imagination. In *Facing the Music,* ed. Simon Frith. New York: Pantheon. 8–50.

3496 Barnett, Steven and Morrison, David. 1989. *The Listener Speaks: The Radio Audience and the Future of Radio.* London: HMSO.

3497 Batel, Günther. 1981. Mass Media and Contemporary Musical Life ('Funkkolleg Musik'). In *Stock-Taking of Musical Life: Sociography and Music Education,* ed. Desmond Mark. Wien: Doblinger. 52–55.

3498 Berland, Jody. 1990. Radio Space and Industrial Time: Music Formats, Local Narratives and Technological Mediation. *Popular Music* 9(2): 179–92.

3499 Chapman, Robert. 1990. The 1960s Pirates: A Comparative Analysis of Radio London and Radio Caroline. *Popular Music* 9(2): 165–78.

3500 Chapman, Robert. 1992. *Selling the Sixties: The Pirates and Pop Music Radio.* London: Routledge.

3501 Denisoff, R. Serge. 1974. The Evolution of Pop Music in Broadcasting: 1920–1972. *Popular Music & Society* 2: 202–26.

3502 Eberly, Philip K. 1982. *Music in the Air: America's Changing Tastes in Popular Music, 1920–1980.* New York: Hastings House.

3503 Fowler, Gene and Crawford, Bill. 1987. *Border Radio.* Austin, TX: Texas Monthly Press.

3504 Gambaccini, Paul. 1976. American Radio Today. In *Rock File 4,* ed. Charlie Gillett and Simon Frith. St. Alban's: Granada. 47–56.

3505 Garner, Ken. 1990. New Gold Dawn: The Traditional English Breakfast Show in 1989. *Popular Music* 9(2): 193–202.

3506 Grenier, Line. 1990. Radio Broadcasting in Canada: The Case of 'Transformat' Music. *Popular Music* 9(2): 221–34.

3507 Hamm, Charles. 1991. 'The Constant Companion of Man': Separate Development, Radio Bantu and Music. *Popular Music* 10(2) (May): 147–74.

3508 Hennion, Antoine and Méadel, Cécile. 1986. Programming Music: Radio as Mediator. *Media, Culture and Society* 8(3): 281–304. (First published in *Vibrations* 1 (1985): 54–70.)

3509 Hesbacher, Peter. 1974. Sound Exposure in Radio: The Misleading Nature of the Playlist. *Popular Music & Society* 2: 189–201.

3510 Hind, John and Mosco, Stephen. 1985. *Rebel Radio.* London: Pluto Press.

3511 Julien, Jean-Rémy. 1985. The Use of Folklore and Popular Music in Radio Advertising. In *Popular Music Perspectives, 2,* ed. David Horn. Göteborg and Exeter: IASPM. 417–27.

3512 Kloosterman, Robert C. and Quispel, Chris. 1990. Not Just the Same Old Show on My Radio: An Analysis of the Role of Radio in the Diffusion of Black Music Among Whites in the South of the United States, 1920 to 1960. *Popular Music* 9(2): 151–64.

3513 Kramarz, Volkmar. 1994. The Kids and the Radio. In *Populäre Musik und Pädagogik - Grundlagen und Praxismaterialien,* ed. Jürgen Terhag.

Oldershausen: Institut für Didaktik der
populären Musik. 202–206.

3514 MacFarland, David T. 1979. *The Development of the Top Forty Radio Format.* New York: Arno Press.

3515 Mackenzie, Harry and Polomski, Lothar. 1991. *One Night Stand Series, 1–1001.* Westport and London: Greenwood Press.

3516 Melton, Gary W. and Galician, Mary-Lou. 1987. A Sociological Approach to the Pop Music Phenomenon: Radio and Music Video Utilization for Expectation, Motivation and Satisfaction. *Popular Music & Society* 11(3): 35–46.

3517 Münch, Thomas. 1991. *Pop-Fit. Musikdramaturgie in Servicewellen: Eine Fallstudie.* Pfaffenweiler: Centaurus-Verlagsgesellschaft.

3518 Negus, Keith. 1993. Plugging and Programming: Pop Radio and Record Promotion in Britain and the United States. *Popular Music* 12(1): 57–68.

3519 Newman, Mark. 1988. *Entrepreneurs of Profit and Pride: From Black Appeal to Radio Soul.* New York: Praeger.

3520 Nysten, Leif. 1992. Rundradions svenskspråkiga radiokanal: en musikpolitisk betraktelse. In *Toosa Soi. Musiiki radion kilpailuvälineenä,* ed. Kimmo Salminen and Arí Alm. Helsinki: YLE Tutkimus ja kehitysosasto. 97–101.

3521 Packwald, Peter. 1987. *Rock 'n' Roll Is on the Air: Dreißig Jahre Jugendmusik im Hörfunk.* Heidelberg: Rüdiger Eggert.

3522 Potts, J. 1992. Heritage Rock: Pop Music on Australian Radio. In *From Pop to Punk to Postmodernism: Popular Music and Australian Culture from the 1960s to the 1990s,* ed. Philip Hayward. Sydney: Allen & Unwin.

3523 Redd, Lawrence N. 1974. *Rock Is Rhythm and Blues: The Impact of Mass Media.* East Lansing, MI: Michigan State University Press.

3524 Rothenbuhler, Eric W. 1987. Commercial Radio and Popular Music: Processes of Selection and Factors of Influence. In *Popular Music & Communication,* ed. James Lull. Newbury Park, CA: Sage. 78–95.

3525 Saucier, Robert. 1985. Programmation musicale et radio communautaire: l'exemple de Channel #5. *Communication Information* 7(3) (Autumn).

3526 Scannell, Paddy. 1981. Music for the Multitudes? The Dilemmas of the BBC's Music Policy, 1923–1946. *Media, Culture and Society* 3(3): 243–60.

3527 Sklar, Rick. 1984. *Rocking America: An Insider's Story. How the All-Hit Radio Stations Took Over.* New York: St. Martin's Press.

3528 Stockwell, Richard P. 1983. The Evolution of Country Radio Format. *Journal of Popular Culture* 16(4): 144–51.

3529 Straw, Will. 1995. Dance Music on North American Radio. In *Popular Music Perspectives III,* ed. Peter Wicke. Berlin: Zyankrise. 224–31.

3530 Wallis, Roger and Malm, Krister. 1982. The Interdependency of Broadcasting and the Phonogram Industry: Events in Kenya, March 1980. In *Popular Music Perspectives, 1,* ed. David Horn and Philip Tagg. Göteborg and Exeter: IASPM. 93–110.

3531 Warne, Steve. 1987. Beyond the Echoes: A Look at Public Radio. In *Missing in Action: Australian Popular Music,* ed. Marcus Breen. Melbourne: Verbal Graphics Pty. 167–83.

RECORD COMPANIES

3532 Aldridge, Benjamin. 1964. *The Victor Talking Machine Co.* New York: RCA Victor.

3533 Andrews, Frank. 1985. *Columbia 10-inch Records, 1904–30.* Rugby: City of London Phonograph and Gramophone Society.

3534 Brooks, Tim. 1978. Columbia Records in the 1890s: Founding the Record Industry. *Association for Recorded Sound Journal* 1: 3–36.

3535 Dixon, Robert M.W. and Godrich, John. 1970. *Recording the Blues.* London: November Books.

3536 Escott, Colin and Hawkins, Martin. 1987. *Sun Records: The Discography.* Vollersode: Bear Family Records.

3537 Escott, Colin and Hawkins, Martin. 1992. *Good Rockin' Tonight: Sun Records and the Birth of Rock 'n' Roll.* New York: St. Martin's Press.

3538 Fagan, Ted and Moran, William R. 1983. *The Encyclopedic Discography of Victor Recordings: Pre-Matrix Series (1900–37).* Westport, CT: Greenwood Press.

3539 Fagan, Ted and Moran, William R. 1986. *The Encyclopedic Discography of Victor Recordings: Matrix Series 1 through 4999 (1903–08).* New York: Greenwood Press.

3540 *Free Music Production: Twenty Years Free Music Production, 1969–1989.* 1989. Berlin: FMP.

3541 Gart, Galen. 1989. *The American Record Label Directory and Dating Guide, 1940–1959.* Milford, NH: Big Nickel Publications.

3542 Gillett, Charlie. 1975. *Making Tracks: The Story of Atlantic Records.* London: Panther.

3543 Jones, Geoffrey. 1985. The Gramophone Company: An Anglo-American Multi-National, 1898–1931. *Business History Review* 59(1): 76–100.

3544 Kennedy, Rick. 1994. *Jelly Roll, Bix and Hoagy: Gennett Studios and the Birth of Recorded Jazz.* Bloomington, IN: Indiana University Press.

3545 Knoedelseder, William. 1993. *Stiffed: A True Story of MCA, the Music Business and the Mafia.* New York: HarperCollins.

3546 Leadbitter, Mike. 1968. *Crowley, Louisiana Blues: The Story of J.D. Miller and His Blues Artists.* Bexhill-on-Sea: Blues Unlimited.

3547 Leadbitter, Mike and Shuler, Eddie. 1969. *From the Bayou: The Story of Goldband Records.* Bexhill-on-Sea: Blues Unlimited.

3548 Lombardi, John. 1986. King of the Schmooze (Walter Yetnikoff). *Esquire* (November): 118–29.

3549 Muirhead, Bert. 1983. *Stiff: The Story of a Label.* Poole: Blandford Press.

3550 Picardie, Justine and Wade, Dorothy. 1993. *Atlantic and the Godfathers of Rock and Roll.* London: Fourth Estate.

3551 Ruppli, Michel. 1980. *The Prestige Label: A Discography.* Westport, CT: Greenwood Press.

3552 Ruppli, Michel. 1980. *The Savoy Label: A Discography.* Westport, CT: Greenwood Press.

3553 Ruppli, Michel. 1983. *The Chess Labels: A Discography.* Westport and London: Greenwood Press.

3554 Ruppli, Michel. 1985. *The King Labels: A Discography.* Westport, CT: Greenwood Press.

3555 Ruppli, Michel. 1986. *The Clef/Verve Labels: A Discography*. New York and London: Greenwood Press.

3556 Ruppli, Michel. 1991. *The Aladdin-Imperial Labels: A Discography*. New York: Greenwood Press.

3557 Rust, Brian. 1973. *The American Record Label Book: From the Nineteenth Century through 1942*. Rochelle, NY: Arlington House.

3558 Seroff, Doug. 1989. Shifty Record Company. *Keskidee: A Journal of Black Musical Traditions* 2: 22–26.

RECORD INDUSTRY

3559 Beishuizen, J., ed. 1959. *The Industry of Human Happiness*. London: IFPI (International Federation of the Phonographic Industry).

3560 Blaukopf, Kurt. 1982. *The Strategies of the Record Industries*. Strasbourg: Council for Cultural Co-operation.

3561 Burnett, Robert C. 1990. *Concentration and Diversity in the International Phonogram Industry*. Göteborg: Department of Journalism and Mass Communication, University of Gothenburg.

3562 Burnett, Robert C. 1996. *The Global Jukebox*. London: Routledge.

3563 d'Angelo, Mario. 1989. *La Renaissance du disque: les mutations mondiales d'une industrie culturelle. Notes et études documentaires, no 4890*. Paris: La documentation française.

3564 Davis, Clive. 1975. *Inside the Record Business*. New York: Morrow.

3565 Denisoff, R. Serge. 1974. The Vinyl Crap Game: The Pop Record Industry. *Journal of Jazz Studies* 1(2): 3–26.

3566 Denisoff, R. Serge. 1975. *Solid Gold: The Popular Record Industry*. New Brunswick, NJ: Transaction.

3567 Denisoff, R. Serge. 1986. *Tarnished Gold: The Record Industry Revisited*. New Brunswick, NJ: Transaction.

3568 Faulkner, Robert R. 1971. *Hollywood Studio Musicians: Their Work and Career in the Recording Industry*. Chicago: Aldine-Atherton.

3569 Ferland, Yvon and Anderson, Robert D. 1982. The Recording Industry Survey Conducted in Canada. In *The Phonogram in Cultural Communication*, ed. Kurt Blaukopf. Wien: Springer-Verlag. 19–42.

3570 Frith, Simon. 1976. The A&R Men. In *Rock File 4*, ed. Charlie Gillett and Simon Frith. St. Alban's: Granada. 25–46.

3571 Frith, Simon. 1981. *Sound Effects: Youth, Leisure and the Politics of Rock 'n' Roll*, revised edition. New York: Pantheon. First published London: Constable, 1978.

3572 Frith, Simon. 1987. The Making of the British Record Industry, 1920–1964. In *Impacts and Influences*, ed. J. Curran, A. Smith and P. Wingate. London: Methuen. 278–91.

3573 Gillett, Charlie. 1983. (1970) *The Sound of the City*, revised edition. London: Souvenir Press.

3574 Gottleib, Anthony. 1991. Almost Grown: A Survey of the Music Business. *The Economist* 21 (December): 1–18.

3575 Gronow, Pekka. 1981. The Record Industry Comes to the Orient. *Journal of the Society for Ethnomusicology* 25 (2 May): 251–84.

3576 Gronow, Pekka. 1983. The Record Industry: The Growth of a Mass Medium. *Popular Music* 3: 53–76.

3577 Hardy, Phil. 1984. *The British Record Industry*. Exeter: IASPM UK.

3578 Harker, Dave. 1980. *One for the Money: Politics and Popular Song*. London: Hutchinson.

3579 Hennion, Antoine. 1981. *Les Professionnels du disque*. Paris: A.-M. Métailié.

3580 Hennion, Antoine. 1982. Popular Music as Social Production. In *Popular Music Perspectives, 1*, ed. David Horn and Philip Tagg. Göteborg and Exeter: IASPM. 32–40.

3581 Hennion, Antoine and Vignolle, Jean-Pierre. 1978. *L'Économie du disque en France*. Paris: La Documentation française.

3582 Hung, Michèle, and Garcia Morencos, Estaban. 1990. *World Record Sales, 1969–1990: A Statistical History of the World Recording Industry*. London: IFPI (International Federation of the Phonographic Industry).

3583 Joshi, G.N. 1988. A Concise History of the Phonography Industry in India. *Popular Music* 7(2): 147–56.

3584 Kawabata, Shigeru. 1991. The Japanese Record Industry. *Popular Music* 10(3): 327–45.

3585 Lange, André. 1987. *Stratégies de la musique*. Brussels: Mardaga.

3586 Lopes, Paul. 1992. Innovation and Diversity in the Popular Music Industry. *American Sociological Review* 57: 56–71.

3587 Luigi, Mario de. 1985. Mercato del disco in Italia: ieri, oggi, domani. In *Musica e sistema dell'informazione in Europa*, ed. Francesco Rampi. Milano: Unicopli. 41–50.

3588 Malm, Krister. 1982. Phonograms and Cultural Policy in Sweden. In *The Phonogram in Cultural Communication*, ed. Kurt Blaukopf. Wien: Springer-Verlag. 43–74.

3589 Negus, Keith. 1992. *Producing Pop: Culture and Conflict in the Popular Music Industry*. London: Edward Arnold.

3590 O'Shea, Shad. 1987. *Just for the Record*. Cincinnati: Positive Feedback.

3591 Peterson, Richard A. and Berger, David G. 1990. (1975) Cycles in Symbol Production: The Case of Popular Music. In *On Record: Rock, Pop and the Written Word*, ed. Simon Frith and Andrew Goodwin. London: Routledge. 140–59. (First published in *American Sociological Review* 40 (1975): 158–73.)

3592 Rust, Brian. 1977. The Development of the Record Industry: Part 1 The United States of America. Part 2 Europe. *The Gramophone* (April, May): 1521–22, 1527.

3593 Schulz-Köhn, Dietrich. 1940. *Die Schallplatte auf dem Weltmarkt*. Berlin: Reher.

3594 Segal, Ariane. 1985. Comunicazione sulla fonografica in Francia. In *Musica e sistema dell'informazione in Europa*, ed. Francesco Rampi. Milano: Unicopli. 80–84.

3595 Stokes, Geoffrey. 1976. *Star-Making Machinery: The Odyssey of an Album*. Indianapolis, IN: Bobbs-Merrill.

3596 Stratton, Jon. 1983. Capitalism and Romantic Ideology in the Record Business. *Popular Music* 3: 143–56.

3597 Wallis, Roger and Malm, Krister. 1982. The Interdependency of Broadcasting and the Phonogram Industry: Events in Kenya, March 1980. In *Popular Music Perspectives, 1*, ed. David Horn and Philip Tagg. Göteborg and Exeter: IASPM. 93–110.

3598 Wallis, Roger and Malm, Krister. 1988. Push-Pull for the Video Clip: A Systems Approach to the Relationship Between the Phonogram/Videogram Industry and Music Television. *Popular Music* 7(3): 267–84.

3599 Wexler, Jerry, and Ritz, David. 1994. *Rhythm and the Blues*. London: Jonathan Cape.

3600 Zeppenfeld, Werner. 1979. The Economics and Structure of the Record and Tape Industry: The Example of West Germany. In *Entertainment: A Cross-Cultural Examination*, ed. H. Fischer and S. Melnik. Hastings, NY: Communication Arts Books. 248–57.

3601 Zeppenfeld, Werner. 1979. *Tonträger in der Bundesrepublik Deutschland. Anatomie eines medialen Massenmarkts*. Bochum: Studienverlag Brockmeyer.

RECORD/PHONOGRAM

3602 Blaukopf, Kurt. 1970. *Technik, Wirtschaft und Ästhetik der Schallplatte*. Karlsruhe: Braun.

3603 Blaukopf, Kurt, ed. 1982. *The Phonogram in Cultural Communication*. Wien: Springer-Verlag.

3604 Bruch, Walter. 1983. *Von der Tonwalze zur Bildplatte. Ein Jahrhundert Ton- und Bildspeicherung*. München: Fancis.

3605 Dean, Roger and Thorgerson, Storm, eds. 1977. *Album Cover Album*. New York: A. & W. Visual Library.

3606 Dean, Roger and Howells, David, comps. 1987. *The Ultimate Album Cover Album*. New York: Prentice-Hall.

3607 Eisenberg, Evan. 1987. *The Recording Angel: Music, Records and Culture from Aristotle to Zappa*. New York: McGraw-Hill.

3608 Elste, Martin. 1981. A Plea for Historically Oriented Appreciation of Sound Recordings. In *Stock-Taking of Musical Life: Sociography and Music Education*, ed. Desmond Mark. Wien: Doblinger.

3609 Golovinskii, Grigoriy L. 1982. On Some Music Sociological Aspects of the Phonogram: The Record in Soviet Musical Culture. In *The Phonogram in Cultural Communication*, ed. Kurt Blaukopf. Wien: Springer-Verlag. 123–32.

3610 Hirsch, Hans. 1987. *Schallplatten zwischen Kunst und Kommerz. Fakten, Tendenzen und Überlegungen zur Produktion und Verbreitung von Tonträgern*. Wilhelmshaven: Noetzel.

3611 Koenigsberg, Allen. 1992. *The Patent History of the Phonograph*. New York: Antique Phonographs.

3612 Marsh, Graham. 1991. *The Cover Art of 'Blue Note'*. London: Collins & Brown.

3613 Peellaert, Guy and Cohn, Nik. 1973. *Rock Dreams*. London: Pan Books.

3614 Plasketes, George. 1992. Romancing the Record: The Vinyl De-Evolution and Subcultural Evolution. *Journal of Popular Culture* 26(1): 109–22.

3615 Seibold, Andreas. 1994. Zur Preisgestaltung von Tonträgern. *PopScriptum* 2: 121–30.

3616 Sörensen, Jens Erik. 1981. Vis mig dine covers og jeg skal sige dig hvem du er! Nogle typer. In *Skivomslag*. Stockholm: Nationalmuseum. 63–70.

3617 Stokes, Geoffrey. 1976. *Star-Making Machinery: The Odyssey of an Album*. Indianapolis, IN: Bobbs-Merrill.

3618 Thorgerson, Storm, ed. 1989. *Classic Album Covers of the 60s*. London: Paper Tiger/Dragon's World.

SHEET MUSIC

3619 Damon, S. Foster, ed. 1931. *Series of Old American Songs.* Providence, RI: Brown University Press.

3620 Davison, Nancy. 1973. *American Sheet Music Illustration: Reflections of the Nineteenth Century.* Ann Arbor, MI: University of Michigan Press.

3621 Dichter, Harry and Shapiro, Elliott. 1941. *Early American Sheet Music: Its Lure and Its Lore.* New York: Bowker Co.

3622 Dichter, Harry and Shapiro, Elliott. 1977. *Handbook of Early American Sheet Music, 1768–1889.* New York: Dover Publications, Inc.

3623 Dillon, Debbie. 1984. *Collectors Guide to Sheet Music.* Gas City: L-W Promotions.

3624 Floyd, Samuel A. 1974. Black Music in the Driscoll Collection. *The Black Perspective in Music* 2(2): 158–73.

3625 Fuld, James J. 1957. *A Pictorial Bibliography of the First Editions of Stephen C. Foster.* Philadelphia: Musica Americana.

3626 Henson, Brian and Morgan, Colin, comps. 1989. *First Hits: The Book of Sheet Music, 1946–1959.* London: Boxtree.

3627 Hoogerwerf, Frank. 1984. *Confederate Sheet-Music Imprints.* Brooklyn, NY: Institute for Studies in American Music, Monograph #21.

3628 Klamkin, Marian. 1975. *Old Sheet Music: A Pictorial History.* New York: Hawthorne Books.

3629 Lawrence, Vera Brodsky. 1975. *Music for Patriots, Politicians and Presidents: Harmonies and Discords of the First Hundred Years.* New York: Macmillan.

3630 Levy, Lester S. 1967. *Grace Notes in American History: Popular Sheet Music from 1820 to 1900.* Norman, OK: University of Oklahoma Press.

3631 Levy, Lester S. 1975. *Give Me Yesterday: American History in Song, 1890–1920.* Norman, OK: University of Oklahoma Press.

3632 Levy, Lester S. 1976. *Picture the Songs: Lithographs from the Sheet Music of Nineteenth-Century America.* Baltimore, MD: Johns Hopkins University Press.

3633 Levy, Lester S. 1983. Sheet Music Buffs and Their Collections: A Personal Memoir. *American Music* 1(4): 90–99.

3634 Pearsall, Ronald. 1972. *Victorian Sheet Music Covers.* Detroit, MI: Gale Research.

3635 Spellman, Doreen and Spellman, Sidney. 1969. *Victorian Music Covers.* London: Evelyn, Adams and Mackay.

3636 Stubblebine, Donald. 1991. *Cinema Sheet Music: A Comprehensive Listing of Published Film Music from 'Squaw Man' (1914) to 'Batman' (1989).* Jefferson, NC: McFarland.

3637 Wenzel, Lynn and Binkowski, Carol J. 1989. *I Hear America Singing: A Nostalgic Tour of Popular Sheet Music.* New York: Crown.

3638 Wilk, Max, ed. 1973. *Memory Lane: Ragtime, Jazz, Foxtrot and Other Popular Music Covers.* London: Studioart.

3639 Wilson, Bernard E., ed. 1982. *The Newberry Library Catalog of Early American Printed Sheet Music.* Boston, MA: G.K. Hall.

SHEET MUSIC COVERS

3640 Levy, Lester S. 1976. *Picture the Songs: Lithographies from the Sheet Music of Nineteenth Century America.* Baltimore and London: Johns Hopkins University Press.

3641 Locatro, Tony. 1985. *Some Girls Do and Some Girls Don't: Sheet Music Covers*. London and New York: Quartet.

3642 Pearsall, Ronald. 1972. *Victorian Sheet Music Covers*. Newton Abbot: David & Charles.

3643 Wilk, Max, ed. 1973. *Memory Lane: Ragtime, Jazz, Foxtrot and Other Popular Music Covers*. London: Studioart.

SOUND ENGINEERING

3644 Alten, Stanley R. 1994. *Audio in Media*, 4th edition. Belmont, CA: Wadsworth.

3645 Borwick, John, ed. 1980. *Sound Recording Practice*, 2nd edition. Oxford: Oxford University Press.

3646 Eargle, John. 1980. (1976) *Sound Recording*, 2nd edition. New York: Van Nostrand Reinhold.

3647 Emerick, Geoff. 1988. Recording Techniques. In *Making Music: The Essential Guide to Writing, Performing & Recording*, ed. George Martin. London: Barrie & Jenkins. 256–65. First published New York: Quill, 1983.

3648 Nisbett, Alec. 1995. *The Sound Studio*, 6th edition. Oxford: Focal Press.

3649 Ross-Trevor, Mike. 1980. The Recording Engineer. In *The Music Goes Round & Round*, ed. Peter Gammond and Raymond Horricks. London: Quartet. 117–34.

3650 Runstein, Robert E. and Huber, David Miles. 1989. (1974) *Modern Recording Techniques*, 3rd edition. Carmel, IN: Howard W. Sams & Company.

3651 Woram, John M. 1989. *The New Recording Studio Handbook*, revised edition. Commack, NY: ELAR Pub. Co. First published Plainview: Sagamore Pub. Co., 1976.

SOUND RECORDING

3652 Adorno, Theodor W. 1991. The Curves of the Needle. *October* 55: 49–55. (First published in *Musikblätter des Anbruch* 10 (1928): 47–50.)

3653 Attali, Jacques. 1985. (1977) Repeating. In *Noise: The Political Economy of Music*. Minneapolis, MN: University of Minnesota Press. 87–132. First published Paris: Presses Universitaires de France, 1977.

3654 Bennett, H. Stith. 1983. Notation and Identity in Contemporary Popular Music. *Popular Music* 3: 215–34.

3655 Borwick, John. 1977. A Century of Recording: Parts 1 and 2. *The Gramophone* (April, May): 1621–22, 1761–65.

3656 Brolinson, Per-Erik and Larsen, Holger. 1981. *Rock . . . Aspekter på industri, elektronik och sound*. Stockholm: Esselte Studium.

3657 Brophy, Philip. 1990. The Architecsonic Object: Stereo Sound, Cinema & Colors. In *Culture, Technology and Creativity in the Late Twentieth Century*, ed. Philip Hayward. London: John Libbey & Co. 91–110.

3658 Chanan, Michael. 1995. *Repeated Takes: A Short History of Recording and Its Effects on Music*. London: Verso.

3659 Clark, Ronald W. 1977. *Edison: The Man Who Made the Future*. New York: Putnam.

3660 Clarke, Paul. 1983. A 'Magic Science': Rock Music as a Recording Art. *Popular Music* 3: 195–213.

3661 Corenthal, Michael G. 1986. *The Iconography of Recorded Sound, 1886–1986: One Hundred Years of Commercial Entertainment and Collecting Opportunity*. Milwaukee, WI: Yesterday's Memories.

3662 Dearling, Robert and Dearling, Celia. 1984. *The Guinness Book of Recorded Sound.* Enfield: Guinness Books.

3663 Dolan, Robert E. 1967. *Music in the Modern Media: Techniques in Tape, Disc and Film Recording, Motion Picture and Television Scoring and Electronic Music.* New York: Schirmer.

3664 Eno, Brian. 1983. The Studio as Compositional Tool, Parts I & II. *Down Beat* 50(7&8): 56–57; 50–53.

3665 Fox, Ted. 1986. *In the Groove.* New York: St. Martin's Press.

3666 Frith, Simon. 1986. Art Versus Technology: The Strange Case of Popular Music. *Media, Culture and Society* 8(3): 263–79.

3667 Gelatt, Roland. 1977. *The Fabulous Phonograph, 1877–1977.* London: Cassell. First published London: Cassell, 1955.

3668 Gerzon, Michael. 1987. A Question of Balance: A Critical Look at the Mixdown Process. *Re Records Quarterly* 2(2): 45–48.

3669 Gronow, Pekka. 1981. The Record Industry Comes to the Orient. *Ethnomusicology* 25(2): 251–84.

3670 Hosokawa, Shuhei. 1984. The Walkman Effect. *Popular Music* 4: 165–80.

3671 Hunter, Mark. 1987. The Beat Goes Off: How Technology Has Gummed Up Rock's Grooves. *Harper's* 274 (May): 53–57.

3672 Jones, Steve. 1992. *Rock Formation: Music, Technology, and Mass Communication.* Newbury Park, CA: Sage.

3673 Kealy, Edward R. 1990. (1979) From Craft to Art: The Case of Sound Mixers and Popular Music. In *On Record: Rock, Pop and the Written Word,* ed. Simon Frith and Andrew Goodwin. London:
Routledge. 207–20. (First published in *Sociology of Work and Occupation* 6 (1979): 3–29.)

3674 Keil, Charles. 1984. Music Mediated and Live in Japan. *Ethnomusicology* 28(1): 91–96.

3675 Lubar, Stephen. 1993. *Infoculture: The Smithsonian Book of Information Age Inventions.* Boston, MA: Houghton Mifflin.

3676 MacLeod, Bruce. 1979. Facing the Muzak. *Popular Music & Society* 7(1): 18–31.

3677 Manuel, Peter. 1993. *Cassette Culture: Popular Music and Technology in North India.* Chicago: University of Chicago Press.

3678 Millard, Andre. 1995. *America on Record: A History of Recorded Sound.* Cambridge: Cambridge University Press.

3679 Moogk, Edward B. 1975. *Roll Back the Years: A History of Canadian Recorded Sound and Its Legacy, Genesis to 1930.* Ottawa: National Library of Canada.

3680 Moore, Jerrold Northrop. 1976. *A Matter of Records: Fred Gaisberg and the Golden Era of the Gramophone.* New York: Taplinger Publishing Co.

3681 Mowitt, John. 1987. The Sound of Music in the Era of Its Electronic Reproducibility. In *Music and Society: The Politics of Composition, Performance and Reception,* ed. Richard Leppert and Susan McClary. Cambridge: Cambridge University Press. 173–97.

3682 Mullin, John T. 1976. Creating the Craft of Tape Recording. *High Fidelity Magazine* 26(4): 62–67.

3683 Porcello, Thomas. 1991. The Ethics of Digital Audio-Sampling: Engineers' Discourse. *Popular Music* 10(1): 69–84.

3684 Qualen, John. 1985. *The Music Industry: The End of Vinyl?* London: Comedia.

3685 Read, Oliver and Welch, Walter L. 1976. *From Tin Foil to Stereo: The Evolution of the Phonograph*, 2nd edition. Indianapolis/New York: Howard Sams/Bobbs-Merrill.

3686 Rose, Tricia. 1994. Soul Sonic Forces: Technology, Orality, and Black Cultural Practice in Rap Music. In *Black Noise: Rap Music and Black Culture in Contemporary America*. Hanover, NH: Wesleyan University Press. 62–96.

3687 Schicke, C.A. 1974. *Revolution in Sound: A Biography of the Recording Industry*. Boston, MA: Little, Brown and Co.

3688 Schlemm, W. 1982. On the Position of the Tonmeister (Sound Recordist) in the Musical Communication Process. In *The Phonogram in Cultural Communication*, ed. Kurt Blaukopf. Wien: Springer-Verlag. 139–57.

3689 Tallmadge, William H. 1979. Equipment Failure and Audio Distortion in the Acoustic Recording and Remastering of Early Jazz. *Journal of Jazz Studies* 5(2): 61–75.

3690 Tankel, Jonathan David. 1990. The Practice of Recording Music: Remixing as Recoding. *Journal of Communication* 40(3): 34–46.

3691 Théberge, Paul. 1989. The 'Sound' of Music: Technological Rationalization and the Production of Popular Music. *New Formations* 8: 99–111.

3692 Wadhams, Wayne. 1988. *Dictionary of Music Production and Engineering Terminology*. New York and London: Schirmer/Collier Macmillan.

3693 Wurtzler, Steve. 1992. 'She Sang Live, But the Microphone Was Turned Off': The Live, the Recorded and the Subject of Representation. In *Sound Theory/Sound Practice*, ed. Rick Altman. New York: Routledge. 87–103.

3694 Zwick, Edward. 1973. An Interview with the Father of Hi-Fi: Dr. Peter Goldmark. *Rolling Stone* (27 September).

SPECIALIST SHOWS

3695 Blacknell, Steve. 1985. *The Story of Top of the Pops*. London: BBC/Patrick Stephens.

3696 Cubitt, Sean. 1984. Top of the Pops: The Politics of the Living Room. In *Television Mythologies: Stars, Shows and Signs*, ed. Len Masterman. London: Comedia. 46–48.

3697 Endres, Clifford. 1987. *Austin City Limits: The Story Behind Television's Most Popular Country Music Program*. Austin, TX: University of Texas Press.

3698 Flippo, Chet. 1981. Hank Williams Hits the Opry: 1949. *Journal of Country Music* 8(3): 5–17.

3699 Garner, Ken. 1987. Blasts from the Past (The Rock 'n' Roll Years). *The Listener* 117(3017) (25 June): 33–34.

3700 Keillor, Garrison. 1974. Onward and Upward with the Arts at the Opry. *The New Yorker* 50(11) (6 May): 46–70.

3701 Peterson, Richard A. and DiMaggio, Paul. 1974. The Early Opry: Its Hillbilly Image in Fact and Fancy. *Journal of Country Music* 4 (Summer): 38–51.

3702 Shore, Michael and Clark, Dick. 1985. *The History of American Bandstand: It's Got a Great Beat and You Can Dance to It*. New York: Ballantine Books.

3703 Tassin, Myron. 1975. *Fifty Years at the Grand Ole Opry*. Gretna, LA: Pelican Publishing.

3704 Tucker, Stephen R. 1977. The Louisiana Hayride, 1948–56. *North Louisiana Historical Association Journal* 8(5) (Fall): 187–201.

THE INDUSTRY

3705 Wolfe, Arnold S. 1985. Pop on Video: Narrative Modes in the Visualisation of Popular Music on 'Your Hit Parade' and 'Solid Gold'. In *Popular Music Perspectives, 2,* ed. David Horn. Göteborg and Exeter: IASPM. 428–44.

3706 Wolfe, Charles K. 1975. *The Grand Ole Opry: The Early Years, 1925–35.* London: Old Time Music, Booklet 1.

TAPE AND CASSETTE

3707 Chambers, Iain. 1990. A Miniature History of the Walkman. *New Formations* 11: 1–4.

3708 El-Shawan Castelo-Branco, Salwa. 1987. Some Aspects of the Cassette Industry in Egypt. *The World of Music* 29(2): 32–45.

3709 Hosokawa, Shuhei. 1984. The Walkman Effect. *Popular Music* 4: 165–80.

3710 Manuel, Peter. 1991. The Cassette Industry and Popular Music in North India. *Popular Music* 10(2): 189–204.

3711 Manuel, Peter. 1993. *Cassette Culture: Popular Music and Technology in North India.* Chicago and London: University of Chicago Press.

3712 Millard, Andre. 1995. *America on Record: A History of Recorded Sound.* Cambridge: Cambridge University Press.

TELEVISION

3713 Barnouw, Eric. 1970. *The Image Empire: A History of Broadcasting in the United States.* New York: Oxford University Press.

3714 Caps, John. 1980. TV Music: Music Makes All the Difference. In *Motion Picture Music,* ed. Luc van de Ven. Mechelen: Soundtrack. 64–68.

3715 Clark, Dick. 1978. *Rock, Roll and Remember.* New York: Popular Library.

3716 Corner, John. 1984. Olympic Myths: The Flame, the Night and the Music. In *Television Mythologies: Stars, Shows and Signs,* ed. Len Masterman. London: Comedia. 58–62.

3717 Dolan, Robert E. 1967. *Music in the Modern Media: Techniques in Tape, Disc and Film Recording, Motion Picture and Television Scoring and Electronic Music.* New York: Schirmer.

3718 Gelfand, Steve. 1985. *Television Theme Recordings: A Discography.* Bronx, NY: Television Music Archives.

3719 Harris, Steve. 1988. *Film Television and Stage Music on Phonograph Records: A Discography.* Jefferson, NC: McFarland.

3720 Jelinek, H. 1968. Musik in Film und Fernsehen. *Österreichische Musikzeitschrift* 23: 122–35.

3721 Krashoborski, W.F. 1980. TV Music: Roots and Offshoots. In *Motion Picture Music,* ed. Luc van de Ven. Mechelen: Soundtrack. 60–63.

3722 Lubar, Stephen. 1993. *Infoculture: The Smithsonian Book of Information Age Inventions.* Boston, MA: Houghton Mifflin.

3723 McLuhan, Marshall. 1965. *Understanding Media.* New York: McGraw-Hill.

3724 Pattillo, Craig W. 1990. *TV Theme Soundtrack Directory and Discography with Cover Versions.* Portland, OR: Braemar Books.

3725 Preston, Mike. 1995. *Tele-tunes.* Morecambe: Mike Preston.

3726 Redd, Lawrence N. 1974. *Rock Is Rhythm and Blues: The Impact of Mass Media.* East Lansing, MI: Michigan State University Press.

3727 Stockbridge, Sally. 1989. Programming Rock 'n' Roll: The Australian Version. *Cultural Studies* 3(1): 73–88.

3728 Tagg, Philip. 1990. An Anthropology of Television Music? *Svensk tidskrift för musikforskning* 1989: 19–42.

3729 Williams, Raymond. 1974. *Television: Technology and Cultural Form*. London: Fontana.

UNIONS

3730 Faulkner, Robert R. 1971. *Hollywood Studio Musicians: Their Work and Career in the Recording Industry*. Chicago: Aldine-Atherton.

3731 Halker, Clark. 1988. A History of Local 208 and the Struggle for Racial Equality in the American Federation of Musicians. *Black Music Research Journal* 8(2): 207–22.

3732 Seltzer, George. 1989. *Music Matters: The Performer and the American Federation of Musicians*. Metuchen and London: Scarecrow Press.

VIDEO

3733 Abt, Dean. 1987. Music Video: The Impact of the Visual Dimension. In *Popular Music & Communication*, ed. James Lull. Newbury Park, CA: Sage. 96–111.

3734 Aufderheide, Paul. 1986. Music Videos: The Look of the Sound. *Journal of Communication* 36(1): 57–78.

3735 Berland, Jody. 1986. Sound, Image and the Media. *Parachute* 41: 12–19.

3736 Berland, Jody. 1986. Sound, Image, and Social Space: Rock Video and Media Reconstruction. *Journal of Communication Inquiry* 10(1) (Winter): 34–47.

3737 Björnberg, Alf. 1992. Music Video and the Semiotics of Popular Music. In *Secondo Convegno Europeo di Analisi Musicale, Vol. I*, ed. Rossana Dalmonte and Mario Baroni. Trento: Università di Trento. 378–88.

3738 Björnberg, Alf. 1994. Structural Relationship of Music and Images in Music Video. *Popular Music* 13(1): 51–73.

3739 Burnett, Robert. 1990. From a Whisper to a Scream: Music Video and Cultural Form. In *Popular Music Research*, ed. Keith Roe and Ulla Karlsson. Göteborg: NORDICOM-Sweden, No. 1–2. 21–28.

3740 Burns, Gary. 1988. Dreams and Mediation in Music Video. *Wide Angle* 10(2): 41–61.

3741 Burns, Gary and Thompson, Robert. 1987. Music, Television and Video: Historical and Aesthetic Considerations. *Popular Music & Society* 11(3) (Fall): 11–25.

3742 Carlin, Dan. 1990. *Music in Film and Video Production*. London: Focal Press.

3743 Chang, Briankle G. 1986. A Hypothesis on the Screen: MTV and/as (Postmodern) Signs. *Journal of Communication Inquiry* 10(1) (Winter): 70–73.

3744 Denisoff, R. Serge. 1988. *Inside MTV*. New Brunswick and Oxford: Transaction.

3745 Fenster, Mark. 1988. Country Music Video. *Popular Music* 7(3): 285–302.

3746 Fiske, John. 1986. Post-Structural Post-Modern. *Journal of Communication Inquiry* 10(1) (Winter): 74–79.

3747 Frith, Simon. 1988. Making Sense of Video: Pop into the Nineties. In *Music for Pleasure: Essays in the Sociology of Pop*, ed. Simon Frith. New York: Routledge. 205–25.

THE INDUSTRY

3748 Frith, Simon. 1989. Video Pop: Picking Up the Pieces. In *Facing the Music*, ed. Simon Frith. New York: Pantheon. 88–130.

3749 Frith, Simon, Andrew Goodwin and Lawrence Grossberg, eds. 1993. *Sound and Vision: The Music Video Reader*. London: Routledge.

3750 Goodwin, Andrew. 1987. Music Video in the (Post) Modern World. *Screen* 28(3) (Summer): 36–55.

3751 Goodwin, Andrew. 1993. *Dancing in the Distraction Factory: Music Television and Popular Culture*. London: Routledge.

3752 Gorham, R. and Nakache, A. 1993. Star Moves: Choreography, Choreographers and Australian Music Video. *Perfect Beat* 1(3): 23–37.

3753 Gow, Joe. 1992. Music Video as Communication: Popular Formulas and Emerging Genres. *Journal of Popular Culture* 26(2): 41–70.

3754 Grigat, Nicoläa. 1995. *Madonnenbilder. Dekonstruktive Ästhetik in den Videobildern Madonnas*. Frankfurt am Main, Berlin, New York, Paris and Wien: Peter Lang.

3755 Harvey, Lisa St. Clair. 1990. Temporary Insanity: Fun, Games, and Transformational Ritual in American Music Video. *Journal of Popular Culture* 24(1): 39–64.

3756 Hausheer, Cecilia and Schönholzer, Annette, eds. 1994. *Visueller Sound. Musikvideos zwischen Avantgarde und Populärkultur*. Luzern: Zyklop.

3757 Holdstein, D. 1984. Music Video: Messages and Structure. *Jump/Cut* 1: 13–14.

3758 Hurley, Jennifer M. 1994. Music Video and the Construction of Gendered Subjectivity (Or How Being a Music Video Junkie Turned Me into a Feminist). *Popular Music* 13(3): 327–38.

3759 Hustwitt, Mark. 1985. *Sure Feels Like Heaven: Consideration on Promotional Videos*. Exeter: IASPM UK.

3760 Kaplan, E. Ann. 1987. *Rocking Around the Clock: Music Television, Postmodernism & Consumer Culture*. New York: Methuen.

3761 Kinder, Martha. 1984. Music Video and the Spectator: Television, Ideology and Dream. *Film Quarterly* 38(1): 2–15.

3762 Laing, Dave. 1985. Music Video: Industrial Product, Cultural Form. *Screen* 26(2): 78–83.

3763 Lewis, Lisa A. 1987. Form and Female Authorship in Music Video. *Communication* 9: 355–77.

3764 Lewis, Lisa A. 1990. Being Discovered: Female Address on Music Television. *Jump/Cut* 35: 2–15.

3765 Lewis, Lisa A. 1990. *Gender Politics and MTV: Voicing the Difference*. Philadelphia: Temple University Press.

3766 Lynch, Joan D. 1984. Music Videos: From Performance to Dada-Surrealism. *Journal of Popular Culture* 18(1): 53–57.

3767 Melton, Gary W. and Galician, Mary-Lou. 1987. A Sociological Approach to the Pop Music Phenomenon: Radio and Music Video Utilization for Expectation, Motivation and Satisfaction. *Popular Music & Society* 11(3): 35–46.

3768 Meyer, Filip de. 1986. *Muziek in Beelden: een erste verkenning in de wereld van de videoclip*. Leuven: Centrum voor Communicatiewetenschap.

3769 Mitchell, Tony. 1993. Treaty Now! Indigenous Music and Music Television in Australia. *Media, Culture and Society* 15: 299–308.

3770 Morse, Margaret. 1986. Postsynchronizing Rock Music and Television. *Journal of Communication Inquiry* 10(1) (Winter): 15–28.

3771 Rabinowitz, Lauren. 1989. Animation, Postmodernism and MTV. *The Velvet Light Trap* 24 (Fall): 99–129.

3772 Shore, Michael. 1985. *The Rolling Stone Book of Rock Video*. London: Sidgwick & Jackson.

3773 Shore, Michael. 1987. *Music Video: A Consumer's Guide*. New York: Ballantine.

3774 Straw, Will. 1988. Music Video in Its Contexts: Popular Music and Post-Modernism in the 1980s. *Popular Music* 7(3): 247–66.

3775 Szemere, Anna. 1989. Il fascino delle lotte tra bande di teppisti in una civiltà decadente: le considerazioni intorno a un 'video' musicale da parte di alcuni gruppi di giovani ungheresi. *Quaderni di Musica/Realtà* 23: 292–312.

3776 Waite, Bradley M. 1987. *Popular Music Videos: A Content Analysis and Social-Developmental Investigation of Their Effects on Gender Orientation and Attitudes*. Ann Arbor, MI: Universal Microfilms International, NEX86–21641.

3777 Wallis, Roger, and Malm, Krister. 1988. Push-Pull for the Video Clip: A Systems Approach to the Relationship Between the Phonogram/Videogram Industry and Music Television. *Popular Music* 7(3): 267–84.

3778 Wicke, Peter. 1988. Splendore e miseria della videomusic. *Musica/Realtà* XI(25): 91–104.

3779 Wicke, Peter. 1989. Musikvideo – Videopop. Geschichte eines Mediums. *Neues Leben* XXXIX(12): 22–27.

3780 Wicke, Peter. 1989. Video Killed the Radio Star: splendore e miseria della videomusic. *Quaderni di Musica/Realtà* 23: 278–91.

3781 Wicke, Peter. 1994. 'Video Killed the Radio Star': Popvideos - Videopop. *Positionen. Beiträge zur Neuen Musik* 18: 7–13.

3782 Wolfe, Arnold S. 1985. Pop on Video: Narrative Modes in the Visualisation of Popular Music on 'Your Hit Parade' and 'Solid Gold'. In *Popular Music Perspectives, 2*, ed. David Horn. Göteborg and Exeter: IASPM. 428–44.

3783 Wollen, Peter. 1986. Ways of Thinking About Music Video (and Post-Modernism). *Critical Quarterly* 28(1/2) (Spring/Summer): 167–70.

WALKMAN

3784 Abruzzese, A., Iain Chambers and Emilio Ghezzi. 1990. *Estetiche del Walkman*. Napoli: Flavio Pagano Editore.

3785 Hosokawa, Shuhei. 1983. The Walkman Effect. *Popular Music* 3: 151–64.

SOCIAL AND CULTURAL CONTEXTS

ADVERTISING (POPULAR MUSIC IN)

3786 Ala, Nemesio and Ghezzi, Emilio. 1985. Music and Advertising on Italian Television. In *Popular Music Perspectives, 2*, ed. David Horn. Göteborg and Exeter: IASPM. 405–16.

3787 Bjurström, Erling and Lilliestam, Lars. 1993. *Sälj det i toner . . . Om musik i TV-reklam*. Stockholm: Konumentverket.

3788 Buxton, Frank, and Owen, Bill. 1972. *The Big Broadcast, 1920–1950*. New York: Viking.

3789 Cole, Matthew. 1988. C'mon Everybody. *Music Week* (13 February): 12.

3790 Cook, Nicholas. 1994. Music and Meaning in the Commercials. *Popular Music* 13(1): 27–40.

3791 Cooper, Mark. 1987. Pop Has Been Taken Over by TV. *Q* 1(5) (February): 11–12.

3792 Dietz, Lawrence. 1973. *Soda Pop: The History, Advertising, Art and Memorabilia of Soft Drinks in America*. New York: Simon & Schuster.

3793 Edel, Herman. 1988. The Jingle Business. In *Making Music: The Essential Guide to Writing, Performing & Recording*, ed. George Martin. London: Barrie & Jenkins. 326–27.

3794 Frith, Simon. 1988. *Music for Pleasure: Essays in the Sociology of Pop*. Cambridge: Polity.

3795 Garrard, Maggie. 1988. Creating a Commercial. In *Making Music: The Essential Guide to Writing, Performing & Recording*, ed. George Martin. London: Barrie & Jenkins. 328–29.

3796 Grein, P. 1984. Coke Backing Duran Duran Tour. *Billboard* (28 January): 4.

3797 Helms, Siegmund. 1981. *Musik in der Werbung*. Wiesbaden: Breitkopf & Härtel.

3798 Julien, Jean-Rémy. 1985. The Use of Folklore and Popular Music in Radio Advertising. In *Popular Music Perspectives, 2*, ed. David Horn. Göteborg and Exeter: IASPM. 417–27.

3799 Julien, Jean-Rémy. 1989. *Musique et publicité: du Cri de Paris aux messages publicitaires radiophoniques et télévisés*. Paris: Flammarion.

3800 Karmen, Steve. 1989. *Through the Jingle Jungle: The Art and Business of Making Music for Commercials*. New York: Billboard Books.

3801 Klempe, Hroar. 1992. On the Mythical Repetitions in Music, Text and Image in the Coca-Cola Commercial. In *Secondo Convegno Europeo di Analisi Musicale, Vol. I*, ed. Rossana Dalmonte and Mario Baroni. Trento: Università di Trento. 401–406.

3802 Klempe, Hroar. 1993. Music, Text and Image in Commercials for Coca-Cola. In *Communication Studies: An Introductory Reader*, ed. John Corner and Jeremy Hawthorn, 4th edition. London/New York/Melbourne/Auckland: Edward Arnold. 245–54.

3803 Larsen, Peter. 1985. Hinsides fortællingen: Musikvideoer og moderne billedfiktion. Læsning, oplevelse and Excitements. *Argos* 2: 21–40.

3804 Lockhart, Ron and Weissman, Dick. 1982. *Audio in Advertising: A Practical Guide to Producing and Recording Music*,

Voiceovers and Sound Effects. New York: Ungar.

3805 Louis, J.C. and Yazijian, Harvey Z. 1980. *The Cola Wars.* New York: Everest House.

3806 Malm, Krister and Wallis, Roger. 1992. *Media Policy and Music Activity.* London: Routledge.

3807 Meyers, William. 1984. *The Imagemakers: Power and Persuasion on Madison Avenue.* New York: Times Books.

3808 Miller, Fred. 1985. *Music in Advertising.* New York: Amsco.

3809 Munsey, Cecil. 1972. *The Illustrated Guide to the Collectibles of Coca-Cola.* New York: Hawthorne Books.

3810 Oliver, Brian. 1987. Playing for High Stakes on TV. *Music Week* (22 November): 23, 24, 26.

3811 Pallazini, F.S. 1988. *Coca-Cola Superstar: The Drink That Became a Business Empire.* London: Columbus Books.

3812 Prendergrast, Mark. 1993. *For God, Country and Coca-Cola: The Unauthorized History of the Great American Soft Drink and the Company That Makes It.* New York: Charles Scribner's Sons.

3813 Ransom, Phil. 1980. *By Any Other Name: A Guide to the Popular Names and Nicknames of Classical Music and to Theme Music in Films, Radio, Television and Broadcast Adverts.* Newcastle: Northern Regional Library Systems.

3814 Rösing, Helmut. 1975. Funktion und Bedeutung von Musik in der Werbung. *Archiv für Musikwissenschaft* 32(3): 139–55.

3815 Rösing, Helmut. 1982. Music in Advertising. In *Popular Music Perspectives, 1,* ed. David Horn and Philip Tagg. Göteborg and Exeter: IASPM. 41–51.

3816 Savage, Jon. 1996. Leave My History Alone: Pop in Ads. In *Time Travel. From the Sex Pistols to Nirvana: Pop, Media and Sexuality, 1977–96.* London: Chatto & Windus. 231–32. (First published in *New Statesman* 115 (25 March) (1988).)

3817 Scott, Linda M. 1990. Understanding Jingles and Needledrop: A Rhetorical Approach to Music in Advertising. *Journal of Consumer Research* 17 (September): 223–36.

3818 Sippel, John. 1981. Singles 'Sneak Previews' to Air in Coke Ad Push. *Billboard* (20 June): 1.

3819 Spitalsky, B. 1981. The Sound That Refreshes. *Billboard* (4 July): 16.

3820 Steiner-Hall, Daniele. 1987. *Musik in der Fernsehwerbung.* Frankfurt am Main: Fischer.

3821 Tauchnitz, Jürgen. 1990. *Werbung mit Musik.* Heidelberg: Physika.

3822 Teixeira, Antonio, Jr. 1974. *Music to Sell By: The Craft of Jingle Writing.* Boston, MA: Berklee Press.

3823 Watters, Pat. 1978. *Coca-Cola: An Illustrated History.* New York: Doubleday.

3824 Wüsthoff, Klaus. 1978. *Die Rolle der Musik in der Film-, Funk- und Fernsehwerbung.* Berlin: Merseburger.

AUTHENTICITY

3825 Bloomfield, Terry. 1993. Resisting Songs: Negative Dialectics in Pop. *Popular Music* 12(1): 13–31.

3826 Buckley, David. 1993. David Bowie: Still Pop's Faker? In *The Bowie Companion,* ed. Elizabeth Thomson and David Gutman. London: Macmillan. 3–11.

SOCIAL AND CULTURAL CONTEXTS

3827 Fornäs, Johan. 1994. Listen to Your Voice! Reflexivity and Authenticity in Rock, Rap and Techno Music. *New Formations* 24: 155–73.

3828 Frith, Simon. 1981. *Sound Effects: Youth, Leisure and the Politics of Rock 'n' Roll.* New York: Pantheon.

3829 Frith, Simon, ed. 1988. *Music for Pleasure: Essays in the Sociology of Pop.* New York: Routledge.

3830 Gilroy, Paul. 1991. Sounds Authentic: Black Music, Ethnicity, and the Challenge of the Changing Same. *Black Music Research Journal* 11(2): 111–36.

3831 Gilroy, Paul. 1993. 'Jewels Brought from Bondage': Black Music and the Politics of Authenticity. In *The Black Atlantic: Modernity and Double Consciousness.* London: Verso. 72–110.

3832 Jensen, Joli. 1993. Honky-Tonking: Mass-Mediated Culture Made Personal. In *All That Glitters: Country Music in America,* ed. George H. Lewis. Bowling Green, OH: Bowling Green University Popular Press. 119–31.

3833 Laing, Dave. 1985. *One Chord Wonders: Power and Meaning in Punk Rock.* Milton Keynes: Open University Press.

3834 Savage, Jon. 1985. Humpty Dumpty and the New Authenticity. *The Face* 63 (July): 80.

3835 Stratton, Jon. 1982. Between Two Worlds: Art and Commercialism in the Record Industry. *The Sociological Review* 30: 267–85.

3836 Stratton, Jon. 1983. What Is 'Popular Music'? *The Sociological Review* 22(2) (May): 293–309.

3837 Tetzlaff, D. 1993. Music for Meaning: Reading the Discourse of Authenticity in Rock. *Journal of Communication Inquiry* 18(1): 95–117.

3838 Thornton, Sarah. 1995. Authenticities from Record Hops to Raves. In *Club Cultures: Music, Media and Subcultural Capital.* London: Verso.

CARNIVAL

3839 Aharonián, Coriún. 1971. Sobre carnaval, tamboril y negritudes. *Marcha* (19 February).

3840 Alencar, Edigar. 1965. *O carnaval através da música.* Rio de Janeiro: Freitas Bastos.

3841 Cohen, Abner. 1993. *Masquerade Politics: Explorations in the Structure of Urban Cultural Movements.* Oxford: Berg.

3842 Cowley, John. 1985. Carnival in Trinidad. *Musical Traditions* 4: 4–8.

3843 Cowley, John. 1991. *Carnival and Other Seasonal Festivals in the West Indies, USA and Britain: A Selected Bibliographical Index.* Coventry: Warwick Centre for Research in Ethnic Relations.

3844 Cowley, John. 1996. *Carnival, Canboulay and Calypso: Traditions in the Making.* Cambridge: Cambridge University Press.

3845 Crook, Larry N. 1993. Black Consciousness, Samba Reggae, and the Re-Africanization of Bahian Carnival Music in Brazil. *The World of Music* 35(2): 70–84.

3846 Hill, Donald. 1993. *Calypso Calaloo: Early Carnival Music in Trinidad.* Gainesville, FL: University Press of Florida.

3847 Hill, Errol. 1972. *The Trinidad Carnival.* Austin, TX: University of Texas Press.

3848 Hill, Errol. 1975. The Trinidad Carnival: Cultural Change and Synthesis. *Cultures* 3(1): 54–86.

172

3849 Juneja, Renu. 1988. The Trinidad Carnival: Ritual, Performance, Spectacle, and Symbol. *Journal of Popular Culture* 21(4): 87–100.

3850 Kohl, Paul R. 1993. Looking Through a Glass Onion: Rock and Roll as Modern Manifestation of Carnival. *Journal of Popular Culture* 27(1): 143–62.

3851 Leal, Néstor. 1992. *Boleros. La canción romántica del Caribe (1930–1960)*. Caracas: Grijalbo.

3852 Lipsitz, George. 1990. Mardi Gras Indians: Carnival and Counter-Narrative in Black New Orleans. In *Time Passages: Collective Memory and American Popular Culture*. Minneapolis, MN: University of Minnesota Press. 233–53.

3853 Maior, Mario, ed. 1991. *Antologia do Carnaval do Recife*. Recife: FUNDAJ/Massangana.

3854 Patton, John H. 1994. Calypso as Rhetorical Performance: Trinidad Carnival 1993. *Latin American Music Review* 15(1): 55–74.

3855 Pearse, Andrew. 1956. Carnival in Nineteenth Century Trinidad. *Caribbean Quarterly* 4(3) & 4(4): 175–93.

3856 Pescatello, Ann M. 1976. Music Fiestas and Their Social Role in Brazil: Carnival in Rio. *Journal of Popular Culture* 9(4): 833–39.

CENSORSHIP

3857 Abraham, Gerald. 1983. Censoring Music. *Index on Censorship* 12(1): 3–4.

3858 Biafra, Jello. 1987. The Far Right and the Censorship of Music. *Harvard Law Review* (17 April): 10–16.

3859 Cloonan, Martin. 1992. *Censorship and Popular Music*. Liverpool: Institute of Popular Music, University of Liverpool.

3860 Cloonan, Martin. 1995. 'I Fought the Law': Popular Music and the British Obscenity Law. *Popular Music* 14(3): 349–64.

3861 Cloonan, Martin. 1996. *Banned! Censorship of Popular Music in Britain, 1967–92*. Aldershot: Arena.

3862 Cohen, Stanley. 1980. (1972) *Folk Devils and Moral Panics: The Creation of Mods and Rockers*. Oxford: Martin Robertson. First published London: MacGibbon & Kee, 1972.

3863 Davis, Tracy C. 1991. The Moral Sense of the Majorities: Indecency and Vigilance in Late-Victorian Music Halls. *Popular Music* 10(1): 21–38.

3864 Dümling, Albrecht and Girth, Peter, eds. 1988. *Entartete Musik: Eine kommentierte Rekonstruktion zur Düsseldorfer Ausstellung von 1938*. Düsseldorf: Landeshauptstadt Düsseldorf.

3865 Hoffmann, Frank. 1989. *Intellectual Freedom and Censorship: An Annotated Bibliography*. Metuchen, NJ: Scarecrow Press.

3866 Jones, Steve. 1991. Banned in the USA: Popular Music and Censorship. *Journal of Communications* 15(1): 71–87.

3867 Kennedy, David. 1990. Frankenchrist Versus the State: The New Right, Rock Music and the Case of Jello Biafra. *Journal of Popular Culture* 24(1): 131–48.

3868 Marshall, Kate. 1985. *Moral Panics and Victorian Values*. London: Junus.

3869 Martin, Linda and Segrave, Kerry. 1993. *Anti-Rock: The Opposition to Rock 'n' Roll*. New York: Da Capo Press.

3870 McDonald, James. 1988. Censoring Rock Lyrics: A Historical Analysis of the Debate. *Youth and Society* 19(3): 294–313.

SOCIAL AND CULTURAL CONTEXTS

3871 Parents Music Resource Center. 1990. *Let's Talk About Rock Music.* Arlington, VA: PMRC.

3872 Peterson, Richard A. 1972. Market and Moralist Censors of a Black Art Form: Jazz. In *The Sounds of Social Change: Studies in Popular Culture,* ed. R. Serge Denisoff and Richard A. Peterson. Chicago: Rand McNally & Co. 236–47.

3873 Ruby, Jay. 1970. Censorship, Nudity and Obscenity in American Popular Music. In *Giants of Rock Music,* ed. Pauline Rivelli and Robert Levin. New York: Da Capo Press.

3874 Street, John. 1986. *Rebel Rock: The Politics of Popular Music.* Oxford: Blackwell.

3875 Sullivan, Mark. 1987. More Popular Than Jesus: The Beatles and the Religious Far Right. *Popular Music* 6(3): 313–26.

3876 Walser, Robert. 1993. Professing Censorship: Academic Attacks on Heavy Metal. *Journal of Popular Music Studies* 5: 68–79.

3877 Willett, Ralph. 1989. Hot Swing and the Dissolute Life: Youth, Style and Popular Music in Europe, 1939–49. *Popular Music* 8(2): 157–64.

CHARITY EVENTS

3878 Berger, Gilda. 1987. *USA for Africa: Rock Aid in the Eighties.* New York: Watts.

3879 Garofalo, Reebee. 1992. Understanding Mega-Events: If We Are the World, Then How Do We Change It? In *Rockin' the Boat: Mass Music and Mass Movements,* ed. Reebee Garofalo. Boston, MA: South End Press. 15–36.

3880 Hillmore, Peter. 1985. *Live Aid World-Wide Concert Book.* Parsipany, NJ: Unicorn.

3881 Marcus, Greil. 1986. We Are the World? *Re Records Quarterly* 1(4): 27–36.

3882 McGuire, William, ed. 1986. *Live Aid Captured Moments.* Monmouth Junction: Unicorn Books.

3883 Rijven, Stan and Straw, Will. 1989. Rock for Ethiopia. In *World Music, Politics and Social Change,* ed. Simon Frith. Manchester: Manchester University Press. 198–209.

3884 Rijven, Stan, Greil Marcus and Will Straw. 1986. *Rock for Ethiopia: Papers from the Third International Conference on Popular Music Studies, Montreal 1986.* Exeter: IASPM.

3885 Ullestad, Neal. 1984. Rock and Rebellion: Subversive Effects of Live Aid and 'Sun City'. *Popular Music* 4: 67–76.

3886 Ullestad, Neal. 1992. Diverse Rock Rebellions Subvert Media Hegemony. In *Rockin' the Boat: Mass Music and Mass Movements,* ed. Reebee Garofalo. Boston, MA: South End Press. 37–54.

CLASS

3887 Ballantine, Christopher. 1995. The Identities of Race, Class and Gender in the Repression of Early Black South African Jazz and Vaudeville (ca. 1920–1944). In *Popular Music: Style and Identity,* ed. Will Straw, et al. Montréal: The Centre for Research on Canadian Cultural Industries and Institutions. 9–12.

3888 Colls, Robert. 1977. *The Collier's Rant: Songs and Culture in the Industrial Village.* London: Croom Helm.

3889 Coplan, David. 1982. The Urbanisation of African Music: Some Theoretical Observations. *Popular Music* 2: 113–29.

3890 Cutler, Chris. 1984. Technology, Politics and Contemporary Music: Necessity and Choice in Musical Forms. *Popular Music* 4: 279–300.

174

3891 Dancis, Bruce. 1978. Safety Pins and Class Struggle: Punk Rock and the American Left. *Socialist Review* 8(2) (May-June): 156–81.

3892 Fuhr, Werner. 1977. *Proletarische Musik in Deutschland 1928–1933.* Göppingen: Alfred Kümmerle.

3893 Gammon, Vic. 1984. 'Not Appreciated in Worthing?': Class Expression and Popular Song Texts in Mid-Nineteenth-Century Britain. *Popular Music* 4: 5–24.

3894 Graf, Hans-Peter. 1987. Concertina- und Bandoneonkultur: Organisierte Arbeiterfreizeit in Deutschland zwischen 1870 und dem Ende der Weimarer Republik. In *Ich will aber gerade vom Leben singen ... Über populäre Musik vom ausgehenden 19. Jahrhundert bis zum Ende der Weimarer Republik*, ed. Sabine Schutte. Reinbek bei Hamburg: Rowohlt. 213–35.

3895 Hall, Stuart and Jefferson, Tony, eds. 1976. *Resistance Through Rituals: Youth Subcultures in Post-War Britain.* London: Hutchinson.

3896 Harker, Dave. 1980. *One for the Money: Politics and Popular Song.* London: Hutchinson.

3897 Hebdige, Dick. 1979. *Subculture: The Meaning of Style.* London: Methuen.

3898 Herbert, Trevor, ed. 1991. *Bands: The Brass Band Movement in the 19th and 20th Centuries.* Milton Keynes: Open University Press.

3899 Hoeher, Dagmar. 1986. The Composition of Music Hall Audiences, 1850–1900. In *Music Hall: The Business of Pleasure*, ed. Peter Bailey. Milton Keynes: Open University Press. 73–92.

3900 Kurkela, Vesa. 1983. Worker's Music in a Finnish Industrial Town. *Suomen antropologi* 4: 218–23.

3901 Lee, Edward. 1982. *Folksong and Music Hall.* London: Routledge & Kegan Paul.

3902 Levine, Robert. 1984. Elite Intervention in Urban Popular Culture in Modern Brazil. *Luso-Brazilian Review* 21(2): 9–23.

3903 Lieberman, Robbie. 1989. *'My Song Is My Weapon': People's Songs, American Communism, and the Politics of Culture, 1930–1950.* Champaign, IL: University of Illinois Press.

3904 Lipsitz, George. 1994. 'Ain't Nobody Here But Us Chickens': The Class Origins of Rock and Roll. In *Rainbow at Midnight: Labor and Culture in the 1940s.* Urbana and Chicago: University of Illinois Press. 303–33.

3905 Malone, Bill C. 1982. Honky Tonk: The Music of the Southern Working Class. In *Folk Music and Modern Sound*, ed. William R. Ferris and Mary L. Hart. Jackson, MS: University Press of Mississippi. 119–28.

3906 Manuel, Peter. 1989. Andalusian, Gypsy and Class Identity in the Contemporary Flamenco Complex. *Ethnomusicology* 33(1): 47–65.

3907 Maróthy, János. 1974. *Music and the Bourgeois, Music and the Proletarian.* Budapest: Akadémiai Kiadó.

3908 Middleton, Richard. 1985. Popular Music, Class Conflict and the Music-Historical Field. In *Popular Music Perspectives, 2*, ed. David Horn. Göteborg and Exeter: IASPM. 24–46.

3909 Pacini Hernandez, Deborah. 1989. Social Identity and Class in Bachata, an Emerging Dominican Popular Music. *Latin American Music Review* 10(1): 69–91.

3910 Peña, Manuel. 1985. From Ranchero to Jaitón: Ethnicity and Class in Texas-Mexican Music (Two Styles in the Form of a Pair). *Ethnomusicology* 29(1): 29–55.

3911 Peña, Manuel. 1985. *The Texas-Mexican Conjunto: History of a Working Class*

Music. Austin, TX: University of Texas Press.

3912 Pestalozza, Luigi. 1986. Lavoro e musica. *Musica/Realtà* 20: 8–12.

3913 Peterson, Richard A. and DiMaggio, Paul. 1975. From Region to Class: The Changing Locus of Country Music. *Social Forces* 53: 497–506.

3914 Russell, Dave. 1987. *Popular Music in England, 1840–1914: A Social History*. Manchester: Manchester University Press.

3915 Scott, Derek B. 1989. *The Singing Bourgeois: Songs of the Victorian Drawing Room and Parlour*. Milton Keynes: Open University Press.

3916 Seeger, Charles. 1957. Music and Class Structure in the United States. *American Quarterly* 9(3): 281–94.

3917 Shepherd, John. 1982. A Theoretical Model for the Sociomusicological Analysis of Popular Musics. *Popular Music* 2: 145–77.

3918 Small, Christopher. 1987. Performance as Ritual: Sketch for an Enquiry into the True Nature of a Symphony Concert. In *Lost in Music: Culture, Style and the Musical Event*, ed. Avron Levine White. London: Routledge. 6–32.

3919 Stedman-Jones, Gareth. 1974. Working-Class Culture and Working-Class Politics in London, 1870–1900: Notes on the Remaking of a Working Class. *Journal of Social History* 7(4): 460–508.

3920 Traies, Jane. 1986. Jones and the Working Girl: Class Marginality in Music-Hall Song, 1869–1900. In *Music Hall: Performance and Style*, ed. J.S. Bratton. Milton Keynes: Open University Press. 23–48.

3921 Weber, William. 1975. *Music and the Middle Class*. London: Croom Helm.

3922 Wicke, Peter. 1990. *Rock Music: Culture, Aesthetics and Sociology*. Cambridge: Cambridge University Press.

3923 Willis, Paul. 1978. *Profane Culture*. London: Routledge & Kegan Paul.

3924 Wilson, Pamela. 1995. Mountains of Contradiction: Gender, Class and Region in the Star Image of Dolly Parton. *South Atlantic Quarterly* 94(1) (Winter): 109–34.

3925 Yeo, Eileen, and Yeo, Stephen, eds. 1981. *Popular Culture and Class Conflict, 1590–1914: Explorations in the History of Labour and Leisure*. Brighton: Harvester Press.

COMMERCIALIZATION/ COMMERCIALISM

3926 Chapple, Steve and Garofalo, Reebee. 1977. *Rock 'n' Roll Is Here to Pay: The History and Politics of the Music Industry*. Chicago: Nelson-Hall.

3927 Denisoff, R. Serge. 1976. Massification and Popular Music: A Review. *Journal of Popular Culture* 9: 886–94.

3928 Denisoff, R. Serge. 1981. Folk-Rock: Folk Music, Protest, or Commercialism? *Journal of Popular Culture* 3(2): 214–30.

3929 Eliot, Marc. 1989. *Rockonomics*, revised edition. New York: Citadel Press.

3930 Fenster, Mark. 1995. Commercial (and/ or?) Folk: The Bluegrass Industry and Bluegrass Traditions. *South Atlantic Quarterly* 94(1) (Winter): 81–108.

3931 Harker, Dave. 1980. *One for the Money: Politics and Popular Song*. London: Hutchinson.

3932 Ivey, William. 1982. Commercialization and Tradition in the Nashville Sound. In *Folk Music and Modern Sound*, ed. William R. Ferris and Mary L. Hart. Jackson, MS: University Press of Mississippi. 129–38.

3933 Jensen, Joli. 1993. Honky-Tonking: Mass-Mediated Culture Made Personal. In *All That Glitters: Counry Music in America*, ed. George H. Lewis. Bowling Green, OH: Bowling Green University Popular Press. 119–31.

3934 Plasketes, George. 1992. Taking Care of Business: The Commercialization of Rock Music. In *America's Musical Pulse: Popular Music in Twentieth-Century Society*, ed. Kenneth Bindas. Westport, CT: Greenwood Press. 149–63.

3935 Siefert, M. 1995. How the Phonograph Became a Musical Instrument: Technology, Aesthetics, and the Capitalization of Culture. *Science in Context* (Summer).

3936 Stratton, Jon. 1982. Between Two Worlds: Art and Commercialism in the Record Industry. *Sociological Review* 30: 267–85.

3937 Stratton, Jon. 1983. Capitalism and Romantic Ideology in the Record Business. *Popular Music* 3: 143–56.

3938 Wicke, Peter. 1992. Stil als kommerzielle Kategorie – Zum Stilbegriff in der populären Musik. In *Stil in der Musik – Innovationsquellen der Musik des 20. Jahrhunderts*, ed. P. Macek. Brno: Mazaryk University. 225–41.

3939 Wicke, Peter. 1994. Jugendkultur zwischen Industrie und Politik. In *Zukunftsforum Jugendkulturarbeit 20000 – Zur gesellschaftspolitischen Verantwortung kultureller Bildung.* Remscheid: Bundesvereinigung kulturelle Jugendbildung. 133–38.

3940 Wicke, Peter. 1995. Popmusik – Konsumfetischismus oder kulturelles Widerstandspotential. In *Yesterday. Today. Tomorrow*, ed. M. Heuger and M. Prell. Regensburg: ConBrio Verlagsgesellschaft. 21–35.

3941 Wicke, Peter and Erlmann, Veit. 1992. Das Eigene und das Fremde. *Positionen* 12: 2–7.

CRIME

3942 Allsop, Kenneth. 1961. *The Bootleggers: The Story of Prohibition*. New Rochelle, NY: Arlington House.

3943 Haskins, Jim. 1977. *The Cotton Club*. London: Robson.

3944 Hines, Earl. 1949. How Gangsters Ran the Nightclub Business. *Ebony* (September).

3945 Morris, Ronald L. 1980. *Wait until Dark: Jazz and the Underworld, 1880–1940*. Bowling Green, OH: Bowling Green University Popular Press.

3946 Oliver, Paul. 1990. (1960) *Blues Fell This Morning: Meaning in the Blues*. Cambridge: Cambridge University Press.

3947 Russell, Ross. 1971. *Jazz Style in Kansas City and the Southwest*. Berkeley, CA: University of California Press.

3948 Tunnell, Kenneth D. 1992. 99 Years Is Almost for Life: Punishment for Violent Crime in Bluegrass Music. *Journal of Popular Culture* 26(3): 165–83.

CULTURAL IMPERIALISM

3949 Acosta, Leonardo. 1982. *Música y Descolonización*. La Habana: Editorial Arte y Literatura.

3950 Barrett, James. 1996. World Music, Nation and Postcolonialism. *Cultural Studies* 10(2): 237–47.

3951 Cooper, Laura E. and Cooper, B. Lee. 1993. The Pendulum of Cultural Imperialism: Popular Music Between the United States and Britain, 1943–1967. *Journal of Popular Culture* 27(3): 61–78.

3952 Erlmann, Veit. 1996. The Aesthetics of the Global Imagination: Reflections on World Music in the 1990s. *Public Culture* 8: 467–87.

3953 Garofalo, Reebee. 1993. Whose World, What Beat: The Transnational Music Industry, Identity and Cultural Imperialism. *The World of Music* 35(2): 16–32.

3954 Iwamura, Takuya. 1995. The Overview of the Modern Western Music Paradigm and Some Conditions of Its Counteractions: Some Japanese Borderline Cases. In *Popular Music Perspectives III*, ed. Peter Wicke. Berlin: Zyankrise. 232–39.

3955 Jones, Steve. 1995. Who Fought the Law? Popular Music, Cultural Production and the International Popular Music Industry. In *Popular Music Perspectives III*, ed. Peter Wicke. Berlin: Zyankrise. 190–203.

3956 Laing, Dave. 1986. The Music Industry and the 'Cultural Imperialism' Thesis. *Media, Culture and Society* 8(3): 331–42.

3957 No entry.

3958 Malm, Krister and Wallis, Roger. 1984. Transculturation and the Rise of National Pop and Rock in Small Countries. In *Tvärspel: 31 artiklar om musik. Festskrift till Jan Ling.* Göteborg: Skrifter från Musikvetenskapliga institutionen, 9. 79–90.

3959 Mattelart, A., X. Delcourt and M. Mattelart. 1984. *International Image Markets: In Search of an Alternative Perspective.* London: Comedia.

3960 Roberts, Martin. 1992. 'World Music' and the Global Cultural Economy. *Diaspora* 2(2) (Fall): 249–52.

3961 Robinson, Deanna Campbell, Elizabeth B. Buck and Marlene Cuthbert, eds. 1991. *Music at the Margins: Popular Music and Global Cultural Diversity.* Newbury Park, CA: Sage.

3961a Wallis, Roger and Malm, Krister. 1984. *Big Sounds from Small Peoples: The Music Industry in Small Countries.* London: Constable.

CULTURAL INTERCHANGE, ACCULTURATION, HYBRIDITY

3962 Baker, Houston A., Jr. 1991. Hybridity, the Rap Race, and Pedagogy for the 1990s. *Black Music Research Journal* 11(2): 217–28.

3963 Bane, Michael. 1992. *White Boy Singin' the Blues: The Black Roots of White Rock.* New York: Da Capo Press.

3964 Beaud, Paul and Willener, Alfred, eds. 1973. *Musique et vie quotidienne: Essai de sociologie d'une nouvelle culture.* Paris: Mame.

3965 BIPE. 1987. *Crise et mutation du domaine musical.* Paris: La Documentation française.

3966 Bloemeke, Rüdiger. 1996. *Roll Over Beethoven. Wie der Rock 'n' Roll nach Deutschland kam.* Andrä-Wördern: Hannibal.

3967 Boggs, Vernon. 1991. Musical Transculturation: From Afro-Cuban to Afro-Cubanism. *Popular Music & Society* 15(4): 71–83.

3968 Chambers, Iain. 1977. (1975) A Strategy for Living: Black Music and White Subcultures. In *Resistance Through Rituals: Youth Subcultures in Post-War Britain,* ed. Stuart Hall and Tony Jefferson. London: Hutchinson. 157–66.

3969 Chambers, Iain. 1995. Travelling Sounds: Whose Centre, Whose Periphery? In *Popular Music Perspectives III*, ed. Peter Wicke. Berlin: Zyankrise. 160–65.

3970 Dauer, Alfons M. 1994. Don't Call My Music Jazz. Zum Musiktransfer von der Alten zur Neuen Welt und dessen Folgen. In *Populäre Musik und Pädagogik – Grundlagen und Praxismaterialien,* ed. Jürgen Terhag. Oldershausen: Institut für Didaktik der populären Musik. 13–25.

3971 Feldmann-Bürgers, Johannes. 1996. *Tango und Jazz. Kulturelle Wechselbeziehungen?* Münster: Lit Verlag.

3972 Gilroy, Paul. 1993. Between Afro-Centrism and Euro-Centrism: Youth Culture and the Problem of Hybridity. *Young* 1(2): 2–13.

3973 Guilbault, Jocelyne. 1994. Créolité and the New Cultural Politics of Difference in Popular Music of the French West Indies. *Black Music Research Journal* 14(2): 161–78.

3974 Guilbault, Jocelyne. 1995. A World Music Back Home: The Power of Mediations. In *Popular Music Perspectives III*, ed. Peter Wicke. Berlin: Zyankrise. 147–59.

3975 Heckman, Don. 1970. Black Music and White America. In *Black Americans*, ed. John F. Szwed. Washington, DC: Voice of America Forum Lectures. 171–84.

3976 Hoare, Ian. 1975. Mighty, Mighty Spade and Whitey: Black Lyrics and Soul's Interaction with White Culture. In *The Soul Book*, ed. Ian Hoare. London: Methuen. 117–89.

3977 Kartomi, Margaret. 1981. The Processes and Results of Musical Culture Contact: A Discussion of Terminology and Concepts. *Ethnomusicology* 25(2): 227–49.

3978 Kearns, William. 1974. From Black to White: A Hillbilly Version of Gussie Davis's 'The Fatal Wedding'. *The Black Perspective in Music* 1(3): 29–36.

3979 Klein, Jean-Claude. 1985. Borrowing, Syncretism, Hybridisation: The Parisian Revue of the 1920's. *Popular Music* 5: 175–88.

3980 Kloosterman, Robert C. and Quispel, Chris. 1990. Not Just the Same Old Show on My Radio: An Analysis of the Role of Radio in the Diffusion of Black Music Among Whites in the South of the United States, 1920 to 1960. *Popular Music* 9(2): 151–64.

3981 Knauer, Wolfram. 1996. Emanzipation woven? Zum Verhbältnis des amerikanischen und des deutschen Jazz in der 50er und 60er Jahren. In *Jazz in Deutschland*, ed. Wolfram Knauer. Hofheim: Wolke. 141–58.

3982 Lee, C.J.W.-L. 1996. Staging the New Asia: Singapore's Dick Lee, Pop Music, and a Counter-Modernity. *Public Culture* 8: 489–510.

3983 Lilliestam, Lars. 1990. Musical Acculturation: 'Hound Dog' from Blues to Swedish Rock and Roll. In *Popular Music Research*, ed. Keith Roe and Ulla Karlsson. Göteborg: NORDICOM-Sweden, No. 1–2. 133–44.

3984 Ling, Jan and Ramsten, Märta. 1985. The Gärdeby Folk Melody: A Musical Migrant. In *Popular Music Perspectives, 2*, ed. David Horn. Göteborg and Exeter: IASPM. 119–41.

3985 Murphy, Dennis. 1972. The Americanization of Three African Musical Instruments. *African Music* 5(2): 105–11.

3986 Mutsaers, Lutgard. 1990. Indorock: An Early Eurorock Style. *Popular Music* 9(3): 307–20.

3987 Narváez, Peter. 1994. The Influences of Hispanic Music Cultures on African-American Blues Musicians. *Black Music Research Journal* 14(2): 203–24.

3988 Oliver, Paul, ed. 1990. *Black Music in Britain: Essays on the Afro-Asian Contribution to Popular Music.* Milton Keynes: Open University Press.

3989 Paysan, Marko. 1993. Transatlantic Rhythm. Jazzkuntakte zwischen Deutschland und den USA vor 1945. In *Jazz in Europa*, ed. Wolfram Knauer. Hofheim: Wolke. 13–42.

3990 Rhodes, Willard. 1952. Acculturation in North American Indian Music. In *Acculturation in the Americas, 2,* ed. Sol Tax. Chicago: Chicago University Press. 127–32.

3991 Rhodes, Willard. 1963. North American Indian Music in Transition: A Study of Songs with English Words as an Index of Acculturation. *Journal of the International Folk Music Council* 15: 9–14.

3992 Ridgeway, Cecilia L. and Roberts, John. 1976. Urban Popular Music and Interaction: A Semantic Relationship. *Ethnomusicology* 20(2): 233–52.

3993 Rirzei, Fred. 1987. 'Hatte der Kaiser Jazz getanzt . . . ' US-Tanzmusik in Deutschland vor und nach dem Erster Weltkrieg. In *Ich will aber gerade vom Leben singen . . . Über populäre Musik vom ausgehenden 19. Jahrhundert bis zum Ende der Weimarer Republik,* ed. Sabine Schutte. Reinbek bei Hamburg: Rowohlt. 265–96.

3994 Russell, Tony. 1970. *Blacks, Whites and Blues.* London: Studio Vista.

3995 Slobin, Mark. 1992. Micromusics of the West: A Comparative Approach. *Ethnomusicology* 36(1) (Winter): 1–87.

3996 Tawa, Nicholas E. 1982. *A Sound of Strangers: Musical Culture, Acculturation and the Post-Civil War Ethnic American.* Metuchen, NJ: Scarecrow Press.

3997 Waterman, Richard. 1952. African Influence on the Music of the Americas. In *Acculturation in the Americas, 2,* ed. Sol Tax. Chicago: University of Chicago Press. 207–18.

3998 Waterman, Richard. 1963. On Flogging a Dead Horse: Lessons Learnt from the Africanisms Controversy. *Ethnomusicology* 7(2): 83–88.

3999 Wertenstein-Zulawski, Jerzy. 1995. Communication and Social Change. In *Popular Music Perspectives III,* ed. Peter Wicke. Berlin: Zyankrise. 55–58.

4000 Westcott, Robert B. and Kaufman, Elias J. 1994. Minstrel and Classic Banjo: American and English Connections. *American Music* 12(1): 1–30.

4001 Winans, William. 1977. Ideas of Afro-American Musical Acculturation in the USA: 1900 to the Present. *Journal of the Steward Anthropological Society* 8(2): 107–36.

CULTURAL POLICY/REGULATION

4002 Alaja-Browne, Afolabi. 1995. Popular Music Policy. In *Popular Music Perspectives III,* ed. Peter Wicke. Berlin: Zyankrise. 312–19.

4003 Bennett, Tony, et al., eds. 1993. *Rock and Popular Music: Politics, Policies, Institutions.* London: Routledge.

4004 Blaukopf, Kurt, ed. 1982. *The Phonogram in Cultural Communication.* Wien: Springer-Verlag.

4005 Cohen, Sara. 1991. Popular Music and Urban Regeneration: The Music Industries of Merseyside. *Cultural Studies* 5(3): 332–46.

4006 Fenger, Pim. 1981. Music in Cultural, Educational and Communication Policies in the Netherlands. In *Stock-Taking of Musical Life: Sociography and Music Education,* ed. Desmond Mark. Wien: Doblinger. 89–96.

4007 Garnham, Nicholas. 1983. *Concepts of Culture, Public Policy and Cultural Industries.* London: Greater London Council.

4008 Jogschies, Rainer. 1991. *Rock & Pop '89. Kritische Analysen. Kulturpolitische Alternativen, II.* Hagen: Kulturpolitische Gesellschaft, Dokumentation 37.

4009 Ketting, Knud. 1983. Rock Music at Government Level: A Report from the First Nordic Rock Music Seminar. *Nordic Sounds* 1983/4: 3–5.

4010 Levine, Faye. 1976. *The Culture Barons: An Analysis of Power and Money in the Arts*. New York: Crowell.

4011 Malm, Krister. 1982. Phonograms and Cultural Policy in Sweden. In *The Phonogram in Cultural Communication*, ed. Kurt Blaukopf. Wien: Springer-Verlag. 43–74.

4012 Malm, Krister and Wallis, Roger. 1993. *Media Policy and Music Activity*. London: Routledge.

4013 Mattelart, A., X. Delcourt and M. Mattelart. 1984. *International Image Markets: In Search of an Alternative Perspective*. London: Comedia.

4014 Muikku, Jari. 1995. Cultural Policy of a State and Popular Music. In *Popular Music Perspectives III*, ed. Peter Wicke. Berlin: Zyankrise. 369–72.

4015 Mulgan, Geoff and Worpole, Ken. 1986. *Saturday Night or Sunday Morning? From Arts to Industry: New Forms of Cultural Policy*. London: Comedia.

4016 Natoli, Dario. 1985. Musica e politica dei media. In *Musica e sistema dell'informazione in Europa*, ed. Francesco Rampi. Milano: Unicopli. 179–84.

4017 Rutten, Paul. 1994. Popular Music Policy: A Contested Area. The Dutch Experience. In *Rock and Popular Music: Politics, Policies, Institutions*, ed. Tony Bennett, et al. London and New York: Routledge. 37–51.

4018 Straw, Will and Laroche, Karyna. 1989. Radio and Sound Recording Policy in Canada. *Australian-Canadian Studies* 7(1–2): 163–66.

4019 Street, John. 1993. Local Differences? Popular Music and the Local State. *Popular Music* 12(1): 43–55.

4020 Tapper, Karl-Herman. 1981. Regional Music Policy in Sweden: Problems and Projects. In *Stock-Taking of Musical Life: Sociography and Music Education*, ed. Desmond Mark. Wien: Doblinger. 104–107.

4021 Wallis, Roger and Malm, Krister. 1990. The Implications of Structural Changes in the Music Industry for Media Policy and Music Activity: A Research Framework. In *Popular Music Research*, ed. Keith Roe and Ulla Karlsson. Göteborg: NORDICOM-Sweden, No. 1–2. 11–20.

4022 Whisnant, David E. 1983. *All That Is Native and Fine: The Politics of Culture in an American Region*. Chapel Hill and London: University of North Carolina Press.

4023 Wicke, Peter. 1990. Kulturstaat statt Staatskultur. *Bulletin* XVII(1): 8–17.

4024 Wicke, Peter. 1993. Kooperativer Kulturaustausch. In *Kulturelle Modernisierung in Europa. Regionale Identitäten und soziokulturelle Konzepte*, ed. Olaf Schwencke, H. Schwengel and N. Sievers. Hagen: Kulturpolitische Gesellschaft. 135–47.

4025 Wicke, Peter. 1994. Aggressive Jugendstile – ein Problem der Jugendkultur (arbeit)? In *Gratwanderungen. Jugendkulturarbeit als Gewaltprävention?* Bonn: BMBW. 87–93.

4026 Wicke, Peter. 1994. Jugendkultur zwischen Industrie und Politik. In *Zukunftsforum Jugendkulturarbeit 20000 – Zur gesellschaftspolitischen Verantwortung kultureller Bildung*. Remscheid: Bundesvereinigung kulturelle Jugendbildung. 133–38.

4027 Wicke, Peter. 1994. Kultur in der Krise. *Kulturstrecke* 12(1): 13–18.

4028 Wicke, Peter. 1994. Neue Ökonomische Politik. *Neue Kultur* 1: 5–9.

4029 Wicke, Peter. 1994. Recht auf Rock 'n' Roll. *Evangelische Kommentare* 6: 357–62.

4030 Wicke, Peter. 1995. Zwischen Staat, Markt und Kulturszene. Kulturpolitik als intermediäres Konzept. In *Was ist und die Kultur wert? Kulturpolitik und Kulturelle Bildung im gesellschaftlichen Umbruch*. Bonn: BMBW. 33–40.

4031 Wicke, Peter. 1996. Das Dilemma der Quote. *Kulturpolitische Mitteilungen* 72/73(I/II): 12–13.

4032 Wicke, Peter. 1996. Popular Music and Processes of Social Transformation: The Case of Rock Music in Former East Germany. In *Socio-Cultural Aspects of Music in Europe*, ed. Paul Rutten. Brussels: European Music Office/Directorate General X. 77–84.

4033 Wicke, Peter. 1996. Zwischen Förderung und Reglementierung – Rockmusik im System der DDR-Kulturbürokratie. In *Rockmusik und Politik. Analysen, Interviews und Dokumente*, ed. Peter Wicke and Lothar Müller. Berlin: Ch. Links. 11–27.

4034 Wicke, Peter and Shepherd, John. 1993. 'The Cabaret Is Dead': Rock Culture as State Enterprise – The Political Organization of Rock in East Germany. In *Culture and Politics: The Politics of Culture*, ed. Tony Bennett. Sydney, London and Boston: Routledge & Kegan Paul. 25–36.

DANCE AND DANCING

4035 Anderson, Jack. 1987. *The American Dance Festival*. Durham, NC: Duke University Press.

4036 Banes, Sally. 1980. *Terpsichore in Sneakers: Post-Modern Dance*. Boston, MA: Houghton Mifflin.

4037 Berger, Renato. 1984. *Africa Dance: Afrikanischer Tanz in Vergangenheit und Zukunft Ursprung und Diaspora: Afrika, Karibik, Brasilien*. Wilhelmshaven: Heinrichshofen.

4038 *The Black Tradition in American Modern Dance*. 1988. Durham, NC: American Dance Festival.

4039 Blackford, Andy. 1979. *Disco Dancing Tonight: Clubs, Dances, Fashions, Music*. London: Octopus Books.

4040 Blum, Lucille Hollander. 1966/67. The Discotheque and the Phenomenon of Alone-Togetherness: A Study of the Young Person's Response to the Frug and Comparable Current Dances. *Adolescence* 1(4) (Winter): 351–66.

4041 Bradby, Barbara. 1993. Sampling Sexuality: Gender, Technology and the Body in Dance Music. *Popular Music* 12(2): 155–76.

4042 Braun, D. Duane. 1969. *Toward a Theory of Popular Culture: The Sociology and History of American Music and Dance, 1920–1968*. Ann Arbor, MI: Ann Arbor Publications.

4043 Breathnach, Brendan. 1971. *Folk Music and Dances of Ireland*. Dublin and Cork: The Mercier Press.

4044 Buckman, Peter. 1978. *Let's Dance: Social, Ballroom & Folk Dancing*. New York: Paddington Press.

4045 Buonaventura, Wendy. 1989. *Serpent of the Nile: Women and Dance in the Arab World*. London: Saqi.

4046 Casey, Betty. 1985. *Dance Across Texas*. Austin, TX: University of Texas Press.

4047 Cayou, Dolores Kirton. 1971. *Modern Jazz Dance*. Palo Alto, CA: Mayfield.

4048 Chujoy, Anatole and Manchester, P.W., eds. 1967. (1949) *The Dance Encyclopedia*, revised edition. New York: Simon & Schuster.

4049 Coe, Robert. 1985. *Dance in America*. New York: Dutton.

4050 Cowan, Jane K. 1990. *Dance and the Body Politic in Northern Greece.* Princeton, NJ: Princeton University Press.

4051 Craddock, J.R. 1937. The Cowboy Dance. *Texas Folklore Society Publications* 2: 31–37.

4052 Cressey, Paul. 1932. *The Taxi-Dance Hall.* New York: Greenwood Press.

4053 Dawson, Jim. 1995. *The Twist: The Story of the Song and Dance That Changed the World.* Boston and London: Faber & Faber.

4054 Delamater, Jerome. 1981. *Dance in the Hollywood Musical.* Ann Arbor, MI: UMI Research Press.

4055 De Mille, Agnes. 1980. *American Dances.* New York and London: Collier Macmillan.

4056 Dyer, Richard. 1990. (1979) In Defense of Disco. In *On Record: Rock, Pop and the Written Word,* ed. Simon Frith and Andrew Goodwin. London: Routledge. 410–18.

4057 Emery, Lynne Fauley. 1988. *Black Dance in the United States: From 1619 to Today,* 2nd revised edition. Manchester, NH: Ayer.

4058 Emmerson, George Sinclair. 1972. *A Social History of Scottish Dance.* Montréal: McGill-Queen's University Press.

4059 Erlmann, Veit. 1989. 'Horses in the Race Course': The Domestication of Ingoma Dancing in South Africa, 1929–39. *Popular Music* 8(3): 259–74.

4060 Fallon, Dennis J. 1980. *The Art of Disco Dancing.* Reston, VA: National Dance Association.

4061 Feldman, Walter. 1994. Bulgareasa/ Bulgarish/Bulgar: The Transformation of a Klezmer Dance Genre. *Ethnomusicology* 38(1): 1–35.

4062 Fenger, Sven. 1982. Keep Dancing. *Modspil* 4(6): 21–26.

4063 Forbes, Fred R., comp. 1986. *Dance: An Annotated Bibliography, 1965–1982.* New York: Garland.

4064 Frank, Rusty E. 1990. *The Greatest Tap Dance Stars and Their Stories, 1900–1955.* New York: William Morrow.

4065 Franks, Arthur Henry. 1963. *Social Dance: A Short History.* London: Routledge & Kegan Paul.

4066 Gaffney, Floyd. 1979. Evolution and Revolution of Afro-Brazilian Dance. *Journal of Popular Culture* 13(1): 98–105.

4067 Garfias, Robert. 1984. Dance Among the Urban Gypsies of Romania. *Yearbook for Traditional Music* 16: 84–96.

4068 Gorer, Geoffrey. 1962. (1935) *Africa Dances: A Book About West African Negroes.* New York: Norton.

4069 Gotfrit, Leslie. 1991. Women Dancing Back: Disruption and the Politics of Pleasure. In *Postmodernism, Feminism, and Cultural Politics,* ed. Henry A. Giroux. Albany, NY: State University of New York Press. 174–95.

4070 Günther, Helmut. 1970. *Grundphänomene und Grundbegriffe des afrikanischen und afro-amerikanischen Tanzes.* Wien: Universal Edition.

4071 Günther, Helmut. 1980. *Jazzdance: Geschichte, Theorie, Praxis.* Berlin: Henschel.

4072 Günther, Helmut. 1982. *Die Tänze und Riten der Afro-Amerikaner. Vom Kongo bis Samba und Soul.* Bonn: Dance Motion.

4073 Günther, Helmut and Haag, Hubert. 1976. *Von Rock 'n' Roll bis Soul. Die modernen Poptänze.* Stuttgart: Ifland.

4074 Günther, Helmut and Schäfer, Helmut. 1975. *Vom Schamanentanz zur Rumba.* Stuttgart: Ifland.

4075 Hazzard-Gordon, Katrina. 1990. *Jookin': The Rise of Social Dance Formation in African-American Culture.* Philadelphia: Temple University Press.

4076 Horst, Louis. 1969. *Modern Dance Forms in Relation to the Other Modern Arts.* New York: Dance Horizons.

4077 Hughes, Walter. 1994. In the Empire of the Beat: Discipline and Disco. In *Microphone Fiends: Youth Music and Youth Culture,* ed. Andrew Ross and Tricia Rose. London: Routledge.

4078 Hustwitt, Mark. 1983. Caught in a Whirlpool of Aching Sound: The Production of Dance Music in Britain in the 1920s. *Popular Music* 3: 7–32.

4079 Jones, Betty, ed. 1983. *Dance as Cultural Heritage.* New York: Congress on Research on Dance.

4080 Jordan, Stephanie and Allen, Dave, eds. 1993. *Parallel Lines: Media Representations of Dance.* London: John Libbey & Co.

4081 Kaeppler, Adrienne. 1991. American Approaches to the Study of Dance. *Yearbook for Traditional Music* 23: 11–22.

4082 Katz, Ruth. 1983. *What Is Dance? Readings in Criticism and Theory,* ed. R. Copeland and M. Cohen. Toronto: Oxford University Press.

4083 Kilbride, Ann T. and Algoso, A. 1979. *The Complete Book of Disco and Ballroom Dancing.* Los Alamitos, CA: Hwong Pub. Co.

4084 Kimball, James. 1988. Country Dancing in Central and Eastern New York State. *New York Folklore* 14(3–4): 71–88.

4085 Kislan, Richard. 1987. *Hoofing on Broadway: A History of Show Dancing.* New York: Prentice-Hall.

4086 Koebner, Franz W. 1921. *Jazz und Shimmy.* Berlin: Eysler.

4087 Kovalcsik, Katalin. 1984. Popular Dance Music Elements in the Folk Music of Gypsies in Hungary. *Popular Music* 4: 45–66.

4088 Krich, John. 1993. *Why Is This Country Dancing?* New York: Simon & Schuster.

4089 Kurth, Ulrich. 1987. 'Ich pfeif auf Tugend und Moral' Zum Foxtrott in den zwanziger Jahren. In *Ich will aber gerade vom Leben singen . . . Über populäre Musik vom ausgehenden 19. Jahrhundert bis zum Ende der Weimarer Republik,* ed. Sabine Schutte. Reinbek bei Hamburg: Rowohlt. 365–84.

4090 LaPointe-Crump, Janice and Staley, Kimberly. 1992. *Discovering Jazz Dance: America's Energy and Soul.* Dubuque, IA: Brown and Benchmark.

4091 Lawson, Joan. 1953. *European Folk Dance: Its National and Musical Characteristics.* London: Pitman Publishing.

4092 Long, Richard A. 1989. *The Black Tradition in American Modern Dance.* New York: Rizzoli.

4093 Lustgarten, Karen. 1978. *The Complete Guide to Disco Dancing.* New York: Warner Books.

4094 Magriel, Paul David, comp. 1966. *A Bibliography of Dancing: A List of Books and Articles on the Dance and Related Subjects.* New York: B. Blom.

4095 McCarthy, Albert. 1974. (1971) *The Dance Band Era: The Dancing Decades from Ragtime to Swing, 1910–1950.* London: Spring Books.

4096 McRobbie, Angela. 1984. Dance and Social Fantasy. In *Gender and*

Generation, ed. Angela McRobbie and Mica Nava. London: Macmillan. 130–61.

4097 Mead, Margaret. 1943. (1928) The Role of the Dance. In *Coming of Age in Samoa*. London: Pelican.

4098 Moore, Alex. 1978. *Gesellschaftstanz*. Stuttgart: Ifland.

4099 Mosco, Carner. 1950. *The Waltz*. London: Max Parrish.

4100 Müller, Renate. 1995. Rocktanz im Unterricht als soziale Realität. In *Popular Music Perspectives III*, ed. Peter Wicke. Berlin: Zyankrise. 363–68.

4101 Nettl, Paul. 1989. *The Story of Dance Music*. New York: Greenwood Press.

4102 O'Grady, Terence. 1979. 'Rubber Soul' and the Social Dance Tradition. *Ethnomusicology* 23(1): 87–94.

4103 Otterbach, Friedemann. 1980. *Die Geschichte der europäischen Tanzmusik. Einführung*. Wilhelmshaven: Heinrichshofen.

4104 Peel, Barbara. 1986. *Dancing and Social Assemblies in York in the Eighteenth and Nineteenth Centuries*. National Resource Centre for Dance, University of Surrey.

4105 Piedra, José. 1991. Poetics for the Hip. *New Literary History* 22: 633–75.

4106 Poveda, Pablo. 1981. Danza de Concheros en Austin, Texas: Entrevista con Andrés Segura Granados. *Latin American Music Review* 2(2): 280–99.

4107 Raffé, W.G. 1964. *Dictionary of the Dance*. New York and London: Barnes.

4108 Renault, Patrick. 1978. *Les bals en France*. Paris: Music et Promotion/ S.A.C.E.M.

4109 Rirzei, Fred. 1987. 'Hatte der Kaiser Jazz getanzt . . . ' US-Tanzmusik in Deutschland vor und nach dem Erster Weltkrieg. In *Ich will aber gerade vom Leben singen . . . Über populäre Musik vom ausgehenden 19. Jahrhundert bis zum Ende der Weimarer Republik*, ed. Sabine Schutte. Reinbek bei Hamburg: Rowohlt. 265–96.

4110 Roman, Leslie G. 1988. Intimacy, Labor and Class: Ideologies of Feminine Sexuality in the Punk Slam Dance. In *Becoming Feminine: The Politics of Popular Culture*. London: Falmer Press.

4111 Rust, Frances. 1969. *Dance in Society: An Analysis of the Relationship Between the Social Dance and Society in England from the Middle Ages to the Present Day*. London: Routledge.

4112 Sachs, Curt. 1937. *World History of the Dance*. New York: W.W. Norton & Co.

4113 Santa-Cruz, César. 1977. *El Waltz y el valse criollo*. Lima: Instituto Nacional de la Cultura.

4114 Savigliano, Marta E. 1995. *Tango and the Political Economy of Passion*. Boulder, CO: Westview Press.

4115 Schleman, Hilton R. 1978. (1936) *Rhythm on Record: A Complete Survey and Register of All the Principal Recorded Dance Music, 1906–1936*. Westport, CT: Greenwood Press. First published London: Melody Maker, 1936.

4116 Schlundt, Christena L., et al. 1989. *Dance in the Musical Theatre: Jerome Robbins and His Peers, 1934–1965*. New York: Garland.

4117 Schutte, Sabine. 1970. *Der Ländler. Untersuchungen zur musikalischen Struktur ungeradtaktiger österreichischer Volkstänze*. Baden-Baden: Heitz.

4118 Seebass, Tilman. 1991. Iconography and Dance Research. *Yearbook for Traditional Music* 23: 33–52.

4119 Sellers-Young, Barbara. 1992. Raks El Sharki: Transculturation of a Folk Form.

Journal of Popular Culture 26(2): 141–52.

4120 Shaw, Lloyd. 1939. *Cowboy Dances.* Caldwell, ID: Caxton Printers.

4121 Spencer, Paul, ed. 1985. *Society and Dance: The Social Anthropology of Process and Performance.* New York: Cambridge University Press.

4122 Stearns, Marshall, and Stearns, Jean. 1964. *Jazz Dance.* New York: Macmillan.

4123 Stibal, Mary E. 1977. Disco: Birth of a New Marketing System. *Journal of Marketing* (October): 82–88.

4124 Stone, Martha. 1975. *At the Sign of Midnight: The Concheros Dance Cult of Mexico.* Tucson, AZ: University of Arizona Press.

4125 Straw, Will. 1995. Dance Music on North American Radio. In *Popular Music Perspectives III*, ed. Peter Wicke. Berlin: Zyankrise. 224–31.

4126 Thomas, Helen, ed. 1993. *Dance, Gender and Culture.* London: Macmillan.

4127 Thomas, Helen. 1995. *Dance, Modernity & Culture: Explorations in the Sociology of Dance.* New York and London: Routledge.

4128 Thornton, Sarah. 1995. *Club Cultures: Music, Media and Subcultural Capital.* Cambridge: Polity.

4129 Thornton, Sarah. 1995. Dancing to Discs: The Public Life of a Commodity. In *Popular Music Perspectives III*, ed. Peter Wicke. Berlin: Zyankrise. 266–71.

4130 Thorpe, Edward. 1989. *Black Dance.* London: Chatto & Windus.

4131 Torp, Lisbet. 1986. Hip Hop Dances: Their Adoption and Function Among Boys in Denmark, 1983–1984. *Yearbook for Traditional Music* 18: 29–86.

4132 Tracey, Hugh. 1952. *African Dances of the Witwatersrand Gold Mines.* Johannesburg: African Music Society.

4133 Valle, Gianni. 1980. *Il manuale di ballo.* Roma: Lato Side.

4134 Van Zile, Judy. 1976. *Dance in Africa, Asia and the Pacific: Selected Readings.* New York: MSS Information Corp.

4135 Vega, Carlos. 1952. *Las Dansas Populares Argentinas.* Buenos Aires: Instituto de Musicologia.

4136 Vloet, Rosita van der and Borgers, Berdien. 1984. *Jazzdans: oude vormen, nieuwe stijlen.* Amsterdam: Sua.

4137 Wees, Inga van der and Thiem, Andrea. 1993. *Shimmy & Charleston. Die Jazztänze der zwanziger Jahre.* Frankfurt am Main: Fischer.

4138 Whiteman, Paul. 1974. (1926) *Jazz.* New York: Arno Press.

DEATH

4139 Clayson, Alan. 1992. *Death Discs.* London: Gollancz.

4140 Dallas, Karl. 1971. *Singers of an Empty Day: Last Sacraments for the Superstars.* London: Kahn & Averill.

4141 Denisoff, R. Serge. 1983. 'Teen Angel': Resistance, Rebellion and Death – Revisited. *Journal of Popular Culture* 16(4): 116–22.

4142 Duncan, Robert. 1986. *Only the Good Die Young: The Rock 'n' Roll Book of the Dead.* New York: Harmony Books.

4143 Marcus, Greil. 1994. Rock Death in the 1970s: A Sweepstakes. In *In the Fascist Bathroom: Writings on Punk, 1977–1992.* New York: Penguin. 57–78.

4144 Tagg, Philip. 1985. Musiken: språket som alla förstår? Fallet med 'dödsmusiken'. In *Tvärkulturell kommunikation*, ed. Jens Allwood. Göteborg: Lingvistiska institutionen, PAL 12. 220–48.

4145 Tagg, Philip. 1990. 'Universal' Music and the Case of Death. In *La musica come linguaggio universale*, ed. Raffaele Pozzi. Firenze: Leo S. Olschki. 227–66.

DRUGS

4146 Baumeister, Roy. 1984. Acid Rock: A Critical Reappraisal and Psychological Commentary. *Journal of Psychoactive Drugs* 16(4): 339–45.

4147 Beckley, Robert and Chalfant, H. Paul. 1979. Contrasting Images of Alcohol and Drug Use in Country and Rock Music. *Journal of Alcohol and Drug Education* 25(1): 44–51.

4148 Douse, Mike. 1973. Contemporary Music, Drug Attitudes and Drug Behaviour. *Australian Journal of Social Issues* 8(1): 74–80.

4149 Hawes, Hampton and Asher, Don. 1979. (1974) *Raise Up Off Me: A Portrait of Hampton Hawes*. New York: Da Capo Press. First published New York: Coward, McCann, 1974.

4150 Hentoff, Nat. 1962. *The Jazz Life*. London: Peter Davies.

4151 Herman, Gary. 1994. *Rock 'n' Roll Babylon*. London: Plexus.

4152 Joynson, Vernon. 1984. *The Acid Trip*. Todmorden, W. Yorks: Babylon Books.

4153 McKenna, Terrence. 1992. *Food of the Gods: The Search for the Original Tree of Knowledge*. New York: Bantam.

4154 Mezzrow, Milton, and Wolfe, Bernard. 1946. *Really the Blues*. New York: Random House.

4155 O'Day, Anita and Eells, George. 1983. *High Times, Hard Times*. London: Corgi.

4156 Pepper, Art and Pepper, Laurie. 1979. *Straight Life: The Story of Art Pepper*. New York: Schirmer.

4157 Robinson, John P. and Pilskaln, Robert. 1976. Protest Rock and Drugs. *Journal of Communications* 26(4): 125–36.

4158 Russell, Ross. 1973. *Bird Lives!* London: Quartet.

4159 Saporita, Jay. 1980. *Pourin' It All Out*. Secaucus, NJ: Citadel Press.

4160 Shapiro, Harry. 1988. *Waiting for the Man: The Story of Drugs and Popular Music*. London: Quartet.

4161 Sugarman, Danny. 1989. *Wonderland Avenue: Tales of Glamour and Excess*. New York: New American Library.

4162 Taylor, Arthur. 1993. *Notes and Tones: Musician-to-Musician Interviews*. New York: Da Capo Press. First published New York: Perigee Books, 1982.

4163 Taylor, Rogan. 1985. *The Death and Resurrection Show: From Shaman to Superstar*. London: Anthony Blond.

4164 Winick, Charles. 1959. The Use of Drugs by Jazz Musicians. *Social Problems* 7: 240–53.

4165 Winick, Charles. 1961. How High the Moon: Jazz and Drugs. *Antioch Review* (Spring): 53–68.

EDUCATION

4166 Baroni, Mario and Nanni, Franco. 1989. *Crescere con il rock. L'educazione musicale nella societa dei mass-media*. Bologna: Clueb.

4167 Birkett, James. 1992. Popular Music Education: The Dawning of a New Age. *Popular Music* 11(2): 239–41.

4168 Björnberg, Alf. 1993. 'Teach You to Rock?': Popular Music in the University

SOCIAL AND CULTURAL CONTEXTS

Music Department. *Popular Music* 12(1): 69–77.

4169 Björnberg, Alf. 1995. School's Out? Popular Music in Academic Music Education. In *Popular Music Perspectives III*, ed. Peter Wicke. Berlin: Zyankrise. 331–39.

4170 Boyer, Régine, et al. 1986. *Les Lycéens et la musique*. Paris: INRP.

4171 Chambers, Iain. 1989. Per un insegnamento della pop music. *Quaderni di Musica/Realtà* 23: 113–31.

4172 De Lerma, Dominique-René, ed. 1970. *Black Music in Our Culture: Curricular Ideas on the Subjects, Materials and Problems*. Kent, OH: Kent State University Press.

4173 De Lerma, Dominique-René. 1984. *Bibliography of Black Music, Vol. 4. Theory, Education and Related Studies*. Westport and London: Greenwood Press.

4174 Ellison, Mary. 1990. Teaching Popular Music. *Popular Music* 9(3): 371–73.

4175 Faulstich, Werner. 1978. *Rock – Pop – Beat – Folk. Grundlagen der Text-Musik-Analyse*. Tübingen: Gunter Narr.

4176 Green, Lucy. 1988. *Music on Deaf Ears: Musical Meaning, Ideology, Education*. Manchester: Manchester University Press.

4177 Hartwich-Wiechell, Dörte. 1974. *Pop-Musik: Analysen und Interpretationen*. Köln: Arno Volk Verlag.

4177a Hartwich-Wiechell, Dörte. 1975. *Didaktik und Methodik der Popmusik*. Frankfurt am Main: Diesterweg.

4178 Hennion, Antoine, ed. 1988. Apprendre la musique. *Vibrations* 6 (September).

4179 Hodek, Johannes and Niermann, Franz. 1984. *Rockmusik – Rockkultur*. Stuttgart: J.B. Metzlersche Verlagsbuchhandlung.

4180 Horn, David. 1995. Instituting Popular Music Studies. In *Popular Music Perspectives III*, ed. Peter Wicke. Berlin: Zyankrise. 392–401.

4181 Huber, Harald. 1985. Popularmusik an der Hochschule für Musik und darstellende Kunst in Wien. *Jazzforschung* 17: 57–60.

4182 Jerrentrup, Ansgar. 1994. Die Vermittlung Populärer Musik durch Erwachsene. In *Populäre Musik und Pädagogik – Grundlagen und Praxismaterialien*, ed. Jürgen Terhag. Oldershausen: Institut für Didaktik der populären Musik. 173–74.

4183 Josephs, Norman. 1982. Popular Music Research: Its Uses in Education. In *Popular Music Perspectives, 1*, ed. David Horn and Philip Tagg. Göteborg and Exeter: IASPM. 243–45.

4184 Knauf, Diethelm and Watson, Ian. 1985. Populäre Musik im Englischunterricht: Probleme und Perspektiven. *Jazzforschung* 17: 42–48.

4185 Konrad, Bernd. 1990. Auf einige Probleme der Jazzpädagogik hingewiesen. In *Darmstädter Jazzforum 89: Beiträge zur Jazzforschung*, ed. Ekkehard Jost. Hofheim: Wolke. 152–60.

4186 Kramarz, Volkmar. 1994. The Kids and the Radio. In *Populäre Musik und Pädagogik – Grundlagen und Praxismaterialien*, ed. Jürgen Terhag. Oldershausen: Institut für Didaktik der populären Musik. 202–206.

4187 Lartigot, Jean-Claude and Sprogis, Eric. 1975. *Libérer la musique*. Paris: Ed. universitaires.

4188 Lee, Johnnie V., et al. 1973. Black Music in the Undergraduate Curriculum. In *Reflections on Afro-American Music*, ed. Dominique-René De Lerma. Kent, OH: Kent State University Press. 51–75.

4189 Linke, Rainer. 1985. Jazz und Popularmusik an der Musikhochschule Köln. *Jazzforschung* 17: 53–54.

4190 Lugert, Wulf-Dieter. 1985. The Beat Goes On: Zur gegenwärtigen Stand einer Didaktik der Pop- und Rockmusik. *Jazzforschung* 17: 24–29.

4191 Maas, Georg. 1995. Der lange Marsch durch die Institutionen: Konzeption, Situation und Problematik einer Popularmusikdidaktik im Musikunterricht an Allgemeinbildenden Schulen. In *Popular Music Perspectives III*, ed. Peter Wicke. Berlin: Zyankrise. 351–62.

4192 Maas, Georg and Schmidt-Brunner, Wolfgang. 1988. *Pop/Rock im Unterricht: Eine kommentierte Bibliographie, Diskographie, Filmographie (Primarstufe und Sekundarstufe I und II)*. Mainz: Schott.

4193 Mark, Desmond, ed. 1981. *Stock-Taking of Musical Life: Sociography and Music Education*. Wien: Doblinger.

4194 Miller, Manfred. 1978. Ein E für ein U vorgemacht. Musikpädagogik und Rockmusik. *Anschläge. Zeitschrift des Archivs für Populäre Musik* I(1): 124–39.

4195 Müller, Renate. 1995. Rocktanz im Unterricht als soziale Realität. In *Popular Music Perspectives III*, ed. Peter Wicke. Berlin: Zyankrise. 363–68.

4196 Neitmann, Erich. 1982. *Das politische Lied im schulischen Musikunterricht der DDR*. Bern: Lang.

4197 Niermann, Franz. 1987. *Rockmusik und Unterricht. Eigene Wege für den Alltag mit Musik*. Stuttgart: J.B. Metzler.

4198 Ostleitner, Elena. 1985. Popmusik und Lernen: Ein interdiziplinärer und -kultureller Ansatz (Lateinamerikanische Popmusik). *Jazzforschung* 17: 39–42.

4199 Pape, Winfried. 1974. *Musikkonsum und Musikunterricht*. Düsseldorf: Schwann.

4200 Paynter, John. 1974. Music Education and the Emotional Needs of Young People: Towards a New Type of Research. In *New Patterns of Musical Behaviour*, ed. Irmgard Bontinck. Wien: Universal Edition. 159–66.

4201 Rauhe, Hermann. 1985. Grundprobleme der Ausbildung und Fortbildung von Künstlern und Pädagogen im Popularmusikbereich. *Jazzforschung* 17: 15–24.

4202 Roe, Keith and Löfgren, Monica. 1987. Music Video Use and Educational Achievement. *Popular Music* 7(3): 303–14.

4203 Rösing, Helmut. 1985. Jazz und Popularmusik: Aspekte der Ausbildung im Hochschulbereich. *Jazzforschung* 17: 49–51.

4204 Rösing, Helmut, Alenka Barber-Kersovan and Armin Fuchs, eds. 1985. Popmusik und Lernen: Beiträge einer Tagung der IASPM (BRD) 10–12 Okt. 1984 (Hamburg). *Jazzforschung* 17: 9–14.

4205 Scharrer, Wolfgang. 1985. Didaktisches Modell zum (re-)produktiven Gestalten populärer Musikstücke im Unterricht. *Jazzforschung* 17: 29–33.

4206 Schütz, Volker. 1982. *Rockmusik – eine Herausforderung für Schüler und Lehrer*. Oldenburg: Isensee.

4207 Shepherd, John. 1985. Prolegomena for the Critical Study of Popular Music. *Canadian Journal of Communication* 11(1): 17–34, 141–44.

4208 Shepherd, John. 1989. Estetica, valore e influenza africana nella popular music: implicazioni interculturali per l'educazione musicale. *Musica/Realtà* 29 (August): 81–92.

4209 Shepherd, John. 1993. Music and the Last Intellectuals. In *Philosopher, Teacher, Musician: Perspectives on Music Education*, ed. Estelle R. Jorgensen.

Urbana and Chicago: University of Illinois Press. 95–114.

4210 Shepherd, John and Vulliamy, Graham. 1983. A Comparative Sociology of School Knowledge. *British Journal of Sociology of Education* 4(1): 3–10.

4211 Shepherd, John and Vulliamy, Graham. 1984. The Application of a Critical Sociology to Music Education. *British Journal of Music Education* 1: 247–66.

4212 Shepherd, John and Vulliamy, Graham. 1994. The Struggle for Culture: A Sociological Case Study of the Development of a National Music Curriculum. *British Journal of Sociology of Education* 15(1): 27–40.

4213 Small, Christopher. 1977. *Music – Society – Education: A Radical Examination of the Prophetic Function of Music in Western, Eastern and African Cultures.* London: Calder.

4214 Straarup, Ole. 1982. Popular Music Research: Needs and Uses in Education. In *Popular Music Perspectives, 1*, ed. David Horn and Philip Tagg. Göteborg and Exeter: IASPM. 246–48.

4215 Swanwick, Keith. 1968. *Popular Music and the Teacher.* Oxford: Pergamon Press.

4216 Swanwick, Keith. 1979. *A Basis for Music Education.* Slough: NFER.

4217 Swanwick, Keith. 1984. A Further Note on Sociology of Music Education. *British Journal of Sociology of Education* 5(3): 303–307.

4218 Swanwick, Keith. 1984. Problems of a Sociological Approach to Pop Music in Schools. *British Journal of Sociology of Education* 5(1): 49–56.

4219 Tagg, Philip. 1982. Music Teacher Training Problems and Popular Music Research. In *Popular Music Perspectives, 1*, ed. David Horn and Philip Tagg. Göteborg and Exeter: IASPM. 232–42.

4220 Tagg, Philip. 1990. Music in Mass Media Studies: Reading Sounds, for Example. In *Popular Music Research*, ed. Keith Roe and Ulla Karlsson. Göteborg: NORDICOM-Sweden, No. 1–2. 103–14.

4221 Taylor, Dorothy. 1979. *Music Now: A Guide to Recent Developments and Current Opportunities in Music Education.* Milton Keynes: Open University Press.

4222 Taylor, Dorothy. 1981. Trends and Developments in Music Education: A British Perspective. In *Stock-Taking of Musical Life: Sociography and Music Education*, ed. Desmond Mark. Wien: Doblinger. 108–20.

4223 Terhag, Jürgen, ed. 1994. *Populäre Musik und Pädagogik – Grundlagen und Praxismaterialien.* Oldershausen: Institut für Didaktik der populären Musik.

4224 Vulliamy, Graham. 1975. Music Education: Some Critical Comments. *Journal of Curriculum Studies* 7: 18–25.

4225 Vulliamy, Graham. 1976. What Counts as School Music? In *Explorations in the Politics of School Knowledge*, ed. G. Whitty and M.F.D. Young. Driffield: Nafferton. 19–34.

4226 Vulliamy, Graham. 1977. Music as a Case Study in the 'New Sociology of Education'. In *Whose Music? A Sociology of Musical Languages.* London: Latimer. 201–32.

4227 Vulliamy, Graham. 1978. Culture Clash and School Music: A Sociological Analysis. In *Sociological Interpretations of Schooling and Classrooms: A Reappraisal*, ed. L. Barton and R. Meighan. Driffield: Nafferton. 115–27.

4228 Vulliamy, Graham. 1980. Music Education and Musical Languages. *Australian Journal of Music Education* 26: 25–28.

4229 Vulliamy, Graham. 1985. A Sociological View of Music Education: An Essay in the Sociology of Knowledge. *Canadian University Music Review* 1984/5: 17–37.

4230 Vulliamy, Graham and Lee, Edward. 1976. *Pop Music in School.* Cambridge: Cambridge University Press.

4231 Vulliamy, Graham and Lee, Edward, eds. 1982. *Pop, Rock and Ethnic Music in School.* London: Cambridge University Press.

4232 Vulliamy, Graham and Shepherd, John. 1984. Sociology and Music Education: A Response to Swanwick. *British Journal of Sociology of Education* 5(1): 57–76.

4233 Vulliamy, Graham and Shepherd, John. 1985. Sociology and Music Education: A Further Response to Swanwick. *British Journal of Sociology of Education* 6(2): 225–29.

4234 Whigham, Jiggs. 1994. Theorie und Praxis des Unterrichts in Jazz. In *Populäre Musik und Pädagogik – Grundlagen und Praxismaterialien,* ed. Jürgen Terhag. Oldershausen: Institut für Didaktik der populären Musik. 175–82.

4235 Wicke, Peter. 1993. *Vom Umgang mit Popmusik.* Berlin: Volk und Wissen.

4236 Wicke, Peter. 1994. Aggressive Jugendstile – ein Problem der Jugendkultur (arbeit)? In *Gratwanderungen. Jugendkulturarbeit als Gewaltprävention?* Bonn: BMBW. 87–93.

4237 Wicke, Peter. 1994. Recht auf Rock 'n' Roll. *Evangelische Kommentare* 6: 357–62.

4238 Wicke, Peter. 1996. Auf der Suche nach dem verlorengegangenem Sinn – Popmusik und Sinnerfahrung. In *Verwerfungen in der Gesellschaft – Verwandlungen in der Schule. Musikunterricht – Lehrplan – Studium,* ed. D. Knolle. Augsburg: Wißner-Verlag. 29–37.

4239 No entry.

4240 Wilkinson, Christopher. 1994. The Influence of West African Pedagogy upon the Education of New Orleans Jazz Musicians. *Black Music Research Journal* 14(1): 25–42.

4241 Zenkl, Ludek and Chyba, Milos, eds. 1982. *Hudební sociologie a hudební vychova.* Prague: Ceská hudební spolecnost.

4242 Zimmerschied, Dieter. 1971. *Beat – Background – Beethoven.* Frankfurt am Main, Berlin and München: Diesterweg.

ETHNICITY

4243 Allinson, E. 1994. It's a Black Thing: Hearing How Whites Can't. *Cultural Studies* 8(3): 438–56.

4244 Ballantine, Christopher. 1995. The Identities of Race, Class and Gender in the Repression of Early Black South African Jazz and Vaudeville (ca. 1920–1944). In *Popular Music: Style and Identity,* ed. Will Straw, et al. Montréal: The Centre for Research on Canadian Cultural Industries and Institutions. 9–12.

4245 Béhague, Gerard H., ed. 1994. *Music and Black Ethnicity: The Caribbean and South America.* New Brunswick and London: Transaction.

4246 Berry, Venise T. 1993. Crossing Over: Musical Perceptions Within Black Adolescent Culture. *Journal of Popular Music Studies* 5: 26–38.

4247 Bibliography of Ethnic Musics in America. 1978. *Selected Reports in Ethnomusicology* 3(1): 241–59.

4248 Carvalho, José Jorge de. 1993. *Black Music of All Colors: The Construction of Black Ethnicity in Ritual and Popular Genres of Afro-Brazilian Music.* Brasília: Departamento de Antropologia/

Universidade de Brasília, Série Antropologia, No. 145.

4249 Carvalho, José Jorge de. 1994. *The Multiplicity of Black Identities in Brazilian Popular Music*. Brasília: Departamento de Antropologia/Universidade de Brasília, Série Antropologia, No. 163.

4250 Cayer, David A. 1974. Black and Blue and Black Again: Three Stages of Racial Imagery in Jazz Lyrics. *Journal of Jazz Studies* 1(2): 38–71.

4251 Cross, Brian. 1993. *It's Not About a Salary: Rap, Race and Resistance in Los Angeles*. London and New York: Verso.

4252 Erenberg, Lewis. 1984. (1981) *Steppin' Out: New York Nightlife and the Transformation of American Culture, 1890–1930*. Chicago: University of Chicago Press.

4253 Ethnic Literature and Music. 1983. *Melus* 10(1): 1–114.

4254 *Ethnic Recordings in America: A Neglected Heritage*. 1982. Washington, DC: American Folklife Center, Library of Congress.

4255 Ferris, William R. 1970. Racial Repertoires Among Blues Performers. *Ethnomusicology* 14(3): 439–49.

4256 George, Nelson. 1993. *Buppies, B-Boys, Baps and Bohos: Notes on Post-Soul Culture*. New York: HarperCollins.

4257 Glasser, Ruth. 1990. Paradoxical Ethnicity: Puerto Rican Musicians in Post World War I New York City. *Latin American Music Review* 11(1): 63–72.

4258 Greene, Victor. 1993. *A Passion for Polka: Old Time Ethnic Music in America*. Berkeley and Los Angeles: University of California Press.

4259 Hirschberg, Jehoash. 1989. *The Role of Music in the Renewed Self-Identity of Karaite Jewish Refugee Communities from Cairo*. New York: International Council for Traditional Music.

4260 Hisama, Ellie M. 1993. Postcolonialism on the Make: The Music of John Mellencamp, David Bowie and John Zorn. *Popular Music* 12(2): 91–104.

4261 Irving, Katrina. 1993. 'I Want Your Hands On Me': Building Equivalences Through Rap Music. *Popular Music* 12(2): 105–21.

4262 Jones, LeRoi (Imamu Amiri Baraka). 1963. *Blues People: Negro Music in White America*. New York: Morrow.

4263 Jones, Simon. 1988. *Black Culture, White Youth: The Reggae Tradition from JA to UK*. Basingstoke: Macmillan Education.

4264 Keil, Charles. 1994. 'Ethnic' Music Traditions in the USA (Black Music; Country Music; Others; All). *Popular Music* 13(2): 175–78.

4265 Krasnow, Carolyn. 1993. Fear and Loathing in the 70s: Race, Sexuality and Disco. *Stanford Humanities Review* 3(2): 37–45.

4266 Krehbiel, Henry Edward. 1962. *Afro-American Folk-Songs: A Study in Racial and National Music*. New York: Ungar.

4267 Lipsitz, George. 1990. *Time Passages: Collective Memory and American Popular Culture*. Minneapolis, MN: University of Minnesota Press.

4268 Loza, Steven, ed. 1994. *Musical Aesthetics and Multiculturism in Los Angeles*. Los Angeles: Selected Reports in Ethnomusicology, 10.

4269 Lusane, Clarence. 1993. Rap, Race and Politics. *Race and Class* 35(1): 41–56.

4270 Morton, David and Wolfe, Charles K. 1991. *De Ford Bailey: A Black Star in Early Country Music*. Knoxville, TN: University of Tennessee Press.

4271 Oliver, Paul, ed. 1990. *Black Music in Britain: Essays on the Afro-Asian Contribution to Popular Music.* Milton Keynes: Open University Press.

4272 Ostendorf, Berndt. 1983. *Ethnicity and Popular Music: On Immigrants and Blacks in American Music, 1830–1900.* Exeter: IASPM UK.

4273 Peña, Manuel. 1985. From Ranchero to Jaitón: Ethnicity and Class in Texas-Mexican Music (Two Styles in the Form of a Pair). *Ethnomusicology* 29(1): 29–55.

4274 Rose, Tricia. 1994. *Black Noise: Rap Music and Black Culture in Contemporary America.* Hanover and London: Wesleyan University Press.

4275 Slobin, Mark. 1983. Tenement Songs: The Popular Music of Jewish Immigrants. *Popular Music* 3: 289–92.

4276 Slobin, Mark. 1984. Klezmer Music: An American Ethnic Genre. *Yearbook for Traditional Music* 16: 34–41.

4277 Spottswood, Richard K. 1990. *Ethnic Music on Records: A Discography of Ethnic Recordings Produced in the United States, 1893–1942.* 7 vols. Urbana, IL: University of Illinois Press.

4278 Statelova, Rosemary. 1995. Strastite na edna muzika. Po problema za etnicheskata identichnost. *Bulgarski folklor* 5: 42–56.

4279 Stokes, Martin, ed. 1994. *Ethnicity, Identity and Music: The Musical Construction of Place.* Oxford: Berg.

4280 Tawa, Nicholas E. 1982. *A Sound of Strangers: Musical Culture, Acculturation and the Post-Civil War Ethnic American.* Metuchen, NJ: Scarecrow Press.

FASCISM

4281 Beck, Earl R. 1985. The Anti-Nazi 'Swing Youth'. *Journal of Popular Culture* 19(3): 45–54.

4282 Bender, Otto. 1993. *Swing unterm Hakenkreuz in Hamburg 1933–1943.* Hamburg: Christians.

4283 Dümling, Albrecht and Girth, Peter, eds. 1988. *Entartete Musik: Eine kommentierte Rekonstruktion zur Düsseldorfer Ausstellung von 1938.* Düsseldorf: Landeshauptstadt Düsseldorf.

4284 Fahr, Margitta. 1996. Odins Erben. Nordheldentum und nordische Mythologie in Rechtsrock-Texten an ausgewählten Beispielen der Britischen Band 'Skrewdriver'. *PopScriptum* 5: 90–105.

4285 Kater, Michael H. 1992. *Different Drummers: Jazz in the Culture of Nazi Germany.* New York: Oxford University Press.

4286 Kersten, Martin. 1996. Jugendkulturen und NS-Vergangenheit. Der schmale Plad zwischen Provokation, Spiel, Inszenierung und erneuter Faszination vom Punk bis zum Nazi-Rock. *PopScriptum* 5: 58–89.

4287 Mayer, Günter. 1984. Popular music e ideologia nazionalfascista nel Terzo Reich. *Musica/Realtà* 13: 45–58.

4288 Meyer, Michael. 1977. The SA Song Industry: A Singing Ideological Posture. *Journal of Popular Culture* 11(3): 568–80.

4289 Nicolodi, Fiamma. 1984. *Musica e musicisti nel ventennio fascista.* Fiesole: Discanto Edizioni.

4290 Polster, Bernd, ed. 1989. *Swing Heil: Jazz im Nationalsozialismus.* Berlin: Transit.

4291 Warren, Roland L. 1972. The Nazi Use of Music as an Instrument of Social Control. In *The Sounds of Social Change: Studies in Popular Culture*, ed. R. Serge Denisoff and Richard A. Peterson. Chicago: Rand McNally & Co. 72–78.

SOCIAL AND CULTURAL CONTEXTS

4292 Wicke, Peter. 1984. Zwischen Sentimentalität und Pathos. Populäre Musik im faschistischen Deutschland. *Unterhaltungskunst* 11: 5–11.

4293 Wicke, Peter. 1985. Sentimentality and High Pathos: Popular Music in Fascist Germany. *Popular Music* 5: 149–58.

4294 Wicke, Peter. 1986. Das Ende: Populäre Musik im faschistischen Deutschland. In *Ich will aber gerade vom Leben singen . . . Über populäre Musik vom ausgehenden 19. Jahrhundert bis zum Ende der Weimarer Republik*, ed. Sabine Schutte. Reinbek bei Hamburg: Rowohlt. 418–31.

4295 Willett, Ralph. 1989. Hot Swing and the Dissolute Life: Youth, Style and Popular Music in Europe, 1939–49. *Popular Music* 8(2): 157–64.

4296 Zwerin, Mike. 1985. *Tristesse de St. Louis: Swing Under the Nazis*. London and New York: Quartet.

FASHION

4297 Chibnall, Steve. 1986. Whistle and Zoot: The Changing Meaning of a Suit of Clothes. *History Workshop* 20: 57–81.

4298 Cosgrove, Stuart. 1984. The Zoot Suit and Style Warfare. *History Workshop* 18: 77–90.

4299 Jones, Mablen. 1987. *Getting It On: The Clothing of Rock and Roll*. New York: Abbeville Press.

4300 McRobbie, Angela, ed. 1989. *Zoot-Suits and Second-Hand Dresses: An Anthology of Fashion and Music*. London: Macmillan.

4301 Polhemus, Ted. 1994. *Street Style*. London: Thames and Hudson.

4302 Rose, Cynthia. 1991. *Design After Dark: The Story of Dancefloor Style*. London: Thames and Hudson.

4303 Thorne, Tony. 1993. *Fads, Fashions and Cults*. London: Bloomsbury.

4304 York, Peter. 1980. *Style Wars*. London: Sidgwick & Jackson.

4305 York, Peter, and Jennings, Charles. 1995. *Peter York's Eighties*. London: BBC Books.

FESTIVALS

4306 Agostinelli, Anthony J. 1977. *The Newport Jazz Festival: Rhode Island, 1954–1971. A Bibliography, Discography and Filmography*. Providence, RI: Agostinelli.

4307 Anderson, Jack. 1987. *The American Dance Festival*. Durham, NC: Duke University Press.

4308 Barsamian, Jacques and Jouffa, François. 1986. *L'Age d'or de la rock music. Blues, country, rock'n'roll, soul, San Francisco sound, underground, hippies, festivals*. Paris: Ramsay.

4309 Bettelheim, Judith, ed. 1993. *Cuban Festivals: An Illustrated Anthology*. New York: Garland.

4310 Cantwell, Robert. 1993. *Ethnomimesis: Folklife and the Representation of Culture*. Chapel Hill, NC: University of North Carolina Press.

4311 Chang, Paolo. 1988. Festival Musical de Chantenay. Dixième anniversaire Chantenay Villedieu. *Musiche* 1: 33–41.

4312 Clarke, Michael. 1982. *The Politics of Pop Festivals*. London: Harrap.

4313 Cobbold, Christine. 1986. *Knebworth Rock Festivals*. London: Omnibus.

4314 Davis, Martha Ellen. 1972. The Social Organization of a Musical Event: The Fiesta de Cruz in San Juan, Puerto Rico. *Ethnomusicology* 16(1): 38–62.

4315 Denselow, Robin. 1989. *When the Music's Over: The Story of Political Pop.* London: Faber.

4316 Drage, Frank, Philip Sweeney and Peter Gabriel. 1990. *The Sounds of Music: WOMAD.* London: Virgin.

4317 Evers, Paul, ed. 1994. *25 Jaar Pinkpop.* Amsterdam: Bonaventura.

4318 Goldblatt, Burt. 1977. *Newport Jazz Festival: The Illustrated History.* New York: Dial Press.

4319 Hinton, Brian. 1995. *Message to Love: The Isle of Wight Festival.* Chessington: Castle Communications.

4320 Landy, Elliott. 1984. *Woodstock Vision.* Reinbek bei Hamburg: Rowohlt.

4321 Lang, Michael and Young, Jean. 1979. *Woodstock Festival Remembered.* New York: Ballantine Books.

4322 Makower, Joel. 1989. *Woodstock: The Oral Story.* New York: Doubleday.

4323 Monestel, Manuel. 1987. A Song for Peace in Central America. *Popular Music* 6(2): 227–31.

4324 Pilpel, Robert, John Roberts and Joel Rosenman. 1974. *Young Men with Unlimited Capital.* New York: Harcourt Brace Jovanovich.

4325 Sandberg, Larry and Weissman, Dick. 1989. (1976) *The Folk Music Source Book.* New York: Da Capo Press. First published New York: Alfred Knopf, 1976.

4326 Santelli, Robert. 1980. *Aquarius Rising: The Rock Festival Years.* New York: Dell Publishing.

4327 Schmidt, Eric von and Rooney, Jim. 1979. *Baby, Let Me Follow You Down: The Illustrated Story of the Cambridge Folk Years.* Garden City, NY: Anchor Books.

4328 Sia, Joseph J. 1970. *Woodstock '69: Summer Pop Festivals.* New York: Scholastic Book Services.

4329 Spitz, Robert Stephen. 1979. *Barefoot in Babylon: The Creation of the Woodstock Music Festival, 1969.* New York: Viking.

4330 Whisnant, David E. 1978. *Folk Festival Issues: Report from a Seminar, March 2–3, 1978 Sponsored by the National Council for the Traditional Arts.* Los Angeles: John Edwards Memorial Foundation.

GENDER/SEXUALITY

4331 Adler, Henrik. 1982. Rock-billeder: Nogle historisk hop over temaet rock-musik och seksualitet. *Modspil* 4(6): 7–15.

4332 Allen, Robert C. 1991. *Horrible Prettiness: Burlesque and American Culture.* Chapel Hill, NC: University of North Carolina Press.

4333 Asante-Darko, Nimrod and van der Geest, Sjaak. 1983. Male Chauvinism: Men and Women in Ghanaian Highlife Songs. In *Female and Male in West Africa,* ed. Christine Oppong. London: George Allen and Unwin. 242–55.

4334 Baker, Roger. 1994. *Drag: A History of Female Impersonation in the Performing Arts.* London: Cassell.

4335 Ballantine, Christopher. 1995. The Identities of Race, Class and Gender in the Repression of Early Black South African Jazz and Vaudeville (ca. 1920–1944). In *Popular Music: Style and Identity,* ed. Will Straw, et al. Montréal: The Centre for Research on Canadian Cultural Industries and Institutions. 9–12.

4336 Bayton, Mavis. 1993. Feminist Musical Practice: Problems and Contradictions. In *Rock and Popular Music: Politics, Policies, Institutions,* ed. Tony Bennett, et al. London: Routledge.

4337 Berry, Venise T. 1994. Feminine or Masculine: The Conflicting Nature of Female Images in Rap Music. In *Cecilia Reclaimed: Feminist Perspectives on Gender and Music*, ed. Susan C. Cook and Judy S. Tsou. Chicago: University of Illinois Press. 183–201.

4338 Binas, Susanne. 1992. 'Keep It Heavy, Keep It Hard': Zu einigen Aspekten soziokorporeller Kommunikationsmuster im Prozeß der Geschlechtersozialisation – Heavy-Metal in der 'ehemaligen' DDR. *PopScriptum* I(1): 96–111.

4339 Bloß, Monika. 1994. Weiblichkeit als Kulturbarriere?: '. . . so spielen wie ein Mann'. Eine Untersuchung mit Berliner Musikerinnen. In *Zwischen Rausch und Ritual*, ed. Konstanze Kriese, et al. Berlin: Zyankrise. 70–79.

4340 Bowers, Jane, and Bareis, Urba. 1991. Bibliography on Music and Gender: Women in Music. *The World of Music* 33(2): 65–103.

4341 Bradby, Barbara. 1990. (1988) Do-Talk and Don't-Talk: The Division of the Subject in Girl-Group Music. In *On Record: Rock, Pop and the Written Word*, ed. Simon Frith and Andrew Goodwin. London: Routledge. 341–68.

4342 Bradby, Barbara. 1993. Lesbians and Popular Music: Does It Matter Who Is Singing? In *Outwrite: Lesbianism and Popular Culture*, ed. Gabriele Griffin. London: Pluto Press. 148–71.

4343 Bradby, Barbara. 1993. Sampling Sexuality: Gender, Technology and the Body in Dance Music. *Popular Music* 12(2): 155–76.

4344 Brett, Philip, Gary Thomas and Elizabeth Wood, eds. 1994. *Queering the Pitch: The New Gay and Lesbian Musicology*. London: Routledge.

4345 Carby, Hazel V. 1990. 'It Jus Be's Dat Way Sometime': The Sexual Politics of Women's Blues. In *Unequal Sisters: A Multicultural Reader in U.S. Women's History*, ed. Ellen Carol DuBois and Vicki L. Ruiz. London: Routledge. 238–49. (First published in *Radical America* 20(4) (1986): 9–24.)

4346 Christenson, Peter, and Peterson, Jon Brian. 1988. Genre and Gender in the Structure of Music Preferences. *Communication Research* 15(3) (June).

4347 Cowan, Jane K. 1990. *Dance and the Body Politic in Northern Greece*. Princeton, NJ: Princeton University Press.

4348 Craig, Steve, ed. 1992. *Men, Masculinity and the Media*. Newbury Park, CA: Sage.

4349 Dhu Shapiro, Ann. 1991. A Critique of Current Research on Music and Gender. *The World of Music* 33(2): 5–13.

4350 Doty, Alexander. 1993. *Making Things Perfectly Queer*. Minneapolis, MN: University of Minnesota Press.

4351 Drukman, Steven. 1995. The Gay Gaze, or Why I Want My MTV. In *A Queer Romance: Lesbians, Gay Men and Popular Culture*, ed. Paul Burston and Colin Richardson. London: Routledge. 81–95.

4352 Dyer, Richard. 1990. (1979) In Defense of Disco. In *On Record: Rock, Pop and the Written Word*, ed. Simon Frith and Andrew Goodwin. London: Routledge. 410–18.

4353 Dyer, Richard. 1992. Getting Over the Rainbow: Identity and Pleasure in Gay Cultural Politics. In *Only Entertainment*. London: Routledge.

4354 Ehrenreich, Barbara, et al. 1992. Beatlemania: Girls Just Want to Have Fun. In *The Adoring Audience: Fan Culture and Popular Media*, ed. Lisa A. Lewis. London: Routledge.

4355 Elder, J.D. 1968. The Male/Female Conflict in Calypso. *Caribbean Quarterly* 14: 23–41.

4356 Endres, Kathleen L. 1984. Sex Role Standards in Popular Music. *Journal of Popular Culture* 18(1): 9–18.

4357 Evans, Liz, ed. 1994. *Women, Sex and Rock 'n' Roll: In Their Own Words.* London: Pandora.

4358 Fenger, Sven. 1982. Keep Dancing. *Modspil* 4(6): 21–26.

4359 Flinn, Caryl. 1992. *Strains of Utopia: Gender, Nostalgia and Hollywood Film Music.* Princeton, NJ: Princeton University Press.

4360 Frank, Lisa and Smith, Paul, eds. 1993. *Madonnarama: Essays on Sex and Popular Culture.* Pittsburgh, PA: Cleis Press.

4361 Frith, Simon, ed. 1988. *Music for Pleasure: Essays in the Sociology of Pop.* London: Polity.

4362 Frith, Simon. 1990. (1985) Afterthoughts. In *On Record: Rock, Pop and the Written Word*, ed. Simon Frith and Andrew Goodwin. London: Routledge. 419–24.

4363 Frith, Simon and McRobbie, Angela. 1990. Rock and Sexuality. In *On Record: Rock, Pop, and the Written Word*, ed. Simon Frith and Andrew Goodwin. London: Routledge. 371–89.

4364 Garratt, Sheryl. 1990. (1984) Teenage Dreams. In *On Record: Rock, Pop and the Written Word*, ed. Simon Frith and Andrew Goodwin. London: Routledge. 399–409.

4365 No entry.

4366 Gill, John. 1995. *Queer Noises.* London: Cassell.

4367 Hadleigh, Boze. 1991. *The Vinyl Closet: Gays in the Music World.* San Diego: Los Hombres Press.

4368 Huffman, James R. and Huffman, Julie L. 1987. Sexism and Cultural Lag: The Rise of the Jailbait Song, 1955–1985. *Journal of Popular Culture* 21(2): 65–83.

4369 Irving, Katrina. 1993. 'I Want Your Hands On Me': Building Equivalences Through Rap Music. *Popular Music* 12(2): 105–21.

4370 Kaplan, E. Ann. 1987. Gender Address and the Gaze in MTV. In *Rocking Around the Clock: Music Television, Postmodernism, and Consumer Culture.* London: Methuen. 89–142.

4371 Keightley, Keir. 1996. 'Turn It Down!' She Shrieked: Gender, Domestic Space, and High Fidelity, 1948–59. *Popular Music* 15(2): 149–78.

4372 Koskoff, Ellen, ed. 1989. *Women and Music in Cross-Cultural Perspective.* Chicago: University of Illinois Press.

4373 Krasnow, Carolyn. 1993. Fear and Loathing in the 70s: Race, Sexuality and Disco. *Stanford Humanities Review* 3(2): 37–45.

4374 Laing, Dave and Taylor, Jenny. 1979. Disco– Pleasure– Discourse: On 'Rock and Sexuality'. *Screen Education* 31: 43–48.

4375 Lance, Larry M. and Berry, Christina Y. 1985. Has There Been a Sexual Revolution? Human Sexuality in Popular Music, 1968–1977. *Journal of Popular Culture* 19(1): 65–73.

4376 Lewis, Lisa A. 1990. *Gender Politics and MTV: Voicing the Difference.* Philadelphia: Temple University Press.

4377 Lewis, Lisa A. 1992. *The Adoring Audience: Fan Culture and Popular Media.* London: Routledge.

4378 Malmros, Anna-Lise. 1982. Rock-scene som könspolitisk slagmark. *Modspil* 4(6): 31–34.

4379 McClary, Susan. 1991. *Feminine Endings: Music, Gender and Sexuality.*

Minneapolis, MN: University of Minnesota Press.

4380 McDonnell, Evelyn and Powers, Ann, eds. 1995. *Rock, She Wrote: Women Write about Rock, Pop and Rap*. London: Plexus.

4381 McRobbie, Angela. 1994. Shut Up and Dance: Youth Culture and Changing Modes of Femininity. In *Postmodernism and Popular Culture*. London: Routledge. 155–76.

4382 McRobbie, Angela. 1995. Zitta e balla: cultura giovanile e forme del femminile in mutamento. In *Annali Istituto Gramsci Emilia-Romagna 2/1995, dossier: Rock Steady/Rock Study: sulle culture del rock . . .*, ed. Franco Minganti. Bologna: Istituto Gramsci Emilia-Romagna. 176–97.

4383 Medevoi, Leerom. 1991–92. Mapping the Rebel Image: Postmodernism and the Masculinist Politics of Rock in the U.S.A. *Cultural Critique* 20 (Winter): 153–88.

4384 Meyer, Moe, ed. 1994. *The Politics and Poetics of Camp*. London: Routledge.

4385 Oliven, Ruben George. 1988. 'The Woman Makes (and Breaks) the Man': The Masculine Imagery in Brazilian Popular Music. *Latin American Music Review* 9(1): 90–108.

4386 Pacini Hernandez, Deborah. 1990. Cantando la cama vacia: Love, Sexuality and Gender Relationships in Dominican 'Bachata'. *Popular Music* 9(3): 351–67.

4386a Peterson-Lewis, Sonja. 1991. A Feminist Analysis of the Defenses of Obscene Rap Lyrics. *Black Sacred Music* 5(1): 68–79.

4387 Ransby, Barbara and Matthews, Tracye. 1993. Black Popular Culture and the Transcendence of Patriarchal Illusions. *Race and Class* 35(1): 57–68.

4388 Reynolds, Simon and Press, Joy. 1995. *The Sex Revolts: Gender, Rebellion and Rock 'n' Roll*. London: Serpent's Tail.

4389 Roman, Leslie G. 1988. Intimacy, Labor and Class: Ideologies of Feminine Sexuality in the Punk Slam Dance. In *Becoming Feminine: The Politics of Popular Culture*. London: Falmer Press.

4390 Rose, Tricia. 1991. Never Trust a Big Butt and a Smile. *Camera Obscura* 23 (May).

4391 No entry.

4392 Saucier, Karen A. 1986. Healers and Heartbreakers: Images of Women and Men in Country Music. *Journal of Popular Culture* 20(3): 147–66.

4393 Savage, Jon. 1980. The Gender Bender. *The Face* 7 (November): 16–20.

4394 Savage, Jon. 1983. Androgyny. *The Face* 38 (June): 20–23.

4395 Savage, Jon. 1988. The Enemy Within: Sex, Rock and Identity. In *Facing the Music*, ed. Simon Frith. New York: Pantheon. 131–72.

4396 Savage, Jon. 1996. *Time Travel: Pop, Media and Sexuality, 1976–96*. London: Chatto & Windus.

4397 Scott, J. 1986. Gender: A Useful Category of Historical Analysis. *The American Historical Review* 91(5): 1053–75.

4398 Shepherd, John. 1991. Music and Male Hegemony. In *Music as Social Text*. Cambridge: Polity. 152–73.

4399 Simels, Steven. 1985. *Gender Chameleons: Androgyny in Rock 'n' Roll*. New York: Arbor House.

4400 Simpson, Mark. 1994. *Male Impersonators*. London: Cassell.

4401 Sinfield, Alan. 1994. *Cultural Politics: Queer Reading*. London: Routledge.

4402 Singer, June. 1977. *Androgyny: Towards a New Theory of Sexuality*. London: Routledge.

4403 Skeggs, Beverley. 1993. Two Minute Brother: Contestation Through Gender, 'Race' and Sexuality. *Innovation* 6(3): 299–322.

4404 Skelton, Tracey. 1995. 'Boom, Bye, Bye': Jamaican Ragga and Gay Resistance. In *Mapping Desire: Geographies of Sexualities*, ed. David Bell and Gill Valentine. London: Routledge. 264–83.

4405 Sontag, Susan. 1967. Notes on 'Camp'. In *Against Interpretation and Other Essays*. London: Eyre & Spottiswoode. 275–92.

4406 Steward, Sue and Garratt, Sheryl. 1984. *Signed, Sealed and Delivered: True Life Stories of Women in Pop*. London: Pluto Press.

4407 Straats, Gregory R. 1979. Sexual Imagery in Blues Music: A Basis for Black Stereotypes. *Journal of Jazz Studies* 5(2): 40–60.

4408 Straw, Will. 1993. Characterising Rock Music Culture: The Case of Heavy Metal. In *The Cultural Studies Reader*, ed. Simon During. London: Routledge. 379–81.

4409 Studer, Wayne. 1994. *Rock on the Wild Side: Gay Male Images in Popular Music of the Rock Era*. San Francisco: Leyland Publications.

4410 Thornton, Sarah. 1995. Exploring the Meaning of the Mainstream: Or Why Sharon and Tracy Dance Around Their Handbags. In *Club Cultures: Music, Media and Subcultural Capital*. Cambridge/Hanover: Polity/Wesleyan University Press.

4411 Torp, Lisbet. 1986. Hip Hop Dances: Their Adoption and Function Among Boys in Denmark, 1983–1984. *Yearbook for Traditional Music* 18: 29–86.

4412 Walser, Robert. 1993. Forging Masculinity: Heavy Metal Sounds and Images of Gender. In *Sound and Vision: The Music Video Reader*, ed. Simon Frith, Andrew Goodwin and Lawrence Grossberg. London and New York: Routledge. 153–81.

4413 Walser, Robert. 1993. *Running with the Devil: Power, Gender, and Madness in Heavy Metal Music*. Hanover, NH: Wesleyan University Press.

4414 Weeks, J. 1981. *Sex, Politics and Society: The Regulation of Sexuality Since 1800*. Essex: Longman.

4415 Wilson, Pamela. 1995. Mountains of Contradiction: Gender, Class and Region in the Star Image of Dolly Parton. *South Atlantic Quarterly* 94(1) (Winter): 109–34.

4416 Wise, Sue. 1990. (1984) Sexing Elvis. In *On Record: Rock, Pop and the Written Word*. ed. Simon Frith and Andrew Goodwin. London: Routledge. 390–98.

4417 Zillman, Dolf and Bhatia, Azra. 1989. Effects of Associating with Musical Genres on Heterosexual Attraction. *Communication Research* 16(2) (April).

GENRE

4418 Ala, Nemesio and Fabbri, Franco. 1985. Generi musicali, schemi di consumo, gusti del pubblico: 'popular music' e ricerca in Italia. In *Musica e sistema dell'informazione in Europa*, ed. Francesco Rampi. Milano: Unicopli. 153–66.

4419 Ala, Nemesio, et al. 1985. *La musica che si consuma*. Milano: Unicopli.

4420 Ala, Nemesio, et al. 1985. Patterns of Music Consumption in Milan and Reggio Emilia from April to May 1983. In *Popular Music Perspectives, 2*, ed. David Horn. Göteborg and Exeter: IASPM. 464–500.

4421 Altman, Rick, ed. 1981. *Genre: The Musical. A Reader*. London: Routledge & Kegan Paul.

4422 Broere, Bernard J. 1989. El Chambù: A Study of Popular Musics in Nariño, South Colombia. In *World Music, Politics and Social Change*, ed. Simon Frith. Manchester: Manchester University Press. 103–21.

4423 Christenson, Peter and Peterson, Jon Brian. 1988. Genre and Gender in the Structure of Music Preferences. *Communication Research* 15(3) (June).

4424 Fabbri, Franco. 1982. A Theory of Musical Genres: Two Applications. In *Popular Music Perspectives, 1*, ed. David Horn and Philip Tagg. Göteborg and Exeter: IASPM. 52–81.

4425 Fabbri, Franco. 1982. What Kind of Music? *Popular Music* 2: 131–43.

4426 Fabbri, Franco. 1983. Musical Genres and Their Metalanguages. *International Society for Music Education Yearbook* 10: 24–30.

4427 Fabbri, Franco. 1985. Nota di cura. In *What Is Popular Music? 41 saggi, ricerche, interventi sulla musica diogni giorno*, ed. Franco Fabbri. Milano: Unicopli. 11–14.

4428 Fabbri, Franco. 1989. Comunicazione e ascolto (ai margini e sui margini della musica contemporanea). In *Musiche/Realtà. Generi musicali/Media/Popular Music*, ed. Franco Fabbri. Milano: Unicopli. 209–26. (First published in *Musica/Realtà* 17 (1985): 149–66.)

4429 Fabbri, Franco. 1989. I generi musicali, una questione da riaprire. In *Musiche/Realtà. Generi musicali/Media/Popular Music*, ed. Franco Fabbri. Milano: Unicopli. 11–33. (First published in *Musica/Realtà* 4 (1981): 43–65.)

4430 Fabbri, Franco. 1989. Introduzione. In *Musiche/Realtà. Generi musicali/Media/Popular Music*, ed. Franco Fabbri. Milano: Unicopli. 7–10.

4431 Fabbri, Franco. 1989. The System of Canzone in Italy Today. In *World Music, Politics and Social Change*, ed. Simon Frith. Manchester: Manchester University Press. 122–42.

4432 Fabbri, Franco. 1996. *Il suono in cui viviamo. Inventare, produrre e diffondere musica*. Milano: Giangiacomo Feltrinelli Editore.

4433 Fornäs, Johan. 1995. The Future of Rock: Discourses That Struggle to Define a Genre. *Popular Music* 14(1): 111–25.

4435 Gridley, Mark C. 1983. Clarifying Labels: Jazz, Rock, Funk and Jazz-Rock. *Popular Music & Society* 9(2): 27.

4436 Hamm, Charles. 1994. Genre, Performance and Ideology in the Early Songs of Irving Berlin. *Popular Music* 13(2): 143–50.

4437 Hennion, Antoine and Klein, Jean-Claude, eds. 1985. Métissage et musiques métissées. *Vibrations* 1.

4438 Marchi, Luca. 1992. Il liscio: pratica sociale e genere musicale. In *Dal blues al liscio: Studi sull'esperienza musicale comune*, ed. Gino Stefani. Verona: Ianua. 135–65.

4439 Middleton, Richard. 1990. *Studying Popular Music*. Milton Keynes: Open University Press.

4440 Moore, Allan F. 1993. *Rock: The Primary Text*. Buckingham: Open University Press.

4440a Orozco, Danilo. 1992. Pocesos socioculturales y rasgos de identidad en los generos musicales con reference especial a la música cubana. *Latin American Music Review* 13(2): 158–78.

4441 Regev, Motti. 1989. The Field of Popular Music in Israel. In *World Music, Politics and Social Change*, ed. Simon Frith. Manchester: Manchester University Press. 143–55.

4442 Stefani, Chiara. 1996. Febbre e altre affezioni del sabato sera. In *Intense emozioni in mca*, ed. Gino Stefani. Bologna: Clueb. 35–54.

4443 Straw, Will. 1985. Characterizing Rock Music Cultures: The Case of Heavy Metal. *Canadian University Music Review* 1984/5: 104–22.

4444 Vignolle, Jean-Pierre. 1980. Mixing Genres and Reaching the Public: The Production of Popular Music. *Social Science Information* 19(1): 79–105.

4445 Wicke, Peter. 1982. Rock Music: A Musical-Aesthetic Study. *Popular Music* 2: 219–44.

4446 Wicke, Peter. 1992. Stil als kommerzielle Kategorie – Zum Stilbegriff in der populären Musik. In *Stil in der Musik – Innovationsquellen der Musik des 20. Jahrhunderts*, ed. P. Macek. Brno: Mazaryk University. 225–41.

HUMOR

4447 Levy, Lester S. 1971. *Flashes of Merriment: A Century of Humorous Songs in America, 1805–1905*. Norman, OK: University of Oklahoma Press.

4448 Loesser, Arthur, comp. 1942. *Humor in American Song*. New York: Howell, Soskin.

4449 Mahabir, Cynthia. 1996. Wit and Popular Music: The Calypso and the Blues. *Popular Music* 15(1): 55–81.

4450 Prato, Paolo. 1991. Il comico in musica: dalla tradizione colta al rock. *Musica/ Realtà* 34: 69–79.

4451 Speaight, George, comp. 1975. *Bawdy Songs of the Early Music Hall*. Newton Abbot: David & Charles.

IDENTITY

4452 Banfi, Emanuele and Winkler, Daniele. 1996. Riflessi dell' 'italiano in movimento' in un *corpus* di canzoni italiane di area alto-atesina. In *Analisi e canzoni*, ed. Rossana Dalmonte. Trento: Università di Trento. 125–44.

4453 Bennett, H. Stith. 1983. Notation and Identity in Contemporary Popular Music. *Popular Music* 3: 215–34.

4454 Berland, Jody. 1988. Locating Listening: Technological Space, Popular Music, Canadian Meditations. *Cultural Studies* 2(3): 343–58.

4455 Blum, Lucille Hollander. 1966/67. The Discotheque and the Phenomenon of Alone-Togetherness: A Study of the Young Person's Response to the Frug and Comparable Current Dances. *Adolescence* 1(4) (Winter): 351–66.

4456 Bradby, Barbara. 1990. Do-Talk and Don't Talk: The Division of the Subject in Girl-Group Music. In *On Record: Rock, Pop and the Written Word*, ed. Simon Frith and Andrew Goodwin. London: Routledge. 341–68.

4457 Bradby, Barbara and Torode, Brian. 1984. Pity Peggy Sue. *Popular Music* 4: 183–206.

4458 Cubitt, Sean. 1984. 'Maybellene': Meaning and the Listening Subject. *Popular Music* 4: 207–24.

4459 Dyer, Richard. 1992. Getting Over the Rainbow: Identity and Pleasure in Gay Cultural Politics. In *Only Entertainment*. London: Routledge.

4460 Fikentscher, Kai. 1995. 'Old School – New School': An Examination of Changes in the Production and Consumption of Post-Disco Underground Dance Music in New York City. In *Popular Music: Style and Identity*, ed. Will Straw, et al. Montréal: The Centre for Research on Canadian

Cultural Industries and Institutions. 89–93.

4461 Fornäs, Johan. 1990. Moving Rock: Youth and Pop in Late Modernity. *Popular Music* 9(3): 291–306.

4462 Fox, Aaron A. 1992. The Jukebox of History: Narratives of Loss and Desire in the Discourse of Country Music. *Popular Music* 11(1): 53–72.

4463 Gaunt, Kyra D. 1995. The Veneration of James Brown and George Clinton in Hip-Hop Music: Is It Live? Or Is It Re-Memory? In *Popular Music: Style and Identity*, ed. Will Straw, et al. Montréal: The Centre for Research on Canadian Cultural Industries and Institutions. 117–22.

4464 Hebdige, Dick. 1987. *Cut 'n' Mix: Culture, Identity and Caribbean Music.* London and New York: Comedia/Methuen.

4465 Hirschberg, Jehoash. 1989. *The Role of Music in the Renewed Self-Identity of Karaite Jewish Refugee Communities from Cairo.* New York: International Council for Traditional Music.

4466 Kopytko, Tanya. 1986. Breakdance as an Identity Marker in New Zealand. *Yearbook for Traditional Music* 18: 20–26.

4467 Kruse, Holly. 1993. Subcultural Identity in Alternative Music Culture. *Popular Music* 12(1): 33–41.

4468 Larkey, Edward. 1992. Austropop: Popular Music and National Identity in Austria. *Popular Music* 11(2): 151–86.

4469 Larkey, Edward. 1993. *Pungent Sounds: Constructing Identity with Popular Music in Austria.* New York: Peter Lang.

4470 Leppert, Richard and Lipsitz, George. 1990. 'Everybody's Lonesome for Somebody': Age, the Body and Experience in the Music of Hank

Williams. *Popular Music* 9(3) (October): 259–74.

4471 Levine, Lawrence. 1971. Slave Songs and Slave Consciousness. In *Anonymous Americans*, ed. Tamara Hareven. Englewood Cliffs, NJ: Prentice-Hall. 99–130.

4472 Levine, Lawrence. 1977. *Black Culture and Black Consciousness: Afro-American Folk Thought from Slavery to Freedom.* Oxford and New York: Oxford University Press.

4473 Ling, Jan. 1992. From 'Empfindsamer' Style to Down Home Village Nostalgia. In *Secondo Convegno Europeo di Analisi Musicale, Vol. I*, ed. Rossana Dalmonte and Mario Baroni. Trento: Università di Trento. 321–40.

4474 MacKinnon, Niall. 1993. *The British Folk Scene: Musical Performance and Social Identity.* Buckingham: Open University Press.

4475 Manuel, Peter. 1989. Andalusian, Gypsy and Class Identity in the Contemporary Flamenco Complex. *Ethnomusicology* 33(2): 47–65.

4476 Menezes Bastos, Rafael José de. 1995. A Origem do Samba como Invenção do Brasil: Sobre o 'Feitio de Oração' de Vadico e Noel Rosa (Por Que as Canções têm Música?). *Cadernos de Estudo – Análise Musical* 8(9): 1–29.

4477 Middleton, Richard. 1995. Authorship, Gender and the Construction of Meaning in The Eurythmics' Hit Recordings. *Cultural Studies* 9(3): 465–85.

4478 Moore, John. 1989. 'The Hieroglyphics of Love': The Torch Singers and Interpretation. *Popular Music* 8(1): 31–58.

4479 Moore, Sylvia. 1982. Social Identity in Popular Mass Media Music. In *Popular Music Perspectives, 1*, ed. David Horn and Philip Tagg. Göteborg and Exeter: IASPM. 196–222.

4480 Narváez, Peter. 1995. Sonny's Dream: Popularity, Folksongs and Regional Anthems. In *Popular Music Perspectives III*, ed. Peter Wicke. Berlin: Zyankrise. 99–112.

4481 Nurse, George T. 1964. Popular Songs and National Identity in Malawi. *African Music* 3(3): 101–106.

4482 Opekar, Ales. 1995. The Influence of Czech Folklore on Czech Rock Music. In *Popular Music: Style and Identity*, ed. Will Straw, et al. Montréal: The Centre for Research on Canadian Cultural Industries and Institutions. 229–31.

4483 Pring-Mill, Robert. 1983. Cantas Canto Cantemos: las canciones de lucha y esperanza como signos de reunión e identidad. *Romanistisches Jahrbuch* 34: 318–54.

4484 Reily, Suzel-Ana. 1992. *Música Sertaneja* and Migrant Identity: The Stylistic Development of a Brazilian Genre. *Popular Music* 11(3): 337–58.

4485 Roman, Leslie G. 1988. Intimacy, Labor and Class: Ideologies of Feminine Sexuality in the Punk Slam Dance. In *Becoming Feminine: The Politics of Popular Culture*. London: Falmer Press.

4486 Rose, Tricia. 1994. *Black Noise: Rap Music and Black Culture in Contemporary America*. Hanover and London: Wesleyan University Press.

4487 Rosenberg, Neil V. 1983. Image and Stereotype: Bluegrass Sound Tracks. *American Music* 1 (Fall): 1–22.

4488 Seitz, Barbara. 1991. Songs, Identity, and Women's Liberation in Nicaragua. *Latin American Music Review* 12(1): 21–41.

4489 Shank, Barry. 1994. *Dissonant Identities: The Rock 'n' Roll Scene in Austin, Texas*.

Hanover, NH: Wesleyan University Press.

4490 Shepherd, John. 1986. Music Consumption and Cultural Self-Identities: Some Theoretical and Methodological Reflections. *Media, Culture and Society* 8(3): 305–30.

4491 Shepp, Archie. 1983. Music and Black Identity. In *Laulu ottaa kantaa: aineistoa 1970-luvun lauliliikkeestä*. Helsinki: Työväenenmusiikki-institutti. 173–80.

4492 Stokes, Martin, ed. 1994. *Ethnicity, Identity and Music: The Musical Construction of Place*. Oxford: Berg.

4493 Sweeney-Turner, Steve. 1995. Dictated by Tradition? Identity and Difference in Queen's Innuendo: The Mercurial Case of Farookh Bulsara. *Popular Musicology* 2: 43–58.

4494 Thornton, Sarah. 1995. *Club Cultures: Music, Media and Subcultural Capital*. Cambridge: Polity.

4495 Tomlinson, Alan, ed. 1990. *Consumption, Identity and Style*. London: Routledge.

4496 Torp, Lisbet. 1986. Hip Hop Dances: Their Adoption and Function Among Boys in Denmark, 1983–1984. *Yearbook for Traditional Music* 18: 29–86.

4497 Turino, Thomas. 1984. The Urban-Mestizo Charango Tradition in Southern Peru: A Statement of Shifting Identity. *Ethnomusicology* 28(2): 252–70.

4498 Walser, Robert. 1993. *Running with the Devil: Power, Gender and Madness in Heavy Metal Music*. Hanover, NH: Wesleyan University Press.

4499 Waterman, Christopher A. 1982. 'I'm a Leader, Not a Boss': Popular Music and Social Identity in Ibadan, Nigeria. *Ethnomusicology* 26(1): 59–72.

4500 Waterman, Christopher A. 1990. 'Our Tradition Is a Very Modern Tradition':

Popular Music and the Construction of Pan-Yoruba Identity. *Ethnomusicology* 34(3): 367–79.

4501 Wicke, Peter. 1990. Rockmusik und Lebensstile. In *Lebensstile und Politik – Politik der Lebensstile,* ed. Olaf Schwencke. Loccum and Hagen: KuPoGe. 175–89.

4502 Winkler, Peter. 1995. In Search of Yaa Amponsah. In *Popular Music: Style and Identity,* ed. Will Straw, et al. Montréal: The Centre for Research on Canadian Cultural Industries and Institutions. 313–23.

JOURNALISM

4503 Breen, Marcus. 1987. Rock Journalism: Betrayal of the Impulse. In *Missing in Action: Australian Popular Music,* ed. Marcus Breen. Melbourne: Verbal Graphics Pty. 202–27.

4504 Denski, Stan. 1989. One Step Up and Two Steps Back: A Heuristic Model for Popular Music and Communication Research. *Popular Music & Society* 13: 9–21.

4505 Draper, Robert. 1990. *The Rolling Stone Story.* Edinburgh: Mainstream.

4506 Flippo, Chet. 1974. The History of Rolling Stone: Part I. *Popular Music & Society* 3: 159–88.

4507 Flippo, Chet. 1974. The History of Rolling Stone: Part II. *Popular Music & Society* 3: 258–80.

4508 Flippo, Chet. 1974. The History of Rolling Stone: Part III. *Popular Music & Society* 3: 281–98.

4509 Fogo, Fred. 1994. *I Read the News Today: The Social Drama of John Lennon's Death.* Lanham, MD: Littlefield Adams.

4510 Gart, Galen. 1986. *First Pressings: Rock History as Chronicled in Billboard Magazine.* Milford, NH: Big Nickel Publications.

4511 Gillett, Charlie. 1972. So You Want to be a Rock'n'Roll Writer (Keep a Carbon). In *Rock File,* ed. Charlie Gillett. London: New English Library. 61–72.

4512 Harley, R. and Botsman, P. 1982. Between No Payola and the Cocktail Set: Rock 'n' Roll Journalism. In *Theoretical Strategies,* ed. P. Botsman. Sydney: Local Consumption Publications. 231–63.

4513 Heylin, Clinton, ed. 1992. *The Penguin Book of Rock & Roll Writing.* London: Penguin.

4514 Jones, Steve. 1992. Re-Viewing Rock Writing: The Origins of Popular Music Criticism. *American Journalism* (Winter-Spring): 87–107.

4515 Jones, Steve. 1993. Popular Music, Criticism, Advertising and the Music Industry. *Journal of Popular Music Studies* 5: 79–91.

4516 Jones, Steve. 1994. Populäre Musik, Musikkritik, Werbung und die Musikindustrie. *PopScriptum* 2: 46–61.

4517 Love, R., ed. 1993. *The Best of Rolling Stone: Twenty-Five Years of Journalism on the Edge.* New York: Doubleday.

4518 Nowell, Robert. 1987. *The Evolution of Rock Journalism at the New York Times and the Los Angeles Times, 1956–1978: A Frame Analysis.* Bloomington, IN: University of Indiana.

4519 Ortner, Lorelies. 1982. *Wortschatz der Pop-/Rockmusik: Das Vokabular der Beiträge über Pop-/Rockmusik.* Düsseldorf: Schwann.

4520 Otto, Ulrich. 1982. *Die historisch-politischen Lieder und Karikaturen des Vormärz und der Revolution von 1848–49.* Köln: Pahl-Rugenstein.

4521 Théberge, Paul. 1991. Musicians' Magazines in the 1980s: The Creation of a Community and a Consumer Market. *Cultural Studies* 5(3): 270–93.

4522 Toynbee, Jason. 1993. Policing Bohemia, Pinning Up Grunge: The Music Press and Generic Change in British Pop and Rock. *Popular Music* 12(3): 289–300.

4523 Vlček, Josef. 1985. A Glimpse Through a Small Crack: The British Music Press from Behind the Iron Curtain. *Re Records Quarterly* 1(2): 32–35.

4524 Wyatt, R. and Hull, G. 1990. The Music Critic in the American Press: A Nationwide Survey of Newspapers and Magazines. *Mass Comm Review* 17(3): 38–43.

KINSHIP/FAMILY

4525 Balfour, Victoria. 1986. *Rock Wives: The Hard Lives and Good Times of the Wives, Girlfriends and Groupies of Rock and Roll.* New York: Beech Tree Books.

4526 Cohen, Sara. 1991. *Rock Culture in Liverpool.* Oxford: Oxford University Press.

4527 Cohen, Sara. 1993. Ethnography and Popular Music Studies. *Popular Music* 12(2): 123–38.

4528 Cohen, Sara, and McManus, Kevin. 1991. *Harmonious Relations: Popular Music in Family Life on Merseyside.* Liverpool: National Museums and Galleries on Merseyside.

4529 Finnegan, Ruth. 1989. *The Hidden Musicians: Music-Making in an English Town.* Cambridge: Cambridge University Press.

4530 Grevatt, Ren. 1963. Offsprings Spring Off on Own. *Billboard* (28 September): 3.

4531 Leach, Joel. 1987. Jazz in the Family. *Jazz Educators Journal* 19(3): 60–62.

4532 Mitz, Rick. 1976. Sibling Rock. *Stereo Review* (December): 88–91.

4533 Rector, Lee. 1979. Nashville's in the Family. *Variety* (21 February): 105.

4534 Robinson, Leroy. 1974. The Family Unit: It Keeps Music Alive, Swinging. *Billboard* (7 September): 28, 31.

4535 The First Family of Pop (The Beach Boys) 1967. *Melody Maker* (6 May): 11.

LAW

4536 Chevigny, Paul. 1992. *Gigs: Jazz and the Cabaret Laws in New York City.* London: Routledge.

4537 Crawford, David. 1977. Gospel Songs in Court: From Rural Music to Urban Industry in the 1950s. *Journal of Popular Culture* 11(3): 551–67.

4538 Lowenthal, Daniel K. 1953. *Trends in the Licensing of Popular Song Hits, 1940–1953.* New York: Bureau of Applied Social Research, Columbia University.

4539 Redhead, Steve. 1995. *Unpopular Cultures: The Birth of Law and Popular Culture.* Manchester: Manchester University Press.

LOCALITY

4540 Breen, Marcus. 1993. Making Music Local. In *Rock and Popular Music: Politics, Policies, Institutions,* ed. Tony Bennett, et al. London: Routledge. 66–82.

4541 Carney, George O. 1974. Bluegrass Grows All Around: The Spatial Dimensions of a Country Music Style. *Journal of Geography* 73: 34–55.

4542 Carney, George O. 1987. *The Sounds of People and Places: Readings in the*

Geography of American Folk and Popular Music. Lanham, MD: University Press of America.

4543 Cohen, Sara. 1991. Popular Music and Urban Regeneration: The Music Industries of Merseyside. *Cultural Studies* 5(3): 332–46.

4544 Cohen, Sara. 1991. *Rock Culture in Liverpool*. Oxford: Oxford University Press.

4545 Cohen, Sara. 1993. Ethnography and Popular Music Studies. *Popular Music* 12(2): 123–38.

4546 Cohen, Sara. 1995. Sounding Out the City: Music and the Sensuous Production of Place. *Transactions of the Institute of British Geographers* 20(4): 434–46.

4547 De Lerma, Dominique-René. 1982. *Bibliography of Black Music, Vol. 3. Geographical Studies*. Westport and London: Greenwood Press.

4548 Fenster, Mark. 1995. Two Stories: Where Exactly Is the Local? In *Popular Music: Style and Identity*, ed. Will Straw, et al. Montréal: The Centre for Research on Canadian Cultural Industries and Institutions. 83–87.

4549 Finnegan, Ruth. 1989. *The Hidden Musicians: Music-Making in an English Town*. Cambridge: Cambridge University Press.

4550 Frith, Simon. 1993. Popular Music and the Local State. In *Rock and Popular Music: Politics, Policies, Institutions*, ed. Tony Bennett, et al. London: Routledge. 14–24.

4551 Gay, Leslie. 1995. Rockin' the Imagined Local: New York Rock in a Reterritorialized World. In *Popular Music: Style and Identity*, ed. Will Straw, et al. Montréal: The Centre for Research on Canadian Cultural Industries and Institutions. 123–26.

4552 Guilbault, Jocelyne. 1993. On Redefining the 'Local' Through World Music. *The World of Music* 35(2): 33–47.

4553 Guilbault, Jocelyne. 1995. Zur Umdeutung das Lokalen durch die World Music. *PopScriptum* 3: 30–44.

4554 Horn, David. 1994. From Catfish Row to Granby Street: Contesting Meaning in *Porgy and Bess*. *Popular Music* 13(2): 165–74.

4555 Järviluomå, Helmi. 1995. Local Construction of Identity: Analysing Category-Work of an Amateur Music Group. In *Popular Music: Style and Identity*, ed. Will Straw, et al. Montréal: The Centre for Research on Canadian Cultural Industries and Institutions. 155–61.

4556 Kong, Lily. 1995. Popular Music in Geographical Analyses. *Progress in Human Geography* 19: 183–98.

4557 Kriese, Konstanze. 1995. Internationaltät im Spiegel lokaler Ironie. In *Popular Music Perspectives III*, ed. Peter Wicke. Berlin: Zyankrise. 143–46.

4558 Kruse, Holly. 1993. Subcultural Identity in Alternative Music Culture. *Popular Music* 12(1): 51–74.

4559 Leyshon, Andrew, David Matless and George Revill. 1995. The Place of Music. *Transactions of the Institute of British Geographers* 20(4): 423–33.

4560 Leyshon, Andrew, David Matless and George Revill. 1996. *The Place of Music: Music, Space and the Production of Place*. New York: Guilford Press.

4561 Lipsitz, George. 1994. *Dangerous Crossroads: Popular Music, Postmodernism and the Poetics of Place*. London and New York: Verso.

4562 Mitchell, Tony. 1996. *Popular Music and Local Identity: Rock, Pop and Rap in*

Europe and Oceania. Leicester: Leicester University Press.

4563 Pegg, Carole. 1983. Factors Affecting the Musical Choices of Audiences in East Suffolk, England. *Popular Music* 4: 51–74.

4564 Pickering, Michael and Green, Tony, eds. 1987. *Everyday Culture: Popular Song and the Vernacular Milieu.* Milton Keynes: Open University Press.

4565 Rutten, Paul. 1994. Lokale Musik und der internationale Markplatz. *PopScriptum* 2: 31–45.

4566 Savage, Jon. 1989. The Escape Artist: Morrissey's Manchester. *Village Voice* (18 July): 8–10.

4567 Shank, Barry. 1994. *Dissonant Identities: The Rock'n'Roll Scene in Austin, Texas.* Hanover, NH: Wesleyan University Press.

4568 Slobin, Mark. 1993. *Subcultural Sounds: Micromusics of the West.* Hanover, NH: Wesleyan University Press.

4569 Stokes, Martin, ed. 1994. *Ethnicity, Identity and Music: The Musical Construction of Place.* Oxford: Berg.

4570 Straw, Will. 1991. Systems of Articulation, Logics of Change: Communities and Scenes in Popular Music. *Cultural Studies* 5(3): 368–88.

4571 Street, John. 1993. Local Differences? Popular Music and the Local State. *Popular Music* 12: 43–55.

4572 Street, John. 1995. (Dis)located? Rhetoric, Politics, Meaning and the Locality. In *Popular Music: Style and Identity,* ed. Will Straw, et al. Montréal: The Centre for Research on Canadian Cultural Industries and Institutions. 255–63.

4573 Wallis, Roger and Malm, Krister. 1984. *Big Sounds from Small Peoples: The Music Industry in Small Countries.* London: Constable.

4574 Wilson, Pamela. 1995. Mountains of Contradiction: Gender, Class and Region in the Star Image of Dolly Parton. *South Atlantic Quarterly* 94(1) (Winter): 109–34.

LOVE/COURTSHIP

4575 Bradby, Barbara. 1990. (1988) Do-Talk and Don't Talk: The Division of the Subject in Girl-Group Music. In *On Record: Rock, Pop and the Written Word,* ed. Simon Frith and Andrew Goodwin. London: Routledge. 341–68.

4576 Carey, James T. 1972. Changing Courtship Patterns in the Popular Song. In *The Sounds of Social Change: Studies in Popular Culture,* ed. R. Serge Denisoff and Richard A. Peterson. Chicago: Rand McNally & Co. 198–212.

4577 Horton, Donald. 1990. (1957) The Dialogue of Courtship in Popular Song. In *On Record: Rock, Pop and the Written Word,* ed. Simon Frith and Andrew Goodwin. London: Routledge. 14–26. (First published in *American Journal of Sociology* 62 (1957).)

4578 Moore, John. 1988. 'The Hieroglyphics of Love': The Torch Singers and Interpretation. *Popular Music* 8(1): 31–58.

4579 Oliver, Paul. 1990. *Blues Fell This Morning: Meaning in the Blues,* 2nd edition. Cambridge: Cambridge University Press. First published London: Cassell, 1960.

4580 Pacini Hernandez, Deborah. 1990. Cantando la cama vacia: Love, Sexuality and Gender Relationships in Dominican 'Bachata'. *Popular Music* 9(3): 351–67.

4581 Spaeth, Sigmund. 1934. *The Facts of Life in Popular Song.* New York: Whittlesey House.

4582 Tawa, Nicholas E. 1976. The Ways of Love in Mid-Nineteenth Century Song. *Journal of Popular Culture* 10(2): 337–52.

4583 Turino, Thomas. 1983. The Charango and the Sirena: Music, Magic, and the Power of Love. *Latin American Music Review* 4(1): 81–119.

LYRICS

4584 Bradby, Barbara. 1990. (1988) Do-Talk and Don't-Talk: The Division of the Subject in Girl-Group Music. In *On Record: Rock, Pop and the Written Word*, ed. Simon Frith and Andrew Goodwin. London: Routledge. 341–68.

4585 Bradby, Barbara and Torode, Brian. 1984. Pity Peggy Sue. *Popular Music* 4: 183–206.

4586 Brahms, Caryl and Sherrin, Ned. 1984. *Song by Song: The Lives and Work of 14 Great Lyric Writers*. Bolton: Ross Anderson.

4587 Cateforis, Theo. 1993. 'Total Trash': Analysis and Post Punk Music. *Journal of Popular Music Studies* 5: 39–57.

4588 Cayer, David A. 1974. Black and Blue and Black Again: Three Stages of Racial Imagery in Jazz Lyrics. *Journal of Jazz Studies* 1(2): 38–71.

4589 Charters, Samuel B. 1970. (1963) *The Poetry of the Blues*. New York: Avon. First published New York: Oak Publications, 1963.

4590 Cooper, B. Lee. 1978. The Image of the Outsider in Contemporary Lyrics. *Journal of Popular Culture* 12(1): 168–78.

4591 Cooper, B. Lee. 1986. *A Resource Guide to Themes in Contemporary American Song Lyrics, 1950–1985*. Westport, CT: Greenwood Press.

4592 Cooper, B. Lee. 1991. *Popular Music Perspectives: Ideas, Themes and Patterns in Contemporary Lyrics*. Bowling Green, OH: Bowling Green State University Press.

4593 Cooper, B. Lee and Haney, Wayne S. 1991. *Response Recordings: An Answer Song Discography, 1950–1990*. Metuchen, NJ: Scarecrow Press.

4594 Coveri, Lorenzo. 1996. Lingua e dialetto nella canzone popolare recente. In *Analisi e canzoni*. ed. Rossana Dalmonte. Trento: Università di Trento. 25–38.

4595 Davis, Sheila. 1985. *The Craft of Lyric Writing*. Cincinnati: Writer's Digest.

4596 Davis, Sheila. 1988. *Successful Lyric Writing: A Step-by-Step Course & Workbook*. Cincinnati: Writer's Digest.

4597 De Lisle, Tim, ed. 1994. *Lives of the Great Songs*. London: Pavilion.

4598 Denisoff, R. Serge and Levine, Mark H. 1971. The One-Dimensional Approach to Popular Music: A Research Note. *Journal of Popular Culture* 4(4): 911–19.

4599 Dennison, Sam. 1982. *Scandalize My Name: Black Imagery in American Popular Music*. New York: Garland.

4600 Fiori, Umberto. 1982. La parola nel rock. *Musica/Realtà* 7: 111–22.

4601 Fiori, Umberto. 1995. 'Servono al rock le parole?' Revisited. In *Annali Istituto Gramsci Emilia-Romagna 2/1995, dossier: Rock Steady/Rock Study: sulle culture del rock . . .*, ed. Franco Minganti. Bologna: Istituto Gramsci Emilia-Romagna. 218–22.

4602 Fox, Aaron A. 1992. The Jukebox of History: Narratives of Loss and Desire in the Discourse of Country Music. *Popular Music* 11(1): 53–72.

4603 Frith, Simon. 1988. Why Do Songs Have Words? In *Music for Pleasure:*

Essays in the Sociology of Pop, ed. Simon Frith. New York: Routledge. 105–28.

4604 Gammon, Vic. 1984. 'Not Appreciated in Worthing?': Class Expression and Popular Song Texts in Mid-Nineteenth-Century Britain. *Popular Music* 4: 5–24.

4605 Graves, Barbara and McBain, Donald J. 1972. *Lyric Voices: Approaches to the Poetry of Contemporary Song*. New York: John Wiley & Sons.

4606 Hischak, Thomas. 1991. *Word Crazy: Broadway Lyricists from Cohan to Sondheim*. New York: Praeger.

4607 Hoare, Ian. 1975. Mighty, Mighty Spade and Whitey: Black Lyrics and Soul's Interaction with White Culture. In *The Soul Book*, ed. Ian Hoare. London: Methuen. 117–89.

4608 Horton, Donald. 1990. (1957) The Dialogue of Courtship in Popular Song. In *On Record: Rock, Pop and the Written Word*, ed. Simon Frith and Andrew Goodwin. London: Routledge. 14–26.

4609 Laing, Dave. 1989. The Grain of Punk: An Analysis of the Lyrics. In *Zoot-Suits and Second-Hand Dresses: An Anthology of Fashion and Music*, ed. Angela McRobbie. London: Macmillan.

4610 Lehman, Engel. 1975. *Their Words Are Music: The Great Theatre Lyricists and Their Lyrics*. New York: Crown.

4611 Macken, Bob, et al. 1981. *The Rock Music Source Book*. Garden City, NY: Anchor Press.

4612 Murphey, T. 1989. The When, Where and Who of Pop Lyrics: The Listener's Prerogative. *Popular Music* 8(2): 185–93.

4613 Oliver, Paul. 1984. *Songsters and Saints: Vocal Traditions on Race Records*. Cambridge: Cambridge University Press.

4614 Peterson, Richard A. 1972. Three Eras in the Manufacture of Popular Music Lyrics. In *The Sounds of Social Change: Studies in Popular Culture*, ed. R. Serge Denisoff and Richard A. Peterson. Chicago: Rand McNally & Co. 282–303.

4615 Peterson, Richard A. and McLaurin, Melton A., eds. 1992. *You Wrote My Life: Lyrical Themes in Country Music (Cultural Perspectives on the American South, Vol. 6)*. Philadelphia: Gordon and Breach.

4616 Potter, John. 1994. The Singer, Not the Song: Women Singers as Composer-Poets. *Popular Music* 13(2): 191–99.

4617 Richmond, W. Edson. 1968. 'Just Sing It Yourself': The American Lyric Tradition. In *American Folklore*, ed. Tristram P. Coffin. Washington, DC: Voice of America Forum Lectures. 105–20.

4618 Riesman, David. 1990. (1957) Listening to Popular Music. In *On Record: Rock, Pop and the Written Word*, ed. Simon Frith and Andrew Goodwin. London: Routledge. 5–13.

4619 Root, Robert L., Jr. 1986. A Listener's Guide to the Rhetoric of Popular Music. *Journal of Popular Culture* 20(1): 15–26.

4620 Thörnvall, Olle. 1981. *Svensk Rocklyrik: analys av fyra svenska rocktexter*. Uppsala: Inst. för litteraturvetenskap.

4621 Urban, Peter. 1979. *Rollende Worte: Die Poesie des Rock. Von der Straßenballade zum Pop-Song*. Frankfurt am Main: Fischer.

4622 Wright, John L. 1983. Croonin' About Cruisin'. In *The Popular Culture Reader*, ed. Christopher D. Geist and Jack Nachbar. Bowling Green, OH: Bowling Green University Popular Press. 102–10.

MIGRATION/DIFFUSION

4623 Bohlman, Philip V. 1984. Central European Jews in Israel: The Reurbanisation of Musical Life in an Immigrant Culture. *Yearbook for Traditional Music* 16: 67–83.

4624 Bythell, Duncan. 1991. The Brass Band in Australia: The Transplantation of British Popular Culture, 1850–1950. In *Bands: The Brass Band Movement in the 19th and 20th Centuries*, ed. Trevor Herbert. Milton Keynes: Open University Press. 145–64.

4625 Correa de Azevedo, Luis Hector. 1981. Music and Musicians of African Origin in Brazil. *The World of Music* 25(2): 53–63.

4626 Cowley, John. 1985. Cultural 'Fusions': Aspects of British West Indian Music in the USA and Britain, 1918–51. *Popular Music* 5: 81–96.

4627 Cowley, John. 1985. *West Indian Gramophone Records in Britain: 1927–1950.* Coventry: Centre for Research in Ethnic Relations, University of Warwick.

4628 Cowley, John. 1985. West Indian Records in Britain. *Musical Traditions* 4: 28–30.

4629 Cowley, John. 1990. London Is the Place: Caribbean Music in the Context of the Empire, 1900–60. In *Black Music in Britain: Essays on the Afro-Asian Contribution to Popular Music*, ed. Paul Oliver. Milton Keynes: Open University Press. 58–76.

4630 Cowley, John. 1994. uBUNGCA (Oxford Bags): Recordings in London of African and West Indian Music in the 1920s and 1930s. *Musical Traditions* 12: 13–27.

4631 Cushman, Thomas. 1991. Rich Rastas and Communist Rockers: A Comparative Study of the Origin, Diffusion and Defusion of Revolutionary Musical Codes. *Journal of Popular Culture* 25(3): 17–62.

4632 Davis, Urula Broschke. 1986. *Paris Without Regret.* Iowa City, IA: University of Iowa Press.

4633 Dyan, Brigitte and Mandel, Jean-Jacques. 1984. *L'Afrique à Paris.* Paris: Editions Rochevignes.

4634 Epstein, Dena J. 1973. African Music in British and French America. *Musical Quarterly* 59(1): 61–91.

4635 Erlmann, Veit. 1990. Migration and Performance: Zulu Migrant Workers' Isicathamiya Performance in South Africa, 1890–1950. *Ethnomusicology* 34(2): 199–219.

4636 Fairley, Jan. 1988. Analysing Performance: Narrative and Ideology in Concerts by ¡Karaxú! *Popular Music* 8(1): 1–30.

4637 Floyd, Samuel A. 1991. Ring Shout! Literary Studies, Historical Studies, and Black Music Inquiry. *Black Music Research Journal* 11(2): 265–78.

4638 Gilroy, Paul. 1993. *The Black Atlantic: Modernity and Double Consciousness.* London: Verso.

4639 Glasser, Ruth. 1990. Paradoxical Ethnicity: Puerto Rican Musicians in Post World War I New York City. *Latin American Music Review* 11(1): 63–72.

4640 Goodey, Brian R. 1968. New Orleans to London: Twenty Years of the New Orleans Jazz Revival in Britain. *Journal of Popular Culture* 2(2): 173–94.

4641 Gronow, Pekka. 1987. The Last Refuge of the Tango. *Finnish Music Quarterly* 3–4: 26–31.

4642 Hebdige, Dick. 1987. *Cut 'n' Mix: Culture, Identity and Caribbean Music.* London and New York: Comedia/Methuen.

4643 Hecht, Paul. 1968. *The Wind Cried: America's Discovery of the World of Flamenco*. New York: Dial Press.

4644 Hirschberg, Jehoash. 1989. *The Role of Music in the Renewed Self-Identity of Karaite Jewish Refugee Communities from Cairo*. New York: International Council for Traditional Music.

4645 Ita, Chief Bassey. 1984. *Jazz in Nigeria: An Outline Cultural History*. Calibar: Radical House.

4646 Jones, Simon. 1988. *Black Culture, White Youth: The Reggae Tradition from JA to UK*. London: Macmillan.

4647 Juste-Constant, Vogeli. 1990. Haitian Popular Music in Montreal: The Effect of Acculturation. *Popular Music* 9(1): 79–86.

4648 Lee, Joanna Ching-Yun. 1995. Brain Drained Cantopop: Songs on Emigration from Hong Kong. In *Popular Music Perspectives III*, ed. Peter Wicke. Berlin: Zyankrise. 248–53.

4649 Ling, Jan and Ramsten, Märta. 1985. The Gärdeby Folk Melody: A Musical Migrant. In *Popular Music Perspectives, 2*, ed. David Horn. Göteborg and Exeter: IASPM. 119–41.

4650 Lipsitz, George. 1994. *Dangerous Crossroads: Popular Music, Postmodernism and the Poetics of Place*. London: Verso.

4651 Lotz, Rainer E. 1990. The Black Troubadours: Black Entertainers in Europe, 1896–1915. *Black Music Research Journal* 10(2): 253–73.

4652 MacDonnel, Margaret. 1982. *The Emigrant Experience: Songs of Highland Emigrants in North America*. Toronto: University of Toronto Press.

4653 Mohren, Michael. 1985. Lieder zur 'emigración'. *Hispanorama* 41: 112–14.

4654 Monson, Ingrid. 1990. Forced Migration, Asymmetrical Power Relations and African-American Music: Reformulation of Cultural Meaning and Form. *The World of Music* 32(3): 22–45.

4655 Moody, Bill. 1993. *The Jazz Exiles: American Musicians Abroad*. Reno, NV: University of Nevada Press.

4656 Mukuna, Kazadi wa. 1979. *Contribuiçao Bantu na música popular brasileira*. Sao Paulo: Global Editora.

4657 Murphy, Jeanette. 1967. The Survival of African Music in America. In *The Negro and His Folklore in Nineteenth-Century Periodicals*, ed. Bruce Jackson. Austin, TX: University of Texas Press. 327–39. (First published in *Popular Science Monthly* 55 (1899): 660–72.)

4658 Mutsaers, Lutgard. 1990. Indorock: An Early Eurorock Style. *Popular Music* 9(3): 307–20.

4659 Mutsaers, Lutgard. 1995. Roots and Recognition: Contributions of Musicians from the Indonesian Archipelago to the Development of Popular Music Culture in the Netherlands. *Perfect Beat* 2(3) (July): 65–81.

4660 O'Connor, Nuala. 1991. *Bringing It All Back Home: The Influence of Irish Music*. London: BBC.

4661 Oliver, Paul. 1970. *Savannah Syncopators: African Retentions in the Blues*. London: Studio Vista.

4662 Oliver, Paul. 1975. Jazz Is Where You Find It: The European Experience of Jazz. In *Superculture: American Popular Culture and Europe*, ed. C.W.E. Bigsby. London: Elek. 140–51.

4663 Ostendorf, Berndt. 1983. *Ethnicity and Popular Music: On Immigrants and Blacks in American Music, 1830–1900*. Exeter: IASPM UK.

4664 Pickering, Michael. 1986. White Skin, Black Masks: 'Nigger' Minstrelsy in

Victorian Britain. In *Music Hall: Performance and Style*, ed. J.S. Bratton. Milton Keynes: Open University Press. 70–91.

4665 Pickering, Michael. 1990. 'A Jet Ornament to Society': Black Music in Nineteenth-Century Britain. In *Black Music in Britain: Essays on the Afro-Asian Contribution to Popular Music*, ed. Paul Oliver. Milton Keynes: Open University Press. 16–33.

4666 Roberts, John Storm. 1974. (1972) *Black Music of Two Worlds*. New York: William Morrow. First published New York/London: Praeger/Allen Lane, 1972.

4667 Ryback, Timothy. 1990. *Rock Around the Bloc: A History of Rock Music in Eastern Europe and the Soviet Union*. New York: Oxford University Press.

4668 Santos, Joao Dos. 1987. The Gangster Reformed: A Study in Musical Parallels. *Musical Traditions* 7: 12–20.

4669 Schlesinger, Michael. 1988. Italian Music in New York City. *New York Folklore* 14(3–4): 129–38.

4670 Singer, Roberta. 1983. Tradition and Innovation in Contemporary Latin American Popular Music in New York City. *Latin American Music Review* 4(2): 183–202.

4671 Singer, Roberta. 1988. Puerto Rican Music in New York City. *New York Folklore* 14(3–4): 139–50.

4672 Slobin, Mark. 1983. Tenement Songs: The Popular Music of Jewish Immigrants. *Popular Music* 3: 289–92.

4673 Stapleton, Chris. 1990. African Connections: London's Hidden Music Scene. In *Black Music in Britain: Essays on the Afro-Asian Contribution to Popular Music*, ed. Paul Oliver. Milton Keynes: Open University Press. 79–86.

4674 Starr, S. Frederick. 1983. *Red and Hot: The Fate of Jazz in the Soviet Union, 1917–1980*. New York and Oxford: Oxford University Press.

4675 Stuckey, Sterling. 1987. *Slave Culture: Nationalist Theory and the Foundations of Black America*. New York: Oxford University Press.

4676 Thompson, Donald. 1975. A New World Mbira: The Caribbean Marimbula. *African Music* 5(4): 140–48.

4677 Torp, Lisbet. 1986. Hip Hop Dances: Their Adoption and Function Among Boys in Denmark, 1983–1984. *Yearbook for Traditional Music* 18: 29–86.

4678 Van der Merwe, Peter. 1989. *Origins of the Popular Style: The Antecedents of Twentieth-Century Popular Music*. Oxford: Clarendon Press.

4679 Welch, David B. 1985. A Yoruba/Nagô 'Melotype' for Religious Songs in the African Diaspora: Continuity of West African Praise Song in the New World. In *More than Drumming: Essays on African and Afro-Latin American Music and Musicians*, ed. Irene V. Jackson. Westport, CT: Greenwood Press. 145–62.

4680 Wilcken, Lois E. 1988. Haiti Chérie: Journey of an Immigrant Music in New York City. *New York Folklore* 14(3–4): 179–89.

4681 Winans, Robert B. and Kaufman, Elias J. 1994. Minstrel and Classic Banjo: American and English Connections. *American Music* 12(1): 1–30.

MUSIC IN SPORT

4682 Bowman, John, and Zoss, Joel. 1989. The Music of the Game. In *Diamonds in the Rough: The Untold History of Baseball*. New York: Macmillan. 366–84.

4683 Corner, John. 1984. Olympic Myths: The Flame, the Night and the Music. In

Television Mythologies: Stars, Shows and Signs, ed. Len Masterman. London: Comedia. 58–62.

4684 Mote, James. 1989. Baseball in Music and Song. In *Everything Baseball*. New York: Prentice-Hall. 275–384.

4685 Rowe, David. 1995. *Popular Cultures: Rock Music, Sport and the Politics of Pleasure*. London: Sage.

4686 Thorn, John, Bob Carroll and David Reuther, comps. 1990. Baseball Music. In *The Whole Baseball Catalogue: The Ultimate Guide to the Baseball Marketplace*. New York: Fireside Books/ Simon & Schuster. 1–15.

NATIONALISM

4687 Hodek, Johannes, and Niermann, Franz. 1984. *Rockmusik – Rockkultur*. Stuttgart: J.B. Metzlersche Verlagsabuchhandlung.

4688 Lahusen, Christian. 1993. The Aesthetic of Radicalism: The Relationship Between Punk and the Patriotic Nationalist Movement of the Basque Country. *Popular Music* 12(3): 263–80.

4689 León, Argeliers. 1991. Of the Axe and the Hinge: Nationalism, Afro-Cubanism and Music in Pre-Revolutionary Cuba. In *Essays on Cuban Music: North American and Cuban Perspectives*, ed. Peter Manuel. Lanham, MD: University Press of America. 267–82.

4690 Manuel, Peter. 1987. Marxism, Nationalism and Popular Music in Revolutionary Cuba. *Popular Music* 6(2): 151–78.

4691 Pekacz, Jolanta. 1995. European Culture Community and Nationalism. In *Popular Music Perspectives III*, ed. Peter Wicke. Berlin: Zyankrise. 38–47.

4692 Wicke, Peter. 1985. Dialektika sootnashenyja nazionalnovo y internationalnovo na primeryje populjarnoy muzyka GDR. In

Rasvlekatelnyje Formy iskustro v rasvitom obtschestro, ed. Evgenij Dukow, et al. Moskva: Progress. 51–76.

4693 Zook, Kristal Bent. 1992. Reconstructions of Nationalist Thought in Black Music and Culture. In *Rockin' the Boat: Mass Music and Mass Movements*, ed. Reebee Garofalo. Boston, MA: South End Press. 255–66.

PERFORMANCE

4694 Abrahams, Roger D. 1983. *The Man of Words in the West Indies*. Baltimore, MD: Johns Hopkins University Press.

4695 Bauman, Richard. 1984. *Verbal Art as Performance*. Prospect Heights, IL: Waveland Press.

4696 Béhague, Gerard, ed. 1984. *Performance and Practice: Ethnomusicological Perspectives*. Westport, CT: Greenwood Press.

4697 Bennett, H. Stith. 1990. (1980) The Realities of Practice. In *On Record: Rock, Pop and the Written Word*, ed. Simon Frith and Andrew Goodwin. London: Routledge. 221–37.

4698 Blacking, John. 1976. *How Musical Is Man?* London: Faber.

4699 Brace, Tim. 1993. Symbolic Rhetoric and the Struggle for Meaning: A Popular Music Performance in Beijing, China. *Journal of Popular Music Studies* 5(3): 8–25.

4700 Dorf, Michael Ethan and Appel, Robert. 1986. *A Guide to Gigging in North America*. New York: Flaming Pie Records.

4701 Fabbri, Franco, ed. 1985. *What Is Popular Music? 41 saggi, ricerche, interventi sulla musica di ogni giorno*. Milano: Unicopli.

4702 Fabbri, Franco. 1989. Musica contemporanea e media: la 'fallacia concertocentrica'. *Quaderni di Musica/Realtà* 23: 227–42.

4703 Fairley, Jan. 1985. Karaxú and Incantation: When Does 'Folk' Music Become 'Popular'? In *Popular Music Perspectives, 2*, ed. David Horn. Göteborg and Exeter: IASPM. 278–86.

4704 Fairley, Jan. 1988. Analysing Performance: Narrative and Ideology in Concerts by ¡Karaxú! *Popular Music* 8(1): 1–30.

4705 Goodall, H.L., Jr. 1990. *Living in the Rock 'n' Roll Mystery: Reading Context, Self and Others as Clues*. Carbondale, IL: Southern Illinois University Press.

4706 Gottfried, Martin. 1985. *In Person: The Great Entertainers*. New York: Abrams.

4707 Herndon, Marcia and Brunyate, Roger, eds. 1976. *Proceedings of a Symposium on Form in Performance, Hard-Core Ethnography*. Austin, TX: University of Texas, Office of the College of Fine Arts.

4708 Keil, Charles. 1966. *Urban Blues*. Chicago: University of Chicago Press.

4709 Laing, Dave. 1985. *One Chord Wonders: Power and Meaning in Punk Rock*. Milton Keynes: Open University Press.

4710 McLeod, Norma and Herndon, Marcia, eds. 1980. *The Ethnography of Musical Performances*. Norwood, PA: Norwood Editions.

4711 Midgett, Douglas K. 1977. Performance Roles and Musical Change in a Caribbean Society. *Ethnomusicology* 21(1): 55–73.

4712 Pickering, Michael and Green, Tony, eds. 1987. *Everyday Culture: Popular Song and the Vernacular Milieu*. Milton Keynes: Open University Press.

4713 Small, Christopher. 1987. Performance as Ritual: Sketch for an Enquiry into the True Nature of a Symphony Concert. In *Lost in Music: Culture, Style and the Musical Event*, ed. Avron Levine White. London: Routledge. 6–32.

4714 Szwed, John F. 1970. Afro-American Musical Adaptation. In *Afro-American Anthropology: Contemporary Perspectives*, ed. Norman E. Whitten and John F. Szwed. New York: Free Press. 219–30.

4715 Taylor, Rogan. 1985. *The Death and Resurrection Show: From Shaman to Superstar*. London: Anthony Blond.

4716 Tetzlaff, D. 1993. Music for Meaning: Reading the Discourse of Authenticity in Rock. *Journal of Communication Inquiry* 18(1): 95–117.

4717 Turner, Victor. 1986. *The Anthropology of Performance*. New York: PAJ Publications.

4718 Turner, Victor. 1990. Liminality and Community. In *Culture and Society: Contemporary Debates*, ed. Jeffrey C. Alexander and Steven Seidman. Cambridge: Cambridge University Press. 147–54.

4719 Van Zile, Judy. 1988. Examining Movement in the Context of the Music Event: A Working Model. *Yearbook for Traditional Music* 20: 125–33.

4720 Washabaugh, William. 1994. The Flamenco Body. *Popular Music* 13(1): 75–90.

4721 White, Avron Levine, ed. 1987. *Lost in Music: Culture, Style and the Musical Event*. London: Routledge.

4722 Wills, Geoff, and Cooper, Cary L. 1988. *Pressure Sensitive: Popular Musicians under Stress*. London: Sage.

POLITICS

4723 Agnew, Spiro. 1972. Talking Brainwashing Blues. In *The Sounds of Social Change: Studies in Popular Culture*, ed. R. Serge Denisoff and Richard A.

Peterson. Chicago: Rand McNally & Co. 307–10.

4724 Allen, Lara. 1995. The Effect of Repressive State Policies on the Development and Demise of Kwela Music in Africa, 1955–1965. In *Popular Music Perspectives III*, ed. Peter Wicke. Berlin: Zyankrise. 326–30.

4725 Ballantine, Christopher. 1995. Fact, Ideology and Paradox: African Elements in Early Black South African Jazz and Vaudeville. In *Papers Presented at the Tenth Symposium on Ethnomusicology, Rhodes University, 30 September-2 October, 1991*, ed. Carol Muller. International Library of African Music, Rhodes University. 5–9.

4726 Ballantine, Christopher. 1995. 'Gateway to Liberty': Reflections on the Social Role of Black South African Jazz and Vaudeville Before the Mid-1940s. In *Popular Music Perspectives III*, ed. Peter Wicke. Berlin: Zyankrise. 305–11.

4727 Ballantine, Christopher. 1995. Politics in Music: Towards an African Style in Black South African Jazz and Vaudeville in the Early 1940s. In *Papers Presented at the Ninth Symposium on Ethnomusicology, University of Namibia, 23–26 August, 1990*, ed. Carol Muller. International Library of African Music, Rhodes University. 5–7.

4727a Bennett, Tony, et al., eds. 1993. *Rock and Popular Music: Politics, Policies, Institutions*. London: Routledge.

4728 Birch, Michael. 1987. 'I've Got Class and I've Got Style': The Politics of Popular Music. In *Missing in Action: Australian Popular Music*, ed. Marcus Breen. Melbourne: Verbal Graphics Pty. 146–66.

4729 Blacking, John. 1981. Political and Musical Freedom of Some Black South African Churches. In *The Structure of Folk Models*, ed. L. Holy and M. Stuchlik. London: Academic Press. 35–62.

4730 Carles, Philippe and Comolli, Jean-Louis. 1971. *Free Jazz/Black Power*. Paris: Edition Champ Libre.

4731 Chapple, Steve and Garofalo, Reebee. 1977. *Rock 'n' Roll Is Here to Pay: The History and Politics of the Music Industry*. Chicago: Nelson-Hall.

4732 Coulonges, Georges. 1985. *La commune en chantant*. Paris: Messidor/Temps Actuels.

4733 Cushman, Thomas. 1991. Rich Rastas and Communist Rockers: A Comparative Study of the Origin, Diffusion and Defusion of Revolutionary Musical Codes. *Journal of Popular Culture* 25(3): 17–62.

4734 Cutler, Chris. 1984. Technology, Politics and Contemporary Music: Necessity and Choice in Musical Forms. *Popular Music* 4: 279–300.

4735 Denisoff, R. Serge. 1971. *A Great Day Coming: Folk Music and the American Left*. Urbana, IL: University of Illinois Press.

4736 Denisoff, R. Serge. 1972. *Sing a Song of Social Significance*. Bowling Green, OH: Bowling Green State University Press.

4737 Denisoff, R. Serge and Peterson, Richard A., eds. 1972. *The Sounds of Social Change: Studies in Popular Culture*. Chicago: Rand McNally & Co.

4738 Denselow, Robin. 1989. *When the Music's Over: The Story of Political Pop*. London and Boston: Faber & Faber.

4739 Derksen, Annete, et al., eds. 1983. *Muziek & Politiek*. Leiden: Stichting Burgerschapskunde.

4740 Dunaway, David King. 1987. Music and Politics in the United States. *Folk Music Journal* 5(3): 268–94.

4741 Dunaway, David King and Larsen, Peter. 1987. Music as Political Communication in the United States. In

Popular Music & Communication, ed. James Lull. Newbury Park, CA: Sage. 36–52.

4742 Dunson, Josh. 1980. *Freedom in the Air: Song Movements of the Sixties.* Westport, CT: Greenwood Press.

4743 Elderen, P. Louis van. 1985. Songs for the Little Man, 1930 and 1980: Popular Music and the Crisis of the Welfare State. In *Popular Music Perspectives, 2,* ed. David Horn. Göteborg and Exeter: IASPM. 148–65.

4744 Elflein, Dietmar. 1995. State Control & Rock 'n' Roll. In *Popular Music Perspectives III,* ed. Peter Wicke. Berlin: Zyankrise. 138–42.

4745 Erlmann, Veit. 1985. Black Political Song in South Africa: Some Research Perspectives. In *Popular Music Perspectives, 2,* ed. David Horn. Göteborg and Exeter: IASPM. 187–209.

4746 Erlmann, Veit. 1993. The Politics and Aesthetics of Transnational Musics. *The World of Music* 35(2): 3–15.

4747 Erlmann, Veit. 1996. *Nightsong: Performance, Power, and Practice in South Africa.* Chicago and London: University of Chicago Press.

4748 Fabbri, Franco and Fiori, Umberto. 1989. Crisi e prospettive della canzone politica italiana. *Quaderni di Musica/ Realtà* 23: 331–46.

4749 Fiori, Umberto. 1983. Rock Music and Politics in Italy. *Popular Music* 3: 261–78.

4750 Floh de Cologne, ed. 1980. *Rock gegen Rechts. Beiträge zu einer Bewegung.* Dortmund: Weltkreis.

4751 Frith, Simon. 1981. *Sound Effects: Youth, Leisure, and the Politics of Rock 'n' Roll.* New York: Pantheon Books.

4752 Frith, Simon, ed. 1989. *World Music, Politics and Social Change.* Manchester

and New York: Manchester University Press.

4753 Garofalo, Reebee. 1986. How Autonomous Is Relative?: Popular Music, the Social Formation and Cultural Struggle. *Popular Music* 6(1): 77–92.

4754 Garofalo, Reebee, ed. 1992. *Rockin' the Boat: Mass Music and Mass Movements.* Boston, MA: South End Press.

4755 Gilroy, Paul. 1987. *There Ain't No Black in the Union Jack: The Cultural Politics of Race and Nation.* London: Hutchinson.

4756 Grossberg, Lawrence. 1989. Rock 'n' Reagan. *Quaderni di Musica/Realtà* 23: 459–77.

4757 Grossberg, Lawrence. 1991. Rock, Territorialization and Power. *Cultural Studies* 5(3): 358–67.

4758 Grossberg, Lawrence. 1992. *We Gotta Get Out of This Place: Popular Conservatism and Postmodern Culture.* London: Routledge.

4759 Haase, Ellionor and Wiener, Bibiana. 1985. Canción y revolucción en Nicaragua. *Hispanorama – Sonderdruck* (November): 84–88.

4760 Hall, James W. 1968. Concepts of Liberty in American Broadside Ballads, 1850–1870: A Study of the Mind of American Mass Culture. *Journal of Popular Culture* 2(2): 252–77.

4761 Hamm, Charles. 1989. 'Graceland' Revisited. *Popular Music* 8(3): 299–303.

4762 Hamm, Charles. 1991. 'The Constant Companion of Man': Separate Development, Radio Bantu and Music. *Popular Music* 10(2): 147–73.

4763 Hamm, Charles. 1995. *Putting Popular Music in Its Place.* Cambridge: Cambridge University Press.

4764 Hampton, Wayne. 1986. *Guerrilla Minstrels: John Lennon, Joe Hill, Woody Guthrie, and Bob Dylan.* Knoxville, TN: University of Tennessee Press.

4765 Harker, Dave. 1980. *One for the Money: Politics and Popular Song.* London: Hutchinson.

4766 Harker, Dave. 1995. Popular Music Doesn't Matter. In *Popular Music Perspectives III,* ed. Peter Wicke. Berlin: Zyankrise. 451–66.

4767 Hebdige, Dick. 1979. *Subculture: The Meaning of Style.* London and New York: Methuen.

4768 Kaiser, Charles. 1988. *1968 in America: Music, Politics, Chaos, Counterculture, and the Shaping of a Generation.* New York: Weidenfeld & Nicolson.

4769 Keating, Kenneth B. 1967. Mine Enemy, the Folksinger. In *The American Folk Scene: Dimensions of the Folk Song Revival,* ed. David De Turk and A. Poulin. New York: Dell Publishing. 103–11.

4770 Keil, Charles and Feld, Steven. 1994. *Music Grooves.* Chicago and London: University of Chicago Press.

4771 Kerkhof, Ian. 1989. Music in the Revolution. *Keskidee: A Journal of Black Musical Traditions* 2: 10–21.

4772 Kofsky, Frank. 1970. *Black Nationalism and the Revolution in Music.* New York: Pathfinder Press.

4773 *La chitarra e il potere: Gli autori della canzone politica contemporanea.* 1976. Roma: Savelli.

4774 Leukert, Bernd, ed. 1980. *Thema: Rock gegen Rechts. Musik als politisches Instrument.* Frankfurt am Main: Fischer.

4775 Levine, Lawrence. 1988. *Highbrow/Lowbrow: The Emergence of Cultural Hierarchy in America.* Cambridge and London: Harvard University Press.

4776 Lewis, Lisa A. 1990. *Gender Politics and MTV: Voicing the Difference.* Philadelphia: Temple University Press.

4777 Lieberman, Robbie. 1989. *'My Song Is My Weapon': People's Songs, American Communism, and the Politics of Culture, 1930–50.* Urbana and Chicago: University of Illinois Press.

4778 Lipsitz, George. 1994. *Dangerous Crossroads: Popular Music, Postmodernism, and the Poetics of Place.* London and New York: Verso.

4779 Lusane, Clarence. 1993. Rap, Race and Politics. *Race and Class* 35(1): 41–56.

4780 Madhlope-Phillips, James. 1983. Music Marches with the People's Revolution. In *Laulu ottaa kantaa: aineistoa 1970-luvun lauliliikkeestä.* Helsinki: Työväenenmusiikki-institutti. 167–72.

4781 Manuel, Peter. 1991. Musical Pluralism in Revolutionary Cuba. In *Essays on Cuban Music: North American and Cuban Perspectives,* ed. Peter Manuel. Lanham, MD: University Press of America. 283–311.

4782 Martin, Linda and Segrave, Kerry. 1993. (1988) *Anti-Rock: The Opposition to Rock 'n' Roll.* New York: Da Capo Press. First published Hamden: The Shoe String Press, 1988.

4783 McClary, Susan and Leppert, Richard, eds. 1987. *Music and Society: The Politics of Composition, Performance and Reception.* Cambridge: Cambridge University Press.

4784 McClary, Susan. 1991. *Feminine Endings: Music, Gender, and Sexuality.* Minneapolis and Oxford: University of Minnesota Press.

4785 Meintjes, Louise. 1990. Paul Simon's 'Graceland', South Africa, and the Mediation of Musical Meaning. *Ethnomusicology* 34(1): 37–73.

SOCIAL AND CULTURAL CONTEXTS

4786 Mitchell, Tony. 1992. Mixing Pop and Politics: Rock Music in Czechoslovakia Before and After the Velvet Revolution. *Popular Music* 11(2): 187–203.

4787 Mossman, Walter and Schleuning, Peter. 1980. *Alte und neue politische Lieder: Entstehung und Gebrauch; Text und Noten.* Reinbek bei Hamburg: Rowohlt.

4788 Muikku, Jari. 1995. Cultural Policy of a State and Popular Music. In *Popular Music Perspectives III*, ed. Peter Wicke. Berlin: Zyankrise. 369–72.

4789 Noebel, David A. 1974. *The Marxist Minstrels: A Handbook on Communist Subversion of Music.* Tulsa, OK: American Christian College Press.

4790 Norman, Philip. 1992. Nazi Chic. *Weekend Guardian* (30–31 May): 4–6.

4791 Olivera, Rubén. 1986. La canción política. *La del taller* 5(6): 2–9.

4792 Orman, John M. 1984. *The Politics of Rock Music.* Chicago: Nelson-Hall.

4793 Otto, Ulrich. 1982. *Die historisch-politischen Lieder und Karikaturen des Vormärz und der Revolution von 1848–49.* Köln: Pahl-Rugenstein.

4794 Pacini Hernandez, Deborah. 1995. *Bachata: A Social History of a Dominican Popular Music.* Philadelphia: Temple University Press.

4795 Palmer, Roy. 1988. *The Sound of History: Songs and Social Comment.* New York: Oxford University Press.

4796 Peinemann, Steve B. 1980. *Die Wut, die du im Bauch hast: Politische Rockmusik.* Reinbek bei Hamburg: Rowohlt.

4797 Pekacz, Jolanta. 1992. On Some Dilemmas of Polish Post-Communist Rock Culture. *Popular Music* 11(2): 205–208.

4798 Pekacz, Jolanta. 1994. Did Rock Smash the Wall? The Role of Rock in Political Transition. *Popular Music* 13(1): 41–49.

4799 Perris, Arnold. 1983. Music as Propaganda: Art at the Command of Doctrine in the People's Republic of China. *Ethnomusicology* 27(1): 1–28.

4800 Pickens, Donald K. 1982. The Historical Images in Republican Campaign Songs, 1860–1900. *Journal of Popular Culture* 15(3): 165–74.

4801 Pomerance, Alan. 1988. *Repeal of the Blues: How Black Entertainers Influenced Civil Rights.* Secaucus, NJ: Citadel Press.

4802 Pratt, Ray. 1994. *Rhythm and Resistance: The Political Uses of American Popular Music.* Washington and London: Smithsonian Institution Press. First published New York: Praeger, 1990.

4803 Pring-Mill, Robert. 1987. The Role of Revolutionary Song: A Nicaraguan Assessment. *Popular Music* 6(2): 179–89.

4804 Ramet, Sabrina Petra, ed. 1994. *Rocking the State: Rock Music and Politics in Eastern Europe and Russia.* Boulder, CO: Westview Press.

4805 Redhead, Steve and Street, John. 1989. Have I the Right? Legitimacy, Authenticity and Community in Folk's Politics. *Popular Music* 8(2): 177–84.

4806 Richards, Sam. 1992. *Sonic Harvest: Towards Musical Democracy.* Oxford: Amber Lane Press.

4807 Rose, Tricia. 1994. *Black Noise: Rap Music and Black Culture in Contemporary America.* Hanover and London: University Press of New England.

4808 Saffioti, Tito. 1978. *Enciclopedia della canzone popolare e della nuova canzone politica.* Milano: Longanesi.

4809 Schoenebeck, Mechthild von, Jürgen Brandhorst and H. Joachim Gerke.

1992. *Politik und gesellschaftlicher Wertewandel im Spiegel populärer Musik.* Essen: Blaue Eule.

4809a Schoenebeck, Mechthild von, Jürgen Brandhorst and H. Joachim Gerke. 1995. Das DFG-Forschungsprojekt: Politischer Wertewandel und Populäre Musik. In *Popular Music Perspectives III*, ed. Peter Wicke. Berlin: Zyankrise. 441–50.

4810 Shepherd, John. 1995. Popular Music Matters. In *Popular Music Perspectives III*, ed. Peter Wicke. Berlin: Zyankrise. 467–81.

4811 Sinclair, John, and Levin, Robert. 1971. *Music and Politics.* New York: World.

4812 Small, Christopher. 1996. *Music-Society-Education.* Hanover and London: University Press of New England. First published London: John Calder, 1980.

4813 Starr, S. Frederick. 1983. *Red and Hot: The Fate of Jazz in the Soviet Union, 1917–1980.* New York and Oxford: Oxford University Press.

4814 Stokes, Martin. 1992. Islam, the Turkish State and Arabesk. *Popular Music* 11(2): 213–27.

4815 Street, John. 1986. *Rebel Rock: The Politics of Popular Music.* Oxford: Blackwell.

4816 Street, John. 1995. In the Neighbourhood: The Local State and Popular Music Consumption. In *Popular Music Perspectives III*, ed. Peter Wicke. Berlin: Zyankrise. 373–86.

4817 Tokaji, András. 1985. Leftist Political Songs in Hungary Before and After 1948. In *Popular Music Perspectives, 2*, ed. David Horn. Göteborg and Exeter: IASPM. 307–16.

4818 Vila, Pablo. 1987. *Rock nacional* and the Dictatorship in Argentina. *Popular Music* 6(2): 129–48.

4819 Vincent, Ted. 1995. *Keep Cool: The Black Activists Who Built the Jazz Age.* London and New Haven: Pluto Press.

4820 No entry.

4821 Wallis, Roger and Malm, Krister. 1984. *Big Sounds from Small Peoples: The Music Industry in Small Countries.* London: Constable.

4822 Walser, Robert. 1993. *Running with the Devil: Power, Gender, and Madness in Heavy Metal Music.* Hanover, NH: University Press of New England.

4823 Wicke, Peter. 1982. Rock Music as a Phenomenon of Progressive Mass Culture. In *Popular Music Perspectives, 1*, ed. David Horn and Philip Tagg. Göteborg and Exeter: IASPM. 223–31.

4824 Wicke, Peter. 1985. Rock 'n' Revolution. Sul significato della musica rock in una cultura di massa progressista. *Musica/Realtà* VI(17): 5–12.

4825 Wicke, Peter. 1990. Zwischen Anpassung und Verweigerung. Pop und Politik in der DDR. *Politicum* 47: 25–28.

4826 Wicke, Peter. 1992. 'The Times They Are A-Changin'': Rock Music and Political Change in East Germany. In *Rockin' the Boat: Mass Music and Mass Movements*, ed. Reebee Garofalo. Boston, MA: South End Press. 81–92.

4827 Wicke, Peter, and Erlmann, Veit. 1992. Das Eigene und das Fremde. *Positionen* 12: 2–7.

4828 Wicke, Peter and Shepherd, John. 1993. 'The Cabaret Is Dead': Rock Culture as State Enterprise – The Political Organization of Rock in East Germany. In *Culture and Politics: The Politics of Culture*, ed. Tony Bennett. Sydney, London and Boston: Routledge & Kegan Paul. 25–36.

4829 Wicke, Peter and Frevel, Bernd. 1996. 'Wenn die Musik sich ändert zittern die Mauern der Stadt'. Rockmusik als

Medium des politischen Diskurses im DDR-Kulturbetrieb. In *Musik und Politik*. Regensburg: Coda. 120–42.

4830 Widgery, David. 1986. *Beating Time: Riot 'n' Race 'n' Rock 'n' Roll*. London: Chatto & Windus.

POPULARITY

4831 Aharonián, Coriún. 1985. A Latin-American Approach in a Pioneering Essay. In *Popular Music Perspectives, 2*, ed. David Horn. Göteborg and Exeter: IASPM. 52–65.

4832 Birrer, Frans A.J. 1985. Definitions and Research Orientation: Do We Need a Definition of Popular Music? In *Popular Music Perspectives, 2*, ed. David Horn. Göteborg and Exeter: IASPM. 99–105.

4833 Blacking, John. 1981. Making Artistic Popular Music: The Goal of True Folk. *Popular Music* 1: 9–14.

4834 Brackett, David. 1994. The Politics and Practice of 'Crossover' in American Popular Music, 1963–65. *Musical Quarterly* 78(4): 774–97.

4835 Charosh, Paul. 1992. 'Popular' and 'Classical' in the Mid-Nineteenth Century. *American Music* 10(2): 110–35.

4836 Cutler, Chris. 1985. What Is Popular Music? In *Popular Music Perspectives, 2*, ed. David Horn. Göteborg and Exeter: IASPM. 3–12.

4837 Fairley, Jan. 1985. Karaxú and Incantation: When Does 'Folk' Music Become 'Popular'? In *Popular Music Perspectives, 2*, ed. David Horn. Göteborg and Exeter: IASPM. 278–86.

4838 Galden, Manfred P. 1985. 'Popular Music' in the Terminology of Communication and Information Theory. In *Popular Music Perspectives, 2*, ed. David Horn. Göteborg and Exeter: IASPM. 106–16.

4839 Hamm, Charles. 1982. Some Thoughts on the Measurement of Popularity in Music. In *Popular Music Perspectives, 1*, ed. David Horn and Philip Tagg. Göteborg and Exeter: IASPM. 3–15.

4840 Harker, Dave. 1980. *One for the Money: Politics and Popular Song*. London: Hutchinson.

4841 Harker, Dave. 1992. Still Crazy After All These Years: What *Was* Popular Music in the 1960s? In *Cultural Revolution? The Challenge of the Arts in the 1960s*, ed. Bart Moore-Gilbert and John Seed. London and New York: Routledge. 236–54.

4842 Harker, Dave. 1994. Blood on the Tracks: Popular Music in the 1970s. In *The Arts in the 1970s: Cultural Closure?* ed. Bart Moore-Gilbert. London and New York: Routledge. 240–58.

4843 Hennion, Antoine. 1981. *Les Professionnels du disque*. Paris: A.-M. Métailié.

4844 Jones, Gaynor and Rahn, Jay. 1981. Definitions of Popular Music: Recycled. In *Breaking the Sound Barrier: A Critical Anthology of the New Music*, ed. Gregory Battcock. New York: E.P. Dutton. 38–52.

4845 Middleton, Richard. 1990. *Studying Popular Music*. Milton Keynes: Open University Press.

4846 Negus, Keith. 1993. Plugging and Promotion: Pop Radio and Record Promotion in Britain and the United States. *Popular Music* 12(1): 57–68.

4847 Parker, Martin. 1991. Reading the Charts: Making Sense with the Hit Parade. *Popular Music* 10(2): 205–17.

4848 Shepherd, John. 1985. Definition as Mystification: A Consideration of Labels as a Hindrance to Understanding Significance in Music. In *Popular Music Perspectives, 2*, ed. David Horn. Göteborg and Exeter: IASPM. 84–98.

4849 Vega, Carlos. 1966. 'Mesomusic': An Essay on the Music of the Masses. *Ethnomusicology* 10(1): 1–17.

4850 Wicke, Peter. 1985. Popularity in Music: Some Aspects of a Historical Materialist Theory for Popular Music. In *Popular Music Perspectives, 2*, ed. David Horn. Göteborg and Exeter: IASPM. 47–51.

4851 Wicke, Peter. 1992. Populäre Musik als theoretisches Konzept. *PopScriptum* 1: 6–42.

4852 Wicke, Peter and Schneider, Frank. 1986. Popularität oder ästhetischer Anspruch? *Musik und Gesellschaft* XXXVI(3): 119–25.

PROTEST/RESISTANCE

4853 Allen, Gary. 1972. More Subversion Than Meets the Ear. In *The Sounds of Social Change: Studies in Popular Culture*, ed. R. Serge Denisoff and Richard A. Peterson. Chicago: Rand McNally & Co. 151–66.

4854 Ames, Russell. 1950. Protest and Irony in Negro Folksong. *Science & Society* 14(3): 193–213.

4855 Artigas, Gustavo and Moncada, Perla Valencia, eds. 1973. *Antología de canciones de lucha y esperanza.* Santiago de Chile: Empresa Editora Nacional Quimantu Ltda.

4856 Bartnik, Norbert and Bordon, Frieda. 1981. *Keep on Rockin': Rockmusik zwischen Protest und Profit.* Weinheim (Basel): Beltz.

4857 Beck, Earl R. 1985. The Anti-Nazi 'Swing Youth'. *Journal of Popular Culture* 19(3): 45–54.

4858 Blankertz, Stefan and Alsmann, Götz. 1979. *Rock 'n' Roll Subversiv.* Wetzlar: Büchse der Pandora.

4859 Brace, Tim and Friedlander, Paul. 1992. Rock and Roll on the New Long March: Popular Music, Cultural Identity, and Political Opposition in the People's Republic of China. In *Rockin' the Boat: Mass Music and Mass Movements*, ed. Reebee Garofalo. Boston, MA: South End Press. 115–28.

4860 Brown, M.P. 1994. Funk Music as Genre: Black Aesthetics, Apocalyptic Thinking and Urban Protest in Post-1965 African-American Pop. *Cultural Studies* 8(3): 484–508.

4861 Calvet, Louis-Jean. 1976. *La Production révolutionnaire. Slogans, affiches, chansons.* Paris: Payot.

4862 Carawan, Guy and Carawan, Candie, eds. 1990. *Sing for Freedom: The Story of the Civil Rights Movement Through Its Songs.* Bethlehem, PA: Sing Out.

4863 Denisoff, R. Serge. 1969. Folk-Rock: Folk Music, Protest or Commercialism? *Journal of Popular Culture* 3(2): 214–30.

4864 Denisoff, R. Serge. 1972. *Sing a Song of Social Significance.* Bowling Green, OH: Bowling Green State University Press.

4865 Denisoff, R. Serge and Reuss, Richard. 1972. The Protest Songs and Skits of American Trotskyists. *Journal of Popular Culture* 6(2): 407–24.

4866 Denselow, Robin. 1989. *When the Music's Over: The Story of Political Pop.* London and Boston: Faber & Faber.

4867 Dunson, Josh. 1980. *Freedom in the Air: Song Movements of the Sixties.* Westport, CT: Greenwood Press.

4867a Dyson, Michael Eric. 1991. Performance, Protest, and Prophecy in the Culture of Hip-Hop. *Black Sacred Music* 5(1): 12–24.

4868 Eaklor, Vicki L. 1988. *American Antislavery Songs: A Collection and Analysis.* Westport, CT: Greenwood Press.

4869 Elkins, Charles. 1980. The Voice of the Poor: The Broadside as a Medium of Popular Culture and Dissent in Victorian England. *Journal of Popular Culture* 14(2): 262–74.

4870 Ellison, Mary. 1989. *Lyrical Protest: Black Music's Struggle Against Discrimination*. London: Greenwood/Praeger.

4871 Frith, Simon and Street, John. 1992. Rock Against Racism and Red Wedge: From Music to Politics, From Politics to Music. In *Rockin' the Boat: Mass Music and Mass Movements*, ed. Reebee Garofalo. Boston, MA: South End Press. 67–80.

4872 Garofalo, Reebee. 1987. How Autonomous Is Relative?: Popular Music, the Social Formation and Cultural Struggle. *Popular Music* 6(1): 77–92.

4873 Garofalo, Reebee. 1992. Nelson Mandela, the Concerts: Mass Culture as Contested Terrain. In *Rockin' the Boat: Mass Music and Mass Movements*, ed. Reebee Garofalo. Boston, MA: South End Press. 55–66.

4874 Garofalo, Reebee. 1992. Popular Music and the Civil Rights Movement. In *Rockin' the Boat: Mass Music and Mass Movements*, ed. Reebee Garofalo. Boston, MA: South End Press. 231–40.

4875 Gellert, Lawrence. 1934. Negro Songs of Protest. In *Negro Anthology*, ed. Nancy Cunard. London: Nancy Cunard.

4876 Gellert, Lawrence and Siegmeister, Elie. 1936. *Negro Songs of Protest*. New York: Carl Fischer.

4877 Granjon, Marie-Christine. 1985. *L'Amérique de la contestation: les années soixante aux États-Unis*. Paris: Fondation nationale des Sciences Politiques.

4878 Greenway, John. 1967. (1953) The Position of Songs of Protest in Folk Literature. In *The American Folk Scene:*

Dimensions of the Folk Song Revival, ed. David De Turk and A. Poulin. New York: Dell Publishing. 112–29.

4879 Greenway, John. 1977. (1953) *American Folk Songs of Protest*. New York: Octagon. First published Philadelphia: University of Pennsylvania Press, 1953.

4880 Grossberg, Lawrence. 1992. *We Gotta Get Out of This Place: Popular Conservatism and Postmodern Culture*. London and New York: Routledge.

4881 Guthrie, Woody. 1970. (1943) *Bound for Glory*. New York: New American Library. First published New York: E.P. Dutton & Co., 1943.

4882 Hall, Stuart and Jefferson, Tony, eds. 1976. *Resistance Through Rituals: Youth Subcultures in Post-War Britain*. London: Hutchinson.

4883 Hebdige, Dick. 1979. *Subculture: The Meaning of Style*. London: Methuen.

4884 Kaiser, Charles. 1988. *1968 in America: Music, Politics, Chaos, Counterculture, and the Shaping of a Generation*. New York: Weidenfeld & Nicholson.

4885 Lacroix, Bernard. 1981. *L'Utopie communautaire: histoire sociale d'une révolte*. Paris: Presses universitaires de France.

4886 Lewis, George H. 1991. Storm Blowing from Paradise: Social Protest and Oppositional Ideology in Popular Hawaiian Music. *Popular Music* 10(1): 53–67.

4887 Makeba, Miriam. 1988. *Makeba: My Story*, ed. James Hall. London: Bloomsbury.

4888 Marsh, Dave. 1986. *Sun City, by Artists Against Apartheid: The Struggle for Freedom in South Africa; the Making of a Record*. New York: Penguin.

4889 McRobbie, Angela. 1980. Settling Accounts with Subcultures. *Screen Education* 34: 37–49.

4890 Miller, Lloyd and Skipper, James K. 1972. Sounds of Black Protest in Avant-Garde Jazz. In *The Sounds of Social Change: Studies in Popular Culture*, ed. R. Serge Denisoff and Richard A. Peterson. Chicago: Rand McNally & Co. 26–37.

4891 Mitchell, Tony. 1992. Mixing Pop and Politics: Rock Music in Czechoslovakia Before and After the Velvet Revolution. *Popular Music* 11(2): 187–203.

4892 Pankake, John and Nelson, Paul. 1967. P for Protest. In *The American Folk Scene: Dimensions of the Folk Song Revival*, ed. David De Turk and A. Poulin. New York: Dell Publishing. 140–49.

4893 Pekacz, Jolanta. 1994. Did Rock Smash the Wall? The Role of Rock in Political Transition. *Popular Music* 13(1): 41–49.

4894 Philibin, Marianne. 1983. *Give Peace a Chance: Music and the Struggle for Peace. A Catalog of the Exhibit at the Peace Museum, Chicago*. Chicago: Chicago Review Press.

4895 Pratt, Ray. 1990. *Rhythm and Resistance: Explorations in the Political Uses of Popular Music*. London: Praeger.

4896 Pring-Mill, Robert. 1979. The Nature and the Functions of Spanish American Poesia de Compromiso. *Bulletin of the Society for Latin American Studies* 31: 4–21.

4897 Pring-Mill, Robert. 1983. Cantas Canto Cantemos: las canciones de lucha y esperanza como signos de reunión e identitad. *Romanistisches Jahrbuch* 34: 318–54.

4898 Pring-Mill, Robert. 1987. The Roles of Revolutionary Song: A Nicaraguan Assessment. *Popular Music* 6(2): 179–89.

4899 Robinson, John P. and Hirsch, Paul M. 1972. Teenage Response to Rock and Roll Protest Song. In *The Sounds of Social Change: Studies in Popular Culture* ed. R. Serge Denisoff and Richard A. Peterson. Chicago: Rand McNally & Co. 222–31.

4900 Rodnitzky, Jerome L. 1969. The Evolution of the American Protest Song. *Journal of Popular Culture* 3(1): 35–45.

4901 Rodnitzky, Jerome L. 1976. *Minstrels of the Dawn: The Folk-Protest Singer as a Cultural Hero*. Chicago: Nelson-Hall.

4902 Rosen, David M. 1972. *Protest Songs in America*. Westlake, CA: Aware.

4903 No entry.

4904 Street, John. 1986. *Rebel Rock: The Politics of Popular Music*. Oxford: Blackwell.

4905 Thiessen, Rudi. 1981. *It's Only Rock 'n' Roll But I Like It: Zu Kult und Mythos einer Protestbewegung*. Berlin: Medusa.

4906 Ullestad, Neal. 1987. Rock and Rebellion: Subversive Effects of Live Aid and 'Sun City'. *Popular Music* 6(1): 67–76.

4907 Ullestad, Neal. 1992. Diverse Rock Rebellions Subvert Media Hegemony. In *Rockin' the Boat: Mass Music and Mass Movements*, ed. Reebee Garofalo. Boston, MA: South End Press. 37–54.

4908 Vail, Leroy and White, Landeg. 1983. Forms of Resistance: Songs and Perceptions of Power in Colonial Mozambique. *The American Historical Review* 88(4): 883–919.

4909 Vila, Pablo. 1987. *Rock nacional* and the Dictatorship in Argentina. *Popular Music* 6(2): 129–48.

4910 Wicke, Peter. 1981. Rock in Opposition. *Musik und Gesellschaft* XXXI(7): 410–17.

SOCIAL AND CULTURAL CONTEXTS

4911 Wicke, Peter. 1983. Rock 'n' Revolution. *Musik und Gesellschaft* XXXIII(9): 538–43.

4912 Wicke, Peter. 1985. Rock in Opposition. Neue Tendenzen in der internationalen Rockmusik. *Beilage zur Zeitschrift 'Unterhaltungskunst'* 2.

4913 Wicke, Peter. 1985. Rock 'n' Revolution. Sul significato della musica rock in una cultura di massa progressista. *Musica/Realtà* VI(17): 5–12.

4914 Wicke, Peter. 1992. (1987) The Role of Rock Music in Processes of Political Change in the GDR. In *Popular Music & Communication,* ed. James Lull. Newbury Park, CA: Sage.

4915 Wicke, Peter. 1992. 'The Times They Are A-Changin'': Rock Music and Political Change in East Germany. In *Rockin' the Boat: Mass Music and Mass Movements,* ed. Reebee Garofalo. Boston, MA: South End Press. 81–92.

RACISM

4916 Berger, Morroe. 1972. Jazz: Resistance to the Diffusion of a Culture Pattern. In *American Music: From Storyville to Woodstock,* ed. Charles Nanry. New Brunswick, NJ: Transaction.

4917 The Chronic . . . (Harassment by Police of Black Musicians). 1993. *R & R* 104 (February-March): 2.

4918 Cloud, L.V. 1993. The Miseducation – and Missed Education – of Musicians about Afro-American Music and Musicians. *Quarterly (CRIMLAT)* 4(2): 12–22.

4919 Dennison, Sam. 1982. *Scandalize My Name: Black Imagery in American Popular Music.* New York: Garland.

4920 Ellison, Mary. 1989. *Lyrical Protest: Black Music's Struggle Against Discrimination.* London and New York: Greenwood/Praeger.

4921 Garner, C. 1991. The Agony and the Agony: James Lincoln Collier's Jazz Writing. *Jazz Studies* 5: 81–89.

4922 Gerard, J. 1993. Noises Off: Rolling Along (Paul Robeson, Jr. Attacks Songs 'Ol' Man River' and Musical 'Show Boat'). *Variety* 351 (7 June): 47.

4923 Grant, J. 1993. Ain't Gonna Study War No More (John 20: 19–23). *Black Sacred Music* 7(1): 62–70.

4924 Halker, Clark. 1988. A History of Local 208 and the Struggle for Racial Equality in the American Federation of Musicians. *Black Music Research Journal* 8(2): 207–22.

4925 Heckman, Don. 1970. Black Music and White America. In *Black Americans,* ed. John F. Szwed. Washington, DC: Voice of America Forum Lectures. 171–84.

4926 Hodek, Johannes and Niermann, Franz. 1984. *Rockmusik – Rockkultur.* Stuttgart: J.B. Metzlersche Verlagsabuchhandlung.

4927 No entry.

4928 Lott, Eric. 1993. *Love and Theft: Blackface Minstrelsy and the American Working Class.* New York and Oxford: Oxford University Press.

4929 Lusane, Clarence. 1993. Rap, Race and Politics. *Race and Class* 35(1): 41–56.

4930 Meltzer, David, ed. 1993. *Reading Jazz.* San Francisco: Mercury House.

4931 Morton, David and Wolfe, Charles K. 1991. *De Ford Bailey: A Black Star in Early Country Music.* Knoxville, TN: University of Tennessee Press.

4932 Pickering, Michael. 1986. White Skin, Black Masks: 'Nigger' Minstrelsy in Victorian Britain. In *Music Hall: Performance and Style,* ed. J.S. Bratton. Milton Keynes: Open University Press. 70–91.

4933 Rehin, George S. 1981. Blackface Street Minstrels in Victorian London and Its Resorts: Popular Culture and Its Racial Connotations as Revealed in Polite Opinion. *Journal of Popular Culture* 15(1): 19–38.

4934 Rodman, G.B. 1994. A Hero to Most?: Elvis, Myth and the Politics of Race. *Cultural Studies* 8(3): 457–84.

4935 Rusch, B. 1993. Steve Kuhn Interview, Part Two (Discrimination Against White Jazz Musicians). *Cadence* 19: 11–15.

4936 Schurk, William L. 1967. Record Review: Ku Klux Klan Songs. *Journal of Popular Culture* 1(3): 315–16.

4937 Teel, L.R. 1993. Execute Jazzmen Says Black History Week Founder. *IAJRC* 26(2): 67–68.

4938 Tyler, B.M. 1992. *From Harlem to Hollywood: The Struggle for Racial and Cultural Democracy, 1920–1943.* New York: Garland.

4939 Widgery, David. 1986. *Beating Time: Riot 'n' Race 'n' Rock 'n' Roll.* London: Chatto & Windus.

4940 Wilson, P.N. 1993. Schwarzmaler & Weißwäscher: Jazz und Rassismus. *Jazz Podium* 42: 3–6.

RECEPTION AND CONSUMPTION

4941 Abrams, Mark. 1959. *The Teenage Consumer.* London: London Press Exchange.

4942 Adler, Bill. 1964. *Love Letters to the Beatles.* London: Blond & Briggs.

4943 Aizlewood, John, ed. 1994. *Love Is the Drug.* Harmondsworth: Penguin.

4944 Ala, Nemesio and Fabbri, Franco. 1985. Generi musicali, schemi di consumo, gusti del pubblico: 'popular music' e ricerca in Italia. In *Musica e sistema dell'informazione in Europa,* ed.

Francesco Rampi. Milano: Unicopli. 153–66.

4945 Ala, Nemesio, et al. 1985. Patterns of Music Consumption in Milan and Reggio Emilia from April to May 1983. In *Popular Music Perspectives, 2,* ed. David Horn. Göteborg and Exeter: IASPM. 464–500.

4946 *Beatlefan: The Authoritative Publication of Record for Fans of The Beatles.* 1985. 2 vols. (Reprint of fanzine). Ann Arbor, MI: Pierian Press.

4947 Becker, Howard. 1972. The Professional Jazz Musician and His Audience. In *The Sounds of Social Change: Studies in Popular Culture,* ed. R. Serge Denisoff and Richard A. Peterson. Chicago: Rand McNally & Co. 248–60. (First published in *American Journal of Sociology* 57 (1951): 136–44.)

4948 Buxton, David. 1983. Rock Music, the Star System and the Rise of Consumerism. *Telos* 57: 93–106.

4949 Collier, James L. 1988. *The Reception of Jazz in America: A New View.* New York: Institute for Studies in American Music.

4950 Crafts, Susan D., Daniel Cavicchi and Charles Keil. 1993. *My Music.* Hanover and London: Wesleyan University Press.

4951 Cubitt, Sean. 1984. 'Maybellene': Meaning and the Listening Subject. *Popular Music* 4: 207–24.

4952 Dollase, Rainer. 1978. *Das Jazzpublikum: Zur Sozialpsychologie einer kulturellen Minderheit.* Mainz: Schott.

4953 Dollase, Rainer, Michael Rüsenberg and Hans J. Stollenwerk. 1975. *Rock People oder die befragte Szene.* Frankfurt am Main: Fischer.

4954 du Gay, Paul and Negus, Keith. 1994. The Changing Sites of Sound: Music Retailing and the Composition of Consumers. *Media, Culture and Society* 16: 395–413.

4955 Fenster, Mark. 1989. Preparing the
Audience, Informing the Performers:
John A. Lomax and *Cowboy Songs and
Other Frontier Ballads. American Music* 7
(Fall): 260–77.

4956 Fikentscher, Kai. 1995. 'Old School –
New School': An Examination of
Changes in the Production and
Consumption of Post-Disco
Underground Dance Music in New
York City. In *Popular Music: Style and
Identity*, ed. Will Straw, et al. Montréal:
The Centre for Research on Canadian
Cultural Industries and Institutions. 89–
93.

4957 Garrett, Sheryl. 1994. All of Me Loves
All of You: The Bay City Rollers. In *Love
Is the Drug*, ed. John Aizlewood. London
and New York: Penguin. 72–85.

4958 Grossberg, Lawrence. 1984. Another
Boring Day in Paradise: Rock and Roll
and the Empowerment of Everyday Life.
Popular Music 4: 225–58.

4959 Grossberg, Lawrence. 1985. If Rock and
Roll Communicates, Then Why Is It So
Noisy? Pleasure and the Popular. In
Popular Music Perspectives, 2, ed. David
Horn. Göteborg and Exeter: IASPM.
451–63.

4960 Grossberg, Lawrence. 1987. Rock and
Roll in Search of an Audience. In
Popular Music & Communication, ed.
James Lull. Newbury Park, CA: Sage.
175–97.

4961 Hartwich-Wiechell, Dörte. 1977.
Musikalisches Verhalten Jugendlicher.
Frankfurt am Main, Berlin and
München: Diesterweg.

4962 Holbrook, Morris B. 1979. The Spatial
Representation of Responses Toward
Jazz: Applications of Consumer
Esthetics to Mapping the Market for
Music. *Journal of Jazz Studies* 5(2): 3–
22.

4963 Jost, Ekkehard. 1976.
*Sozialpsychologische Faktoren der
Popmusik-Rezeption.* Mainz: Schott.

4964 Kapustin, Yuri. 1976. *Muzykant i
publika.* Leningrad: Znanie.

4965 Kapustin, Yuri. 1985. *Muzykant-
ispolnitel' i publika: Sotsiologicheskie
problemy sovremennoi kontsertoi zhizni.*
Leningrad: Muzyka.

4966 Kramarz, Volkmar. 1994. The Kids and
the Radio. In *Populäre Musik und
Pädagogik – Grundlagen und
Praxismaterialien*, ed. Jürgen Terhag.
Oldershausen: Institut für Didaktik der
populären Musik. 202–206.

4967 Lewis, Lisa A., ed. 1992. *The Adoring
Audience: Fan Culture and Popular
Media.* London: Routledge.

4968 Lull, James. 1987. Listeners'
Communicative Uses of Popular Music.
In *Popular Music & Communication*, ed.
James Lull. Newbury Park, CA: Sage.
140–74.

4969 Meintjes, Louise. 1990. Paul Simon's
'Graceland', South Africa, and the
Mediation of Musical Meaning.
Ethnomusicology 34(1): 37–73.

4970 Miller, Manfred. 1978. Shakin' All Over:
Zur Rock'n'Roll-Rezeption in England.
Anschläge 1(2): 5–24.

4971 Negus, Keith. 1994. Zwischen
Unternehmen und Verbraucher.
PopScriptum 2: 62–81.

4972 Pegg, Carole. 1983. Factors Affecting
the Musical Choices of Audiences in
East Suffolk, England. *Popular Music* 4:
51–74.

4973 Philippot, Michel. 1974. Observations
on Sound Volume and Music Listening.
In *New Patterns of Musical Behaviour*, ed.
Irmgard Bontinck. Wien: Universal
Edition. 54–59.

4974 Roberts, Chris, ed. 1994. *Idle Worship*. London: HarperCollins.

4975 Robinson, J. Bradford. 1992. Zur 'Jazz' Rezeption der Weimarer Periode: Eine stilhistorische Jagd nach einer Rhythmus-Floskel. In *Jazz und Komposition*, ed. Wolfram Knauer. Hofheim: Wolke. 11–26.

4976 Rösing, Helmut. 1981. Musik und ihre Wirkungen auf den Rezipienten: Versuch einer Standortbestimmung. *International Review of the Aesthetics and Sociology of Music* 12: 3–20.

4977 Rösing, Helmut. 1983. Listening Behaviour and Musical Preferences in the Age of 'Transmitted' Music. *Popular Music* 3: 119–50.

4978 Schmücker, Fritz. 1993. *Das Jazzkonzertpublikum. Das Profil einer kulturellen Minderheit im Zeitvergleich*. Münster and Hamburg: Lit Verlag.

4979 Shepherd, John. 1986. Music Consumption and Cultural Self-Identities: Some Theoretical and Methodological Reflections. *Media, Culture and Society* 8(3): 305–30.

4980 Sonner, Rudolf. 1978. (1930) Der Typus des großstädtischen Musikverbrauchers. *Musik und Gesellschaft* 1(3): 73–76.

4981 Straw, Will. 1990. (1983) Characterizing Rock Music Culture: The Case of Heavy Metal. In *On Record: Rock, Pop and the Written Word*, ed. Simon Frith and Andrew Goodwin. London: Routledge. 97–110.

4982 Street, John. 1995. In the Neighbourhood: The Local State and Popular Music Consumption. In *Popular Music Perspectives III*, ed. Peter Wicke. Berlin: Zyankrise. 373–86.

4983 Thornton, Sarah. 1995. *Club Cultures: Music, Media and Subcultural Capital*. Oxford: Polity.

4984 Tomlinson, Alan, ed. 1990. *Consumption, Identity and Style*. London: Routledge.

4985 Vermorel, Fred, and Vermorel, Judy. 1985. *Starlust: The Secret Fantasies of Fans*. London: Comedia.

4986 Vermorel, Fred and Vermorel, Judy. 1989. *Fandemonium!: The Book of Fan Cults and Dance Crazes*. London: Comedia.

4987 Wells, Alan. 1990. Popular Music: Emotional Use and Management. *Journal of Popular Culture* 24(1): 105–18.

4988 Wicke, Peter. 1982. Musik und alltägliche Lebensprozesse. *Musik und Gesellschaft* XXXII(12): 712–17.

4989 Wicke, Peter. 1990. Rockmusik und Lebensstile. In *Lebensstile und Politik – Politik der Lebensstile*, ed. Olaf Schwencke. Loccum and Hagen: KuPoGe. 175–89.

RELIGION/SPIRITUALITY

4990 Aranza, Jacob. 1983. *Backward Masking Unmasked: Backward Satanic Messages of Rock and Roll Exposed*. Shreveport, LA: Huntington House.

4991 Breen, Marcus. 1987. Fundamentalist Music: The Popular Music Impulse. In *Missing in Action: Australian Popular Music*, ed. Marcus Breen. Melbourne: Verbal Graphics Pty. 8–31.

4992 Bubmann, Peter. 1990. *Sound zwischen Himmel und Erde. Populäre christliche Musik*. Stuttgart: Quell.

4993 Buschmann, Michael. 1989. *Rock im Rückwärtsgang: Manipulation durch 'Backward Masking'*. Asslar: Schulte/Gerth.

4994 Cornelius, Steven. 1990. Encapsulating Power: Meaning and Taxonomy of the Musical Instruments of Santeria in New

York City. *Selected Reports in Ethnomusicology* 8: 125–41.

4995 Davis, Gerald L. 1985. *I Got the Word in Me and I Can Sing It, You Know: A Study of the Performed African-American Sermon.* Philadelphia: University of Pennsylvania Press.

4996 Elbers, Alfons. 1984. *Rockmusik und ihre Bedeutung für den Religionsunterricht: Eine anthropologische Grundlagentheorie religiöser Sozialisationsmöglichkeiten.* Bern: Lang.

4997 Howard, Jay R. 1992. Contemporary Christian Music: Where Rock Meets Religion. *Journal of Popular Culture* 26(1): 123–30.

4998 Kögler, Ilse. 1994. *Die Sehnsucht nach mehr. Rockmusik, Jugend und Religion.* Graz, Wien and Köln: Styria.

4999 Larson, Bob. 1988. *Your Kids and Rock.* Wheaton, IL: Tynedale House.

5000 Lawhead, Stephen. 1987. *Rock of This Age: The Real and Imagined Dangers of Rock Music.* Downers Grove, IL: Intervarsity Press.

5001 Leonard, Neil. 1987. *Jazz: Myth and Religion.* New York and Oxford: Oxford University Press.

5002 Lund, Jens. 1972. Fundamentalism, Racism, and Political Reaction in Country Music. In *The Sounds of Social Change: Studies in Popular Culture*, ed. R. Serge Denisoff and Richard A. Peterson. Chicago: Rand McNally & Co. 79–91.

5003 Marshall, Howard Wight. 1974. *Keep on the Sunny Side of Life: Pattern and Religious Expression in Bluegrass Gospel Music.* Los Angeles: John Edwards Memorial Foundation.

5004 Martin, Linda, and Segrave, Kerry. 1988. *Anti-Rock: The Opposition to Rock 'n' Roll.* Hamden, CT: The Shoe String Press.

5004a Nelson, Angela Spence. 1991. Theology in the Hip-Hop of Public Enemy and Kool Moe Dee. *Black Sacred Music* 5(1): 51–59.

5005 Peck, Richard. 1985. *Rock: Making Musical Choices.* Greenville, SC: Bob Jones University Press.

5006 No entry.

5007 Peters, Dan, and Peters, Steve. 1984. *Why Knock Rock?* Minneapolis, MN: Bethany House.

5008 Peters, Dan, et al. 1986. *What About Christian Rock?* Minneapolis, MN: Bethany House.

5009 Qureshi, Regula Burckhardt. 1992. 'Muslim Devotional': Popular Religious Music and Muslim Identity under British, Indian and Pakistani Hegemony. *Asian Music* 24(1): 111–21.

5010 Seay, Davin and Neely, Mary. 1986. *Stairway to Heaven: The Spiritual Roots of Rock 'n' Roll; From the King and Little Richard to Prince and Amy Grant.* New York: Ballantine/Epiphany Press.

5011 Taylor, Rogan. 1985. *The Death and Resurrection Show: From Shaman to Superstar.* London: Anthony Blond.

5012 Tucker, Stephen R. 1982. Pentecostalism and Popular Culture in the South: A Study of Four Musicians. *Journal of Popular Culture* 16(3): 68–80.

5013 Turner, Steve. 1995. *Hungry for Heaven: Rock and Roll and the Search for Redemption.* London: Hodder and Stoughton.

5014 Ventura, Michael. 1985. *Shadow Dancing in the USA.* Los Angeles: Jeremy P. Tarcher.

5015 Welch, David B. 1985. A Yoruba/Nagô 'Melotype' for Religious Songs in the African Diaspora: Continuity of West African Praise Song in the New World. In *More than Drumming: Essays on*

African and Afro-Latin American Music and Musicians, ed. Irene V. Jackson. Westport, CT: Greenwood Press. 145–62.

5016 Wilcken, Lois E. 1992. Power, Ambivalence, and the Remaking of Haitian Vodoun Music in New York. *Latin American Music Review* 13(1): 1–32.

SCENE

5017 Gay, Leslie. 1995. Rockin' the Imagined Local: New York Rock in a Reterritorialized World. In *Popular Music: Style and Identity*, ed. Will Straw, et al. Montréal: The Centre for Research on Canadian Cultural Industries and Institutions. 123–26.

5018 Kruse, Holly. 1993. Subcultural Identity in Alternative Music Culture. *Popular Music* 12(1): 33–41.

5019 Shank, Barry. 1994. *Dissonant Identities: The Rock and Roll Scene in Austin, Texas.* Hanover, NH: Wesleyan University Press.

5020 Stokes, Martin, ed. 1994. *Ethnicity, Identity and Music: The Musical Construction of Place.* Oxford: Berg.

5021 Straw, Will. 1991. Systems of Articulation, Logics of Change: Communities and Scenes in Popular Music. *Cultural Studies* 5(3): 368–88.

SLANG

5022 Baugh, John. 1983. *Black Street Speech: Its History, Structure and Survival.* Austin, TX: University of Texas Press.

5023 Brophy, John and Partridge, Eric, comps. 1930. *Songs and Slang of the British Soldier, 1914–1918.* London: Eric Partridge.

5024 Calloway, Cab. 1976. *Of Minnie the Moocher and Me.* New York: Crowell.

5025 Gold, Robert S. 1975. *Jazz Talk.* Indianapolis, IN: Bobbs-Merrill.

5026 Hibbert, Tom. 1981. *The Dictionary of Rock Terms.* London: Omnibus.

5027 Irwin, Godfrey, comp. 1931. *American Tramp and Underworld Slang, with a Collection of Tramp Songs.* London: Eric Partridge.

5028 Levet, Jean-Paul. 1992. *Talkin' That Talk: le langage du blues et du jazz.* Paris: Hatier.

5029 Major, Clarence. 1970. *Black Slang: A Dictionary of Afro-American Talk.* New York: International Publishers.

5030 Wilmeth, Don B., ed. 1981. *The Language of American Popular Entertainment: A Glossary of Argot, Slang and Terminology.* Westport, CT: Greenwood Press.

STARDOM

5031 Alberoni, Fred. 1972. The Powerless 'Elite': Theory and Sociological Research on the Phenomenon of the Stars. In *Sociology of Mass Communication*, ed. Denis McQuail. London: Faber & Faber. 75–98.

5032 Bogle, Donald. 1980. *Brown Sugar: Eighty Years of America's Black Female Superstars.* New York: Harmony Books.

5033 Buxton, David. 1990. (1983) Rock Music, the Star System, and the Rise of Consumerism. In *On Record: Rock, Pop and the Written Word*, ed. Simon Frith and Andrew Goodwin. London: Routledge. 427–40.

5034 Dallas, Karl. 1971. *Singers of an Empty Day: Last Sacraments for the Superstars.* London: Kahn & Averill.

5035 Dyer, Richard. 1979. *Stars.* London: BFI Publishing.

5036 Gledhill, Christine, ed. 1991. *Stardom: Industry of Desire*. London: Routledge.

5037 Gubernick, Lisa Rebecca. 1993. *Get Hot or Got Home – Trisha Yearwood: The Making of a Nashville Star*. New York: William Morrow & Co.

5038 Herman, Gary. 1994. *Rock 'n' Roll Babylon*. London: Plexus.

5039 Hill, Dave. 1986. *Designer Boys and Material Girls*. Poole: Blandford Press.

5040 James, Clive. 1993. *Fame in the Twentieth Century*. Harmondsworth: Penguin.

5041 Kriese, Konstanze. 1994. Die Inflation des Stars: Industrialisierung der göttlichen Einmaligkeit. In *Zwischen Rausch und Ritual*, ed. Konstanze Kriese, et al. Berlin: Zyankrise. 100–24.

5042 Kruse, Holly. 1990. (1988) In Praise of Kate Bush. In *On Record: Rock, Pop and the Written Word*, ed. Simon Frith and Andrew Goodwin. London: Routledge. 450–65.

5043 Lawrence, Sharon. 1983. (1976) *So You Want To Be a Rock and Roll Star*. New York: McGraw-Hill.

5044 Riemann-Al Batrouny, Silke. 1994. Forever Young, auch noch mit fünfzig? Alternde Rockstars. In *Populäre Musik und Pädagogik – Grundlagen und Praxismaterialien*, ed. Jürgen Terhag. Oldershausen: Institut für Didaktik der populären Musik. 41–49.

5045 Wise, Sue. 1990. (1984) Sexing Elvis. In *On Record: Rock, Pop and the Written Word*, ed. Simon Frith and Andrew Goodwin. London: Routledge. 390–98.

SUBCULTURE

5046 Beaud, Paul. 1974. Musical Subcultures in France. In *New Patterns of Musical Behaviour*, ed. Irmgard Bontinck. Wien: Universal Edition. 212–18.

5047 Beaud, Paul and Willener, Alfred, eds. 1973. *Musique et vie quotidienne: Essai de sociologie d'une nouvelle culture*. Paris: Mame.

5048 Brake, Mike. 1980. *The Sociology of Youth Culture and Youth Subcultures: Sex and Drugs and Rock 'n' Roll?* London: Routledge & Kegan Paul.

5049 Cagle, Van M. 1995. *Reconstructing Pop/Subculture: Art, Rock and Andy Warhol*. Thousand Oaks, CA: Sage.

5050 Calvet, Louis-Jean. 1976. *La Production révolutionnaire. Slogans, affiches, chansons*. Paris: Payot.

5051 Carr, Roy. 1986. *The Hip: Hipsters, Jazz and the Beat Generation*. London: Faber.

5052 Cifuentes, Luis. 1989. *Fragmentos de un sueño. Inti-illimani y la generación de los 60*. Santiago: Ediciones Logos.

5053 Clarke, Gary. 1990. (1981) Defending Ski-Jumpers: A Critique of Theories of Youth Subcultures. In *On Record: Rock, Pop and the Written Word*, ed. Simon Frith and Andrew Goodwin. London: Routledge. 81–96.

5054 Clarke, John. 1977. (1975) Style. In *Resistance Through Rituals: Youth Subcultures in Post-War Britain*, ed. Stuart Hall and Tony Jefferson. London: Hutchinson. 175–91.

5055 Clarke, Mike. 1974. On the Concept of Subculture. *British Journal of Sociology* 25(4): 428–41.

5056 Cohen, Stanley. 1980. (1972) *Folk Devils and Moral Panics: The Creation of Mods and Rockers*. Oxford: Martin Robertson. First published London: MacGibbon & Kee, 1972.

5057 Cook, Bruce. 1971. *The Beat Generation*. New York: Watts.

5058 Elms, R. 1985. All You Have To Do Is Win. *The Face* (May): 50–56.

5059 Epstein, Jonathan, ed. 1994. *Adolescents and Their Music: If It's Too Loud, You're Too Old.* New York: Garland.

5060 Frith, Simon. 1988. The Art of Posing. In *Music for Pleasure: Essays in the Sociology of Pop*, ed. Simon Frith. New York: Routledge. 176–79.

5061 Granjon, Marie-Christine. 1985. *L'Amérique de la contestation: les années soixante aux États-Unis.* Paris: Fondation nationale des Sciences Politiques.

5062 Grieves, Jim. 1982. Style as Metaphor for Symbolic Action: Teddy Boys, Authenticity and Identity. *Theory, Culture & Society* 1(2) (Autumn): 35–49.

5063 Gross, Robert L. 1990. Heavy Metal Music: A New Subculture in American Society. *Journal of Popular Culture* 24(1): 119–30.

5064 Hebdige, Dick. 1979. Posing . . . Threats, Striking . . . Poses: Youth, Surveillance, and Display. *SubStance* 37/38: 68–88.

5065 Hebdige, Dick. 1979. *Subculture: The Meaning of Style.* London: Routledge.

5066 Kneif, Tibor. 1977. Rockmusik und Subkultur. In *Rockmusik*, ed. Wolfgang Sandner. Mainz: Schott. 37–52.

5067 Kruse, Holly. 1993. Subcultural Identity in Alternative Music Culture. *Popular Music* 12(1): 33–41.

5068 Lacroix, Bernard. 1981. *L'Utopie communautaire: histoire sociale d'une révolte.* Paris: Presses universitaires de France.

5069 Laing, Dave. 1994. *Scrutiny* to Subcultures: Notes on Literary Criticism and Popular Music. *Popular Music* 13(2): 179–90.

5070 No entry.

5071 McRobbie, Angela. 1990. (1980) Settling Accounts with Subcultures: A Feminist Critique. In *On Record: Rock, Pop and the Written Word*, ed. Simon Frith and Andrew Goodwin. London: Routledge. 66–80.

5072 McRobbie, Angela. 1994. Shut Up and Dance: Youth Culture and Changing Modes of Femininity. In *Postmodernism and Popular Culture.* London: Routledge. 155–76.

5073 Middleton, Richard and Muncie, John. 1981. Pop Culture, Pop Music and Post-War Youth: Countercultures. In *Politics, Ideology and Popular Culture (1).* Milton Keynes: Open University Press. 63–92.

5074 Nehring, Neil. 1993. *Flowers in the Dustbin: Culture, Anarchy and Postwar England.* Ann Arbor, MI: University of Michigan Press.

5075 Polhemus, Ted. 1994. *Street Style.* London: Thames and Hudson.

5076 Redhead, Steve. 1990. *The End-of-the-Century Party: Youth and Pop Towards 2000.* Manchester: Manchester University Press.

5077 Slobin, Mark. 1993. *Subcultural Sounds: Micromusics of the West.* Hanover and London: University Press of New England/Wesleyan University Press.

5078 Stuart, Johnny. 1987. *Rockers!* London: Plexus.

5079 Szemere, Anna. 1992. The Politics of Marginality: A Rock Musical Subculture in Socialist Hungary in the Early 1980s. In *Rockin' the Boat: Mass Music and Mass Movements*, ed. Reebee Garofalo. Boston, MA: South End Press. 93–114.

5080 Taylor, Ian and Wall, David. 1976. Beyond Skinheads: Comments on the Emergence and Significance of the Glamrock Cult. In *Working Class Youth Culture*, ed. Geoff Mungham and

Geoffrey Pearson. London: Routledge. 105–23.

5081 Thorne, Tony. 1993. *Fads, Fashions and Cults*. London: Bloomsbury.

5082 Thornton, Sarah. 1995. *Club Cultures: Music, Media and Subcultural Capital*. Cambridge: Polity.

5083 Wicke, Peter. 1991. Die Entwicklung der Jugendszenen in der DDR. In *Rock & Pop '89. Kritische Analysen, Kulturpolitische Alternativen II*. Hagen: Kulturpolitische Gesellschaft. 23–33.

5084 Wicke, Peter. 1995. Popmusik – Konsumfetischismus oder kulturelles Widerstandspotential. In *Yesterday. Today. Tomorrow*, ed. M. Heuger and M. Prell. Regensburg: ConBrio Verlagsgesellschaft. 21–35.

5085 Willis, Paul. 1978. *Profane Culture*. London: Routledge.

5086 Willis, Paul. 1990. *Common Culture*. Buckingham: Open University Press.

5087 York, Peter. 1980. *Style Wars*. London: Sidgwick & Jackson.

TASTE

5088 Brooks, William. 1982. On Being Tasteless. *Popular Music* 2: 9–18.

5089 Carrera, Alessandro. 1980. *Musica e pubblico giovanile: l'evoluzione del gusto musicale dagli anni sessanta ad oggi*. Milano: Feltrinella Economica.

5090 Christenson, Peter, and Peterson, Jon Brian. 1988. Genre and Gender in the Structure of Music Preferences. *Communication Research* 15(3) (June).

5091 Crafts, Susan D., et al. 1993. *My Music*. Hanover, NH: Wesleyan University Press.

5092 Dyer, Richard. 1992. Getting Over the Rainbow: Identity and Pleasure in Gay Cultural Politics. In *Only Entertainment*. London: Routledge.

5093 Hornby, Nick. 1995. *High Fidelity*. London: Victor Gollancz.

5094 Lewis, George H. 1977. Taste Cultures and Culture Classes in Mass Society. *International Review of the Aesthetics and Sociology of Music* 8: 39–48.

5095 Lewis, George H. 1987. Patterns of Meaning and Choice: Taste Cultures in Popular Music. In *Popular Music & Communication*, ed. James Lull. Newbury Park, CA: Sage. 198–211.

5096 Lewis, George H. 1992. Who Do You Love?: The Dimensions of Musical Taste. In *Popular Music & Communication*, ed. James Lull, 2nd edition. Newbury Park, CA: Sage.

5097 Mooney, H.F. 1972. Popular Music Since the 1920s: The Significance of Shifting Taste. In *The Sounds of Social Change: Studies in Popular Culture*, ed. R. Serge Denisoff and Richard A. Peterson. Chicago: Rand McNally & Co. 181–97.

5098 Nylöf, Göran. 1990. Trends in Popular Music Preferences in Sweden, 1960–1988. In *Popular Music Research*, ed. Keith Roe and Ulla Karlsson. Göteborg: NORDICOM-Sweden, No. 1–2. 87–102.

5099 Pelinski, Ramón. 1985. From Tango to 'Rock Nacional': A Case Study of Changing Popular Taste in Buenos Aires. In *Popular Music Perspectives, 2*, ed. David Horn. Göteborg and Exeter: IASPM. 287–95.

5100 Rösing, Helmut. 1983. Listening Behaviour and Musical Preferences in the Age of 'Transmitted' Music. *Popular Music* 3: 119–50.

5101 Salminen, Kimmo. 1992. Finnish Taste in Music and Musical Preferences. In *Broadcasting Research Review, 1992*, ed. Heikki Kasari. Helsinki: Yleisradio. 114–22.

5102 Stipp, Horst. 1985. Children's Knowledge of and Taste in Popular Music. *Popular Music & Society* 10(2): 1–17.

5103 Thornton, Sarah. 1995. *Club Cultures: Music, Media and Subcultural Capital.* Cambridge: Polity.

5104 Trondman, Mats. 1990. Rock Taste: On Rock as Symbolic Capital. A Study of Young People's Music Taste and Music Making. In *Popular Music Research,* ed. Keith Roe and Ulla Karlsson. Göteborg: NORDICOM-Sweden, No. 1–2. 71–86.

5105 Valkman, Otto. 1974. Some Methodological Aspects of Preferences in Pop Music. In *New Patterns of Musical Behaviour,* ed. Irmgard Bontinck. Wien: Universal Edition. 33–43.

URBANIZATION

5106 Chambers, Iain. 1988. Contamination, Coincidence and Collusion: Pop Music, Urban Culture and the Avant-Garde. In *Marxism and the Interpretation of Culture,* ed. Lawrence Grossberg and Cary Nelson. Urbana, IL: University of Illinois Press. 607–11.

5107 Coplan, David. 1982. The Urbanisation of African Music: Some Theoretical Observations. *Popular Music* 2: 113–29.

5108 Fujie, Linda. 1983. Effects of Urbanization on 'Matsuri-Bayashi' in Tokyo. *Yearbook for Traditional Music* 15: 38–44.

5109 Koetting, James T. 1975. The Effects of Urbanization: The Music of the Kasena People of Ghana. *The World of Music* 17(4): 23–31.

5110 L'Armand, Kathleen and L'Armand, Adrian. 1978. Music in Madras: The Urbanization of a Cultural Tradition. In *Eight Urban Musical Cultures: Tradition and Change,* ed. Bruno Nettl. Urbana and London: University of Illinois Press. 115–45.

5111 L'Armand, Kathleen and L'Armand, Adrian. 1983. One Hundred Years of Music in Madras: A Case Study in Secondary Urbanization. *Ethnomusicology* 27(3): 411–38.

5112 Nettl, Bruno, ed. 1978. *Eight Urban Musical Cultures: Tradition and Change.* Urbana and London: University of Illinois Press.

5113 Ostransky, Leroy. 1971. *Jazz City: The Impact of Our Cities in the Development of Jazz.* Englewood Cliffs, NJ: Prentice-Hall.

5114 Ridgeway, Cecilia L. and Roberts, John. 1976. Urban Popular Music and Interaction: A Semantic Relationship. *Ethnomusicology* 20(2): 233–52.

5115 Shiloah, Amnon. 1986. The Traditional Artist in the Limelight of the Modern City. *The World of Music* 28(1): 87–98.

5116 Torres, Rodrigo. 1985. La Urbanización de la Canción Folklórica. *Literatura Chilena. Creación y Crítica* 9(33–34): 25–29.

5117 Wicke, Peter. 1995. 'Der King vom Prenzlauer Berg'. Vom Mythos des Rock in einer sozialistischen Metropole. In *Berlin – Hauptstadt der DDR 1949–1989: Utopie und Realität,* ed. Bernd Wilzek. Zürich and Baden Baden: Elster-Verlag. 236–47.

VENUES

5118 Beckman, Dieter and Martens, Klaus. 1980. *Star-Club.* Reinbek bei Hamburg: Rowohlt.

5119 Chevigny, Paul. 1991. *Gigs: Jazz and the Cabaret Laws in New York City.* London and New York: Routledge.

5120 Claypool, Bob. 1980. *Saturday Night at Gilley's.* New York: Grove Press.

5121 Dorf, Michael Ethan and Appel, Robert. 1986. *A Guide to Gigging in North*

America. New York: Flaming Pie Records.

5122 Finnegan, Ruth. 1989. *The Hidden Musicians: Music-Making in an English Town.* Cambridge: Cambridge University Press.

5123 Fordham, John. 1986. *Let's Join Hands and Celebrate the Living: The Story of Ronnie Scott and His Club.* London: Elm Tree Books.

5124 Gordon, Max. 1980. *Live at the Village Vanguard.* New York: St. Martin's Press.

5125 Grime, Kitty. 1979. *Jazz at Ronnie Scott's.* London: Robert Hale.

5126 Haskins, Jim. 1977. *The Cotton Club: A Pictorial and Social History of the Most Famous Symbol of the Jazz Era.* New York: Random House.

5127 Imes, Birney. 1990. *Juke Joint: Photographs by Birney Imes.* Jackson, MS: University Press of Mississippi.

5128 Neißer, Horst F., Werner Mezger and Günter Verdin. 1981. *Jugend in Trance? Diskotheken in Deutschland.* Heidelberg: Quelle & Meyer.

5129 Reed, Harry A. 1979. The Black Bar in the Making of a Jazz Musician: Bird, Mingus and Stan Hope. *Journal of Jazz Studies* 5(2): 76–90.

5130 Riddle, Ronald. 1978. Music Clubs and Ensembles in San Francisco's Chinese Community. In *Eight Urban Musical Cultures: Tradition and Change,* ed. Bruno Nettl. Urbana and London: University of Illinois Press. 223–59.

5131 Street, John. 1993. Local Differences? Popular Music and the Local State. *Popular Music* 12(1): 43–56.

5132 White, Avron Levine, ed. 1987. *Lost in Music: Culture, Style and the Musical Event.* London: Routledge.

5133 Whitelaw, Graham. 1985. *Disco Management.* Stirling: Mandel Press and Music.

5134 Woliver, Robbie. 1986. *Bringing It All Home: 25 Years of American Music at Folk City.* New York: Pantheon Books.

5135 Zozak, Roman. 1988. *This Ain't No Disco: The Story of CBGBs.* Boston, MA: Faber & Faber.

WOMEN

5136 Alessandrini, Marjorie. 1980. *Le rock au féminin.* Paris: Albin Michel.

5137 Alloy, Evelyn. 1976. *Working Women's Music: The Songs and Struggle of Women in the Cotton Mills, Textile Plants and Needle Trade.* Somerville, MA: New England Free Press.

5138 Balfour, Victoria. 1986. *Rock Wives: The Hard Lives and Good Times of the Wives, Girlfriends and Groupies of Rock and Roll.* New York: Beech Tree Books.

5139 Barwick, Linda. 1990. Central Australian Women's Ritual Music: Knowing Through Analysis Versus Knowing Through Performance. *Yearbook for Traditional Music* 22: 60–79.

5140 Bayton, Mavis. 1990. (1988) How Women Become Musicians. In *On Record: Rock, Pop and the Written Word,* ed. Simon Frith and Andrew Goodwin. London: Routledge. 238–57.

5141 Bayton, Mavis. 1993. Feminist Musical Practice: Problems and Contradictions. In *Rock and Popular Music: Politics, Policies, Institutions,* ed. Tony Bennett, et al. London: Routledge.

5142 Becker, Audrey. 1990. New Lyrics by Women: A Feminist Alternative. *Journal of Popular Culture* 24(1): 1–22.

5143 Betrock, Alan. 1982. *Girl Groups: The Story of a Sound.* New York: Delilah.

5144 Bloß, Monika. 1994. Weiblichkeit als Kulturbarriere?: '. . . so spielen wie ein Mann'. Eine Untersuchung mit Berliner Musikerinnen. In *Zwischen Rausch und Ritual*, ed. Konstanze Kriese, et al. Berlin: Zyankrise. 70–79.

5145 Bogle, Donald. 1980. *Brown Sugar: Eighty Years of America's Black Female Superstars*. New York: Harmony Books.

5146 Bowers, Jane and Bareis, Urba. 1991. Bibliography on Music and Gender: Women in Music. *The World of Music* 33(2): 65–103.

5147 Bradby, Barbara and Torode, Brian. 1984. Pity Peggy Sue. *Popular Music* 4: 183–206.

5148 Bufwack, Mary A. and Oermann, Robert K. 1993. *Finding Her Voice: The Saga of Women in Country Music*. New York: Crown.

5149 Buonaventura, Wendy. 1989. *Serpent of the Nile: Women and Dance in the Arab World*. London: Saqi.

5150 Carby, Hazel V. 1992. In Body and Spirit: Representing Black Women Musicians. *Black Music Research Journal* 11(2): 177–92.

5151 Cooper, Sarah, ed. 1995. *Girls! Girls! Girls!: Essays on Women and Music*. London: Cassell.

5152 Dahl, Linda. 1984. *Stormy Weather: The Music and Lives of a Century of Jazz Women*. New York: Pantheon Books.

5153 Davis, Angela. 1990. Black Women and Music: A Historical Legacy of Struggle. In *Wild Women in the Whirlwind: Afro-American Culture and the Contemporary Literary Renaissance*, ed. Joanne Braxton and Andree McLaughlin. New Brunswick, NJ: Rutgers University Press.

5154 Ehrenreich, Barbara, et al. 1992. Beatlemania: Girls Just Want to Have Fun. In *The Adoring Audience: Fan Culture and Popular Media*, ed. Lisa A. Lewis. London: Routledge.

5155 Evans, Liz, ed. 1994. *Women, Sex and Rock 'n' Roll: In Their Own Words*. London: Pandora.

5156 Farin, Klaus and Kuckuck, Anke. 1987. *ProEmotion: Frauen im Rock Business; Begegnungen, Gespräche Reportagen*. Reinbek bei Hamburg: Rowohlt.

5157 Gaar, Gillian G. 1993. *She's a Rebel: The History of Women in Rock and Roll*. London: Blandford Press.

5158 Garbutt, Bob. 1979. *Rockabilly Queens*. Toronto: Ducktail Press.

5159 Gottlieb, Joanne and Wald, Gayle. 1994. Smells Like Teen Spirit: Riot Grrrls, Revolution and Women in Independent Rock. In *Microphone Fiends: Youth Music and Youth Culture*, ed. Andrew Ross and Tricia Rose. London: Routledge.

5160 Gratton, Virginia L. 1983. *American Women Songwriters: A Biographical Dictionary*. Westport and London: Greenwood Press.

5161 Greig, Charlotte. 1989. *Will You Still Love Me Tomorrow?: Girl Groups from the 50s On . . .* London: Virago.

5162 Handy, D. Antoinette. 1981. *Black Women in American Bands and Orchestras*. Metuchen and London: Scarecrow Press.

5163 Harrison, Daphne Duval. 1988. *Black Pearls: Blues Queens of the 1920s*. New Brunswick, NJ: Rutgers University Press.

5164 Jones, Hettie. 1974. *Big Star Fallin' Mama: Five Women in Black Music*. New York: Viking.

5165 Juge, Pascale. 1982. *Rockeuses: les heroïnes de Juke-Box*. Paris: Grancher.

SOCIAL AND CULTURAL CONTEXTS

5166 Kent, Greta. 1983. *A View from the Bandstand*. London: Sheba Feminist Publications.

5167 Kingsbury, Paul. 1992. Women in Country: A Special Report. *Journal of Country Music* 15(1): 12–35.

5168 Koskoff, Ellen, ed. 1987. *Women and Music in Cross-Cultural Perspective*. Westport, CT: Greenwood Press.

5169 Leder, Jan. 1985. *Women in Jazz: A Discography of Instrumentalists, 1913–1968*. Westport and London: Greenwood Press.

5170 Lont, Cynthia M. 1992. Women's Music: No Longer a Small Private Party. In *Rockin' the Boat: Mass Music and Mass Movements*, ed. Reebee Garofalo. Boston, MA: South End Press. 241–54.

5171 McDonnell, Evelyn and Powers, Ann. 1995. *Rock, She Wrote: Women Write about Rock, Pop and Rap*. London: Plexus.

5172 Meade, Marion. 1972. The Degradation of Women. In *The Sounds of Social Change: Studies in Popular Culture*, ed. R. Serge Denisoff and Richard A. Peterson. Chicago: Rand McNally & Co. 173–77.

5173 Mellers, Wilfrid. 1986. *Angels of the Night: Popular Female Singers of Our Time*. Oxford: Blackwell.

5174 Moore, John. 1988. 'The Hieroglyphics of Love': The Torch Singers and Interpretation. *Popular Music* 8(1): 31–58.

5175 O'Brien, Karen. 1995. *Hymn to Her: Women Musicians Talk*. London: Virago.

5176 O'Brien, Lucy. 1995. *She Bop: The Definitive History of Women in Rock, Pop and Soul*. London: Penguin.

5177 Pendle, Karin, ed. 1991. *Women and Music: A History*. Indianapolis, IN: Indiana University Press.

5178 Placksin, Sally. 1985. *Jazzwomen: 1900 to the Present. Their Words, Lives and Music*. London: Pluto Press.

5179 Potter, John. 1994. The Singer, Not the Song: Women Singers as Composer-Poets. *Popular Music* 13(2): 191–99.

5180 Raphael, Amy. 1995. *Never Mind the Bollocks: Women Rewrite Rock*. London: Virago.

5181 Roberts, Robin. 1991. Music Videos, Performance and Resistance: Feminist Rappers. *Journal of Popular Culture* 25(2): 141–52.

5182 Rowley, Eddie. 1993. *A Woman's Voice*. Dublin: O'Brien Press.

5183 Rumley, Gina and Little, Hilary. 1989. Women and Pop: A Series of Lost Encounters. In *Zoot-Suits and Second-Hand Dresses: An Anthology of Fashion and Music*, ed. Angela McRobbie. London: Macmillan.

5184 Scheurer, Timothy E. 1990. Goddesses and Golddiggers: Images of Women in Popular Music of the 1930s. *Journal of Popular Culture* 24(1): 23–38.

5185 Schien, Gina. 1987. Female Notes: Women's Music. In *Missing in Action: Australian Popular Music*, ed. Marcus Breen. Melbourne: Verbal Graphics Pty. 78–97.

5186 Seitz, Barbara. 1991. Songs, Identity, and Women's Liberation in Nicaragua. *Latin American Music Review* 12(1): 21–41.

5187 Sordo, María del Carmen. 1982. Compositoras mexicanas de música comercial. *Heterofonía* 15(78): 16–20.

5188 Steward, Sue and Garratt, Sheryl. 1984. *Signed, Sealed and Delivered: True Life Stories of Women in Pop*. London: Pluto Press.

5189 Thomson, Elizabeth, ed. 1982. *New Women in Rock*. London: Omnibus.

5190 Thornton, Sarah. 1995. Exploring the Meaning of the Mainstream: Or Why Sharon and Tracy Dance Around Their Handbags. In *Club Cultures: Music, Media and Subcultural Capital.* Cambridge/Hanover: Polity/Wesleyan University Press.

5191 Unterbrink, Mary. 1983. *Jazz Women at the Keyboard.* Jefferson, NC: McFarland.

5192 Walenberg, Pauli. 1990. Meisjes en popcultuur. *Vrijetijd en samenleving* 8(3/4): 19–32.

YOUTH

5193 Abrams, Mark. 1959. *The Teenage Consumer.* London: London Press Exchange.

5194 Agardy, S., et al. 1985. *Young Australians and Music.* Melbourne: Australian Broadcasting Tribunal Research Branch.

5195 Alekseev, Eduard Y. and Golovinskii, Grigoriy L. 1974. From the Experience of the Moscow Youth Music Club: On the Question of the Socio-Psychological. In *New Patterns of Musical Behaviour,* ed. Irmgard Bontinck. Wien: Universal Edition. 91–102.

5196 Allinson, Francesca. 1979. *Die Jugendmusikbewegung: Gemeinschaftsmusik, Theorie und Praxis.* Stuttgart: Metzler.

5197 Andersson, Tony and Bergendahl, Elisabet. 1982. *Låt tusen stenar rulla – kuratorgruppens musikverksamhet: teori och praktik.* Göteborg: Socialhögskolan.

5198 Anson, Robert S. 1981. *Gone Crazy and Back Again: The Rise and Fall of the Rolling Stones Generation.* New York: Doubleday.

5199 Arnichand, Jean-François. 1990. *Représentations et ontologie de la jeunesse.* Aix: Université de Provence, Aix-Marseille I.

5200 Axelsen, Doris. 1981. Swedish Adolescents and the Phonogram. In *Stock-Taking of Musical Life: Sociography and Music Education,* ed. Desmond Mark. Wien: Doblinger. 47–51.

5201 Baacke, Dieter. 1968. *Beat – die sprachlose Opposition.* München: Juventa.

5202 Baacke, Dieter. 1972. *Jugend und Subkultur.* München: Juventa.

5203 Beaud, Paul and Willener, Alfred, eds. 1973. *Musique et vie quotidienne: Essai de sociologie d'une nouvelle culture.* Paris: Mame.

5204 Benson, Dennis C. 1976. *The Rock Generation.* Nashville, TN: Abingdon.

5205 Betrock, Alan. 1986. *The I Was A Teenage Juvenile Delinquent Rock 'n' Roll Beach Party Movie Book: A Complete Guide to the Teen Exploitation Film, 1954–1969.* New York: St. Martin's Press.

5206 Blake, C. Fred. 1979. Love Songs and the Great Leap: The Role of a Youth Culture in the Revolutionary Phase of China's Economic Development. *American Ethnologist* 6(1): 41–54.

5207 Blum, Lucille Hollander. 1966/67. The Discotheque and the Phenomenon of Alone-Togetherness: A Study of the Young Person's Response to the Frug and Comparable Current Dances. *Adolescence* 1(4) (Winter): 351–66.

5208 Bontinck, Irmgard, ed. 1974. *New Patterns of Musical Behaviour.* Wien: Universal Edition.

5209 Brake, Mike. 1980. *The Sociology of Youth Culture and Youth Subcultures: Sex and Drugs and Rock 'n' Roll?* London: Routledge & Kegan Paul.

5210 Carrera, Alessandro. 1980. *Musica e pubblico giovanile. L'evoluzione del gusto musicale dagli anni sessanta ad oggi.* Milano: Feltrinella Economica.

5211 Carter, Angela. 1977. (1967) Notes for a Theory of Sixties Style. *New Society* 22: 803–807.

5212 Cashmore, E. Ellis. 1987. Shades of Black, Shades of White. In *Popular Music & Communication*, ed. James Lull. Newbury Park, CA: Sage. 245–65.

5213 Coleman, Arthur. 1961. *The Adolescent Society*. Chicago: Free Press Glencoe.

5214 Denisoff, R. Serge. 1983. 'Teen Angel': Resistance, Rebellion and Death – Revisited. *Journal of Popular Culture* 16(4): 116–22.

5215 Dobrotrorskva, Ekaterina. 1992. Soviet Teens of the 1970s: Rock Generation, Rock Refusal, Rock Context. *Journal of Popular Culture* 26(3): 145–50.

5216 Doherty, Thomas. 1988. *Teenagers and Teenpics: The Juvenilization of American Movies in the 1950s*. Winchester, MA: Unwin Hyman Books.

5217 Dubet, François. 1987. *La Galère: jeunes en survie*. Paris: Fayard.

5218 Fornäs, Johan. 1990. Moving Rock: Youth and Pop in Late Modernity. *Popular Music* 9(3): 291–306.

5219 Fornäs, Johan. 1990. Popular Music and Youth Culture in Late Modernity. In *Popular Music Research*, ed. Keith Roe and Ulla Karlsson. Göteborg: NORDICOM-Sweden, No. 1–2. 29–40.

5220 Fornäs, Johan, Ulf Lindberg and Ove Sernhede. 1988. *Under Rocken: Musikins Roll i Tre Ungar Band*. Stockholm and Lund: Symposium Bokforlag.

5221 Frith, Simon. 1978. Youth Culture/ Youth Cults: A Decade of Rock Consumption. In *Rock File 5*, ed. Charlie Gillett and Simon Frith. St. Alban's: Granada. 9–20.

5222 Frith, Simon. 1983. *Sound Effects: Youth, Leisure and the Politics of Rock 'n' Roll*. London: Constable.

5223 Gantz, Walter, et al. 1978. Gratifications and Expectations Associated with Pop Music Among Adolescents. *Popular Music & Society* 6: 81–89.

5224 Geerts, Claude. 1974. The Share of Music in the Time Budget of Young People in Belgium. In *New Patterns of Musical Behaviour*, ed. Irmgard Bontinck. Wien: Universal Edition. 201–204.

5225 Gilroy, Paul. 1993. Between Afro-Centrism and Euro-Centrism: Youth Culture and the Problem of Hybridity. *Young* 1(2): 2–13.

5226 Green, Anne-Marie. 1987. *Les Jeunes et la musique*. Paris: EAP.

5227 Greenberg, B.S., et al., eds. 1994. *Young People and Their Orientation to the Mass Media: An International Study. Study #20: Comparisons Among Belgium, Flanders, West Germany, the Netherlands, Spain and Sweden*. East Lansing, MI: Michigan State University.

5228 Grossberg, Lawrence. 1983. The Politics of Youth Culture: Some Observations on Rock and Roll in America. *Social Text* 8: 104–26.

5229 Hafen, Roland. 1994. Jugend und Populäre Musik. In *Populäre Musik und Pädagogik – Grundlagen und Praxismaterialien*, ed. Jürgen Terhag. Oldershausen: Institut für Didaktik der populären Musik. 122–26.

5230 Hartwich-Wiechell, Dörte. 1974. Musikalisches Verhalten Jugendlicher: Ergebnisse empirischer musiksoziologischer Untersuchungen. *Forschung in der Musikerziehung*: 39–62.

5231 Lagrée, Jean-Charles. 1982. *Les Jeunes chantent leurs cultures*. Paris: L'Harmattan.

5232 Martin, Bernice. 1981. *A Sociology of Contemporary Cultural Change*. Oxford: Blackwell.

5233 Martinengo, M. and Nuciari, M. 1986. *I giovani della musica*. Milano: Angeli.

5234 Meyer, Gust de, A. Hendriks and G. Fauconnier. 1980. *Jeugd en popmuziek*. Leuven: Centrum voor Communicatiewetenschappen.

5235 Middleton, Richard and Muncie, John. 1981. Pop Culture, Pop Music and Post-War Youth: Countercultures. In *Politics, Ideology and Popular Culture (1)*. Milton Keynes: Open University Press. 63–92.

5236 Mungham, Geoff. 1976. Youth in Pursuit of Itself. In *Working Class Youth Culture*, ed. Geoff Mungham and Geoffrey Pearson. London: Routledge.

5237 Neißer, Horst F., Werner Mezger and Günter Verdin. 1981. *Jugend in Trance? Diskotheken in Deutschland*. Heidelberg: Quelle & Meyer.

5238 Redhead, Steve. 1990. *The End-of-the-Century Party: Youth and Pop Towards 2000*. Manchester: Manchester University Press.

5239 Redhead, Steve, ed. 1993. *Rave Off: Politics and Deviance in Contemporary Youth Culture*. Aldershot: Avebury.

5240 Robinson, John P. and Hirsch, Paul M. 1972. Teenage Response to Rock and Roll Protest Song. In *The Sounds of Social Change: Studies in Popular Culture*, ed. R. Serge Denisoff and Richard A. Peterson. Chicago: Rand McNally & Co. 222–31.

5241 Roe, Keith. 1990. Adolescents' Music Use: A Structural-Cultural Approach. In *Popular Music Research*, ed. Keith Roe and Ulla Karlsson. Göteborg: NORDICOM-Sweden, No. 1–2. 41–52.

5242 Rosenbaum, Jill and Prinsky, Lorraine. 1987. Sex, Violence and Rock 'n' Roll: Youth's Perception of Popular Music. *Popular Music & Society* 11(2): 78–91.

5243 Ross, Andrew and Rose, Tricia, eds. 1994. *Microphone Fiends: Youth Music and Youth Culture*. London: Routledge.

5244 Scherman, Robert. 1969. What Are Our Kids Buying? *Journal of Popular Culture* 3(2): 274–80.

5245 Simek, Milan. 1974. Musical Interests of the Czech Youth in the Light of Research Findings. In *New Patterns of Musical Behaviour*, ed. Irmgard Bontinck. Wien: Universal Edition. 140–41.

5246 Spengler, Peter. 1987. *Rockmusik und Jugend: Bedeutung und Funktion einer Musikkultur für die Identitätsuche im Jugendalter*. Frankfurt: Brandes and Aspel.

5247 Szemere, Anna. 1989. Il fascino delle lotte tra bande di teppisti in una civiltà decadente: le considerazioni intorno a un 'video' musicale da parte di alcuni gruppi di giovani ungheresi. *Quaderni di Musica/Realtà* 23: 292–312.

5248 Thoveron, Gabriel. 1974. Leisure Time Behaviour and Cultural Attitude of the Youth: International Research. In *New Patterns of Musical Behaviour*, ed. Irmgard Bontinck. Wien: Universal Edition. 226–29.

5249 Tillekens, Ger. 1993. Het patroon van de popmuziek: de vier dimensies van. jeugdstijlen[The Pattern of Popular Music: The Four Dimensions of Youth Styles]. *Tijdschrift voor Sociologie en Sociaal Onderzoek* 40(2): 177–94.

5250 Trimillos, Ricardo. 1986. Music and Ethnic Identity: Strategies Among Overseas Filipino Youth. *Yearbook for Traditional Music* 18: 9–20.

5251 Trondman, Mats. 1990. Rock Taste: On Rock as Symbolic Capital. A Study of Young People's Music Taste and Music Making. In *Popular Music Research*, ed. Keith Roe and Ulla Karlsson. Göteborg: NORDICOM-Sweden, No. 1–2. 71–86.

5252 Urbanski, Janusz. 1974. Sweet Beat and Other Forms of Youth Music in Poland. In *New Patterns of Musical Behaviour*, ed. Irmgard Bontinck. Wien: Universal Edition. 80–83.

5253 Wicke, Peter. 1985. Jugend und populäre Musik. *Bulletin* XXI(2): 9–12.

5254 Wicke, Peter. 1985. Young People and Popular Music in East Germany: Focus on a Scene. *Communication Research* XII(3): 319–27.

5255 Wicke, Peter. 1989. Jugendszene DDR. Zur Situation der Rock– und Popmusik. *Kulturpolitische Mitteilungen (Zeitschrift der Kulturpolitischen Gesellschaft)* 47: 18–21.

5256 Wicke, Peter. 1990. Rockmusik und Lebensstile. In *Lebensstile und Politik – Politik der Lebensstile*, ed. Olaf Schwencke. Loccum and Hagen: KuPoGe. 175–89.

5257 Wicke, Peter. 1991. Die Entwicklung der Jugendszenen in der DDR. In *Rock & Pop '89. Kritische Analysen, Kulturpolitische Alternativen II.* Hagen: Kulturpolitische Gesellschaft. 23–33.

5258 Wicke, Peter. 1993. Born in the GDR. Zur Situation von Jugendkultur und Rockmusik. In *Woher – Wohin? Kinder – und Jugendkulturarbeit in Ostdeutschland.* Remscheid: Bundesvereinigung kulturelle Jugendbildung.

5259 Wicke, Peter. 1994. Aggressive Jugendstile – ein Problem der Jugendkultur(arbeit)? In *Gratwanderungen. Jugendkulturarbeit als Gewaltprävention?* Bonn: BMBW. 87–93.

5260 Wicke, Peter. 1994. Jugendkultur zwischen Industrie und Politik. In *Zukunftsforum Jugendkulturarbeit 20000 – Zur gesellschaftspolitischen Verantwortung kultureller Bildung.* Remscheid: Bundesvereinigung kulturelle Jugendbildung. 133–38.

5261 Wicke, Peter. 1995. La culture-jeunes on transition. Ruptures et mutations. *Allemagne d'aujourd'hui* 132 (June): 68–76.

5262 Willis, Paul. 1974. Youth Groups in Birmingham and Their Specific Relation to Pop Music. In *New Patterns of Musical Behaviour.* ed. Irmgard Bontinck. Wien: Universal Edition. 108–13.

5263 Willis, Paul. 1990. Music and Symbolic Creativity. In *Common Culture.* Milton Keynes: Open University Press. 59–83.

MUSICAL PRACTISES

MUSICAL GROUPS

Big Bands

5264 Bernhardt, Clyde E.B. and Harris, Sheldon. 1986. *I Remember: Eighty Years of Black Entertainment, Big Bands and the Blues*. Philadelphia: University of Pennsylvania Press.

5265 Crowther, Bruce. 1988. *The Big Band Years*. Newton Abbot: David & Charles.

5266 Edelhagen, Viola and Edelhagen-Holtz, Joachim. 1988. *Die Big Band Story nach 1945 in der BRD*. Frankfurt am Main: Eisenbletter u. Naumann.

5267 Gammond, Peter and Horricks, Raymond, eds. 1981. *Big Bands*. Cambridge: Stephens.

5268 Walker, Leo. 1978. *The Big Band Almanac*. Pasadena, CA: Ward Ritchie Press.

Brass Bands

5269 Bainbridge, Cyril. 1980. *Brass Triumphant*. London: Frederick Muller Ltd.

5270 Booth, Gregory D. 1990. Brass Bands: Tradition, Change and the Mass Media in Indian Wedding Music. *Ethnomusicology* 34(2): 245–61.

5271 Brand, Violet and Brand, Geoffrey. 1986. *The World of Brass Bands*. Baldock, Herts.: Egon.

5272 Bythell, Duncan. 1991. The Brass Band in Australia: The Transplantation of British Popular Culture. In *Bands: The Brass Band Movement in the 19th and 20th Centuries*, ed. Trevor Herbert. Milton Keynes: Open University Press. 145–64.

5273 Camus, Raoul F. 1975. *Military Music of the American Revolution*. Westerville, OH: Integrity Press.

5274 Dudgeon, Ralph T. 1993. *The Keyed Bugle*. Metuchen and London: Scarecrow Press.

5275 Fasman, Mark J. 1990. *Brass Bibliography: Sources on the History, Literature, Pedagogy, Performance and Acoustics of Brass Instruments*. Bloomington, IN: Indiana University Press.

5276 Hazen, Margaret Hindle and Hazen, Robert M. 1987. *The Music Men: An Illustrated History of Brass Bands in America, 1800–1920*. Washington, DC: Smithsonian Institution Press.

5277 Herbert, Trevor. 1990. The Repertory of a Provincial Brass Band. *Popular Music* 9(1): 117–32.

5278 Herbert, Trevor, ed. 1991. *Bands: The Brass Band Movement in the 19th and 20th Centuries*. Milton Keynes: Open University Press.

5279 Herbert, Trevor. 1992. Victorian Brass Bands: The Establishment of a 'Working-Class Musical Tradition'. *Historic Brass Society Journal* 4: 1–11.

5280 Martin, Stephen H. 1991. Brass Bands and the Beni Phenomena in Urban East Africa. *African Music* 7(1): 72–81.

5281 Mortimer, Harry. 1981. *On Brass*. Sherborne: Alphabooks.

5282 Rose, Algernon S. 1995. (1895) *Talks with Bandsmen: A Popular Handbook for Brass Instrumentalists*. London: Tony Bingham. First published London: William Rider & Son, Ltd., 1895.

5283 Ruhr, Peter. 1987. 'Mit klingendem Spiel' - badische Blasmusik zwischen der Revolution 1848 und dem Ersten Weltkrieg. In *Ich will aber gerade vom Leben singen . . . Über populäre Musik vom ausgehenden 19. Jahrhundert bis zum Ende der Weimarer Republik*, ed. Sabine Schutte. Reinbek bei Hamburg: Rowohlt. 115–36.

5284 Russell, Dave. 1987. *Popular Music in England, 1840–1914: A Social History.* Manchester: Manchester University Press.

5285 Russell, J.F. and Elliot, J.H. 1936. *The Brass Band Movement.* London: J.M. Dent & Sons Ltd.

5286 Schafer, William J. and Allen, Richard B. 1977. *Brass Bands and New Orleans Jazz.* Baton Rouge, LA: Louisiana State University Press.

5287 Suppan, Wolfgang. 1983. *Blasmusik in Baden: Geschichte und Gegenwart einer traditionsreichen Blasmusiklandschaft.* Freiburg: Musikverlag Fritz Schulz.

5288 Suppan, Wolfgang. 1988. (1973) *Lexikon des Blasmusikwesens*, 2nd edition. Freiburg im Breisgau: Musikverlag Fritz Schulz. First published Freiburg im Breisgau: Musikverlag Fritz Schulz, 1973.

5289 Taylor, Arthur. 1979. *Brass Bands.* St. Alban's: Granada.

5290 Taylor, Arthur. 1983. *Love and Lore: An Oral History of the Brass Band Movement.* London: Elm Tree Press.

5291 Wright, Frank, ed. 1957. *Brass Today.* London: Besson & Co. Ltd.

Dance Bands

5292 Averill, Gage. 1989. Haitian Dance Bands, 1915–1970: Class, Race and Authenticity. *Latin American Music Review* 10(2): 203–35.

5293 Becker, Howard. 1972. The Culture and Career of the Dance Musician. In *American Music: From Storyville to Woodstock*, ed. Charles Nanry. New Brunswick, NJ: Transaction. 65–98.

5294 Colin, Sid. 1977. *And the Bands Played On.* London: Hamish Hamilton.

5295 Fernett, Gene. 1970. *A Thousand Golden Horns: The Exciting Age of America's Greatest Dance Bands.* Midland, MI: Pendell.

5296 Fernett, Gene. 1970. *Swing Out: The Great Negro Dance Bands.* Midland, MI: Pendell.

5297 McCarthy, Albert. 1974. (1971) *The Dance Band Era: The Dancing Decades from Ragtime to Swing, 1910–1950.* London: Spring Books.

5298 Ritzel, Fred and Stroh, Wolfgang Martin. 1985. Deutsche Tanzmusiker: Zu einer Sozialgeschichte der populären Musik in Deutschland. *Jazzforschung* 17: 69–75.

5299 Scott, Derek B. 1994. Incongruity and Predictability in British Dance Bands of the 1920s and 1930s. *Musical Quarterly* 78(2): 290–315.

5300 Specht, Paul L. 1941. *How They Became Name Bands: The Modern Technique of a Danceband Maestro.* New York: Fine Art Publications.

5301 Thomson, Raymond A. 1989. Dance Bands and Dance Halls in Greenock, 1945–55. *Popular Music* 8(2): 143–55.

5302 Walker, Leo. 1972. *The Wonderful World of the Great Dance Bands.* New York: Doubleday.

5303 Welk, Lawrence and McGeehan, Bernice. 1971. *Wunnerful, Wunnerful!: The Autobiography of Lawrence Welk.* Englewood Cliffs, NJ: Prentice-Hall.

Military Bands

5304 Adkins, H.E. 1945. *Treatise on the Military Band*. London: Boosey.

5305 Foster, Robert E. 1994. The Contribution of Bands During World War II. *The Instrumentalist* 49 (November): 79–80.

5306 Railsback, Tomas C. and Longellier, John P. 1987. *The Drums Would Roll: A Pictorial History of US Army Bands on the American Frontier, 1866–1900*. Poole: Blandford Press.

5307 Schwartz, H.W. 1957. *Bands of America*. New York: Doubleday & Co.

5308 Strand, Sigfrid. 1974. *Militärmusikern i svenskt musikliv*. Stockholm: Sohlmans.

5309 Trendell, John. 1991. *Colonel Bogey to the Fore*. Deal: Blue Band Magazine.

5310 Turner, Gordon and Turner, Alwyn. 1995. *The History of British Military Bands. Vol. 1: Cavalry and Corps*. Staplehurst: Spellmount.

5311 Turner, Gordon and Turner, Alwyn. 1995. *The History of British Military Bands. Vol. 2: Guards and Scottish Division*. Staplehurst: Spellmount.

Rock Bands

5312 Gorman, Clem. 1978. *Backstage Rock: Behind the Scenes with the Bands*. London: Pan.

5313 Tennstedt, Florian. 1979. *Rockmusik und Gruppenprozesse: Aufstieg und Abstieg der Petards*. München: Wilhelm Fink Verlag.

Steel Bands

5314 Aho, William R. 1987. Steel Band Music in Trinidad and Tobago: The Creation of a People's Music. *Latin American Music Review* 8(1): 26–58.

5315 Borde, Percival. 1973. The Sound of Trinidad: The Development of the Steel-Drum Bands. *The Black Perspective in Music* 1(1): 45–49.

5316 Chatburn, Thomas. 1990. Trinidad All Stars: The Steel Pan Movement in Britain. In *Black Music in Britain: Essays on the Afro-Asian Contribution to Popular Music*, ed. Paul Oliver. Milton Keynes: Open University Press. 102–17.

Traveling Shows

5317 Albertson, Chris. 1972. *Bessie*. New York/London: Stein and Day/Barrie & Jenkins.

5318 Anderson, Jervis. 1982. *Harlem: The Great Black Way, 1900–1950*. London: Orbis Publishing.

5319 Beaton, Josephine and Rye, Howard. 1977. Sam Wooding in England and France. *Storyville* 74: 47–49.

5320 Behncke, Bernhard H. 1975. Sam Wooding and the Chocolate Kiddies at the Thalia Theatre in Hamburg, 28th July 1925 to 24th August 1925. *Storyville* 60: 214–21.

5321 Bergmeier, Horst J.P. 1977. Sam Wooding Recapitulated. *Storyville* 74: 44–47.

5322 Bernhardt, Clyde E.B. and Harris, Sheldon. 1986. *I Remember: Eighty Years of Black Entertainment, Big Bands, and the Blues*. Philadelphia: University of Pennsylvania Press.

5323 Biagioni, Egino. 1977. *Herb Flemming: A Jazz Pioneer Around the World*. Alphen Aan De Rijn: Micrography.

5324 Bricktop (Ada Smith) and Haskins, James. 1983. *Bricktop*. New York: Atheneum Press.

5325 Darensbourg, Joe. 1987. *Telling It Like It Is*, ed. Peter Vacher. London: Macmillan.

5326 Englund, Björn. 1975. Chocolate Kiddies: The Show That Brought Jazz to

Europe and Russia in 1925. *Storyville* 62: 44–50.

5327 Fox, Ted. 1983. *Showtime at the Apollo.* New York: Holt, Rinehart & Winston.

5328 Goddard, Chris. 1979. *Jazz Away from Home.* New York and London: Paddington Press.

5329 Hammond, Bryan and O'Connor, Patrick. 1988. *Josephine Baker.* Boston, Toronto and London: Little, Brown & Co.

5330 Harris, Sheldon. 1979. *Blues Who's Who.* New Rochelle, NY: Arlington House.

5331 Kimball, Robert and Bolcom, William. 1973. *Reminiscing with Sissle and Blake.* New York: Viking.

5332 Kukla, Barbara J. 1991. *Swing City: Newark Nightlife, 1925–50.* Philadelphia: Temple University Press.

5333 Larsen, John and Larsen, Hans. 1965. The Chocolate Kiddies in Copenhagen. *Record Research* 67: 3–5.

5334 Lieb, Sandra R. 1981. *Mother of the Blues: A Study of Ma Rainey.* Amherst, MA: University of Massachusetts Press.

5335 Lotz, Rainer E. 1986. Will Garland and His Negro Operetta Company. In *Under the Imperial Carpet: Essays in Black History, 1780–1950,* ed. Rainer E. Lotz and Ian Pegg. Crawley: Rabbit Press. 130–44.

5336 Mazzoletti, Adriano. 1983. *Il Jazz in Italia, Dalle Origini Al Dopoguerra.* Roma-Bari: Laterza.

5337 Oliver, Paul. 1984. *Songsters and Saints: Vocal Traditions on Race Records.* Cambridge and London: Cambridge University Press.

5338 Rye, Howard. 1978. How Come: Sidney Bechet's Brief Career as Chinese Laundryman/Police Chief. *Storyville* 76: 138–39.

5339 Rye, Howard. 1982. Visiting Firemen 6: Teddy Hill & the Cotton Club Revue. *Storyville* 100: 144–46.

5340 Rye, Howard. 1984. Visiting Firemen 9/ 10: The Blackbirds and Their Orchestras. *Storyville* 112; 114: 132–47; 216–17.

5341 Rye, Howard and Green, Jeffrey P. 1995. Black Musical Internationalism in England in the 1920s. *Black Music Research Journal* 15(1): 93–107.

5342 Schoener, Allon, ed. 1968. *Harlem on My Mind: Cultural Capital of Black America, 1900–1968.* New York: Random House.

5343 Seroff, Doug. 1983. Blues Itineraries. *Whiskey, Women, and . . .* 11: 33–35.

5344 Stearns, Marshall and Stearns, Jean. 1968. *Jazz Dance: The Story of American Vernacular Dance.* New York and London: Macmillan.

5345 Waters, Ethel and Samuels, Charles. 1959. (1951) *His Eye Is on the Sparrow.* New York: Bantam Books. First published New York/London: Doubleday/W.H. Allen, 1951.

5346 zur Heide, Karl. 1977. Clyde, Mike & the Whitman Sisters. *Footnote* 8(3): 16–22.

Wind Bands

5347 Dauer, Alfons M. 1985. *Tradition afrikanischer Blasorchester und Entstehung des Jazz.* Graz: Akademische Druck- und Verlagsanstalt.

5348 Suppan, Wolfgang. 1983. *Blasmusik in Baden: Geschichte und Gegenwart einer traditionsreichen Blasmusiklandschaft.* Freiburg: Musikverlag Fritz Schulz.

MUSIC ANALYSIS AND THEORY

Music Analysis

5349 Agostini, Roberto. 1992. Studiare la 'popular music'. In *Dal blues al liscio: Studi sull'esperienza musicale comune*, ed. Gino Stefani. Verona: Ianua. 169–89.

5350 Agostini, Roberto. 1996. *Lucy in the Sky with Diamonds:* un'analisi. In *Analisi e canzoni*, ed. Rossana Dalmonte. Trento: Università di Trento. 263–91.

5351 Alencar-Pinto, Guilherme de. 1985. Análisis: *Deus lhe pague. La del taller* 4 (December): 19–26.

5352 Asriel, Andre. 1985. *Jazz: Analysen und Aspekte*. Berlin: Lied der Zeit.

5353 Ballantine, Christopher. 1995. Fact, Ideology and Paradox: African Elements in Early Black South African Jazz and Vaudeville. In *Papers Presented at the Tenth Symposium on Ethnomusicology, Rhodes University, 30 September-2 October, 1991*, ed. Carol Muller. International Library of African Music, Rhodes University. 5–9.

5354 Ballantine, Christopher. 1995. Politics in Music: Towards an African Style in Black South African Jazz and Vaudeville in the Early 1940s. In *Papers Presented at the Ninth Symposium on Ethnomusicology, University of Namibia, 23–26 August, 1990*, ed. Carol Muller. International Library of African Music, Rhodes University. 5–7.

5355 Banfi, Emanuele and Winkler, Daniele. 1996. Riflessi dell' 'italiano in movimento' in un *corpus* di canzoni italiane di area alto-atesina. In *Analisi e canzoni*, ed. Rossana Dalmonte. Trento: Università di Trento. 125–44.

5356 Baroni, Mario. 1996. Analisi musicale e giudizio di valore nella musica leggera. In *Analisi e canzoni*, ed. Rossana Dalmonte. Trento: Università di Trento. 81–102.

5357 Bauer, William R. 1993. Billie Holiday and Betty Carter: Emotion and Style in the Jazz Vocal Line. *Annual Review of Jazz Studies* 6: 99–152.

5358 Björnberg, Alf. 1990. Sounding the Mainstream: An Analysis of the Songs Performed in the Swedish Eurovision Song Contest Semi-Finals, 1959–1983. In *Popular Music Research*, ed. Keith Roe and Ulla Karlsson. Göteborg: NORDICOM-Sweden, No. 1–2. 121–31.

5359 Björnberg, Alf. 1994. Structural Relationships of Music and Images in Music Video. *Popular Music* 13(1): 51–74.

5360 Bohländer, Carlo. 1986. *Die Anatomie des Swing*. Frankfurt am Main: Schmitt.

5361 Bolelli, Roberto. 1992. Il rock è blu? In *Secondo Convegno Europeo di Analisi Musicale, Vol. I*, ed. Rossana Dalmonte and Mario Baroni. Trento: Università di Trento. 629–30.

5362 Bowman, Rob. 1995. The Stax Sound: A Musicological Analysis. *Popular Music* 14(3): 285–320.

5363 Brackett, David. 1992. James Brown's 'Superbad' and the Double-Voiced Utterance. *Popular Music* 11(3): 309–24.

5364 Brackett, David. 1994. The Politics and Practice of 'Crossover' in American Popular Music, 1963 to 1965. *Musical Quarterly* 78(4): 774–97.

5365 Brackett, David. 1995. *Interpreting Popular Music*. Cambridge: Cambridge University Press.

5366 Bradby, Barbara and Torode, Brian. 1984. Pity Peggy Sue. *Popular Music* 4: 183–206.

5367 Braha, Liviu von. 1983. *Phänomene der Rockmusik*. Wilhelmshaven: Heinrichshofen.

5368 Brofsky, Howard. 1994. Response to Robert Walser's 'Out of Notes: Signification, Interpretation, and the Problem of Miles Davis'. *Musical Quarterly* 78(2): 417.

5369 Brownell, John. 1994. Analytical Models of Jazz Improvisation. *Jazzforschung/ Jazz Research* 26: 9–30.

5370 Burbat, Wolfgang. 1988. *Die Harmonik des Jazz*. Kassel: dtv/Bärenreiter.

5371 Burns, Gary. 1987. A Typology of 'Hooks' in Popular Music. *Popular Music* 6(1): 1–20.

5372 Byrnside, Ronald. 1975. The Formation of a Musical Style: Early Rock. In *Contemporary Music and Music Cultures*, ed. Charles Hamm, Bruno Nettl and Ronald Byrnside. Englewood Cliffs, NJ: Prentice-Hall. 159–92.

5373 Cipelli, Roberto. 1993. Il linguaggio di Elmo Hope. *Nerosubianco* 1(2): 55–101.

5374 Clynes, Manfred. 1985. Secrets of Life in Music. In *Analytica: Studies in the Description and Analysis of Music*. Stockholm: Kungliga Musikaliska Akademien. 3–16.

5375 Cogan, Robert. 1993. Mingus: Oppositional Design, Composition, and Improvisation. *Sonus* 14(1): 29–54.

5376 Cook, Nicholas. 1994. Music and Meaning in the Commercial. *Popular Music* 13(1): 27–40.

5377 Cook, Nicholas. 1995. *Analysing Musical Multimedia*. Oxford: Oxford University Press.

5378 Corrado, Gabriele. 1992. Swing: senso, tecnica, condotta. In *Dal blues al liscio: Studi sull'esperienza musicale comune*, ed. Gino Stefani. Verona: Ianua. 77–101.

5379 Costamagna, Lidia. 1996. La canzone e la didattica dell'italiano come lingua straniera. In *Analisi e canzoni*, ed.

Rossana Dalmonte. Trento: Università di Trento. 337–55.

5380 Covach, John. 1995. We Can Work It Out: Musical Analysis and Rock Music. In *Popular Music: Style and Identity*, ed. Will Straw, et al. Montréal: The Centre for Research on Canadian Cultural Industries and Institutions. 69–71.

5381 Coveri, Lorenzo. 1996. Lingua e dialetto nella canzone popolare recente. In *Analisi e canzoni*, ed. Rossana Dalmonte. Trento: Università di Trento. 25–38.

5382 Crook, Larry N. 1982. A Musical Analysis of the Cuban Rumba. *Latin American Music Review* 3(1): 93–123.

5383 Dalmonte, Rossana. 1994. Cinque buone ragioni pert analizzare la popular music. *Vox Popular, Bollettino della IASPM Italiana* 2: 7.

5384 Dalmonte, Rossana, ed. 1996. *Analisi e canzoni*. Trento: Università di Trento.

5385 Dalmonte, Rossana. 1996. Metodi di analisi per la canzone. In *Analisi e canzoni*, ed. Rossana Dalmonte. Trento: Università di Trento. 11–23.

5386 Dauer, Alfons M. 1983. *Blues aus 100 Jahren: 43 Beispiele zur Typologie der vokalen Bluesformen*. Frankfurt am Main: Fischer.

5387 Dean, Roger Thornton. 1991. *New Structures in Jazz and Improvised Music: From the 1960s into the 1980s*. New York: Taylor and Francis.

5388 Diadori, Pierangela. 1996. Le canzoni e la musica nella glottodidattica. In *Analisi e canzoni*, ed. Rossana Dalmonte. Trento: Università di Trento. 357–72.

5389 Diettrich, Eva. 1979. *Tendenzen der Pop-Musik. Dargestellt am Beispiel der Beatles*. Tutzing: Schneider.

5390 Erra, Andrea. 1996. La struttura del rap italiano. In *Analisi e canzoni*, ed. Rossana Dalmonte. Trento: Università di Trento.

317–36. (First published in *Musica/Realtà* 48 (1995): 155–70.)

5391 Everett, Walter. 1985. Text-Painting in the Foreground and Middleground of Paul McCartney's Beatle Song 'She's Leaving Home': A Musical Study of Psychological Conflict. *In Theory Only* 9: 5–13.

5392 Everett, Walter. 1986. Fantastic Remembrance in John Lennon's 'Strawberry Fields Forever' and 'Julia'. *Musical Quarterly* 72(3): 360–85.

5393 Fabbri, Franco. 1991. Analizzare la popular music: perché? In *L'analisi musicale*, ed. Rossana Dalmonte and Mario Baroni. Milano: Unicopli. 84–95.

5394 Fabbri, Franco. 1996. Che genere di musica? In *Il suono in cui viviamo. Inventare, produrre e diffondere musica.* Milano: Feltrinelli. 7–32.

5395 Fabbri, Franco. 1996. Forme e modelli delle canzoni dei Beatles. In *Analisi e canzoni*, ed. Rossana Dalmonte. Trento: Università di Trento. 169–96.

5396 Fabich, R. 1993. *Musik für den Stimmfilm: Analysierende Beschreibung originaler Film Komposition.* Frankfurt: Lang.

5397 Faulstich, Werner. 1978. *Rock - Pop - Beat - Folk. Grundlagen der Textmusik-Analyse.* Tübingen: Gunter Narr.

5398 Fiori, Umberto. 1996. 'In un supremo anelito'. L'idea di poesia nella canzone italiana. In *Analisi e canzoni*, ed. Rossana Dalmonte. Trento: Università di Trento. 145–59.

5399 Fiori, Umberto and Ghezzi, Emilio. 1989. I Have the Touch di Peter Gabriel: un'analisi. In *Musiche/Realtà*, ed. Franco Fabbri. Milano: Unicopli. 363–80. (First published in *Musica/Realtà* 17 (1985): 87–104. Published in English as 'Listening to Peter Gabriel's *I Have the Touch*'. *Popular Music* 6(1) (1986).)

5400 Fitzgerald, Jon. 1995. Black or White? Stylistic Analysis of Early Motown 'Crossover' Hits: 1963–1966. In *Popular Music: Style and Identity*, ed. Will Straw, et al. Montréal: The Centre for Research on Canadian Cultural Industries and Institutions. 95–98.

5401 Forte, Allen. 1995. *The American Popular Ballad of the Golden Era, 1924–1950.* Princeton, NJ: Princeton University Press.

5402 Gorbman, Claudia. 1987. *Unheard Melodies: Narrative Film Music.* London/Bloomington/Indianapolis: B.F.I. Publishing/Indiana University Press.

5403 Grässer, Hanno. 1994. Stéphane Grappellis Violintechnik. Transkription und Analyse einer Videoaufzeichnung. *Jazzforschung/Jazz Research* 26: 133–42.

5404 Griffiths, David. 1988. Three Tributaries of 'The River'. *Popular Music* 7(1): 27–34.

5405 Griffiths, David. 1992. Talking About Popular Song: In Praise of Anchorage. In *Secondo Convegno Europeo di Analisi Musicale, Vol. I*, ed. Rossana Dalmonte and Mario Baroni. Trento: Università di Trento. 351–58.

5406 Hartwich-Wiechell, Dörte. 1974. *Pop-Musik: Analysen und Interpretationen.* Köln: Arno Volk Verlag.

5407 Hatch, David and Millward, Stephen. 1987. *From Blues to Rock: An Analytical History of Pop Music.* Manchester: Manchester University Press.

5408 Hawkins, Stan. 1992. Prince: Harmonic Analysis of 'Anna Stesia'. *Popular Music* 11(3): 325–35.

5409 Hawkins, Stan. 1995. Being Banal: The Pet Shop Boys. *Popular Musicology* 2: 29–42.

5410 Hawkins, Stan. 1995. New Perspectives in Musicology: Musical Structures, Codes and Meaning in 1990s Pop. In

Popular Music: Style and Identity, ed. Will Straw, et al. Montréal: The Centre for Research on Canadian Cultural Industries and Institutions. 131–36.

5411 Hawkins, Stan. 1996. Perspectives in Popular Musicology: Music, Lennox and Meaning in 1990s Pop. *Popular Music* 15(1): 17–36.

5412 Hellhund, Herbert. 1990. Konzept und spontaner Prozeß. Zu einigen Strukturprinzipien improvisierter Avantgardemusik. In *Darmstädter Jazz forum 89: Beiträge zur Jazzforschung*, ed. Ekkehard Jost. Hofheim: Wolke. 225–34.

5413 Jaffe, Andrew. 1983. *Jazz Theory*. Dubuque, IA: Wm. C. Brown.

5414 Jerrentrup, Ansgar. 1981. *Entwicklung der Rockmusik von den Anfängen bis zum Beat*. Regensburg: Bosse.

5415 Johns, Donald. 1993. Funnel Tonality in American Popular Music, ca. 1900–70. *American Music* 11(4): 458–72.

5416 Johnson, Bruce. 1994. Klactoveesedstene: Music, Soundscape and Me. In *Soundscapes: Essays on Vroom and Moo*, ed. Helmi Järviluoma. Tampere: Department of Folk Tradition. 39–47.

5417 Josephson, Nors S. 1992. Bach Meets Liszt: Traditional Formal Structures and Performance Practices in Progressive Rock. *Musical Quarterly* 76(1): 67–92.

5418 Jost, Ekkehard. 1975. *Free Jazz. Stilistische Untersuchungen zum Jazz der 60er Jahre*. Mainz: Schott.

5419 Kjellberg, Erik. 1985. Rena Rama and Lisa's Piano: An Essay in Jazz Analysis. In *Analytica: Studies in the Description and Analysis of Music*. Stockholm: Kungliga Musikaliska Akademien. 323–36.

5420 Knauer, Wolfram. 1991. *Jazz und Komposition*. Hofheim: Wolke.

5421 Kramarz, Volkmar. 1985. Rockmusik und Musiktheorie. *Jazzforschung* 17: 99–101.

5422 La Polla, Franco. 1996. Cambiare la costituzione (o la testa?): i Beatles fra pop e letteratura. In *Analisi e canzoni*, ed. Rossana Dalmonte. Trento: Università di Trento. 291–97.

5423 Lawn, R.J. and Hellmer, J.L. 1993. *Jazz Theory and Practice*. Belmont, CA: Wadsworth.

5424 Ling, Jan. 1992. From 'Empfindsamer' Style to Down Home Village Nostalgia. In *Secondo Convegno Europeo di Analisi Musicale, Vol. I*, ed. Rossana Dalmonte and Mario Baroni. Trento: Università di Trento. 321–40.

5425 Marconi, Luca. 1996. Baglioni e i Beatles: solo un piccola grande amore? In *Analisi e canzoni*, ed. Rossana Dalmonte. Trento: Università di Trento. 299–316.

5426 Mellers, Wilfrid. 1973. *Twilight of the Gods: The Beatles in Retrospect*. London: Faber & Faber.

5427 Mellers, Wilfrid. 1984. *A Darker Shade of Pale: A Backdrop to Bob Dylan*. London: Faber & Faber.

5428 Meyer, Gust de. 1985. Minimal and Repetitive Aspects in Pop Music. In *Popular Music Perspectives, 2*, ed. David Horn. Göteborg and Exeter: IASPM. 387–96.

5429 Miceli, Sergio, ed. 1990. *Chigiana XLII(22) (Atti del Convegno Internazionale di Studi 'Musica & Cinema')*. Firenze: Olschki.

5430 Miceli, Sergio. 1994. Analizzare la musica per film. Una risposta dalla teoria dei livelli. *Rivista Italiana di Musicologia* 29(2): 517–44.

5431 Miceli, Sergio. 1994. *Morricone, la musica, il cinema*. Milano: Ricordi/Mucchi.

5432 Middleton, Richard. 1983. 'Play It Again Sam': Some Notes on the Productivity of Repetition in Popular Music. *Popular Music* 3: 235–70.

5433 Middleton, Richard. 1990. *Studying Popular Music*. Milton Keynes: Open University Press.

5434 Middleton, Richard. 1992. Toward a Theory of Gesture in Popular Song Analysis. In *Secondo Convegno Europeo di Analisi Musicale, Vol. I*, ed. Rossana Dalmonte and Mario Baroni. Trento: Università di Trento. 345–50.

5435 Middleton, Richard. 1993. Popular Music Analysis and Musicology: Bridging the Gap. *Popular Music* 12(2): 177–90.

5436 Middleton, Richard. 1995. Authorship, Gender and the Construction of Meaning in The Eurythmics' Hit Recordings. *Cultural Studies* 9(3): 465–85.

5437 Minganti, Franco. 1996. I Beatles 'americani' della BBC. In *Analisi e canzoni*, ed. Rossana Dalmonte. Trento: Università di Trento. 235–54.

5438 Monson, Ingrid. 1994. Doubleness and Jazz Improvisation: Irony, Parody and Ethnomusicology. *Critical Inquiry* 20(2): 283–313.

5439 Montecchi, Giordano. 1996. Aspetti di intertestualità nella musica rock degli anni Sessanta. In *Analisi e canzoni*, ed. Rossana Dalmonte. Trento: Università di Trento. 39–57.

5440 Moore, Allan F. 1992. The Texture of Rock. In *Secondo Convegno Europeo di Analisi Musicale, Vol. I*, ed. Rossana Dalmonte and Mario Baroni. Trento: Università di Trento. 341–44.

5441 Moore, Allan F. 1993. *Rock: The Primary Text*. Buckingham: Open University Press.

5442 Moore, Allan F. 1995. The So-Called 'Flattened Seventh' in Rock. *Popular Music* 14(2): 185–201.

5443 Okada, Maki. 1991. Musical Characteristics of *Enka*. *Popular Music* 10(3): 283–303.

5444 Oliver, Paul. 1982. Blues and the Binary Principle. In *Popular Music Perspectives, 1*, ed. David Horn and Philip Tagg. Göteborg and Exeter: IASPM. 163–73.

5445 Olshausen, U., W. Sandner and Hans-Jürgen Feurich. 1977. Chuck Berry: Johnny B Goode - Analyse. In *Rockmusik*, ed. Wolfgang Sandner. Mainz: Schott. 162–67.

5446 Opekar, Ales. 1992. Analysis of a Rock Album *Straka v hrstí* by the Group Pražský výběr. In *Secondo Convegno Europeo di Analisi Musicale, Vol. I*, ed. Rossana Dalmonte and Mario Baroni. Trento: Università di Trento. 359–65.

5447 Owens, Thomas. 1974. Applying the Melograph to 'Parker's Mood'. *Selected Reports in Ethnomusicology* 2(1): 167–75.

5448 Pasolini, Pier Paolo. 1979. La musica del film. In *Teoria e tecnica del film in Pasolini*, ed. A. Bertini. Roma: Bulzoni. 169–75.

5449 Pasquali, Augusto. 1996. Persistenza del mito dei Beatles ed il loro uso nella didattica musicale. In *Analisi e canzoni*, ed. Rossana Dalmonte. Trento: Università di Trento. 161–68.

5450 Pérez, Rolando. 1986. Il metodo comparativo e la binarizzazione dei ritmi ternari africani in America Latina. *Musica/Realtà* 20: 129–47.

5451 Perlman, Alan M. and Greenblatt, Daniel. 1981. Miles Davis Meets Noam Chomsky: Some Observations on Jazz Improvisation and Language Structure. In *The Sign in Music and Literature*, ed. Wendy Steiner. Austin, TX: University of Texas Press. 169–83.

5452 Pestalozza, Luigi, et al. 1996. Tavola rotonda su 'From Me To You' dei Beatles. In *Analisi e canzoni*, ed. Rossana Dalmonte. Trento: Università di Trento. 373–407.

5453 Radano, Ronald M. 1994. *New Musical Figurations: Anthony Braxton's Cultural Critique.* Chicago and London: University of Chicago Press.

5454 Raljevic, Sania. 1992. A Case of 'New Composed Folk Music' in Yugoslavia. In *Secondo Convegno Europeo di Analisi Musicale, Vol. I*, ed. Rossana Dalmonte and Mario Baroni. Trento: Università di Trento. 671–73.

5455 Russo, Marco. 1996. La prassi dell'arrangiamento nelle canzoni: esempi ed osservazioni. In *Analisi e canzoni*, ed. Rossana Dalmonte. Trento: Università di Trento. 197–233.

5456 Schuler, Manfred. 1978. Rockmusik und Kunstmusik der Vergangenheit: Ein analytischer Versuch. *Archiv für Musikwissenschaft* 35(2): 135–50.

5457 Schutte, Sabine. 1970. *Der Ländler. Untersuchungen zur musikalischen Struktur ungeradtaktiger österreichischer Volkstänze.* Baden-Baden: Heitz.

5458 Scott, Derek B. 1994. Incongruity and Predictability in British Dance Bands of the 1920s and 1930s. *Musical Quarterly* 78(2): 290–315.

5459 Shepherd, John. 1982. A Theoretical Model for the Sociomusicological Analysis of Popular Musics. *Popular Music* 2: 145–77.

5460 Simeon, Ennio. 1987. La nascita di una drammaturgia della musica per film: il ruolo di Giuseppe Becce. *Musica/Realtà* 24: 103–20.

5461 Simeon, Ennio. 1992. Programmi narrativi e stratificazioni di senso nella musica per film. Il caso di 'Entr'acte'. In *Secondo Convegno Europeo di Analisi Musicale, Vol. I*, ed. Rossana Dalmonte and Mario Baroni. Trento: Università di Trento. 389–99.

5462 Simeon, Ennio. 1992. Proposte per una teoria analitica di tipo narratologico applicata alla musica da film. 'Mission' di Joffé - Morricone. *Cinema* 102: 18–27.

5463 Simeon, Ennio. 1995. *Per un pugno di note. Storia, teoria, estetica della musica per il cinema, la televisione e il video.* Milano: Reggimenti.

5464 Smith, Gregory E. 1991. In Quest of a New Perspective on Improvised Jazz: A View from the Balkans. *The World of Music* 33(3): 29–52.

5465 Stefani, Gino. 1996. Dire fare cantare. In *Analisi e canzoni*, ed. Rossana Dalmonte. Trento: Università di Trento. 255–61.

5466 Stefani, Gino, Luca Marconi and Franca Ferrari. 1990. *Gli intervalli musicali.* Milano: Bompiani.

5467 Stumpo, Francesco Domenico. 1992. Assimilazioni 'colte' nella pop music. In *Secondo Convegno Europeo di Analisi Musicale, Vol. I*, ed. Rossana Dalmonte and Mario Baroni. Trento: Università di Trento. 683–85.

5468 Tagg, Philip. 1979. *Kojak: 50 Seconds of Television Music. Towards the Analysis of Affect in Popular Music.* Göteborg: Skrifter från Göteborgs universitet, Musikvetenskapliga institutionen, 2.

5469 Tagg, Philip. 1982. Analysing Popular Music: Theory, Method and Practice. *Popular Music* 2: 37–67.

5470 Tagg, Philip. 1984. Understanding 'Time Sense': Concepts, Sketches, Consequences. In *Tvärspel: 31 artiklar om musik. Festskrift till Jan Ling.* Göteborg: Skrifter från Musikvetenskapliga institutionen, 9. 21–43.

5471 Tagg, Philip. 1985. La musicologie et la sémantique de la musique populaire. In *Analytica: Studies in the Description and Analysis of Music*. Stockholm: Kungliga Musikaliska Akademien. 77–96.

5472 Tagg, Philip. 1985. Zur Analyse von populärer Musik. *Beiträge zur Musikwissenschaft* 3–4: 241–64.

5473 Tagg, Philip. 1990. Music for Moving Pictures: Academia, Education and Independent Thought. In *Chigiana XLII(22) (Atti del Convegno Internazionale di Studi 'Musica & Cinema')*, ed. Sergio Miceli. Firenze: Olschki. 351–80.

5474 Tagg, Philip. 1990. Music in Mass Media Studies: Reading Sounds, For Example. In *Popular Music Research*, ed. Keith Roe and Ulla Karlsson. Göteborg: NORDICOM-Sweden, No. 1–2. 103–14.

5475 Tagg, Philip. 1990. Reading Sounds. *Re Records Quarterly* 3(2): 4–11. First published Göteborg: IASPM Norden Working Papers, 1987.

5476 Tagg, Philip. 1991. *Fernando the Flute: Analysis of Musical Meaning in an Abba Mega-Hit*. Liverpool: Institute of Popular Music, University of Liverpool.

5477 Tagg, Philip. 1992. Toward a Sign Typology in Music. In *Secondo Convegno Europeo di Analisi Musicale, Vol. I*, ed. Rossana Dalmonte and Mario Baroni. Trento: Università di Trento. 369–78.

5478 Tagg, Philip. 1993. 'Universal' Music and the Case of Death. In *La musica come linguaggio universale. Genesi e storia di un'idea*, ed. Raffaele Pozzi. Firenze: Olschki. 227–65.

5479 Tagg, Philip. 1994. From Refrain to Rave: The Decline of Figure and the Rise of Ground. *Popular Music* 13(2): 209–22.

5480 Tagg, Philip. 1994. *Popular Music: Da Kojak al Rave*, ed. Roberto Agostini and Luca Marconi. Bologna: Clueb.

5481 Tagg, Philip. 1994. Subjectivity and Soundscape, Motorbikes and Music. In *Soundscapes: Essays on Vroom and Moo*, ed. Helmi Järviluoma. Tampere: Department of Folk Tradition. 48–66.

5482 Tagg, Philip. 1995. Dal ritornello al 'rave': tramonta la figura emerge lo sfondo. In *Annali Istituto Gramsci Emilia-Romagna 2/1995, dossier: Rock Steady/ Rock Study: sulle culture del rock . . .*, ed. Franco Minganti. Bologna: Istituto Gramsci Emilia-Romagna. 158–75.

5483 Taylor, Timothy D. 1992. His Name Was in Lights: Chuck Berry's 'Johnny B. Goode'. *Popular Music* 11(1): 27–40.

5484 Van Der Lek, Robert. 1994. Concert Music as Reused Film Music: E.-W. Korngold's Self-Arrangements. *Acta Musicologica* LXVI(II): 78–112.

5485 Van der Merwe, Peter. 1989. *Origins of the Popular Style: The Antecedents of Twentieth-Century Popular Music*. Oxford: Clarendon Press.

5486 Walser, Robert. 1992. Eruptions: Heavy Metal Appropriations of Classical Virtuosity. *Popular Music* 11(3): 263–308.

5487 Walser, Robert. 1993. Forging Masculinity: Heavy Metal Sounds and Images of Gender. In *Sound and Vision: The Music Video Reader*, ed. Simon Frith, Andrew Goodwin and Lawrence Grossberg. London and New York: Routledge. 153–81.

5488 Walser, Robert. 1993. Out of Notes: Signification, Interpretation, and the Problem of Miles Davis. *Musical Quarterly* 77(2): 343–65.

5489 Walser, Robert. 1993. *Running with the Devil: Power, Gender and Madness in Heavy Metal Music*. Hanover and London: Wesleyan University Press.

5490 Walser, Robert. 1995. Rhythm, Rhyme, and Rhetoric in the Music of Public

MUSICAL PRACTISES

Enemy. *Ethnomusicology* 39(2): 193–217.

5491 Whiteley, Sheila. 1990. Progressive Rock and Psychedelic Coding in the Work of Jimi Hendrix. *Popular Music* 9(1): 37–60.

5492 Whiteley, Sheila. 1992. *The Space Between the Notes: Rock and the Counter-Culture*. London: Routledge.

5493 Wicke, Peter. 1975. Versuch über populäre Musik. *Beiträge zur Musikwissenschaft* XV(4): 225–41.

5494 Wicke, Peter. 1978. 'Licht in das Dunkel' - Popmusik in der Analyse. *Beiträge zur Musikwissenschaft* XX(1): 3–15.

5495 Wicke, Peter. 1982. Rock Music: A Musical-Aesthetic Study. *Popular Music* 2: 219–43.

5496 Wicke, Peter. 1993. *Vom Umgang mit Popmusik*. Berlin: Volk und Wissen.

5497 Wilder, Alec. 1972. *American Popular Song: The Great Innovators, 1900–1950*. New York: Oxford University Press.

5498 Williams, Martin. 1992. What Kind of Composer Was Thelonious Monk? *Musical Quarterly* 76(3): 433–41.

5499 Winkler, Peter. 1978. Toward a Theory of Popular Harmony. *In Theory Only* 4(2): 3–26.

5500 Winkler, Peter. 1988. Randy Newman's Americana. *Popular Music* 7(1): 1–26.

5501 Winkler, Peter. 1995. In Search of Yaa Amponsah. In *Popular Music: Style and Identity*, ed. Will Straw, et al. Montréal: The Centre for Research on Canadian Cultural Industries and Institutions. 313–23.

5502 Worbs, Hans Christoph. 1963. *Der Schlager. Bestandsaufnahme, Analyse, Dokumentation*. Bremen: Schünemann.

5503 Zak, Vladimir. 1979. *O melodike masovoy repi, Opit analyza*. Moskva: Sovjetskij kompositor.

Harmony

5504 Abbott, Lynn. 1992. 'Play That Barbershop Chord': A Case for the African-American Origin of Barbershop Harmony. *American Music* 10(3): 289–325.

5505 Baptista, Todd R. 1996. *Group Harmony: Behind the Rhythm and the Blues*. New Bedford, MA: TRB Enterprises.

5506 Baresel, Alfred. 1963. *Jazz-Harmonielehre*. Trossingen: Hohner.

5507 Björnberg, Alf. 1984. 'There's Something Going On' - om eolisk harmoni i nutida rockmusik. In *Tvärspel: 31 artiklar om musik. Festskrift till Jan Ling*. Göteborg: Skrifter från Musikvetenskapliga institutionen, 9. 371–86.

5508 Block, Steven. 1990. Pitch-Class Transformation in Free Jazz. *Music Theory Spectrum* 12(2): 181–202.

5509 Block, Steven. 1993. Organized Sound: Pitch-Class Relations in the Music of Ornette Coleman. *Annual Review of Jazz Studies* 6: 229–52.

5510 Bobbitt, R. 1976. *Harmonic Techniques in the Rock Idiom: The Theory and Practice of Rock Harmony*. Belmont, CA: Wadsworth.

5511 Bohländer, Carlo. 1961. *Harmonielehre*. Mainz: Schott.

5512 Bohländer, Carlo. 1979. *Akkorde und Akkordverbindungen der populären Musik. Kurze Anleitung zum Harmonisieren und Liedermachen*. Mainz: Schott.

5513 Brown, Charles T. 1992. (1983) *The Art of Rock and Roll*. Englewood Cliffs, NJ: Prentice-Hall.

5514 Burbat, Wolfgang. 1988. *Die Harmonik des Jazz*. Kassel: dtv/Bärenreiter.

5515 Burns, Gary. 1987. A Typology of 'Hooks' in Popular Music. *Popular Music* 6: 1–20.

5516 Demsey, D. 1991. Chromatic Third Relations in the Music of John Coltrane. *Annual Review of Jazz Studies* 5: 145–80.

5517 Fikentscher, Kai. 1995. The Decline of Functional Harmony in Popular Dance Music. In *Popular Music Perspectives III*, ed. Peter Wicke. Berlin: Zyankrise. 420–23.

5518 Forte, Allen. 1995. *The American Popular Ballad of the Golden Era, 1924–1950*. Princeton, NJ: Princeton University Press.

5519 Hawkins, Stan. 1992. Prince: Harmonic Analysis of 'Anna Stesia'. *Popular Music* 11(3): 325–35.

5520 Haywood, Mark. 1991. The Harmonic Role of Melody in Vertical and Horizontal Jazz. *Annual Review of Jazz Studies* 5: 1–35.

5521 Kaplan, Max, ed. 1993. *Barbershopping: Musical and Social Harmony*. London: Associated University Presses.

5522 Kramarz, Volkmar. 1983. *Harmonieanalyse der Rockmusik: Von Folk und Blues zu Rock und New Wave*. Mainz: Schott.

5523 Liebmann, David. 1991. *A Chromatic Approach to Jazz Harmony and Melody*. Rottenburg: Advance Music.

5524 Manuel, Peter. 1989. *Modal Harmony in Andalusian, Eastern European and Turkish Syncretic Musics*. New York: International Council for Traditional Music.

5525 Markewich, Reese. 1967. *Inside Outside: Substitute Harmony in Modern Jazz and Pop Music*. Riverdale, NY: The author.

5526 McClary, Susan. 1991. Living to Tell: Madonna's Resurrection of the Fleshly. In *Feminine Endings: Music, Gender, and Sexuality*. Minneapolis, MN: University of Minnesota Press. 148–66.

5527 Middleton, Richard. 1983. 'Play It Again Sam': Some Notes on the Productivity of Repetition in Popular Music. *Popular Music* 3: 235–70.

5528 Miller, Ron. 1992. *Modal Jazz Composition and Harmony*. Rottenburg: Advance Music.

5529 Moore, Allan F. 1992. Patterns of Harmony. *Popular Music* 11(1): 73–106.

5530 Moore, Allan F. 1993. *Rock: The Primary Text*. Buckingham: Open University Press.

5531 Moore, Allan F. 1995. The So-Called 'Flattened Seventh' in Rock. *Popular Music* 14(2): 185–201.

5532 Pressing, Jeff. 1982. Pitch-Class Set Structures in Contemporary Jazz. *Jazzforschung/Jazz Research* 14: 18–32.

5533 Steedman, Mark. 1984. A Generative Grammar for Jazz Chord Sequences. *Music Perception* 2(1): 52–77.

5534 Wilder, Alec. 1972. *American Popular Song: The Great Innovators, 1900–1950*. New York: Oxford University Press.

5535 Winkler, Peter. 1978. Toward a Theory of Popular Harmony. *In Theory Only* 4(2): 3–26.

5536 Winkler, Peter. 1983. *The Harmonic Language of Rock*. New York: Music Department, SUNY.

Melody

5537 Baily, John. 1983. A System of Modes Used in the Urban Music of Afghanistan. *Ethnomusicology* 27(1): 1–39.

MUSICAL PRACTISES

5538 Bradby, Barbara and Torode, Brian.
1984. Pity Peggy Sue. *Popular Music* 4:
183–206.

5539 Brothers, Thomas. 1994. Solo and Cycle
in Afro-American Jazz. *Musical
Quarterly* 78(3): 479–509.

5540 Brown, Charles T. 1992. (1983) *The Art
of Rock and Roll*. Englewood Cliffs, NJ:
Prentice-Hall.

5541 Burns, Gary. 1987. A Typology of
'Hooks' in Popular Music. *Popular
Music* 6: 1–20.

5542 Di Pisa, G. Alessandro. 1992. Riff:
tattica e modelli. In *Dal blues al liscio:
Studi sull'esperienza musicale comune*, ed.
Gino Stefani. Verona: Ianua. 50–72.

5543 Everett, Walter. 1985. Text-Painting in
the Foreground and Middleground of
Paul McCartney's Beatle Song 'She's
Leaving Home': A Musical Study of
Psychological Conflict. *In Theory Only* 9:
5–13.

5544 Everett, Walter. 1986. Fantastic
Remembrance in John Lennon's
'Strawberry Fields Forever' and 'Julia'.
Musical Quarterly 72(3): 360–91.

5545 Fabbri, Franco. 1980. Abbiamo un riff.
Laboratorio musica II(14/15): 48–50.

5546 Fabbri, Franco. 1995. Abbiamo un riff, o
due. In *Annali Istituto Gramsci Emilia-
Romagna 2/1995, dossier: Rock Steady/
Rock Study: sulle culture del rock . . .*, ed.
Franco Minganti. Bologna: Istituto
Gramsci Emilia-Romagna. 209–17.

5547 Ferrari, Franca. 1994. Acchiappa lo
hook: traccia didattica per un lavoro
cooperativo sulla melodia. In
Imparerock? A scuola con la popular music,
ed. Franca Ferrari and Enrico Strobino.
Milano: Ricordi. 52–64.

5548 Forte, Allen. 1993. Secrets of Melody:
Line and Design in the Songs of Cole
Porter. *Musical Quarterly* 77(4): 607–47.

5549 Haywood, Mark. 1991. The Harmonic
Role of Melody in Vertical and
Horizontal Jazz. *Annual Review of Jazz
Studies* 5: 1–35.

5550 Kerschbaumer, Franz. 1995.
Improvisation modale dans la musique
de Miles Davis. *Musurgia* 2(2): 45–52.

5551 Kulenovich, Vuk. 1993. The Lydian
Concept. *Sonus* 14(1): 55–76.

5552 Kwan, Kelina. 1992. Textual and
Melodic Contour in Cantonese Popular
Song. In *Secondo Convegno Europeo di
Analisi Musicale, Vol. I*, ed. Rossana
Dalmonte and Mario Baroni. Trento:
Università di Trento. 179–87.

5553 Liebmann, David. 1991. *A Chromatic
Approach to Jazz Harmony and Melody*.
Rottenburg: Advance Music.

5554 Miani, Guido. 1992. Gesti melodici del
blues. In *Dal blues al liscio: Studi
sull'esperienza musicale comune*, ed. Gino
Stefani. Verona: Ianua. 13–46.

5555 Middleton, Richard. 1983. 'Play It Again
Sam': Some Notes on the Productivity of
Repetition in Popular Music. *Popular
Music* 3: 235–70.

5556 Moore, Allan F. 1993. *Rock: The
Primary Text*. Buckingham: Open
University Press.

5557 Postacchini, Pier Luigi. 1996. La
melodia ossessiva. Intense esperienze
emotive con la musica. In *Analisi e
canzoni*, ed. Rossana Dalmonte. Trento:
Università di Trento. 59–80.

5558 Spitzer, John. 1994. 'Oh Susanna': Oral
Transmission and the Tune
Transformation. *Journal of the American
Musicological Society* XLVII(1): 90–136.

5559 Stefani, Gino. 1985. La melodia: una
prospettiva popolare. *Musica/Realtà* 17:
105–24.

5560 Stefani, Gino. 1987. Melody: A Popular
Perspective. *Popular Music* 6(1): 21–35.

5561 Stefani, Gino and Marconi, Luca. 1992. *La melodia.* Milano: Bompiani.

5562 Stefani, Gino, Luca Marconi and Franca Ferrari. 1990. *Gli intervalli musicali.* Milano: Bompiani.

5563 Tagg, Philip. 1981. The Analysis of Theme Tunes as a Method of Decoding Implicit Ideologies in the Mass Media. In *Mass Communications & Culture,* 5, ed. Gunnar Andrén and Hans Strand. Stockholm: Akademi Litteratur. 90–105.

5564 Van der Merwe, Peter. 1989. *Origins of the Popular Style: The Antecedents of Twentieth-Century Popular Music.* Oxford: Clarendon Press.

5565 Vaughn, Kathryn. 1990. Exploring Emotion in Sub-Structural Aspects of Karelian Lament: Application of Time Series Analysis to Digitized Melody. *Yearbook for Traditional Music* 22: 106–22.

Rhythm

5566 Baresel, Alfred. 1955. *Der Rhythmus in der Jazz- und Tanzmusik.* Trossingen: Hohner.

5567 Bohländer, Carlo. 1979. *Jazz - Geschichte und Rhythmus.* Mainz: Schott.

5568 Burns, Gary. 1987. A Typology of 'Hooks' in Popular Music. *Popular Music* 6: 1–20.

5569 Byrnside, Ronald. 1975. The Formation of a Musical Style: Early Rock. In *Contemporary Music and Music Cultures,* ed. Charles Hamm, Bruno Nettl and Ronald Byrnside. Englewood Cliffs, NJ: Prentice-Hall. 159–92.

5570 Chernoff, John M. 1979. *African Rhythm and African Sensibility: Aesthetics and Social Action in African Musical Idioms.* Chicago: University of Chicago Press.

5571 Durgnat, R. 1971. Rock, Rhythm and Dance. *British Journal of Aesthetics* 11: 28–47.

5572 Graham, James D. 1971. Rhythms in Rock Music. *Popular Music & Society* 1(1): 33–43.

5573 Jaedtke, Wolfgang. 1995. Zur Bedeutung afrikanischer Rhythmik für den Erfolg von Jazz, Rock- und Popmusik in der abendländischen Kultur. *Acta Musicologica* LXVII: 20–38.

5574 Keil, Charles. 1994. Motion and Feeling Through Music. In *Music Grooves,* ed. Steven Feld and Charles Keil. Chicago: University of Chicago Press. 53–76. (First published in *Journal of Aesthetics and Art Criticism* 24 (1966): 337–49.)

5575 Man, Henrik de. 1978. (1930) Die Wirkung des Rhythmus im Vollzug industrialisierter Werkarbeit. *Musik und Gesellschaft* 1(2): 41–43.

5576 Martin, Randy. 1986. The Shuffle. *Modern Drummer* 10(2): 38, 41.

5577 Moore, Allan F. 1993. *Rock: The Primary Text.* Buckingham: Open University Press.

5578 Pérez, Rolando. 1986. *La binarización de los ritmos ternarios africanos en América Latina.* La Habana: Casa de las Américas.

5579 Petreni, Francesco. 1993. Elementi di poliritmia in Max Roach. *Nerosubianco* 1(2): 45–53.

5580 Prögler, J.A. 1995. Searching for Swing: Participatory Discrepancies in the Jazz Rhythm Section. *Ethnomusicology* 39(1): 21–54.

5581 Robinson, J. Bradford. 1992. Zur 'Jazz' Rezeption der Weimarer Periode: Eine stilhistorische Jagd nach einer Rhythmus-Floskel. In *Jazz und Komposition,* ed. Wolfram Knauer. Hofheim: Wolke. 11–26.

5582 Roland-Manuel, Claude. 1987. Rhythme cinématographique et musical. *Vibrations* 4: 11–22.

5583 Strobino, Enrico. 1994. Un metro e i suoi dialetti: il 4/4. In *Imparerock? A scuola con la popular music*, ed. Franca Ferrari and Enrico Strobino. Milano: Ricordi. 32–51.

5584 Walser, Robert. 1995. Rhythm, Rhyme and Rhetoric in the Music of Public Enemy. *Ethnomusicology* 39(2): 193–217.

5585 Wilson, Olly. 1974. The Significance of the Relationship Between Afro-American and West African Music. *The Black Perspective in Music* 2: 3–22.

Timbre

5586 Barthes, Roland. 1990. The Grain of the Voice. In *On Record: Rock, Pop and the Written Word*, ed. Simon Frith and Andrew Goodwin. London: Routledge. 293–300.

5587 Brackett, David. 1995. *Interpreting Popular Music*. Cambridge: Cambridge University Press.

5588 Moore, Allan F. 1992. The Texture of Rock. In *Secondo Convegno Europeo di Analisi Musicale, Vol. I*, ed. Rossana Dalmonte and Mario Baroni. Trento: Università di Trento. 341–44.

5589 Shepherd, John. 1991. Music and Male Hegemony. In *Music as Social Text*. Cambridge: Polity. 152–73.

5590 Tamm, Eric. 1989. *Brian Eno: His Music and the Vertical Color of Sound*. Boston and London: Faber & Faber.

MUSICAL INSTRUMENTS

Instruments (Various)

5591 Acosta, Leonardo. 1983. *Del Tambor al Sintetizador*. La Habana: Editorial Letras Cubanas.

5592 Bacon, Tony, ed. 1981. *Rock Hardware: The Instruments and Technology of Rock*. Poole: Blandford Press.

5593 Beck, John H., ed. 1994. *Encyclopedia of Percussion Instruments*. New York: Garland.

5594 Blades, James. 1984. *Percussion Instruments and Their History*, 3rd edition. London: Faber.

5595 Brincard, M.T., ed. 1989. *Sounding Forms: African Musical Instruments*. New York: American Federation of Arts.

5596 Chester, Galina and Jegede, Tunde. 1996. *The Silenced Voice: Hidden Music of the Kora*. London: Diabaté Kora Arts.

5597 Evans, David. 1970. Afro-American One-Stringed Instruments. *Western Folklore* 29(4): 229–45.

5598 Field, Kim. 1993. *Harmonicas, Harps, and Heavy Breathers: The Evolution of the People's Instrument*. New York: Fireside Books/Simon & Schuster.

5599 Geller, Janna M. and Geller, Mallory. 1993. *Exploring Folk Harp*. Pacific, MT: Mel Bay Publications.

5600 Glaser, Matt and Grappelli, Stephane. 1981. *Jazz Violin*. New York: Oak Publications.

5601 Groce, Nancy. 1983. *The Hammered Dulcimer in America*. Washington, DC: Smithsonian Institution Press.

5602 Hennion, Antoine, ed. 1985. A la recherche de l'instrument. *Vibrations* 2 (special issue).

5603 Jones, A.M. 1971. *Africa and Indonesia: The Evidence of the Xylophone and Other Musical and Cultural Factors*. Leiden: E.J. Brill.

5604 Jones, Trevor A. 1967. The Dijeridu: Some Comparisons of Its Typology and Musical Functions with Similar Instruments Throughout the World. *Studies in Music* 1: 22–25.

5605 Kirby, Percival R. 1968. *The Musical Instruments of the Native Races of South*

Africa. Johannesburg: Witwatersrand University Press.

5606 *L'Instrument de musique populaire: usages et symboles*. 1980. Paris: Ed. de la Réunion des Musées de France.

5607 Locke, David. 1990. *Drum Damba: Talking Drum Lessons*. Crown Point, IN: White Cliffs Media Co.

5608 Morales, H. 1954. *Latin American Rhythm Instruments*, 2nd edition. New York.

5609 Murphy, Dennis. 1972. The Americanization of Three African Musical Instruments. *African Music* 5(2): 105–11.

5610 Oliveira, Ernest Veija de. 1982. *Instrumentos musicais populares portugueses*. Lisbon: Fundaçâo Calousta Gulbenkian.

5611 Oliver, Paul. 1988. Ethnomusicological Approaches to Musical Instruments. *Popular Music* 7(2): 216–18.

5612 Ortiz, Fernando. 1952. *Los instrumentos de la música afro-cubana*. 5 vols. La Habana: Ministerio de Educación.

5613 Schellberg, Dirk. 1993. *Didgeridoo: Ritual Origins and Playing Techniques*. Diever: Binkey Kok.

5614 Sulsbrück, Birger. 1991. *Latin-American Percussion. Rhythmen und Rhythmusinstrumente aus Kuba und Brasilien*. Rottenburg: Advance Music.

5615 Tosi, E. 1990. *La kora e il sax: Forme e protagonisti della musica africana moderna*. Bologna: E.M.I.

5616 Yacoub, Gabriel. 1986. *Les Instruments de musique populaire et leurs anecdotes*. Paris: MA.

Mechanical Instruments

5617 Bowers, Q. David. 1966. *Put Another Nickel In: A History of Coin Operated*

Pianos and Orchestrions. New York: Vestal.

5618 Enders, Bernd. 1987. Von Drehorgeln, Spieldosen und musikalischen Kunstmaschinen oder: Mechanische Musikautomaten und ihre Musik im 19. Jahrhundert. In *Ich will aber gerade vom Leben singen . . . Über populäre Musik vom ausgehenden 19. Jahrhundert bis zum Ende der Weimarer Republik*, ed. Sabine Schutte. Reinbek bei Hamburg: Rowohlt. 85–114.

5619 Ord-Hume, Arthur W.J.G. 1970. *Player-Piano: The History of the Mechanical Piano*. New York: A.S. Barnes.

5620 Roehl, Harvey. 1972. *Player Piano Treasury: The Scrapbook History of the Mechanical Piano in America*. New York: Vestal.

Synthesizers and Sequencers

5621 Crombie, David. 1982. *The Complete Synthesizer: A Comprehensive Guide*. London: Omnibus.

5622 Crombie, David. 1984. *The Synthesiser and Electronic Keyboard Handbook*. London: Dorling Kindersley.

5623 Darter, Tom, ed. 1985. *The Whole Synthesizer Catalogue*. Milwaukee, WI: Leonard.

5624 Friedman, Dean. 1986. *Synthesizer Basics*. New York: Amsco.

5625 Friedman, Dean. 1987. *The Complete Guide to Synthesizers, Sequencers and Drum Machines*. New York: Amsco.

5626 Howe, J. and Hubert, S. 1975. *Electronic Music Synthesis*. New York: Norton.

5627 Leyman, Johannes. 1986. *Synthesizer: En bok om elektroniska musikinstrument*. Stockholm: Akademiförlaget.

5628 Myers, David. 1989. A 'Personal' System for Electronic Music. *Re Records Quarterly* 2(3): 5–8.

5629 Norman, Michael and Dickey, Ben. 1984. *The Complete Synthesiser Handbook*. London: Zomba Books.

5630 Penfold, L.A. 1988. *Synthesizers for Musicians*. Edenbridge: PC Publishing.

5631 Pressing, Jeff. 1992. *Synthesizer Performance and Real-Time Techniques*. Oxford: Oxford University Press.

5632 Yelton, Gary. 1986. *The Rock Synthesizer Manual: A Revised Guide for the Electronic Musician*. Woodstock, GA: Rock Tech Publications.

Accordion

5633 Billard, François and Roussin, Didier. 1991. *Histoires de l'accordéon*. Castelnau-le-Lez: Climats.

5634 Helistö, Paavo. 1989. Matti Rantanen, Apostle of the Finnish Accordion. *Finnish Music Quarterly* 89(2): 32–35.

5635 Kolehmainen, Ilkka. 1989. The Accordion in Finnish Folk Music. *Finnish Music Quarterly* 89(2): 29–31.

5636 Lyon, George W. 1980. The Accordion in Cajun, Zydeco and Norteno Music. *Sing Out!* 28(4): 14–18.

5637 Wagner, Christoph. 1993. *Das Akkordeon: Eine wilde Karriere*. Berlin: Transit.

Banjo

5638 Epstein, Dena J. 1975. The Folk Banjo: A Documentary History. *Ethnomusicology* 19(3) (September): 347–71.

5639 Heier, Uli and Lotz, Rainer E., eds. 1993. *The Banjo on Record: A Bio-Discography*. Westport, CT: Greenwood Press.

5640 Kubik, Gerhard. 1989. The Southern African Periphery: Banjo Traditions in Zambia and Malawi. *The World of Music* 31(3): 3–29.

5641 Linn, Karen. 1991. *That Half-Barbaric Twang: The Banjo in American Popular Culture*. Urbana, IL: University of Illinois Press.

5642 Shrubsall, Wayne. 1987. Banjo as Icon. *Journal of Popular Culture* 20(4): 31–60.

5643 Trischka, Tony and Wernick, Pete. 1988. *Masters of the 5-String Banjo: In Their Own Words and Music*. New York: Oak Publications.

5644 Winans, Robert B. and Kaufman, Elias J. 1994. Minstrel and Classic Banjo: American and English Connections. *American Music* 12(1): 1–30.

Drums

5645 Akpabot, Samuel. 1971. Standard Drum Patterns in Nigeria. *African Music* 5(1): 37–39.

5646 Breithaupt, Robert B. 1995. The Drum Set: A History. In *Encyclopedia of Percussion*, ed. John H. Beck. New York: Garland. 173–85.

5647 Chernoff, John M. 1985. The Artistic Challenge of African Music: Thoughts on the Absence of Drum Orchestras in Black American Music. *Black Music Research Journal* 5: 1–20.

5648 Cobbson, Felix. 1982. African Drumming. In *Pop, Rock and Ethnic Music in Schools*, ed. Graham Vulliamy and Edward Lee. London: Cambridge University Press. 171–86.

5649 Coplan, David. 1991. Notes on New and Old World African Drumming. *African Music* 7(1): 105–109.

5650 Cornelius, Steven. 1991. Drumming for the Orishas: Reconstruction of Tradition in New York City. In *Essays on Cuban Music: North American and Cuban*

Perspectives, ed. Peter Manuel. Lanham, MD: University Press of America. 136–56.

5651 Erskine, Peter and Mattingly, Rick. 1986. Focus on Hi-Hat. *Modern Drummer* 10(6): 38–41.

5652 Fampou, François. 1986. *Ku sa: introduction à la percussion africaine.* Paris: L'Harmattan.

5653 Fish, Scott K. 1982. The History of Rock Drumming: The Blues Influence. *Modern Drummer* 6(4): 18–21, 84–91.

5654 Fish, Scott K. 1982. The History of Rock Drumming: The Country Influence. *Modern Drummer* 6(5): 16–19, 62–65.

5655 Fish, Scott K. 1982. The History of Rock Drumming: The Sixties. *Modern Drummer* 6(6): 18–21, 88–93.

5656 Fish, Scott K. 1982. The History of Rock Drumming: The Sixties Continued. *Modern Drummer* 6(7): 20–23, 96–100.

5657 Fish, Scott K. 1982. The History of Rock Drumming: The Final Chapter. *Modern Drummer* 6(8): 16–19, 70–75.

5658 The Great Jazz Drummers: Part 1. 1980. *Modern Drummer* 4(3): 16–20, 56.

5659 The Great Jazz Drummers: Part 2. 1980. *Modern Drummer* 4(4): 16–19, 51–55, 77.

5660 The Great Jazz Drummers: Part 3. 1980. *Modern Drummer* 4(5): 22–25, 79–80.

5661 The Great Jazz Drummers: Part 4. 1980. *Modern Drummer* 4(6): 20–23, 65, 68, 74.

5662 Hart, Mickey. 1990. *Drumming at the Edge of Magic: A Journey into the Spirit of Percussion.* New York: HarperCollins.

5663 Hart, Mickey, Frederic Lieberman and B.A. Sonneborn. 1991. *Planet Drum: A Celebration of Percussion and Rhythm.* New York: HarperCollins.

5664 Herskovits, Melville J. 1944. Drums and Drummers in Afro-Brazilian Cult Life. *Musical Quarterly* 30: 477–92.

5665 Johnson, Hafiz Shabazz Farel and Chernoff, John M. 1991. Basic Conga Drum Rhythms in African-American Musical Styles. *Black Music Research Journal* 11(1): 55–73.

5666 Jones, A.M. 1934. African Drumming. *Bantu Studies* 8: 1–16.

5667 Jones, A.M. 1957. Drums Down the Centuries. *African Music Society* 14(4): 4–10.

5668 King, Anthony. 1976. *Yoruba Sacred Drums.* Ibadan: Caxton Press.

5669 Nketia, J.H. Kwabena. 1968. *Our Drums and Drummers.* Accra: State Publishing Corporation.

5670 Weinberg, Max. 1991. (1984) *The Big Beat: Conversations with Rock's Great Drummers.* New York: Billboard Books.

Fiddle

5671 Alburger, Mary Anne. 1983. *Scottish Fiddlers and Their Music.* London: Gollancz.

5672 Bronner, Simon. 1988. The Anglo-American Fiddle Tradition in New York State. *New York Folklore* 14(3–4): 33–38.

5673 Burman-Hall, Linda C. 1975. Southern American Folk Fiddle Styles. *Ethnomusicology* 19(1): 47–65.

5674 Cauthen, Joyce H. 1989. *With Fiddle and Well Rosined Bow: Old-Time Fiddling in Alabama.* Tuscaloosa, AL: University of Alabama Press.

5675 Cooke, Peter. 1987. *The Fiddle Tradition in the Shetland Isles.* Cambridge: Cambridge University Press.

5676 Guntharp, Matthew G. 1980. *Learning the Fiddler's Ways*. University Park, PA: Pennsylvania State University Press.

5677 Johnson, David. 1984. *Scottish Fiddle Music in the 18th Century: A Musical Collection and Historical Study*. Edinburgh: John Donald.

5678 Orr, Jay. 1989. Fiddle and Fiddlers' Conventions. In *Encyclopedia of Southern Culture, Vol. 3*, ed. Charles Reagan Wilson and William R. Ferris. New York: Doubleday Anchor. 379–80.

5679 Quigley, Colin. 1988. A French-Canadian Fiddler's Musical World View: The Violin is 'Master of the World'. *Selected Reports in Ethnomusicology* 7: 99–121.

5680 Schroedter, Ulrich. 1985. Die Geige in Jazz und Rock. *Beiträge zur Musikwissenschaft* 3–4: 265–84.

5681 Wiggins, Gene. 1979. Popular Music and the Fiddle. *John Edwards Memorial Foundation Quarterly* 15(55) (Fall): 144–52.

5682 Wiggins, Gene. 1986. *Fiddlin' Georgia Crazy: Fiddlin' John Carson, His Real World and the World of His Songs*. Urbana/Chicago: University of Illinois Press.

Guitar

5683 Achard, Ken. 1979. *The History and Development of the American Guitar*. London: Musical New Services.

5684 Anderton, Craig. 1987. *Guitar Gadgets*. New York: Amsco.

5685 Angeletti, Maurizio. 1982. *American Guitar*. Milano: Gammalibri.

5686 Bacon, Tony and Day, Paul. 1991. *The Ultimate Guitar Book*. New York: Alfred A. Knopf.

5687 Bacon, Tony and Day, Paul. 1992. *The Fender Book: A Complete History of Fender Electric Guitars*. Woodford Green: International Music Publications.

5688 Bacon, Tony and Day, Paul. 1993. *The Gibson Les Paul Book: A Complete History of Les Paul Guitars*. San Francisco: G.P.I. Books/Miller Freeman.

5689 Bacon, Tony and Day, Paul. 1994. *The Rickenbacker Book: A Complete History of Rickenbacker Electric Guitars*. London: Balafon Books.

5690 Bacon, Tony and Moorhouse, Barry. 1994. *The Bass Guitar Book: The First Complete Illustrated History of the Bass Guitar*. London: Balafon Books.

5691 Bellow, Alexander. 1970. *The Illustrated History of the Guitar*. Long Island, NY: Franco Columbo Publications.

5692 Berle, Arnie. 1994. *Patterns, Scales and Modes for Jazz Guitar*. New York: Amsco.

5693 Bishop, Ian Courtney. 1979. *The Gibson Guitar: From 1950*. London: Musical New Services.

5694 Bosman, Lance. 1978. *Harmony for Guitar*. London: Musical New Services.

5695 Britt, Stan. 1984. *The Jazz Guitarists*. Poole: Blandford Press.

5696 Brosnac, Donald. 1975. *The Electric Guitar*. San Francisco: Panjandrum Press.

5697 Brosnac, Donald. 1975. *The Steel String Guitar: Its Construction, Origin & Design*. Los Angeles: Panjandrum Press.

5698 Brosnac, Donald. 1983. *Guitar Electronics for Musicians*. New York: Amsco.

5699 Brozman, Bob, et al. 1993. *The History and Artistry of National Resonator Instruments*. Fullerton, CA: Centerstream Publishing.

5700 Chapman, Richard. 1993. *The Complete Guitarist.* New York: Dorling Kindersley.

5701 Denyer, Ralph. 1992. *The Guitar Handbook,* revised edition. New York: Alfred A. Knopf. First published New York: Alfred A. Knopf, 1982.

5702 Duarte, John W. 1965. *The Guitarist's ABC of Music: Rudiments for Students.* Borough Green: Novello & Company.

5703 Duarte, John W. 1980. *Melody and Harmony for the Guitarist.* London: Universal Editions.

5704 Duchossoir, André R. 1983. *Guitar Identification: Fender, Gibson, Martin.* Paris: Mediapresse.

5705 Erlewine, Dan. 1994. *The Guitar Player Repair Guide: How to Set Up, Maintain, and Repair Electrics and Acoustics,* revised edition. Cupertino, CA: Miller Freeman. First published Cupertino: Miller Freeman, 1990.

5706 Evans, Tom and Evans, Mary Anne. 1977. *Guitars: Music, History, Construction and Players from the Renaissance to Rock.* New York: Paddington Press.

5707 George, David. 1982. *The Flamenco Guitar.* Shaftesbury: Musical New Series.

5708 Goodrick, Mick. 1987. *The Advancing Guitarist: Applying Guitar Concepts and Techniques.* Milwaukee, WI: Third Earth Productions.

5709 Greci, Juan. 1973. *La Guitarra Flamenca.* Madrid: Union Musical Española.

5710 Greene, Ted. 1971. *Chord Chemistry.* Melville: Dale Zdenek.

5711 Greene, Ted. 1978. *Jazz Guitar Single Note Soloing, Vols. 1–2.* Melville: Dale Zdenek.

5712 Grossman, Stefan. 1972. *The Book of Guitar Tunings.* New York: Amsco.

5713 Grunfeld, Frederic V. 1969. *The Art and Times of the Guitar: An Illustrated History of Guitars and Guitarists.* London: Macmillan.

5714 Hill, Thomas A. 1973. *The Guitar: An Introduction to the Instrument.* New York: Franklin Watts.

5715 Hood, Mantle. 1983. Musical Ornamentation as History: The Hawaiian Steel Guitar. *Yearbook for Traditional Music* 15: 141–48.

5716 Jansson, Erik V., ed. 1983. *Function, Construction and Quality of the Guitar.* Stockholm: Royal Swedish Academy of Music.

5717 Kaiser, Rolf. 1987. *Gitarrenlexikon.* Reinbek bei Hamburg: Rowohlt.

5718 Kienzle, Rich. 1985. *Great Guitarists: The Most Influential Players in Jazz, Country, Blues and Rock.* New York: Facts on File.

5719 Kozinn, Allan, et al. 1984. *The Guitar: The History, the Music, the Players.* Bromley, Kent: Columbus.

5720 Leavitt, William G. 1966. *A Modern Method for Guitar, Vols. 1–3.* Boston, MA: Berklee Press.

5721 Longworth, Mike. 1975. *Martin Guitars.* Cedar Knolls, NJ: Colonial Press Division.

5722 Low, John. 1982. A History of Kenyan Guitar Music: 1945–1980. *African Music* 6(2): 17–36.

5723 Mongan, Norman. 1983. *The History of the Guitar in Jazz.* New York: Oak Publications.

5724 Montanaro, Bruno. 1983. *Les guitares hispano-américaines.* Aix-en-Provence: Edisud.

MUSICAL PRACTISES

5725 Nicholson, Geoff. 1991. *Big Noises: Rock Guitar in the 1990s*. London: Quartet.

5726 Picart, Hervé and Gassian, Claude. 1983. *Guitar Heroes*. Paris: Grancher.

5727 Sallis, James. 1982. *The Guitar Players: One Instrument and Its Masters in American Music*. New York: Quill.

5728 Schneider, John. 1985. *The Contemporary Guitar*. Berkeley, CA: University of California Press.

5729 Schwartz, Jeff. 1993. Writing Jimi: Rock Guitar Pedagogy as Postmodern Folkloric Practice. *Popular Music* 12(3): 281–88.

5730 Sievert, Jon. 1978. Les Paul. In *The Guitar Player Book*, ed. Jim Ferguson. New York: Grove. 184–90.

5731 Siminoff, Roger H. 1986. *Constructing a Solid-Body Guitar*. Milwaukee, WI: Hal Leonard.

5732 Sloane, Irving. 1973. *Guitar Repair: A Manual of Repair for Guitars and Fretted Instruments*. New York: E.P. Dutton.

5733 Smith, Richard. 1987. *Rickenbacker*. Fullerton, CA: Centerstream Publishing.

5734 Summerfield, Maurice J. 1978. *The Jazz Guitar: Its Evolution and Its Players*. Milwaukee, WI: Hal Leonard.

5735 Tedesco, Tommy. 1981. *For Guitar Players Only: Short Cuts in Technique, Sight Reading and Studio Playing*. Melville: Dale Zdenek.

5736 Tobler, John and Grundy, Stuart. 1983. *The Guitar Greats*. London: BBC.

5737 Trynka, Paul, ed. 1993. *The Electric Guitar*. London: Virgin.

5738 Wheeler, Tom. 1978. *The Guitar Book: A Handbook for Electric and Acoustic Guitarists*, revised edition. New York: Harper & Row. First published New York: Harper & Row, 1974.

5739 Wheeler, Tom. 1982. *American Guitars: An Illustrated History*. London: Harper & Row.

5740 Wheeler, Tom, ed. 1987. *Guitar Player: 20th Anniversary* 21(1) (January).

5741 Winston, Winnie and Keith, Bill. 1979. *Pedal Steel Guitar*. New York: Oak Publications.

Lute

5742 Alvey, R. Gerald. 1984. *Dulcimer Maker: The Craft of Homer Ledford*. Louisville, KY: University Press of Kentucky.

5743 Baily, John. 1988. Amin-e Diwaneh: The Musician as Madman. *Popular Music* 7(2): 133–46.

5744 Murphy, John. 1991. The Charanga in New York and the Persistence of the Tipico Style. In *Essays on Cuban Music: North American and Cuban Perspectives*, ed. Peter Manuel. Lanham, MD: University Press of America. 115–35.

5745 Tosi, E. 1990. *La kora e il sax: forme e protagonisti della musica africana moderna*. Bologna: E.M.I.

Organ

5746 Foort, Reginald. 1970. *The Cinema Organ*, 2nd edition. New York: Vestal.

5747 Palm, Johann. 1982. *Es war einmal ein Kölner Husar: Die Lebensgeschichte des 'Orgel-Palm'*. Köln: Bachen.

5748 Whitworth, Reginald. 1932. *The Cinema and Theater Organ*. London: Musical Opinion.

Piano

5749 Kriss, Eric. 1973. *Six Blues-Roots Pianists: A Thorough Guide to Early Blues Piano Styles*. New York: Oak Publications.

5750 Kriss, Eric. 1974. *Barrelhouse and Boogie Piano*. New York: Oak Publications.

5751 Lyons, Len. 1983. *The Great Jazz Pianists Speaking of Their Lives and Music*. New York: Quill.

5752 Newberger, Eli H. 1976. Archetypes and Antecedents of Piano Blues and Boogie-Woogie Style. *Journal of Jazz Studies* 4(1): 84–109.

5753 Newberger, Eli H. 1976. The Transition from Ragtime to Improvised Piano Style. *Journal of Jazz Studies* 3(2): 3–18.

5754 Newberger, Eli H. 1977. The Development of New Orleans and Stride Piano Styles. *Journal of Jazz Studies* 4(2): 43–71.

5755 Taylor, Billy. 1983. *Jazz Piano: A Jazz History*. Dubuque, IA: W.C. Brown & Co. Publishers.

5756 Unterbrink, Mary. 1983. *Jazz Women at the Keyboard*. Jefferson, NC: McFarland.

5757 Waite, Brian. 1986. *Modern Jazz Piano: A Study in Harmony and Improvisation*. Tunbridge Wells: Spellmount.

5758 Wildman, Joan M. 1979. The Function of the Left Hand in the Evolution of Jazz Piano. *Journal of Jazz Studies* 5(2): 23–39.

Trumpet

5759 Johnson, Keith. 1981. *The Art of Trumpet Playing*. Ames, IA: Iowa State University Press.

5760 McCarthy, Albert. 1967. (1945) *The Trumpet in Jazz*. London: Dent.

PERSONNEL

Disk Jockey

5761 Hadley, Daniel J. 1993. 'Ride the Rhythm': Two Approaches to DJ Practice. *Journal of Popular Music Studies* 5: 58–67.

5762 Langlois, Tony. 1992. Can You Feel It? DJs and House Music Culture in the UK. *Popular Music* 11(2).

5763 Shannon, Doug. 1985. *Off the Record: Everything Related to Playing Recorded Dance Music in the Nightclub Industry*. Cleveland, OH: Pacesetting Publishing House.

Engineer

5764 Kealy, Edward R. 1979. From Craft to Art: The Case of Sound Mixers and Popular Music. *Sociology of Work and Occupation* 6: 3–29.

5765 Porcello, Thomas. 1991. The Ethics of Digital Audio Sampling: Engineers' Discourse. *Popular Music* 10(1): 69–84.

5766 Schlemm, W. 1982. On the Position of the Tonmeister. In *The Phonogram in Cultural Communication*, ed. Kurt Blaukopf. Wien: Springer-Verlag. 151–64.

Musician

5767 Becker, Howard. 1972. The Culture and Career of the Dance Musician. In *American Music: From Storyville to Woodstock*, ed. Charles Nanry. New Brunswick, NJ: Transaction. 65–98.

5768 Becker, Howard. 1972. The Professional Jazz Musician and His Audience. In *The Sounds of Social Change: Studies in Popular Culture*, ed. R. Serge Denisoff and Richard A. Peterson. Chicago: Rand McNally & Co. 248–60. (First published in *American Journal of Sociology* 57 (1951): 136–44.)

5769 Bennett, H. Stith. 1980. *On Becoming a Rock Musician*. Amherst, MA: University of Massachusetts Press.

5770 Breen, Marcus. 1986. The Bands and the Media. *Arena* 74: 12–16.

5771 Coffman, James T. 1972. 'So You Want to Be a Rock & Roll Star!': Role Conflict and the Rock Musician. In *The Sounds of*

Social Change: Studies in Popular Culture, ed. R. Serge Denisoff and Richard A. Peterson. Chicago: Rand McNally & Co. 261–73.

5772 Faulkner, Robert R. 1971. *Hollywood Studio Musicians: Their Work and Careers in the Recording Industry.* New York: Aldine-Atherton.

5773 Faulkner, Robert R. 1972. Hollywood Studio Musicians: Making It in the Los Angeles Film and Recording Industry. In *American Music: From Storyville to Woodstock,* ed. Charles Nanry. New Brunswick, NJ: Transaction. 200–22.

5774 Fornäs, Johan, Ulf Lindberg and Ove Sernhede. 1988. *Under Rocken: Musikins Roll i Tre Ungar Band.* Stockholm and Lund: Symposium Bokforlag.

5775 Gottfried, Martin. 1985. *In Person: The Great Entertainers.* New York: Abrams.

5776 Hentoff, Nat. 1972. Paying Dues: Changes in the Jazz Life. In *American Music: From Storyville to Woodstock,* ed. Charles Nanry. New Brunswick, NJ: Transaction. 99–114.

5777 Hentoff, Nat. 1978. (1961) *The Jazz Life.* New York: Da Capo Press. First published New York: Dial, 1961.

5778 Hernandez, Prisco. 1993. Décima, Seis, and the Art of the Puertorican Trovador Within the Modern Social Context. *Latin American Music Review* 14(1): 20–51.

5779 Hobsbawm, Eric John. 1989. (1959) *The Jazz Scene.* London: Weidenfeld and Nicolson. Originally published under pseudonym of Francis Newton.

5780 Horowitz, Irving Louis. 1978. Style and Stewardship: Sociological Considerations on the Professionalization of Music. *Journal of Jazz Studies* 5(1): 4–18.

5781 Jost, Ekkehard. 1981. *Jazzmusiker: Materialien zur Soziologie der afro-amerikanischen Musik.* Berlin: Ullstein.

5782 Kapustin, Yuri. 1976. *Muzykant i publika.* Leningrad: Znanie.

5783 Kapustin, Yuri. 1985. *Muzykant-ispolnitel' i publika: Sotsiologicheskie problemy sovremennoi kontsertoi zhizni.* Leningrad: Muzyka.

5784 Knauer, Wolfram. 1993. 'Musicianer' oder: Der Jazzmusiker als Musikant. Anmerkungen zum Verhältnis von Jazz und Folklore. In *Jazz in Europa,* ed. Wolfram Knauer. Hofheim: Wolke. 185–200.

5785 Köhler, Peter and Schacht, Konrad. 1983. *Die Jazzmusiker: Zur Soziologie einer kreativen Randgruppe.* Freiburg: Peter Weininger, Roter Punkt Verlag.

5786 Lees, Gene. 1989. *Meet Me at Jim and Andy's: Jazz Musicians and Their World.* Oxford: Oxford University Press.

5787 Lewis, George H. 1985. Beyond the Reef: Role Conflict and the Professional Musician in Hawaii. *Popular Music* 5: 189–98.

5788 Ludman, Kim. 1987. *Make a Living as a Rock Musician.* London: Kogan.

5789 Lyons, Len. 1983. *The Great Jazz Pianists Speaking of Their Lives and Music.* New York: Quill.

5790 Nketia, J.H. Kwabena. 1979. Performing Musicians in a Changing Society. *The World of Music* 21(2): 65–70.

5791 Palm, Johann. 1982. *Es war einmal ein Kölner Husar: die Lebensgeschichte des 'Orgel-Palm'.* Köln: Bachen.

5792 Preston, Katherine K. 1983. Popular Music in the 'Gilded Age': Musicians' Gigs in Late 19th Century Washington DC. *Popular Music* 3: 25–50.

5793 Quigley, Colin. 1988. A French-Canadian Fiddler's Musical World View: The Violin is 'Master of the World'. *Selected Reports in Ethnomusicology* 7: 99–121.

5794 Reed, Harry A. 1979. The Black Bar in the Making of a Jazz Musician: Bird, Mingus and Stan Hope. *Journal of Jazz Studies* 5(2): 76–90.

5795 Ritzel, Fred and Stroh, Wolfgang Martin. 1985. Deutsche Tanzmusiker: Zu einer Sozialgeschichte der populären Musik in Deutschland. *Jazzforschung* 17: 69–75.

5796 Seltzer, George. 1989. *Music Matters: The Performer and the American Federation of Musicians*. Metuchen and London: Scarecrow Press.

5797 Shiloah, Amnon. 1986. The Traditional Artist in the Limelight of the Modern City. *The World of Music* 28(1): 87–98.

5798 Statelova, Rosemary. 1989. Profesionalizmat v njakoi muzikalni zhanrove za masovo uchastie. Sociologicheski i psihologicheski aspekti na roka. *Muzikalni horizonti* 12–13: 250–59.

5799 Stebbins, Robert A. 1972. A Theory of the Jazz Community. In *American Music: From Storyville to Woodstock*, ed. Charles Nanry. New Brunswick, NJ: Transaction. 115–34.

5800 Stockmann, Erich. 1985. Zum Professionalismus instrumentaler Volksmusikanten. In *Wegzeichen: Studien zur Musikwissenschaft*, ed. Jürgen Mainka and Peter Wicke. Berlin: Verlag Neue Musik. 331–41.

5801 Taylor, Rogan. 1985. *The Death and Resurrection Show*. London: Blond.

Producer

5802 Batten, J. 1956. *Joe Batten's Book*. London: Rockcliff.

5803 Culshaw, J. 1981. *Putting the Record Straight*. New York: Viking.

5804 Eargle, John. 1980. (1976) *Sound Recording*, 2nd edition. New York: Van Nostrand Reinhold.

5805 Gillett, Charlie. 1980. The Producer as Artist. In *The Phonograph and Our Musical Life*, ed. H. Wiley Hitchcock. Brooklyn, NY: Institute for Studies in American Music/CUNY. 51–56.

5806 Martin, George, ed. 1983. *Making Music*. New York: Quill.

5807 Muikku, Jari. 1990. On the Role and Tasks of a Record Producer. *Popular Music & Society* 14(1): 25–33.

5808 Tamm, Eric. 1989. *Brian Eno: His Music and the Vertical Color of Sound*. Boston and London: Faber & Faber.

Songwriter

5809 Bennett, Roy C. 1983. *The Songwriter's Guide to Writing and Selling Hit Songs*. Englewood Cliffs, NJ: Prentice-Hall.

5810 Berger, Robert Alan. 1983. *Songwriting: A Structured Approach*. San Diego, CA: Beer Flat Music.

5811 Boye, Henry. 1970. *How to Make Money by $elling the $ongs You Write*. New York: Fell Inc.

5812 Brahms, Caryl and Sherrin, Ned. 1984. *Song by Song: The Lives and Work of 14 Great Lyric Writers*. Bolton: Ross Anderson.

5813 Cahn, Sammy. 1983. *The Songwriter's Dictionary*. New York: Facts on File.

5814 Carter, Walter. 1988. *The Songwriter's Guide to Collaboration*. Cincinnati: Writer's Digest.

5815 Citron, Stephen. 1985. *Songwriting: A Complete Guide to the Craft*. New York: Morrow.

5816 Davis, Sheila. 1985. *The Craft of Lyric Writing*. Cincinnati: Writer's Digest.

5817 Davis, Sheila. 1988. *Successful Lyric Writing: A Step-by-Step Course & Workbook*. Cincinnati: Writer's Digest.

5818 Etzkorn, K. Peter. 1963. Social Context of Songwriting in the United States. *Ethnomusicology* 7(2): 96–107.

5819 Furia, Philip. 1991. *The Poets of Tin Pan Alley: A History of America's Greatest Lyricists*. New York: Oxford University Press.

5820 Gratton, Virginia L. 1983. *American Women Songwriters: A Biographical Dictionary*. Westport and London: Greenwood Press.

5821 Josefs, Jai. 1989. *Writing Music for Hit Songs*. Cincinnati: Writer's Digest.

5822 Lehman, Engel. 1972. *Words with Music*. New York: Macmillan.

5823 Liggett, Mark and Liggett, Cathy. 1985. *The Complete Handbook of Songwriting: An Insider's Guide to Making It in the Music Industry*. New York: New American Library.

5824 Pollock, Bruce, ed. 1992. *In Their Own Words: Twenty Successful Songwriters Tell How They Write Their Songs*. New York: Collier/Macmillan.

Singer-Songwriter

5825 Ankli, Ruedi and Burri, Peter. 1985. *Cantautore Républic: die italienischen Rockpoetik, ihre Geschichte, ihre Texte*. Basel: Lenos.

5826 Carrera, Alessandro. 1989. I cantautori in Italia e il loro pubblico. *Quaderni di Musica/Realtà* 23: 313–30.

5827 DiMartino, Dave. 1994. *Singer-Songwriters: Pop Music's Performer-Composers, from A to Zevon*. New York: Billboard Books.

5828 Fiori, Umberto. 1989. Tra quaresima e carnevale. Pratiche e strategie della canzone d'autore. *Quaderni di Musica/Realtà* 23: 347–62.

5829 Potter, John. 1994. The Singer, Not the Song: Women Singers as Composer-Poets. *Popular Music* 13(2): 191–99.

5830 Stenzl, Jürg. 1986. La 'canzone d'autore' da Gilles a Yvette Théraulaz. *Musica/Realtà* 20: 12–19.

5831 Swann, Mike. 1989. *How Many Roads? History and Guide of American Singer Songwriters*. Lewes, East Sussex: Book Guild.

5832 Takeda, Seiji. 1989. *New Music no bishintachi*. Tokyo: Asuka-shinsha.

PRACTISES

Improvisation

5833 Aebersold, Jamey. 1979. *A New Approach to Jazz Improvisation*, 5th edition. New Albany, IN: Selbstverlag.

5834 Bailey, Derek. 1991. *Improvisation: Its Nature and Practice in Music*. London: British Library.

5835 Baker, David. 1968–71. *Techniques of Improvisation*. 4 vols. Chicago: Mahler Publications.

5836 Baker, David. 1972. *Advanced Improvisations*. Bloomington, IN: Frangipani Press.

5837 Baker, David. 1983. (1969) *Jazz Improvisation: A Comprehensive Method of Study for All Players*. Rottenburg: Advance Music. First published Chicago: University of Chicago Press, 1969.

5838 Benward, Bruce and Wildman, Joan M. 1984. *Jazz Improvisation in Theory and Practice*. Dubuque, IA: Wm. C. Brown.

5839 Berlin, Edward E. 1977. Ragtime and Improvised Jazz: Another View. *Journal of Jazz Studies* 4(2): 4–10.

5840 Berliner, Paul F. 1994. *Thinking in Jazz: The Infinite Art of Improvisation.* Chicago and London: University of Chicago Press.

5841 Coker, Jerry. 1964. *Improvizing Jazz.* Englewood Cliffs, NJ: Prentice-Hall.

5842 Dean, Roger Thornton. 1989. *Creative Improvisation.* Milton Keynes: Open University Press.

5843 Dean, Roger Thornton. 1992. *New Structures in Jazz and Improvised Music Since 1960.* Buckingham: Open University Press.

5844 Gerber, Alain. 1973. L'improvisation instrumentale. In *Musique et vie quotidienne: Essai de sociologie d'une nouvelle culture,* ed. Paul Beaud and Alfred Willener. Paris: Mame. 153–204.

5845 Gillespie, L.O. 1991. Literacy, Orality, and the Parry-Lord 'Formula': Improvisation and the Afro-American Jazz Tradition. *International Review of the Aesthetics and Sociology of Music* 22(2): 147–64.

5846 Hartman, Charles O. 1991. *Jazz Text: Voice and Improvisation in Poetry, Jazz, and Song.* Princeton, NJ: Princeton University Press.

5847 Hellhund, Herbert. 1990. Konzept und spontaner Prozeß. Zu einigen Strukturprinziplen improvisierter Avantgardemusik. In *Darmstädter Jazzforum 89: Beiträge zur Jazzforschung,* ed. Ekkehard Jost. Hofheim: Wolke. 225–34.

5848 Hodgkinson, Tim. 1984. Sulla libera improvvisazione. *Musica/Realtà* 15: 107–28.

5849 Kerschbaumer, Franz. 1995. Improvisation modale dans la musique de Miles Davis. *Musurgia* 2(2): 45–52.

5850 Kynaston, Trent P. 1978. *Jazz Improvisation.* Englewood Cliffs, NJ: Prentice-Hall.

5851 LaPorta, John. 1966. *A Guide to Improvisation.* Boston, MA: Berklee Press.

5852 Neitzert, Lutz. 1992. Der Komponist, sein Werk und die subversive Kraft des Extempore. Über das problematische Verhältnis der bürgerlichen Musikkultur zu improvisierter Musik. In *Jazz und Komposition,* ed. Wolfram Knauer. Hofheim: Wolke. 37–53.

5853 Newberger, Eli H. 1976. The Transition from Ragtime to Improvised Piano Style. *Journal of Jazz Studies* 3(2): 3–18.

5854 Noglik, Bert. 1990. Improvisierte Musik in der Folge des Free Jazz. Kontinuum - Beliebigkeit - Stilpluralismus. In *Darmstädter Jazzforum 89: Beiträge zur Jazzforschung,* ed. Ekkehard Jost. Hofheim: Wolke. 14–27.

5855 Noglik, Bert. 1992. Komposition und Improvisation - Anmerkungen zu einem spannungsreichen Verhältnis. In *Jazz und Komposition,* ed. Wolfram Knauer. Hofheim: Wolke. 203–20.

5856 Russell, George. 1959. *The Lydian Chromatic Concept of Tonal Organization for Improvisation.* New York: Concept Publishing.

5857 Schomerus, Hilko. 1994. Polyrhythmik, Improvisation und Sprache. In *Populäre Musik und Pädagogik - Grundlagen und Praxismaterialien,* ed. Jürgen Terhag. Oldershausen: Institut für Didaktik der populären Musik. 133–41.

5858 Similä, Jussi. 1983. Suavecito: Verbal Improvisation in Cuban Son Singing. *Suomen antropologi* 4: 244–49.

5859 Sutherland, Roger. 1990. Improvised Music. *Re Records Quarterly* 3(2): 35–48.

5860 Trimillos, Ricardo. 1987. Time-Distance and Melodic Models in Improvisation Among the Tausug of the Southern Philippines. *Yearbook for Traditional Music* 19: 23–36.

5861 Willener, Alfred and Ganty, Alex. 1973. L'improvisation non-instrumentale. Le groupe Faire: exploration, improvisation, construction. In *Musique et vie quotidienne: Essai de sociologie d'une nouvelle culture*, ed. Paul Beaud and Alfred Willener. Paris: Mame. 205–67.

Karaoke

5862 Allison, Anne. 1994. *Nightwork: Sexuality, Pleasure, and Corporate Masculinity in a Tokyo Hostess Club*. Chicago: University of Chicago Press.

5863 Drew, Robert S. 1995. American Karaoke Performers as Amateurs and Professionals. In *Popular Music: Style and Identity*, ed. Will Straw, et al. Montréal: The Centre for Research on Canadian Cultural Industries and Institutions. 77–78.

5864 Fornäs, Johan. 1994. Karaoke: Subjectivity, Play and Interactive Media. *The Nordicom Review of Nordic Research on Media and Communication* 1: 87–103.

5865 Fornäs, Johan. 1995. Listen to Your Voice! Authenticity and Reflexivity in Karaoke, Rock, Rap and Techno Music. In *Popular Music: Style and Identity*, ed. Will Straw, et al. Montréal: The Centre for Research on Canadian Cultural Industries and Institutions. 99–102.

5866 Fujie, Linda. 1989. Popular Music. In *Handbook of Japanese Popular Culture*, ed. Richard Gid Powers and Hidetoshi Kato. Westport, CT: Greenwood Press. 197–220.

5867 Hosokawa, Shuhei. 1995. *Sanba no kuni ni enka wa nagareru*. Tokyo: Chuo Kouronsha, Chukou Shinshou #1263.

5868 Hosokawa, Shuhei. 1995. Singing Not Together: Karaoke in Sao Paolo. In *Popular Music: Style and Identity*, ed. Will Straw, et al. Montréal: The Centre for Research on Canadian Cultural Industries and Institutions. 149–53.

5869 Kelly, William H. 1995. The Adaptability of Karaoke in the United Kingdom. In *Popular Music: Style and Identity*, ed. Will Straw, et al. Montréal: The Centre for Research on Canadian Cultural Industries and Institutions. 177–80.

5870 Kogawa, Tetsuo. 1988. New Trends in Japanese Popular Music. In *The Japanese Trajectory: Modernization and Beyond*, ed. G. McCormack and Y. Sugimoto. Cambridge: Cambridge University Press. 54–66.

5871 Kunihiro, Narumi. 1994. The Electric Geisha. In *The Electric Geisha: Exploring Japan's Popular Culture*, ed. Atsushi Ueda. Tokyo: Kodansha International. 60–67.

5872 Linhart, Sepp. 1988. From Industrial to Postindustrial Society: Changes in Japanese Leisure-Related Values and Behavior. *Journal of Japanese Studies* 14(2): 271–307.

5873 Lum, Casey Man Kong. 1996. *In Search of Voice: Karaoke, Communication and the Construction of Identity*. Mahwah, NJ: Erlbaum.

5874 Macaw, Heather. 1995. A Comparison of the Use and Appeal of Karaoke in Japan and Australia: How Has Karaoke Adapted to the Australian Culture? In *Popular Music: Style and Identity*, ed. Will Straw, et al. Montréal: The Centre for Research on Canadian Cultural Industries and Institutions. 201–203.

5875 Mitsui, Torû. 1995. Karaoke: How the Combination of Technology and Music Evolved. In *Popular Music Perspectives III*, ed. Peter Wicke. Berlin: Zyankrise. 216–23.

5876 Ogawa, Hiroshi. 1990. The Karaoke Way. *Pacific Friend* 18(6): 32.

5877 Ogawa, Hiroshi. 1993. Unstoppable Karaoke. *Pacific Friend*: 17–21.

5878 Ogawa, Hiroshi. 1995. Karaoke in Japan: A Sociological Overview. In *Popular Music: Style and Identity*, ed. Will Straw, et al. Montréal: The Centre for Research on Canadian Cultural Industries and Institutions. 225–27.

5879 Sakurai, Tetsuo. 1993. Karaoke juushichi nen. *Minpaku Tsuushin* 62: 2–7.

5880 Satou, Tsuyoshi, ed. 1993. Jouhouka to taishuu bunka - 'video game' to karaoke. *Gendai no Esprit* 312.

Mbira

5881 Berliner, Paul F. 1979. *The Soul of Mbira*. Berkeley, CA: University of California Press.

5882 Maraire, Dumisani. 1971. *The Mbira Music of Rhodesia*. Seattle, WA: University of Washington Press.

5883 Thompson, Donald. 1975. A New World Mbira: The Caribbean Marimbula. *African Music* 5(4): 140–48.

Performance (Gospel)

5884 Allen, Ray. 1991. *Singing in the Spirit: African-American Sacred Quartets in New York City*. Philadelphia: University of Pennsylvania Press.

5885 Boyer, Horace Clarence. 1979. Contemporary Gospel Music, Part 2: Characteristics and Style. *The Black Perspective in Music* 7(1) (Spring): 22–58.

5886 Feintuch, Burt. 1980. A Noncommercial Black Gospel Group in Context: We Live the Life We Sing About. *Black Music Research Journal* 1: 37–50.

5887 Lornell, Kip. 1988. 'Happy in the Service of the Lord': Afro-American Gospel Music Quartets in Memphis. Urbana, IL: University of Illinois Press.

5888 Seroff, Doug. 1985. On the Battlefield: Gospel Quartets in Jefferson County, Alabama. In *Repercussions: A Celebration of African-American Music*, ed. Geoffrey Haydon and Denis Marks. London: Century. 30–53.

5889 Tallmadge, William H. 1961. Dr. Watts and Mahalia Jackson: The Development, Decline, and Survival of a Folk Style in America. *Ethnomusicology* 5(2): 95–100.

5890 Tallmadge, William H. 1968. The Responsorial and Antiphonal Practice in Gospel Singing. *Ethnomusicology* 12(2): 219–38.

Performance Techniques

5891 Béhague, Gerard H., ed. 1984. *Performance Practice: Ethnomusicological Perspectives*. Westport, CT: Greenwood Press.

5892 Berliner, Paul F. 1994. *Thinking in Jazz: The Infinite Art of Improvisation*. Chicago: University of Chicago Press.

5893 Buckley, David. 1993. David Bowie: Still Pop's Faker? In *The Bowie Companion*, ed. Elizabeth Thomson and David Gutman. London: Macmillan. 3–11.

5894 Davies, Nollene. 1994. The Guitar in Zulu Maskanda Tradition. *The World of Music* 36(2): 118–37.

5895 Guilbault, Jocelyne. 1993. *Zouk: World Music in the West Indies*. Chicago: University of Chicago Press.

5896 Josephson, Nors S. 1992. Bach Meets Liszt: Traditional Formal Structures and Performance Practices in Progressive Rock. *Musical Quarterly* 76(1): 67–92.

5897 Kubik, Gerhard. 1975. *The Kachamba Brothers' Band: A Study of Neo-Traditional Music in Malawi*. Manchester: Manchester University Press.

5898 Lilliestam, Lars. 1996. On Playing by Ear. *Popular Music* 15(2): 195–216.

5899 Metfessel, Milton. 1981. (1926) *Phonophotography in Folk Music: American Negro Songs in New Notation.* Durham, NC: University of North Carolina Press.

5900 Olmstead, Frederick Law. 1976. (1856) Negro Jodling: The Carolina Yell. *The Black Perspective in Music* 4(2): 140–41.

5901 Seeger, Charles. 1954. Singing Style. *Western Folklore* 8(1).

5902 Wicks, Sammie Ann. 1988. A Belated Salute to the 'Old Way' of 'Snaking' the Voice on Its (ca) 345th Birthday. *Popular Music* 8(1): 59–96.

Recording Practises

5903 Borwick, John. 1987. *Sound Recording Practice.* New York: Oxford University Press.

5904 Clarke, Paul. 1983. A 'Magic Science': Rock Music as a Recording Art. *Popular Music* 3: 195–213.

5905 Cutler, Chris. 1985. The Studio as Instrument (2): Whose Future of Music? *Re Records Quarterly* 1(2): 28–30.

5906 Durant, Alan. 1990. A New Day for Music? Digital Technologies in Contemporary Music-Making. In *Culture, Technology and Creativity in the Late Twentieth Century,* ed. Philip Hayward. London: John Libbey & Co. 175–96.

5907 Everard, Chris. 1985. *The Home Recording Handbook.* London: Virgin.

5908 Kealy, Edward R. 1990. From Craft to Art: The Case of Sound Mixers and Popular Music. In *On Record: Rock, Pop and the Written Word,* ed. Simon Frith and Andrew Goodwin. London: Routledge. 207–20. (First published in *Sociology of Work and Occupation* 6 (1979): 3–29.)

5909 Miller, Fred. 1981. *Studio Recording for Musicians.* New York: Amsco.

5910 Moore, Steve. 1985. The Recording Studio as a Musical Instrument. *Re Records Quarterly* 1(2): 32–33.

5911 Moylan, W. 1992. *The Art of Recording: The Creative Resources of Music Production and Audio.* New York: Van Nostrand Reinhold.

5912 Nisbett, Alec. 1987. *The Technique of the Sound-Studio.* London: Focal Press.

5913 Siefert, M. 1995. Image/Music/Voice: Song Dubbing in Hollywood Musicals. *Journal of Communications* 45(1).

5914 Woram, John M. 1982. *The Recording Studio Handbook.* New York: ELAR.

Sampling

5915 Beadle, Jeremy J. 1993. *Will Pop Eat Itself?: Pop Music in the Soundbite Era.* London: Faber & Faber.

5916 Christgau, Robert. 1986. Down by Law. *Village Voice* 31(12) (25 March): 39–40, 42.

5917 Considine, J.D. 1990. Larcenous Art? *Rolling Stone* 580 (14 June): 107–108.

5918 DeCurtis, Anthony. 1986. Who Owns a Sound? *Rolling Stone* 488 (4 December): 13.

5919 Durant, Alan. 1990. A New Day for Music? Digital Technologies in Contemporary Music-Making. In *Culture, Technology and Creativity in the Late Twentieth Century,* ed. Philip Hayward. London: John Libbey & Co. 175–96.

5920 Goodwin, Andrew. 1990. (1988) Sample and Hold: Pop Music in the Digital Age of Reproduction. In *On Record: Rock, Pop and the Written Word,* ed. Simon Frith and Andrew Goodwin. London: Routledge. 258–73. (First published in *Critical Quarterly* 30(3) (1988): 34–49.)

5921 Hartley, Ross. 1993. Beat in the System. In *Rock and Popular Music: Politics, Policies, Institutions,* ed. Tony Bennett, et al. London: Routledge. 210–30.

5922 Jones, Steve. 1992. Technology, Music, and Copyright. In *Rock Formation.* Newbury Park, CA: Sage. 95–118.

5923 Oswald, John. 1990. Taking Sampling 50 Times Beyond the Expected. *Musicworks* 47: 4–10.

5924 Porcello, Thomas. 1991. The Ethics of Digital Audio Sampling: Engineers' Discourse. *Popular Music* 10(1): 69–84.

5925 Ressner, J. 1990. Sampling Amok? *Rolling Stone* 580 (14 June): 103–105.

5926 Rose, Tricia. 1994. Soul Sonic Forces: Technology, Orality, and Black Cultural Practice in Rap Music. In *Black Noise: Rap Music and Black Culture in Contemporary America.* Hanover, NH: Wesleyan University Press. 62–96.

5927 Théberge, Paul. 1993. Technology, Economy and Copyright Reform in Canada. In *Music and Copyright,* ed. Simon Frith. Edinburgh: Edinburgh University Press. 40–66.

Street Music (Busking)

5928 Cohen, David and Greenwood, Ben. 1981. *The Buskers: A History of Street Entertainment.* Newton Abbot and London: David & Charles.

5929 Engelke, Kai, ed. 1984. *Das Straßenmusikbuch; mit vielen Tips, Berichten, Erfahrungen, juristischen Hinweisen.* Hannoversch-Münden: Gauke.

5930 Hill, Donald. 1987. Two Street Musicians: Roy Brown and Daddy Stovepipe. *Cadence* (February): 17–19.

5931 Mayhew, Henry. 1967. *London Labour and the London Poor, Vols. 1–4.* London: Frank Cass. First published London: Griffin, Bohn & Co., 1861–62.

5932 Prato, Paolo. 1984. Music in the Streets: The Example of Washington Square Park in New York City. *Popular Music* 4: 151–63.

5933 Rehin, George S. 1981. Blackface Street Minstrels in Victorian London and Its Resorts: Popular Culture and Its Racial Connotations as Revealed in Polite Opinion. *Journal of Popular Culture* 15(1): 19–38.

5934 Richter, Lukas. 1970. *Die Berliner Gassenhauer. Darstellung, Dokumente, Sammlung.* Leipzig: Deutscher Verlag für Musik.

5935 Richter, Lukas, ed. 1977. *Mutter, der Mann mit dem Koks ist da: Berliner Gassenhauer.* Leipzig: Deutscher Verlag für Musik.

5936 Zucchi, John F. 1992. *The Little Slaves of the Harp: Italian Child Street Musicians in Nineteenth-Century Paris, London and New York.* Montréal: McGill-Queen's University Press.

Two-Tone

5937 Cashmore, E. Ellis. 1987. Shades of Black, Shades of White. In *Popular Music & Communication,* ed. James Lull. Newbury Park, CA: Sage. 245–65.

5938 Hebdige, Dick. 1987. *Cut 'n' Mix: Culture, Identity and Caribbean Music.* London and New York: Comedia/Methuen.

SINGING

Jazz Singer

5939 Büchter-Römer, Ute. 1995. Aspekte des Vocal-Jazz. Untersuchungen zur zeitgenössischen Improvisierten Musik mit der Stimme. In *Popular Music*

Perspectives III, ed. Peter Wicke. Berlin: Zyankrise. 424–28.

5940 Crowther, Bruce. 1986. *The Jazz Singers: From Ragtime to the New Wave.* Poole: Blandford Press.

5941 Federighi, Luciano. 1986. *Cantare il jazz: l'universo vocale afroamericano.* Rome: Laterza.

5942 Friedwald, Will. 1992. (1990) *Jazz Singing: America's Great Voices from Bessie Smith to Bebop and Beyond.* New York: Collier. First published New York: Scribner, 1990.

5943 Gourse, Leslie. 1984. *Louis' Children: American Jazz Singers.* New York: Quill.

5944 Lees, Gene. 1987. *Singers and the Song.* New York: Oxford University Press.

Singing

5945 Abbott, Lynn and Seroff, Doug. 1993. America's Blue Yodel. *Musical Traditions* 11: 2–11.

5946 Busch, Hermann J. 1987. 'Gesangfest' zwischen 1845 und 1871 im Spiegel der Zeitschrift 'Euterpe'. In *Ich will aber gerade vom Leben singen . . . Über populäre Musik vom ausgehenden 19. Jahrhundert bis zum Ende der Weimarer Republik*, ed. Sabine Schutte. Reinbek bei Hamburg: Rowohlt. 60–84.

5947 Gottfried, Martin. 1985. *In Person: The Great Entertainers.* New York: Abrams.

5948 Jewell, Derek. 1980. *The Popular Voice: A Musical Record of the 60s & 70s.* London: Deutsch.

5949 Lomax, Alan. 1968. *Folk Song Style and Culture: A Staff Report on Cantometrics.* New Brunswick, NJ: Transaction.

5950 Lomax, Alan. 1976. *Cantometrics: An Approach to the Anthropology of Music.* Berkeley, CA: University of California Extension Media Center.

5951 Marks, Edward B. 1935. *They All Sang: From Tony Pastor to Rudy Vallee (1890–1930).* New York: Viking.

5952 Mellers, Wilfrid. 1986. *Angels of the Night: Popular Female Singers of Our Time.* Oxford: Blackwell.

5953 Moore, John. 1988. 'The Hieroglyphics of Love': The Torch Singers and Interpretation. *Popular Music* 8(1): 31–58.

5954 Ottenheimer, Harriet. 1979. Catharsis, Communication and Evocation: Alternative View of the Sociopsychological Functions of Blues Singing. *Ethnomusicology* 23(1): 75–86.

5955 Pavletich, Aida. 1983. *Sirens of Song: The Popular Female Vocalist in America.* New York: Da Capo Press.

5956 Pleasants, Henry. 1974. *The Great American Popular Singers.* New York: Simon & Schuster.

5957 Seeger, Charles. 1954. Singing Style. *Western Folklore* 8(1).

5958 Warner, Jay. 1992. *The Billboard Book of American Singing Groups: A History, 1940–1990.* New York: Watson-Guptill.

Voice

5959 Barthes, Roland. 1990. (1977) The Grain of the Voice. In *On Record: Rock, Pop and the Written Word*, ed. Simon Frith and Andrew Goodwin. London: Routledge. 293–300.

5960 Bernhardt, Clyde E.B. and Harris, Sheldon. 1986. *I Remember: Eighty Years of Black Entertainment, Big Bands and the Blues.* Philadelphia: University of Pennsylvania Press.

5961 Brackett, David. 1992. James Brown's 'Superbad' and the Double-Voiced Utterance. *Popular Music* 11(3): 309–24.

5962 Brolinson, Per-Erik and Larsen, Holger. 1981. *. . . and roll: Aspekter på text och*

vokal gestaltning. Stockholm: Esselte
Studium.

5963 Hartman, Charles O. 1991. *Jazz Text:
Voice and Improvisation in Poetry, Jazz,
and Song.* Princeton, NJ: Princeton
University Press.

5964 Hoskyns, Barney. 1991. *From a Whisper
to a Scream: The Great Voices of Popular
Music.* London: Fontana.

5965 Laing, Dave. 1990. (1971) Listen to Me.
In *On Record: Rock, Pop and the Written
Word,* ed. Simon Frith and Andrew
Goodwin. London: Routledge. 326–40.

5966 Lomax, Alan. 1968. *Folk Song Style and
Culture: A Staff Report on Cantometrics.*
New Brunswick, NJ: Transaction.

5967 Lomax, Alan. 1976. *Cantometrics: An
Approach to the Anthropology of Music.*
Berkeley, CA: University of California
Extension Media Center.

5968 Olmstead, Frederick Law. 1976. (1856)
Negro Jodling: The Carolina Yell. *The
Black Perspective in Music* 4(2): 140–41.

5969 Similä, Jussi. 1983. Suavecito: Verbal
Improvisation in Cuban Son Singing.
Suomen antropologi 4: 244–49.

5970 Wicks, Sammie Ann. 1988. A Belated
Salute to the 'Old Way' of 'Snaking' the
Voice on Its (ca) 345th Birthday.
Popular Music 8(1): 59–96.

TECHNOLOGIES

Electronic Technologies

5971 Bacon, Tony, ed. 1981. *Rock Hardware:
The Instruments, Equipment and
Technology of Rock.* London: Quill.

5972 Breithaupt, Robert B. 1995. The Drum
Set: A History. In *Encyclopedia of
Percussion,* ed. John H. Beck. New York:
Garland. 173–85.

5973 Clarke, Paul. 1983. A 'Magic Science':
Rock Music as a Recording Art. *Popular
Music* 3: 195–213.

5974 Crombie, David. 1987. *The Complete
Electronic Percussion Book.* New York:
Amsco.

5975 Cutler, Chris. 1984. Technology,
Politics and Contemporary Music:
Necessity and Choice in Musical Forms.
Popular Music 4: 279–300.

5976 Cutler, Chris. 1985. *File under Popular:
Theoretical and Critical Writings on
Music.* London: November Books.

5977 Cutler, Chris. 1985. The Studio as
Instrument (2): Whose Future of Music?
Re Records Quarterly 1(2): 28–30.

5978 Darter, Tom and Armbruster, Greg.
1984. *The Art of Electronic Music.* New
York: G.P.I.

5979 Doerschuk, Bob. 1985. *Rock Keyboard.*
New York: G.P.I.

5980 Durant, Alan. 1985. Rock Revolution or
Time-No-Changes: Visions of Change
and Continuity in Rock Music. *Popular
Music* 5: 97–121.

5981 Eco, Umberto. 1964. La musica e la
macchina. In *Apocalittici e integrati.*
Milano: Bompiani. 295–307.

5982 Fabbri, Franco. 1984. *Elettronica e
musica.* Milano: Fabbri Editori.

5983 Fabbri, Franco. 1987. Skill: The Positive
Case (or: In Praise of Learning). *Re
Records Quarterly* 2(1): 37–40.

5984 Fabbri, Franco. 1996. *Il suono in cui
viviamo. Inventare, produrre e diffondere
musica.* Milano: Giangiacomo Feltrinelli
Editore.

5985 Gerzon, Michael. 1986. The Politics of
P.A. *Re Records Quarterly* 1(4): 21–25.

5986 Gerzon, Michael. 1987. The Electronic
Music Tradition: Influences from

Classical on Popular Music. *Re Records Quarterly* 2(1): 17–22.

5987 Gorges, Peter and Merck, Alex. 1993. *Keyboards, MIDI, Homerecording*, 3rd edition. München: Carstensen.

5988 Hoffman, Alan Neil. 1983. *On the Nature of Rock and Roll: An Enquiry into the Aesthetic of a Musical Vernacular.* Ann Arbor, MI: University Microfilms International.

5989 Holmes, Thomas B. 1985. *Electronic and Experimental Music: History, Instruments, Technique, Performers, Recordings.* New York: Charles Scribner's Sons.

5990 Mackay, Andy. 1982. *Electronic Music.* Minneapolis, MN: Control Data.

5991 Manning, Peter. 1987. *Electronic & Computer Music.* Oxford: Clarendon Press.

5992 Martin, George. 1979. *All You Need Is Ears.* London: Macmillan.

5993 Matthews, Robert. 1986. Analogue versus Digital. *Re Records Quarterly* 1(4): 27–36.

5994 Mitsui, Torû. 1995. Karaoke: How the Combination of Technology and Music Evolved. In *Popular Music Perspectives III*, ed. Peter Wicke. Berlin: Zyankrise. 216–23.

5995 Moore, Steve. 1985. The Recording Studio as a Musical Instrument. *Re Records Quarterly* 1(1): 32–33.

5996 Oswald, John. 1987. Plunderphonics, or Audio Piracy as a Compositional Prerogative. *Re Records Quarterly* 2(1): 24–29.

5997 Porcello, Thomas. 1991. The Ethics of Digital Audio Sampling: Engineers' Discourse. *Popular Music* 10(1): 69–84.

5998 Schaefer, John. 1990. *New Sounds: The Virgin Guide to New Music.* London: Virgin.

5999 Vilardi, Frank and Tarshis, Steve. 1985. *Electronic Drums.* New York: Amsco.

6000 Yelton, Gary. 1986. *The Rock Synthesizer Manual: A Revised Guide for the Electronic Musician.* Woodstock, GA: Rock Tech Publications.

Notation

6001 Bennett, H. Stith. 1983. Notation and Identity in Contemporary Popular Music. *Popular Music* 3: 215–34.

6002 Haywood, Mark. 1993. Melodic Notation in Jazz Transcription. *Annual Review of Jazz Studies* 6: 271–75.

6003 Metfessel, Milton. 1981. (1926) *Phonophotography in Folk Music: American Negro Songs in New Notation.* Durham, NC: University of North Carolina Press.

LOCATIONS

AFRICA (SUB-SAHARAN)

General

6004 Adamo, Giorgio. 1989. Tradizioni musicali in Africa: Conversazione con Gerhard Kubik (II). *Musica/Realtà* 28: 75–88.

6005 Alaja-Browne, Afolabi. 1989. A Diachronic Study of Change in JuJu Music. *Popular Music* 9(3): 231–42.

6006 Aning, B.A. 1975. *An Annotated Bibliography of Music and Dance in English-Speaking Africa*. Legon: University of Ghana.

6007 Ankerman, Bernhard. 1901. *Die afrikanischen Musikinstrumente*. Berlin: A. Haack.

6008 Bebey, Francis. 1975. *African Music: A People's Art*. Westport, CT: Lawrence Hill.

6009 Bebey, Francis. 1979. African Musical Tradition in the Face of Foreign Influence. *Cultures* 6(2): 134–40.

6010 Bender, Wolfgang. 1985. *Sweet Mother: Modern African Music*. Chicago: University of Chicago Press.

6011 Bensignor, Francis. 1988. *Sons d'Afrique*. Paris: Marabout.

6012 Berger, Renato. 1984. *Africa Dance: Afrikanischer Tanz in Vergangenheit und Zukunft, Ursprung und Diaspora: Afrika, Karibik, Brasilien*. Wilhelmshaven: Heinrichshofen.

6013 Bergman, Billy. 1985. *African Pop: Goodtime Kings*. Poole: Blandford Press.

6014 Blacking, John. 1959. Continuity and Change in African Culture. *African Music* 2(2): 15–23.

6015 Brincard, M.T., ed. 1989. *Sounding Forms: African Musical Instruments*. New York: American Federation of Arts.

6016 Chernoff, John M. 1979. *African Rhythm and African Sensibility: Aesthetics and Social Action in African Musical Idioms*. Chicago: University of Chicago Press.

6017 Collins, John. 1985. *African Pop Roots: The Inside Rhythms of Africa*. ed. Sylvia Moore. London: Foulsham.

6018 Collins, John. 1989. The Early History of West African Highlife Music. *Popular Music* 8(3): 221–30.

6019 Collins, John. 1992. Some Anti-Hegemonic Aspects of African Popular Music. In *Rockin' the Boat: Mass Music and Mass Movements*, ed. Reebee Garofalo. Boston, MA: South End Press. 185–94.

6020 Coplan, David. 1981. Popular Music. In *The Cambridge Encyclopaedia of Africa*, ed. R. Oliver and M. Crowder. Cambridge: Cambridge University Press. 446–50.

6021 Coplan, David. 1982. The Urbanisation of African Music: Some Theoretical Observations. *Popular Music* 2: 113–29.

6022 Coplan, David. 1991. Notes on New and Old World African Drumming. *African Music* 7(1): 105–109.

6023 Correa de Azevedo, Luis Hector. 1981. Music and Musicians of African Origin in Brazil. *The World of Music* 25(2): 53–63.

6024 Cowley, John. 1994. uBUNGCA (Oxford Bags): Recordings in London of African and West Indian Music in the 1920s and 1930s. *Musical Traditions* 12: 13–27.

6025 Dauer, Alfons M. 1985. *Tradition afrikanischer Blasorchester und Entstehung des Jazz*. Graz: Akademische Druck- und Verlagsanstalt.

6026 De Lerma, Dominique-René. 1981. *Bibliography of Black Music, Vol. 1. Reference Materials*. Westport and London: Greenwood Press.

6027 Djedje, Jacqueline Cogdell, and Carter, William G., eds. 1989. *African Musicology: Current Trends, Vol. 1*. Los Angeles: University of California Press.

6028 Dyan, Brigitte and Mandel, Jean-Jacques. 1984. *L'Afrique à Paris*. Paris: Editions Rochevignes.

6029 Epstein, Dena J. 1973. African Music in British and French America. *Musical Quarterly* 59(1): 61–91.

6030 Euba, Akin. 1988. *Essays on Music in Africa*. Bayreuth: Bayreuth University.

6031 Euba, Akin. 1989. *Essays on Music in Africa: Intercultural Perspectives, Vol. 2*. Lagos: Elekoto Music Centre.

6032 Evans, David. 1972. Africa and the Blues. *Living Blues* 10: 27–29.

6033 Ewens, Graeme. 1991. *Africa O-Ye! A Celebration of African Music*. Enfield: Guinness Publishing.

6034 Fabian, Johannes. 1978. Popular Culture in Africa: Findings and Conjectures. *Africa* 48(4): 315–34.

6035 Fampou, François. 1986. *Ku sa: introduction à la percussion africaine*. Paris: L'Harmattan.

6036 Gaskin, L.J.P. 1957. *A Select Bibliography of Music in Africa, Compiled at the International African Institute*. London: International African Institute.

6037 Graham, Ronnie. 1988. *Stern's Guide to Contemporary African Music*. London: Zwan and 'Off the Record Press' Culture.

6038 Graham, Ronnie. 1992. *The World of African Music: Stern's Guide to Contemporary African Music*. London: Pluto Press.

6039 Gray, John, ed. 1991. *African Music: A Bibliographical Guide to the Traditional, Popular, Art and Liturgical Musics of Sub-Saharan Africa*. Westport, CT: Greenwood Press.

6040 Harrev, Flemming. 1989. Bibliography of Books on Popular Music in Africa. *Popular Music* 8(3): 317–18.

6041 Jahn, Janheinz. 1990. Residual African Elements in the Blues. In *Mother Wit from the Laughing Barrel*, ed. Alan Dundes. Jackson, MS: University Press of Mississippi. 95–103.

6042 Jones, A.M. 1934. African Drumming. *Bantu Studies* 8: 1–16.

6043 Jones, A.M. 1957. Drums Down the Centuries. *African Music Society* 14(4): 4–10.

6044 Jones, A.M. 1959. *Studies in African Music*. Oxford: Oxford University Press.

6045 Jones, A.M. 1971. *Africa and Indonesia: The Evidence of the Xylophone and Other Musical and Cultural Factors*. Leiden: E.J. Brill.

6046 Kebede, Ashenafi. 1982. *Roots of Black Music: The Vocal, Instrumental and Dance Heritage of Africa and Black America*. Englewood Cliffs, NJ: Prentice-Hall.

6047 Kubik, Gerhard. 1970. *La Musique Africaine*. UNESCO: Reunion de Yaounde.

6048 Kubik, Gerhard. 1973. Verstehen in afrikanischen Musikkulturen. In *Musik und Verstehen*, ed. Peter Faltin and Hans-Peter Reinecke. Köln: Gerig. 171–88.

6049 Kubik, Gerhard. 1986. Stability and Change in African Musical Traditions. *The World of Music* 28(1): 44–68.

6050 Lems-Dworkin, Carol, ed. 1991. *African Music: A Pan-African Annotated Bibliography*. Munich: Hans Zell Publishers.

6051 Manuel, Peter. 1988. Africa. In *Popular Musics of the Non-Western World*. New York: Oxford University Press. 84–114.

6052 Mensah, A.A. 1980. Music South of the Sahara. In *Musics of Many Cultures*, ed. Elizabeth May. Berkeley and London: University of California Press. 172–94.

6053 Merriam, Alan P. 1984. (1981) *African Music in Perspective*. New York: Garland.

6054 Moore, Sylvia. 1982. Social Identity in Popular Mass Media Music. In *Popular Music Perspectives, 1*, ed. David Horn and Philip Tagg. Göteborg and Exeter: IASPM. 196–222.

6055 Mukuna, Kazadi wa, ed. 1980. *African Urban Studies* 6 (Special Issue on African Urban Music).

6056 Murphy, Dennis. 1972. The Americanization of Three African Musical Instruments. *African Music* 5(2): 105–11.

6057 Murphy, Jeanette. 1967. The Survival of African Music in America. In *The Negro and His Folklore in Nineteenth-Century Periodicals*, ed. Bruce Jackson. Austin, TX: University of Texas Press. 327–39. (First published in *Popular Science Monthly* 55 (1899): 660–72.)

6058 Nketia, J.H. Kwabena. 1968. *Our Drums and Drummers*. Accra: State Publishing Corporation.

6059 Nketia, J.H. Kwabena. 1973. The Study of African and Afro-American Music. *The Black Perspective in Music* 1(1): 7–15.

6060 Nketia, J.H. Kwabena. 1974. *The Music of Africa*. New York: Norton.

6061 Nketia, J.H. Kwabena. 1982. On the Historicity of Music in African Cultures. *Journal of African Studies* 9: 91–100.

6062 Roberts, John Storm. 1974. (1972) *Black Music of Two Worlds*. New York: William Morrow. First published New York/London: Praeger/Allen Lane, 1972.

6063 Schmidt, Cynthia. 1994. The Guitar in Africa: Issues and Research. *The World of Music* 36(2): 3–20.

6064 Seck, Nago and Clerfeuille, Sylvie. 1986. *Musiciens africains des années 80*. Paris: L'Harmattan.

6065 Simon, Artur, ed. 1983. *Musik in Afrika*. Berlin: Staatliche Museen.

6066 Southern, Eileen. 1982. *Biographical Dictionary of Afro-American and African Musicians*. Westport, CT: Greenwood Press.

6067 Stapleton, Chris. 1990. African Connections: London's Hidden Music Scene. In *Black Music in Britain: Essays on the Afro-Asian Contribution to Popular Music*, ed. Paul Oliver. Milton Keynes: Open University Press. 79–86.

6068 Stapleton, Chris and May, Chris. 1987. *African All-Stars: The Pop Music of a Continent*. London: Quartet.

6069 Stewart, Gary. 1992. *Breakout: Profiles in African Rhythm*. Chicago: University of Chicago Press.

6070 Taylor, Jeremy. 1992. *Ag Pleez Daddy!: Songs and Reflections*. Jeremy Taylor Publishing.

6071 Templeton, Ray. 1994. African Musical History on Record. *Musical Traditions* 12: 36–38.

6072 Tosi, E. 1990. *La kora e il sax. Forme e protagonisti della musica africana moderna*. Bologna: E.M.I.

6073 Van Zile, Judy. 1976. *Dance in Africa, Asia and the Pacific: Selected Readings.* New York: MSS Information Corp.

6074 Wachsmann, Klaus. 1971. *Essays on Music and History in Africa.* Evanston, IL: Northwestern University Press.

6075 Warren, Fred and Warren, Lee. 1970. *The Music of Africa: An Introduction.* Englewood Cliffs, NJ: Prentice-Hall.

6076 Waterman, Richard. 1952. African Influence on the Music of the Americas. In *Acculturation in the Americas, 2.* ed. Sol Tax. Chicago: University of Chicago Press. 207–18.

6077 Waterman, Richard. 1963. On Flogging a Dead Horse: Lessons Learnt from the Africanisms Controversy. *Ethnomusicology* 7(2): 83–88.

Central Africa

6078 Brandel, Rose. 1973. (1961) *The Music of Central Africa: An Ethnomusicological Study – Former French Equatorial Africa, the Former Belgian Congo, Ruanda-Urundi, Uganda, Tanginyika.* The Hague: Nijhoff.

Zaire

6079 Bebey, Francis. 1984. *50 Ans de Musique du Zaire-Congo.* Paris: Présence africaine.

6080 Bemba, Sylvain. 1984. *Cinquante ans de musique du Congo-Zaire, 1920–1970.* Paris: Présence africaine.

6081 Ewens, Graeme. 1994. *Congo Colossus: The Life and Legacy of Franco and OK Jazz.* Norfolk: Buku Press.

6082 Low, John. 1982. *Shaba Diary: A Trip to Rediscover the Katanga Guitar Styles and Songs of the 1950s and 1960s.* Vienna: Acta Ethnologica et Linguistica.

6083 Matondo ne Mansangaza, Kanza. 1972. *Musique zaïroise moderne.* Kinshasa: Publications du CNMA.

6084 No entry.

6085 Mukuna, Kazadi wa. 1980. The Origin of Zairean Modern Music: A Socioeconomic Aspect. *African Urban Studies* 6: 31–39.

6086 Mukuna, Kazadi wa. 1994. The Changing Role of the Guitar in the Urban Music of Zaire. *The World of Music* 36(2): 62–72.

6087 Prince, Rob. 1989. Zaire and Now. *Folk Roots* 73 (July): 21–27.

6088 Rycroft, David. 1961. The Guitar Improvisations of Mwenda Jean Bosco. *African Music* 2(4): 81–98.

6089 Rycroft, David. 1962. The Guitar Improvisations of Mwenda Jean Bosco. *African Music* 3(1): 79–85.

East Africa

6090 Kubik, Gerhard. 1981. Neo-Traditional Popular Music in East Africa Since 1945. *Popular Music* 1: 83–104.

6091 Martin, Stephen H. 1991. Brass Bands and the Beni Phenomena in Urban East Africa. *African Music* 7(1): 72–81.

6092 Martin, Stephen H. 1991. Popular Music in Urban East Africa: From Historical Perspective to a Contemporary Hero. *Black Music Research Journal* 11(1): 39–53.

6093 Ranger, T.O. 1975. *Dance and Society in East Africa, 1890–1970.* London: Heinemann.

6094 Topp Fargion, Janet. 1993. The Role of Women in Taarab in Zanzibar: An Historical Examination of a Process of 'Africanisation'. *The World of Music* 35(2): 109–25.

Kenya

6095 Low, John. 1982. A History of Kenyan Guitar Music: 1945–1980. *African Music* 6(2): 17–36.

6096 Roberts, John Storm. 1965. Kenya's Pop Music. *Transition* 4(19): 40–43.

6097 Roberts, John Storm. 1968. Popular Music in Kenya. *African Music* 4(2): 53–55.

6098 Wallis, Roger and Malm, Krister. 1982. The Interdependency of Broadcasting and the Phonogram Industry: Events in Kenya, March 1980. In *Popular Music Perspectives, 1*, ed. David Horn and Philip Tagg. Göteborg and Exeter: IASPM. 93–110.

Horn of Africa

Ethiopia

6099 Kebede, Ashenafi. 1976. Zemenawi Muzika: Modern Trends in Traditional Secular Music of Ethiopia. *The Black Perspective in Music* 4(3): 289–302.

6100 Shelemay, Kay Kaufman. 1989. *Music, Ritual, and Falasha History.* East Lansing, MI: Michigan State University Press.

6101 Silfverberg, Paul. 1986. Etiopialainen populaarimusiikki. *Musiikin suunta* 8(4): 120–24.

Southern Africa

6102 Rycroft, David. 1958. The New 'Town' Music of Southern Africa. *Recorded Folk Music* 1: 54–57.

6103 No entry.

6104 Tracey, Hugh. 1954. The State of Folk Music in Bantu Africa. *African Music* 1(1): 8–11.

Botswana

6105 Mitchell, Clyde. 1956. *The Kalela Dance: Aspects of Social Relationships Among Urban Africans in Northern Rhodesia.* Manchester: Manchester University Press.

Malawi

6106 Kubik, Gerhard. 1974. *The Kachamba Brothers Band: A Study of Neo-Traditional Music in Malawi.* Manchester: Manchester University Press.

6107 Kubik, Gerhard. 1988. Daniel Kachamba, 1947–1987: Malawian Musician-Composer. *Jazzforschung* 20: 174–79.

6108 Kubik, Gerhard. 1989. The Southern African Periphery: Banjo Traditions in Zambia and Malawi. *The World of Music* 31(3): 3–29.

6109 Nurse, George T. 1964. Popular Songs and National Identity in Malawi. *African Music* 3(3): 101–106.

Mozambique

6110 No entry.

6111 Vail, Leroy and White, Landeg. 1986. Forms of Resistance: Songs and Perceptions of Power in Colonial Mozambique. In *Banditry, Rebellion, and Social Protest in Africa*, ed. Donald Crummey. London: James Currey. 193–227.

South Africa

6112 Allen, Lara. 1995. The Effect of Repressive State Policies on the Development and Demise of Kwela Music in Africa, 1955–1965. In *Popular Music Perspectives III*, ed. Peter Wicke. Berlin: Zyankrise. 326–30.

6113 Andersson, Muff. 1981. *Music in the Mix: The Story of South African Popular Music.* Johannesburg: Ravan Press.

6114 Ballantine, Christopher. 1989. A Brief History of South African Popular Music. *Popular Music* 8(3): 304–10.

6115 Ballantine, Christopher. 1991. 'Concert and Dance': The Foundations of Black Jazz in South Africa Between the

Twenties and Early Forties. *Popular Music* 10(3): 121–46.

6116 Ballantine, Christopher. 1993. *Marabi Nights: Early South African Jazz and Vaudeville*. Johannesburg: Ravan Press.

6117 Berliner, Paul F. 1981. *The Soul of Mbira*. Berkeley and Los Angeles: University of California Press.

6118 Blacking, John. 1980. Trends in the Black Music of South Africa, 1959–1969. In *Musics of Many Cultures*, ed. Elizabeth May. Berkeley and London: University of California Press. 195–215.

6119 Chilvers, Garth. 1994. *History of Contemporary Music of South Africa*. Braamfontein: Toga Publishing.

6120 Clegg, Jonathan. 1981. The Music of Zulu Immigrant Workers in Johannesburg: A Focus on Concertina and Guitar. In *Papers Presented at the Symposium on Ethnomusicology*. Grahamstown: International Library of African Music. 2–9.

6121 Cockrell, Dale. 1987. Of Gospel Hymns, Minstrel Shows, and Jubilee Singers: Toward Some Black South African Musics. *American Music* 5(4): 417–32.

6122 Coplan, David. 1979. The African Musician and the Development of the Johannesburg Entertainment Industry: 1900–1960. *Journal of Southern African Studies* 5(2): 135–64.

6123 Coplan, David. 1979. The African Performer and the Jo'burg Entertainment Industry: Struggle for African Culture on the Witwatersrand. In *Labour, Townships and Protest*. Johannesburg: Ravan Press.

6124 Coplan, David. 1985. *In Township Tonight! South Africa's Black City Music and Theatre*. London and New York: Longman.

6125 Coplan, David. 1994. *In the Time of Cannibals: The Word Music of South Africa's Basotho Migrants*. Chicago: University of Chicago Press.

6126 Dargie, David. 1988. *Xhosa Music: Its Techniques and Instruments, with a Collection of Songs*. Cape Town and Johannesburg: David Philip.

6127 Davies, Nollene. 1994. The Guitar in Zulu Maskanda Tradition. *The World of Music* 36(2): 118–37.

6128 Erlmann, Veit. 1985. Black Political Song in South Africa: Some Research Perspectives. In *Popular Music Perspectives, 2*, ed. David Horn. Göteborg and Exeter: IASPM. 187–209.

6129 Erlmann, Veit. 1989. A Conversation with Joseph Shabalala of Ladysmith Black Mambazo: Aspects of African Performers' Life Stories. *The World of Music* 33(1): 31–58.

6130 Erlmann, Veit. 1989. 'Horses in the Race Course': The Domestication of Ingoma Dancing in South Africa, 1929–39. *Popular Music* 8(3): 259–74.

6131 Erlmann, Veit. 1990. Migration and Performance: Zulu Migrant Workers' Isicathamiya Performance in South Africa, 1890–1950. *Ethnomusicology* 34(2): 199–219.

6132 Erlmann, Veit. 1991. *African Stars: Studies in Black South African Performance*. Chicago: University of Chicago Press.

6133 Erlmann, Veit. 1996. *Nightsong: Performance, Power and Practice in South Africa*. Chicago: University of Chicago Press.

6134 Hamm, Charles. 1985. Rock 'n' Roll in a Very Strange Society. *Popular Music* 5: 159–74.

6135 Hamm, Charles. 1988. *Afro-American Music, South Africa and Apartheid*.

Brooklyn, NY: Institute for Studies in American Music.

6136 Hamm, Charles. 1991. 'The Constant Companion of Man': Separate Development, Radio Bantu, and Music. *Popular Music* 10(2): 147–73.

6137 Hamm, Charles. 1992. Privileging the Moment of Reception: Music and Radio in South Africa. In *Music and Text: Critical Inquiries*, ed. Steven Scher. Cambridge: Cambridge University Press.

6138 Huskisson, Yvonne. 1969. *The Bantu Composers of Southern Africa*. Johannesburg: The South African Broadcasting Corporation.

6139 Jackson, Melveen. 1989. Tiger Dance, Tango and Tchaikovsky: A Politico-Cultural View of Indian South African Music Before 1948. *The World of Music* 31(1): 59–75.

6140 Jackson, Melveen. 1991. Popular Indian South African Music: Division in Diversity. *Popular Music* 10(2): 175–88.

6141 Kerkhof, Ian. 1985. Music in South Africa: Censorship and Repression. *Re Records Quarterly* 1(2): 9–15.

6142 Kerkhof, Ian. 1989. Music in the Revolution. *Keskidee: A Journal of Black Musical Traditions* 2: 10–21.

6143 Kirby, Percival R. 1968. *The Musical Instruments of the Native Races of South Africa*. Johannesburg: Witwatersrand University Press.

6144 Kivnick, Helen. 1990. *Where Is the Way: Song and Struggle in South Africa*. London and New York: Penguin.

6145 No entry.

6146 Makeba, Miriam. 1988. *Makeba: My Story*, ed. James Hall. London: Bloomsbury.

6147 Marsh, Dave. 1986. *Sun City, by Artists Against Apartheid: The Struggle for Freedom in South Africa; the Making of a Record*. New York: Penguin.

6148 Martin, Denis-Constant. 1992. Music Beyond Apartheid? In *Rockin' the Boat: Mass Music and Mass Movements*, ed. Reebee Garofalo. Boston, MA: South End Press. 195–208.

6149 Matshikiza, Todd. 1982. (1961) *Chocolates for My Wife*. Cape Town: Africasouth Paperbacks.

6150 Meintjes, Louise. 1990. Paul Simon's 'Graceland', South Africa, and the Mediation of Musical Meaning. *Ethnomusicology* 34(1): 37–73.

6151 Mensah, A.A. 1973. Problems of Pitch, Pattern and Harmony in the Ocarini Music of the Venda. *Jazz Research* 3(4).

6152 Rörich, Mary. 1989. Shebeens, Slumyards and Sophiatown: Black Women, Music and Cultural Change in Urban South Africa, 1920–1960. *The World of Music* 31(1): 78–101.

6153 Rycroft, David. 1956. Melodic Imports and Exports: A Byproduct of Recording in South Africa. *Bulletin of the British Institute of Recorded Sound* 1: 19–21.

6154 Rycroft, David. 1959. African Music in Johannesburg: African and Non-African Features. *Journal of the International Folk Music Council* 9: 25–36.

6155 Rycroft, David. 1977. Evidence of Stylistic Continuity in Zulu 'Town' Music. In *Essays for a Humanist: An Offering to Klaus Wachsmann*. New York: The Town House Press. 216–60.

6156 Rycroft, David. 1991. Black South African Urban Music Since the 1890s: Reminiscences of A.A. Kumalo (1879–1966). *African Music* 7(1): 5–31.

6157 Seroff, Doug. 1986. The Zulu Choirs: A Brief Introduction. *Keskidee: A Journal of Black Musical Traditions* 1: 20–26.

6158 Seroff, Doug. 1989. Shifty Record Company. *Keskidee: A Journal of Black Musical Traditions* 2: 22–26.

6159 Seroff, Doug. 1990. A Brief Introduction to Zulu Choirs. *Black Music Research Journal* 10(1): 54–57.

6160 Tracey, Hugh. 1952. *African Dances of the Witwatersrand Gold Mines*. Roodepoort: African Music Society.

6161 Trewela, Ralph. 1980. *Song Safari: A Journey Through Light Music in South Africa*. Johannesburg: Limelight Press.

6162 Zindi, Fred. 1985. *Roots Rocking in Zimbabwe*. Gweru: Mambo Press.

Zambia

6163 Kubik, Gerhard. 1989. The Southern African Periphery: Banjo Traditions in Zambia and Malawi. *The World of Music* 31(3): 3–29.

6164 Malamusia, Moya Aliya. 1984. The Zambian Popular Music Scene. *Jazzforschung* 16: 189–98.

Zimbabwe

6165 Brown, Ernest D. 1994. The Guitar and the Mbira: Resilience, Assimilation, and Pan-Africanism in Zimbabwean Music. *The World of Music* 36(2): 73–117.

6166 Kauffman, Robert. 1980. Tradition and Innovation in the Urban Music of Zimbabwe. *African Urban Studies* 6: 41–48.

6167 Maraire, Dumisani. 1971. *The Mbira Music of Rhodesia*. Seattle, WA: University of Washington Press.

6168 Pongweni, Alec. 1982. *Songs That Won the Liberation War*. Harare: The College Press.

6169 Zindi, Fred. 1985. *Roots Rocking in Zimbabwe*. Gweru: Mambo Press.

West Africa

6170 Charry, Eric. 1994. The Grand Mande Guitar Tradition of the Western Sahel and Savannah. *The World of Music* 36(2): 21–61.

6171 Charters, Samuel B. 1981. *The Roots of the Blues*. London: Quartet.

6172 Chernoff, John M. 1985. *Africa Come Back: The Popular Music of West Africa*, ed. Geoffrey Haydon and Denis Marks. London: Century.

6173 Collins, John. 1977. Post-War Popular Band Music in West Africa. *African Arts* 10(3): 53–60.

6174 Collins, John. 1985. *Music Makers of West Africa*. Washington, DC: Three Continents Press.

6175 Collins, John. 1992. (1985) *West African Pop Roots*, revised edition. Philadelphia: Temple University Press. First published London: Foulsham, 1985.

6176 Collins, John and Richards, Paul. 1982. Popular Music in West Africa: Suggestions for an Interpretative Framework. In *Popular Music Perspectives, 1*, ed. David Horn and Philip Tagg. Göteborg and Exeter: IASPM. 111–41.

6177 Fosu-Mensah, Kwabena, Lucy Durán and Chris Stapleton. 1987. On Music in Contemporary West Africa. *African Affairs* 86(343): 227–40.

6178 Gorer, Geoffrey. 1962. (1935) *Africa Dances: A Book About West African Negroes*. New York: Norton.

6179 Kinney, Esi Sylvia. 1970. Urban West African Music and Dance. *African Urban Notes* 5(4): 3–10.

6180 Oliver, Paul. 1970. *Savannah Syncopators: African Retentions in the Blues*. London: Studio Vista.

6181 Smith, Edna M. 1962. Popular Music of West Africa. *African Music* 3(1): 11–17.

6182 Van Dam, Theodore. 1954. The Influence of West African Songs of Derision in the New World. *African Music* 1(1): 53–56.

6183 Welch, David B. 1985. A Yoruba/Nagô 'Melotype' for Religious Songs in the African Diaspora: Continuity of West African Praise Song in the New World. In *More than Drumming: Essays on African and Afro-Latin American Music and Musicians*, ed. Irene V. Jackson. Westport, CT: Greenwood Press. 145–62.

6184 Wiggins, Trevor. 1993. *Music of West Africa*. London: Heinemann Educational.

6185 Wilson, Olly. 1974. The Significance of the Relationship Between Afro-American Music and West African Music. *The Black Perspective in Music* 1(3): 3–22.

Ghana

6186 Collins, John. 1985. The Concert Party in Ghana. *Musical Traditions* 4: 37–39.

6187 Koetting, James T. 1975. The Effects of Urbanization: The Music of the Kasena People of Ghana. *The World of Music* 17(4): 23–31.

6188 Lee, Hélène. 1988. *Rockers d'Afrique: Stars et légendes du rock mandingue*. Paris: Albin Michel.

6189 McAllester, David P., ed. 1971. Modern Trends in Ghana Music. In *Readings in Ethnomusicology*. New York: Johnson Reprint Company. 330–35. (First published in *African Music* 1(4) (1957): 13–17.)

6190 Mensah, A.A. 1966. The Impact of Western Music on the Musical Traditions of Ghana. *Composer* 19: 19–22.

6191 Nketia, J.H. Kwabena. 1956. The Gramophone and Contemporary African Music in the Gold Coast. *Proceedings of the West African Institute of Social and Economic Research* 5: 189–200.

6192 Nketia, J.H. Kwabena. 1957. Modern Trends in Ghana Music. *African Music* 1(4): 11–13.

6193 Schmidt, Cynthia. 1994. An Interview with John Collins on Cultural Policy, Folklore and the Recording Industry in Ghana. *The World of Music* 36(2): 138–47.

Mali

6194 Durán, Lucy. 1989. Djely Mousso. *Folk Roots* 75 (September): 34–39.

6195 Durán, Lucy. 1995. Birds of Wasulu: Freedom of Expression and Expressions of Freedom in the Popular Music of Southern Mali. *British Journal for Ethnomusicology* 4: 101–34.

Nigeria

6196 Abimbola, W. 1975. The Interrelationship of Poetry and Music in Yoruba Tradition. In *Yoruba Oral Tradition: Poetry in Music, Dance and Drama*. Ife: Department of African Languages and Literature, University of Ife. 471–87.

6197 Aig-Imoukhuede, Frank. 1975. Contemporary Culture. In *Lagos: The Development of an African City*. Lagos: Longman Nigeria. 197–226.

6198 Ajibola, J.O. 1974. *Yoruba Songs*. Ife: University of Ife Press.

6199 Akpabot, Samuel. 1971. Standard Drum Patterns in Nigeria. *African Music* 5(1): 37–39.

6200 Akpabot, Samuel. 1973. The Conflict Between Foreign and Traditional Culture in Nigeria. In *Reflections on Afro-*

American Music. Kent, OH: Kent State University Press. 124–30.

6201 Alaja-Browne, Afolabi. 1991. On Music, Emotions and Mobilization. *Worldbeat* 1: 46–54.

6202 Ames, David W. 1970. Urban Hausa Music. *African Urban Notes* 5(4): 19–24.

6203 Bucknor, Segun. 1976. The Big Battle: Pop vs. Juju. *Drum Magazine* (20 September).

6204 Ita, Chief Bassey. 1984. *Jazz in Nigeria: An Outline Cultural History*. Calibar: Radical House.

6205 Keil, Charles. 1979. *Tiv Song*. Chicago: Chicago University Press.

6206 King, Anthony. 1976. *Yoruba Sacred Drums*. Ibadan: Caxton Press.

6207 Waterman, Christopher A. 1982. 'I'm a Leader, Not a Boss': Popular Music and Social Identity in Ibadan, Nigeria. *Ethnomusicology* 26(1): 59–72.

6208 Waterman, Christopher A. 1990. 'Our Tradition is a Very Modern Tradition': Popular Music and the Construction of Pan-Yoruba Identity. *Ethnomusicology* 34(3): 367–79.

6209 Waterman, Christopher A. 1995. Full Garbage in Destiny World, or Is Yoruba Pop Po-Mo? In *Popular Music Perspectives III*, ed. Peter Wicke. Berlin: Zyankrise. 166–73.

Sierra Leone

6210 Dowu Horton, Christian. 1984. Popular Bands of Sierra Leone: 1920 to the Present. *The Black Perspective in Music* 21(2): 183–92.

6211 No entry.

6212 Oven, C. van. 1981. *An Introduction to the Music of Sierra Leone*. London: Evans.

6213 Ware, Naomi. 1970. Popular Musicians in Freetown. *African Urban Notes* 5(4): 11–18.

6214 Ware, Naomi. 1978. Popular Music and African Identity in Freetown, Sierra Leone. In *Eight Urban Musical Cultures: Tradition and Change*, ed. Bruno Nettl. Urbana and London: University of Illinois Press.

ASIA

General

6215 Khe, Tran Van. 1990. A propos des notions dualistes dans les traditions musicales des pays d'Asie. In *La musica come linguaggio universale*, ed. Raffaele Pozzi. Firenze: Leo S. Olschki. 215–26.

Central Asia

6216 Krishnaswami, S. 1974. Musical Changes in Uzbekhistan. *Journal of the Indian Musicological Society* 5(2): 13–17.

6217 Levin, Theodore C. 1979. Music in Modern Uzbekistan: The Convergence of Marxist Aesthetics and Central Asian Tradition. *Asian Music* 12(1): 149–63.

6218 Zemtovsky, Izaly. 1990. Music and Ethnic History: An Attempt to Substantiate a Eurasian Hypothesis. *Yearbook for Traditional Music* 22: 20–28.

China

6219 Birrell, Anne, ed. 1988. *Popular Songs and Ballads of Han China*. London: Unwin Hyman.

6220 Brace, Tim and Friedlander, Paul. 1992. Rock and Roll on the New Long March: Popular Music, Cultural Identity, and Political Opposition in the People's Republic of China. In *Rockin' the Boat: Mass Music and Mass Movements*, ed. Reebee Garofalo. Boston, MA: South End Press. 115–28.

6222 Lee, Gregory. 1995. The 'East Is Red' Goes Pop: Commodification, Hybridity and Nationalism in Chinese Popular Song and Its Televised Performance. *Popular Music* 14(1): 95–110.

6223 Lee, Joanna Ching-Yun. 1992. All for the Music: The Rise of Patriotic/Pro-Democratic Popular Music in Hong Kong in Response to the Chinese Student Movement. In *Rockin' the Boat: Mass Music and Mass Movements*, ed. Reebee Garofalo. Boston, MA: South End Press. 129–48.

6224 Lee, Joanna Ching-Yun. 1992. Cantopop Songs on Emigration from Hong Kong. *Yearbook for Traditional Music* 24: 14–23.

6225 Mao Chun, Liang. 1995. History of Chinese Popular Music in Historical Discographies: Music and Social Relations. In *Popular Music Perspectives III*, ed. Peter Wicke. Berlin: Zyankrise. 283–88.

6226 Perris, Arnold. 1973. Music as Propaganda: Art at the Command of Doctrine in the People's Republic of China. *Ethnomusicology* 17(1).

6227 Qi-hong, Ju. 1991. La Musique populaire de la Chine du XXe siècle dans le contexte des relations complexes entre la révolution et la démocratie. *Worldbeat* 1: 13–21.

6228 Steen, Andreas. 1995. Rockmusik in der VR China. *PopScriptum* 3: 80–100.

6229 Sui-jin, Zeng. 1991. Un étude sociologique de la chanson populaire de la Chine contemporaine. *Worldbeat* 1: 22–33.

6230 No entry.

Hong Kong

6231 Lee, Joanna Ching-Yun. 1992. All for the Music: The Rise of Patriotic/Pro-Democratic Popular Music in Hong Kong in Response to the Chinese Student Movement. In *Rockin' the Boat: Mass Music and Mass Movements*, ed. Reebee Garofalo. Boston, MA: South End Press. 129–48.

6232 Lee, Joanna Ching-Yun. 1992. Cantopop Songs on Emigration from Hong Kong. *Yearbook for Traditional Music* 24: 14–23.

6233 Lee, Joanna Ching-Yun. 1995. Brain Drained Cantopop: Songs on Emigration from Hong Kong. In *Popular Music Perspectives III*, ed. Peter Wicke. Berlin: Zyankrise. 248–53.

Tibet

6234 Doukas, James. 1969. *Electric Tibet: The Chronicles and Sociology of the San Francisco Rock Musicians*. North Hollywood, CA: Dominion.

Indian Subcontinent

6235 Bhattacharya, Deben. 1969. *The Mirror of the Sky: Songs of the Bâuls from Bengal*. London: George Allen and Unwin.

6236 Qureshi, Regula Burckhardt. 1986. *Sufi Music of India and Pakistan: Sound, Context and Meaning*. Cambridge: Cambridge University Press.

6237 Qureshi, Regula Burckhardt. 1992. 'Muslim Devotional': Popular Religious Music and Muslim Identity under British, Indian and Pakistani Hegemony. *Asian Music* 24(1): 111–21.

India

6238 Arnold, Alison E. 1988. Popular Film Song in India: A Case of Mass Market Musical Eclecticism. *Popular Music* 7(2): 177–88.

6239 Arnold, Alison E. 1992. Aspects of Production and Consumption in the Popular Hindi Film Song Industry. *Asian Music* 24(1): 122–36.

6240 Arora, V.N. 1986. Popular Songs in Hindi Films. *Journal of Popular Culture* 20(2): 143–66.

6241 Booth, Gregory D. 1991. Disco Laggi: Modern Repertoire and Traditional Performance Practice in North Indian Popular Music. *Asian Music* 23(1): 61–84.

6242 Capwell, Charles. 1988. The Popular Expression of Religious Syncretism: The Bauls of Bengal as Apostles of Brotherhood. *Popular Music* 7(2): 123–32.

6243 Coppola, Carlo. 1977. Politics, Social Criticism and Indian Film Songs: The Case of Sahir Ludhianvi. *Journal of Popular Culture* 10(4): 896–901.

6244 Farrell, Gerry. 1988. Reflecting Surfaces: Indian Music in Popular Music and Jazz. *Popular Music* 7(2): 189–206.

6245 Grandin, Ingemar. 1989. *Music and Media in Local Life: Music Practice in a Newar Neighbourhood in Nepal.* Linköping: Linköping University, Department of Communication Studies.

6246 Joshi, G.N. 1987. A Concise History of the Phonograph Industry in India. *Popular Music* 7(2): 28–32.

6247 Kuppuswamy, Gowri. 1981. *Indian Dance and Music Literature: A Selected Bibliography.* New Delhi: Biblia Impex.

6248 L'Armand, Kathleen and L'Armand, Adrian. 1978. Music in Madras: The Urbanization of a Cultural Tradition. In *Eight Urban Musical Cultures: Tradition and Change,* ed. Bruno Nettl. Urbana and London: University of Illinois Press. 115–45.

6249 L'Armand, Kathleen and L'Armand, Adrian. 1983. One Hundred Years of Music in Madras: A Case Study in Secondary Urbanization. *Ethnomusicology* 27(3): 411–38.

6250 Manuel, Peter. 1988. Popular Music in India, 1901–86. *Popular Music* 7(2): 157–76.

6251 Manuel, Peter. 1992. Popular Music and Media Culture in South Asia: Prefatory Considerations. *Asian Music* 24(1): 91–100.

6252 Manuel, Peter. 1993. *Cassette Culture: Popular Music and Technology in North India.* Chicago and London: University of Chicago Press.

6253 Marcus, Scott. 1992. Recycling Indian Film-Songs: Popular Music as a Source of Melodies for North Indian Folk Musicians. *Asian Music* 24(1): 101–10.

6254 Menon, Narayana. 1974. Music and Culture Change in India. *Cultures* 1(3): 59–73.

6255 Miner, Allyn Jayne. n.d. *Hindustani Instrumental Music in the Early Modern Period: A Study of the Sitar and Sarod in the Eighteenth and Early Nineteenth Centuries.* Banaras: Hindu University.

6256 Neuman, Daniel M. 1978. Gharanas: The Rise of Musical 'Houses' in Delhi and Neighbouring Cities. In *Eight Urban Musical Cultures: Tradition and Change.* ed. Bruno Nettl. Urbana and London: University of Illinois Press. 187–222.

6257 Ojha, J.M. 1985. *The Phonogram and Cultural Communication in India.* New Delhi: Behavioural Sciences Centre.

6258 Oliver, Paul. 1988. Movie Mahal: Indian Cinema on ITV Channel 4. *Popular Music* 7(2): 215–16.

6259 Oliver, Paul. 1988. The Tagore Collection of Indian Musical Instruments. *Popular Music* 7(2): 218–20.

6260 Rosenthal, Ethel. 1980. (1928) *The Story of Indian Music and Its Instruments: A Study of the Present and a Record of the Past.* New Delhi: Oriental Books Reprint Corp.

6261 Skillman, Teri. 1986. The Bombay Hindi Film Song Genre: A Historical Survey. *Yearbook for Traditional Music* 18: 133–44.

6262 Virgilio, Domenico Di. 1989. Espressione colta ed espressione popolare in India oggi: alcune riflessioni. *Musica/Realtà* 30: 71–96.

6263 Wade, Bonnie C. 1982. *Performing Arts in India: Essays on Music, Dance and Drama.* Berkeley, CA: University of California Press.

Sri Lanka

6264 Amunugama, Sarath. 1980. *Notes on Sinhala Culture.* Colombo: Gunasena.

Japan

6265 Aikura, Hisato. 1982. *Toshi no irodori, toshi no oto.* Tokyo: Tôju-sha.

6266 Aikura, Hisato. 1986. *An Introduction to Japanese Rockology.* Tokyo: Shincho-Sha.

6267 Anderson, Ian. 1992. Katcharsee Kings. *Folk Roots* 103–104 (January-February): 36–37.

6268 Asakura, Takashi. 1989. *Hayari uta no tanjo.* Tokyo: Seiku-sha.

6269 Cahoon, Keith. 1992. Popular Music in Japan. In *Japan: An Illustrated Encyclopedia, Vol. 1.* Tokyo: Kodansha. 286–87.

6270 Clewley, John. 1995. Enka, Okinawa and the Masters of Clone: The Japanese Are Coming!!. In *World Music: The Rough Guide,* ed. Simon Broughton, et al. London: The Rough Guides. 459–68.

6271 Fujie, Linda. 1992. East Asia/Japan. In *Worlds of Music: An Introduction to the Music of the World's Peoples,* ed. Jeff Todd Titon. New York: Schirmer Books. 318–75.

6272 Gekkan Onstage, ed. 1990. *Nippon rock taikei 57–59.* Tokyo: Byakuya-shobô.

6273 Groemer, Gerald. 1995. *Popular Songs in the Closing Days of the Tokugawa Shogunate* [translation of original Japanese title]. Tokyo: Meicho-shuppan.

6274 Havens, Thomas R.H. 1982. *Artist and Patron in Post-War Japan: Dance, Music, Theater and the Visual Arts, 1955–1980.* Princeton, NJ: Princeton University Press.

6275 Herd, Judith Anne. 1984. Trends and Taste in Japanese Popular Music: A Case-Study of the 1982 Yamaha World Popular Music Festival. *Popular Music* 4: 75–96.

6276 Hosokawa, Shuhei. 1994. East of Honolulu: Hawaiian Music in Japan from the 1920s to the 1940s. *Perfect Beat* 2(1): 51–67.

6277 Iwamura, Takuya. 1995. The Overview of the Modern Western Music Paradigm and Some Conditions of Its Counteractions: Some Japanese Borderline Cases. In *Popular Music Perspectives III,* ed. Peter Wicke. Berlin: Zyankrise. 232–39.

6278 Kawabata, Shigeru. 1991. The Japanese Record Industry. *Popular Music* 10(3): 327–45.

6279 Kikumura, Norihiko. 1989. *A History of Chansons in Japan* [translation of original Japanese title]. Tokyo: Yuzankaku.

6280 Kimura, Atsuko. 1991. Japanese Corporations and Popular Music. *Popular Music* 10(3): 317–26.

6281 Kitagawa, Junko. 1991. Some Aspects of Japanese Popular Music. *Popular Music* 10(3): 305–15.

6282 Komota, Nobuo, et al. 1994–95. *A History of Popular Songs in Japan* [translation of original Japanese title]. 3 vols. Tokyo: Shakaishiso-sha.

6283 Kurata, Yoshihiro. 1979. *A History of Phonograph Culture in Japan* [translation of original Japanese title]. Tokyo: Tokyo-shoseki.

6284 Kurosawa, Susumu. 1989. *All About 1960s Rock in Japan* [translation of original Japanese title]. Tokyo: Beat-shiryo kanko-kai.

6285 Kurosawa, Susumu, ed. 1995. *Roots of Japanese Pops: 1955–1970* [translation of original Japanese title]. Tokyo: Shinko Music.

6286 Maeda, Hirotake and Hirahara, Koji, eds. 1993. *The Age of Folk in the 1960s* [translation of original Japanese title]. Tokyo: Shinko Music.

6287 Maeda, Hirotake and Hirahara, Koji, eds. 1993. *The Age of New Music* [translation of original Japanese title]. Tokyo: Shinko Music.

6288 Masui, Keiji. 1990. *A Story of Asakusa Opera* [translation of original Japanese title]. Tokyo: Gendaigeijutsu-sha.

6289 Mita, Munesuke. 1967. *A History of Sentiments in Modern Japan* [translation of original Japanese title]. Tokyo: Kodansha.

6290 Mitsui, Torû. 1983. Japan in Japan: Notes on an Aspect of the Popular Music Record Industry in Japan. *Popular Music* 3: 107–20.

6291 Mitsui, Torû, ed. 1990. *Popular ongaku no kenkyu*. Tokyo: Ongakunotomo-sha.

6292 Mitsui, Torû. 1993. The Reception of the Music of American Southern Whites in Japan. In *Transforming Tradition: Folk Music Revivals Examined.*, ed. Neil V. Rosenberg. Champaign, IL: University of Illinois Press. 275–93.

6293 Mori, Akihide. 1988. *The Japanese Blues*. Tokyo: Shônen-sha.

6294 Murata, Hisao and Kojima, Satoshi, eds. 1991. *Talking About Japanese 'Popular'*

[translation of original Japanese title]. Tokyo: Shinko Music.

6295 Nakamura, Toyo. 1991. Early Pop Song Writers and Their Backgrounds. *Popular Music* 10(3): 263–82.

6296 Nishizawa, So. 1990. *A History of Modern Songs in Japan* [translation of original Japanese title]. 3 vols. Tokyo: Ofusha.

6297 Ogawa, Hiroshi. 1988. *Ongaku suru shakai*. Tokyo: Keiso Shobo.

6298 Ogawa, Hiroshi. 1990. Idol Industry Hits the Skids. *Pacific Friend* 18(1).

6299 Ogawa, Hiroshi. 1990. New Band Boom. *Pacific Friend* 18(4).

6300 Ogawa, Hiroshi. 1990. The Rise and Fall of the Red-and-White Show. *Pacific Friend* 18(8).

6301 Okada, Maki. 1991. Musical Characteristics of *Enka*. *Popular Music* 10(3): 283–303.

6302 Okano, Ben. 1988. *Enka genryuu ko*. Tokyo: Gakugei Shorin.

6303 Powers, Richard Gid and Kato, Hidetoshi, eds. 1989. *Handbook of Japanese Popular Culture*. Westport, CT: Greenwood Press.

6304 Savigliano, Marta E. 1992. Tango in Japan and the World Economy of Passion. In *Re-made in Japan: Everyday Life and Consumer Taste in a Changing Society*, ed. Joseph J. Tobin. New Haven, CT: Yale University Press. 235–52.

6305 Signell, Karl L. 1976. The Modernization Process in Two Oriental Music Cultures: Turkish and Japanese. *Asian Music* 7(2): 72–102.

6306 Tagawa, Tadasu. 1982. *Nihon no folk & rock shi*. Tokyo: Ongaku-no-tono-Sha.

6307 Tenku-kikaku. 1992. *Uchina Pop* [translation of original Japanese title]. Tokyo: Tokyo-shoseki.

6308 Yano, Christine. 1995. *Shaping of Tears of a Nation: An Ethnography of Emotion in Japanese Popular Song*. Hawaii: University of Hawaii Press.

South-East Asia

Indonesia

6309 Anderson-Sutton, R. 1986. The Crystallization of a Marginal Tradition: Music in Banyumas, West Central Java. *Yearbook for Traditional Music* 18: 115–32.

6310 Feld, Steven. 1982. *Sound and Sentiment: Birds, Weeping and Poetics in Kaluli Expression*. Philadelphia: University of Pennsylvania Press.

6311 Frederick, William. 1982. Rhoma Irama and the Dangdut Style: Aspects of Contemporary Indonesian Popular Culture. *Indonesia* 34: 102–30.

6312 Haryadi, Frans. 1978. Modern Music in Java. *The World of Music* 20: 100–102.

6313 Hatch, Martin. 1985. Popular Music in Indonesia. In *Popular Music Perspectives, 2*, ed. David Horn. Göteborg and Exeter: IASPM. 210–27.

6314 Heins, Ernst. 1975. Two Cases of Urban Folk Music in Jakarta: Kroncong and Tanjidor. *Asian Music* 7(1): 20–32.

6315 Jones, A.M. 1971. *Africa and Indonesia: The Evidence of the Xylophone and Other Musical and Cultural Factors*. Leiden: E.J. Brill.

6316 Kartomi, Margaret. 1970. Conflict in Javanese Music. *Studies in Music* 4: 62–80.

6317 Kartomi, Margaret. 1980. *Minangkabau Musical Culture: The Contemporary Scene and Recent Attempts at Its Modernisation*. New Haven, CT: Yale University Press.

6318 Mutsaers, Lutgard. 1990. Indorock: An Early Eurorock Style. *Popular Music* 9(3): 307–20.

6319 Sanger, Annette. 1989. *Music and Musicians, Dance and Dancers: Socio-Musical Interrelationships in Balinese Performance*. New York: International Council for Traditional Music.

Korea

6320 Lee, Kang-sook. 1980. Certain Experiences in Korean Music. In *Musics of Many Cultures*, ed. Elizabeth May. Berkeley and London: University of California Press. 32–47.

6321 Pak, Chanho. 1987. *Kankoku Kayo Shi 1895–1945*. Tokyo: Shobunsha.

Philippines

6322 Trimillos, Ricardo. 1986. Music and Ethnic Identity: Strategies Among Overseas Filipino Youth. *Yearbook for Traditional Music* 18: 9–20.

6323 Trimillos, Ricardo. 1987. Time-Distance and Melodic Models in Improvisation Among the Tausug of the Southern Philippines. *Yearbook for Traditional Music* 19: 23–36.

6324 Valdes, Carlos J., et al. 1982. *Rationalization of the Popular Music Industry in the Philippines*. 3 vols. Manila: Carlos J. Valdes for the Popular Music Foundation of the Philippines.

Thailand

6325 Morton, David. 1960. *Thai Musical Instruments*. Bangkok: Department of Fine Arts.

6326 Morton, David. 1980. The Music of Thailand. In *Musics of Many Cultures*, ed. Elizabeth May. Berkeley and London: University of California Press. 63–82.

6327 Myers-Moro, Pamela A. 1986. Songs for Life: Leftist Thai Popular Music in the

1970s. *Journal of Popular Culture* 20(3): 93–113.

6328 Siriyuvasak, Ubonrat. 1990. Commercialising the Sound of the People: Pleng Luktoong and the Thai Pop Music Industry. *Popular Music* 9(1): 61–78.

Vietnam

6329 Duy, Pham. 1975. *Musics of Vietnam.* Carbondale, IL: Southern Illinois University Press.

6330 Khe, Tran Van. 1983. A propos des publications sur la musique vietnamienne aux cours des 10 dernières années. *Yearbook for Traditional Music* 15: 149–51.

6331 Trainor, John. 1975. Significance and Development in the Vong Cô of South Vietnam. *Asian Music* 7(1): n.p.

CARIBBEAN

General

6332 Abrahams, Roger D. 1970. Patterns of Performance in the British West Indies. In *Afro-American Anthropology: Contemporary Perspectives,* ed. Norman E. Whitten and John F. Szwed. New York: Free Press. 163–79.

6333 Abrahams, Roger D. 1974. *Deep the Water, Shallow the Shore: Three Essays on Shantying in the West Indies.* Austin and London: University of Texas Press.

6334 Acosta, Leonardo. 1987. *From the Drum to the Synthesizer.* Havana: José Martí.

6335 Arteaga, José. 1994. *Música del Caribe.* Bogotá: Editorial Voluntad.

6336 Béhague, Gerard H., ed. 1994. *Music and Black Ethnicity: The Caribbean and South America.* Miami, FL: University of Miami, North-South Center.

6337 Bergman, Billy, et al. 1985. *Reggae and Latin Pop: Hot Sauces.* Poole: Blandford Press.

6338 Bilby, Kenneth. 1985. Caribbean Crucible. In *Repercussions: A Celebration of African-American Music,* ed. Geoffrey Haydon and Denis Marks. London: Century. 128–51.

6339 Bilby, Kenneth. 1985. The Caribbean as a Musical Region. In *Caribbean Contours,* ed. Sidney Mintz and Sally Price. Baltimore and London: Johns Hopkins University Press. 81–218.

6340 Boggs, Vernon, ed. 1992. *Salsiology: Afro-Cuban Music and the Evolution of Salsa in New York City.* New York: Greenwood Press.

6341 Cally-Lezin, Sully. 1990. *Musiques et danses afro-caraibes: Martinique.* Gros-Morne: The author.

6342 Cárdenas, Rocío. 1992. *Música caribeña.* Cali: Ediciones Universidad del Valle.

6343 Carpentier, Alejo. 1946. *La Música en Cuba.* Mexico City: Fondo de Cultura Económica.

6344 Cowley, John. 1985. Cultural 'Fusions': Aspects of British West Indian Music in the USA and Britain, 1918–51. *Popular Music* 5: 81–96.

6345 Cowley, John. 1985. *West Indian Gramophone Records in Britain: 1927–1950.* Coventry: Centre for Research in Ethnic Relations, University of Warwick.

6346 Cowley, John. 1985. West Indian Records in Britain. *Musical Traditions* 4: 28–30.

6347 Cowley, John. 1990. London Is the Place: Caribbean Music in the Context of the Empire, 1900–60. In *Black Music in Britain: Essays on the Afro-Asian Contribution to Popular Music,* ed. Paul Oliver. Milton Keynes: Open University Press. 58–76.

6348 Cowley, John. 1991. *Carnival and Other Seasonal Festivals in the West Indies, USA and Britain: A Selected Bibliographical Index*. Coventry: Centre for Research in Ethnic Relations, University of Warwick.

6349 Cowley, John. 1993. L'Année Passée: Selected Repertoire in English-Speaking West Indian Music, 1900–1960. *Keskidee: A Journal of Black Musical Traditions* 3: 2–44.

6350 Cowley, John. 1994. uBUNGCA (Oxford Bags): Recordings in London of African and West Indian Music in the 1920s and 1930s. *Musical Traditions* 12: 13–27.

6351 Cushman, Thomas. 1991. Rich Rastas and Communist Rockers: A Comparative Study of the Origin, Diffusion and Defusion of Revolutionary Musical Codes. *Journal of Popular Culture* 25(3): 17–62.

6352 De Lerma, Dominique-René. 1981. *Bibliography of Black Music, Vol. 1. Reference Materials*. Westport and London: Greenwood Press.

6353 Fiehrer, Thomas. 1991. From Quadrille to Stomp: The Creole Origins of Jazz. *Popular Music* 10(1): 21–38.

6354 Flores, Juan. 1991. Cortijo's Revenge. *Centro de Estudios Puertorriqueños-Boletín* 3(2): 8–21.

6355 Guilbault, Jocelyne. 1993. *Zouk: World Music in the West Indies*. Chicago: University of Chicago Press.

6356 Guralnick, Peter. 1979. *Lost Highway: Journeys and Arrivals of American Musicians*. Boston, MA: David R. Godine.

6357 Hebdige, Dick. 1987. *Cut 'n' Mix: Culture, Identity and Caribbean Music*. London and New York: Comedia/Methuen.

6358 Leal, Néstor. 1992. *Boleros. La canción romántica del Caribe (1930–1960)*. Caracas: Grijalbo.

6359 Lent, John, ed. 1990. *Caribbean Popular Culture*. Bowling Green, OH: Bowling Green State University Press.

6360 León, Argeliers. 1984. *Del canto y el tiempo*. Havana: Editorial Letras.

6361 Lucas, Maria Elizabeth, comp. 1989. Directory of Latin American and Caribbean Music Theses and Dissertations (1984–1988). *Latin American Music Review* 10(1): 148–76.

6362 Malavet Vega, Pedro. 1988. *Del bolero a la nueva canción*. Ponce: Editoria Corripio.

6363 Manuel, Peter, Kenneth Bilby and Michael Largey. 1995. *Caribbean Currents: Caribbean Music from Rumba to Reggae*. Philadelphia: Temple University Press.

6364 Midgett, Douglas K. 1977. Performance Roles and Musical Change in a Caribbean Society. *Ethnomusicology* 21(1): 55–73.

6365 Pacini Hernandez, Deborah. 1993. A View from the South: Spanish Caribbean Perspectives on World Beat. *The World of Music* 35(2): 48–69.

6366 Pinckney, Warren R., Jr. 1992. Jazz in the US Virgin Islands. *American Music* 10(4): 441–67.

6367 Roberts, John Storm. 1974. (1972) *Black Music of Two Worlds*. New York: William Morrow. First published New York/London: Praeger/Allen Lane, 1972.

6368 Roberts, John Storm. 1979. *The Latin Tinge: The Impact of Latin American Music on the United States*. New York: Oxford University Press.

6369 Rosemain, Jacqueline. 1987. *La musique dans la société antillaise, 1635–1902*,

Martinique, Guadeloupe. Paris: L'Harmattan.

6370 Sealy, John and Malm, Krister. 1982. *Music in the Caribbean.* London: Routledge & Kegan Paul.

6371 Van Dam, Theodore. 1954. The Influence of West African Songs of Derision in the New World. *African Music* 1(1): 53–56.

6372 Waterman, Richard. 1952. African Influence on the Music of the Americas. In *Acculturation in the Americas, 2,* ed. Sol Tax. Chicago: University of Chicago Press. 207–18.

6373 Waxer, Lise. 1994. Of Mambo Kings and Songs of Love: Dance Music in Havana and New York from the 1930s to the 1950s. *Latin American Music Review* 15(2): 139–76.

Cuba

6374 Acosta, Leonardo. 1993. *Elige tu, que canto yo.* La Habana: Editorial Letras Cubanas.

6375 Alén Rodriguez, Olavo. 1991. Center for the Research and Development of Cuban Music. *Worldbeat* 1: 186–93.

6376 Alén Rodriguez, Olavo. 1994. *De lo Afrocubano a la Salsa: Géneros Musicales de Cuba.* Havana: Ediciones Artex.

6377 Andacht, Fernando. 1986. El canto popular: su público, su crisis. *La del taller* 7: 28–36.

6378 Boggs, Vernon. 1991. Musical Transculturation: From Afro-Cuban to Afro-Cubanism. *Popular Music & Society* 15(4): 71–83.

6379 Boggs, Vernon. 1992. *Salsiology: Afro-Cuban Music and the Evolution of Salsa in New York City.* New York: Excelsior Music Publishing Company.

6380 Brouwer, Leo. 1991. La musica, il cubano e l'innovazione. *Musica/Realtà* 36: 103–16.

6381 Cañizares, Dulcila. 1992. *La trova tradicional cubana.* La Habana: Editorial Letras Cubanas.

6382 Carpentier, Alejo. 1984. (1946) *La Musica en Cuba.* Mexico: Fondo de Cultura Económica. First published Mexico: Fondo de Cultura Económica, 1946.

6383 Contreras, Félix. 1989. *Porque tienen filin.* Santiago de Cuba: Editorial Oriente.

6384 Cornelius, Steven. 1990. Encapsulating Power: Meaning and Taxonomy of the Musical Instruments of Santeria in New York City. *Selected Reports in Ethnomusicology* 8: 125–41.

6385 Cornelius, Steven. 1991. Drumming for the Orishas: Reconstruction of Tradition in New York City. In *Essays on Cuban Music: North American and Cuban Perspectives,* ed. Peter Manuel. Lanham, MD: University Press of America. 136–56.

6386 Courlander, Harold. 1942. Musical Instruments of Cuba. *Musical Quarterly* 28: 227–40.

6387 Daniel, Yvonne. 1995. *Rumba: Dance and Social Change in Contemporary Cuba.* Bloomington and Indianapolis: Indiana University Press.

6388 Díaz Ayala, Cristobal. 1981. *Discografía de la música cubana: volumen 1, 1898 a 1925.* San Juan: Fundación Musicalia.

6389 Díaz Ayala, Cristobal. 1981. *Música cubana del areyto a la nueva trova,* revised edition. San Juan: Editorial Cubanacan.

6390 Eli, Victoria and Gómez, Zoila. 1989. *Haciendo música cubana.* La Habana: Editorial Pueblo y Educación.

6391 Febles, Jorge. 1990. Popular Song as Degrading Text: Two 'Sones' by Miguel Matamoros. *Journal of Popular Culture* 24(1): 79–86.

6392 Galan, Natalio. 1983. *Cuba y sus sones.* Valencia: Pre-Textos.

6393 Garcíaporrúa, Jorge. 1987. Síntesis, el rock cubano. *Clave* 5: 12–15.

6394 No entry.

6395 Hellqvist, Per-Anders. 1978. *Röster på Cuba: Om musik, kultur, samhälle.* Stockholm: Sveriges Radios Förlag.

6396 Kaden, Christian. 1989. Cultural Diversity: A Challenge to the World of Music. *The World of Music* 31(2): 114–40.

6397 León, Argeliers. 1984. *Del canto y el tiempo.* La Habana: Editorial Letras Cubanas.

6398 Manuel, Peter. 1985. The Anticipated Bass in Cuban Popular Music. *Latin American Music Review* 6(2): 249–61.

6399 Manuel, Peter. 1987. Marxism, Nationalism and Popular Music in Revolutionary Cuba. *Popular Music* 6(2): 161–78.

6400 Manuel, Peter, ed. 1991. *Essays on Cuban Music: North American and Cuban Perspectives.* Lanham, MD: University Press of America.

6401 Orovio, Hélio. 1981. *Diccionario de la música cubana: Biográfico y técnico.* La Habana: Editorial Letras Cubanas.

6401a Orozco, Danilo. 1992. Pocesos socioculturales y rasgos de identidad en los generos musicales con reference especial a la música cubana. *Latin American Music Review* 13(2): 158–78.

6402 Ortiz, Fernando. 1952. *Los instrumentos de la música afro-cubana.* 5 vols. La Habana: Ministerio de Educación.

6403 Perez Firmat, Gustavo. 1994. *Life on the Hyphen: The Cuban-American Way.* Austin, TX: University of Texas Press.

6404 Pérez Sanjurjo, Elena. 1986. *Historia de la Música Cubana.* Miami, FL: Moderna Poesía.

6405 Robbins, James. 1989. Practical and Abstract Taxonomy in Cuban Music. *Ethnomusicology* 33(3): 379–89.

6406 Robbins, James. 1991. Institutions, Incentives, and Evaluations in Cuban Music-Making. In *Essays on Cuban Music: North American and Cuban Perspectives*, ed. Peter Manuel. Lanham, MD: University Press of America. 215–48.

6407 Rodriguez, Victora Elí. 1989. Apuntes sobre la creación musical actuel en Cuba. *Latin American Music Review* 10(2): 287–97.

6408 Suco, Idalberto. 1986. ¿Jazz latino o música cubana? *Clave* 1: 16–22.

6409 Whites, Charles W. 1992. Report on Music in Cuba Today. *Latin American Music Review* 13(2): 234–42.

Dominica

6410 González, Almanzor. 1989. *Recopilación de la música popular dominicana.* Santo Domingo: Taller.

6411 Pacini Hernandez, Deborah. 1991. La lucha sonora: Dominican Popular Music in the Post-Trujillo Era. *Latin American Music Review* 12(2): 105–23.

6412 Sistachs, Enriqueta. 1985. La situazione musicale nella Repubblica Dominicana. *Musica/Realtà* 17: 167–76.

Haiti

6413 Averill, Gage. 1989. Haitian Dance Bands, 1915–1970: Class, Race and Authenticity. *Latin American Music Review* 10(2): 203–35.

LOCATIONS

6414 Courlander, Harold. 1960. *The Drum and the Hoe: Life and Lore of the Haitian People*. Berkeley, CA: University of California Press.

6415 Courlander, Harold. 1973. (1939) *Haiti Singing*. New York: Cooper Square.

6416 Juste-Constant, Vogeli. 1990. Haitian Popular Music in Montreal: The Effect of Acculturation. *Popular Music* 9(1): 79–86.

6417 Wilcken, Lois E. 1992. Power, Ambivalence, and the Remaking of Haitian Vodoun Music in New York. *Latin American Music Review* 13(1): 1–32.

Jamaica

6418 Boot, Adrian and Thomas, Michael. 1976. *Jamaica, Babylon on a Thin Wire*. London: Thames and Hudson.

6419 Clarke, Sebastian. 1980. *Jah Music: The Evolution of the Popular Jamaican Song*. London: Heinemann Educational Books.

6420 Cooper, Carolyn. 1993. *Noises in the Blood: Orality, Gender and the 'Vulgar' Body of Jamaican Popular Culture*. London: Macmillan.

6421 Jones, Simon. 1988. *Black Culture, White Youth: The Reggae Tradition from JA to UK*. Basingstoke: Macmillan Education.

6422 Weber, Tom. 1992. *Reggae Island: Jamaican Music in the Digital Age*. Kingston: Kingston Publications.

6423 White, Garth. 1982. *The Development of Jamaican Popular Music, with Special Reference to the Music of Bob Marley: A Bibliography*. Kingston: African-Caribbean Institute of Jamaica.

6424 Witmer, Robert. 1987. 'Local' and 'Foreign': The Popular Music Culture of Kingston, Jamaica, Before Ska, Rocksteady and Reggae. *Latin American Music Review* 8(1): 1–25.

Puerto Rico

6425 Block, Peter. 1973. *La-le-lo-lai: Puerto Rican Music and Its Performers*. New York: Plus Ultra Ed. Publishers, Inc.

6426 Canino Salgado, Marcelino. 1986. (1974) *El Cantar Folklórico de Puerto Rico*. Rio Piedras: Editorial de la Universidad de Puerto Rico.

6427 Cortez, Felix, Angel Facon and Juan Flores. 1976. The Cultural Expression of Puerto Ricans in New York: A Theoretical Perspective and Critical Review. *Latin American Perspective* 3(3): 117–52.

6428 Davis, Martha Ellen. 1972. The Social Organization of a Musical Event: The Fiesta de Cruz in San Juan, Puerto Rico. *Ethnomusicology* 16(1): 38–62.

6429 Duany, Jorge. 1984. Popular Music in Puerto Rico: Toward an Anthropology of Salsa. *Latin American Music Review* 5(2): 186–216.

6430 Duany, Jorge. 1990. Salsa, Plena and Danza: Recent Materials on Puerto Rican Popular Music. *Latin American Music Review* 11(2): 286–96.

6431 Glasser, Ruth. 1990. Paradoxical Ethnicity: Puerto Rican Musicians in Post World War I New York City. *Latin American Music Review* 11(1): 63–72.

6432 Glasser, Ruth. 1995. *My Music Is My Flag: Puerto Rican Musicians and Their New York Communities: 1917–1940*. Berkeley, CA: University of California Press.

6433 Hernandez, Prisco. 1993. Décima, Seis, and the Art of the Puertorican Trovador Within the Modern Social Context. *Latin American Music Review* 14(1): 20–51.

6434 López Cruz, Francisco. 1967. *La Música Folklórica de Puerto Rico*. Sharon, CT: Troutman.

294

6435 Malavet Vega, Pedro. 1988. *Del Bolero a la Nueva Canción*. Ponce.

6436 Manuel, Peter. 1994. Puerto Rican Music and Cultural Identity: Creative Appropriation of Cuban Sources from Danza to Salsa. *Ethnomusicology* 38(2): 249–80.

6437 Ortiz, Pablo. 1991. *A tres voces y guitarras: Los tríos en Puerto Rico*, ed. Pablo Ortiz. San Juan: Pablo Ortiz.

6438 Pinckney, Warren R., Jr. 1989. Puerto Rican Jazz and the Incorporation of Folk Music: An Analysis of New Musical Directions. *Latin American Music Review* 10(2): 236–66.

6439 Roseman, Marina. 1983. The New Rican Village: Artists in Control of the Image-Making Machinery. *Latin American Music Review* 4(1): 132–67.

6440 Singer, Roberta. 1988. Puerto Rican Music in New York City. *New York Folklore* 14(3–4): 139–50.

6441 Thompson, Annie Figueroa, comp. 1977. *Bibiografia anotada sobre la meusica en Puerto Rico*. San Juan: Instituto de Cultura Puertorriqueña.

St. Vincent

6442 Abrahams, Roger D. 1972. Christmas and Carnival in St. Vincent. *Western Folklore* 31(4).

Trinidad and Tobago

6443 Aho, William R. 1987. Steel Band Music in Trinidad and Tobago: The Creation of a People's Music. *Latin American Music Review* 8(1): 26–58.

6444 Campbell, Susan. 1989. Carnival, Calypso and Class Struggle in Nineteenth Century Trinidad. *History Workshop* 26: 1–27.

6445 Cowley, John. 1985. Carnival in Trinidad. *Musical Traditions* 4: 4–8.

6446 Cowley, John. 1996. *Carnival, Canboulay and Calypso: Traditions in the Making*. Cambridge: Cambridge University Press.

6447 Elder, J.D. 1966. Kalinda: Son of the Battling Troubadors of Trinidad. *Journal of the Folklore Institute* 3(2).

6448 Hill, Errol. 1972. *The Trinidad Carnival*. Austin, TX: University of Texas Press.

6449 Hill, Errol. 1975. The Trinidad Carnival: Cultural Change and Synthesis. *Cultures* 3(1): 54–86.

6450 Juneja, Renu. 1988. The Trinidad Carnival: Ritual, Performance, Spectacle, and Symbol. *Journal of Popular Culture* 21(4): 87–100.

6451 Myers, Helen. 1978. The Process of Change in Trinidad East Indian Music. *Journal of the Indian Musicological Society* 9(3): 11–16.

6452 Patton, John H. 1994. Calypso as Rhetorical Performance: Trinidad Carnival, 1993. *Latin American Music Review* 15(1): 55–74.

6453 Pearse, Andrew. 1956. Carnival in Nineteenth Century Trinidad. *Caribbean Quarterly* 4(3) & 4(4): 175–93.

6454 Quevedo, Raymond. 1983. *Attila's Kaiso: A Short History of Trinidad Calypso*, ed. Errol Hill. St. Augustine: University of the West Indies.

6455 Rohlehr, Gordon. 1990. *Calypso & Society in Pre-Independence Trinidad*. Port of Spain: Gordon Rohlehr.

6456 *Trinidad Carnival*. 1988. (1956) Port of Spain: Paria Publishing Company. (First published in *Caribbean Quarterly* 4(3&4) (1956).)

6457 Warner, Keith. 1985. *Kaiso! The Trinidad Calypso: A Study of the Calypso as Oral Literature*. Washington, DC: Three Continents Press.

LOCATIONS

EASTERN AND SOUTH-EASTERN EUROPE

General

6458 Bausch, Armando. 1985. *Jazz in Europa*. Trier: Editions Phi.

6459 Humann, Klaus and Reichert, Carl-Ludwig, eds. 1981. *EuroRock. Länder und Szenen. Ein Überblick*. Reinbek bei Hamburg: Rowohlt.

6460 Jost, Ekkehard. 1993. Über das Europäische im europäischen Jazz. In *Jazz in Europa*, ed. Wolfram Knauer. Hofheim: Wolke. 233–49.

6461 Knauer, Wolfram, ed. 1993. *Jazz in Europa*. Hofheim: Wolke.

6462 Kotek, Josef. 1975. *Kronika èeské synkopy. Pùstoletí èeského jazzu a moderní populární hudby v obrazech a svedìctvich souèasnikù, 1903–1938*. Praha: Supraphon.

6463 Kurkela, Vesa. 1993. Deregulation of Popular Music in the European Post-Communist Countries: Business Identity and Cultural Collage. *The World of Music* 35(3): 80–196.

6464 Lotz, Rainer E. 1990. The Black Troubadours: Black Entertainers in Europe, 1896–1915. *Black Music Research Journal* 10(2): 253–73.

6465 Manuel, Peter. 1989. *Modal Harmony in Andalusian, Eastern European and Turkish Syncretic Musics*. New York: International Council for Traditional Music.

6466 Noglik, Bert. 1993. Osteuropäischer Jazz im Umbruch der Verhältnisse: Vom Wandel der Sinne im Prozeß gesellschaftlicher Veränderungen. In *Jazz in Europa*, ed. Wolfram Knauer. Hofheim: Wolke. 147–68.

6467 Otterbach, Friedemann. 1980. *Die Geschichte der europäischen Tanzmusik*.

Einführung. Wilhelmshaven: Heinrichshofen.

6468 Pekacz, Jolanta. 1991. 'Gott erhalte unsern Kaiser': The Image of the World in Galician School Songbooks in the Second Half of the Nineteenth Century. *Worldbeat* 1: 95–108.

6469 Polednak, Ivan. 1985. Zur Problematik der nonartifiziellen Musik slawischer Völker. *Beiträge zur Musikwissenschaft* 3–4: 285–94.

6470 Ryback, Timothy. 1990. *Rock Around the Bloc: A History of Rock Music in Eastern Europe and the Soviet Union*. New York and London: Oxford University Press.

6471 Watts, Michael. 1975. The Call and Response of American Popular Music: The Impact of American Pop Music in Europe. In *Superculture: American Popular Culture and Europe*, ed. C.W.E. Bigsby. London: Elek. 123–39.

6472 Young, James. 1995. *A Hard Place*. London: Century.

Balkan Countries (former Yugoslavia)

6473 Ambrozic-Paic, Arlette. 1974. Mass Media and Pop Groups in Yugoslavia. In *New Patterns of Musical Behaviour*, ed. Irmgard Bontinck. Wien: Universal Edition. 119–28.

6474 Barbarich, Peter. 1982. Prekriti z listjem. Intervju z Elektricnim Orgazmom. *Revija Glasbene Mladine Slovenije* 3/10/12.

6475 Barber-Kersovan, Alenka. 1982. Tradition and Acculturation as Polarities of Slovenian Popular Music. In *Popular Music Perspectives, 1*, ed. David Horn and Philip Tagg. Göteborg and Exeter: IASPM. 174–89.

6476 Barber-Kersovan, Alenka. 1995. Etablierte Alternative. In *Popular Music Perspectives III*, ed. Peter Wicke. Berlin: Zyankrise. 59–71.

6477 Kolar, Walter W. 1981. *An Introduction to Croatian Musical Folklore.* Pittsburgh, PA: Tamburitza Press.

6478 Kos, K. 1972. New Dimensions in Folk Music: A Contribution to the Study of Musical Tastes in Contemporary Yugoslav Society. *International Review of the Aesthetics and Sociology of Music* 3(1): 61–73.

6479 Lockwood, Yvonne R. 1983. *Text and Context: Folksong in a Bosnian Muslim Village.* Columbus, OH: Slavica Publishers.

6480 Maleckar, Nez and Mastnak, Tomaz. 1985. *Punk pod Slovenci.* Ljubljana: KRT.

6481 Ramet, Sabrina Petra. 1994. Shake, Rattle, and Self-Management: Making the Scene in Yugoslavia. In *Rocking the State: Rock Music and Politics in Eastern Europe and Russia,* ed. Sabrina Petra Ramet. Boulder, CO: Westview Press. 103–40.

6482 Simic, Andrei. 1976. Country 'n' Western Yugoslav Style: Folk Music as a Mirror of Social Sentiment. *Journal of Popular Culture* 10(1): 156–66.

6483 Smith, Gregory E. 1991. In Quest of a New Perspective on Improvised Jazz: A View from the Balkans. *The World of Music* 33(3): 29–52.

6484 Vidic Rasmussen, Ljerka. 1991. Gypsy Music in Yugoslavia: Inside the Popular Culture Tradition. *Journal of the Gypsy Lore Society* 5(1): 127–39.

6485 Vidic Rasmussen, Ljerka. 1995. From Source to Commodity: Newly Composed Folk Music of Yugoslavia. *Popular Music* 14(2): 241–56.

Bulgaria

6486 Ashley, Stephen. 1994. The Bulgarian Rock Scene Under Communism (1962–1990). In *Rocking the State: Rock Music and Politics in Eastern Europe and Russia,* ed. Sabrina Petra Ramet. Boulder, CO: Westview Press. 141–64.

6487 Bakalov, Todor. 1992. *Svatbarskite orkestri.* Sofia: Muzika.

6488 Dainov, Evgeni. 1991. *Zabavlenijata na drugata polovina: rokat i savremennata kulturna situacia.* Sofia: Kliment Ohridski University Press.

6489 Djokanov, Sergei and Rupchev, Jordan. 1994. *Pop rok dzhaz – leksikon.* Sofia: Prosveta.

6490 Gaitandjiev, Gencho. 1973. Uchilishteto i njakoi projavi na muzikalnite interesi i na muzikalnija vkus na uchenicite. *Bulgarsko muzikoznanie* 2: 32–92.

6491 Gaitandjiev, Gencho. 1982. Detckoto muzikalno tvorchesto – sredstvo, a ne cel. *Bulgarsko muzikoznanie* 2: 42–49.

6492 Gaitandjiev, Gencho. 1986. 'Vecherjai Rado' na rokscenata. *Mladezh* 10: 62–65.

6493 Levy, Claire. 1981. Sashtnost, zadachi i funkcija na savremennata politicheska pesen kato osoben tip javlenie v oblastta na kulturata. *Bulgarsko muzikoznanie* 1: 49–64.

6494 Levy, Claire. 1990. Vavedenie kam problema za vzaimodeistvijata v rokmuzikata. *Bulgarsko muzikoznanie* 2: 16–28.

6495 Levy, Claire. 1991. Za rokmuzikata i neinata ekspanzija: opit za postavjane na problema za nacionalnata identichnost v uslovijata na dominirashtata pop kultura. *Bulgarsko muzikoznanie* 3: 44–54.

6496 Levy, Claire. 1992. The Influence of British Rock in Bulgaria. *Popular Music* 11(2): 209–12.

6497 Levy, Claire. 1993. Rokmuzikata v Bulgarija: Nachaloto. *Bulgarsko muzikoznanie* 3: 9–16.

6498 Levy, Claire. 1994. The Cork's Popped Out of the Bottle . . . So What Do We Do Now the Champagne's Jetting All Over the Place? US Influence in the Light of Bulgarian Realities. In *Central European Popular Music*, ed. Ales Opekar. Prague: Institute of Musicology, Academy of Sciences of Czech Republic. 36–40.

6499 Pekkilä, Erkki. 1985. Culture, Non-Culture and Myth in Bulgarian Music-Folklorism. *Musiikin suunta* 7: 45–53.

6500 Rupchev, Jordan, and Hofmann, Heinz P. 1987. *ABeVe na popmuzikata*. Sofia: Muzika.

6501 Spasov, Rumen and Nedeva-Voeva, Neli. 1990. *Ambiciata, Narecena BG-Rock*. Sofia.

6502 Statelova, Rosemary. 1987. Die populäre Musik in Bulgarien. *Beilage zur Zeitschrift 'Unterhaltungskunst'* 1: 2–4.

6503 Statelova, Rosemary. 1989. Iz istorijata na zabavnata muzika. *Bulgarsko muzikoznanie* 3: 58–73.

6504 Statelova, Rosemary. 1993. *Obarnatata piramida. Aspekti na populjarnata muzika*. Sofia: Edem.

6505 Statelova, Rosemary. 1994. Das Elementare. *PopScriptum* 2: 82–93.

6506 Statelova, Rosemary. 1994. The Process of Americanisation of Bulgarian Pop Music: Development, Forcible Interruption and New Assertation. In *Central European Popular Music*, ed. Ales Opekar. Prague: Institute of Musicology, Academy of Sciences of Czech Republic. 32–36.

6507 Statelova, Rosemary. 1995. Das populäre Tagebuch: Der Verlust einer Funktion. In *Popular Music Perspectives III*, ed. Peter Wicke. Berlin: Zyankrise. 48–51.

6508 Statelova, Rosemary. 1995. Dinamika v razvitieto na populjarno-muzikalnite zhanrove v Bulgaria v parvata polovina na 90-te godini. *Bulgarsko muzikoznanie* 2: 59–86.

6509 Statelova, Rosemary. 1995. *Prezhivjano v Bulgaria. Rok, pop, folk 1990–1994*. Sofia: Riva.

6510 Statelova, Rosemary. 1996. Cennostno-smislovi aspekti na populjarnata muzika v Bulgaria. *Bulgarsko muzikoznanie* 2: 64–91.

6511 Statelova, Rosemary and Chendov, Chavdar. 1983. *Popmuzikata*. Sofia: Muzika.

6512 Stojanova, Svetla. 1990. Njakoi nabljudenija varhu bulgarskata filmova muzika prez perioda ot 1944 do kraja na 60-te godini. *Bulgarsko muzikoznanie* 2: 3–15.

6513 Tschernokoscheva, Elka. 1995. Populäre Musik und Aneignung des Alltags Umgang mit Musik als Form der Lebensbewältigung. In *Popular Music Perspectives III*, ed. Peter Wicke. Berlin: Zyankrise. 52–54.

6514 Valchinova, Elisaveta. 1982. Za repertoara na voennite duhovi orkestri v Bulgaria (1879–1944) i mjastoto na bulgarskoto muzikalno tvorchestvo v nego. *Bulgarsko muzikoznanie* 3: 66–71.

Czechoslovakia (including the recently created countries of the Czech Republic and Slovakia)

6515 Doruška, Lubomír. 1978. *Populárna hudba – priemysel, obchod, umenie*. Bratislava: Opus.

6516 Doruška, Lubomír. 1993. Jazz in der Tschechoslowakei 1945 bis 1993. In *Jazz in Europa*, ed. Wolfram Knauer. Hofheim: Wolke. 129–46.

6517 Doruška, Lubomír and Doruška, Peter. 1981. *Panorama populární hudby, 1918–1978*. Praha: Mladá Fronta.

6518 Kotek, Josef. 1975. *Kronika èeské synkopy. Vol. 1. 1903–1938. Pùlstoleti èeského jazzu a moderní populární hudby v obrazech a svedìctvich souèasnìkù.* Prague: Supraphon.

6519 Mitchell, Tony. 1992. Mixing Pop and Politics: Rock Music in Czechoslovakia Before and After the Velvet Revolution. *Popular Music* 11(2): 187–204.

6520 Opekar, Ales. 1995. Functions and Situations of Popular Music in Czechoslovakia Between Two Revolutions. In *Popular Music Perspectives III*. ed. Peter Wicke. Berlin: Zyankrise. 127–30.

6521 Opekar, Ales. 1995. The Influence of Czech Folklore on Czech Rock Music. In *Popular Music: Style and Identity*, ed. Will Straw, et al. Montréal: The Centre for Research on Canadian Cultural Industries and Institutions. 229–31.

6522 Ramet, Sabrina Petra. 1994. Rock Music in Czechoslovakia. In *Rocking the State: Rock Music and Politics in Eastern Europe and Russia*, ed. Sabrina Petra Ramet. Boulder, CO: Westview Press. 55–72.

6523 Simek, Milan. 1974. Musical Interests of the Czech Youth in the Light of Research Findings. In *New Patterns of Musical Behaviour*, ed. Irmgard Bontinck. Wien: Universal Edition. 140–41.

German Democratic Republic

6524 Binas, Susanne. 1992. 'Keep It Heavy, Keep It Hard': Zu einigen Aspekten soziokorporeller Kommunika-tionsmuster im Prozeß der Geschlechtersozialisation – Heavy-Metal in der 'ehemaligen' DDR. *PopScriptum* I(1): 96–111.

6525 Binas, Susanne. 1996. Die 'anderen Bands' und ihre Kassettenproduktionen: Zwischen organisiertem Kulturbetrieb und selbstorganisierten Kulturformen. In *Rockmusik und Politik. Analysen,*

Interviews und Dokumente, ed. Peter Wicke and Lothar Müller. Berlin: Ch. Links. 48–62.

6526 Bloß, Monika. 1995. Veränderte soziale Realität: Fallbeispiel DDR. In *Popular Music Perspectives III*, ed. Peter Wicke. Berlin: Zyankrise. 77–84.

6527 Leitner, Olaf. 1983. *Rockszene DDR: Aspekte einer Massenkultur im Sozialismus.* Reinbek bei Hamburg: Rowohlt.

6528 Mayer, Günter. 1984. Popular Music in the GDR. *Journal of Popular Culture* 18(3): 145–58.

6529 Neitmann, Erich. 1982. *Das politische Lied im schulischen Musikunterricht der DDR.* Bern: Lang.

6530 Noglik, Bert. 1996. Hürdenlauf zum freien Spiel. Ein Rückblick auf den Jazz der DDR. In *Jazz in Deutschland*, ed. Wolfram Knauer. Hofheim: Wolke. 205–22.

6531 Ojakäär, Walter. 1993. Jazz in Estland. Hoffnungen und Wirklichkeit. In *Jazz in Europa*, ed. Wolfram Knauer. Hofheim: Wolke. 95–106.

6532 Osang, Alexander. 1994. Beatmusik – Staatlich gepflegt. Levis, Springsteen, Coca Cola und Herbstrevolution im Osten. In *Puhdys. Eine Kultband aus dem Osten*, ed. Peter Wicke and Irmela Hannover. Berlin: Elephanten Press. 55–60.

6533 Penzel, Katrin. 1994. Unter der Käseglocke. Kulturverwaltung und DDR-Rockszene. In *Puhdys. Eine Kultband aus dem Osten*, ed. Peter Wicke and Irmela Hannover. Berlin: Elephanten Press. 61–66.

6534 Rauhut, Michael. 1993. *Beat in der Grauzone. DDR-Rock 1964 bis 1972 – Politik und Alltag.* Berlin: BasisDruck.

6535 Rauhut, Michael. 1995. Von der Utopie zum Original. Kulturpolitische

Koordinaten früher DDR-Rockentwicklung. In *Popular Music Perspectives III*, ed. Peter Wicke. Berlin: Zyankrise. 387–91.

6536 Rauhut, Michael. 1996. Ohr an Masse – Rockmusik im Fadenkreuz der Stasi. In *Rockmusik und Politik. Analysen, Interviews und Dokumente*, ed. Peter Wicke and Lothar Müller. Berlin: Ch. Links. 28–47.

6537 Sommer, Günter. 1990. Über einige Besonderheiten der Jazzszene in der DDR. In *Darmstädter Jazzforum 89: Beiträge zur Jazzforschung*, ed. Ekkehard Jost. Hofheim: Wolke. 120–34.

6538 Wicke, Peter. 1981. Rockmusik in der DDR. Erfahrungen – Tendenzen – Perspektiven. *Beilage zur Zeitschrift 'Unterhaltungskunst'* 2.

6539 Wicke, Peter. 1981. Rockmusik in der DDR. Stationen einer Entwicklung. *Bulletin* XVII(2–3): 4–9.

6540 Wicke, Peter. 1982. Les avatars du rock. *Connaissance de la RDA* 14: 59–72.

6541 Wicke, Peter. 1985. Dialektika sootnashenyja nazionalnovo y internationalnovo na primeryje populjarnoy muzyka GDR. In *Rasvlekatelnyje Formy iskustro v rasvitom obtschestro*, ed. Evgenij Dukow, et al. Moskva: Progress. 51–76.

6542 Wicke, Peter. 1985. Jugend und populäre Musik. *Bulletin* XXI(2): 9–12.

6543 Wicke, Peter. 1985. Young People and Popular Music in East Germany: Focus on a Scene. *Communication Research* XII(3): 319–27.

6544 Wicke, Peter. 1989. Back in the DDR. Poponderzoek in Oostduitsland. *Link* V(90–4): 12–18.

6545 Wicke, Peter. 1989. Jugendszene DDR. Zur Situation der Rock– und Popmusik. *Kulturpolitische Mitteilungen (Zeitschrift der Kulturpolitischen Gesellschaft)* 47: 18–21.

6546 Wicke, Peter. 1990. Zwischen Anpassung und Verweigerung. Pop und Politik in der DDR. *Politicum* 47: 25–28.

6547 Wicke, Peter. 1991. Die Entwicklung der Jugendszenen in der DDR. In *Rock & Pop '89. Kritische Analysen, Kulturpolitische Alternativen II*. Hagen: Kulturpolitische Gesellschaft. 23–33.

6548 Wicke, Peter. 1992. (1987) The Role of Rock Music in Processes of Political Change in the GDR. In *Popular Music & Communication*, ed. James Lull, 2nd edition. Newbury Park, CA: Sage.

6549 Wicke, Peter. 1992. 'The Times They Are A-Changin'': Rock Music and Political Change in East Germany. In *Rockin' the Boat: Mass Music and Mass Movements*, ed. Reebee Garofalo. Boston, MA: South End Press. 81–92.

6550 Wicke, Peter. 1993. Born in the GDR. Zur Situation von Jugendkultur und Rockmusik. In *Woher – Wohin? Kinder- und Jugendkulturarbeit in Ostdeutschland*. Remscheid: Bundesvereinigung kulturelle Jugendbildung.

6551 Wicke, Peter. 1994. 'Wenn Träume sterben . . .' Die Puhdys und der Alltag in der DDR. In *Puhdys. Eine Kultband aus dem Osten*, ed. Peter Wicke and Irmela Hannover. Berlin: Elephanten Press. 17–22.

6552 Wicke, Peter. 1995. 'Der King vom Prenzlauer Berg'. Vom Mythos des Rock in einer sozialistischen Metropole. In *Berlin – Hauptstadt der DDR 1949–1989: Utopie und Realität*, ed. Bernd Wilzek. Zürich and Baden Baden: Elster-Verlag. 236–47.

6553 Wicke, Peter. 1996. Pop Music in the GDR: Between Conformity and Resistance. In *Changing Identities in East Germany (Studies in GDR Culture and Society 14(15))*, ed. M. Gerber and R.

Wood. Lanham, MD: University Press of America. 25–37.

6554 Wicke, Peter. 1996. Rock Around Socialism. Jugend und ihre Musik in einer gescheiterten Gesellschaft. In *Jugend und ihre Musik*, ed. Dieter Baacke. München: Juventus. 26–41.

6555 Wicke, Peter. 1996. Zwischen Förderung und Reglementierung – Rockmusik im System der DDR-Kulturbürokratie. In *Rockmusik und Politik. Analysen, Interviews und Dokumente*, ed. Peter Wicke and Lothar Müller. Berlin: Ch. Links. 11–27.

6556 Wicke, Peter and Frevel, Bernd. 1996. 'Wenn die Musik sich ändert zittern die Mauern der Stadt'. Rockmusik als Medium des politischen Diskurses im DDR-Kulturbetrieb. In *Musik und Politik*. Regensburg: Coda. 120–42.

6557 Wicke, Peter, and Shepherd, John. 1993. 'The Cabaret Is Dead': Rock Culture as State Enterprise – The Political Organization of Rock in East Germany. In *Culture and Politics: The Politics of Culture*, ed. Tony Bennett. Sydney, London and Boston: Routledge & Kegan Paul. 25–36.

Greece

6558 Baud-Bovy, Samuel. 1983. *Essai sur la Chanson Populaire Grecque*. Navplion: Fondation ethnographique du Péleponèse.

6559 Butterworth, Katherine. 1975. *Rembetika: Songs from the Old Greek Underworld*. Athens: Komboloi.

6560 Cowan, Jane K. 1990. *Dance and the Body Politic in Northern Greece*. Princeton, NJ: Princeton University Press.

6561 Harrison, John. 1984. Damn Society: An Introduction to Greek Rembetika. *Musical Traditions* 3: 17–21.

6562 Holst, Gail. 1977. *Road to Rembetika: Music from a Greek Subculture; Songs of Love, Sorrow and Hashish*. Athens: Anglo-Hellenic Publishing.

6563 Zannos, Iannis. 1990. Intonation in Theory and Practice of Greek and Turkish Music. *Yearbook for Traditional Music* 22: 42–59.

Hungary

6564 Kadar, Péter C. 1984. *Diszkónica (a rockzene és a diskó technikája)*. Budapest: Lapés Könyvkiadó.

6565 Kovalcsik, Katalin. 1984. Popular Dance Music Elements in the Folk Music of Gypsies in Hungary. *Popular Music* 4: 45–66.

6566 Kürti, László. 1994. 'How Can I Be a Human Being?' Culture, Youth, and Musical Opposition in Hungary. In *Rocking the State: Rock Music and Politics in Eastern Europe and Russia*, ed. Sabrina Petra Ramet. Boulder, CO: Westview Press. 73–102.

6567 Malecz, Attila. 1981. *A jazz Magyarországon*. Budapest: Tömegkommunikácios Kutatóközpont.

6568 Sagi, Mária. 1982. Music on Records in Hungary. In *The Phonogram in Cultural Communication*, ed. Kurt Blaukopf. Wien: Springer-Verlag. 111–22.

6569 Sarosi, Bálint. 1971. Gypsy Musicians and Hungarian Peasant Music. In *1970 Yearbook of the International Folk Music Council*, ed. Alexander L. Ringer. Urbana, IL: University of Illinois Press. 8–27.

6570 Simon, Géza Gábor. 1985. *Magyar jazzlemezek 1912–1984 diszkográfia*. Budapest: PECS.

6571 Szemere, Anna. 1983. Some Institutional Aspects of Pop and Rock in Hungary. *Popular Music* 3: 121–42.

6572 Szemere, Anna. 1985. Das Petöfi-Theater ein Musical-Theater? *Beiträge zur Musikwissenschaft* 3–4: 295–302.

6573 Szemere, Anna. 1985. On Avant-Garde Rock in Hungary. In *Popular Music Perspectives, 2*, ed. David Horn. Göteborg and Exeter: IASPM. 183–86.

6574 Szemere, Anna. 1985. Pop Scene in Hungary. *Communication Research* 12(3): 401–11.

6575 Szemere, Anna. 1989. Il fascino delle lotte tra bande di teppisti in una civiltà decadente: le considerazioni intorno a un 'video' musicale da parte di alcuni gruppi di giovani ungheresi. *Quaderni di Musica/Realtà* 23: 292–312.

6576 Szemere, Anna. 1992. The Politics of Marginality: A Rock Musical Subculture in Socialist Hungary in the Early 1980s. In *Rockin' the Boat: Mass Music and Mass Movements*, ed. Reebee Garofalo. Boston, MA: South End Press. 93–114.

6577 Tokaji, András. 1985. Leftist Political Songs in Hungary Before and After 1948. In *Popular Music Perspectives, 2*, ed. David Horn. Göteborg and Exeter: IASPM. 307–16.

6578 Turi, Gábor. 1983. *Azt mondom: jazz; interjúk magyar jazz muzsikusokkal*. Budapest: Zenemükiado.

6579 Vitanyi, Ivan. 1974. The Musical and Social Influence of Beat Music in Hungary. In *New Patterns of Musical Behaviour*, ed. Irmgard Bontinck. Wien: Universal Edition. 69–79.

Poland

6580 Baranczak, Anna. 1984. (1983) *Slowo w piosence: poetyka wspolczesnej piosenki estradowej*. Wroklaw: Zaklad Narodowy im Ossolinskich.

6581 Kan, Alex and Hayes, Nick. 1994. Big Beat in Poland. In *Rocking the State: Rock Music and Politics in Eastern Europe and Russia*, ed. Sabrina Petra Ramet. Boulder, CO: Westview Press. 41–54.

6582 Pekacz, Jolanta. 1992. On Some Dilemmas of Polish Post-Communist Rock Culture. *Popular Music* 11(2): 205–208.

6583 Sasinska-Klas, Teresa. 1992. 'Turbulenzen der Massen': Rockmusik in Polen als soziologisches Phänomen. *PopScriptum* I(1): 112–25.

6584 Urbanski, Janusz. 1974. Sweet Beat and Other Forms of Youth Music in Poland. In *New Patterns of Musical Behaviour*, ed. Irmgard Bontinck. Wien: Universal Edition. 80–83.

Romania

6585 Garfias, Robert. 1984. Dance Among the Urban Gypsies of Romania. *Yearbook for Traditional Music* 16: 84–96.

6586 Mihaiu, Virgil. 1993. Entwicklung und Probleme des Jazz in Rumänien 1965 bis 1993. In *Jazz in Europa*, ed. Wolfram Knauer. Hofheim: Wolke. 107–28.

6587 Petric, Gabriel. 1995. Popular Music in Romania: Music ad usum delphini in Romania. In *Popular Music Perspectives III*, ed. Peter Wicke. Berlin: Zyankrise. 72–76.

Russia

6588 Cuker, A. 1993. *Y rok, y synfonya*. Moskva: Kompositor.

6589 Feigin, Leo. 1986. (1985) *Russian Jazz: New Identity*. London: Quartet.

6590 Ovtschinikov, E. 1994. *Istoria dzaza*. Moskva: Muzyka.

6591 Ramet, Sabrina Petra, ed. 1994. *Rocking the State: Rock Music and Politics in Eastern Europe and Russia*. Boulder, CO: Westview Press.

6592 Rothstein, Robert A. 1995. Homeland, Home Town, and Battlefield: The Popular Song. In *Culture in Wartime Russia*, ed. Richard Stites. Bloomington, IN: Indiana University Press. 77–107.

6593 Sigalow, Michael. 1995. Die Rockmusik in der Sowjetunion von Breshnjew bis Gorbatschow. In *Popular Music Perspectives III*, ed. Peter Wicke. Berlin: Zyankrise. 254–60.

6594 Smirnov, I. 1994. *Vremja kolokolchikov. Shisn i smert sovjetskovo roka.* Moskva: INTO.

6595 Stites, Richard. 1992. *Russian Popular Culture: Entertainment and Society Since 1900.* Cambridge: Cambridge University Press.

6596 Tichwinskaya, L. 1995. *Kabare y teatr miniatjur v Rossya 1908–1917.* Moskva: Kultura.

6597 Tzerbakova, T. 1984. *Cyganskoye muzykalnoye ispolnitelstvo y tvordzestvo v Rossya.* Moskva: Muzyka.

6598 Uvarova, E., ed. 1976. *Ruskoye sovjetskoye estradnovo iskusstva, Vol. I: 1917–1929.* Moskva: Iskusstvo.

6599 Uvarova, E., ed. 1977. *Ruskoye sovjetskoye estradnovo iskusstva, Vol. II: 1930–1945.* Moskva: Iskusstvo.

6600 Uvarova, E., ed. 1981. *Ruskoye sovjetskoye estradnovo iskusstva, Vol. III: 1946–1977.* Moskva: Iskusstvo.

6601 Zak, Vladimir. 1979. *O melodike masovoy repi, Opit analyza.* Moskva: Sovjetskij kompositor.

USSR

6602 Alekseev, Eduard Y. 1986. Fol'klor v gorodye. *Muzikalni khorizonti* 1986/9.

6603 Alekseev, Eduard Y. and Golovinskii, Grigoriy L. 1974. From the Experience of the Moscow Youth Music Club: On the Question of the Socio-Psychological.

In *New Patterns of Musical Behaviour*, ed. Irmgard Bontinck. Wien: Universal Edition. 91–102.

6604 Alexeev, A., A. Burlaka and A. Sidorov, eds. 1991. *Kto est kto v sovjetsky roke. Ilustrirovanaya encyklopedya otetzestvenovo roka.* Moskva: Ostankino.

6605 Bataschev, Aleksej. 1973. *Sovjetskij dschaz.* Moskva: Muzyka.

6606 Bright, Terry. 1985. Soviet Crusade Against Pop. *Popular Music* 5: 123–48.

6607 Bright, Terry. 1986. Pop Music in the USSR. *Media, Culture and Society* 8(3).

6608 Dobrotrorskva, Ekaterina. 1992. Soviet Teens of the 1970s: Rock Generation, Rock Refusal, Rock Context. *Journal of Popular Culture* 26(3): 145–50.

6609 Druzhkin, Yu S. 1985. Statovlenie otechestvennyh VIA: pereintonirovanie kak tradicionnyi vzaimodistvia muzyka. Hudozhestvennaya samodeyat. *Sbornik nauchnyh trudov* 14: 67–86.

6610 Druzhkin, Yu S. 1985. Vokal 'no-instrumental' nye ansambli i diskoteka kak molodezhnye formi samodeyatel 'novo. *Molodezh i kul'tura. Sbornik nauchnyh trudov* 137: 21–41.

6611 Feigin, Leo. 1986. (1985) *Russian Jazz: New Identity.* London: Quartet.

6612 Golovinskii, Grigoriy L. 1982. On Some Music Sociological Aspects of the Phonogram: The Record in Soviet Musical Culture. In *The Phonogram in Cultural Communication*, ed. Kurt Blaukopf. Wien: Springer-Verlag. 123–32.

6613 Gronow, Pekka. 1987. Searching for 78s in Samarkand. *Musical Traditions* 7: 38–41.

6614 Kudinova, T. 1982. *Ot vodevil do muzykal.* Moskva: Sovjetskij kompositor.

6615 Kumpf, Hans. 1990. Sowjetischer Jazz. Erlebnisse und Bestandsaufnahme. In *Darmstädter Jazz forum 89: Beiträge zur Jazzforschung*, ed. Ekkehard Jost. Hofheim: Wolke. 49–66.

6616 Logan, Wendell. 1992. The Development of Jazz in the Former Soviet Union: An Interview with Victor Lebedev. *Black Music Research Journal* 12(2): 225–32.

6617 Medvedevm, Aleksandr and Medvedeva, Olga, eds. 1987. *Sovietskii Jazz: problemy sobytiya mastera*. Moskva: Sovietskii Kompozitor.

6618 Nestiev, Israel. 1982. Popular Music in the USSR: Problems and Opinions. In *Popular Music Perspectives, 1*, ed. David Horn and Philip Tagg. Göteborg and Exeter: IASPM. 155–62.

6619 Pestalozza, Luigi. 1988. *La musica in USSR: cronaca di un viaggio*. Milano: Unicopli.

6620 Ramet, Pedro and Zamascikov, Sergei. 1990. The Soviet Rock Scene. *Journal of Popular Culture* 24(1): 149–74.

6621 Smirnov, I. 1994. *Vremja kolokolchikov. Shisn i smert sovjetskovo roka*. Moskva: INTO.

6622 Smith, Gerald Stanton. 1984. *Songs to Seven Strings: Russian Guitar Poetry and Soviet 'Mass Song'*. Bloomington, IN: Indiana University Press.

6623 Starr, S. Frederick. 1983. *Red and Hot: The Fate of Jazz in the Soviet Union, 1917–1980*. New York and Oxford: Oxford University Press.

6624 Troitzky, Artemy. 1987. *Back in the USSR: The True Story of Rock in Russia*. London: Omnibus.

6625 Troitzky, Artemy. 1990. (1987) *Tusovka: Who's Who in the New Soviet Rock Culture*. London: Omnibus.

6626 Troitzky, Artemy. 1994. *Rok v SSSR*. Moskva: Knigi.

6627 Tzerednitzenko, T. 1994. *Tipologyja sovjetskoy masovoy kultury: mezdy 'Breznev' y 'Pugatzevoy'*. Moskva: Kultura.

6628 Uvarova, E., ed. 1976. *Ruskoye sovjetskoye estradnovo iskusstva, Vol. I: 1917–1929*. Moskva: Iskusstvo.

6629 Uvarova, E., ed. 1977. *Ruskoye sovjetskoye estradnovo iskusstva, Vol. II: 1930–1945*. Moskva: Iskusstvo.

6630 Uvarova, E., ed. 1981. *Ruskoye sovjetskoye estradnovo iskusstva, Vol. III: 1946–1977*. Moskva: Iskusstvo.

6631 Vickers, M., ed. 1985. Soviet Pop Lyrics. *Re Records Quarterly* 1(2): 25ff.

LATIN AMERICA

General

6632 Aharonián, Coriún. 1991. Revolution and Dependency in Latin America. *Worldbeat* 1: 115–28.

6633 Ayala, María Ignez. 1988. Cantoria nordestina (Northeastern Folk Singing): Its Spheres of Performance and Its Relationship to the Cultural Industry. *Studies in Latin-American Popular Culture* 7: 183–90.

6634 Béhague, Gerard H. 1979. *Music in Latin America: An Introduction*. Englewood Cliffs, NJ: Prentice-Hall.

6635 Béhague, Gerard H. 1980. Latin America: Popular Music. In *The New Grove Dictionary of Music and Musicians, Vol. 10*, ed. Stanley Sadie. London: Macmillan. 529–54.

6636 Béhague, Gerard H. 1985. Popular Music. In *The Handbook of Latin American Popular Culture*, ed. Harold Hinds and Charles Tatum. Westport, CT: Greenwood Press.

6637 Béhague, Gerard H. 1986. Popular Music in Latin America. *Studies in Latin American Popular Culture* 5: 41–67.

6638 Díaz Ayala, Cristobal. 1988. *Si te quieres por el pico divertir: Historia del pregón musical latinoamericano*. San Juan: Editorial Cubanacan.

6639 Durán, Gustavo. 1950. *Recordings of Latin American Songs and Dances: An Annotated and Selective List of Popular and Folk-Popular Music*. Washington, DC: Pan-American Union.

6640 Fairley, Jan. 1985. Annotated Bibliography of Latin-American Popular Music with Particular Reference to Chile and to Nueva Canción. *Popular Music* 5: 305–56.

6641 González, Juan-Pablo. 1986. Hacia el Estudio Musicológico de la Música Popular Latinoamericana. *Revista Musical Chilena* 40(165): 59–84.

6642 Horvath, Ricardo. 1982. *Los rockeros*. Buenos Aires: Centro Editor de América Latina.

6643 Llerena, Rito. 1985. *Memoria cultural en el vallenato*. Medellín: Editorial Universidad de Antioquía.

6644 Olivera, Rubén. 1986. La canción política. *La del taller* 5(6): 2–9.

6645 Pérez, Rolando. 1986. Il metodo comparativo e la binarizzazione dei ritmi ternari africani in America Latina. *Musica/Realtà* 20: 129–47.

6646 Pérez, Rolando. 1986. *La binarización de los ritmos ternarios africanos en América Latina*. La Habana: Casa de las Américas.

6647 Pring-Mill, Robert. 1979. The Nature and the Functions of Spanish American Poesia de Compromiso. *Bulletin of the Society for Latin American Studies* 31: 4–21.

6648 Pring-Mill, Robert. 1983. Cantas Canto Cantemos: las canciones de lucha y esperanza como signos de reunión e identitad. *Romanistisches Jahrbuch* 34: 318–54.

6649 Prudencio, Cergio. 1986. La música contemporánea y el público en América Latina. *La del taller* 5(6): 29–32.

6650 Roberts, John Storm. 1974. (1972) *Black Music of Two Worlds*. New York: William Morrow. First published New York/London: Praeger/Allen Lane, 1972.

6651 Roberts, John Storm. 1979. *The Latin Tinge: The Impact of Latin American Music on the United States*. New York and Oxford: Oxford University Press.

6652 Salazar, Max. 1975. Latin Music's Rivalries and Battles. *Latin New York Magazine* (November): 30–52.

6653 Schecter, John. 1983. Corona y Baile: Music in the Child's Wake of Ecuador and Hispanic South America, Past and Present. *Latin American Music Review* 4(1): 1–80.

6654 Schreiner, Claus. 1982. *Musica Latina. Musikfolklore zwischen Kuba und Feuerland*. Frankfurt am Main: Fischer.

6655 Singer, Roberta. 1983. Tradition and Innovation in Contemporary Latin American Popular Music in New York City. *Latin American Music Review* 4(2): 183–202.

6656 Waterman, Richard. 1952. African Influence on the Music of the Americas. In *Acculturation in the Americas, 2*, ed. Sol Tax. Chicago: University of Chicago Press. 207–18.

Central America

6657 Monestel, Manuel. 1987. A Song for Peace in Central America. *Popular Music* 6(2): 227–31.

6658 Smith, Ronald R. 1982. Latin American Ethnomusicology: A Discussion of Central America and Northern South America. *Latin American Music Review* 3(1): 1–16.

Belize

6659 Foster, Byron. 1986. *Heart Drum: Spirit Possession in the Garifuna Communities of Belize*. Belize City: Cubola Productions.

6660 Hadel, Richard. 1976. Black Carib Folk Music. *Caribbean Quarterly* 22(2/3) (June-September): 84–96.

Costa Rica

6661 Acevedo Vargas, Jorge L. 1986. *La Música en Guanacaste*, 2nd edition. San José: Editorial Universidad de Costa Rica.

6662 Chang, Giselle. 1989. La canción criolla en la discografía folklórica costarricense. *Folklore Americano* (July-December): 51–68.

6663 No entry.

6664 Flores, Bernal. 1978. *La música en Costa Rica*. San José: Editorial Costa Rica.

6665 Fonseca, Jaime. 1977. *Communication Policies in Costa Rica: A Study*. Paris: UNESCO.

6666 Fonseca, Julio. 1950. Referencia sobre música costarricense. *Revista de estudios musicales* 1: 75–97.

6667 Salazar Salvatierra, Rodrigo. 1985. *La música popular afrolimonense*. San José: Organización de Estados Americanos, Ministerio de Cultura, Juventud y Deportes.

6668 Salazar Salvatierra, Rodrigo. 1988. *La marimba: empleo, diseño y construcción*. San José: Editorial Universidad de Costa Rica.

6669 Salazar Salvatierra, Rodrigo. 1992. *Los instrumentos de la música folclórica costarricense*. Cartago: Editorial Instituto Technólogico de Costa Rica.

El Salvador

6670 Calderón E., Francisco, ed. 1983. El Salvador: comunicación en la revolución. *Plural (Mexico)* 12(137): 64–65.

6671 Escobar, Francisco Andres. 1990. Valoración de 'Xolotl'. *ECA – Estudios Centroamericanos* 45(503): 783–85.

6672 Kirk, John. 1985. Revolutionary Music, Salvadoran Style: 'Yolacamba Ita'. In *Literature and Contemporary Revolutionary Culture*, ed. Hernán Vidal. Minneapolis, MN: Society for the Study of Contemporary Hispanic and Lusophone Revolutionary Literature. 338–52.

6673 López Vigil, José Ignacio. 1994. *Rebel Radio: The Story of El Salvador's Radio Venceremos*. Willimantic, CT: Curbstone Press.

6674 Scruggs, T.M. 1985. Review of *Escuchen Nuestras Voces* (Recordings), Compiled by Grupo Sabiá, 1984. *Latin American Music Review* 6(2) (Fall/Winter): 292–94.

6675 Vladimirskaia, Tatiana. 1984. Encuentro con la canción de la revolución. *América Latina (USSR)* 7: 53–59.

Guatemala

6676 Arivillaga Cortés, Alfonso. 1990. La Música Tradicional Garífuna en Guatemala. *Latin American Music Review* 11(2): 253–80.

6677 Chenoweth, Vida. 1964. *The Marimbas of Guatemala*. Lexington, KY: University of Kentucky Press.

6678 Monsato Dardón, Carlos Hugo. 1970. *La marimba*. Guatemala: Piedra Santa.

6679 Monsato Dardón, Carlos Hugo. 1982. Guatemala a través de su Marimba.

Latin American Music Review 3(1): 60–72.

6680 O'Brien, Linda. 1981. Marimbas of Guatemala: The African Connection. *The World of Music* 25(2): 99–103.

6681 Taracena Arriola, Arturo. 1983. La marimba: espejo de una sociedad. *Araucaria de Chile* 22: 139–50.

6682 Vela, David. 1962. *La marimba: estudio sobre el instrumento nacional.* Guatemala: Ministerio de Educación Pública.

Honduras

6683 Agerkop, Terry. 1977. Música de los Miskitos de Honduras. *Folklore Americano* 23: 7–37.

6684 Cargalv, H. (Héctor C. Gálvez). 1983. *Historia de la música de Honduras y sus símbolos nacionales.* Tegucigalpa.

6685 Cristano Meléndez, Armando. 1988. Instrumentos musicales pertenecientes a la cultura Garífuna. In *Organología del Folklore Hondureño,* ed. Jesús Muñoz Tábora. Tegucigalpa: Secretaría del Turismo y Cultura. 65–124.

6686 Manzanares Aguilar, Rafael. 1960. *Canciones de Honduras.* Washington, DC: Unión Panamericana.

6687 Manzanares Aguilar, Rafael. 1967. *Canciones de Honduras. Colección popular #2.* Tegucigalpa.

6688 Miller, Amy. 1991. Teaching the World to Punta. *The Beat* 10(4): 38–41, 54.

6689 Muñoz Tábora, Jesús, ed. 1988. *Organología del Folklore Hondureño.* Tegucigalpa: Secretaría del Turismo y Cultura.

6690 Scruggs, T.M. 1991. Review of *Patria: Music from Honduras and Nicaragua* (Recordings), Compiled by David Blair Stiffler, Lyrichord Records. *Latin American Music Review* 12(1): 84–96.

6691 Sletto, Jacqueline. 1991. Ancestral Ties That Bind. *Americas* 43(1): 20–27.

6692 Velásquez, Ronny. 1987. *Chamanismo, Mito y Religión en Cuarto Naciones Étnicas de América Aborigen.* Caracas: Biblioteca de la Academia Nacional de la Historia.

Mexico

6693 Civeira, Miguel. 1978. *Sensibilidad Yucateca en la Canción Romántica.* Toluca: Fonapas.

6694 Farquarson, Mary. 1990. Blondes and Fiestas. *Folk Roots* 79/80 (January-February): 29–30.

6695 Garrido, Juan S. 1974. *Historia de la música popular en México: 1896–1973.* Mexico: Editorial Extemporáneos.

6696 Geijerstam, Claes. 1976. *Popular Music in Mexico.* Albuquerque, NM: University of New Mexico Press.

6697 Gradante, William. 1982. El Hijo del Pueblo': José Alfredo Jiménez and the Mexican Canción Ranchera. *Latin American Music Review* 3(1): 36–59.

6698 Hermes, Rafael. 1983. *Origen e historia del mariachi,* second edition. Mexico City: Editorial Katún.

6699 Mendoza, Vicente. 1961. *La canción mexicana: ensayo de clasificación y antología.* Mexico: Universidad Nacional Autónoma de México.

6700 Mendoza, Vicente. 1982. *La canción mexicana: ensayo de clasificación y antología.* Mexico: Fondo de Cultura Economica.

6701 Moreno, Yolanda. 1979. *Historia de la Música Popular Mexicana.* Mexico: Alianza Editorial.

6702 Reuter, Jas. 1981. *La Música Popular de Mexico.* Mexico City: Panorama Editorial.

6703 Reyes, Judith. 1978. Wir müssen von dem singen, was heute passiert Gespräch mit Judith Reyes. *Anschläge* 1(1): 38–52.

6704 Solis, Theodore. 1980. Muñecas de Chiapaneco: The Economic Importance of Self-Image in the World of Mexican Marimba. *Latin American Music Review* 1(1): 34–46.

6705 Sordo, María del Carmen. 1982. Compositoras mexicanas de música comercial. *Heterofonía* 15(78): 16–20.

6706 Stigberg, David. 1978. Jaracho, Tropical, and 'Pop': Aspects of Musical Life in Veracruz, 1971–72. In *Eight Urban Musical Cultures: Tradition and Change*, ed. Bruno Nettl. Urbana and London: University of Illinois Press. 260–95.

6707 Stigberg, David. 1985. Foreign Currents During the '60s and '70s in Mexican Popular Music: Rock and Roll, the Romantic Ballad and the Cumbia. *Studies in Latin American Popular Culture* 4: 170–84.

6708 Stone, Martha. 1975. *At the Sign of Midnight: The Concheros Dance Cult of Mexico*. Tucson, AZ: University of Arizona Press.

Nicaragua

6709 Ciechanower, Mauricio. 1985. Carlos Mejía Godoy: la canción en Nicaragua; otra herramienta. *Plural (Mexico)* 14(2a)(167): 21–24.

6710 Ciechanower, Mauricio. 1985. Carlos Mejía Godoy: Nicaragua en constante combustión. *Plural (Mexico)* 14(2a)(168): 45–51.

6711 Ciechanower, Mauricio. 1988. Nicaragua: una cultura de resistencia; entrevista con Luis Enrique Mejía Godoy. *Plural (Mexico)* 18(2a)(207): 61–65.

6712 Craven, David. 1989. *The New Concept of Art and Popular Culture in Nicaragua Since the Revolution in 1979: An Analytical Essay and Compendium of Illustrations*. Lewiston and Queenston: Edwin Mellen Press.

6713 Haase, Ellionor and Wiener, Bibiana. 1985. Canción y revolucción en Nicaragua. *Hispanorama – Sonderdruck* (November): 84–88.

6714 Mejía Sánchez, Ernesto. 1946. *Romances y corridos nicaragüenses*. Mexico City: Imprenta Universitaria.

6715 Pring-Mill, Robert. 1987. The Uses of Revolutionary Song: A Nicaraguan Assessment. *Popular Music* 6(2): 179–90.

6716 Scruggs, T.M. 1991. Review of ¡Nicaragua . . . Presente! – Music from Nicaragua Libre. *Latin American Music Review* 12(1): 84–96.

6717 Scruggs, T.M. 1994. *The Nicaraguan baile de la marimba and the Empowerment of Identity*. Ann Arbor, MI: University Microfilms.

6718 Seitz, Barbara. 1991. Songs, Identity, and Women's Liberation in Nicaragua. *Latin American Music Review* 12(1): 21–41.

Panama

6719 Cheville, Lila R. and Cheville, Richard A. 1977. *Festivals and Dances of Panama*. Panama: L.R. Cheville.

6720 Ciechanower, Mauricio. 1992. Ruben Blades: frente al publico. *Plural (Mexico)* 21(248): 74.

6721 Parker, Robert A. 1985. The Vision of Ruben Blades. *Americas* 37 (March/April): 15–19.

6722 Randel, Don Michael. 1991. Crossing Over with Ruben Blades. *Journal of the American Musicological Society* 44: 301–23.

6723 Randel, Don Michael. 1992. The Rap on the Raperos. *Americas* 44(5): 4.

6724 Smith, Ronald R. 1985. They Sing with the Voice of the Drum: Afro-Panamanian Musical Traditions. In *More than Drumming: Essays on African and Afro-Latin American Music and Musicians*, ed. Irene V. Jackson. Westport, CT: Greenwood Press. 163–98.

6725 Smith, Ronald R. 1991. Street Music of Panama: Cumbias, Tamoritos, and Mejoranas. *Latin American Music Review* 12(2): 216–20.

6726 Zárate, Dora Pérez de. 1971. *Textos del tamborito panameño: un estudio folklórico-literario de los textos del tamborito en Panamá*. Panama: D.P. de Zárate.

6727 Zárate, Manuel F. and Zárate, Dora Pérez de. 1968. *Tambor y socavon: un estudio comprensivo de dos temas del folklore panameño, y de sus implicaciones históricas y culturales*. Panama: Ediciones del Ministerio de Educación, Dirección Nacional.

South America

Argentina

6728 Andacht, Fernando. 1986. El canto popular: su público, su crisis. *La del taller* 7: 28–36.

6729 Benavides, Washington. 1965. *Las milongas*. Montevideo: Ediciones de la Banda Oriental.

6730 Fernández, Marcelo. 1993. *Historia del rock en Argentina*. Buenos Aires: Editorial Distal.

6731 Gravano, Ariel. 1983. La música de proyección folclórica argentina. *Folklore Americano* 35 (January-June): 5–71.

6732 Grinberg, Miguel. 1977. *La Música Progresiva Argentina*. Buenos Aires: Editorial Convergencia.

6733 Hidalgo, M. and Salton, R.D. 1987. Argentina (Sources and Resources). *Popular Music* 6(2): 219–26.

6734 Hidalgo, M., O. G. Brunelli and R. D. Salton. 1985. The Evolution of Rock in Argentina. In *Popular Music Perspectives, 2*, ed. David Horn. Göteborg and Exeter: IASPM. 296–306.

6735 Marzallo, Osvaldo and Munez, Pancho. 1986. *El rock en la Argentina: la historia y sus protagonistas*. Buenos Aires: Editorial Galerna.

6736 Pelinski, Ramón. 1985. From Tango to 'Rock Nacional': A Case Study of Changing Popular Music Taste in Buenos Aires. In *Popular Music Perspectives, 2*, ed. David Horn. Göteborg and Exeter: IASPM. 287–95.

6737 Pinnell, Richard. 1984. The Guitarist-Singer of Pre-1900 Gaucho Literature. *Latin American Music Review* 5(2): 243–62.

6738 Pisano, Juan Carlos. 1983. *Reportaje al rock*. Buenos Aires: Ediciones Paulinas.

6739 Pujol, Sergio. 1989. *Las canciones del inmigrante*. Buenos Aires: Editorial Almagesto.

6740 Serrano Redonnet, Ana. 1964. *Cancionero Music Argentino*. Buenos Aires: Ediciones Culturales Argentinas.

6741 Vega, Carlos. 1936. *Danzas y canciones argentinas: teormas e investigaciones. Un ensayo sobre el tango*. Buenos Aires: Ricordi.

6742 Vega, Carlos. 1941. *La música populár argentina, tomo II: Fraselogía. Proposición de uno nuevo método para la escritura y análisis de las ideas musicales y sa*. Buenos Aires: Facultad de Filosofia y Letras de la Universidad de Buenos Aires.

6743 Vega, Carlos. 1944. *Panorama de la música popular Argentina*. Buenos Aires: Editorial Losada.

LOCATIONS

6744 Vega, Carlos. 1952. *Las Dansas Populares Argentinas*. Buenos Aires: Instituto de Musicologia.

6745 Vega, Carlos. 1981. *Apuntes para la historia del movimiento tradicionalista argentino*. Buenos Aires: Instituto Nacional de Musicología.

6746 Vila, Pablo. 1982. Música popular y auge del folklore en la decada del '60. *Crear en la cultura nacional* 10 (September/October): 24–27.

6747 Vila, Pablo. 1985. Rock Nacional: ¿Creación o consumo? *Crear* 3.

6748 Vila, Pablo. 1987. *Rock nacional* and the Dictatorship in Argentina. *Popular Music* 6(2): 129–48.

6749 Vila, Pablo. 1989. Argentina's Rock Nacional: The Search for Meaning. *Latin American Music Review* 10(1): 1–28.

6750 Vila, Pablo. 1991. Tango to Folk: Hegemony, Construction and Popular Identities in Argentina. *Studies in Latin American Popular Culture* 10: 107–39.

Bolivia

6751 Auza, Atiliano. 1989. *La simbiosis cultural de la música boliviana*. La Paz: Cima.

6752 Chazarreta, Manuel. 1985. Bolivia: música popular y caricaturas trágicas. *La del taller* 2 (February-March): 4–6.

6753 Leichtman, Ellen. 1989. Musical Interaction: A Bolivian Mestizo Perspective. *Latin American Music Review* 10(1): 29–52.

6754 Prudencio, Cergio. 1988. Insonancias, una visión critica de la música culta en Bolivia. *La del taller* 8(9): 15–20.

6755 Wara-Céspedes, Gilka. 1984. New Currents in Música Folklórica in La Paz, Bolivia. *Latin American Music Review* 5(2): 217–42.

6756 Wara-Céspedes, Gilka. 1993. Huayno, Chaya and Chuntunqui: Bolivian Identity in the Music of Los Kjarkas. *Latin American Music Review* 14(1): 52–101.

Brazil

6756a Alencar-Pinto, Guilherme de. 1988. Música en el bolsillo. *La del taller* 8(9): 39–42.

6757 Alvarenga, Oneyda. 1946. A influencia negra na música brasileira. *Boletín Latinoamericano de Música* 6: 357–407.

6758 Alvarenga, Oneyda. 1982. (1950) *Música populár brasileira*. Sao Paulo: Livraria Duas Cidades. First published Rio de Janeiro: Editora Globo, 1950.

6759 Andrade, Mário de. 1987. *As Melodias de boi e otras peças*. Sao Paulo: Duas Cidades.

6760 Andrade, Mário de. 1989. *Dicionário Musical Brasileiro*. ed. Oneyda Alvarenga and Flávia Camargo Toni. Belo Horizonte: Editora Itatiaia Limitada, Ministério da Cultura, Instituto de Estudos Brasileiros, Editora da Universidade de Sao Paulo.

6761 Appleby, David P. 1983. *The Music of Brazil*. Austin, TX: University of Texas Press.

6762 Araújo, Samuel. 1988. Brega: Music and Conflict in Urban Brazil. *Latin American Music Review* 9(1): 50–89.

6763 Bangel, Tasso. 1989. *O estilo gaucho na musica brasileira*. Porto Alegre-RS: Movimento.

6764 Béhague, Gerard H. 1973. Bossa and Bossas: Recent Changes in Brazilian Urban Popular Music. *Ethnomusicology* 17(2): 209–33.

6765 Béhague, Gerard H. 1980. Brazilian Musical Values of the 1960s and 1970s: Popular Urban Music from Bossa Nova to Tropicalia. *Journal of Popular Culture* 14(3): 437–52.

6766 Béhague, Gerard H. 1986. Musical Change: A Case Study from South America. *The World of Music* 28(1): 16–25.

6767 Borges, Beatriz (Bia). 1990. *Música Popular do Brasil.* Sao Paulo: B. Borges.

6768 Cabral, Sérgio. 1974. *As Escolas de Samba: O Quê, Quem, Como, Quando e Por Quê?* Rio de Janeiro: Editora Fontana Ltda.

6769 Cabral, Sérgio. 1990. *No tempo de Almirante: uma historia do radio e da MPB.* Rio de Janeiro: F. Alves.

6770 Cabral, Sérgio. ca. 1991. *No tempo de Ari Barroso.* Rio de Janeiro: Luminar Editora.

6771 Caldas, Waldenyr. 1977. *Acorde na Aurora: Música Sertaneja e Indústria Cultural.* Sao Paulo: Companhia Editora Nacional.

6772 Carvalho, Herminio Bello de. 1988. *O canto do paje: Villa-Lobos e a musica popular brasileira.* Santiago de Chile: Las Ediciones del Ornitorrinco.

6773 Carvalho, José Jorge de. 1993. *Black Music of All Colors: The Construction of Black Ethnicity in Ritual and Popular Genres of Afro-Brazilian Music.* Brasília: Departamento de Antropologia/ Universidade de Brasília, Série Antropologia, No. 145.

6774 Carvalho, José Jorge de. 1994. *The Multiplicity of Black Identities in Brazilian Popular Music.* Brasília: Departamento de Antropologia/Universidade de Brasília, Série Antropologia, No. 163.

6775 Carvalho, Martha de Ulhôa. 1990. Cançao da América: Style and Emotion in Brazilian Popular Song. *Popular Music* 9(3): 321–50.

6776 Cascudo, Luís da Câmara. 1979. *Dicionário do Folclore Brasileiro,* 5th revised edition. Sao Paulo: Companhia Melhoramentos. First published Rio de Janeiro: Instituto Nacional do Livro, 1954.

6777 Cáurio, Rita, ed. 1988. *Brasil Musical: Viagem pelos Sons e Ritmos Populares.* Rio de Janeiro: Art Bureau.

6778 Cleary, David. 1994. Meu Brasil Brasileiro: If They Had a World Cup for Music, Brazil Would Give Anyone a Game. In *World Music: The Rough Guide,* ed. Simon Broughton, et al. London: Rough Guides. 557–69.

6779 Correa de Azevedo, Luis Hector. 1981. Music and Musicians of African Origin in Brazil. *The World of Music* 25(2): 53–63.

6780 Crook, Larry N. 1993. Black Consciousness, Samba Reggae, and the Re-Africanization of Bahian Carnival Music in Brazil. *The World of Music* 35(2): 70–84.

6781 Dantas, Marcelo. 1994. *Olodum: De Bloco Afro a Holding Cultural.* Salvador: Grupo Cultural Olodum/Fundaçao Casa de Jorge Amado.

6782 Dapieve, Arthur. 1995. *Brock: O Rock Brasileiro dos Anos 80.* Rio de Janeiro: Editora 34.

6783 Dolabela, Marcelo. 1987. *ABZ do Rock Brasileiro.* Sao Paulo: Estrela do Sul Editora.

6784 Duarte, Ruy. n.d. *História Social do Frevo.* Rio de Janeiro: Editôra Leitura S.A.

6785 Dunn, Christopher. 1993. It's Forbidden to Forbid (The Impact of the 1960's Art Movement Tropicalismo on Brazilian Culture). *Americas* 45(5): 14–22.

6786 Efegê, Jota. 1978. *Figuras e Coisas da Música Popular Brasileira*, Vol. 1. Rio de Janeiro: Fundaçao Nacional de Arte.

6787 Efegê, Jota. 1980. *Figuras e Coisas da Música Popular Brasileira*, Vol. 2. Rio de Janeiro: Fundaçao Nacional de Arte.

6788 Favaretto, Celso. 1979. *Tropicália: alegoria alegria*. Sao Paulo: Kairós.

6789 Ferretti, Mundicarmo Maria Rocha. 1988. *Baiao dos Dois: A Música de Zedantas e Luiz Gonzaga no seu Contexto de Produçao e sua Atualizaçao na Década de 70*. Recife: Fundaçao Joaquim Nabuco.

6790 Franceschi, Humberto M. 1984. *Registro Sonoro por Meios Mecânicos no Brasil*. Rio de Janeiro: Studio HMF.

6791 Gaffney, Floyd. 1979. Evolution and Revolution of Afro-Brazilian Dance. *Journal of Popular Culture* 13(1): 98–105.

6792 Goldfeder, Miriam. 1980. *Por Trás das Ondas da Rádio Nacional*. Rio de Janeiro: Editora Paz e Terra.

6793 Herskovits, Melville J. 1944. Drums and Drummers in Afro-Brazilian Cult Life. *Musical Quarterly* 30.

6794 Homem de Mello, José Eduardo. 1976. *Música Popular Brasileira*. Sao Paulo: Melhoramentos.

6795 Khallyhabby, Tonyan. 1976. A influencia africana na música brasileira. *Cultura* 23 (October-December): 44–51.

6796 Krausche, Valter Antonio. 1983. *Música popular brasileira: da cultura de roda à música de massa*. Sao Paolo: Brasiliense.

6797 Krich, John. 1993. *Why Is This Country Dancing? A One-Man Samba to the Beat of Brazil*. New York: Simon & Schuster.

6798 Levine, Robert. 1984. Elite Intervention in Urban Popular Culture in Modern Brazil. *Luso-Brazilian Review* 21(2): 9–23.

6799 Madeira, Angelica. 1991. Rhythm and Irreverence (Notes about the Rock Music Movement in Brasilia). *Popular Music & Society* 15(4): 57–70.

6800 Marcondes, Marcos-Antonio, ed. 1977. *Enciclopédia da Música Brasileira: Erudita, Popular e Folclórica*. 2 vols. Sao Paulo: Art Editora.

6801 Mariz, Vasco. 1980. *A cançao brasileira: erudita, folclórica, popular*. Rio de Janeiro: Civilizacâo, Brasileira.

6802 Martins, J.B. 1978. *Antropologia da musica brasileira: natureza, ritmo, texto, cultura*. Sao Paulo: Obelisco.

6803 Maurício, Ivan, Marcos Cirano and Ricardo de Almeida, eds. 1978. *Arte popular e dominaçao: O caso de Pernambuco – 1961/77*. Recife: Editora Alternativa Ltda.

6804 McGowan, Chris. 1991. *The Billboard Book of Brazilian Music: Samba, Bossa Nova and the Popular Sounds of Brazil*. Enfield: Guinness.

6805 McGowan, Chris and Pessanha, Ricardo. 1991. *The Brazilian Sound: Samba, Bossa Nova, and the Popular Music of Brazil*. New York: Billboard Books.

6806 Menezes Bastos, Rafael José de. 1977. Situación del músico en la sociedad. In *América Latina en su música*, ed. Isabel Aretz. México: Siglo XXI. 103–38.

6807 Menezes Bastos, Rafael José de. 1982. Música y sociedad en Brasil: una introducción al lenguaje musical. *Culturas* 8(2): 53–72.

6808 Menezes Bastos, Rafael José de. 1995. A Origem do Samba como Invenção do Brasil: Sobre o 'Feitio de Oração' de Vadico e Noel Rosa (Por Que as Canções têm Música?). *Cadernos de Estudo – Análise Musical* 8(9): 1–29.

6809 Morelli, Rita C.L. 1991. *Indústria Fonográfica: Um Estudo Antropológico.* Campinas: Editora da Universidade de Campinas.

6810 Moreno, Albrecht. 1982. Bossa nova: nova Brasil: The Significance of Bossa Nova as a Brazilian Popular Music. *Latin American Research Review* 17(2): 129–41.

6811 Moura, Roberto. 1983. *Tia Ciata e a Pequena Africa no Rio de Janeiro.* Rio de Janeiro: Fundaçao Nacional de Arte.

6812 Mukuna, Kazadi wa. 1979. *Contribuiçao Bantu na música popular brasileira.* Sao Paulo: Global Editora.

6813 No entry.

6814 Oliveira Pinto, Tiago de, ed. 1986. *Brasilien. Einführung in Musiktraditionen Brasiliens.* Mainz: Schott.

6815 Oliveira Pinto, Tiago de. 1991. 'Making Ritual Drama': Dance, Music and Representation in Brazilian Candomblé and Umbanda. *The World of Music* 33(1): 70–88.

6816 Oliveira Pinto, Tiago de. 1995. Forró in Brasilien. Musik für Dienstmädchen und Taxifahrer? *PopScriptum* 3: 52–79.

6816a Oliven, Ruben George. 1984. A malandragem na música popular brasileira. *Latin American Music Review* 5(1): 66–96.

6817 Oliven, Ruben George. 1988. 'The Woman Makes (and Breaks) the Man': The Masculine Imagery in Brazilian Popular Music. *Latin American Music Review* 9(1): 90–108.

6818 Perrone, Charles. 1982. A Música Popular num Romance Brasileiro de Trinta: Das 'Memórias de um Sargento de Milícias' a 'Marafa'. *Latin American Music Review* 3(1): 73–91.

6819 Perrone, Charles. 1985. From Noigrandres to 'Milagre da Algeria': The Concrete Poets and Contemporary Brazilian Popular Music. *Latin American Music Review* 6(1): 58–79.

6820 Perrone, Charles. 1986. An Annotated Interdisciplinary Bibliography and Discography of Brazilian Popular Music. *Latin American Music Review* 7(2): 302–40.

6821 Perrone, Charles. 1987. Brazil (Sources and Resources). *Popular Music* 6(2): 219–26.

6822 Perrone, Charles. 1989. *Masters of Contemporary Brazilian Song: MPB, 1965–1985.* Austin, TX: University of Texas Press.

6823 No entry.

6824 Pescatello, Ann M. 1976. Music Fiestas and Their Social Role in Brazil: Carnival in Rio. *Journal of Popular Culture* 9(4): 833–39.

6825 Pessanha, José Américo Motta, ed. 1976. (1970) *Nova História da Música Popular Brasileira,* 2nd revised edition. Sao Paulo: Abril Cultural.

6826–7 No entries.

6828 Rangel, Lúcio. 1962. *Sambistas e choroes.* Sao Paulo: Francisco Alves.

6829 Reily, Suzel-Ana. 1992. *Música Sertaneja* and Migrant Identity: The Stylistic Development of a Brazilian Genre. *Popular Music* 11(3): 337–58.

6830 Reily, Suzel-Ana. 1994. Macunaíma's National Identity and Ethnomusicological Research in Brazil. In *Ethnicity, Identity and Music: The Musical Construction of Place,* ed. Martin Stokes. Oxford: Berg. 71–96.

6831 Romano, Alfonso. 1980. *Musica Popular e Moderna Poesia Brasileira.* Petrópolis: Vozes.

6832 Sá Reg, Enylton de and Perrone, Charles. 1985. *MPB: Contemporary*

Brazilian Popular Music. Albuquerque, NM: University of New Mexico/Latin American Institute, Brazilian Curriculum Guide Series.

6833 Schönberger, Axel. 1985. *Música Popular Brasileira. Hispanorama* 41: 105–10.

6834 Schreiner, Claus. 1985. (1979) *Musica Popular Brasileira. Handbuch der populären und folkloristischen Musik Brasiliens.* Marburg: Tropical Music.

6835 Schreiner, Claus. 1993. (1977) *Música Brasileira: A History of Popular Music and the People of Brazil,* revised edition. New York and London: Marion Boyars.

6836 Souza, Tárik de. 1983. *O Som Nosso de Cada Dia.* Porto Alegre: L & PM Editores.

6837 Souza, Tárik de, et al. 1988. *Brasil musical: viagem pelos sons e ritmos populares.* Rio de Janeiro: Art Bureau/ Banco Chase Manhattan.

6838 Tatit, Luiz. 1996. *O Cancionista: Composiçao de Cançoes no Brasil.* Sao Paulo: Editora da Universidade de Sao Paulo.

6839 Tinhorao, José Ramos. 1969. (1966) *Música Popular, Um Tema em Debate.* Rio de Janeiro: Editôra Saga.

6840 Tinhorao, José Ramos. 1972. *Música popular, Teatro & Cinema.* Petrópolis: Editora Vozes.

6841 Tinhorao, José Ramos. 1974. *Pequena História da Música Popular: da Modinha à Cançao de Protesto.* Petrópolis: Vozes.

6842 Tinhorao, José Ramos. 1981. *Música popular: do gramofone ao rádio e TV.* Sao Paulo: Atica.

6843 Tinhorao, José Ramos. 1986. *Pequena História da Música Popular: da Modinha ào Tropicalismo,* revised edition. Sao Paulo: Art Editora. First published Petrópolis: Vozes, 1974.

6844 Tinhorao, José Ramos. 1990. *História Social da Música Popular Brasileira.* Lisbon: Editorial Caminho, S.A.

6845 Tinhorao, José Ramos. 1991. (1974) *Pequena História da Música Popular: da Modinha à Lambada,* 6th revised edition. Sao Paulo: Art Editora Ltda.

6846 No entry.

6847 Vasconcelos, Ary. 1977. *Raízes da Música Popular Brasileira.* Sao Paulo and Brasília: Martins/Instituto Nacional do Livro.

6848 Vasconcelos, Gilberto. 1977. *Música Popular: De Olho na Fresta.* Rio de Janeiro: Ediçoes do Graal.

6849 Vianna, Hermano. 1988. *O Mundo Funk Carioca.* Rio de Janeiro: Jorge Zahar Editor.

6850 Vivacqua, Renato. 1984. *Música popular brasileira (historias de sua gente).* Brasilia: Thesaurus.

6851 Waddey, Ralph C. 1980. Viola de Samba and Samba de Viola in the Recôncavo of Bahia. *Latin American Music Review* 1(2): 196–212.

6852 Waddey, Ralph C. 1981. Samba de Viola (Part II). *Latin American Music Review* 2(2): 252–79.

6853 Yúdice, George. 1994. The Funkification of Rio. In *Microphone Fiends: Youth Music and Youth Culture,* ed. Andrew Ross and Tricia Rose. London: Routledge.

Chile

6854 Advis, Luis and González, Juan-Pablo, comps. 1994. *Clásicos de la Música Popular Chilena, 1900–1960.* Santiago: Ediciones Universidad Católica.

6855 Artigas, Gustavo and Moncada, Perla Valencia, eds. 1973. *Antología de canciones de lucha y esperanza.* Santiago de Chile: Empresa Editora Nacional Quimantu Ltda.

6856 Cánepa, Gina. 1987. Violeta Parra and Los Jaivas: Unequal Discourse or Successful Integration? *Popular Music* 6(2): 235–40.

6857 Escárate, Héctor. ca. 1994. *Historia del rock chileno*. Santiago: Héctor Escárate.

6858 Fairley, Jan. 1985. Annotated Bibliography of Latin-American Popular Music with Particular Reference to Chile and to Nueva Canción. *Popular Music* 5: 305–56.

6859 Fairley, Jan. 1985. Karaxú and Incantation: When Does 'Folk' Music Become 'Popular'? In *Popular Music Perspectives, 2*, ed. David Horn. Göteborg and Exeter: IASPM. 278–86.

6860 Fairley, Jan. 1989. Analysing Performance: Narrative and Ideology in Concerts by ¡Karaxú! *Popular Music* 8(1): 1–30.

6861 Godoy, Alvaro and González, Juan-Pablo, eds. 1995. *Música Popular Chilena 20 años: 1970–1990*. Santiago: Ministerio de Educación.

6862 González, Juan-Pablo. 1989. Inti-illimani and the Artistic Treatment of Folklore. *Latin American Music Review* 10(2): 267–86.

6863 González, Juan-Pablo. 1991. Hegemony and Counter-Hegemony of Music in Latin-America: The Chilean Pop. *Popular Music & Society* 15(2): 63–78.

6864 Pring-Mill, Robert. 1990. *'Gracias a la vida': The Power and Poetry of Song*. London: Queen Mary and Westfield College.

6865 Salas, Fabio. 1993. *Utopía: Antología del Rock Chileno*. Santiago: Bravo y Allende.

6866 Torres, Rodrigo. 1980. *Perfil de la creación musical en la nueva canción chilena desde sus orígenes hasta 1973*. Santiago: Ceneca.

Colombia

6867 Abadía Morales, Guillermo. 1973. *La música folklórica colombiana*. Bogota: Universidad Nacional de Colombia.

6868 Alzate, Alberto. 1980. *El músico de banda: aproximación a su realidad social*. Montería: Editorial América Latina.

6869 Añez, Jorge. 1951. *Canciones y recuerdos: conceptos acerca del origen del bambuco y de noestros instrumentos t'ipices y sobre la evoluci'on de la canci'on colombiana*. Bogota: Imprenta Nacional.

6870 Araújo de Molina, Consuelo. 1973. *Vallenatología: orígenes y fundamentos de la música vallenata*. Bogota: Tercer Mundo.

6871 Araujonoguera, Consuelo. 1988. *Rafael Escalona: hombre y mito*. Bogota: Planeta.

6872 Arteaga, José. 1990. *La salsa*. Bogota: Intermedio.

6873 Benavides, Iván. 1992. *Música popular colombiano: compositores jóvenes*. Bogota: Centro Colombo-Americano.

6874 Bermúdez, Egberto. 1985. *Los instrumentos musicales de Colombia*. Bogota: Universidad Nacional de Colombia.

6875 Bermúdez, Egberto, et al. 1987. *Música tradicional y popular colombiana*. Bogota: Procultura.

6876 Betancur Alvarez, Fabio. 1993. *Sin clave y bongó no hay son: música afrocubana y confluencias musicales de Colombia y Cuba*. Medellín: Editorial Universidad de Antioquia.

6877 Briceño, Arnulfo. 1988. La música llanera como punto de encuentro entre Colombia y Venezuela. *Correo de los Andes* 49 (January-February): 85–88.

6878 Broere, Bernard J. 1985. El Chambú: A Study of Popular Music in Nariño (South Colombia). In *Popular Music Perspectives, 2,* ed. David Horn. Göteborg and Exeter: IASPM. 235–51.

6879 Fortich Díaz, William. 1994. *Con bombos y platillos: origen del porro, approximación al fandango y las bandas pelayeras.* Montería: Domus Libri.

6880 García Usta, Jorge and Salcedo Ramos, Alberto. 1994. *Diez juglares en su patio.* Bogota: Ecoe Ediciones.

6881 Gilard, Jacques. 1987. Vallenato: ¿cuál tradición narrativa? *Huellas* 19: 59–67.

6882 Gilard, Jacques. 1993. ¿Crescencio o don Toba? Falsos interrogantes y verdaderas respuestas sobre el vallenato. *Huellas* 37: 28–34. (First published in *Cahiers du Monde Hispanique et Luso-Brésilien, Caravelle* 48 (1987): 69–80.)

6883 Gómez, Néstor. 1988. *Deformaciones de la cumbia.* Barranquilla: Editorial Don Bosco.

6884 González Henríquez, Adolfo. 1987. La música costeña en la obra de Fals Borda. *Anuario Científico* 6: 57–92.

6885 González Henríquez, Adolfo. 1988. La música costeña en la tercera década del siglo XIX. *Latin American Music Review* 9(2): 187–206.

6886 González Henríquez, Adolfo. 1989. La rumba costeña en los años 20. *Revista Diners* 228: 86–91.

6887 Jaramillo, Luis Felipe, ed. 1992. *Música tropical y salsa en Colombia.* Medellín: Discos Fuentes.

6888 Jiménez Urriola, Roque. 1992. *Breve historia de la música costeña.* Barranquilla: Ediciones Antillas.

6889 List, George. 1983. *Music and Poetry in a Colombian Village.* Bloomington, IN: Indiana University Press.

6890 Llerena, Rito. 1985. *Memoria cultural en el vallenato.* Medellín: Editorial Universidad de Antioquía.

6891 Londoño, María Eugenia. 1983. *Estudio de la realidad musical en Colombia.* 5 vols. Bogota: Colcultura.

6892 Londoño, Patricia and Londoño, Santiago. 1989. Vida diaria en las ciudades colombianas. In *Nueva Historia de Colombia, Vol. 4. Educación, ciencias, luchas de la mujer, vida diaria,* ed. Alvaro Tirado Mejía. Bogota: Planeta. 313–97.

6893 Lotero Botero, Amparo. 1989. El porro pelayero: de las gaitas y tambores a las bandas de viento. *Boletín Cultural y Bibliográfico* 26(19): 39–53.

6894 Ocampo López, Javier. 1984. *Música y folclor de Colombia.* Bogota: Plaza y Janes.

6895 Pacini Hernandez, Deborah. 1993. The Picó Phenomenon in Cartagena, Colombia. *América Negra* 6: 69–115.

6896 Perdomo Escobar, José Ignacio. 1963. *La historia de la música en Colombia.* Bogota: Editorial ABC.

6897 Posada, Consuelo. 1986. *Canción vallenata y tradición oral.* Medellín: Universidad de Antioquia.

6898 Quiroz Otero, Ciro. 1982. *Vallenato: hombre y canto.* Bogota: Icaro Editores.

6899 Restrepo Duque, Hernán. 1971. *Lo que cuentan las canciones: un cronicón musical.* Bogota: Tercer Mundo.

6900 Restrepo Duque, Hernán. 1986. *A mí cántenme un bambuco.* Medellín: Ediciones Autores Antioqueños.

6901 Restrepo Duque, Hernán. 1991. *Las 100 mejores canciones colombianas y sus autores.* Bogota: RCN, Sonolux.

6902 Ruiz Hernández, Alvaro. 1983. *Personajes y episodios de la canción popular.* Barranquilla: Luz Negra.

6903 Schwegler, Armin. 1991. Africa en América: los 'juegos de velorio' y otros cantos funerarios afrohispanos remanentes en la Costa Atlántica de Colombia. In *Akten des 7. Essener Kolloquium über Sprachminoritäten/ Minoritätensprachen*, ed. James R. Dow and Thomas Stolz. Bochum: Studienverlag Brockmeyer. 189–221.

6904 Simon, Alissa. 1994. *The Costeño Hip Movement: A Conceptual Framework for Understanding Sexuality in Afro-Colombian Folkloric Music and Dance.* Los Angeles: Department of Ethnomusicology, UCLA.

6905 Triana, Gloria. 1987. El litoral caribe. *La música tradicional y popular colombiana* 5–7.

6906 Ulloa Sanmiguel, Alejandro. 1992. *La salsa en Cali*. Cali: Ediciones Universidad del Valle.

6907 Valverde, Umberto. 1995. *Afran Paso: Historia de las Orquestas Femeninas de Cali*. ed. Rafael Quintero. Cali: Ediciones Universidad del Valle.

6908 Villegas, Jorge and Grisales, Hernando. 1976. *Crescencio Salcedo: mi vida.* Medellín: Ediciones Hombre Nuevo.

6909 Wade, Peter. 1995. Black Music and Cultural Syncretism in Colombia. In *Slavery and Beyond: The African Impact on Latin America and the Caribbean*, ed. Darien J. Davis. Wilmington, DE: Scholarly Resources. 121–46.

6910 Whitten, Norman E. 1968. Personal Networks and Musical Contexts in the Pacific Lowlands of Colombia and Ecuador. *Man* 3(1): 50–63.

6911 Whitten, Norman E. 1986. *Black Frontiersmen: Afro-Hispanic Culture of Ecuador and Colombia*. Prospect Heights, IL: Waveland Press.

6912 Zapata Cuencar, Heriberto. 1962. *Compositores colombianos*. Medellín: Carpel.

Ecuador

6913 Belzner, William. 1981. Music, Modernization and Westernization Among the Macuma Shuar. In *Cultural Transformations and Ethnicity in Ecuador, 1.* Urbana, IL: University of Illinois Press. 731–48.

6914 Gabor, Charles. 1981. *Antología: Introducción a la música folklórica del Ecuador*. Quito: PNUD/UNESCO.

6915 Moreno, Segund Luis. 1972. *Historia de la música en al Ecuador*. Quito: Editorial casa de al cultura ecuatoriana.

6916 Riedel, Johannes. 1986. (1985) The Ecuadorean Pasillo: Is It 'Música Popular', 'Música Nacional' or 'Música Folklórica'? *Latin American Music Review* 7(1): 1–25.

6917 Schecter, John. 1983. Corona y Baile: Music in the Child's Wake of Ecuador and Hispanic South America, Past and Present. *Latin American Music Review* 4(1): 1–80.

6918 Whitten, Norman E. 1968. Personal Networks and Musical Contexts in the Pacific Lowlands of Colombia and Ecuador. *Man* 3(1): 50–63.

6919 Whitten, Norman E. 1986. *Black Frontiersmen: Afro-Hispanic Culture of Ecuador and Colombia*. Prospect Heights, IL: Waveland Press.

Peru

6920 Arguedas, José-Maria. 1977. *Nuestra Música Popular y sus Intérpretes*. Lima: Mosca Azul & Horizonte Editores.

6921 Arnold, Pierre. 1985. La música popular en el Perú. *La del taller 2* (February-March): 9–13.

6922 Bradby, Barbara. 1987. Symmetry Around a Centre: Music of an Andean Community. *Popular Music* 6(2): 197–218.

6923 Bullen, Margaret. 1993. Chicha in the Shanty Towns of Arequipa, Peru. *Popular Music* 12(3): 229–44.

6924 Degregori, Carlos. 1984. Huayno, 'chicha': el nuevo rostro de la música peruana. *Cultura Popular* 13–14 (November): 187–92.

6925 Lengwinat, Katrin. 1991. La 'chicha': Identidad chola en la gran ciudad. *Ibero-Amerikanisches Archiv* 17(4): 431–38.

6926 Lloréns, José-Antonio. 1983. *Música popular en Lima: criollos y andinos*. Lima: Instituto de Estudios Peruanos.

6927 Lloréns, José-Antonio. 1987. Introducción al estudio de la música popular criolla en Lima, Perú. *Latin American Music Review* 8(2): 262–68.

6928 Lloréns, José-Antonio. 1991. Andean Voices on Lima Airwaves: Highland Migrants and Radio Broadcasting in Peru. *Studies in Latin American Popular Culture* 10: 177–89.

6929 Lloréns, José-Antonio and Oliart, Patricia. 1985. Perú: la nueva canción. *La del taller* 4: 4–11.

6930 Turino, Thomas. 1983. The Charango and the Sirena: Music, Magic, and the Power of Love. *Latin American Music Review* 4(1): 81–119.

6931 Turino, Thomas. 1984. The Urban-Mestizo Charango Tradition in Southern Peru: A Statement of Shifting Identity. *Ethnomusicology* 28(2): 253–70.

6932 Turino, Thomas. 1988. The Music of Andean Migrants in Lima, Peru: Demographics, Social Process, Power, and Style. *Latin American Music Review* 9(2): 127–50.

6933 Turino, Thomas. 1989. The Coherence of Social Style and Musical Creation Among the Aymara in Southern Peru. *Ethnomusicology* 33(1): 1–30.

Uruguay

6934 Andacht, Fernando. 1986. El canto popular: su público, su crisis. *La del taller* 7: 28–36.

6935 Artigas, Gustavo and Moncada, Perla Valencia, eds. 1973. *Antología de canciones de lucha y esperanza*. Santiago de Chile: Empresa Editora Nacional Quimantu Ltda.

6936 Ayestarán, Lauro. 1953. *La música en el Uruguay*. Montevideo: SODRE.

6937 Ayestarán, Lauro. 1965. *El minue montonero: danzas, canciones e instrumentos del pueblo del Uruguay*. Montevideo: Ediciones de la Banda Oriental.

6938 Benavides, Washington. 1965. *Las milongas*. Montevideo: Ediciones de la Banda Oriental.

6939 Bonaldi, Jorge. 1985. El canto popular uruguayo. *Boletín de Música Casa de las Américas* 106 (July-December): 5–12.

6940 Dabezies, Antonio and Fabregat, Aquiles. 1983. *Canto Popular Uruguayo*. Buenos Aires: El Juglar.

6941 Echeverriarza-Espinola, Maria Paz. 1987. *Uruguayan Popular Song under the Dictatorship (1973–1984)*. Albuquerque, NM: New Mexico State University.

6942 Martins, Carlos Alberto. 1986. *Música popular uruguaya 1973–1982*. Montevideo: Centro Latinoamericana de Economía Humana.

6943 Martins, Carlos Alberto. 1988. *Communication, Morphogenèse et Identité Culturelle*. Belgium: Ciaco éditeur.

6944 Martins, Carlos Alberto. 1988. Popular Music as Alternative Communication: Uruguay, 1973–82. *Popular Music* 7(1): 77–94.

Venezuela

6945 Briceño, Arnulfo. 1988. La música llanera como punto de encuentro entre Colombia y Venezuela. *Correo de los Andes* 49 (January-February): 85–88.

6946 Ramón y Rivera, Luis Felipe. 1967. *Música Indígena Folklorica y Popular de Venezuela.* Buenos Aires: Ricordi Americana, Sociedad Anónima Editorial y Comercial.

OCEANIA

General

6947 Hannan, Michael. 1996. Music Archive for the Pacific. *Perfect Beat* 2(4) (January): vii–ix.

6948 Malm, William. 1977. *Music Cultures of the Pacific, the Near East and Asia.* Englewood Cliffs, NJ: Prentice-Hall.

6949 Marshall-Dean, Deidre. 1996. Cross-Cultural Connections: An Overview of Musical Exchange on the Yap Islands of Micronesia. *Perfect Beat* 2(4) (January): 89–97.

6950 McLean, M. 1977. *An Annotated Bibliography of Oceanic Music and Dance.* Wellington: The Polynesian Society.

Australia (Settler)

6951 Agardy, S., et al. 1985. *Young Australians and Music.* Melbourne: Australian Broadcasting Tribunal Research Branch.

6952 Barwick, Linda. 1990. Central Australian Women's Ritual Music: Knowing Through Analysis Versus Knowing Through Performance. *Yearbook for Traditional Music* 22: 60–79.

6953 Beilby, P. and Roberts, M., eds. 1981. *Australian Music Directory.* Melbourne: Australian Music Directory.

6954 Bennett, Tony, ed. 1988. *Rock Music: Politics and Policy.* Griffith: Institute for Cultural Policy Studies, Division of Humanities, Griffith University.

6955 Bissett, Andrew. 1979. *Black Roots, White Flowers: A History of Jazz in Australia.* Sydney: Golden Press.

6956 Breen, Marcus, ed. 1987. *Missing in Action: Australian Popular Music.* Melbourne: Verbal Graphics Pty.

6957 Breen, Marcus. 1987. Musica Rock 'indipendente' e cultura popolare in Australia. *Musica/Realtà* 22: 7–14.

6958 Bythell, Duncan. 1991. The Brass Band in Australia: The Transplantation of British Popular Culture, 1850–1950. In *Bands: The Brass Band Movement in the 19th and 20th Centuries,* ed. Trevor Herbert. Milton Keynes: Open University Press. 145–64.

6959 Canova, Gianni and Malagini, Fabio. 1984. *Australia New Wave.* Milano: Gammalibri.

6960 Centre for Studies in Australian Music. 1996. *Register of Theses in Australian Music.* Melbourne: The University of Melbourne.

6961 Covell, Roger. 1967. *Australia's Music. Themes of a New Society.* Melbourne: Sun Books.

6962 Cox, Peter. 1996. The Ambonese Connection: Lou Casch, Johnny O'Keefe and the Development of Australian Rock and Roll. *Perfect Beat* 2(4) (January): 1–17.

6963 Crisp, Deborah. 1982. *Bibliography of Australian Music: An Index to Monographs, Journal Articles and Theses.* Armidale: Australian Music Studies Project.

6964 Fahey, W. 1984. *Eureka: The Songs That Made Australia.* Sydney: Omnibus.

6965 Grieve, Ray. 1995. *A Band in a Waistcoat Pocket: The Story of the Harmonica in Australia*. Sydney: Currency Press.

6966 Harrison, Gillian, ed. 1988. *Strike a Light: Contemporary Songs of Australian Working Life*. Marrickville: Hale & Iremonger.

6967 Hayward, Philip, ed. 1992. *From Pop to Punk to Postmodernism: Popular Music and Australian Culture from the 1960s to the 1990s*. North Sydney: Allen & Unwin.

6968 Hutchison, Tracee. 1992. *Your Name's on the Door: Ten Years of Australian Music*. Sydney: ABC Enterprises.

6969 Johnson, Bruce. 1987. *The Oxford Companion to Australian Jazz*. Melbourne: Oxford University Press.

6970 Kent, David. 1993. *Australian Chart Book: 1970–1992*. St. Ives: Australian Chart Book.

6971 Latta, David. 1991. *Australian Country Music*. Sydney: Random House.

6972 Magoffin, Richard. 1983. *Waltzing Matilda, Songs of Australia: A Folk-History*. Charters Towers: Mimosa.

6973 McGrath, Noel. 1984. *Noel McGrath's Australian Encyclopedia of Rock & Pop*. Adelaide: Rigby.

6974 McGregor, Craig. 1984. *Pop Goes the Culture*. London: Pluto Press. First published Sydney: Hodder and Stoughton, 1983.

6975 Meredith, John and Anderson, Hugh. 1967. *Folk Songs of Australia, Vol. 1*. Sydney: Ure Smith.

6976 Meredith, John, Roger Covell and P. Brown. 1987. *Folk Songs of Australia, Vol. 2*. Kensington: New South Wales University Press.

6977 Milsom, W. and Thomas, H. 1986. *Pay to Play: The Australian Rock Music Industry*. Ringwood: Penguin.

6978 Mitchell, Tony. 1996. Real Wild Child: Australian Popular Music and National Identity. In *Popular Music and Local Identity: Rock, Pop and Rap in Europe and Oceania*. Leicester: Leicester University Press. 173–214.

6979 Pearce, Harry Hastings. 1971. *On the Origins of Waltzing Matilda*. Melbourne: The Hawthorn Press.

6980 Rogers, Robert Barton. 1975. *Rock 'n' Roll Australia: The Australian Pop Scene, 1954–1964*, ed. Denis O'Brien. Stanmore: Cassell Australia.

6981 Ryan, Michael. 1995. Brazilian Music in Sydney, Australia: Analysing Change in Urban Ethnic Music. In *Popular Music Perspectives III*, ed. Peter Wicke. Berlin: Zyankrise. 91–98.

6982 Sly, Leslie. 1993. *The Power and the Passion: A Guide to the Australian Music Industry*. North Sydney: Warner Chappell Music.

6983 Smith, James 'Jazzer'. 1984. *The Book of Australian Country Music*. Gordon: BFT Publishing Group.

6984 Snell, Kenneth R. 1987. *Australian Popular Music*. East Malvern: Quick Trick Press.

6985 Spencer, Chris and Nowara, Zbig. 1993. *Who's Who of Australian Rock and Roll*, revised edition. Fitzroy: Five Mile Press. First published Fitzroy: Five Mile Press, 1987.

6986 St. Leon, Mark. 1983. *Spangles and Sawdust: The Circus in Australia*. Melbourne: Greenhouse Publications.

6987 Stockbridge, Sally. 1989. Programming Rock 'n' Roll: The Australian Version. *Cultural Studies* 3(1): 73–88.

6988 Sturma, Michael. 1991. *Australian Rock 'n' Roll: The First Wave.* Kenthurst: Kangaroo Press.

6989 Sturma, Michael. 1992. The Politics of Dancing: When Rock 'n' Roll Came to Australia. *Journal of Popular Culture* 25(4): 123–42.

6990 Walker, Clinton. 1984. *The Next Thing: Contemporary Australian Rock.* Kenthurst: Kangaroo Press.

6991 Waterhouse, Richard. 1990. *From Minstrel Show to Vaudeville: The Australian Popular Stage, 1788–1914.* Kensington: New South Wales University Press.

6992 Waterhouse, Richard. 1990. The Minstrel Show and Australian Culture. *Journal of Popular Culture* 24(2): 147–66.

6993 Watson, Eric. 1982/83. *Country Music in Australia, Vols. 1 & 2.* Australia: Angus & Robertson. First published Kensington: Rodeo Press, 1975.

6994 Watson, Eric. 1987. Country Music: The Voice of Rural Australia. In *Missing in Action: Australian Popular Music,* ed. Marcus Breen. Melbourne: Verbal Graphics Pty. 47–77.

6995 Williams, Mike. 1981. *The Australian Jazz Explosion.* Sydney: Angus & Robertson.

6996 Wilmoth, Peter. 1993. *Glad All Over: The Countdown Years, 1974–87.* Ringwood: McPhee Gribble.

6997 Zion, Lawrence. 1989. Disposable Icons: Pop Music in Australia, 1955–1962. *Popular Music* 8(2): 165–75.

Fiji

6998 Saumaiwai, Chris. 1994. Urban Fijian Musical Attitudes and Ideas: Has Intercultural Contact Through Music and Dance Changed Them? In *Music-Cultures in Contact: Convergences and Collisions,* ed. Margaret Kartomi and Stephen Blum. Sydney: Currency Press. 93–99.

Hawaii

6999 Bambrick, Nikki, and Miller, Jeremy. 1994. Exotic Hula: Hawaiian Dance Entertainment in Post-War Australia. *Perfect Beat* 2(1): 68–87.

7000 Barrere, D., M. K. Pukui and M. Kelly. 1980. *Hula: Historical Perspectives.* Honolulu: Bishop Museum.

7001 Cooper, Mike. 1992. Brothers in Paradise. *Folk Roots* 117 (March): 33–37.

7002 Coyle, Jackey and Coyle, Rebecca. 1995. Aloha Australia: Hawaiian Music in Australia. *Perfect Beat* 2(2): 32–58.

7003 Elbert, Samuel and Mahoe, Noelani. 1970. *Na Mele O Hawaii Nei.* Honolulu: University of Hawaii Press.

7004 Hayatsu, T. 1982. *Buckie Shirakata, Hawaiian Paradise.* Tokyo: Sun Create.

7005 Hosokawa, Shuhei. 1994. East of Honolulu: Hawaiian Music in Japan from the 1920s to the 1940s. *Perfect Beat* 2(1): 51–67.

7006 Kamohalu, Robert and Burlingame, Burt, eds. 1978. *Da Kine Sound: Conversations with the People Who Create Hawaiian Music.* Honolulu: Press Pacifica.

7007 Kanahele, George. 1979. *Hawaiian Music and Musicians: An Illustrated History.* Honolulu: University of Hawaii Press.

7008 Lewis, George H. 1985. Beyond the Reef: Role Conflict and the Professional Musician in Hawaii. *Popular Music* 5: 189–98.

7009 Lewis, George H. 1991. Storm Blowing from Paradise: Social Protest and Oppositional Ideology in Popular

Hawaiian Music. *Popular Music* 10(1): 53–67.

7010 Lewis, George H. 1992. Don't Go Down Waikiki: Social Protest and Popular Music in Hawaii. In *Rockin' the Boat: Mass Music and Mass Movements*, ed. Reebee Garofalo. Boston, MA: South End Press. 171–83.

7011 McNeil, Adrian. 1995. A Mouse, a Frog, the Hawaiian Guitar and World Music Aesthetics: Vishwa Mohan Bhatt and Ry Cooder Meet by the River. *Perfect Beat* 2(3) (July): 82–97.

7012 Mutsaers, Lutgard. 1992. *Haring & Hawaii, hawaiianmuziek in Nederland 1925–1992*. Amsterdam: Poparchief Nederland (Dutch Rock Archives, #1).

7013 Owens, Harry. 1970. *Sweet Leilani*. Pacific Palisades, CA: Hula House.

7014 Weintraub, Andrew. 1993. Jamaican and Local Cultural Identity in Hawaii. *Perfect Beat* 1(2): 78–89.

7015 Whiteoak, John. 1995. Hawaiian Music and Jazzing. *Perfect Beat* 2(3): 115–18.

Indigenous Australian

7016 Berndt, Ronald M. 1976. *Three Faces of Love: Traditional Aboriginal Song Poetry*. Melbourne: Nelson.

7017 Breen, Marcus. 1989. *Our Place, Our Music*. Canberra: Aboriginal Studies Press.

7018 Breen, Marcus. 1992. Desert Dreams, Media, and Interventions in Reality: Australian Aboriginal Music. In *Rockin' the Boat: Mass Music and Mass Movements*, ed. Reebee Garofalo. Boston, MA: South End Press. 149–70.

7019 Castles, J. 1992. Tjungaringanyi: Aboriginal Rock. In *From Pop to Punk to Postmodernism: Popular Music and Australian Culture from the 1960s to the 1990s*, ed. Philip Hayward. North Sydney: Allen & Unwin. 25–39.

7020 No entry.

7021 Dixon, Robert M.W. and Koch, Grace. 1996. *Dyirbal Song Poetry: The Oral Literature of an Australian Rainforest People*. Saint Lucia: Queensland University Press.

7022 Dunbar-Hall, Peter. 1995. *Discography of Aboriginal and Torres Strait Islander Performers*. Sydney: Australian Music Centre.

7023 Ellis, Catherine. 1966. Aboriginal Songs of South Australia. *Miscellanea Musicologica: Adelaide Studies in Musicology* 1: 137–90.

7024 Ellis, Catherine. 1985. *Aboriginal Music: Education for Living. Cross-Cultural Experiences from South Australia*. Brisbane: University of Queensland Press.

7025 Ellis, Catherine, M. Brunton and Linda Barwick. 1988. From the Dreaming Rock to Reggae Rock. In *From Colonel Light into the Footlights: The Performing Arts in S.A. from 1836 to the Present*, ed. A.D. McCredie. Adelaide: Pagel Books. 151–72.

7026 Hayward, Philip. 1992. Music Video, the Bicentenary (and After). In *From Pop to Punk to Postmodernism: Popular Music and Australian Culture from the 1960s to the 1990s*, ed. Philip Hayward. North Sydney: Allen & Unwin. 160–71.

7027 Hayward, Philip. 1993. Safe, Exotic and Somewhere Else: Yothu Yindi, Treaty and the Mediation of Aboriginality. *Perfect Beat* 1(2) (January): 33–42.

7028 Isaacs, Jennifer, ed. 1979. *Australian Aboriginal Music*. Sydney: Aboriginal Artists Agency.

7029 Johnson, Rob. 1993. Looking Out: An Interview with Kev Carmody. *Perfect Beat* 1(2) (January): 43–47.

7030 Jones, Trevor A. 1967. The Dijeridu: Some Comparisons of Its Typology and

Musical Functions with Similar Instruments Throughout the World. *Studies in Music* 1: 22–25.

7031 Jones, Trevor A. 1980. The Traditional Music of the Australian Aborigines. In *Musics of Many Cultures*, ed. Elizabeth May. Berkeley and London: University of California Press. 154–71.

7032 Koch, Grace. 1987. A Bibliography of Publications on Australian Aboriginal Music: 1975–1985. *Musicology Australia* 10: 58–71.

7033 Lawe Davies, Chris. 1988. Looking for Signs of Style in Contemporary Popular Aboriginal Music. *Australian Journal of Communications* 16: 74–86.

7034 Lawe Davies, Chris. 1993. Aboriginal Rock Music: Place and Space. In *Rock and Popular Music: Politics, Policies, Institutions*, ed. Tony Bennett, et al. London and New York: Routledge. 249–65.

7035 Lawe Davies, Chris. 1993. Black Rock and Broome: Musical and Cultural Specificities. *Perfect Beat* 1(2) (January): 48–59.

7036 Magowen, Fiona. 1994. 'The Land Is Our Marr (Essence), It Stays Forever': The Yothu Yindi Relationship in Australian Aboriginal Traditional and Popular Musics. In *Ethnicity, Identity and Music: The Musical Construction of Place*, ed. Martin Stokes. Oxford: Berg. 135–56.

7037 Mitchell, Ewen. 1996. *Contemporary Aboriginal Music*. Port Melbourne: Ausmusic.

7038 Mitchell, Tony. 1992. World Music, Indigenous Music and Music Television in Australia. *Perfect Beat* 1(1) (July): 1–16.

7039 Mitchell, Tony. 1993. Treaty Now! Indigenous Music and Music Television in Australia. *Media, Culture and Society* 15: 299–308.

7040 Mitchell, Tony. 1996. Real Wild Child: Australian Popular Music and National Identity. In *Popular Music and Local Identity: Rock, Pop and Rap in Europe and Oceania*. Leicester: Leicester University Press. 173–214.

7041 Neuenfeldt, Karl. 1993. The Didjeridu and the Overdub: Technologising and Transposing Aural Images of Aboriginality. *Perfect Beat* 1(2) (January): 60–77.

7042 Neuenfeldt, Karl. 1993. Yothu Yindi and Ganma: The Cultural Transposition of the Aboriginal Agenda Through Metaphor and Music. *Journal of Australian Studies* 38: 1–11.

7043 Neuenfeldt, Karl. 1994. The Essentialistic, the Exotic, the Equivocal and the Absurd: The Cultural Production and Use of the Didjeridu in World Music. *Perfect Beat* 2(1) (July): 88–104.

7044 Neuenfeldt, Karl, ed. 1996. *The Didjeridu: From Arnhem Land to Internet*. Sydney: Perfect Beat and John Libbey Publications.

7045 Nicol, Lisa. 1993. Culture, Custom and Collaboration: Yothu Yindi's *Treaty*. *Perfect Beat* 1(2) (January): 23–32.

7046 Ryan, Robyn. 1994. Tracing the Urban Songlines: Contemporary Koori Music in Melbourne. *Perfect Beat* 2(1) (July): 20–37.

7047 Ryan, Robyn. 1995. Gnarnyarrhe Waitairie, Claim and Pundulumura. *Perfect Beat* 2(2) (January): 20–30.

7048 Streit-Warburton, J. 1993. Smashing the Silence: A Review of 'With Open Eyes' – The First National Aboriginal and Torres Strait Islander Contemporary Women's Music Festival. *Perfect Beat* 1(3): 86–90.

7049 Stubington, Jill and Dunbar-Hall, Peter. 1995. Yothu Yindi's 'Treaty': *Ganma* in

Music. *Popular Music* 13(3) (Special Australia/New Zealand Issue): 243–60.

7050 Sullivan, C. 1988. Non-Tribal Dance Music and Song: From First Contact to Citizen Rights. *Australian Aboriginal Studies* 1: 34–38.

Maori and Pacific Islander

7051 Bollinger, N. 1992. South of the Border. *Rip It Up* 181 (August).

7052 Bourke, C. 1992. Brothers and Sisters. *Rip It Up* 179 (June).

7053 Buchanan, Kerry. 1989. The Upper Hutt Posse: Music with a Message. *Music in New Zealand* (Summer): 34–35.

7054 Dart, William. 1994. Te Ku Te Whe: Rediscovering a Tradition. *Music in New Zealand* 24 (Autumn): 25–27.

7055 Derby, Mark and Wilson, Helen. 1995. Pacific Islander Radio and Music in Auckland. *Perfect Beat* 2(2) (January): 83–91.

7056 Dix, John. 1988. *Stranded in Paradise: New Zealand Rock 'n' Roll, 1955–1988.* Wellington: Paradise Publications.

7057 Findlay, K. 1993. Maori Radio: Where Is It Going? *Mana* 1(1).

7058 Hannan, Michael. 1996. Music Archive for the Pacific. *Perfect Beat* 2(4) (January): vii–ix.

7059 Hayward, Philip, Tony Mitchell and Roy Shuker, eds. 1994. *North Meets South: Popular Music in Aotearoa/New Zealand.* Umina: Perfect Beat Publications.

7060 Kopytko, Tanya. 1986. Breakdance as an Identity Marker in New Zealand. *Yearbook for Traditional Music* 18: 20–26.

7061 McLean, M. 1977. *An Annotated Bibliography of Oceanic Music and Dance.* Wellington: The Polynesian Society.

7062 Mitcalfe, Barry. 1974. *The Singing Word: Maori Poetry.* Wellington: Victoria University Press.

7063 Mitchell, Tony. 1995. New Urban Polynesians: Once Were Warriors, Proud and the South Auckland Music Scene. *Perfect Beat* 2(3) (July): 1–20.

7064 Mitchell, Tony. 1996. The Sounds of Nowhere? Bicultural Music in Aotearoa/New Zealand. In *Popular Music and Local Identity: Rock, Pop and Rap in Europe and Oceania.* Leicester: Leicester University Press. 215–63.

7065 Morley, Bruce. 1993. The Launching of Nga Matua: A Personal View. *Music in New Zealand* 21 (Spring): 38–41.

7066 Reedy, E. 1993. A Passion for Maori Music. *Mana* 1(1) (January).

7067 Reid, Graham. 1992. New Zealand's Maori Music: A Genre Melange. *Billboard* 104(22) (30 May): 1, 34.

7068 Reid, Graham. 1993. The Kiwi Scene Makes Strong '93 Showing. *Billboard* 105(30) (24 July): 19, 93.

7069 Reid, Graham. 1996. Polygram's OMC Unearths Polynesia. *Billboard* 108(27) (6 July): 1, 16.

7070 Shuker, Roy and Pickering, Michael. 1995. Kiwi Rock: Popular Music and Cultural Identity in New Zealand. *Popular Music* 13(3) (Special Australia/New Zealand Issue): 261–78.

7071 Thomson, Margie. 1991. A New Song: Women's Music in Aotearoa. *Music in New Zealand* (Winter): 22–29.

7072 Vui-Talitu, Sara. 1996. AEIOU Moana and the Moahunters, Music Video and the Communication of Polynesian Cultures in Contemporary New Zealand. *Perfect Beat* 2(4) (January): 78–88.

7073 Walker, Clinton. 1995. Pacific Pride. *Rolling Stone (Australian Edition)* 510 (June): 28–29.

7074 Whaanga, P. 1990. Radio: Capable of Carrying a Bicultural Message? In *Between the Lines: Racism and the New Zealand Media*. Auckland: Heinemann Reid.

7075 Wilson, Helen. 1993. Broadcasting and the Treaty of Waitangi. *Media Information Australia* 67 (February).

New Zealand: Pakeha (European)

7076 Chunn, Mike, and Chunn, Jeremy. 1995. *The Mechanics of Popular Music: A New Zealand Perspective*. Wellington: GP Publications.

7077 Davey, Tim, and Puschmann, Horst. 1996. *Kiwi Rock: A Reference Book*. Dunedin: Kiwi Rock Publications.

7078 Derby, Mark, and Wilson, Helen. 1995. Pacific Islander Radio and Music in Auckland. *Perfect Beat* 2(2) (January): 83–91.

7079 Dix, John. 1988. *Stranded in Paradise: New Zealand Rock 'n' Roll, 1955–1988*. Wellington: Paradise Publications.

7080 Hayward, Philip, Tony Mitchell and Roy Shuker, eds. 1994. *North Meets South: Popular Music in Aotearoa/New Zealand*. Umina: Perfect Beat Publications.

7081 Kopytko, Tanya. 1986. Breakdance as an Identity Marker in New Zealand. *Yearbook for Traditional Music* 18: 20–26.

7082 Lealand, G. 1988. *A Foreign Egg in Our Nest? American Popular Culture in New Zealand*. Wellington: Victoria University Press.

7083 Malm, William. 1977. *Music Cultures of the Pacific, the Near East and Asia*. Englewood Cliffs, NJ: Prentice-Hall.

7084 McDonnell, E. 1990. Green Grass and High Tides Forever: Rock and Roll Is Alive and Well and Living in New Zealand. *Village Voice Rock and Roll Quarterly* 3(2) (Summer): 24–27.

7085 McLeay, Colin. 1994. The 'Dunedin Sound': New Zealand Rock and Cultural Geography. *Perfect Beat* 2(1) (July): 38–50.

7086 Mitchell, Tony. 1996. The Sounds of Nowhere? Bicultural Music in Aotearoa/New Zealand. In *Popular Music and Local Identity: Rock, Pop and Rap in Europe and Oceania*. Leicester: Leicester University Press. 215–63.

7087 Pickering, Michael, and Shuker, Roy. 1993. Radio Gaga: Popular Music and the Radio Quota Debate in New Zealand. *New Zealand Sociology* 8(1): 1–36.

7088 Reid, Graham. 1992. New Zealand Awards Display Diversity. *Billboard* 104(17) (25 April).

7089 Shuker, Roy. 1994. Climbing the Rock: The New Zealand Music Industry. In *North Meets South: Popular Music in Aotearoa/New Zealand*, ed. Philip Hayward, Tony Mitchell and Roy Shuker. Umina: Perfect Beat Publications. 16–27.

7090 Shuker, Roy and Pickering, Michael. 1991. We Want the Airwaves: The New Zealand Music Quota Debate. *Illusions* 18: 40–44.

7091 Shuker, Roy and Pickering, Michael. 1995. Kiwi Rock: Popular Music and Cultural Identity in New Zealand. *Popular Music* 13(3) (Special Australia/New Zealand Issue): 261–78.

7092 Watkins, Roger. 1989. *When Rock Got Rolling*. Wellington: Hazard Press.

7093 Watkins, Roger. 1995. *Hostage to the Beat: The Auckland Scene, 1955–70*. Auckland: Tandem Press.

7094 Yska, Redmer. 1993. *All Shook Up: The Flash Bodgie and the Rise of the New Zealand Teenager in the Fifties.* Auckland: Penguin.

Papua New Guinea

7095 Hayward, Philip. 1993. After the Record: The *Tabaran* Documentary, Papua New Guinea and Intercultural Relations. *Perfect Beat* 1(3) (July): 75–85.

7096 Hayward, Philip. 1995. Titus Tilley and the Development of Music Video in Papua New Guinea. *Perfect Beat* 2(2) (January): 1–19.

7097 Hutton, Tiffany. 1993. Uncertain Identities: Marketing Tabaran. *Perfect Beat* 1(2) (January): 16–22.

7098 Krempl-Pereira, S., ed. 1984. *The Urban Music Situation in Papua New Guinea, 1977–1984.* Waigani: National Arts School.

7099 Niles, Don. 1984. *Commercial Recordings of Papua New Guinea Music, 1949–1983.* Boroko: Institute of Papua New Guinea Studies.

7100 Niles, Don. 1994. Religion, Media and Shows: The Effect of Intercultural Contacts on Papua New Guinean Musicians. In *Music-Cultures in Contact: Convergences and Collisions*, ed. Margaret Kartomi and Stephen Blum. Sydney: Currency Press. 84–92.

7101 Philpott, Malcolm. 1995. Developments in Papua New Guinea's Popular Music Industry: The Media and Technological Change in a Country with Many Cultures. *Perfect Beat* 2(3) (July): 98–114.

7102 Webb, Michael. 1993. *Lokal Musik: Lingua Franca Song and Identity in Papua New Guinea.* Boroko: National Research Institute.

7103 Webb, Michael. 1993. *Tabaran:* Intercultural Exchange, Participation and Collaboration. An Analysis of the Joint Recording Project of Not Drowning, Waving and the Musicians of Rabaul, Papua New Guinea. *Perfect Beat* 1(2) (January): 1–15.

7104 Webb, Michael and Niles, Don. 1986. *Riwain: Papua New Guinea Pop Songs.* Goroka and Boroko: University of Papua New Guinea, Goroka Teachers College.

MIDDLE EAST AND NORTH AFRICA

General

7105 Arafah, Abd al Muncim. 1947. *Tarikh Aclam al Musiqá al Sharqiyyah.* Cairo: Matbacat Anani.

7106 Bizot, Jean-François. 1988. Sex and Soul in the Maghreb. *The Face* 98(6): 86–93.

7107 Buonaventura, Wendy. 1989. *Serpent of the Nile: Women and Dance in the Arab World.* London: Saqi.

7108 Chabrier, Jean-Claude. 1974. Music in the Fertile Crescent: Lebanon, Syria and Iraq. *Cultures* 1(3): 35–58.

7109 Racy, Ali Jihad. 1978. Arabian Music and the Effects of Commercial Recording. *The World of Music* 20: 47–58.

7110 Salvador-Daniel, Francisco. 1987. *Musique et instruments de musique du Maghreb.* Paris: Boîte à Documents.

Afghanistan

7111 Baily, John. 1976. Recent Changes in the Dutar of Herat. *Asian Music* 8(1): 29–64.

7112 Baily, John. 1981. Cross-Cultural Perspectives in Popular Music: The Case of Afghanistan. *Popular Music* 1: 105–22.

7113 Baily, John. 1983. A System of Modes Used in the Urban Music of

Afghanistan. *Ethnomusicology* 27(1): 1–39.

7114 Baily, John. 1988. Amin-e Diwaneh: The Musician as Madman. *Popular Music* 7(2): 131–46.

7115 Baily, John. 1988. *Music of Afghanistan: Professional Musicians in the City of Herat.* Cambridge: Cambridge University Press.

7116 Baily, John. 1994. The Role of Music in the Creation of an Afghan National Identity, 1923–73. In *Ethnicity, Identity and Music: The Musical Construction of Place.* ed. Martin Stokes. Oxford: Berg. 45–60.

7117 Sakata, Hiromi Lorraine. 1983. *Music in the Mind: Concepts of Music and Musicians in Afghanistan.* Kent, OH: Kent State University Press.

7118 Slobin, Mark. 1974. Music in Contemporary Afghan Society. In *Afghanistan in the 1970s,* ed. Louis Dupree and Linette Albert. New York: Praeger. 239–48.

7119 Slobin, Mark. 1976. *Music in the Culture of Northern Afghanistan.* Tucson, AZ: University of Arizona Press, Viking Fund Publications in Anthropology, No. 54.

Algeria

7120 Baghli, Sid-Ahmad. 1978. *Aspects of Algerian Cultural Policy.* Paris: UNESCO.

7121 Elsner, Jürgen. 1983. Ferment nationalen Bewusstseins: Die Musikkultur Algeriens. *Musik und Gesellschaft* 33(8): 456–63.

Egypt

7122 Danielson, Virginia. 1996. New Nightingales of the Nile: Popular Music in Egypt Since the 1970s. *Popular Music* 15(3): 299–312.

7123 El-Shawan Castelo-Branco, Salwa. 1987. Some Aspects of the Cassette Industry in Egypt. *The World of Music* 29(2): 32–45.

7124 Racy, Ali Jihad. 1976. The Record Industry and Egyptian Traditional Music. *Ethnomusicology* 20(1): 23–48.

7125 Racy, Ali Jihad. 1978. Music in Contemporary Cairo: A Comparative Overview. *The World of Music* 20: 4–26.

7126 Racy, Ali Jihad. 1982. Musical Aesthetics in Present-Day Cairo. *Ethnomusicology* 26(3): 391–406.

7127 Racy, Ali Jihad. 1988. Sound and Society: The Takht Music of Early Twentieth Century Cairo. *Selected Reports in Ethnomusicology* 7: 139–69.

Iran

7128 Beeman, William O. 1976. You Can Take the Music Out of the Country, But . . .: The Dynamics of Change in Iranian Musical Tradition. *Asian Music* 7(2): 6–19.

7129 Blum, Stephen. 1978. Changing Roles of Performers in Meshhed and Bojnurd, Iran. In *Eight Urban Musical Cultures: Tradition and Change,* ed. Bruno Nettl. Urbana and London: University of Illinois Press. 19–95.

7130 Nettl, Bruno. 1972. Persian Popular Music in 1969. *Ethnomusicology* 16(2): 718–39.

Iraq

7131 Chabrier, Jean-Claude. 1974. Music in the Fertile Crescent: Lebanon, Syria and Iraq. *Cultures* 1(3): 35–58.

7132 Hassan, Schéhérazade Qassim. 1980. *Les Instruments de Musique en Irak.* Paris: Mouton Éditeur.

Israel

7133 Bayer, Bathja. 1980. Creation and Tradition in Israeli Folksongs. In *Aspects of Music in Israel*. Tel Aviv: Israel Composers' League/National Council for Culture and Art. 61–65.

7134 Ben-Porat, Ziva, ed. 1989. *Lirika ve-lahit*. Tel Aviv: Ha-kibutz ha-meukhad.

7135 Benski, Tova. 1989. Ethnicity and the Shape of Musical State Patterns in an Israeli Urban Community. *Social Forces* 67: 731–50.

7136 Benski, Tova, Joachim Braun and Uri Sharvit. 1986. Towards a Study of Israeli Urban Musical Culture: The Case of Kiryat Ono. *Asian Music* 17: 168–209.

7137 Bohlman, Philip V. 1984. Central European Jews in Israel: The Reurbanisation of Musical Life in an Immigrant Culture. *Yearbook for Traditional Music* 16: 67–83.

7138 Bohlman, Philip V. 1989. *The Land Where Two Streams Flow: Music in the German-Jewish Community of Israel*. Urbana and Chicago: University of Illinois Press.

7139 Cohen, Erik and Shiloah, Amnon. 1985. Major Trends of Change in Jewish Oriental Ethnic Music in Israel. *Popular Music* 5: 199–223.

7140 Halper, Jeff, Edwin Seroussi and Pamela Squires-Kidron. 1989. 'Musica Mizrakhit': Ethnicity and Class Culture in Israel. *Popular Music* 8: 177–84.

7141 Plam, Gila. 1986. Beracha Zefira: A Case in Acculturation in Israeli Song. *Asian Music* 17: 108–25.

7142 Regev, Motti. 1986. 'Oriental Music' and Israeli Popular Music. *Media, Culture and Society* 8(3): 343–56.

7143 Regev, Motti. 1989. The Field of Popular Music in Israel. In *World Music, Politics and Social Change*, ed. Simon Frith. Manchester: Manchester University Press. 143–55.

7144 Regev, Motti. 1992. Israeli Rock, or a Study in the Politics of 'Local Authenticity'. *Popular Music* 11(1): 1–14.

7145 Regev, Motti. 1993. *Ud ve-gitara: Tarbut ha-musica shel arviey israel*. Raanana: The Institute for Israeli Arab Studies, Beit Berl.

7146 Regev, Motti. 1995. Present Absentee: Arab Music in Israeli Culture. *Public Culture* 7: 433–45.

7147 Regev, Motti. 1995. *Rock: musica ve-tarbut*. Tel Aviv: Dvir.

7148 Regev, Motti. 1996. Musica Mizrakhit, Israeli Rock and National Culture in Israel. *Popular Music* 15(3): 275–84.

7149 Seroussi, Edwin. 1995. 'Songs from the Land of Israel': The Origins of Israel's Popular Music in Historical Perspective. In *Popular Music Perspectives III*, ed. Peter Wicke. Berlin: Zyankrise. 272–82.

7150 Seroussi, Edwin. 1996. *Popular Music in Israel: The First Fifty Years*. Cambridge, MA: Harvard College Library.

7151 Shiloah, Amnon and Cohen, Erik. 1983. The Dynamics of Change in Jewish Oriental Ethnic Music in Israel. *Ethnomusicology* 27: 227–51.

7152 Shmueli, Herzl. 1971. *Ha-zemer ha-ivry*. Tel Aviv: Mifaley Tarbut ve-Khinukh.

Lebanon

7153 Chabrier, Jean-Claude. 1974. Music in the Fertile Crescent: Lebanon, Syria and Iraq. *Cultures* 1(3): 35–58.

7154 Racy, Ali Jihad. 1986. Words and Music in Beirut: A Study of Attitudes. *Ethnomusicology* 30(3): 391–496.

Oman

7155 Mallah, Issam El. 1990. Some Observations on the Naming of Musical Instruments and on Rhythm in Oman. *Yearbook for Traditional Music* 22: 123–26.

Saudi Arabia

7156 Al-Mani, Muhammad. 1981. *Cultural Policy in the Kingdom of Saudi Arabia.* Paris: UNESCO.

Syria

7157 Chabrier, Jean-Claude. 1974. Music in the Fertile Crescent: Lebanon, Syria and Iraq. *Cultures* 1(3): 35–58.

Turkey

7158 Kozanoglu, Can. 1995. *Pop Cagi Atesi.* Istanbul: Iletisim.

7159 Manuel, Peter. 1989. *Modal Harmony in Andalusian, Eastern European and Turkish Syncretic Musics.* New York: International Council for Traditional Music.

7160 Signell, Karl L. 1976. The Modernization Process in Two Oriental Music Cultures: Turkish and Japanese. *Asian Music* 7(2): 72–102.

7161 Stokes, Martin. 1992. The Media and Reform: The Saz and Elektrosaz in Turkish Popular Music. *British Journal of Ethnomusicology* 1: 89–102.

7162 Stokes, Martin. 1994. Place, Exchange and Meaning: Black Sea Musicians in the West of Ireland. In *Ethnicity, Identity and Music: The Musical Construction of Place*, ed. Martin Stokes. Oxford: Berg. 97–116.

7163 Zannos, Iannis. 1990. Intonation in Theory and Practice of Greek and Turkish Music. *Yearbook for Traditional Music* 22: 42–59.

NORTH AMERICA

Native North-American

7164 Frisbie, Charlotte. 1977. *Music and Dance Research of Southwestern United States Indians: Past Trends, Present Activities and Suggestions for Future Research.* Detroit, MI: Information Coordinators.

7165 Frisbie, Charlotte. 1977. The Music of American Indians. In *Music in American Society, 1776–1976.* New Brunswick, NJ: Transaction. 95–105.

7166 Keillor, Elaine. 1986. The Role of Youth in the Continuation of Dogrib Musical Traditions. *Yearbook for Traditional Music* 18: 61–76.

7167 Keillor, Elaine. 1995. The Emergence of Postcolonial Musical Expression of Aboriginal Peoples Within Canada. *Cultural Studies* 9(1) (January): 106–24.

7168 Koranda, Lorraine D. 1980. Music of the Alaskan Eskimos. In *Musics of Many Cultures*, ed. Elizabeth May. Berkeley and London: University of California Press. 332–62.

7169 McAllester, David P. 1980. North American Native Music. In *Musics of Many Cultures*, ed. Elizabeth May. Berkeley and London: University of California Press. 307–31.

7170 Morrisseau, Miles. 1996. Buffy's World. *Aboriginal Voices* 3(2) (April, May, June): 18–21.

7171 Pelinski, Ramón. 1982. *La musique des Inuit du Caribou.* Montréal: Presses de l'Université Laval.

7172 Rhodes, Willard. 1952. Acculturation in North American Indian Music. In *Acculturation in the Americas, 2*, ed. Sol Tax. Chicago: Chicago University Press. 127–32.

7173 Rhodes, Willard. 1963. North American Indian Music in Transition: A Study of

Songs with English Words as an Index of Acculturation. *Journal of International Folk Music Council* 15: 9–14.

7174 Underhill, Ruth Murray. 1976. *Singing for Power: The Song Magic of the Papago Indians of Southern Arizona.* Berkeley, CA: University of California Press.

7175 Whidden, Lynn. 1984. How Can You Dance to Beethoven?: Native People and Country Music. *Canadian University Music Review* 5: 87–103.

7176 Wimer, Robert. 1973. Recent Change in the Musical Culture of the Blood Indians. *Yearbook for Inter-American Musical Research* 9.

Canada

7177 Adria, Marco. 1990. *Music of Our Times: Eight Canadian Singer-Songwriters.* Toronto: James Lorimer & Company.

7178 Bell, Leslie. 1955. Popular Music. In *Music in Canada*, ed. Ernest MacMillan. Toronto: University of Toronto Press. 208–15.

7179 Berland, Jody. 1981. A Musician under the Influence. *Canadian Journal of Political and Social Theory* 5(1–2): 174–82.

7180 Berland, Jody. 1988. Locating Listening: Technological Space, Popular Music, Canadian Mediations. *Cultural Studies* 2: 343–58.

7181 Berland, Jody. 1991. Free Trade and Canadian Music: Level Playing Field or Scorched Earth? *Cultural Studies* 5(3): 317–25.

7182 Daigle, Pierre V. 1972. *Tears, Love and Laughter: The Story of the Acadians.* Church Point, LA: Acadian Publishing Enterprise.

7183 Diamond, Beverley and Witmer, Robert, eds. 1994. *Canadian Music: Issues of Hegemony and Identity.* Toronto: Canadian Scholars' Press Inc.

7184 Einarson, John. 1987. *Shakin' All Over: The Winnipeg Sixties Rock Scene.* Winnipeg: John Einarson.

7185 Evans, Chad. 1983. *Frontier Theatre: A History of Theatrical Entertainment in the Canadian Far West and Alaska.* Victoria: Sono Nis Press.

7186 Ferland, Yvon and Anderson, Robert D. 1982. The Recording Industry Survey Conducted in Canada. In *The Phonogram in Cultural Communication*, ed. Kurt Blaukopf. Wien: Springer-Verlag. 19–42.

7187 Fetherling, Doug. 1991. *Some Day Soon.* Kingston: Quarry Press.

7188 Garofalo, Reebee. 1991. The Internationalization of the US Music Industry and Its Impact on Canada. *Cultural Studies* 5(3): 326–31.

7189 Goddard, Peter and Kamin, Philip. 1989. *Shakin' All Over: The Rock 'n' Roll Years in Canada.* Toronto/Montréal: McGraw-Hill Ryerson.

7190 Grant, Barry K. 1986. 'Across the Great Divide': Imitation and Inflection in Canadian Rock Music. *Journal of Canadian Studies* 21(1) (Spring): 116–27.

7191 Grenier, Line. 1990. Radio Broadcasting in Canada: The Case of 'Transformat' Music. *Popular Music* 9(2): 221–34.

7192 Harry, Isobel. 1980. Reggae inna Canada. *Le Compositeur canadien/The Canadian Composer* 152 (June): 4–17.

7193 Jackson, Rick. 1994. *Encyclopedia of Canadian Rock, Pop and Folk Music.* Kingston: Quarry Press.

7194 Jackson, Rick. 1996. *Encyclopedia of Canadian Country Music.* Kingston: Quarry Press.

7195 Kallmann, Helmut and Potvin, Gilles, eds. 1992. (1981) *Encyclopedia of Music in Canada*, 2nd edition. Toronto/

Buffalo/London: University of Toronto Press.

7196 Kivi, K. Linda. 1992. *Canadian Women Making Music*. Toronto: Green Dragon Press.

7197 Litchfield, Jack. 1982. *The Canadian Jazz Discography*. Toronto: University of Toronto Press.

7198 Litchfield, Jack. 1992. *Toronto Jazz, 1948–1950*. Etobicoke: Harmony Printing.

7199 MacDonnel, Margaret. 1982. *The Emigrant Experience: Songs of Highland Emigrants in North America*. Toronto: University of Toronto Press.

7200 McCormick, Chris. 1985. Maritime Folk Song as Popular Culture: An Applied Study in Discourse and Relations. *Canadian University Music Review* 1984/5: 60–86.

7201 McNamara, Helen and Lomax, Jack. 1973. *The Bands Canadians Danced To*. Toronto: Griffen Press.

7202 Melhuish, Martin. 1983. *Heart of Gold: 30 Years of Canadian Pop Music*. Toronto: CBC Enterprises.

7203 Melhuish, Martin. 1996. *Oh What a Feeling: A Vital History of Canadian Music*. Kingston: Quarry Press.

7204 Miller, Mark. 1982. *Jazz in Canada: Fourteen Lives*. Toronto: University of Toronto Press.

7205 Miller, Mark. 1982. The New Improvised Jazz: A National Survey. *Le Compositeur canadien/The Canadian Composer* 170 (April): 24–31.

7206 Miller, Mark. 1987. *Boogie, Pete & the Senator: Canadian Musicians in Jazz, the Eighties*. Toronto: Nightwood Editions.

7207 Mockus, Martha. 1994. Queer Thoughts on Country Music and k.d. lang. In *Queering the Pitch: The New Gay and Lesbian Musicology*, ed. Philip Brett, Elizabeth Wood and Gary Thomas. New York/London: Routledge. 257–74.

7208 Moogk, Edward B. 1975. *Roll Back the Years: A History of Canadian Recorded Sound and Its Legacy, Genesis to 1930*. Ottawa: National Library of Canada.

7209 Rosenberg, Neil V. 1980. 'Folk' and 'Country' Music in the Canadian Maritimes: A Regional Model. In *Country Music in the Maritimes: Two Studies*. St. John's: Memorial University of Newfoundland. 1–11. (First published in *The Journal of Country Music* 5 (1974): 76–83.)

7210 Sévigny, Jean-Pierre. 1994. *Sierra Norteña: The Influence of Latin Music on the French-Canadian Popular Song and Dance Scene*. Montréal: Montreal Vintage Music Society.

7211 Stephens, W. Ray. 1993. *The Canadian Entertainers of World War II*. Oakville/New York/London: Mosaic Press.

7212 Straw, Will. 1993. The English Canadian Recording Industry Since 1970. In *Rock and Popular Music: Politics, Policies, Institutions*, ed. Tony Bennett, et al. London: Routledge. 52–65.

7213 Straw, Will. 1996. Sound Recording. In *The Cultural Industries in Canada*, ed. Michael Dorland. Toronto: James Lorimer and Company. 95–117.

7214 Straw, Will, et al., ed. 1995. *Popular Music: Style and Identity*. Montréal: The Centre for Research on Canadian Cultural Industries and Institutions.

7215 Wright, Robert. 1991. 'Gimme Shelter': Observations on Cultural Protectionism and the Recording Industry in Canada. *Cultural Studies* 5(3): 306–16.

7216 Yorke, Ritchie. 1971. *Axes, Chops, and Hot Licks: The Canadian Rock Music Scene*. Edmonton: Hurtig.

Québec

7217 Baillargeon, Richard and Côté, Christian. 1991. *Destination Ragou: Une histoire de la musique populaire au Québec.* Montréal: Triptyque.

7218 Côté, Gérald. 1992. *Les 101 Blues du Québec (1965–1985).* Montréal: Triptyque.

7219 Day, Pierre. 1991. *Une histoire de La Bolduc.* Montréal: VLB Éditeur.

7220 Destrempes, Josée. 1985. 'Gens du Pays', un simbolo della 'Québécitude'. *What Is Popular Music? Quaderni di Musica/Realtà* 8: 302–305.

7221 Gilmore, John. 1988. *Swinging in Paradise: The Story of Jazz in Montreal.* Montréal: Véhicule.

7222 Gilmore, John. 1989. *Who's Who of Jazz in Montreal.* Montréal: Véhicule.

7223 Juste-Constant, Vogeli. 1990. Haitian Popular Music in Montreal: The Effect of Acculturation. *Popular Music* 9(1): 79–86.

7224 Roy, Bruno. 1978. *Et cette Amérique chante en québécois.* Ottawa: Leméac.

7225 Roy, Bruno. 1989. *Pouvoir chanter: essai d'analyse politique.* Montréal: VLB Éditeur.

7226 Saucier, Robert. 1985. Programmation musicale et radio communautaire: l'exemple de Channel #5. *Communication Information* 7(3) (Autumn).

7227 Tremblay-Matte, Cécile. 1990. *La chanson écrite au féminin: de Madeleine de Verchères à Mitsou, 1730–1990.* Montréal: Éditions Trois.

USA

General

7228 Abrahams, Roger D. and Foss, George. 1968. *Anglo-American Folksong Style.* Englewood Cliffs, NJ: Prentice-Hall.

7229 Atherton, Lewis. 1954. *Main Street on the Middle Border.* Bloomington, IN: Indiana University Press.

7230 Bastin, Bruce. 1986. *Red River Blues: The Blues Tradition in the Southwest.* Urbana, IL: University of Illinois Press.

7231 Bayles, Martha. 1994. *Hole in Our Soul: The Loss of Beauty and Meaning in American Popular Music.* New York: Free Press.

7232 Becker, Bart. 1986. *'Til the Cows Come Home: Rock 'n' Roll Nebraska.* Seattle, WA: Real Gone.

7233 Bindas, Kenneth. 1992. *America's Musical Pulse.* Westport, CT: Greenwood Press.

7234 Bluestein, Gene. 1994. *Poplore: Folk and Pop in American Culture.* Amherst, MA: University of Massachusetts Press.

7235 Boggs, Vernon. 1991. Musical Transculturation: From Afro-Cuban to Afro-Cubanism. *Popular Music & Society* 15(4): 71–83.

7236 Boggs, Vernon. 1992. *Salsiology: Afro-Cuban Music and the Evolution of Salsa in New York City.* New York: Excelsior Music Publishing Company.

7237 Booth, Mark. 1983. *American Popular Music: A Reference Guide.* Westport, CT: Greenwood Press.

7238 Braun, D. Duane. 1969. *Toward a Theory of Popular Culture: The Sociology and History of American Music and Dance, 1920–1968.* Ann Arbor, MI: Ann Arbor Publications.

7239 Carney, Gene, ed. 1994. *The Sounds of People and Places: A Geography of*

American Folk and Popular Music.
Lanham, MD: Rowman and Littlefield.

7240 Chase, Gilbert. 1987. (1955) *America's Music: From the Pilgrims to the Present.* Urbana, IL: University of Illinois Press.

7241 Cohen-Stratyner, Barbara, ed. 1988. *Popular Music, 1900–1919: An Annotated Guide to American Popular Song.* Detroit, MI: Gale Research.

7242 Collier, James L. 1988. *The Reception of Jazz in America: A New View.* New York: Institute for Studies in American Music.

7243 Cook, Bruce. 1971. *The Beat Generation.* New York: Watts.

7244 Dachs, David. 1964. *Anything Goes: The World of Popular Music.* New York: Bobbs-Merrill.

7245 Davis, Elizabeth. 1981. *Index to the New World Recorded Anthology of American Music.* New York: W.W. Norton.

7246 Davis, Ronald L. 1980–82. *A History of Music in American Life.* 3 vols. Malabar, FL: Robert Krieger.

7247 Denisoff, R. Serge. 1971. *A Great Day Coming: Folk Music and the American Left.* Urbana, IL: University of Illinois Press.

7248 Denisoff, R. Serge and Reuss, Richard. 1972. The Protest Songs and Skits of American Trotskyists. *Journal of Popular Culture* 6(2): 407–24.

7249 Dorough, Prince. 1992. *Popular-Music Culture in America.* New York: Ardsley House Publishers.

7250 Dunaway, David King. 1987. Music and Politics in the United States. *Folk Music Journal* 5(3): 268–94.

7251 Dunaway, David King and Larsen, Peter. 1987. Music as Political Communication in the United States. In *Popular Music & Communication*, ed.

James Lull. Newbury Park, CA: Sage. 36–52.

7252 Durant, J.B. 1984. *A Student's Guide to American Jazz and Popular Music: Outlines, Recordings and Historical Commentary.* Scottsdale, AZ: J.B. Durant.

7253 Eberly, Philip K. 1982. *Music in the Air: America's Changing Tastes in Popular Music, 1920–1980.* New York: Hastings House.

7254 Ennis, Philip H. 1992. *The Seventh Stream: The Emergence of Rock 'n' Roll in American Popular Music.* Middletown, CT: Wesleyan University Press.

7255 *Ethnic Recordings in America: A Neglected Heritage.* 1982. Washington, DC: American Folklife Center, Library of Congress.

7256 Ewen, David. 1957. *Panorama of American Popular Music: The Story of Our National Ballads and Folk Songs, the Songs of Tin Pan Alley, Broadway and Hollywood, New Orleans Jazz, Swing, and Symphonic Jazz.* Englewood Cliffs, NJ: Prentice-Hall.

7257 Ewen, David. 1977. *All the Years of American Popular Music.* Englewood Cliffs, NJ: Prentice-Hall.

7258 Ferris, William R. and Hart, Mary L., eds. 1982. *Folk Music and Modern Sound.* Jackson, MS: University Press of Mississippi.

7259 Finson, Jon W. 1994. *Voices That Are Gone: Themes in Nineteenth-Century American Popular Song.* New York: Oxford University Press.

7260 Fuld, James J. 1976. *American Popular Music, 1950–1975.* Philadelphia: Musica Americana.

7261 Garofalo, Reebee. 1996. *Rockin' Out: Popular Music in the USA.* Needham Heights, MA: Allyn and Bacon.

7262 Giddins, Gary. 1981. *Riding on a Blue Note: Jazz and American Pop*. New York: Oxford University Press.

7263 Gilbert, Douglas. 1970. (1942) *Lost Chords: The Diverting Story of American Popular Songs*. New York: Cooper Square. First published New York: Doubleday, 1942.

7264 Goodall, H.L., Jr. 1990. *Living in the Rock 'n' Roll Mystery*. Carbondale, IL: Southern Illinois University Press.

7265 Graf, Christian. 1989. *Rockmusik Lexikon. Amerika, Band 1, A-K. Band 2, L-Z*. Hamburg: Taurus.

7266 Grossberg, Lawrence. 1983. The Politics of Youth Culture: Some Observations on Rock and Roll in America. *Social Text* 8.

7267 Grossberg, Lawrence. 1989. Rock 'n' Reagan. *Quaderni di Musica/Realtà* 23: 459–77.

7268 Guralnick, Peter. 1971. *Feel Like Going Home: Portraits in Blues and Rock & Roll*. New York: Outerbridge & Dienstfrey.

7269 Hamm, Charles. 1979. *Yesterdays: Popular Song in America*. New York: W.W. Norton.

7270 Hamm, Charles. 1983. *Music in the New World*. New York: W.W. Norton.

7271 Horn, David. 1977. *The Literature of American Music in Books and Folk Music Collections: A Fully Annotated Bibliography*. Metuchen, NJ: Scarecrow Press.

7272 Horn, David. 1993. Musical America. In *Modern American Culture: An Introduction*, ed. Mick Gidley. London and New York: Longman. 239–61.

7273 Horn, David, and Jackson, Richard. 1988. *The Literature of American Music in Books and Folk Music Collections: A Fully Annotated Bibliography. Supplement 1*. Metuchen, NJ: Scarecrow Press.

7274 Jasen, David A. 1988. *Tin Pan Alley: The Composers, the Songs, the Performers and Their Times. The Golden Age of American Popular Music from 1886–1956*. New York: D.I. Fine.

7275 Johns, Donald. 1993. Funnel Tonality in American Popular Music, ca. 1900–70. *American Music* 11(4): 458–72.

7276 Joyner, David Lee. 1993. *American Popular Music*. Madison, WI: Brown & Benchmark.

7277 Keller, Kate van Winkle. 1981. *Popular Secular Music in America Through 1800: A Preliminary Checklist of Manuscripts in North American Collections*. Philadelphia: Music Library Association.

7278 Krummel, D.W., et al. 1981. *Resources of American Music History: A Directory of Source Materials from Colonial Times to World War II*. Urbana, IL: University of Illinois Press.

7279 Levy, Lester S. 1967. *Grace Notes in American History: Popular Sheet Music from 1820 to 1900*. Norman, OK: University of Oklahoma Press.

7280 Levy, Lester S. 1975. *Give Me Yesterday: American History in Song, 1890–1920*. Norman, OK: University of Oklahoma Press.

7281 Levy, Lester S. 1976. *Picture the Songs: Lithographies from the Sheet Music of Nineteenth Century America*. Baltimore and London: Johns Hopkins University Press.

7282 Lissauer, Robert. 1996. *Lissauer's Encyclopedia of Popular Music in America: 1888 to the Present*. New York: Facts on File.

7283 Luther, Frank. 1942. *Americans and Their Songs*. New York: Harper & Bros.

7284 MacDonnel, Margaret. 1982. *The Emigrant Experience: Songs of Highland Emigrants in North America*. Toronto: University of Toronto Press.

7285 Mackenzie, Harry and Polomski, Lothar. 1991. *One Night Stand Series, 1–1001.* Westport and London: Greenwood Press.

7286 Marcus, Greil. 1990. (1975) *Mystery Train: Images of America in Rock 'n' Roll Music.* London: Omnibus. First published New York: E.P. Dutton, 1975.

7287 Matlaw, Myron, ed. 1979. *American Popular Entertainment: Papers and Proceedings of the Conference on the History of American Popular Entertainment.* Westport, CT: Greenwood Press.

7288 Mattfeld, Julius. 1971. (1952) *Variety Music Cavalcade, 1620–1969: A Chronology of Vocal and Instrumental Music Popular in the United States.* Englewood Cliffs, NJ: Prentice-Hall.

7289 McCue, George, ed. 1977. *Music in American Society, 1776–1976: From Puritan Hymn to Synthesizer.* New Brunswick, NJ: Transaction.

7290 Mead, Rita H. 1974. *Doctoral Dissertations in American Music: A Classified Bibliography.* New York and Brooklyn: Institute for Studies in American Music.

7291 Mellers, Wilfrid. 1987. *Music in a New Found Land: Themes and Developments in the History of American Music.* London: Faber & Faber.

7292 Miller, Terry E. 1986. *Folk Music in America: A Reference Guide.* New York: Garland.

7293 Mooney, H.F. 1972. Popular Music Since the 1920s: The Significance of Shifting Taste. In *The Sounds of Social Change: Studies in Popular Culture*, ed. R. Serge Denisoff and Richard A. Peterson. Chicago: Rand McNally & Co. 181–97.

7294 Moore, McDonald. 1985. *Yankee Blues: Musical Culture and American Identity.*
Bloomington, IN: Indiana University Press.

7295 Murphy, Jeanette. 1967. The Survival of African Music in America. In *The Negro and His Folklore in Nineteenth-Century Periodicals*, ed. Bruce Jackson. Austin, TX: University of Texas Press. 327–39. (First published in *Popular Science Monthly* 55 (1899): 660–72.)

7296 Nanry, Charles, ed. 1972. *American Music: From Storyville to Woodstock.* New Brunswick, NJ: Transaction.

7297 Ostendorf, Berndt. 1982. *Black Literature in White America.* Brighton: Harvester Press.

7298 Ostendorf, Berndt. 1983. *Ethnicity and Popular Music: On Immigrants and Blacks in American Music, 1830–1900.* Exeter: IASPM UK.

7299 Perez Firmat, Gustavo. 1994. *Life on the Hyphen: The Cuban-American Way.* Austin, TX: University of Texas Press.

7300 Phelps, Richard. 1983. Songs of the American Hobo. *Journal of Popular Culture* 17(2): 1–21.

7301 Podell, Janet, ed. 1987. *Rock Music in America.* New York: H.W. Wilson.

7302 Pound, Louise. 1922. *American Ballads and Songs.* New York: Scribner's & Sons.

7303 Roberts, John Storm. 1979. *The Latin Tinge: The Influence of Latin American Music in the United States.* New York and Oxford: Oxford University Press.

7304 Rosenberg, Bernard and White, David, eds. 1957. *Mass Culture: The Popular Arts in America.* New York: The Free Press.

7305 Rourke, Constance. 1965. (1942) *The Roots of American Culture, and Other Essays.* Port Washington, CT: Kennikat Press. First published New York: Harcourt, Brace, 1942.

7306 Sample, Duane. 1985. The Popular Music of the Spanish-American War: How Popular Was It? In *Popular Music Perspectives*, 2, ed. David Horn. Göteborg and Exeter: IASPM. 360–66.

7307 Sanjek, Russell. 1988. *American Popular Music and Its Business: The First Four Hundred Years*. New York: Oxford University Press.

7308 Sanjek, Russell, and Sanjek, David. 1991. *American Popular Music Business in the 20th Century*. New York: Oxford University Press.

7309 Scheurer, Timothy E., ed. 1989. *American Popular Music: Readings from the Popular Press*. 2 vols. Bowling Green, OH: Bowling Green State University Press.

7310 Scheurer, Timothy E. 1991. *Born in the U.S.A.: The Myth of America in Popular Music from Colonial Times to the Present*. Jackson, MS: University Press of Mississippi.

7311 Seeger, Pete and Reiser, Bob. 1986. *Carry It On: A History in Song and Pictures of the Working Men and Women of America*. Poole: Blandford Press.

7312 Shaw, Arnold. 1986. *Black Popular Music in America: From the Spirituals, Minstrels, and Ragtime to Soul, Disco, and Hip-Hop*. New York: Schirmer.

7313 Shaw, Arnold. 1987. *The Jazz Age: Popular Music in the 1920s*. New York and Oxford: Oxford University Press.

7314 Simon, George T. 1979. *The Best of the Music Makers: From Acuff to Ellington to Presley to Sinatra to Zappa and 279 More of the Most Popular Performers of the Last Fifty Years*. Garden City, NY: Doubleday.

7315 Slobin, Mark. 1983. Tenement Songs: The Popular Music of Jewish Immigrants. *Popular Music* 3: 289–92.

7316 Small, Christopher. 1977. *Music – Society – Education: A Radical Examination of the Prophetic Function of Music in Western, Eastern and African Cultures*. London: Calder.

7317 Sonneck, Oscar G.T. 1969. (1914) *The Star Spangled Banner*. New York: Da Capo Press. First published Washington, DC: Government Printing Office, 1914.

7318 Southern, Eileen. 1983. (1971) *The Music of Black Americans: A History*. New York: W.W. Norton.

7319 Spaeth, Sigmund. 1971. (1948) *A History of Popular Music in America*. New York: Random House.

7320 Spottswood, Richard K. 1990. *Ethnic Music on Records: A Discography of Ethnic Recordings Produced in the United States, 1893–1942*. 7 vols. Urbana, IL: University of Illinois Press.

7321 Tawa, Nicholas E. 1982. *A Sound of Strangers: Musical Culture, Acculturation and the Post-Civil War Ethnic American*. Metuchen, NJ: Scarecrow Press.

7322 Tawa, Nicholas E. 1984. *A Music for the Millions: Antebellum Democratic Attitudes and the Birth of American Popular Music*. New York: Pendragon Press.

7323 Tawa, Nicholas E. 1984. *Serenading the Reluctant Eagle: American Musical Life, 1925–1945*. New York: Schirmer.

7324 Toll, Robert C. 1982. *The Entertainment Machine: American Show Business in the Twentieth Century*. New York and London: Oxford University Press.

7325 Van Dam, Theodore. 1954. The Influence of West African Songs of Derision in the New World. *African Music* 1(1): 53–56.

7326 Vassal, Jacques. 1984. (1971) *Folksong: une histoire de la musique populaire aux Etats-Unis*. Paris: Albin Michel.

7327 Warner, Jay. 1992. *The Billboard Book of American Singing Groups: A History, 1940–1990*. New York: Billboard Books.

7328 Warren, Craig. 1978. *Sweet and Low-Down: America's Popular Song Writers*. Metuchen, NJ: Scarecrow Press.

7329 Waterman, Richard. 1952. African Influence on the Music of the Americas. In *Acculturation in the Americas, 2*, ed. Sol Tax. Chicago: University of Chicago Press. 207–18.

7330 Watts, Michael. 1975. The Call and Response of American Popular Music: The Impact of American Pop Music in Europe. In *Superculture: American Popular Culture and Europe*, ed. C.W.E. Bigsby. London: Elek. 123–39.

7331 Whitburn, Joel. 1986. *Pop Memories, 1890–1954: The History of American Popular Music*. Menomonee Falls, WI: Record Research Inc.

7332 Whitcomb, Ian. 1972. *After the Ball*. London: Penguin.

7333 Wicke, Peter. 1988. Musikindustrie in den USA: Eine Analyse. *Beilage zur Zeitschrift 'Unterhaltungskunst'* 12.

7334 Wicke, Peter. 1991. *Bigger than Life: Musik und Musikindustrie in den USA: Porträt einer Musikszene*. Leipzig: Reclam.

7335 Wilder, Alec. 1972. *American Popular Song: The Great Innovators, 1900–1950*. New York: Oxford University Press.

7336 Wilk, Max. 1976. *Memory Lane: The Golden Age of American Popular Music, 1890–1925*. New York: Ballantine.

7337 Wilson, William A. 1985. The Outlaw Hero in U.S. Legend and Song. *Musiikin suunta* 7: 80–88.

Regions

– Appalachians

7338 Scarborough, Dorothy. 1937. *A Song Catcher in the Southern Mountains: American Folksongs of British Ancestry*. New York: Columbia University Press.

7339 Tribe, Ivan M. 1984. *Mountaineer Jamboree: Country Music in West Virginia*. Lexington, KY: University Press of Kentucky.

7340 Whisnant, David E. 1983. *All That Is Native and Fine: The Politics of Culture in an American Region*. Chapel Hill and London: University of North Carolina Press.

– The South

7341 Booth, Stanley and Eggleston, William. 1991. *Rythm Oil: A Journey Through the Music of the American South*. New York: Pantheon.

7342 Cobb, James C. 1982. From Muskogee to Luckenbach: Country Music and the Southernization of America. *Journal of Popular Culture* 16(3): 81–90.

7343 Evans, David. 1972. Black Fife and Drum Music in Mississippi. *Mississippi Folklore Register* 6: 94–107.

7344 Guralnick, Peter. 1986. *Sweet Soul Music: Rhythm and Blues and the Southern Dream of Freedom*. New York: Harper & Row.

7345 Hoskyns, Barney. 1987. *Say It One Time for the Broken-Hearted: The Country Side of Southern Soul*. London: Country Music Foundation.

7346 Imes, Birney. 1990. *Juke Joint: Photographs by Birney Imes*. Jackson, MS: University Press of Mississippi.

7347 Kennedy, R. Emmett. 1925. *Mellows: A Chronicle of Unknown Singers*. New York: Albert & Charles Boni.

7348 Lund, Jens. 1972. Fundamentalism, Racism, and Political Reaction in

Country Music. In *The Sounds of Social Change: Studies in Popular Culture*, ed. R. Serge Denisoff and Richard A. Peterson. Chicago: Rand McNally & Co. 79–91.

7349 Malone, Bill C. 1979. *Southern Music, American Music*. Lexington, KY: University Press of Kentucky.

7350 Malone, Bill C. 1982. Honky Tonk: The Music of the Southern Working Class. In *Folk Music and Modern Sound*, ed. William R. Ferris and Mary L. Hart. Jackson, MS: University Press of Mississippi. 119–28.

7351 Malone, Bill C. 1993. *Singing Cowboys and Musical Mountaineers: Southern Culture and the Roots of Country Music*. Athens, GA: University of Georgia Press.

7352 Parrish, Lydia. 1965. *Slave Songs of the Georgia Sea Islands*. Hatboro, PA: Folklore Associates.

7353 Patterson, Daniel W., ed. 1991. *Sounds of the South: A Report and Selected Papers from a Conference on the Collecting and Collections of Southern Traditional Music*. Chapel Hill, NC: University of North Carolina Southern Folklife Collection.

7354 Tucker, Stephen R. 1982. Pentecostalism and Popular Culture in the South: A Study of Four Musicians. *Journal of Popular Culture* 16(3): 68–80.

7355 Tullos, Allen. 1977. *Long Journey Home: Folklife in the South*. Chapel Hill, NC: Institute for Southern Studies.

– *Southwest USA*

7356 Arnold, Anita G., ed. 1995. *Legendary Times and Tales of Second Street*. Oklahoma City, OK: Black Liberated Arts Council, Inc.

7357 Casey, Betty. 1985. *Dance Across Texas*. Austin, TX: University of Texas Press.

7358 Ellison, Ralph. 1964. *Shadow and Act*. New York: Random House.

7359 Ellison, Ralph. 1986. *Going to the Territory*. New York: Random House.

7360 Owens, William A. 1983. *Tell Me a Story, Sing Me a Song: A Texas Chronicle*. Austin, TX: University of Texas Press.

7361 Paredes, Américo. 1958. *'With a Pistol in His Hand': A Border Ballad and Its Hero*. Austin, TX: University of Texas Press.

7362 Russell, Ross. 1981. (1971) *Jazz Style in Kansas City and the Southwest*. Berkeley, CA: University of California Press.

7363 Savage, William W., Jr. 1983. *Singing Cowboys and All That Jazz: A Short History of Popular Music in Oklahoma*. Norman, OK: University of Oklahoma Press.

7364 Schuller, Gunther. 1968. The Southwest. In *Early Jazz: Its Roots and Musical Development*. New York: Oxford University Press. 279–317.

7365 Whitlock, E. Clyde and Saunders, Richard Drake, eds. 1950. *Music and Dance in Texas, Oklahoma and the South-West*. Hollywood, CA: Bureau of Musical Research.

7366 Willoughby, Larry. 1984. *Texas Rhythm, Texas Rhyme: A Pictorial History of Texas Music*. Austin, TX: Texas Monthly Press.

Cities
– *Austin*

7367 Endres, Clifford. 1987. *Austin City Limits*. Austin, TX: University of Texas Press.

7368 Green, Archie. 1981. Austin's Cosmic Cowboys: Words in Collision. In *And Other Neighborly Names: Social Process and Cultural Image in Texas Folklore*, ed. Richard Bauman and Roger D. Abrahams. Austin, TX: University of Texas Press.

7369 Machann, Clinton. 1981. Country-Western and the 'Now' Sound in Texas-

Czech Polka Music. *John Edwards Memorial Foundation Quarterly* 19: 3–7.

7370 Nightbyrd, Jeff. 1975. Cosmo Cowboys: Too Much Cowboy and Not Enough Cosmic. *Austin Sun* (3 April): 13, 19.

7371 Poveda, Pablo. 1981. Danza de Concheros en Austin, Texas: Entrevista con Andrés Segura Granados. *Latin American Music Review* 2(2): 280–99.

7372 Reid, Jan. 1974. *The Improbable Rise of Redneck Rock*. Austin, TX: Heidelberg Publishers.

7373 Reid, Jan. 1976. Who Killed Redneck Rock? *Texas Monthly* (December): 210–13, 216.

7374 Shank, Barry. 1994. *Dissonant Identities: The Rock 'n' Roll Scene in Austin, Texas*. Hanover, NH: Wesleyan University Press and University Press of New England.

7375 Spitzer, Nicholas R. 1975. 'Bob Wills Is Still the King': Romantic Regionalism and Convergent Culture in Central Texas. *John Edwards Memorial Foundation Quarterly* 11(40): 191–96.

– Chicago

7376 Baker, Cary and Lind, Jeff. 1976. Sounds of the Sixties: Part Three, Chicago. *Who Put the Bomp!* 15 (Spring): 31–36.

7377 Boehlert, Eric. 1993. Chicago: Cutting Edge's New Capital. *Billboard* (21 August): 1, 68, 76.

7378 Boyd, Joe. 1964. South Side Blues: Blues Lyrics, Chicago-Style. In *ABC TV Hootenanny*. New York: SMP Publishing. 22–23.

7379 Brubaker, Robert L. 1985. *Making Music Chicago Style*. Chicago: Chicago Historical Society.

7380 Dahl, Bill. 1993. City Clubs, Labels, Find Blues Is the Cure. *Billboard* (21 August): 1, 76.

7381 Epstein, Dena J. 1969. *Music Publishing in Chicago Before 1871: The Firm of Root and Cady, 1858–1871*. Detroit, MI: Information Coordinators (Detroit Studies in Music Bibliography).

7382 Grayson, Lisa. 1992. *The History of Chicago's Legendary Old Town School of Folk Music*. Chicago: Old Town School of Folk Music.

7383 Hafferkamp, Jack. 1974. Pop Music in Chicago: This Isn't Where It's At. *Chicago Daily News* (1 June).

7384 Hurst, Jack. 1984. 'Barn Dance' Days: Remembering the Stars of a Pioneering Chicago Radio Show. *Chicago Tribune Sunday* (5 August): 8–13, 15.

7385 Kennedy, Rick. 1994. *Jelly Roll, Bix, and Hoagy: Gennett Studios and the Birth of Recorded Jazz*. Bloomington, IN: Indiana University Press.

7386 Kenney, William Howland. 1993. *Chicago Jazz: A Cultural History, 1904–1930*. New York: Oxford University Press.

7387 Kot, Greg. 1994. A Wax Trax for the '90s. *Chicago Tribune* (23 October).

7388 Langer, Adam. 1989. Glory Days. *Reader* (13 January): 1, 14, 16, 18, 20, 22, 24, 28, 30, 32, 34–35.

7389 Lax, John. 1974. Chicago's Black Jazz Musicians in the Twenties: Portrait of an Era. *Journal of Jazz Studies* 1(2): 107–27.

7390 Ostendorf, Berndt. 1982. *Black Literature in White America*. Brighton: Harvester Press.

7391 Popson, Tom. 1980. Jim Lounsbury and 'Bandstand': A Big Leap for Rock, Small Hop for TV. *Chicago Tribune* (17 November).

7392 Popson, Tom. 1989. Have Platters, Will Travel: Recalling Mar-Vel Records and a Bygone Era. *Chicago Tribune* (17 November).

7393 Pruter, Robert. 1991. *Chicago Soul.* Urbana, IL: University of Illinois Press.

7394 Pruter, Robert. 1996. *Doowop: The Chicago Scene*. Urbana, IL: University of Illinois Press.

7395 Rand, Lawrence. 1994. Old Folkies: A Gathering of the Gate of Horn Crowd. *Reader* (7 October).

7396 Rowe, Mike. 1973. *Chicago Blues: The City and the Music*. New York: Da Capo Press.

7397 Verna, Paul. 1993. Touch and Go Thrives by Keeping Punk Ethic. *Billboard* (21 August): 1, 76–77.

7398 Vincent, Ted. 1992. The Community That Gave Jazz to Chicago. *Black Music Research Journal* 12(1): 42–55.

7399 Wyman, Bill. 1993. Chicago-Area Labels Agree to Disagree. *Billboard* (21 August): 1, 75.

– *Kansas City*

7400 Atkins, Hannah. 1969–70. The Jazzmen: From the Blue Devils Through Bennie Moten to Count Basie. *Oklahoma Today* 20 (Winter): 15–18.

7401 Carney, George O., comp. 1992. *Oklahoma Jazz Artists: A Biographical Dictionary*. Stillwater, OK: Oklahoma State University Printing.

7402 Carney, George O. 1994. Oklahoma Jazz: Deep Second to 52nd Street. *The Chronicles of Oklahoma* 72 (Spring): 4–21.

7403 Driggs, Franklin S. 1975. Kansas City and the Southwest. In *Jazz: New Perspectives on the History of Jazz by Twelve of the World's Foremost Jazz Critics and Scholars*, ed. Nat Hentoff and Albert McCarthy. New York: Da Capo Press. 189–230. First published New York: Rinehart, 1959.

7404 Horricks, Raymond. 1957. Jimmy Rushing. In *Count Basie and His Orchestra: Its Music and Its Musicians*. London: Victor Gollancz. 147–59.

7405 Kirk, Andy and Lee, Amy. 1989. *Twenty Years on Wheels*. Ann Arbor, MI: University of Michigan Press.

7406 Munstedt, Peter A. 1991. Kansas City Music Publishing. *American Music* 9(4): 353–83.

7407 Ostransky, Leroy. 1978. Kansas City: The Development of Its Spirit. In *Jazz City: The Impact of Our Cities on the Development of Jazz*. Englewood Cliffs, NJ: Prentice-Hall. 123–72.

7408 Pearson, Nathan W., Jr. 1987. *Goin' to Kansas City*. Urbana, IL: University of Illinois Press.

7409 Russell, Ross. 1983. (1971) *Jazz Style in Kansas City and the Southwest*. Berkeley, CA: University of California Press.

7410 Schuller, Gunther. 1968. The Southwest. In *Early Jazz: Its Roots and Musical Development*. New York: Oxford University Press. 279–317.

7411 Stowe, David W. 1992. Jazz in the West. *Western Historical Quarterly* 23(1): 53–73.

– *Los Angeles*

7412 Cross, Brian. 1993. *It's Not About a Salary: Rap, Race and Resistance in Los Angeles*. London and New York: Verso.

7413 Djedje, Jacqueline Cogdell. 1989. Gospel Music in the Los Angeles Black Community. *Black Music Research Journal* 9(1): 35–79.

7414 Djedje, Jacqueline Cogdell. 1993. Los Angeles Composers of African American Gospel Music: The First Generations. *American Music* 11(4): 412–57.

7415 Eastman, Ralph. 1989. Central Avenue Blues: The Making of Los Angeles

Rhythm and Blues, 1942–1947. *Black Music Research Journal* 9(1): 19–33.

7416 Faulkner, Robert R. 1971. *Hollywood Studio Musicians: Their Work and Careers in the Recording Industry*. New York: Aldine-Atherton.

7417 Faulkner, Robert R. 1972. Hollywood Studio Musicians: Making It in the Los Angeles Film and Recording Industry. In *American Music: From Storyville to Woodstock*, ed. Charles Nanry. New Brunswick, NJ: Transaction. 200–22.

7418 Fawcett, Anthony. 1978. *California Rock, California Sound: The Music of Los Angeles and Southern California*. Los Angeles: Reed Books.

7419 Gordon, Robert. 1986. *Jazz West Coast: The Los Angeles Jazz Scene of the 1950s*. London: Quartet.

7420 Lewis, Jon. 1988. Punks in LA: It's Kiss or Kill. *Journal of Popular Culture* 22(2): 87–97.

7421 Lipsitz, George. 1990. *Time Passages: Collective Memory and American Popular Culture*. Minneapolis, MN: University of Minnesota Press.

7422 Lipsitz, George. 1992. Chicano Rock: Cruisin' Around the Historical Bloc. In *Rockin' the Boat: Mass Music and Mass Movements*, ed. Reebee Garofalo. Boston, MA: South End Press. 267–80.

7423 Loza, Steven. 1993. *Barrio Rhythm: Mexican American Music in Los Angeles*. Urbana, IL: University of Illinois Press.

7424 Murray, Lyn. 1987. *Musician: A Hollywood Journal; of Wives, Women, Writers, Lawyers, Directors, Producers and Music*. Secaucus, NJ: Lyle Stuart.

– Memphis

7425 Anderson, Clive. 1975. Memphis and the Sounds of the South. In *The Soul Book*, ed. Tony Cummings, Ian Hoare and Simon Frith. London: Methuen. 60–116.

7426 Charters, Samuel B. 1973. *Sweet as the Showers of Rain*. New York: Oak Publications.

7427 Escott, Colin. 1986. *The Sun Country Years: Country Music in Memphis, 1950–1959*. Bremen: Bear Family Records.

7428 Escott, Colin and Hawkins, Martin. 1980. *Sun Records: The Brief History of the Legendary Record Label*. New York: Quick Fox.

7429 Escott, Colin and Hawkins, Martin. 1991. *Good Rockin' Tonight: Sun Records and the Birth of Rock 'n' Roll*. New York: St. Martin's Press.

7430 Gordon, Robert. 1995. *It Came from Memphis*. Boston, MA: Faber & Faber.

7431 Guralnick, Peter. 1986. *Sweet Soul Music: Rhythm and Blues and the Southern Dream of Freedom*. New York: Harper & Row.

7432 Guralnick, Peter. 1994. *Last Train to Memphis: The Rise of Elvis Presley*. Boston, MA: Little, Brown & Co.

7433 Handy, W.C. 1970. (1941) *Father of the Blues*. New York: Collier Books.

7434 Kirby, Edward 'Prince Gabe'. 1983. *From Africa to Beale Street*. Memphis, TN: Musical Management.

7435 Leadbitter, Mike. 1968. *Delta Country Blues*. Bexhill-on-Sea: Blues Unlimited.

7436 Lee, George W. 1969. (1934) *Beale Street: Where the Blues Began*. College Park, MD: McGrath Publishing Co. First published New York: Vail-Ballou, 1934.

7437 Lornell, Kip. 1995. *'Happy in the Service of the Lord': African-American Sacred Vocal Harmony Quartets in Memphis*. Knoxville, TN: University of Tennessee Press. First published Urbana: University of Illinois Press, 1988.

7438 McKee, Margaret and Chisenhall, Fred. 1981. *Beale Black & Blue: Life and Music on Black America's Main Street.* Baton Rouge, LA: Louisiana State University Press.

7439 Olsson, Bengt. 1970. *Memphis Blues and Jug Bands.* London: Studio Vista.

7440 Palmer, Robert. 1979. *A Tale of Two Cities: Memphis Rock and New Orleans Roll.* Brooklyn, NY: Institute for Studies in American Music.

7441 Reagon, Bernice Johnson, ed. 1992. *We'll Understand It Better By and By: Pioneering African American Gospel Composers.* Washington, DC: Smithsonian Institution Press.

– *Nashville*

7442 Acuff, Roy and Neeley, William. 1983. *Roy Acuff's Nashville: The Life and Good Times of Country Music.* New York: Pedigree Books.

7443 Bart, Teddy. 1970. *Inside Music City, USA.* Nashville, TN: Aurora Publishers.

7444 Corbin, Everett J. 1980. *Storm Over Nashville: A Case Against Modern Country Music.* Nashville, TN: Ashlar Press.

7445 Gill, Andy. 1986. Kicking the Horseshit Out of Nashville. *New Musical Express* (6 September): 28–29.

7446 Hemphill, Paul. 1971. *The Nashville Sound: Bright Lights and Country Music.* New York: Simon & Schuster.

7447 Lomax, John, III. 1985. *Nashville: Music City USA.* New York: Abrams.

7448 Wolfe, Charles K. 1973. Nashville and Country Music, 1925–1930: Notes on Early Nashville Media and Its Response to Old-Time Music. *Journal of Country Music* 4: 2–16.

– *New Orleans*

7449 Barker, Danny. 1985. *A Life in Jazz,* ed. Alyn Shipton. London: Macmillan.

7450 Barker, Danny and Buerkle, Jack V., eds. 1973. *Bourbon Street Black: The New Orleans Black Jazzman.* New York: Oxford University Press.

7451 Berry, Jason. 1986. *Up from the Cradle of Jazz: New Orleans Music Since World War II.* Athens, GA: University of Georgia Press.

7452 Berry, Jason. 1988. African Cultural Memory in New Orleans Music. *Black Music Research Journal* 8(1): 3–12.

7453 Borders, Florence E. 1988. Researching Creole and Cajun Music in New Orleans. *Black Music Research Journal* 8(1): 15–31.

7454 Boyer, Horace Clarence. 1988. Tracking the Tradition: New Orleans Sacred Music. *Black Music Research Journal* 8(1): 135–47.

7455 Broven, John. 1974. *Walking to New Orleans: The Story of New Orleans Rhythm and Blues.* Bexhill-on-Sea: Blues Unlimited.

7456 Charters, Samuel B. 1983. *Jazz: New Orleans, 1885–1963. An Index to the Negro Musicians of New Orleans,* revised edition. New York: Da Capo Press. First published Belleville: Walter C. Allen, 1958.

7457 Colyer, Ken. 1968. *New Orleans and Back.* Delph, Yorks.: Brooks and Pratt.

7458 Crawford, Ralston. 1983. *Music in the Street: Photographs of New Orleans.* New Orleans, LA: Historic New Orleans Collection, William Ransom Hogan Archive, Tulane University.

7459 Deffaa, Chip. 1993. *Traditionalists and Revivalists in Jazz.* Metuchen, NJ: Scarecrow Press.

7460 Fiehrer, Thomas. 1991. From Quadrille to Stomp: The Creole Origins of Jazz. *Popular Music* 10(1): 21–38.

7461 Friedlander, Lee. 1992. *The Jazz People of New Orleans*. New York: Pantheon.

7462 Hannusch, Jeff. 1975. *I Hear You Knocking: The Sound of New Orleans Rhythm & Blues*. Ville Platte, LA: Swallow Publications.

7463 Jerde, Curtis D. 1990. Black Music in New Orleans: A Historical Overview. *Black Music Research Journal* 10(1): 18–24.

7464 Kmen, Harry A. 1966. *Music in New Orleans: The Formative Years, 1791–1841*. Baton Rouge, LA: Louisiana State University Press.

7465 Newberger, Eli H. 1977. The Development of New Orleans and Stride Piano Styles. *Journal of Jazz Studies* 4(2): 43–71.

7466 Palmer, Robert. 1979. *A Tale of Two Cities: Memphis Rock and New Orleans Roll*. Brooklyn, NY: Institute for Studies in American Music.

7467 Rose, Al. 1967. *New Orleans Jazz: A Family Album*. Baton Rouge, LA: Louisiana State University Press.

7468 Schafer, William J. 1978. Further Thoughts on Jazz Historiography: That Robert Charles Song. *Journal of Jazz Studies* 5(1): 19–27.

7469 Schafer, William J. and Allen, Richard B. 1977. *Brass Bands and New Orleans Jazz*. Baton Rouge, LA: Louisiana State University Press.

7470 Stagg, Tom and Crump, Charlie. 1973. *New Orleans – The Revival: A Tape and Discography of Negro Traditional Jazz Recorded in New Orleans or by New Orleans Bands, 1937–1972*. Dublin: Bashall Eaves.

7471 Turner, Frederick. 1982. *Remembering Song: Encounters with the New Orleans Jazz Tradition*. New York: Viking.

– *New York City*

7472 Allen, Ray. 1988. African-American Sacred Quartet Singing in New York City. *New York Folklore* 14(3–4): 7–22.

7473 Boggs, Vernon, ed. 1992. *Salsiology: Afro-Cuban Music and the Evolution of Salsa in New York*. London: Greenwood Press.

7474 Charters, Samuel B. and Kunstadt, Leonard. 1981. (1962) *Jazz: A History of the New York Scene*. New York: Da Capo Press. First published New York: Doubleday, 1962.

7475 Chevigny, Paul. 1991. *Gigs: Jazz and the Cabaret Laws in New York City*. London: Routledge.

7476 Cornelius, Steven. 1990. Encapsulating Power: Meaning and Taxonomy of the Musical Instruments of Santeria in New York City. *Selected Reports in Ethnomusicology* 8: 125–41.

7477 Cornelius, Steven. 1991. Drumming for the Orishas: Reconstruction of Tradition in New York City. In *Essays on Cuban Music: North American and Cuban Perspectives*, ed. Peter Manuel. Lanham, MD: University Press of America. 136–56.

7478 Cortez, Felix, Angel Facon and Juan Flores. 1976. The Cultural Expression of Puerto Ricans in New York: A Theoretical Perspective and Critical Review. *Latin American Perspective* 3(3): 117–52.

7479 Dixon, William F. 1969. Music in Harlem. In *Harlem: A Community in Transition*, ed. John Henrik Clarke. New York: Citadel Press. 65–76.

7480 Durante, Jimmy and Koefoed, Jack. 1931. *Nightclubs*. New York: Knopf.

7481 Erenberg, Lewis. 1984. (1981) *Steppin' Out: New York Nightlife and the Transformation of American Culture,*

1890–1930. Chicago: University of Chicago Press.

7482 Feldman, Walter. 1994. Bulgareasa/ Bulgarish/Bulgar: The Transformation of a Klezmer Dance Genre. *Ethnomusicology* 38(1): 1–35.

7483 Floyd, Samuel A., ed. 1993. (1990) *Black Music and the Harlem Renaissance: A Collection of Essays.* Knoxville, TN: University of Tennessee Press. First published New York: Greenwood Press, 1990.

7484 Fox, Ted. 1983. *Showtime at the Apollo.* New York: Holt, Rinehart, and Winston.

7485 Glasser, Ruth. 1990. Paradoxical Ethnicity: Puerto Rican Musicians in Post World War I New York City. *Latin American Music Review* 11(1): 63–72.

7486 Glasser, Ruth. 1995. *My Music Is My Flag: Puerto Rican Musicians and Their New York Communities, 1917–1940.* Berkeley, CA: University of California Press.

7487 Gordon, Max. 1980. *Live at the Village Vanguard.* New York: St. Martin's Press.

7488 Groia, Phil. 1983. *They All Sang on the Corner: A Second Look at New York City's Rhythm and Blues Vocal Groups.* West Hempstead, NY: Phillie Dee Enterprises.

7489 Haskins, Jim. 1977. *The Cotton Club.* New York: Random House.

7490 Johnson, James Weldon. 1988. (1930) *Black Manhattan.* New York: Ayer. First published New York: Knopf, 1930.

7491 Lewis, David Levering. 1981. *When Harlem Was In Vogue.* New York: Knopf.

7492 Murphy, John. 1991. The Charanga in New York and the Persistence of the Tipico Style. In *Essays on Cuban Music: North American and Cuban Perspectives,*

ed. Peter Manuel. Lanham, MD: University Press of America. 115–35.

7493 Prato, Paolo. 1983. Music in the Streets: The Example of Washington Square Park. *Popular Music* 3: 151–64.

7494 Riis, Thomas. 1989. *Just Before Jazz: Black Musical Theater in New York, 1890–1915.* Washington, DC: Smithsonian Institution Press.

7495 Roseman, Marina. 1983. The New Rican Village: Artists in Control of the Image-Making Machinery. *Latin American Music Review* 4(1): 132–67.

7496 Runcie, John. 1987. Black Music and the Garvey Aesthetic. *Afro-Americans in New York Life and History* 11(2): 7–23.

7497 Schiffman, Jack. 1971. *Uptown: The Story of Harlem's Apollo Theatre.* New York: Cowles Book Co.

7498 Schlesinger, Michael. 1988. Italian Music in New York City. *New York Folklore* 14(3–4): 129–38.

7499 Shaw, Arnold. 1971. *The Street That Never Slept: New York's Fabled 52nd Street.* New York: Coward, McGann & Geoghegan.

7500 Singer, Roberta. 1983. Tradition and Innovation in Contemporary Latin American Popular Music in New York City. *Latin American Music Review* 4(2): 183–202.

7501 Singer, Roberta. 1988. Puerto Rican Music in New York City. *New York Folklore* 14(3–4): 139–50.

7502 Slovenz, Madeline. 1988. 'Rock the House': The Aesthetic Dimension of Rap Music in New York City. *New York Folklore* 14(3–4): 151–64.

7503 Smith, Willie ('The Lion') and Hoefer, George. 1978. (1964) *Music on My Mind: The Memoirs of an American Pianist.* New York: Da Capo Press. First published New York: Doubleday, 1964.

7504 Snyder, Robert. 1989. *The Sound of the City: Vaudeville and Popular Culture in New York*. New York: Oxford University Press.

7505 Stowe, David W. 1994. *Swing Changes: Big-Band Jazz in New Deal America*. Cambridge, MA: Harvard University Press.

7506 Toop, David. 1984. *The Rap Attack: African Jive to New York Hip Hop*. Boston, MA: South End Press.

7507 Wilcken, Lois E. 1988. Haiti Chérie: Journey of an Immigrant Music in New York City. *New York Folklore* 14(3–4): 179–89.

7508 Woliver, Robbie. 1986. *Bringing It All Home: 25 Years of American Music at Folk City*. New York: Pantheon.

– *St. Louis*

7509 Chevan, David. 1989. Riverboat Music from St. Louis and the Streckfus Steamboat Line. *Black Music Research Journal* 9(2): 153–80.

7510 Cunningham, Lyn Driggs, and Jones, Jimmy. 1989. *Sweet, Hot and Blues: St. Louis' Musical Heritage*. Jefferson, NC: McFarland & Co.

7511 Evans, David. 1972. Black Fife and Drum Music in Mississippi. *Mississippi Folklore Register* 6: 94–107.

7512 Ottenheimer, Harriet. 1990. The Blues Tradition in St. Louis. *Black Music Research Journal* 9(2): 135–51.

– *San Francisco*

7513 Gleason, Ralph J. 1969. *The Jefferson Airplane and the San Francisco Sound*. New York: Ballantine.

7514 McDonough, Jack. 1985. *San Francisco Rock: The Illustrated History of San Francisco Rock Music*. San Francisco: Chronicle Books.

7515 Perry, Charles. 1984. *The Haight-Ashbury: A History*. New York: Random House.

7516 Riddle, Ronald. 1978. Music Clubs and Ensembles in San Francisco's Chinese Community. In *Eight Urban Musical Cultures: Tradition and Change*, ed. Bruno Nettl. Urbana and London: University of Illinois Press. 223–59.

7517 Riddle, Ronald. 1983. *Flying Dragons, Flowing Streams: Music in the Life of San Francisco's Chinese*. Westport and London: Greenwood Press.

7518 Sculatti, Gene and Seay, Davin. 1985. *San Francisco Nights: The Psychedelic Music Trip, 1965–1968*. New York: St. Martin's Press.

7519 Stoddard, Tom. 1982. *Jazz on the Barbary Coast*. Chigwell: Storyville.

– *Other Major Cities*

7520 Boyd, Herb. 1983. *Detroit Jazz Who's Who*. Detroit, MI: Jazz Research Institute.

7521 Chantry, Art, ed. 1985. *Instant Litter: Concert Posters from Seattle Punk Culture*. Seattle, WA: Real Comet.

7522 Cummings, Tony. 1975. *The Sound of Philadelphia*. London: Methuen.

7523 Preston, Katherine K. 1984. Popular Music in the 'Gilded Age': Musicians' Gigs in Late Nineteenth-Century Washington DC. *Popular Music* 4: 25–50.

WESTERN EUROPE

General

7524 Bausch, Armando. 1985. *Jazz in Europa*. Trier: Editions Phi.

7525 Humann, Klaus, and Reichert, Carl-Ludwig, eds. 1981. *EuroRock. Länder und Szenen. Ein Überblick*. Reinbek bei Hamburg: Rowohlt.

7526 Jost, Ekkehard. 1993. Über das Europäische im europäischen Jazz. In *Jazz in Europa*, ed. Wolfram Knauer. Hofheim: Wolke. 233–49.

7527 Knauer, Wolfram, ed. 1993. *Jazz in Europa*. Hofheim: Wolke.

7528 Lotz, Rainer E. 1990. The Black Troubadours: Black Entertainers in Europe, 1896–1915. *Black Music Research Journal* 10(2): 253–73.

7529 Otterbach, Friedemann. 1980. *Die Geschichte der europäischen Tanzmusik. Einführung*. Wilhelmshaven: Heinrichshofen.

7530 Watts, Michael. 1975. The Call and Response of American Popular Music: The Impact of American Pop Music in Europe. In *Superculture: American Popular Culture and Europe*, ed. C.W.E. Bigsby. London: Elek. 123–39.

7531 Willett, Ralph. 1989. Hot Swing and the Dissolute Life: Youth, Style and Popular Music in Europe, 1939–49. *Popular Music* 8(2): 157–64.

Austria

7532 Brödl, Günter, ed. 1985. *Die guten Kräfte: Neue Rockmusik in Österreich*. Wien: Hannibal.

7533 Bronner, Gerhard. 1995. *Die goldene Zeit des Wiener Cabarets – Anekdoten, Texte, Erinnerungen*. St. Andrä-Wördern: Hannibal.

7534 Gröbchen, Walter, ed. 1995. *Heimspiel – Eine Chronik des Austropop*. St. Andrä-Wördern: Hannibal.

7535 Hadamowsky, Franz and Otte, Heinz. 1947. *Die Wiener Operette*. Wien: Bellaria.

7536 Juhasz, Christiane. 1994. *Kritische Lieder und Politrock in Österreich*. Frankfurt am Main: Peter Lang.

7537 Larkey, Edward. 1992. Austropop: Popular Music and National Identity in Austria. *Popular Music* 11(2): 151–86.

7538 Lohr, Stasi. 1982. *Drum hab i Wean so gern. Wien und seine Lieder*. München: Goldmann.

7539 Maurer, Walter. 1974. Music of Contrasts: Report on the Contests of Austrian Beat Groups. In *New Patterns of Musical Behaviour*, ed. Irmgard Bontinck. Wien: Universal Edition. 129–34.

7540 Schüller, Dietrich and Thiel, Helga. 1985. Between Folk & Pop: Stylistic Plurality in Music Activities in Several Austrian Regions. In *Popular Music Perspectives, 2*, ed. David Horn. Göteborg and Exeter: IASPM. 166–82.

7541 Signitzer, Benno and Wallnöfer, Pierre. 1982. Structures of the Phonographic Industry in Austria. In *The Phonogram in Cultural Communication*, ed. Kurt Blaukopf. Wien: Springer-Verlag. 133–40.

7542 Smudits, Alfred. 1995. I Am from Austria. Austropop: Die Karriere eines musikkulturellen Phänomens von der Innovation zur Etablierung. In *Österreich 1945–1955*. Wien: Verlag für Gesellschaftskritik.

7543 Zink, Wolfgang. 1989. *Austro-Rock-Lexikon – 20 Jahre Austro-Rock von A-Z*. Wien: Eigenverlag.

Basque Region

7544 Barandiaran, G. 1978. El folklore vasco. In *Cultura Vasca*, ed. J.L. Alvarez-Emparanza, et al. 2 vols. San Sebastian: Erein. 379–427.

7545 Lahusen, Christian. 1991. 'Unsere Stimme erwacht . . .': Populäre Musikkultur und nationale Frage im heutigen Spanien. Saarbrücken/Fort Lauderdale: Verlag Breitenbach Publishers.

7546 Lahusen, Christian. 1993. The Aesthetic
of Radicalism: The Relationship
Between Punk and the Patriotic
Nationalist Movement of the Basque
Country. *Popular Music* 12(3): 263–80.

Belgium

7547 Collin, Robert, comp. 1990. *Het Belgisch
Hitboek 1959–1989: meer dan 30 jaar hits
in Vlaanderen.* Zonhoven: Boek.

7548–50 No entries.

7551 Despringre, André-Marie, ed. 1991.
*Poésies chantées de tradition orale en
Flandre et en Bretagne.* Paris: Champion.

7552 Geerts, Claude. 1974. The Share of
Music in the Time Budget of Young
People in Belgium. In *New Patterns of
Musical Behaviour,* ed. Irmgard
Bontinck. Wien: Universal Edition. 201–
204.

7553 Gérardy, Denis. 1988. *Histoire du rock et
de la chanson française à Liège.* Liège-
Bressoux: M. Dricot.

7554 Graef, Jack de. 1980. *De Swingperiode
(1935–1947): Jazz in Belgie.* Antwerp:
Dageraad.

7554a Meyer, Gust de and Trappeniers, Alex.
1994. *De muziekindustrie van A tot Z.*
Leuven: Trappeniers and De Meyer.

7554b Meyer, Gust de and Van Raemdonck,
Olivier. 1995. Concentratie van de
culturele industrie en diversiteit van de
culturele produkten. Het geval van de
(Belgische) populaire muziek.
*Communicatie, Tijdschrift voor
Massamedia en Cultuur* 24(3): 3–22.

7554c Meyer, Gust de, A. Hendriks and G.
Fauconnier. 1980. *Jeugd en popmuziek.*
Leuven: Centrum voor
Communicatiewetenschappen.

Catalonian Region

7555 Van Liew, Maria. 1993. The Scent of
Catalan Rock: *Els Pets'* Ideology and the

Rock and Roll Industry. *Popular Music*
12(3): 245–61.

Denmark

7556 Andresen, Jørn T. 1986. *Regnbuens
Endestation: Provinsrødder & Rockmusik
1958–86.* Århus: Klim.

7557 Björnberg, Alf and Stockfelt, Ola. 1996.
Kristen Klatvask fra Vejle: Danish Pub
Music, Mythscapes and 'Local Camp'.
Popular Music 15(2): 131–47.

7558 Ebbesen, Niels Fink. 1980. *Dansk
Jazzlitteratur – Litteratur om Dansk Jazz:
En Bibliografi.* Copenhagen: Arkiv for
Dansk Jazzhistorie, Musikvidenskabeligt
Institut, Københavns Universitet.

7559 Ellegaard, Lasse. 1975. *Dansk
Rockmusik.* Copenhagen: Information.

7560 Gjedsted, Jens Jørn, ed. 1985. *Dansk
Rock: fra pigtråd til punk, leksikon 1956–
1985.* Copenhagen: Politiken.

7561 Jacobsen, Niels W., Jens Allan Mose and
Egon Nielsen. 1980. *Dansk Rock'n'Roll:
Anderumper, Ekstase og Opposition: En
Analyse af Dansk Rockkultur 1956–63.*
Tappernøje Mjølner

7562 Jacobsen, Niels W., Jens Alan Mose and
Egon Nielsen. 1983. *Dansk Rock'n'Roll
Leksikon.* Præstø: Mjølner.

7563 Ketting, Knud. 1983. Rock Music at
Government Level: A Report from the
First Nordic Rock Music Seminar.
Nordic Sounds 1983/4: 3–5.

7564 Ketting, Knud, ed. 1987. *Music in
Denmark.* Copenhagen: The Danish
Cultural Institute.

7565 Larsen, Charlotte Rørdam. 1994. Dansk
Rock fra Plagiat til Kopy. In *Cæcilia,
Årbog 1994.* Århus: Musikvidenskabeligt
Institut, Aarhus Universitet. 135–200.

7566 Malmros, Anna-Lise. 1974.
Organisational Set-Up and Politico-
Cultural Aspects of Beat in Copenhagen.

LOCATIONS

In *New Patterns of Musical Behaviour*, ed. Irmgard Bontinck. Wien: Universal Edition. 114–18.

7567 Malmros, Anna-Lise. 1982. Rock-scene som könspolitisk slagmark. *Modspil* 4(6): 31–34.

7568 Piil, Beate S. 1981. *Beat på Dansk.* Århus: Publimus.

7569 Skjerne, Godtfred. 1946. (1912) *H.C. Lumbye og Hans Samtid,* revised edition. Copenhagen: Hagerup. First published Copenhagen: Hagerup, 1912.

7570 Torp, Lisbet. 1986. Hip Hop Dances: Their Adoption and Function Among Boys in Denmark, 1983–1984. *Yearbook for Traditional Music* 18: 29–86.

7571 Wiedemann, Erik. 1982. *Jazz i Danmark i tyverne, trediverne og fyrrerne: en musikkulturel undersøgelse.* 3 vols. Copenhagen: Gyldendal.

7572 Wiedemann, Erik. 1993. Jazz in Dänemark 1933 bis 1945. In *Jazz in Europa,* ed. Wolfram Knauer. Hofheim: Wolke. 43–50.

Finland

7573 Alm, Arí. 1992. Radiomafia: The New Business Approach. In *Broadcasting Research Review, 1992,* ed. Heikki Kasari. Helsinki: Yleisradio. 8–19.

7574 Alm, Arí. 1992. Radion musiikkiviestinän muutuvat merkitykset. In *Toosa Soi. Musiiki radion kilpailuvälineenä,* ed. Kimmo Salminen and Arí Alm. Helsinki: YLE Tutkimus ja kehitysosasto. 29–47.

7575 Eerikäinen, Hannu. 1995. Greetings from the Northern Forests: Some Preliminary Observations on Finnish Music Videos. In *Popular Music Perspectives III,* ed. Peter Wicke. Berlin: Zyankrise. 261–65.

7576 Gronow, Pekka. 1987. The Last Refuge of the Tango. *Finnish Music Quarterly* 3–4: 26–31.

7577 Gronow, Pekka. 1989. The Recording Industry in Finland. *Finnish Music Quarterly* 4: 3–9.

7578 Gronow, Pekka. 1995. The Record Industry in Finland, 1945–60. *Popular Music* 14(1): 33–53.

7579 Haapanen, Urpo. 1983. *Suomalaisten äänilevyen luetto/Catalogue of Finnish Records, 1946–1966.* Helsinki: Suomen äänitearkisto.

7580 Jårviluoma, Helmi. 1991. Research on Folk and Popular Music in Finland. In *Finnish-Hungarian Symposium on Music & Folklore Research, 15–21 November 1987,* ed. Antti Koiranen. Tampere: Tampereen Yliopisto Kansanperinteen laitos J 14 1991. 19–38.

7581 Karttunen, Antero. 1989. The Past Two Decades on Records. *Finnish Music Quarterly* 4: 10–26.

7582 Ketting, Knud. 1983. Rock Music at Government Level: A Report from the First Nordic Rock Music Seminar. *Nordic Sounds* 1983/4: 3–5.

7583 Kolehmainen, Ilkka. 1989. The Accordion in Finnish Folk Music. *Finnish Music Quarterly* 89(2): 29–31.

7584 Konttinen, Matti. 1982. *Finnish Jazz.* Helsinki: Finnish Music Information Centre.

7585 Konttinen, Matti. 1987. The Jazz Invasion. *Finnish Music Quarterly* 3–4: 21–25.

7586 Kurkela, Vesa. 1983. Worker's Music in a Finnish Industrial Town. *Suomen antropologi* 4: 218–23.

7587 Kurkela, Vesa. 1995. Long-Term Fusion and Lost Traditions: Toward a Historiography of Finnish Popular Music. In *Popular Music Perspectives III,*

348

ed. Peter Wicke. Berlin: Zyankrise. 297–304.

7588 Lehtonen, Esko. 1983. *Suomalaisen rockin tietosanakirja.* Tampere: Fanzine Oy.

7589 Leisiö, Timo. 1983. Surface and Deep Structure in Music: An Expedition into Finnish Music Culture. *Suomen antropologi* 4: 198–208.

7590 Madhlope-Phillips, James. 1983. Music Marches with the People's Revolution. In *Laulu ottaa kantaa – aineistoa 1970-luvun lauliliikkeestä.* Helsinki: Työväenenmusiikki-institutti. 167–72.

7591 Numminen, Mauri A. 1974. An Inside View of Pop Music in Finland. In *New Patterns of Musical Behaviour,* ed. Irmgard Bontinck. Wien: Universal Edition. 60–65.

7592 Nysten, Leif. 1992. Rundradions svenskspråkiga radiokanal: en musikpolitisk betraktelse. In *Toosa Soi. Musiiki radion kilpailuvälineenä,* ed. Kimmo Salminen and Arí Alm. Helsinki: YLE Tutkimus ja kehitysosasto. 97–101.

7593 Pekkilä, Erkki. 1983. 'Musiikki' and 'Kappalevalikoima': Aspects of the Ethno-Theory of a Finnish Folk Musician. *Suomen antropologi* 4: 209–17.

7594 Ritamäki, Tapani and Söderling, Trygve. 1983. Rock och nationalitet i Finland. *Nordisk Forum* 39–40 (8(3) & 8(4)): 104–109.

7595 Salminen, Kimmo. 1992. Finnish Taste in Music and Musical Preferences. In *Broadcasting Research Review, 1992,* ed. Heikki Kasari. Helsinki: Yleisradio. 114–22.

7596 Similä, Juhani. 1992. Rock, kansanmusiikki ja maailmanmusiikki. In *Toosa Soi. Musiiki radion kilpailuvälineenä,* ed. Kimmo Salminen and Arí Alm. Helsinki: YLE Tutkimus ja kehitysosasto. 177–90.

7597 Tuominen, Harri. 1992. Korvaluomia ei ole! Katsaus paikallisradioden musiikkipolitiikkaan. In *Toosa Soi. Musiiki radion kilpailuvälineenä,* ed. Kimmo Salminen and Arí Alm. Helsinki: YLE Tutkimus ja kehitysosasto. 108–21.

7598 Tuominen, Kalle. 1983. *Suomalaisten äänilevyen luettelo.* Helsinki: Suomen äänitearkisto.

7599 Vaughn, Kathryn. 1990. Exploring Emotion in Sub-Structural Aspects of Karelian Lament: Application of Time Series Analysis to Digitized Melody. *Yearbook for Traditional Music* 22: 106–22.

France

7600 Adison, Fred. 1983. *Dans ma vie y'a d'la musique: histoire du show-biz de 1930 à nos jours.* Paris: Clancier-Guénaud.

7601 Beaud, Paul. 1974. Musical Sub-Cultures in France. In *New Patterns of Musical Behaviour,* ed. Irmgard Bontinck. Wien: Universal Edition. 212–18.

7602 Beaud, Paul and Willener, Alfred, eds. 1973. *Musique et vie quotidienne: Essai de sociologie d'une nouvelle culture.* Paris: Mame.

7603 Bensignor, Francis. 1988. *Sons d'Afrique.* Paris: Marabout.

7604 Boyer, Régine, et al. 1986. *Les Lycéens et la musique.* Paris: INRP.

7605 Chang, Paolo. 1988. Festival Musical de Chantenay. Dixième anniversaire Chantenay Villedieu. *Musiche* 1: 33–41.

7606 Constantin, Philippe. 1971. Pop et profit, le changement dans la continuité. *Musique en jeu* 2: 95–101.

7607 Coulonges, Georges. 1985. *La commune en chantant.* Paris: Messidor/Temps Actuels.

7608 Despringre, André-Marie, ed. 1991. *Poésies chantées de tradition orale en Flandre et en Bretagne.* Paris: Champion.

7609 Fabiani, Jean-Louis. 1986. Carrières improvisées: théories et pratiques de la musique de jazz en France. In *Sociologie de l'art,* ed. Raymonde Moulin. Paris: La Documentation française. 231–45.

7610 Fleouter, Claude. 1988. *Un siècle de chansons.* Paris: PUF.

7611 Gerbod, Paul. 1980. L'Institution orphéonique en France du XIXe au XXe siècle. *Ethnologie française* 10(1): 27–44.

7612 Grosse, Francis and Gueffier, Bernard. 1989. *La discographie du rock français.* Dombasle: Grosse et Gueffier.

7613 Gumplowicz, Philippe. 1987. *Les Travaux d'Orphée: 150 ans de vie musicale amateur en France: harmonies, chorales, fanfares.* Paris: Aubier.

7614 Helian, Jacques. 1984. *Les grands orchestres de music hall en France: souvenirs et témoignages.* Paris: Filipacchi.

7615 Hirsch, Jean-François. 1971. La cause du pop est-elle insaisissable? *Musique en jeu* 2: 66–72.

7616 Hirsch, Jean-François. 1971. La radicalisation pop. *Musique en jeu* 2: 72–74.

7617 Joseph, Jean-Pierre. 1984. *Le show business français, un état dans l'état: l'étouffement dans la création musicale en France.* Paris: La Pensée Sauvage.

7618 Jouffa, François and Barsamian, Jacques. 1983. *L'age d'or du yeye français.* Paris: Ramsay.

7619 Julien, Jean-Rémy. 1989. *Musique et publicité: Du Cri de Paris aux messages publicitaires radiophoniques et télévisés.* Paris: Flammarion.

7620 Locke, Ralph P. 1987. La musica della canzone francese, 1810–1850. *Musica/ Realtà* 22: 67–96.

7621 Lucas, Jean-Michel. 1983. *Rock et politique culturelle: l'exemple de Rennes.* Paris: SER/Ministère de la culture.

7622 Moreira, Paul. 1987. *Rock métis en France.* Paris: Interpublications.

7623 Noyer, Alain-Pierre. 1989. *Dictionnaire des chanteurs francophones de 1900 à nos jours.* Paris: CILF.

7624 Pirot, Christian. 1982. *French Rock.* Paris: Le Vagabond.

7625 Poupart, René. 1988. *Aspects de la chanson poetique.* Paris: Didier.

7626 Renault, Patrick. 1978. *Les bals en France.* Paris: Music et Promotion/ S.A.C.E.M.

7627 Schroeder, Jean-Pol. 1985. *Histoire du jazz à Liège de 1900 à 1980.* Liège: Labor: RTBF-Liège.

7628 Segal, Ariane. 1985. Comunicazione sulla fonografica in Francia. In *Musica e sistema dell'informazione in Europa,* ed. Francesco Rampi. Milano: Unicopli. 80–84.

7629 Wais, Alain. 1983. *Téléphone le livre.* Paris: Love Me Tender.

7630 Yonnet, Paul. 1985. *Jeux, modes et masses. La société française et le moderne, 1945–1985.* Paris: Gallimard.

Bretagne

7631 Giraudon, Daniel, ed. 1985. *Chansons populaires de Basse-Bretagne.* Spezed: Breizh.

7632 Kuter, Lois. 1981. Music and Identity in Brittany, France. In *Discourse in Ethnomusicology II: A Tribute to Alan P. Merriam.* Bloomington, IN: Ethnomusicology Publications Group, Indiana University. 17–41.

7633 Malrieu, Patrick. 1984. *Histoire de la chanson populaire bretonne*. Rennes: Dasturn/Skol.

7634 Marot, Robert. 1987. *La chanson populaire bretonne: reflet de l'évolution culturelle*. Paris: Grassin.

Paris

7635 Dyan, Brigitte and Mandel, Jean-Jacques. 1984. *L'Afrique à Paris*. Paris: Editions Rochevignes.

7636 Klein, Jean-Claude. 1985. Borrowing, Syncretism, Hybridisation: The Parisian Revue of the 1920's. *Popular Music* 5: 175–88.

7637 Knight, Roderic C. 1991. Music Out of Africa: Mande Jaliya in Paris. *The World of Music* 33(1): 52–69.

Germany

7638 Allinson, Francesca. 1979. *Die Jugendmusikbewegung: Gemeinschaftsmusik, Theorie und Praxis*. Stuttgart: Metzler.

7639 Arnold, Herbert A. 1981. Oral Tradition and Critical Song in Contemporary Germany. *Journal of Popular Culture* 15(3): 144–54.

7640 Augustin, Gerhard and Gatter, Nikolaus. 1987. *Die Beat-Jahre: Musik in Deutschland, die sechziger Jahre*. München: Goldmann.

7641 Beck, Earl R. 1985. The Anti-Nazi 'Swing Youth'. *Journal of Popular Culture* 19(3): 45–54.

7642 Blankertz, Stefan and Alsmann, Götz. 1979. *Rock 'n' Roll Subversiv*. Wetzlar: Büchse der Pandora.

7643 Bloemeke, Rüdiger. 1996. *Roll Over Beethoven. Wie der Rock 'n' Roll nach Deutschland kam*. Andrä-Wördern: Hannibal.

7644 Busch, Hermann J. 1987. 'Gesangfest' zwischen 1845 und 1871 im Spiegel der Zeitschrift 'Euterpe'. In *Ich will aber gerade vom Leben singen . . . Über populäre Musik vom ausgehenden 19. Jahrhundert bis zum Ende der Weimarer Republik*, ed. Sabine Schutte. Reinbek bei Hamburg: Rowohlt. 60–84.

7645 Carfi, Pietro and Lutri, Ignazio. 1989. German Rock: From Drums to the Electric Drill/Il rock tedesco dalla batteria al trapano elettrico. In *Music & the Machine/La musica e le macchine*, ed. Paolo Prato. Torino: Progetto Lingotto/FIAT. 16–19.

7646 Dahlhaus, Carl, ed. 1967. *Studien zur Trivialmusik des 19. Jahrhunderts*. Regensburg: Bosse.

7647 Döpfner, M.O. and Garms, Thomas. 1984. *Neue deutsche Welle: Kunst oder Mode? Eine sachliche Polemik für und wider die neudeutsche Popmusik*. Frankfurt am Main: Ullstein.

7648 Dümling, Albrecht and Girth, Peter, eds. 1988. *Entartete Musik: eine kommentierte Rekonstruktion zur Düsseldorfer Ausstellung von 1938*. Düsseldorf: Landeshauptstadt Düsseldorf.

7649 Ebbecke, Klaus and Lüschper, Pit. 1987. *Rockmusiker: Szene intern. Fakten und Anmerkungen zum Musikleben einer industriellen Grossstadt. Befragung Dortmunder Musiker*. Stuttgart: Marohl Musikverlag.

7650 Edelhagen, Viola and Edelhagen-Holtz, Joachim. 1988. *Die Big Band Story nach 1945 in der BRD*. Frankfurt am Main: Eisenbletter u. Naumann.

7651 Ehnert, Günter and Kinsler, Detlef. 1984. *Rock in Deutschland: Lexikon deutscher Rockgruppen und Intepreten*. Hamburg: Taurus.

7652 Fahr, Margitta. 1996. Odins Erben. Nordheldentum und nordische Mythologie in Rechtsrock-Texten an ausgewählten Beispielen der Britischen

Band 'Skrewdriver'. *PopScriptum* 5: 90–105.

7653 Farin, Klaus. 1996. 'Rechtsrock' – eine Bestandsaufnahme. *PopScriptum* 5: 4–13.

7654 Fohrbeck, Karla and Wiesand, Andreas Johannes, eds. 1982. *Musik, Statistik, Kulturpolitik: Daten und Argumente zum Musikleben in der Bundersrepublik Deutschland*. Köln: DuMont.

7655 Fuhr, Werner. 1977. *Proletarische Musik in Deutschland 1928–1933*. Göppingen: Alfred Kümmerle.

7656 Graf, Hans-Peter. 1987. Concertina- und Bandoneonkultur: Organisierte Arbeiterfreizeit in Deutschland zwischen 1870 und dem Ende der Weimarer Republik. In *Ich will aber gerade vom Leben singen . . . Über populäre Musik vom ausgehenden 19. Jahrhundert bis zum Ende der Weimarer Republik*, ed. Sabine Schutte. Reinbek bei Hamburg: Rowohlt. 213–35.

7657 Hamm, Wolfgang. 1985. Crescita e declino dell'indipendenza nel mercato musicale tedesco. In *Musica e sistema dell'informazione in Europa*, ed. Francesco Rampi. Milano: Unicopli. 136–44.

7658 Haring, Hermann. 1983. *Rock aus Deutschland/West: Buch vom neuen Heimatklang*. Reinbek bei Hamburg: Rowohlt.

7659 Haring, Hermann. 1984. *Rock aus Deutschland/West: Von den Rattles bis NENA. Zwei Jahrzehnte Heimatklang*. Reinbek bei Hamburg: Rowohlt.

7660 Hartwich-Wiechell, Dörte. 1974. Musikalisches Verhalten Jugendlicher. Ergebnisse empirischer musiksoziologischer Untersuchungen. *Forschung in der Musikerziehung*: 39–62.

7661 Helm, Roland. 1991. *Saar Rock History*. Saarbrücken: Buchverl. Saarbrücker Zeitung.

7662 Helt, Richard C. 1977. A German Bluegrass Festival: The 'Country-Boom' and Some Notes on the History of American Popular Music in West Germany. *Journal of Popular Culture* 10(4): 821–32.

7663 James, Barbara. 1987. 'Der Kaiser ist ein lieber Mann . . .' Schullieder auf Kaiser Wilhelm. In *Ich will aber gerade vom Leben singen . . . Über populäre Musik vom ausgehenden 19. Jahrhundert bis zum Ende der Weimarer Republik*, ed. Sabine Schutte. Reinbek bei Hamburg: Rowohlt. 169–86.

7664 Jogschies, Rainer. 1991. *Rock & Pop '89. Kritische Analysen. Kulturpolitische Alternativen, II*. Hagen: Kulturpolitische Gesellschaft, Dokumentation 37.

7665 Jost, Ekkehard. 1981. Musical Subcultures in Rural Communities of Hessen. In *Stock-Taking of Musical Life: Sociography and Music Education*, ed. Desmond Mark. Wien: Doblinger. 66–71.

7666 Kater, Michael H. 1992. *Different Drummers: Jazz in the Culture of Nazi Germany*. New York: Oxford University Press.

7667 Kaufmann, Dorothea. 1991. 'Wenn Damen pfeifen, gehen die Gracien flöten'. Die Musikerin in der deutschen Tanz- und Unterhaltungsmusik des 19. Jahrhunderts. *Worldbeat* 1: 81–94.

7668 Keldany-Mohr, Irmgard. 1977. *'Unterhaltungsmusik' als soziokulturelles Phänomen des 19. Jahrhunderts: Untersuchung über den Einfluß der musikalischen Öffentlichkeit auf die Herausbildung eines neuen Musiktypes*. Regensburg: Bosse.

7669 Kersten, Martin. 1996. Jugendkulturen und NS-Vergangenheit. Der schmale Plad zwischen Provokation, Spiel, Inszenierung und erneuter Faszination vom Punk bis zum Nazi-Rock. *PopScriptum* 5: 58–89.

7670 Knauer, Wolfram, ed. 1996. *Jazz in Deutschland*. Hofheim: Wolke.

7671 Koch, Albert. 1987. *Angriff auf's Schlaraffenland: 20 Jahre deutschsprachige Popmusik*. Frankfurt am Main: Ullstein.

7672 Köhler, Peter, and Schacht, Konrad. 1983. *Die Jazzmusiker: Zur Soziologie einer kreativen Randgruppe*. Freiburg: Peter Weininger, Roter Punkt Verlag.

7673 Kuehenbuch, Ludolf. 1990. Notizen zur 'Notation' im Amateurjazz der sechziger und siebziger Jahre. In *Darmstädter Jazzforum 89: Beiträge zur Jazzforschung*, ed. Ekkehard Jost. Hofheim: Wolke. 161–89.

7674 Kurth, Ulrich. 1987. 'Ich pfeif auf Tugend und Moral'. Zum Foxtrott in den zwanziger Jahren. In *Ich will aber gerade vom Leben singen . . . Über populäre Musik vom ausgehenden 19. Jahrhundert bis zum Ende der Weimarer Republik*, ed. Sabine Schutte. Reinbek bei Hamburg: Rowohlt. 365–84.

7675 Lange, Horst H. 1966. *Jazz in Deutschland. Die deutsche Jazz-Chronik 1900–1960*. Berlin: Colloquium.

7676 Longerich, Winfried. 1989. *'Da Da Da' – Zur Standortbestimmung der Neuen Deutschen Welle*. Pfaffenweiler: Centaurus.

7677 Lotz, Rainer E. 1985. *German Ragtime and Prehistory of Jazz, Vol. 1. The Sound Documents*. Chigwell: Storyville.

7678 Mayer, Günter. 1984. Popular music e ideologia nazionalfascista nel Terzo Reich. *Musica/Realtà* 13: 45–58.

7679 Meyer, Michael. 1977. The SA Song Industry: A Singing Ideological Posture. *Journal of Popular Culture* 11(3): 568–80.

7680 Meyer, Thomas. 1995. Aspekte von Rockmusik in der ehemaligen DDR und in der Marktwirtschaft der Bundesrepublik. In *Popular Music Perspectives III*, ed. Peter Wicke. Berlin: Zyankrise. 131–37.

7681 Meyer, Thomas. 1996. 'Rechtsrock' als Messagerock. *PopScriptum* 5: 44–57.

7682 Mezger, Werner. 1975. *Schlager – Versuch einer Gesamtdarstellung unter besonderer Berücksichtigung des Musikmarktes der Bundesrepublik Deutschland*. Tübingen: Tübingen Vereinigung für Volkskunde.

7683 Mossman, Walter and Schleuning, Peter. 1980. *Alte und neue politische Lieder: Entstehung und Gebrauch; Text und Noten*. Reinbek bei Hamburg: Rowohlt.

7684 Ott, Paul and Hollow, Skai, eds. 1983. *Wir waren Helden für einen Tag: Aus deutschsprachigen Punk-Fanzines*. Reinbek bei Hamburg: Rowohlt.

7685 Packwald, Peter. 1987. *Rock 'n' Roll Is on the Air: Dreißig Jahre Jugendmusik im Hörfunk*. Heidelberg: Rüdiger Eggert.

7686 Paysan, Marko. 1993. Transatlantic Rhythm. Jazzkontakte zwischen Deutschland und den USA vor 1945. In *Jazz in Europa*, ed. Wolfram Knauer. Hofheim: Wolke. 13–42.

7687 Polster, Bernd, ed. 1989. *'Swing Heil': Jazz im Nationalsozialismus*. Berlin: Transit Buchverlag.

7688 Richter, Lukas, ed. 1977. *Mutter, der Mann mit dem Koks ist da: Berliner Gassenhauer*. Leipzig: Deutscher Verlag für Musik.

7689 Rirzei, Fred. 1987. 'Hatte der Kaiser Jazz getanzt . . .' US-Tanzmusik in Deutschland vor und nach dem Erster Weltkrieg. In *Ich will aber gerade vom Leben singen . . . Über populäre Musik vom ausgehenden 19. Jahrhundert bis zum Ende der Weimarer Republik*, ed. Sabine Schutte. Reinbek bei Hamburg: Rowohlt. 265–96.

7690 Ritzel, Fred and Stroh, Wolfgang Martin. 1985. Deutsche Tanzmusiker. Zu einer Sozialgeschichte der populären Musik in Deutschland. *Jazzforschung* 17: 69–75.

7691 Robinson, J. Bradford. 1992. Zur 'Jazz' Rezeption der Weimarer Periode Eine stilhistorische Jagd nach einer Rhythmus-Floskel. In *Jazz und Komposition*, ed. Wolfram Knauer. Hofheim: Wolke. 11–26.

7692 Robinson, J. Bradford. 1994. The Jazz Essays of Theodor Adorno: Some Thoughts on Jazz Reception in Weimar Germany. *Popular Music* 13(1): 1–25.

7693 Ruhr, Peter. 1987. 'Mit klingendem Spiel' – badische Blasmusik zwischen der Revolution 1848 und dem Ersten Weltkieg. In *Ich will aber gerade vom Leben singen . . . Über populäre Musik vom ausgehenden 19. Jahrhundert bis zum Ende der Weimarer Republik*, ed. Sabine Schutte. Reinbek bei Hamburg: Rowohlt. 115–36.

7694 Sackett, Robert Eben. 1982. *Popular Entertainment, Class and Politics in Munich, 1900–1923*. Cambridge, MA: Harvard University Press.

7695 Schmidt, Mathias R. 1979. The German Song-Writing Movement of the Late 1960s and 1970s. *Journal of Popular Culture* 13(1): 44–54.

7696 Schmidt, Roland. 1995. African Music – Made in Germany. In *Popular Music Perspectives III*, ed. Peter Wicke. Berlin: Zyankrise. 113–22.

7697 Schmücker, Fritz. 1993. *Das Jazzkonzertpublikum. Das Profil einer kulturellen Minderheit im Zeitvergleich.* Münster and Hamburg: Lit Verlag.

7698 Schoenebeck, Mechthild von, Jürgen Brandhorst and H. Joachim Gerke. 1992. *Politik und gesellschaftlicher Wertewandel im Spiegel populärer Musik.* Essen: Blaue Eule.

7699 Schröder, Rainer M. 1980. *Rock Made in Germany: Die Entwicklung der deutschen Rockmusik.* München: Heyne.

7700 Schulze, Ralf. 1996. *Die Musikwirtschaft. Markstrukturen und Wettbewerbsstrategien der Deutschen Musikindustrie.* Hamburg: Kammerer & Unverzagt.

7701 Schutte, Sabine, ed. 1987. *Ich will aber gerade vom Leben singen . . . Über populäre Musik vom ausgehenden 19. Jahrhundert bis zum Ende der Weimarer Republik.* Reinbek bei Hamburg: Rowohlt.

7702 Schwörer, Werner. 1989. *Jazzszene Frankfurt: Eine musiksoziologische Untersuchung anfangs der achtziger Jahre.* Mainz: Schott.

7703 Siepen, Elmar. 1994. *Untersuchungen zur Geschichte der Rockmusik in Deutschland.* Frankfurt am Main: Peter Lang.

7704 Spaude-Schulze, Edelgard. 1987. 'Ich sah durchs Land im Weltenbrand'. Anti-Kriegs-Lieder in der Weimarer Republik. In *Ich will aber gerade vom Leben singen . . . Über populäre Musik vom ausgehenden 19. Jahrhundert bis zum Ende der Weimarer Republik*, ed. Sabine Schutte. Reinbek bei Hamburg: Rowohlt. 385–406.

7705 Steinel, Roland. 1992. *Zur Lage und Problematik der Musikwirtschaft.* München: Edition Roland/Intermedia.

7706 Suppan, Wolfgang. 1983. *Blasmusik in Baden: Geschichte und Gegenwart einer traditionsreichen Blasmusiklandschaft.* Freiburg: Musikverlag Fritz Schulz.

7707 Warren, Roland L. 1972. The Nazi Use of Music as an Instrument of Social Control. In *The Sounds of Social Change: Studies in Popular Culture*, ed. R. Serge Denisoff and Richard A. Peterson. Chicago: Rand McNally & Co. 72–78.

7708 Wicke, Peter. 1984. Zwischen Sentimentalität und Pathos. Populäre Musik im faschistischen Deutschland. *Unterhaltungskunst* 1: 7–11.

7709 Wicke, Peter. 1985. Sentimentality and High Pathos: Popular Music in Fascist Germany. *Popular Music* 5: 149–58.

7710 Wicke, Peter. 1987. Das Ende: Populäre Musik im faschistischen Deutschland. In *Ich will aber gerade vom Leben singen . . . Über populäre Musik vom ausgehenden 19. Jahrhundert bis zum Ende der Weimarer Republik*, ed. Sabine Schutte. Reinbek bei Hamburg: Rowohlt. 418–31.

7711 Wicke, Peter. 1994. Aggressive Jugendstile – ein Problem der Jugendkultur(arbeit)? In *Gratwanderungen. Jugendkulturarbeit als Gewaltprävention?* Bonn: BMBW. 87–93.

7712 Wicke, Peter. 1994. Jugendkultur zwischen Industrie und Politik. In *Zukunftsforum Jugendkulturarbeit 20000 – Zur gesellschaftspolitischen Verantwortung kultureller Bildung.* Remscheid: Bundesvereinigung kulturelle Jugendbildung. 133–38.

7713 Wicke, Peter. 1994. Kultur in der Krise. *Kulturstrecke* 12(1): 13–18.

7714 Wicke, Peter. 1994. Neue Ökonomische Politik. *Neue Kultur* 1: 5–9.

7715 Wicke, Peter. 1994. Recht auf Rock 'n' Roll. *Evangelische Kommentare* 6: 357–62.

7716 Wicke, Peter. 1995. La culture-jeunes on transition. Ruptures et mutations. *Allemagne d'aujourd'hui* 132 (June): 68–76.

7717 Wicke, Peter. 1996. Popular Music and Processes of Social Transformation: The Case of Rock Music in Former East Germany. In *Socio-Cultural Aspects of Music in Europe*, ed. Paul Rutten. Brussels: European Music Office/ Directorate General X. 77–84.

7718 Wolff, Jochen. 1987. 'Ideologisch verdächtig?' Zur Lübecker Arbeiterchorbewegung. In *Ich will aber gerade vom Leben singen . . . Über populäre*

Musik vom ausgehenden 19. Jahrhundert bis zum Ende der Weimarer Republik, ed. Sabine Schutte. Reinbek bei Hamburg: Rowohlt. 236–51.

7719 Wouters, Kees. 1993. Von den Wandervögeln zum Wanderers Horclub. In *Jazz in Europa*, ed. Wolfram Knauer. Hofheim: Wolke. 51–72.

7720 Zeppenfeld, Werner. 1979. *Tonträger in der Bundesrepublik Deutschland. Anatomie eines medialen Massenmarkts.* Bochum: Studienverlag Brockmeyer.

7721 Zimmerman, Peter. 1984. *Rock 'n' Roller, Beats und Punks: Rockgeschichte und Sozialisation.* Essen: Rigogern Verlag.

Berlin

7722 Danzi, Michael. 1985. *American Musician in Germany, 1924–1939: Memoirs of the Jazz Entertainment and Music World of Berlin During the Weimar Republic and the Nazi Era.* Frankfurt am Main: Rücker.

7723 *Free Music Production: Twenty Years Free Music Production, 1969–1989.* 1989. Berlin: FMP.

7724 Henkel, Oliva and Wolff, Karsten. 1996. *Berlin Underground. Techno und HipHop zwischen Mythos und Ausverkauf.* Berlin: FAB.

7725 Mehlitz, Bernd. 1985. Rock- und Jazzförderung in Berlin. *Jazzforschung* 17: 85–88.

7726 Meier, Uta. 1984. *Unabhängige Musikproduktion in Berlin: Zwischen Subkultur und alternativer Öffentlichkeit.* Nijmegen: University of Nijmegen Department of Mass Communications.

7727 Richter, Lukas. 1970. *Die Berliner Gassenhauer. Darstellung, Dokumente, Sammlung.* Leipzig: Deutscher Verlag für Musik.

LOCATIONS

Ireland

7728 Breathnach, Brendan. 1971. *Folk Music and Dances of Ireland*. Dublin and Cork: The Mercier Press.

7729 Carson, Ciarán. 1986. *Irish Traditional Music*. Belfast.

7730 Carson, Ciarán. 1996. *Last Night's Fun: A Book About Irish Traditional Music*. London: Jonathan Cape.

7731 Clayton-Lea, Tony and Richie, Taylor. 1992. *Irish Rock: Where It's Come From, Where It's At, Where It's Going*. Dublin: Gill & Macmillan.

7732 Curtis, P.J. 1994. *Notes from the Heart: A Celebration of Irish Traditional Music*. Dublin: Torc.

7733 Faolain, Turlough. 1983. *Blood on the Harp: Irish Rebel History in Ballad*. Troy, NY: Whitston Publishing Co.

7734 Galvin, Patrick. 1962. *Irish Songs of Resistance*. New York: Oak Publications.

7735 Gillen, Gerard and White, Harry, eds. 1995. *Music and Irish Cultural History*. Dublin: Irish Academic Press.

7736 O'Connor, Nuala. 1991. *Bringing It All Back Home: The Influence of Irish Music*. London: BBC Books.

7737 O'Neill, Francis. 1910. *Irish Folk Music: A Fascinating Hobby*. Chicago: Regan Printing House.

7738 O'Neill, Francis. 1973. *Irish Minstrels and Musicians, with Numerous Dissertations on Related Subjects*, new edition. Darby, PA: Norwood Editions. First published Chicago: Regan Printing House, 1913.

7739 Power, Vincent. 1990. *Send 'Em Home Sweatin': The Showbands' Story*. Dublin: Kildanore Press.

7740 Prendergast, Mark J. 1987. *Irish Rock: Roots, Personalities, Directions*. Dublin: O'Brien Press.

7741 Rimmer, Joan. 1984. *The Irish Harp: Cláirseach na héireann*. Dublin and Cork: The Mercier Press.

7742 Rowley, Eddie. 1993. *A Woman's Voice*. Dublin: O'Brien Press.

7743 Savage, Jon. 1995. Rough Emeralds: How Much Does British Pop Owe to the Anglo-Irish? *Guardian* (20 March): 9.

7744 Smyth, Gerry. 1992. Who's the Greenest of Them All? Irishness and Popular Music. *Irish Studies Review* 2: 3–5.

7745 Stokes, Martin. 1994. Place, Exchange and Meaning: Black Sea Musicians in the West of Ireland. In *Ethnicity, Identity and Music: The Musical Construction of Place*, ed. Martin Stokes. Oxford: Berg. 97–116.

7746 Wilson, David A. 1995. *Ireland, a Bicycle and a Tin Whistle*. Belfast and Toronto: Blackstaff Press and McGill-Queen's University Press.

7747 Wright, Robert. 1975. *Irish Emigrant Ballads and Songs*. Bowling Green, OH: Bowling Green University Popular Press.

Italy

7748 Ala, Nemesio and Fabbri, Franco. 1985. Generi musicali, schemi di consumo, gusti del pubblico: 'popular music' e ricerca in Italia. In *Musica e sistema dell'informazione in Europa*, ed. Francesco Rampi. Milano: Unicopli. 153–66.

7749 Ala, Nemesio, et al. 1985. *La musica che si consuma*. Milano: Unicopli.

7750 Ala, Nemesio, et al. 1985. Patterns of Music Consumption in Milan and Reggio Emilia from April to May 1983. In *Popular Music Perspectives, 2*, ed.

David Horn. Göteborg and Exeter: IASPM. 464–500.

7751 Ala, Nemesio, et al. 1985. Schemi del consumo musicale a Milano e a Reggio Emilia. *What Is Popular Music?/Quaderni di Musica/Realtà?* 8: 492–527.

7752 Ankli, Ruedi and Burri, Peter. 1985. *Cantautore Républic: die italienischen Rockpoetik, ihre Geschichte, ihre Texte.* Basel: Lenos.

7753 Bermani, Cesare. 1993. Musica popolare e musica colta negli anni Sessanta-Settanta. *Musica/Realtà* 42: 79–101.

7754 Bertrando, Paolo. 1980. *Bologna Rock.* Milano: Re Nudo.

7755 Borgna, Gianni. 1983. *Il tempo della musica.* Bari: Laterza.

7756 Branzaglia, Carlo, Pierfrancesco Pacoda and Alba Solaro. 1992. *Posse italiane: Centri sociali, underground musicale e cultura giovanile degli anni '90 in Italia.* Firenze: Tosca.

7757 Caioli, L., A.R. Calabro and M. Fraboni. 1986. *Banda, un modo di dire. Rockabillies, Mods, Punks.* Milano: Unicopli.

7758 Cammelli, Stefano, ed. 1983. *Musiche da ballo, balli da festa: musiche, balli e suonatori tradizionali della montagna bolognese.* Bologna: Edizioni Alfa.

7759 Carollo, Agostino. 1993. *Il rock in Trentino alto adige: La storia ed il panorama attuale in un'analisi a 360 gradi.* Rovereto: Ritmi Urbani.

7760 Carrera, Alessandro. 1980. *Musica e pubblico giovanile.* Milano: Giangiacomo Feltrinelli Editore.

7761 Carrera, Alessandro. 1989. I cantautori in Italia e il loro pubblico. In *Musiche/ Realtà. Generi musicali/Media/Popular Music.* ed. Franco Fabbri. Milano:

Unicopli. 313–30. (First published in *Musica/Realtà* 2 (1980): 133–50.)

7762 Cinque, Luigi. 1977. *Kunsertu: La musica popolare in Italia.* Milano: Longanesi.

7763 Fabbri, Franco. 1982. A Theory of Musical Genres: Two Applications. In *Popular Music Perspectives, 1,* ed. David Horn and Philip Tagg. Göteborg and Exeter: IASPM. 52–81.

7764 Fabbri, Franco. 1989. The System of Canzone in Italy Today. In *World Music, Politics and Social Change,* ed. Simon Frith. Manchester: Manchester University Press. 122–42.

7765 Fabbri, Franco. 1996. *Il suono in cui viviamo: inventare, produrre e diffondere musica.* Milano: Giangiacomo Feltrinelli Editore.

7766 Fabbri, Franco and Fiori, Umberto. 1988. Il Sessantotto e la canzone: un tabù. *Musica/Realtà* 27: 103–18.

7767 Fabbri, Franco and Fiori, Umberto. 1989. Crisi e prospettive della canzone politica in Italia. In *Musiche/Realtà. Generi musicali/Media/Popular Music.* Milano: Unicopli. 331–46. (First published in *Musica/Realtà* 1 (1980): 161–76.)

7768 Fiori, Umberto. 1984. Rock Music and Politics in Italy. *Popular Music* 4: 261–77.

7769 Fiori, Umberto. 1989. Tra quaresima e carnevale: pratiche e strategie della canzone d'autore. In *Musiche/Realtà. Generi musicali/Media/Popular Music,* ed. Franco Fabbri. Milano: Unicopli. 347–62. (First published in *Musica/Realtà* 3 (1980): 111–26.)

7770 *La chitarra e il potere. Gli autori della canzone politica contemporanea.* 1976. Roma: Savelli.

7771 Lortat-Jacob, Bernard. 1995. *Sardinian Chronicles*. Chicago: University of Chicago Press.

7772 Luigi, Mario de. 1985. Mercato del disco in Italia: ieri, oggi, domani. In *Musica e sistema dell'informazione in Europa*, ed. Francesco Rampi. Milano: Unicopli. 41–50.

7773 Magrini, Tullia. 1982. *Vi no la buonasera: studi sul canto popolare in Romagna: il repertorio lirico*. Bologna: Clueb.

7774 Marchi, Luca. 1992. Il liscio: pratica sociale e genere musicale. In *Dal blues al liscio: Studi sull'esperienza musicale comune*, ed. Gino Stefani. Verona: Ianua. 135–65.

7775 Mitchell, Tony. 1995. Questions of Style: Notes on Italian Hip Hop. *Popular Music* 14(3): 333–48.

7776 Murtas, Clara. 1981. *La canzone italiana*. Roma: Casa Editrice Roberto Napoleone.

7777 Nicolodi, Fiamma. 1984. *Musica e musicisti nel ventennio fascista*. Fiesole: Discanto Edizioni.

7778 Pestalozza, Luigi. 1986. La musica in Italia fra pubblico e privato. *Musica/Realtà* 20: 179–91.

7779 Pestalozza, Luigi. 1986. Lavoro e musica. *Musica/Realtà* 20: 8–12.

7780 Prato, Paolo. 1988. L'editoria della popular music in Italia. *Musica/Realtà* 26: 75–86.

7781 Rosselli, John. 1991. *Music and Musicians in Nineteenth Century Italy*. Portland, OR: Amadeus Press.

7782 Saffioti, Tito. 1978. *Enciclopedia della canzone popolare e della nuova canzone politica*. Milano: Longanesi.

7783 Simone, Roberto De. 1983. Appunti per una disordinata storia della canzone napoletana. *Culture musicali* (Gen.-Giu).

7784 Tortora, Daniela. 1987. Roma e Palermo centri di nuova musica negli anni Sessanta. *Musica/Realtà* 26: 87–105.

7785 Valle, Gianni. 1980. *Il manuale di ballo*. Roma: Lato Side.

The Netherlands

7786 Bajema, Roeland, et al. 1982. *Nederpop: 25 jaar popmuziek in Nederland; compleet overzicht van alle artiesten en hun platen*. Utrecht: Het Spectrum.

7787 Berg, Erik van den, Roy Mantel and Pieter van Adrichem. 1994. *Klare Taal, 15 jaar Nederlandstalige rock*. Groningen: Passage.

7788 Bouwman, Francis, comp. 1994. *Hit Dossier 1939–1994*. Haarlem: Becht.

7789 Bouwman, Francis, and Broekhuizen, C. 1983. *Hitdossier, 1958–1982*. Amsterdam: Becht.

7790 Briel, Robert. 1987. *Hitdossier 1958 to 1987*. Haarlem: Becht.

7791 No entry.

7792 Elderen, P. Louis van. 1983. Music and Meaning Behind the Dykes: The New Wave of Dutch Rock and Its Audiences. *Popular Music* 3: 51–74.

7793 Elderen, P. Louis van. 1985. Songs for the Little Man 1930 and 1980: Popular Music and the Crisis of the Welfare State. In *Popular Music Perspectives, 2*, ed. David Horn. Göteborg and Exeter: IASPM. 148–65.

7794 Evers, Paul, ed. 1994. *25 Jaar Pinkpop*. Amsterdam: Bonaventura.

7795 Fenger, Pim. 1981. Music in Cultural, Educational and Communication Policies in the Netherlands. In *Stock-*

Taking of Musical Life: Sociography and Music Education, ed. Desmond Mark. Wien: Doblinger. 89–96.

7796 Franssen, Pieter. 1992. *Haag(sch)e Bluf, het verhaal van Golden Earring.* The Hague: BZZTOH.

7797 Gelder, Henk van and Carvalho, Hester. 1994. *Gouden Tijden, vijftig jaar Nederlandse popbladen.* Amsterdam: Jan Mets (Dutch Rock Archives, #4).

7798 Gout, Cor. 1989. De struikelgang van de Nederlandse pop. In *De cultuurelite van Nederland: wie maken en breken de kunst,* ed. Theo Stokkink. 113–39.

7799 Janssen, Rienk, ed. 1988. *Say Pardner: Strictly Country in Nederland.* Vlagtwedde: SCR.

7800 Labree, Rob. 1993. *Rock & roll in rood-wit-blauw.* Amsterdam: Jan Mets (Dutch Rock Archives, #2).

7801 Maas, Luc and Sparidans, Rob. 1985. *Het subculturele proces: punk en new wave.* Tilburg: TIAS.

7802 Mol, Pieter Jan. 1985. Paradise Lost: een generatie op drift, Hitweek 1965–1969. *Jeugd & Samenleving* 15: 612–68.

7803 Mutsaers, Lutgard. 1987. *Pop Utrecht 1956–1986.* Utrecht: Matrijs.

7804 Mutsaers, Lutgard. 1989. *Rockin' Ramona, een gekleurde kijk op de bakermat van de Nederpop.* The Hague: SDU-Uitgeverij.

7805 Mutsaers, Lutgard. 1992. *Haring & Hawaii, hawaiianmuziek in Nederland 1925–1992.* Amsterdam: Poparchief Nederland (Dutch Rock Archives, #1).

7806 Mutsaers, Lutgard. 1993. *25 Jaar Paradiso.* Amsterdam: Jan Mets.

7807 Mutsaers, Lutgard. 1995. No Limit: New Dutch Musics Since the 1950s. *Popular Musicology* 2(6): 15–24.

7808 Mutsaers, Lutgard. 1995. Roots and Recognition: Contributions of Musicians from the Indonesian Archipelago to the Development of Popular Music Culture in the Netherlands. *Perfect Beat* 2(3) (July): 65–81.

7809 No entry.

7810 Rutten, Paul. 1992. *Hitmuziek in Nederland 1960–1985.* Amsterdam: Stichting Het Persinstituut; Otto Cramwinckel Uitgever.

7811 Rutten, Paul. 1995. Nederlandstalige popmuziek, een synthese van eigen en mondiale cultuur. *Volkskundig Bulletin* 21(2) (October): 277–98.

7812 Rutten, Paul and Oud, Gerd Jan. 1991. *Nederlandse popmuziek op de binnen- en buitenlandse markt.* Rijswijk: Dutch Ministry of Culture (WVC).

7813 Slootweg, Dick. 1989. *B-kant van de Beat.* The Hague: SDU-Uitgeverij.

7814 Steensma, Frans, ed. 1987. *Oor's eerste nederlandse pop encyclopedie.* Amsterdam: Annoventuna.

7815 Steensma, Frans, ed. 1990. *Encyclopedie van de Nederlandse Popmuziek 1960–1990.* Amsterdam: Bonaventura.

7816 Van Eyle, Wim. 1982. *The Dutch Jazz and Blues Discography, 1916–1980.* Utrecht: Het Spectrum.

7817 van Veen, Gert. 1994. *Welcome to the Future.* Amsterdam: Platina Paperbacks.

7818 Wermuth, Mir. 1991. Meanwhile, at the Other Side of the Ocean: Hip Hop Culture in Holland. *Nothing Bloody Stands Still* 1: 62–65.

7819 Wermuth, Mir. 1993. Let's Talk About Sex, Baby! Fly Girls in de Nederhop Hop Scene. *Lover* 20(4): 224–27.

7820 Wermuth, Mir. 1993. Weri Man! Een studie naar de hiphop-cultuur in

Nederland. *Kunst en Kunstbeleid in Nederland* 6: 63–112.

Norway

7821 Bull-Hansen, Haaken. 1984. *Rock: ni norske historier.* Oslo: J.W. Cappelan.

7822 Johnson, Geir. 1985. Changes in Norwegian Popular Music, 1976–1981. In *Popular Music Perspectives, 2,* ed. David Horn. Göteborg and Exeter: IASPM. 142–47.

7823 Johnson, Geir. 1986. *Norge i Melodi Grand Prix.* Oslo: Forlaget Atheneum.

7824 Ketting, Knud. 1983. Rock Music at Government Level: A Report from the First Nordic Rock Music Seminar. *Nordic Sounds* 1983/4: 3–5.

Portugal

7825 *Coloquio sobre Musica Popular Portuguesa: Communicacoes e conclusoes.* 1984. Lisbon: Instituto Nacional para Aproveitamento dos Tempos Livres dos Trabalhadores.

7826 Correia, Mário. 1984. *Música popular portuguesa: um parto de partida.* Coimbra: Centelha.

7827 Oliveira, Ernest Veija de. 1982. *Instrumentos musicais populares portugueses.* Lisbon: Fundaçâo Calousta Gulbenkian.

Spain

7828 Claudin, Victor. 1981. *Canción de auto en España.* Gijon: Jucar.

7829 Fleury, Jean-Jacques. 1985. Castilla y Leon en la Nueva Canción. *Hispanorama* 41: 81–91.

7830 Fleury, Jean-Jacques. 1985. El indio y el niño en la Nueva Canción. *Hispanorama* (November): 89–94.

7831 Fleury, Jean-Jacques. 1985. La nueva canción en Aragon. *Hispanorama* 41: 75–81.

7832 Lahusen, Christian. 1991. 'Unsere Stimme erwacht . . .': Populäre Musikkultur und nationale Frage im heutigen Spanien. Saarbrücken/Fort Lauderdale: Verlag Breitenbach Publishers.

7833 Manuel, Peter. 1989. Andalusian, Gypsy and Class Identity in the Contemporary Flamenco Complex. *Ethnomusicology* 33(1): 47–65.

7834 Manuel, Peter. 1989. *Modal Harmony in Andalusian, Eastern European and Turkish Syncretic Musics.* New York: International Council for Traditional Music.

7835 Marin, Adolfo. 1984. *La nueva música: del industrial al tecno-pop.* Barcelona: Teorema.

7836 Mohren, Michael. 1985. Lieder zur 'emigración'. *Hispanorama* 41: 112–14.

7837 Ordovás Blasco, Jesus. 1987. *Historia de la música pop española.* Madrid: Alianza.

7838 Palacios Garoz, Miguel Angel. 1984. *Introduccion a la musica popular castellana y leonesa.* Segovia: Consejeria de Educacion y Cultura.

7839 Pedrell, Felipe. 1922. *Cancionero musical popular español.* Barcelona: Casa Editorial de Música, Boileau.

7840 Rehrmann, Norbert. 1985. Die nueva canción in Spanien: Ein Überblick. *Hispanorama* 41: 63–74.

Sweden

7841 Andersson, Tony and Bergendahl, Elisabet. 1982. *Låt tusen stenar rulla: kuratorgruppens musikverksamhet. Teori och praktik.* Göteborg: Socialhögskolan.

7842 Axelsen, Doris. 1981. Swedish Adolescents and the Phonogram. In

Stock-Taking of Musical Life: Sociography and Music Education, ed. Desmond Mark. Wien: Doblinger. 47–51.

7843 Björnberg, Alf. 1990. Sounding the Mainstream: An Analysis of the Songs Performed in the Swedish Eurovision Song Contest Semi-Finals, 1959–1983. In *Popular Music Research*, ed. Keith Roe and Ulla Karlsson. Göteborg: NORDICOM-Sweden, No. 1–2. 121–32.

7844 Bjurström, Erling and Fornäs, Johan. 1983. Svenska musikalternativ på sjuttiotalet/Det kommersiella tomrummet/Inventering. *Nordisk Forum* 39–40 (8(3) & 8(4)): 110–22.

7845 Brolinson, Per-Erik and Larsen, Holger. 1983. *Rockens introduktion i Sverige*. Stockholm: Skrifter från Musikvetenskapliga institutionen, 4.

7846 Brolinson, Per-Erik and Larsen, Holger. 1984. *När rocken slog i Sverige: Svensk rockhistoria, 1955–1965*. Stockholm: Sweden Music Förlags AB.

7847 Burnett, Robert C. 1990. Statistical Profile of Music Consumption in Sweden. In *Popular Music Research* ed. Keith Roe and Ulla Karlsson. Göteborg: NORDICOM-Sweden, No. 1–2. 145–56.

7848 Burnett, Robert C. 1992. Dressed for Success: Sweden from Abba to Roxette. *Popular Music* 11(2): 141–50.

7849 Edström, Olle. 1989. *Schlager i Sverige 1910–1940*. Göteborg: Skrifter från Musikvetenskap, Göteborgs Universitet.

7850 Edström, Olle. 1996. 'Looking on the West Coast': A Contribution from the Swedish West Coast to Contemporary Composition Practice. *Popular Music* 15(1): 83–104.

7851 Eriksson, Bengt. 1975. *Från Rock Ragge till Hoola Bandoola*. Stockholm: Tidens Förlag.

7852 Fornäs, Johan, Ulf Lindberg and Ove Sernhede. 1988. *Under Rocken: Musikins Roll i Tre Ungar Band*. Stockholm and Lund: Symposium Bokforlag.

7853 Haslum, Bengt and Haslum, M., eds. 1982. *Svensk populärmusik: visor, barnvisor, schlager, underhållningsmusik, jazz*. Stockholm: STIM.

7854 Johansson, Carl-Owe. 1979. *Rock Around the Clock – Saturday Night Fever: en 80-sidig sammanställning av vad som schlagit i Sverige 1955–1978*. Vara: Dominique Muzic-Club.

7855 Karlsson, Henrik. 1980. *Musikspelet: Det svenska musiksamhället av idag*. Göteborg: Göteborgs Universitet.

7856 Ketting, Knud. 1983. Rock Music at Government Level: A Report from the First Nordic Rock Music Seminar. *Nordic Sounds* 1983/4: 3–5.

7857 Kjellberg, Erik and Thema, Zum. 1993. 'Old Folklore in Swedish Modern': Volkmusik und Jazz in Schweden. In *Jazz in Europa*, ed. Wolfram Knauer. Hofheim: Wolke. 221–32.

7858 Lilliestam, Lars. 1990. Musical Acculturation: 'Hound Dog' from Blues to Swedish Rock and Roll. In *Popular Music Research*, ed. Keith Roe and Ulla Karlsson. Göteborg: NORDICOM-Sweden, No. 1–2. 133–44.

7859 Ling, Jan. 1986. Folk Music Revival in Sweden: The Lilla Edet Fiddle Club. *Yearbook for Traditional Music* 18: 1–8.

7860 Ling, Jan and Ramsten, Märta. 1985. The Gärdeby Folk Melody: A Musical Migrant. In *Popular Music Perspectives*, 2, ed. David Horn. Göteborg and Exeter: IASPM. 119–41.

7861 Malm, Krister. 1982. Phonograms and Cultural Policy in Sweden. In *The Phonogram in Cultural Communication*, ed. Kurt Blaukopf. Wien: Springer-Verlag. 43–74.

LOCATIONS

7862 Möllerstedt, Gunnar. 1982. *Göteborgsjazz: musiker och dansställen under 50-talet.* Göteborg: Wezäta förlag.

7863 Nicolausson, Harry. 1983. *Swedish Jazz Discography.* Stockholm: Swedish Music Information Centre.

7864 Nylöf, Göran. 1990. Trends in Popular Music Preferences in Sweden, 1960–1988. In *Popular Music Research*, ed. Keith Roe and Ulla Karlsson. Göteborg: NORDICOM-Sweden, No. 1–2. 87–102.

7865 Nysten, Leif. 1992. Rundradions svenskspråkiga radiokanal: en musikpolitisk betraktelse. In *Toosa Soi. Musiiki radion kilpailuvälineenä*, ed. Kimmo Salminen and Arí Alm. Helsinki: YLE Tutkimus ja kehitysosasto. 97–101.

7866 Rehal, Agneta. 1991. Rocksångaren som den offrade sonen och rocken som religion: om rockens funktion utifrån Imperiets sångtexter. In *Ungdomar i rörelse*, ed. Jan Carle and Hans-Erik Hermansson. Göteborg: Daidalos. 181–222.

7867 Roe, Keith. 1985. The Swedish Moral Panic over Video, 1980–1984. *NORDICOM-Information* 2–3: 13–18.

7868 Ronström, Owe. 1989. *Making Use of History: The Revival of the Bagpipe in Sweden in the 1980s.* New York: International Council for Traditional Music.

7869 Strand, Sigfrid. 1974. *Militärmusikern i svenskt musikliv.* Stockholm: Sohlmans.

7870 Tapper, Karl-Herman. 1981. Regional Music Policy in Sweden: Problems and Projects. In *Stock-Taking of Musical Life: Sociography and Music Education*, ed. Desmond Mark. Wien: Doblinger. 104–107.

7871 Tegen, Martin. 1986. *Populärmusik under 1800-talet.* Stockholm: Reimers.

7872 Thörnvall, Olle. 1981. *Svensk Rocklyrik: analys av fyra svenska rocktexter.* Uppsala: Inst. för litteraturvetenskap.

7873 Winqvist, Sven G. 1980. *Musik i svenska ljudfilmer 1929–1939.* Stockholm: STIM.

Switzerland

7874 Bolle-Zemp, Sylvie. 1992. *Le Réenchantement de la montagne: Aspects du folklore musical en haute Gruyère.* Genève: Georg/Société suisse des traditions populaires.

7875 Buser, Ernst W. 1988. *Singing Basel: Basler Bigund Swingbands, 1924–1950.* Basel: Basler Zeitung.

7876 Mäusli, Theo. 1993. Jazz und Geistige Landesverteidigung. Zur Rezeption des Jazz in der Schweiz der Jahre 1933 bis 1945. In *Jazz in Europa*, ed. Wolfram Knauer. Hofheim: Wolke. 73–94.

7877 Stenzl, Jürg. 1986. La 'canzone d'autore' da Gilles a Yvette Théraulaz. *Musica/Realtà* 20: 12–19.

7878 Urbain, Jacques. 1977. *Chanson populaire en Suisse romande, t. 1 & 2.* Yverdon-les-Bains: Thièle.

United Kingdom

7879 Bailey, Peter, ed. 1986. *Music Hall: The Business of Pleasure.* Milton Keynes: Open University Press.

7880 Banerji, Sabita and Baumann, Gerd. 1990. Bhangra 1984–88: Fusion and Professionalization in a Genre of South Asian Dance Music. In *Black Music in Britain: Essays on the Afro-Asian Contribution to Popular Music*, ed. Paul Oliver. Milton Keynes: Open University Press. 137–52.

7881 Banfield, Stephen, ed. 1995. *The Blackwell History of Music in Britain. Vol. 6, The Twentieth Century.* Oxford: Blackwell.

7882 Barnard, Stephen. 1989. *On the Radio: Music Radio in Britain*. Milton Keynes: Open University Press.

7883 Baxendale, John. 1995. ' . . . into another kind of life in which anything might happen . . .': Popular Music and Late Modernity, 1910–1930. *Popular Music* 14(2): 137–54.

7884 Bennett, Anthony. 1982. Sources of Popular Song in Early Nineteenth-Century Britain: Problems and Methods of Research. *Popular Music* 2: 69–89.

7885 Birchall, Ian. 1969. The Decline and Fall of British Rhythm and Blues. In *The Age of Rock*, ed. Jonathan Eisen. New York: Vintage Books. 94–102.

7886 Boulton, David. 1960. (1958) *Jazz in Britain*. London: Jazz Book Club.

7887 Bradley, Dick. 1992. *Understanding Rock 'n' Roll: Popular Music in Britain, 1955–1964*. Buckingham: Open University Press.

7888 Bratton, J.S. 1975. *The Victorian Popular Ballad*. London: Macmillan.

7889 Bratton, J.S., ed. 1986. *Music Hall: Performance and Style*. Milton Keynes: Open University Press.

7890 Broughton, Viv. 1985. *Black Gospel: An Illustrated History of the Gospel Sound*. Poole: Blandford Press.

7891 Brunning, Bob. 1986. *The Blues: The British Connection*. Poole: Blandford Press.

7892 Brunning, Bob. 1995. (1986) *Blues in Britain, The History: 1950s to the Present*. London: Blandford Press. First published London: Blandford Press, 1986.

7893 Burchill, Julie and Parsons, Tony. 1978. *The Boy Looked at Johnny: The Obituary of Rock and Roll*. London: Pluto Press.

7894 Carr, Ian. 1973. *Music Outside: Contemporary Jazz in Britain*. London: Latimer New Dimensions.

7895 Carter, Angela. 1977. (1967) Notes for a Theory of Sixties Style. *New Society* 22: 803–807.

7896 Cashmore, E. Ellis. 1987. Shades of Black, Shades of White. In *Popular Music & Communication*, ed. James Lull. Newbury Park, CA: Sage. 245–65.

7897 Chambers, Iain. 1977. (1975) A Strategy for Living: Black Music and White Subcultures. In *Resistance Through Rituals: Youth Subcultures in Post-War Britain*, ed. Stuart Hall and Tony Jefferson. London: Hutchinson. 157–66.

7898 Chambers, Iain. 1987. British Pop: Some Tracks from the Other Side of the Record. In *Popular Music & Communication*, ed. James Lull. Newbury Park, CA: Sage. 231–45.

7899 Chapman, Robert. 1990. The 1960s Pirates: A Comparative Analysis of Radio London and Radio Caroline. *Popular Music* 9(2): 165–78.

7900 Chapman, Robert. 1992. *Selling the Sixties: The Pirates and Pop Music Radio*. London: Routledge.

7901 Chatburn, Thomas. 1990. Trinidad All Stars: The Steel Pan Movement in Britain. In *Black Music in Britain: Essays on the Afro-Asian Contribution to Popular Music*, ed. Paul Oliver. Milton Keynes: Open University Press. 102–17.

7902 Clarke, Sebastian. 1980. *Jah Music: The Evolution of the Popular Jamaican Song*. London: Heinemann Educational Books.

7903 Clayson, Alan. 1995. *Beat Merchants*. London: Blandford Press.

7904 Cohen, Stanley. 1980. (1972) *Folk Devils and Moral Panics: The Creation of Mods and Rockers*. Oxford: Martin

Robertson. First published London: MacGibbon & Kee, 1972.

7905 Colin, Sid. 1977. *And the Bands Played On*. London: Hamish Hamilton.

7906 Colls, Robert. 1977. *The Collier's Rant: Songs and Culture in the Industrial Village*. London: Croom Helm.

7907 Cowley, John. 1985. Cultural 'Fusions': Aspects of British West Indian Music in the USA and Britain, 1918–51. *Popular Music* 5: 81–96.

7908 Cowley, John. 1985. *West Indian Gramophone Records in Britain: 1927–1950*. Coventry: Centre for Research in Ethnic Relations, University of Warwick.

7909 Cowley, John. 1985. West Indian Records in Britain. *Musical Traditions* 4: 28–30.

7910 Cowley, John. 1991. *Carnival and Other Seasonal Festivals in the West Indies, USA and Britain: A Selected Bibliographical Index*. Coventry: Centre for Research in Ethnic Relations, University of Warwick.

7911 Cowley, John. 1994. uBUNGCA (Oxford Bags): Recordings in London of African and West Indian Music in the 1920s and 1930s. *Musical Traditions* 12: 13–27.

7912 Cross, Colin, Paul Kendall and Mick Farren. 1980. *Encyclopedia of British Beat Groups and Solo Artists of the Sixties*. London: Omnibus.

7913 Dallas, Karl. 1987. *Bricks in the Wall*. New York: Shapolsky Publishers.

7914 Fancourt, Leslie. 1989. *British Blues on Record (1957–1970)*. Faversham, Kent: Privately printed.

7915 Frith, Simon. 1978. *The Sociology of Rock*. London: Constable.

7916 Frith, Simon and Horne, Howard. 1987. *Art into Pop*. London: Methuen.

7917 Frith, Simon and Street, John. 1992. Rock Against Racism and Red Wedge: From Music to Politics, From Politics to Music. In *Rockin' the Boat: Mass Music and Mass Movements*, ed. Reebee Garofalo. Boston, MA: South End Press. 67–80.

7918 Gammon, Vic. 1984. 'Not Appreciated in Worthing?': Class Expression and Popular Song Texts in Mid-Nineteenth-Century Britain. *Popular Music* 4: 5–24.

7919 Gänzl, Kurt. 1986. *The British Musical Theatre*. London: Macmillan.

7920 Godbolt, Jim. 1976. *All This and 10%*. London: Hale.

7921 Godbolt, Jim. 1984. *A History of Jazz in Britain, 1919–1950*. London: Quartet.

7922 Godbolt, Jim. 1989. *A History of Jazz in Britain, 1950–1970*. London: Quartet.

7923 Harker, Dave. 1985. *Fakesong: The Manufacture of British 'Folksong', 1700 to the Present Day*. Milton Keynes: Open University Press.

7924 Hebdige, Dick. 1977. (1975) Reggae, Rastas, Rudies: Style and the Subversion of Form. In *Resistance Through Rituals: Youth Subcultures in Post-War Britain*, ed. Stuart Hall and Tony Jefferson. London: Hutchinson. 135–53.

7925 Hebdige, Dick. 1988. (1979) *Subculture: The Meaning of Style*. London: Routledge.

7926 Heckstall-Smith, Dick. 1989. *The Safest Place in the World: A Personal History of British Rhythm and Blues*. London: Quartet.

7927 Henderson, W., ed. 1937. *Victorian Street Ballads: A Selection of Popular Ballads Sold in the Street in the Nineteenth Century*. London: Country Life.

7928 Herbert, Trevor, ed. 1991. *Bands: The Brass Band Movement in the 19th and*

20th Centuries. Buckingham: Open
University Press.

7929 Hustwitt, Mark. 1983. 'Caught in a
Whirlpool of Aching Sound': The
Production of Dance Music in Britain in
the 1920s. *Popular Music* 3: 7–31.

7930 Jasper, Tony. 1991. *The Top Twenty
Book: The Official British Record Charts,
1955–1990.* Poole: Blandford Press.

7931 Jones, Simon. 1988. *Black Culture, White
Youth: The Reggae Tradition from JA to
UK.* Basingstoke: Macmillan Education.

7932 Kelly, Matthew. 1995. The Unlikely
Popularity of Cajun Music in Britain. In
Popular Music Perspectives III, ed. Peter
Wicke. Berlin: Zyankrise. 85–90.

7933 Laing, Dave. 1972. Roll Over Lonnie
(Tell George Formby the News). In
Rock File, ed. Charlie Gillett. London:
New English Library. 45–51.

7934 Laing, Dave. 1985. *One Chord Wonders:
Power and Meaning in Punk Rock.* Milton
Keynes: Open University Press.

7935 Langlois, Tony. 1992. Can You Feel It?
DJs and House Music Culture in the
UK. *Popular Music* 11(2): 229–38.

7936 Lee, Edward. 1970. *Music of the People:
A Study of Popular Music in Great
Britain.* London: Barrie & Jenkins.

7937 Lee, Edward. 1982. *Folksong and Music
Hall.* London: Routledge & Kegan Paul.

7938 Lemonnier, Bertrand. 1986. *La
révolution pop dans l'Angleterre des années
60.* Paris: Table Ronde.

7939 Levy, Claire. 1992. The Influence of
British Rock in Bulgaria. *Popular Music*
11(2): 209–12.

7940 MacInnes, Colin. 1967. *Sweet Saturday
Night: Pop Song, 1840–1920.* London:
MacGibbon and Kee.

7941 MacKinnon, Niall. 1993. *The British
Folk Scene: Musical Performance and
Social Identity.* Buckingham: Open
University Press.

7942 Mackintosh, Iain and Sell, Michael, eds.
1982. *Curtains!!! or, A New Life for Old
Theatres: Being a Complete Gazetteer of
All the Surviving Pre-1914 Theatres,
Music Halls of Great Britain.* Eastbourne:
Offord.

7943 Martin, Bernice. 1981. *A Sociology of
Contemporary Cultural Change.* Oxford:
Blackwell.

7944 May, Chris and Phillips, Tim. 1974.
British Beat. London: Socion.

7945 Melly, George. 1970. *Revolt into Style:
The Pop Arts in Britain.* London:
Penguin.

7946 Miller, Manfred. 1978. Shakin' All Over:
Zur Rock 'n' Roll-Rezeption in England.
Anschläge 1(2): 5–24.

7947 Mulgan, Geoff and Worpole, Ken.
1986. *Saturday Night or Sunday
Morning? From Arts to Industry: New
Forms of Cultural Policy.* London:
Comedia.

7948 Negus, Keith. 1995. The Discovery and
Development of Recording Artists in the
Music Industry in Britain. In *Popular
Music Perspectives III*, ed. Peter Wicke.
Berlin: Zyankrise. 204–15.

7949 Oliver, Paul, ed. 1990. *Black Music in
Britain: Essays on the Afro-Asian
Contribution to Popular Music.* Milton
Keynes: Open University Press.

7950 Palmer, Roy, ed. 1974. *Poverty Knock: A
Picture of Industrial Life in the 19th
Century Through Songs, Ballads and
Contemporary Accounts.* Cambridge:
Cambridge University Press.

7951 Palmer, Roy. 1976. (1974) *A Touch of
the Times: Songs of Social Change.*
London: Weidenfeld & Nicolson. First
published London: Penguin, 1974.

7952 Palmer, Roy. 1988. *The Sound of History: Songs and Social Comment.* New York: Oxford University Press.

7953 Pearsall, Ronald. 1973. *Victorian Popular Music.* Newton Abbot: David & Charles.

7954 Pearsall, Ronald. 1975. *Edwardian Popular Music.* Newton Abbot: David & Charles.

7955 Pearsall, Ronald. 1976. *Popular Music of the 20s.* Newton Abbot: David & Charles.

7956 Pickering, Michael. 1990. 'A Jet Ornament to Society': Black Music in Nineteenth-Century Britain. In *Black Music in Britain: Essays on the Afro-Asian Contribution to Popular Music,* ed. Paul Oliver. Milton Keynes: Open University Press. 16–33.

7957 Pickering, Michael and Green, Tony, eds. 1987. *Everyday Culture: Popular Song and the Vernacular Milieu.* Milton Keynes: Open University Press.

7958 Rimmer, Dave. 1985. *Like Punk Never Happened.* London: Faber & Faber.

7959 Rouville, Henry de. 1986. *La Musique anglaise.* Paris: PUF.

7960 Savage, Jon. 1995. Rough Emeralds: How Much Does British Pop Owe to the Anglo-Irish? *Guardian* (20 March): 9.

7961 Scannell, Paddy. 1981. Music for the Multitudes?: The Dilemmas of the BBC's Music Policy, 1923–1946. *Media, Culture and Society* 3(3): 243–60.

7962 Scott, Derek B. 1989. *The Singing Bourgeois: Songs of the Victorian Drawing Room and Parlour.* Milton Keynes: Open University Press.

7963 Senelick, Laurence, David F. Cheshire and Ulrich Schneider, . 1981. *British Music Hall, 1840–1923: A Bibliography and Guide to Sources, with a Supplement on European Music-Hall.* Hamden, CT: Archon Books.

7964 Temperley, Nicholas, ed. 1981. *The Athlone History of Music in Britain. Vol. 5, The Romantic Age, 1800–1914.* London: Athlone Press.

7965 Vicinus, Martha. 1974. *The Industrial Muse: A Study of Nineteenth Century British Working-Class Literature.* London: Croom Helm.

7966 Vlček, Josef. 1985. A Glimpse Through a Small Crack: The British Music Press from Behind the Iron Curtain. *Re Records Quarterly* 1(2): 32–35.

7967 Wale, Michael. 1972. *Voxpop: Profiles of the Pop Process.* London: Harrap.

7968 Walker, John A. 1987. *Cross-Overs: Art into Pop, Pop into Art.* London: Comedia.

7969 Watson, Ian. 1983. *Song and Democratic Culture in Britain: An Approach to Popular Culture in Social Movements.* London: Croom Helm.

7970 Widgery, David. 1986. *Beating Time: Riot 'n' Race 'n' Rock 'n' Roll.* London: Chatto & Windus.

7971 Yeo, Eileen and Yeo, Stephen, eds. 1981. *Popular Culture and Class Conflict, 1590–1914: Explorations in the History of Labour and Leisure.* Brighton: Harvester Press.

England

7972 Bailey, Peter. 1987. Rational Recreation and the Entertainment Industry: The Case of the Victorian Music Halls. In *Leisure and Class in Victorian England: Rational Recreation and the Contest for Control, 1830–1885,* revised edition. London and New York: Methuen. First published London: Routledge & Kegan Paul, 1978.

7973 Boyes, Georgina. 1993. *The Imagined Village: Culture, Ideology and the English Folk Revival.* Manchester: Manchester University Press.

7974 Elbourne, Roger. 1980. *Music and Tradition in Early Industrial Lancashire, 1780–1840*. Woodbridge: D.S. Brewer.

7975 Elkins, Charles. 1980. The Voice of the Poor: The Broadside as a Medium of Popular Culture and Dissent in Victorian England. *Journal of Popular Culture* 14(2): 262–74.

7976 Finnegan, Ruth. 1989. *The Hidden Musicians: Music-Making in an English Town*. Cambridge: Cambridge University Press.

7977 Garner, Ken. 1990. New Gold Dawn: The Traditional English Breakfast Show in 1989. *Popular Music* 9(2): 193–202.

7978 Harker, Dave. 1981. The Making of the Tyneside Concert Hall. *Popular Music* 1: 27–56.

7979 Heckstall-Smith, Dick. 1989. *The Safest Place in the World: A Personal History of British Rhythm and Blues*. London: Quartet.

7980 Laing, Dave, and Newman, Richard, eds. 1994. *30 Years of the Cambridge Folk Festival*. Ely: Music Maker Publications.

7981 Lemonnier, Bertrand. 1986. *La Révolution pop dans l'Angleterre des années 60*. Paris: Table Ronde.

7982 Lemonnier, Bertrand. 1995. *L'Angleterre des Beatles: une histoire culturelle des années soixante*. Paris: Kimé.

7983 Lloyd, A.L. 1967. *Folk Song in England*. London: Lawrence and Wishart.

7984 Macan, Edward. 1996. *Rocking the Classics: English Progressive Rock and the Counterculture*. New York: Oxford University Press.

7985 Palmer, Roy. 1979. *A Ballad History of England from 1588 to the Present Day*. London: Batsford.

7986 Palmer, Roy. 1988. *The Sound of History: Songs and Social Comment*. Oxford: Oxford University Press.

7987 Russell, Dave. 1987. *Popular Music in England, 1840–1914: A Social History*. Manchester: Manchester University Press.

7988 Rust, Frances. 1969. *Dance in Society: An Analysis of the Relationship Between the Social Dance and Society in England from the Middle Ages to the Present Day*. London: Routledge.

7989 Savage, Jon. 1991. *England's Dreaming: Sex Pistols and Punk Rock*. London: Faber & Faber.

7990 Sharp, Cecil. 1907. *English Folk Song: Some Conclusions*. Taunton: Barnicott and Pearce.

7991 Smith, Giles. 1995. *Lost in Music*. London: Picador.

7992 Storch, Robert D., ed. 1982. *Popular Culture and Customs in Nineteenth-Century England*. London and Canberra: Croom Helm.

7993 Thornton, Sarah. 1995. *Club Cultures: Music, Media and Subcultural Capital*. Oxford: Polity.

7994 Walker, Edward S. and Walker, Steven, eds. 1971. *English Ragtime: A Discography*. Mastin Moor, Derby: Walker.

7995 Willis, Paul. 1974. Youth Groups in Birmingham and Their Specific Relation to Pop Music. In *New Patterns of Musical Behaviour*, ed. Irmgard Bontinck. Wien: Universal Edition. 108–13.

– Liverpool

7996 Braun, Michael. 1996. *Love Me Do*. Harmondsworth: Penguin.

7997 Cohen, Sara. 1991. Popular Music and Urban Regeneration: The Music Industries of Merseyside. *Cultural Studies* 5(3): 332–46.

7998 Cohen, Sara. 1991. *Rock Culture in Liverpool: Popular Music in the Making.* Oxford: Oxford University Press.

7999 Cohen, Sara. 1994. Identity, Place and the 'Liverpool Sound'. In *Ethnicity, Identity and Music: The Musical Construction of Place*, ed. Martin Stokes. Oxford: Berg. 117–34.

8000 Cohen, Sara. 1995. Popular Music in 20th Century Liverpool: A Case Study. In *Popular Music Perspectives III*, ed. Peter Wicke. Berlin: Zyankrise. 289–96.

8001 Cohen, Sara and McManus, Kevin. 1991. *Harmonious Relations: Popular Music and Family Life on Merseyside.* Liverpool: National Museums and Galleries on Merseyside.

8002 Epstein, Brian. 1981. (1964) *A Cellarful of Music.* London: New English Library. First published London: Souvenir Press, 1964.

8003 Harry, Bill, ed. 1977. *Mersey Beat: The Beginnings of the Beatles.* London: Omnibus.

8004 Jenkins, Tricia. 1995. *Let's Go Dancing: Dance Band Musicians of 1930s Liverpool.* Liverpool: Institute of Popular Music, University of Liverpool.

8005 Leigh, Spencer. 1984. *Let's Go Down the Cavern: The Story of Liverpool's Merseybeat.* London: Vermillion.

8006 McAleer, Dave. 1994. *Beatboom! Pop Go the Sixties.* London: Hamlyn.

8007 McCartney, Mike. 1981. *Thank U Very Much: Mike McCartney's Family Album.* London: Barker.

8008 McManus, Kevin. 1994. *Céilís, Jigs and Ballads: Irish Music in Liverpool.* Liverpool: Institute of Popular Music, University of Liverpool.

8009 McManus, Kevin. 1994. *'Nashville of the North': Country Music in Liverpool.* Liverpool: Institute of Popular Music, University of Liverpool.

8010 Seuss, Jürgen, Gerold Dommermuth and Hans Maier. 1965. *Beat in Liverpool.* Frankfurt am Main: Europäische Verlagsanstalt.

8011 Thompson, Phil. 1995. *The Best of Cellars: A History of the Cavern.* Liverpool: Bluecoat Press.

– London

8012 Back, Les. 1988. Coughing Up Fire: Sound Systems in South-East London. *New Formations* 5: 141–52.

8013 Burton, Peter. 1985. *Parallel Lives.* London: GMP Publishers.

8014 Cowley, John. 1990. London Is the Place: Caribbean Music in the Context of Empire, 1900–1960. In *Black Music in Britain: Essays on the Afro-Asian Contribution to Popular Music*, ed. Paul Oliver. Milton Keynes: Open University Press. 58–76.

8015 Fordham, John. 1986. *Let's Join Hands and Celebrate the Living: The Story of Ronnie Scott and His Club.* London: Elm Tree Books.

8016 Fordham, John. 1995. *Jazz Man: The Amazing Story of Ronnie Scott and His Club*, revised edition. London: Kyle Cathie. First published London: Elm Tree Books, 1986.

8017 Green, Jonathon. 1988. *Days in the Life: Voices from the English Underground, 1961–1971.* London: Heinemann.

8018 Grime, Kitty. 1979. *Jazz at Ronnie Scott's.* London: Robert Hale.

8019 Mayhew, Henry. 1967. *London Labour and the London Poor, Vols. 1–4.* London: Frank Cass. First published London: Griffin, Bohn & Co., 1861–62.

8020 Melly, George. 1966. *Owning Up.* London: MacGibbon and Kee.

8021 Platt, John. 1985. *London's Rock Routes*. London: Fourth Estate.

8022 Repsch, John. 1989. *The Legendary Joe Meek*. London: Woodford House.

8023 Savage, Jon. 1989. *England's Dreaming: The Sex Pistols and Punk Rock*. London: Faber & Faber.

8024 Schneider, Ulrich. 1984. *Die Londoner Music Hall und ihre Songs, 1850–1920*. Tübingen: Max Niemeyer.

8025 Stapleton, Chris. 1990. African Connections: London's Hidden Music Scene. In *Black Music in Britain: Essays on the Afro-Asian Contribution to Popular Music*, ed. Paul Oliver. Milton Keynes: Open University Press. 87–101.

8026 Summerfield, Penelope. 1981. The Effingham Arms and the Empire: Deliberate Selection in the Evolution of Music Hall in London. In *Popular Culture and Class Conflict, 1590–1914: Explorations in the History of Labour and Leisure*, ed. Eileen Yeo and Stephen Yeo. Brighton: Harvester Press. 209–40.

– *Manchester*

8027 Brown, Adam. 1991. Ratfink Reds: Montpellier and Rotterdam 1991. In *The Passion and the Fashion: Football Fandom in the New Europe*, ed. Steve Redhead. Aldershot: Avebury.

8028 Centre for Employment Research. 1989. *The Culture Industry: The Economic Importance of the Arts and Cultural Industries in Greater Manchester*. Manchester: Centre for Employment Research, Manchester Metropolitan University.

8029 Champion, Sarah. 1991. *And God Created Manchester*. Manchester: Wordsmith.

8030 Curtis, Deborah. 1995. *Touching from a Distance*. London: Faber.

8031 Lawson, Alan. n.d. *It Happened in Manchester: The Story of Manchester's Music, 1958–1965*. Bury: Multimedia.

8032 Redhead, Steve. 1991. *Rave Off: Politics and Deviance in Contemporary Youth Culture*. Aldershot: Avebury.

8033 Savage, Jon, ed. 1992. *The Hacienda Must Be Built*. London: International Music Publications.

8034 Savage, Jon. 1993. *England's Dreaming: The Sex Pistols and Punk Rock*. London: Faber & Faber.

8035 Spinoza, Andy, ed. 1992. *Sublime: The Sol Mix: Manchester Music and Design, 1976–1992*. Manchester: Cornerhouse.

Northern Ireland

8036 Graham, Len. 1994. *It's of My Rambles*. Belfast: Harvest Home/Arts Council of Northern Ireland.

8037 Power, Vincent. 1990. *Send 'Em Home Sweatin': The Showbands' Story*. Dublin: Kildanore Press.

8038 Wilson, David A. 1995. *Ireland, a Bicycle and a Tin Whistle*. Belfast and Toronto: Blackstaff Press and McGill-Queen's University Press.

Scotland

8039 Alburger, Mary Anne. 1983. *Scottish Fiddlers and Their Music*. London: Gollancz.

8040 Cooke, Peter. 1987. *The Fiddle Tradition in the Shetland Isles*. Cambridge: Cambridge University Press.

8041 Emmerson, George Sinclair. 1972. *A Social History of Scottish Dance*. Montréal: McGill-Queen's University Press.

8042 Hardie, Ian, ed. 1996. *The Nineties Collection: Contemporary Scottish Music*. Edinburgh: Mainstream.

LOCATIONS

8043 Henderson, Hamish. 1992. *Alias McAlias: Writings on Song, Folk and Literature*. Edinburgh: Polygon.

8044 Hogg, Brian. 1993. *The History of Scottish Rock and Pop: All That Ever Mattered*. London: Guinness.

8045 Imlach, Hamish and McVicker, Ewan. 1992. *Cod Liver Oil and the Orange Juice: Reminiscences of a Fat Folk Singer*. Edinburgh: Mainstream.

8046 Johnson, David. 1984. *Scottish Fiddle Music in the 18th Century: A Musical Collection and Historical Study*. Edinburgh: John Donald.

8047 Kane, Pat. 1992. *Tinsel Show: Pop, Politics and Scotland*. Edinburgh: Polygon.

8048 Lauder, Sir Harry. 1976. (1928) *Roamin' in the Gloamin'*. Wakefield: EP Publishing. First published London: Hutchinson, 1928.

8049 MacDonnel, Margaret. 1982. *The Emigrant Experience: Songs of Highland Emigrants in North America*. Toronto: University of Toronto Press.

8050 Munro, Ailie. 1984. *The Folk Music Revival in Scotland*. London: Kahn & Averill.

8051 Munro, Ailie. 1995. *Democratic Muse: The Folk Music Revival in Scotland*. Edinburgh: Scottish Cultural Press.

8052 Thomson, Raymond A. 1989. *Dance Bands and Dance Halls in Greenock, 1945–55*. Cambridge: Cambridge University Press.

Wales

8053 Crossley-Holland, Peter. 1980. Wales. In *The New Grove Dictionary of Music and Musicians, Vol. 20*, ed. Stanley Sadie. London: Macmillan. 159–71.

8054 Harper, John, ed. 1996. *Welsh Music History/Hanes Cerddoriaeth Cymru, Vol. 1*. Cardiff: University of Wales Press.

8055 Herbert, Trevor. 1988. The Virtuosi of Merthyr. *Llafur: The Journal of Welsh Labour History* 5(1): 60–67.

8056 Herbert, Trevor. 1990. The Repertory of a Victorian Brass Band. *Popular Music* 9(1): 117–32.

8057 Malm, Krister and Wallis, Roger. 1992. *Media Policy and Music Activity*. London: Routledge.

8058 Thomas, Wyn. 1982. *Cerddoriaeth Draddodiadol yng Nghymru: Llyfryddiaeth/A Bibliography: Traditional Music in Wales*. Cardiff: National Museum of Wales (Welsh Folk Museum).

8059 Wallis, Roger and Malm, Krister. 1983. Sain Cymru: The Role of the Welsh Record Industry in the Development of a Welsh-Language Pop/Rock/Folk Scene. *Popular Music* 3: 77–106.

8060 Williams, C. 1977. Non-Violence and the History of the Welsh Language Society. *Welsh History Review* 8(4): 426–55.

8061 Williams, Gareth. 1988. 'How's the Tenors in Dowlais?': Hegemony, Harmony and Popular Culture in England and Wales, 1600–1900. *Llafur: The Journal of Welsh Labour History* 5(1): 70–80.

THEORY AND METHOD

GENERAL WORKS

8062 Frith, Simon and Goodwin, Andrew, eds. 1990. *On Record: Rock, Pop and the Written Word.* London: Routledge.

8063 Horn, David and Tagg, Philip, eds. 1982. *Popular Music Perspectives: Papers from the First International Conference on Popular Music Research, Amsterdam, June 1981.* Göteborg and Exeter: IASPM.

8064 Horn, David, ed. 1985. *Popular Music Perspectives, 2: Papers from the Second International Conference on Popular Music Studies, Reggio Emilia, September 19–24, 1983.* Göteborg and Exeter: IASPM.

8065 Middleton, Richard. 1990. *Studying Popular Music.* Buckingham: Open University Press.

8066 Shuker, Roy. 1994. *Understanding Popular Music.* London: Routledge.

8067 Wicke, Peter, ed. 1995. *Popular Music Perspectives III: Papers from the Sixth International Conference on Popular Music Studies, Berlin, July 1991.* Berlin: Zyankrise.

AESTHETICS

8068 Agostini, Roberto. 1990. *Analizzare la 'popular music': Philip Tagg e l'analisi dell' 'affetto'.* Bologna: D.A.M.S., Facoltà di lettere e filosofia, Università degli Studii.

8069 Agostini, Roberto. 1992. Studiare la 'popular music'. In *Dal blues al liscio: Studi sull' esperienza musicale comune,* ed. Gino Stefani. Verona: Ianua. 167–89.

8070 Attali, Jacques. 1985. *Noise: The Political Economy of Music.* Manchester: Manchester University Press.

8071 Baugh, Bruce. 1993. Prolegomena to Any Aesthetics of Rock Music. *Journal of Aesthetics and Art Criticism* 51(1): 23–29.

8072 Baxter, Ed. 1987. The Setting of Value. *Re Records Quarterly* 2(1): 46–49.

8073 Behrens, Roger. 1996. *Pop Kultur Industrie. Zur Philosophie der populären Musik.* Würzburg: Königshausen & Neumann.

8074 Blacking, John. 1981. Making Artistic Popular Music: The Goal of True Folk. *Popular Music* 1: 9–14.

8075 Booth, Gregory D. 1994. Traditional Practice and Mass Mediated Music in India. *International Review of the Aesthetics and Sociology of Music* 24(2): 159–74.

8076 Brolinson, Per-Erik and Larsen, Holger. 1990. The Meaning of Rock: Some Problems Concerning the Aesthetics of Popular Music. In *Popular Music Research,* ed. Keith Roe and Ulla Karlsson. Göteborg: NORDICOM-Sweden, No. 1–2. 115–20.

8077 Brooks, William. 1982. On Being Tasteless. *Popular Music* 2: 9–18.

8078 Brown, M.P. 1994. Funk Music as Genre: Black Aesthetics, Apocalyptic Thinking and Urban Protest in Post-1965 African-American Pop. *Cultural Studies* 8(3): 484–508.

8079 Carducci, Joe. 1990. *Rock and the Pop Narcotic.* Chicago: Redoubt Press.

8080 Chester, Andrew. 1970. For a Rock Aesthetic. *New Left Review* 59: 82–86.

8081 Chester, Andrew. 1970. Second Thoughts on a Rock Aesthetic: The Band. *New Left Review* 62: 75–82.

8082 Clarke, Paul. 1983. A 'Magic Science': Rock Music as a Recording Art. *Popular Music* 3: 195–213.

8083 Corbett, John. 1994. *Extended Play: Sounding Off from John Cage to Dr. Funkenstein.* Urbana, IL: University of Illinois Press.

8084 Cutler, Chris. 1993. *File under Popular: Theoretical and Critical Writings on Music.* London: ReR Megacorp. First published London: November Books, 1985.

8085 Erlmann, Veit. 1995. Ideologie der Differenz: Zur Ästhetik der World Music. *PopScriptum* 3: 6–29.

8086 Feld, Steven. 1988. Aesthetics as Iconicity of Style, or 'Lift-Up-Over Sounding': Getting into the Kaluli Groove. *Yearbook for Traditional Music* 20: 74–113.

8087 Ferris, William R. 1970. The Blues Aesthetic. *Blues World* 43 (Summer).

8088 Fiori, Umberto. 1985. Popular Music: Theory, Practice, Value. In *Popular Music Perspectives, 2,* ed. David Horn. Göteborg and Exeter: IASPM. 13–23.

8089 Fiori, Umberto. 1987. Listening to Peter Gabriel's 'I Have The Touch'. *Popular Music* 6(1): 37–44.

8090 Flender, Reinhard and Rauhe, Hermann. 1989. *Popmusik: Geschichte, Funktion, Wirkung und Ästhetik.* Darmstadt: Wissenschaftliche Buchgesellschaft.

8091 Frith, Simon. 1986. Art Versus Technology: The Strange Case of Popular Music. *Media, Culture and Society* 8(3): 263–80.

8092 Frith, Simon. 1987. Towards an Aesthetic of Popular Music. In *Music and Society,* ed. Richard Leppert and Susan McClary. Cambridge: Cambridge University Press. 133–49.

8093 Frith, Simon. 1996. *Performing Rites: On the Value of Popular Music.* Oxford/ Cambridge, MA: Oxford University Press/Harvard University Press.

8094 Gioia, Ted. 1988. *The Imperfect Art: Reflections on Jazz and Modern Culture.* New York: Oxford University Press.

8095 Goodwin, Andrew. 1990. Sample and Hold: Pop Music in the Digital Age of Reproduction. In *On Record: Rock, Pop and the Written Word,* ed. Simon Frith and Andrew Goodwin. London: Routledge. 258–74.

8096 Gracyk, T.A. 1992. Adorno, Jazz, and the Aesthetics of Popular Music. *Musical Quarterly* 76(4): 526–42.

8097 Hosokawa, Shuhei. 1990. *Record no bigaku.* Tokyo: Keisô-shobô.

8098 Kealy, Edward R. 1982. Conventions and the Production of the Popular Music Aesthetic. *Journal of Popular Culture* 16(2): 100–15.

8099 Kneif, Tibor. 1977. Ästhetische und nichtästhetische Wertungskriterien der Rockmusik. In *Rockmusik,* ed. Wolfgang Sandner. Mainz: Schott. 101–12.

8100 Kriese, Konstanze. 1994. Rock 'n' Ritual. *PopScriptum* 2: 94–120.

8101 Levin, Theodore C. 1979. Music in Modern Uzbekistan: The Convergence of Marxist Aesthetics and Central Asian Tradition. *Asian Music* 12(1): 149–63.

8102 Loza, Steven, ed. 1994. *Musical Aesthetics and Multiculturism in Los Angeles.* Los Angeles: Selected Reports in Ethnomusicology, 10.

8103 Manuel, Peter. 1995. Music as Symbol, Music as Simulacrum: Postmodern, Pre-Modern, and Modern Aesthetics in Subcultural Popular Music. *Popular Music* 14(2): 227–309.

8104 Meltzer, Richard. 1987. (1970) *The Aesthetics of Rock*. New York: Alfred A. Knopf.

8105 Mischke, Jörg. 1992. Der Pluralismus der ästhetischen Erfahrung oder Wie postmodern ist populäre Musik? *PopScriptum* I(1): 89–95.

8106 Plas, Wim van der. 1985. Can Rock Be Art? In *Popular Music Perspectives, 2*, ed. David Horn. Göteborg and Exeter: IASPM. 397–404.

8107 Regev, Motti. 1995. Popular Music Studies: The Issue of Musical Value. In *Popular Music Perspectives III*, ed. Peter Wicke. Berlin: Zyankrise. 402–405.

8108 Simeon, Ennio. 1995. *Per un pugno di note. Storia, teoria, estetica della musica per il cinema, la televisione e il video*. Milano: Reggimenti.

8109 Slovenz, Madeline. 1988. 'Rock the House': The Aesthetic Dimension of Rap Music in New York City. *New York Folklore* 14(3–4): 151–64.

8110 Smith, Steven G. 1992. Blues and Our Mind-Body Problem. *Popular Music* 11(1): 41–52.

8111 Stefani, Gino. 1993. (1991) Prima dell' 'oggetto' e del 'discorso': l'esperienza musicale. In *Tendenze e metodi della ricerce musicologica*, ed. Raffaele Pozzi. Firenze: Olschki. 122–32.

8112 Tagg, Philip. 1982. Natur i massmediemusik. In *Natur som symbol*, ed. Jens Allwood, Tore Frängsmyr and Uno Svedin. Stockholm: Liber. 161–99.

8113 Wicke, Peter. 1981. Rockmusik - Aspekte einer Faszination. *Weimarer Beiträge* XXVII(9): 89–127.

8114 Wicke, Peter. 1982. Funktion und Wertform. Zu einer marxistschen Ästhetik der Musik. *Beiträge zur Musikwissenschaft* XXIV(2): 161–99.

8115 Wicke, Peter. 1982. Rock Music: A Musical-Aesthetic Study. *Popular Music* 2: 219–44.

8116 Wicke, Peter. 1982. Rock Music as a Phenomenon of Progressive Mass Culture. In *Popular Music Perspectives, 1*, ed. David Horn and Philip Tagg. Göteborg and Exeter: IASPM. 223–31.

8117 Wicke, Peter. 1985. La popularitá in musica. In *What Is Popular Music? 41 saggi, interventi, ricerche sulla musica di ogni giorno*, ed. Franco Fabbri. Milano: Edizioni Unicopli. 146–50.

8118 Wicke, Peter. 1985. Popularity in Music: Some Aspects of a Historical Materialist Theory for Popular Music. In *Popular Music Perspectives, 2*, ed. David Horn. Göteborg and Exeter: IASPM. 47–51.

8119 Wicke, Peter. 1985. Von der Aura der technisch produzierten Klanggestalt. Zur Ästhetik des Pop. In *Wegzeichen. Studien zur Musikwissenschaft*, ed. Peter Wicke and Jürgen Mainka. Berlin: Verlag Neue Musik. 276–89.

8120 Wicke, Peter. 1986. *Rockmusik. Zur Ästhetik und Soziologie eines Massenmeduims*. Leipzig: Reclam.

8121 Wicke, Peter. 1986. Theoretische Probleme der Produktion von Rockmusik. *Beilage zur Zeitschrift 'Unterhaltungskunst'* 3.

8122 Wicke, Peter. 1989. Rockmusik - Dimensionen eines Massenmediums. *Weimarer Beiträge* XXXV(6): 885–907.

8123 Wicke, Peter. 1990. Rock Music: Meaning Production Through Popular Music. *Canadian University Music Review/La revue musicale des universités canadiennes* 10(2): 137–57.

8124 Wicke, Peter. 1995. Popmusik - Konsumfetischismus oder kulturelles Widerstandspotential. In *Yesterday. Today. Tomorrow*, ed. M. Heuger and M. Prell. Regensburg: ConBrio Verlagsgesellschaft. 21–35.

8125 Wicke, Peter and Schneider, Frank. 1986. Popularität oder ästhetischer Anspruch? *Musik und Gesellschaft* XXXVI(3): 119–25.

HISTORIOGRAPHY

8126 Braun, D. Duane. 1969. *Toward a Theory of Popular Culture: The Sociology and History of American Music and Dance, 1920–1968.* Ann Arbor, MI: Ann Arbor Publications.

8127 Cantrick, Robert P. 1965. The Blind Men and the Elephants: Scholars on Popular Music. *Ethnomusicology* 9(2): 100–14.

8128 Chambers, Iain. 1982. Some Critical Tracks. *Popular Music* 2: 19–36.

8129 Floyd, Samuel A. 1991. Ring Shout! Literary Studies, Historical Studies, and Black Music Inquiry. *Black Music Research Journal* 11(2): 265–78.

8130 Floyd, Samuel A. 1993. Troping the Blues: From Spirituals to the Concert Hall. *Black Music Research Journal* 13(1): 31–51.

8131 Gammon, Vic. 1982. Problems of Method in the Historical Study of Popular Music. In *Popular Music Perspectives, 1,* ed. David Horn and Philip Tagg. Göteborg and Exeter: IASPM. 16–31.

8132 Harker, Dave. 1995. Popular Music Doesn't Matter. In *Popular Music Perspectives III,* ed. Peter Wicke. Berlin: Zyankrise. 451–66.

8132a Hartwich-Wiechell, Dörte. 1975. *Didaktik und Methodik der Popmusik.* Frankfurt am Main: Diesterweg.

8133 Jones, Gaynor and Rahn, Jay. 1981. Definitions of Popular Music: Recycled. In *Breaking the Sound Barrier: A Critical Anthology of the New Music,* ed. Gregory Battcock. New York: E.P. Dutton. 38–52.

8134 Karpeles, Maud. 1968. The Distinction Between Folk Music and Popular Music. *Journal of the International Folk Music Council* 20: 9–12.

8135 Kassabian, Anahid. 1995. Feminist Theory and the Study of Popular Music. In *Popular Music Perspectives III,* ed. Peter Wicke. Berlin: Zyankrise. 406–14.

8136 Kimiko, Ohtani. 1991. Japanese Approaches to the Study of Dance. *Yearbook for Traditional Music* 23: 23–32.

8137 Kneif, Tibor. 1982. *Rockmusik: Ein Handbuch zum kritischen Verständnis.* Reinbek bei Hamburg: Rowohlt.

8138 Kurkela, Vesa. 1995. Long-Term Fusion and Lost Traditions: Toward a Historiography of Finnish Popular Music. In *Popular Music Perspectives III,* ed. Peter Wicke. Berlin: Zyankrise. 297–304.

8139 Laing, Dave. 1989. L'acoltatore e la macchina: i più recenti studi marxisti sulla musica popolare in Inghilterra. *Quaderni di Musica/Realtà* 23: 132–46.

8140 Ling, Jan. 1985. Hvad er populærmusik? Refleksioner efter en kongres. *Modspil* 6(25): 12–21.

8141 Middleton, Richard. 1985. Articulating Musical Meaning/Re-Constructing Musical History/Locating the 'Popular'. *Popular Music* 5: 5–44.

8142 Middleton, Richard. 1985. Popular Music, Class Conflict and the Music-Historical Field. In *Popular Music Perspectives, 2,* ed. David Horn. Göteborg and Exeter: IASPM. 24–46.

8143 Minganti, Franco. 1995. Rock Steady! . . . But Study Rock, Too. Introduzione per un convegno. In *Annali Istituto Gramsci Emilia-Romagna 2/1995, dossier: Rock Steady/Rock Study: sulle culture del rock . . .,* ed. Franco Minganti. Bologna: Istituto Gramsci Emilia-Romagna. 107–11.

8144 Oliver, Paul. 1991. That Certain Feeling: Blues and Jazz in 1890? *Popular Music* 10(1): 11–19.

8145 Shepherd, John. 1985. Definition as Mystification: Labels as a Hindrance to Understanding Significance in Music. In *Popular Music Perspectives, 2*, ed. David Horn. Göteborg and Exeter: IASPM. 84–98.

8146 Shepherd, John. 1994. Music, Culture and Interdisciplinarity: Reflections on Relationships. *Popular Music* 13(2): 127–41.

8147 Shepherd, John. 1995. Popular Music Matters. In *Popular Music Perspectives III*, ed. Peter Wicke. Berlin: Zyankrise. 467–81.

8148 Tagg, Philip. 1989. Open Letter: 'Black Music', 'Afro-American Music' and 'European Music'. *Popular Music* 8(3): 285–98.

8149 Tegen, Martin. 1985. Changing Concepts of Western Popular Music Before and After 1900. In *Popular Music Perspectives, 2*, ed. David Horn. Göteborg and Exeter: IASPM. 340–45.

8150 Thornton, Sarah. 1990. Strategies for Reconstructing the Popular Past. *Popular Music* 9(1): 87–96.

8151 Vega, Carlos. 1966. 'Mesomusic': An Essay on the Music of the Masses. *Ethnomusicology* 10(1): 1–17.

8152 Wicke, Peter. 1984. Populäre Musik als Problem der Musikhistoriographie. *Beiträge zur Musikwissenshaft* XXVI(3/4): 208–13.

8153 Wicke, Peter. 1985. Populäre Musik in der Literatur: Aspekte - Tendenzen - Probleme. *Beiträge zur Musikwissenschaft* 3–4: 199–240.

8154 Wicke, Peter. 1985. Popularity in Music: Some Aspects of a Historical Materialist Theory for Popular Music. In *Popular Music Perspectives, 2*, ed. David Horn. Göteborg and Exeter: IASPM. 47–51.

8155 No entry.

MUSICOLOGY

8156 Agostini, Roberto. 1992. Studiare la 'popular music'. In *Dal blues al liscio: Studi sull'esperienza musicale comune*, ed. Gino Stefani. Verona: Ianua. 169–89.

8157 Behrens, Roger. 1996. *Pop Kultur Industrie: Zur Philosophie der populären Musik*. Würzburg: Königshausen & Neumann.

8158 Blacking, John. 1978. Some Problems of Theory and Method in the Study of Musical Change. *Yearbook of the International Folk Music Council* 9: 1–26.

8159 Brackett, David. 1992. James Brown's 'Superbad' and the Double-Voiced Utterance. *Popular Music* 11(3): 309–24.

8160 Brackett, David. 1995. *Interpreting Popular Music*. Cambridge: Cambridge University Press.

8161 Brett, Philip, Gary Thomas and Elizabeth Wood, eds. 1994. *Queering the Pitch: The New Gay and Lesbian Musicology*. London: Routledge.

8162 Djedje, Jacqueline Cogdell and Carter, William G., eds. 1989. *African Musicology: Current Trends, Vol. 1*. Los Angeles: University of California Press.

8163 Fabbri, Franco. 1991. Analizzare la popular music: perché? In *L'analisi musicale*, ed. Rossana Dalmonte and Mario Baroni. Milano: Unicopli. 84–95.

8164 Födermayr, Franz. 1985. Popularmusik als Gegenstand musikwissenschaftlicher Forschung. Ein hermeneutischer Versuch. *Musicologica Austriaca* 5: 49–84.

8165 Hawkins, Stan. 1994. *Lost in Music: Problems Facing Musicologists. Popular Musicology* 1: 6–8.

8166 Hawkins, Stan. 1995. Towards New Analytical Methodologies in Popular Music. In *Popular Music Perspectives III*, ed. Peter Wicke. Berlin: Zyankrise. 340–50.

8167 Hawkins, Stan. 1996. Perspectives in Popular Musicology: Music, Lennox and Meaning in 1990s Pop. *Popular Music* 15(1): 17–36.

8168 Hennion, Antoine. 1983. The Production of Success: An Anti-Musicology of the Pop Song. *Popular Music* 3: 159–93.

8169 Kaufmann, Dorothea. 1991. 'Wenn Damen pfeifen, gehen die Gracien flöten'. Die Musikerin in der deutschen Tanz- und Unterhaltungsmusik des 19. Jahrhunderts. *Worldbeat* 1: 81–94.

8170 Keil, Charles and Feld, Steven. 1994. *Music Grooves: Essays and Dialogues*. Chicago: University of Chicago Press.

8171 Le jazz est-il un objet d'analyse? 1995. *Musurgia* 2(3).

8172 Lomax, Alan. 1968. *Folk Song Style and Culture: A Staff Report on Cantometrics*. New Brunswick, NJ: Transaction.

8173 Lomax, Alan. 1976. *Cantometrics: An Approach to the Anthropology of Music*. Berkeley, CA: University of California Extension Media Center.

8174 McClary, Susan. 1991. *Feminine Endings: Music, Gender and Sexuality*. Minneapolis, MN: University of Minnesota Press.

8175 McClary, Susan and Leppert, Richard, eds. 1987. *Music and Society: The Politics of Composition, Performance and Reception*. Cambridge: Cambridge University Press.

8176 McClary, Susan and Walser, Robert. 1990. (1988) Start Making Sense!: Musicology Wrestles with Rock. In *On Record: Rock, Pop and the Written Word*, ed. Simon Frith and Andrew Goodwin. London: Routledge. 277–92.

8177 Menezes Bastos, Rafael José de. 1995. Esboco de una Teoria da Musica: Para Alem de una Antropologia Sem Musica e de una Musicologia Sem Homem. *Anuario Antropologico*: 9–73.

8178 Metfessel, Milton. 1981. (1926) *Phonophotography in Folk Music: American Negro Songs in New Notation*. Durham, NC: University of North Carolina Press.

8179 Middleton, Richard. 1985. Articulating Musical Meaning/Re-constructing Musical History/Locating the 'Popular'. *Popular Music* 5: 5–43.

8180 Middleton, Richard. 1992. Toward a Theory of Gesture in Popular Song Analysis. In *Secondo Convegno Europeo di Analisi Musicale, Vol. I*, ed. Rossana Dalmonte and Mario Baroni. Trento: Università di Trento. 345–50.

8181 Middleton, Richard. 1993. Popular Music Analysis and Musicology: Bridging the Gap. *Popular Music* 12(2): 177–90.

8182 Moore, Allan F. 1993. *Rock: The Primary Text*. Buckingham: Open University Press.

8183 Robinette, Richard. 1980. *Historical Perspectives on Popular Music*. Dubuque, IA: Kendall/Hunt.

8184 Schoenebeck, Mechthild von. 1987. *Was macht Musik populär? Untersuchungen zu Theorie und Geschichte der populären Musik*. Frankfurt am Main/Bern/New York/Paris: Peter Lang.

8185 Seeger, Charles. 1960. On the Moods of a Music-Logic. *Journal of the American Musicological Society* 13: 224–61.

8186 Shepherd, John. 1982. A Theoretical Model for the Sociomusicological Analysis of Popular Musics. *Popular Music* 2: 145–77.

8187 Shepherd, John. 1988. *La musica come sapere sociale*. Milano: Ricordi/Unicopli.

8188 Shepherd, John. 1991. *Music as Social Text*. Cambridge: Polity.

8189 Shepherd, John. 1992. Warum Popmusikforschung? *PopScriptum* I(1): 43–67.

8190 Shepherd, John. 1993. Popular Music Studies: Challenges to Musicology. *Stanford Humanities Review* 3(2): 17–35.

8191 Shepherd, John. 1995. Popular Music Matters. In *Popular Music Perspectives III*, ed. Peter Wicke. Berlin: Zyankrise. 467–81.

8192 Slobin, Mark. 1992. Micromusic of the West: A Comparative Approach. *Ethnomusicology* 36(1): 1–87.

8193 Statelova, Rosemary. 1994. Das Elementare. *PopScriptum* 2: 82–93.

8194 Stefani, Gino. 1995. Studi (popolari) sulla Musica. In *Annali Istituto Gramsci Emilia-Romagna 2/1994, dossier: Rock Steady/Rock Study: sulle culture del rock ...*, ed. Franco Minganti. Bologna: Istituto Gramsci Emilia-Romagna. 150–57.

8195 Stillman, Amy Ku'uleialoha. 1995. Of What Use Are Published Hawaiian Songbooks? *Perfect Beat* 2(2): 64–82.

8196 Tagg, Philip. 1995. Vers une musicologie de la télévision. In *Frank Martin, musique et esthetique musicale. Actes du colloque de La Chaux-de-Fonds 1990*, ed. Eric Emery. Neuchatel: Revue Musicale de Suisse Romande. 33–60.

8197 Wicke, Peter. 1975. Versuch über populäre Musik. *Beiträge zur Musikwissenschaft* XV(4): 225–41.

8198 Wicke, Peter. 1980. Ein methodologischer Versuch über musikalische Massenkultur. *Wissenschaftliche Zeitschrift der Humboldt-Universität, Gesellschaftswissenschaftliche Reihe* 1: 95–99.

8199 Wicke, Peter. 1983. Pokus a teorii populárni hudby. *Opus Musicum* XV(8): 11–23.

8200 Wicke, Peter. 1983. Versuch zu einer Theorie der populären Musik. *Beilage zur Zeitschrift 'Unterhaltungskunst'* 3(4).

8201 Wicke, Peter. 1985. Populäre Musik in der Literatur. Ein Forschungsbericht. *Beiträge zur Musikwissenschaft* XXVII (1/2): 167–91.

8202 Wicke, Peter. 1986. Populäre Musik. Begriff und Konzept. *Beilage zur Zeitschrift 'Unterhaltungskunst'* 3.

8203 Wicke, Peter. 1992. Populäre Musik als theoretisches Konzept. *PopScriptum* 1: 6–42.

SEMIOTICS

8204 Alencar-Pinto, Guilherme de. 1985. Análisis: *Deus lhe pague. La del taller* 4 (December): 19–26.

8205 Björnberg, Alf. 1992. Music Video and the Semiotics of Popular Music. In *Secondo Convegno Europeo di Analisi Musicale, Vol. I*, ed. Rossana Dalmonte and Mario Baroni. Trento: Università di Trento. 378–88.

8206 Björnberg, Alf. 1994. Structural Relationship of Music and Images in Music Video. *Popular Music* 13(1): 51–73.

8207 Boiles, Charles. 1975. La signification dans la musique de film. *Musique en Jeu* 19: 69–85.

8208 Bradby, Barbara and Torode, Brian. 1984. Pity Peggy Sue. *Popular Music* 4: 183–206.

8209 Brofsky, Howard. 1994. Response to Robert Walser's 'Out of Notes: Signification, Interpretation, and the Problem of Miles Davis'. *Musical Quarterly* 78(2): 417.

8210 Cano, Cristina and Cremonini, Giorgio. 1990. *Cinema e musica. Il racconto per sovrapposizioni*. Bologna: Thema.

8211 Chafee, Steven. 1985. Popular Music and Communication Research: An Editorial Epilogue. *Communication Research* 12(3): 413–24.

8212 Cook, Nicholas. 1994. Music and Meaning in the Commercial. *Popular Music* 13(1): 27–40.

8213 Cook, Nicholas. 1995. *Analysing Musical Multimedia*. Oxford: Oxford University Press.

8214 Cubitt, Sean. 1984. 'Maybellene': Meaning and the Listening Subject. *Popular Music* 4: 207–24.

8215 Dunbar-Hall, Peter. 1991. Semiotics as a Method for the Study of Popular Music. *International Review of the Aesthetics and Sociology of Music* 22(2): 127–32.

8216 Fabbri, Franco. 1982. A Theory of Musical Genres: Two Applications. In *Popular Music Perspectives, 1*, ed. David Horn and Philip Tagg. Göteborg and Exeter: IASPM. 52–81.

8217 Fabbri, Franco. 1982. What Kind of Music? *Popular Music* 2: 131–43.

8218 Fabbri, Franco. 1983. Musical Genres and Their Metalanguages. *International Society for Music Education Yearbook* 10: 24–30.

8219 Fabbri, Franco, ed. 1985. *What Is Popular Music? 41 saggi, ricerche, interventi sulla musica di ogni giorno*. Milano: Unicopli.

8220 Fabbri, Franco. 1989. I generi musicali: una questione di riaprire. *Quaderni di Musica/Realtà* 23: 11–33.

8221 Feld, Steven. 1982. *Sound and Sentiment: Birds, Weeping and Poetics in Kaluli Expression*. Philadelphia: University of Pennsylvania Press.

8222 Fiori, Umberto. 1996. 'In un supremo anelito'. L'idea di poesia nella canzone italiana. In *Analisi e canzoni*, ed. Rossana Dalmonte. Trento: Università di Trento. 145–59.

8223 Galden, Manfred P. 1985. 'Popular Music' in the Terminology of Communication and Information Theory. In *Popular Music Perspectives, 2*, ed. David Horn. Göteborg and Exeter: IASPM. 106–18.

8224 Golianek, Ryszard Daniel. 1992. The Concept of Musical Dramaturgy in Soviet Musicological Research. In *Secondo Convegno Europeo di Analisi Musicale, Vol. I*, ed. Rossana Dalmonte and Mario Baroni. Trento: Università di Trento. 407–12.

8225 Hawkins, Stan. 1995. New Perspectives in Musicology: Musical Structures, Codes and Meaning in 1990s Pop. In *Popular Music: Style and Identity*, ed. Will Straw, et al. Montréal: The Centre for Research on Canadian Cultural Industries and Institutions. 131–36.

8226 Hustwitt, Mark. 1984. Rocker Boy Blues. *Screen* 25(3) (May-June): 89–98.

8227 Johnson, Bruce. 1994. Klactoveesedstene: Music, Soundscape and Me. In *Soundscapes: Essays on Vroom and Moo*, ed. Helmi Järviluoma. Tampere: Department of Folk Tradition. 39–47.

8228 Kohl, Paul R. 1993. Looking Through a Glass Onion: Rock and Roll as Modern Manifestation of Carnival. *Journal of Popular Culture* 27(1): 143–62.

8229 Locatelli, Carla. 1996. Musica e società nella storia del rap: 'non un tentativo di vendita; è un tentativo di presa di parola'. In *Analisi e canzoni*, ed. Rossana Dalmonte. Trento: Università di Trento. 103–24.

8230 Miceli, Sergio. 1982. *La musica nel film. Arte e artigianato*. Firenze: Discanto/Nuova Italia.

8231 Miceli, Sergio, ed. 1990. *Chigiana XLII(22) (Atti del Convegno Internazionale di Studi 'Musica & Cinema')*. Firenze: Olschki.

8232 Miceli, Sergio. 1994. Analizzare la musica per film. Una risposta dalla teoria dei livelli. *Rivista Italiana di Musicologia* 29(2): 517–44.

8233 Miceli, Sergio. 1994. *Morricone, la musica, il cinema*. Milano: Ricordi/Mucchi.

8234 Middleton, Richard. 1981. 'Reading' Popular Music. In *Form and Meaning (2)*. Milton Keynes: Open University Press. 4–41.

8235 Middleton, Richard. 1986. In the Groove, or Blowing Your Mind? The Pleasures of Musical Repetition. In *Popular Culture and Social Relations*, ed. Tony Bennett and Janet Woollacott. Milton Keynes: Open University Press. 159–76.

8236 Monson, Ingrid. 1994. Doubleness and Jazz Improvisation: Irony, Parody and Ethnomusicology. *Critical Inquiry* 20(2): 283–313.

8237 Montecchi, Giordano. 1996. Aspetti di intertestualità nella musica rock degli anni Sessanta. In *Analisi e canzoni*, ed. Rossana Dalmonte. Trento: Università di Trento. 39–57.

8238 Pasolini, Pier Paolo. 1979. La musica del film. In *Teoria e tecnica del film in Pasolini*, ed. A. Bertini. Roma: Bulzoni. 169–75.

8239 Perlman, Alan M. and Greenblatt, Daniel. 1981. Miles Davis Meets Noam Chomsky: Some Observations on Jazz Improvisation and Language Structure. In *The Sign in Music and Literature*, ed. Wendy Steiner. Austin, TX: University of Texas Press. 169–83.

8240 Prato, Paolo. 1992. La censura e il piacere: tra sociologia e musicologia. *Musica/Realtà* 37: 65–77.

8241 Prato, Paolo. 1995. Teoria e metodi della critica rock. In *Annali Istituto Gramsci Emilia-Romagna 2/1995, dossier: Rock Steady/Rock Study: sulle culture del rock . . .*, ed. Franco Minganti. Bologna: Istituto Gramsci Emilia-Romagna. 130–49.

8242 Radano, Ronald M. 1994. *New Musical Figurations: Anthony Braxton's Cultural Critique*. Chicago and London: University of Chicago Press.

8243 Simeon, Ennio. 1987. La nascita di una drammaturgia della musica per film: il ruolo di Giuseppe Becce. *Musica/Realtà* 24: 103–20.

8244 Simeon, Ennio. 1992. Programmi narrativi e stratificazioni di senso nella musica per film. Il caso di 'Entr'acte'. In *Secondo Convegno Europeo di Analisi Musicale, Vol. I*, ed. Rossana Dalmonte and Mario Baroni. Trento: Università di Trento. 389–99.

8245 Simeon, Ennio. 1992. Proposte per una teoria analitica di tipo narratologico applicata alla musica da film. 'Mission' di Joffé - Morricone. *Cinema* 102: 18–27.

8246 Simeon, Ennio. 1995. *Per un pugno di note: Storia, teoria, estetica della musica per il cinema, la televisione e il video*. Milano: Reggimenti.

8247 Stefani, Gino. 1976. Denotazione e connotazione nei caroselli. In *Introduzione alla semiotica della musica*. Palermo: Sellerio. 200–11.

8248 Stefani, Gino. 1976. 'E la vita, la vita'. La canzone cioè l'evasione? In *Introduzione alla semiotica della musica*. Palermo: Sellerio. 159–67. (First published in *Nuova Rivista Musicale Italiana* 1 (1975): 97–105.)

8249 Stefani, Gino. 1977. Codice popolare e codice colto. In *Insegnare la musica*. Firenze: Guaraldi. 27–38.

8250 Stefani, Gino. 1982. *Il linguaggio della musica*. Roma: Edizioni Paoline.

8251 Stefani, Gino. 1982. *La competenza musicale*. Bologna: Clueb.

8252 Stefani, Gino. 1985. La melodia: una prospettiva popolare. *Musica/Realtà* 17: 105–24.

8253 Stefani, Gino. 1987. *Il segno della musica: Saggi di semiotica musicale*. Palermo: Sellerio.

8254 Stefani, Gino. 1989. L'arte di arrangiarsi in musica. In *Musica con coscienza*. Cinisello Balsamo: Edizioni Paoline. 30–56. (First published in *Carte Semiotiche* 2 (1986): 97–114.)

8255 Stefani, Gino. 1989. *Musica con coscienza*. Cinisello Balsamo: Edizioni Paoline.

8256 Stefani, Gino. 1993. (1991) Prima dell' 'oggetto' e del 'discorso': l'esperienza musicale. In *Tendenze e metodi della ricerce musicologica*, ed. Raffaele Pozzi. Firenze: Olschki. 122–32.

8257 Stefani, Gino. 1995. Studi(popolari) sulla musica. In *Annali Istituto Gramsci Emilia-Romagna 2/1995, dossier: Rock Steady/Rock Study: sulle culture del rock . . .*, ed. Franco Minganti. Bologna: Istituto Gramsci Emilia-Romagna. 150–57.

8258 Tagg, Philip. 1979. *Kojak: 50 Seconds of Television Music. Towards the Analysis of Affect in Popular Music*. Göteborg: Skrifter från Göteborgs universitet, Musikvetenskapliga institutionen, 2.

8259 Tagg, Philip. 1981. The Analysis of Theme Tunes as a Method of Decoding Implicit Ideologies in the Mass Media. In *Mass Communications & Culture*, 5, ed. Gunnar Andrén and Hans Strand. Stockholm: Akademi Litteratur. 90–105.

8260 Tagg, Philip. 1982. Analysing Popular Music: Theory, Method and Practice. *Popular Music* 2: 37–67.

8261 Tagg, Philip. 1984. Understanding 'Time Sense': Concepts, Sketches, Consequences. In *Tvärspel: 31 artiklar om musik. Festskrift till Jan Ling*. Göteborg: Skrifter från Musikvetenskapliga institutionen, 9. 21–43.

8262 Tagg, Philip. 1985. La musicologie et la sémantique de la musique populaire. In *Analytica: Studies in the Description and Analysis of Music*. Stockholm: Kungliga Musikaliska Akademien. 77–96.

8263 Tagg, Philip. 1987. Musicology and the Semiotics of Popular Music. *Semiotica* 66(1–3): 279–98.

8264 Tagg, Philip. 1988. Musiken som kommunikationsform. In *Kulturmöten, kommunikation, skola*, ed. Sven Strömqvist and Göran Strömqvist. Stockholm: Nordstedts. 133–53.

8265 Tagg, Philip. 1989. Musica popolare, innovazione, tecnologia. *Quaderni di Musica/Realtà* 23: 34–43.

8266 Tagg, Philip. 1990. Music for Moving Pictures: Academia, Education and Independent Thought. In *Chigiana XLII(22) (Atti del Convegno Internazionale di Studi 'Musica & Cinema')*, ed. Sergio Miceli. Firenze: Olschki. 351–80.

8267 Tagg, Philip. 1990. Music in Mass Media Studies: Reading Sounds, For Example. In *Popular Music Research*, ed. Keith Roe and Ulla Karlsson. Göteborg: NORDICOM-Sweden, No. 1–2. 103–14.

8268 Tagg, Philip. 1990. Reading Sounds. *Re Records Quarterly* 3(2): 4–11.

8269 Tagg, Philip. 1991. *Fernando the Flute: Analysis of Musical Meaning in an Abba Mega-Hit.* Liverpool: Institute of Popular Music, University of Liverpool.

8270 Tagg, Philip. 1992. Toward a Sign Typology in Music. In *Secondo Convegno Europeo di Analisi Musicale, Vol. I,* ed. Rossana Dalmonte and Mario Baroni. Trento: Università di Trento. 369–78.

8271 Tagg, Philip. 1993. 'Universal' Music and the Case of Death. In *La musica come linguaggio universale. Genesi e storia di un'idea,* ed. Raffaele Pozzi. Firenze: Olschki. 227–65.

8272 Tagg, Philip. 1994. From Refrain to Rave: The Decline of Figure and the Rise of Ground. *Popular Music* 13(2): 209–22.

8273 Tagg, Philip. 1994. *Popular Music: Da Kojak al Rave,* ed. Roberto Agostini and Luca Marconi. Bologna: Clueb.

8274 Tagg, Philip. 1994. Subjectivity and Soundscape, Motorbikes and Music. In *Soundscapes: Essays on Vroom and Moo,* ed. Helmi Järviluoma. Tampere: Department of Folk Tradition. 48–66.

8275 Tagg, Philip. 1995. Dal ritornello al 'rave': tramonta la figura emerge lo sfondo. In *Annali Istituto Gramsci Emilia-Romagna 2/1995, dossier: Rock Steady/ Rock Study: sulle culture del rock . . .,* ed. Franco Minganti. Bologna: Istituto Gramsci Emilia-Romagna. 158–75.

8276 Walser, Robert. 1993. Out of Notes: Signification, Interpretation and the Problem of Miles Davis. *Musical Quarterly* 77(2): 343–65.

8277 Walser, Robert. 1995. Rhythm, Rhyme and Rhetoric in the Music of Public Enemy. *Ethnomusicology* 39(2): 193–217.

SOCIOLOGY

8278 Adorno, Theodor W. 1932. Zur gesellschaftlichen Lage der Musik. *Zeitschrift für Sozialforschung* 1/2, 3: 103–24, 356–78.

8279 Adorno, Theodor W. 1955. Zeitlose Mode: Zum Jazz. In *Prismen,* ed. Theodor W. Adorno. Frankfurt am Main: Suhrkamp. 123–37.

8280 Adorno, Theodor W. 1956. Fetischcharakter in der Musik und die Regression des Hörens. In *Dissonanzen.* Göttingen: Vadenhoeck & Ruprecht. (First published in *Zeitschrift für Sozialforschung* VII (1938).)

8281 Adorno, Theodor W. 1962. *Einleitung in die Musiksoziologie: Zwölf theoretische Vorlesungen.* Frankfurt am Main: Suhrkamp.

8282 Adorno, Theodor W. 1964. Über Jazz. In *Moments musicaux,* ed. Theodor W. Adorno. Frankfurt am Main: Suhrkamp.

8283 Adorno, Theodor W. 1967. Perennial Fashion: Jazz. In *Prisms,* ed. Theodor W. Adorno. London: Neville Spearman. First published Frankfurt am Main: Suhrkamp, 1955.

8284 Adorno, Theodor W. 1967. Resume über Kulturindustrie. In *Ohne Leitbild. Parva Aesthetica,* ed. Theodor W. Adorno. Frankfurt am Main: Suhrkamp.

8285 Adorno, Theodor W. 1975. Culture Industry Reconsidered. *New German Critique* 6: 12–19. First published Frankfurt am Main: Suhrkamp, 1967.

8286 Adorno, Theodor W. 1976. *Introduction to the Sociology of Music.* New York: Seabury Press. First published Frankfurt am Main: Suhrkamp, 1962.

8287 Adorno, Theodor W. 1978. On the Social Situation of Music. *Telos* 35 (Spring): 128–64. (First published in *Zeitschrift für Sozialforschung* 1/2, 3 (1932): 103–24, 356–78.)

THEORY AND METHOD

8288 Adorno, Theodor W. and Simpson, George. 1941. On Popular Music. *Studies in Philosophy and Social Sciences* 9: 17–48.

8289 Alaja-Browne, Afolabi. 1991. On Music, Emotions and Mobilization. *Worldbeat* 1: 47–54.

8290 Attali, Jacques. 1985. *Noise: The Political Economy of Music.* Manchester: Manchester University Press.

8291 Ballantine, Christopher. 1995. 'Gateway to Liberty': Reflections on the Social Role of Black South African Jazz and Vaudeville Before the Mid-1940s. In *Popular Music Perspectives III*, ed. Peter Wicke. Berlin: Zyankrise. 305–11.

8292 Beaud, Paul. 1982. Et si l'on reparlait d'Adorno? In *Popular Music Perspectives, 1*, ed. David Horn and Philip Tagg. Göteborg and Exeter: IASPM. 82–92.

8293 Beaud, Paul and Willener, Alfred, eds. 1973. *Musique et vie quotidienne: Essai de sociologie d'une nouvelle culture.* Paris: Mame.

8294 Blaukopf, Kurt. 1979. The Sociography of Musical Life: A Research Task. *The World of Music* 21(3): 78–82.

8295 Bloomfield, Terry. 1993. Resisting Songs: Negative Dialectics in Pop. *Popular Music* 12(1): 13–31.

8296 Born, Georgina. 1987. Modern Music Cultures: On Shock, Pop and Synthesis. *New Formations* 2: 51–78.

8297 Bradley, Dick. 1981. Music and Social Science: A Survey. *Media, Culture and Society* 3(3): 205–18.

8298 Braun, D. Duane. 1969. *Toward a Theory of Popular Culture: The Sociology and History of American Music and Dance, 1920–1968.* Ann Arbor, MI: Ann Arbor Publications.

8299 Cook, Lez. 1983. Popular Culture and Rock Music. *Screen* 24(3): 44–49.

8300 Cutler, Chris. 1985. *File under Popular: Theoretical and Critical Writings on Music.* London: November Books.

8301 Denisoff, R. Serge and Levine, Mark H. 1971. The One-Dimensional Approach to Popular Music: A Research Note. *Journal of Popular Culture* 4(4): 911–19.

8302 Durant, Alan. 1985. Rock Revolution or Time-No-Changes: Visions of Change and Continuity in Rock Music. *Popular Music* 5: 97–122.

8303 Etzkorn, K. Peter. 1969. Die Verwundbarkeit von Berufen und der soziale Wandel. Das Beispiel der Schlagerkomponisten. *Kölner Zeitschrift für Soziologie und Sozialpsychologie* XXI(3): 529–42.

8304 Frith, Simon. 1981. 'The Magic That Can Set You Free': The Ideology of Folk and the Myth of the Rock Community. *Popular Music* 1: 159–68.

8305 Frith, Simon. 1982. The Sociology of Rock: Notes from Britain. In *Popular Music Perspectives, 1*, ed. David Horn and Philip Tagg. Göteborg and Exeter: IASPM. 142–53.

8306 Frith, Simon. 1986. Art Versus Technology: The Strange Case of Popular Music. *Media, Culture and Society* 8(3) (July).

8307 Frith, Simon. 1988. Art Ideology and Pop Practice. In *Marxism and the Interpretation of Culture*, ed. Lawrence Grossberg and Cary Nelson. Urbana, IL: University of Illinois Press. 461–76.

8308 Frith, Simon. 1992. The Cultural Study of Popular Music. In *Cultural Studies*, ed. Lawrence Grossberg, Cary Nelson and Paula A. Treichler. New York and London: Routledge. 174–86.

8309 Frith, Simon. 1996. *Performing Rites: On the Value of Popular Music.* Oxford/ Cambridge, MA: Oxford University Press/Harvard University Press.

8310 Garofalo, Reebee. 1987. How Autonomous Is Relative?: Popular Music, the Social Formation and Cultural Struggle. *Popular Music* 6(1): 77–92.

8311 Gendron, Bernard. 1986. Theodor Adorno Meets the Cadillacs. In *Studies in Entertainment: Critical Approaches to Mass Culture*, ed. Tania Modleski. Bloomington, IN: Indiana University Press. 18–38.

8312 Goodwin, Andrew. 1991. Popular Music and Postmodern Theory. *Cultural Studies* 5(2): 174–90.

8313 Grenier, Line and Guilbault, Jocelyne. 1990. 'Authority' Revisited: The 'Other' in Anthropology and Popular Music Studies. *Ethnomusicology* 34(3): 381–97.

8314 Grossberg, Lawrence. 1992. *We Gotta Get Out of This Place: Popular Conservatism and Postmodern Culture*. New York: Routledge.

8315 Grossberg, Lawrence. 1995. C'è nessuno in ascolto? Frega niente a nessuno? Note sullo 'stato del rock'. In *Annali Istituto Gramsci Emilia-Romagna 2/1995, dossier: Rock Steady/Rock Study: sulle culture del rock . . .*, ed. Franco Minganti. Bologna: Istituto Gramsci Emilia-Romagna. 112–29.

8316 Harker, Dave. 1995. Popular Music Doesn't Matter. In *Popular Music Perspectives III*, ed. Peter Wicke. Berlin: Zyankrise. 451–66.

8317 Hennion, Antoine. 1982. Popular Music as Social Production. In *Popular Music Perspectives, 1*, ed. David Horn and Philip Tagg. Göteborg and Exeter: IASPM. 32–40.

8318 Hennion, Antoine. 1983. The Production of Success: An Anti-Musicology of the Pop-Song. *Popular Music* 3: 159–93.

8319 Hennion, Antoine. 1993. *La Passion musicale. Une sociologie de la médiation*. Paris: Métailié.

8320 Horn, David. 1995. Instituting Popular Music Studies. In *Popular Music Perspectives III*, ed. Peter Wicke. Berlin: Zyankrise. 392–401.

8321 Kassabian, Anahid. 1995. Feminist Theory and the Study of Popular Music. In *Popular Music Perspectives III*, ed. Peter Wicke. Berlin: Zyankrise. 406–14.

8322 Lewis, George L. 1983. The Meaning's in the Music and the Music's in Me: Popular Music as Symbolic Communication. *Theory, Culture & Society: Explorations in Critical Social Science* 1(3): 133–41.

8323 Longhurst, Brian. 1995. *Popular Music and Society*. Oxford: Polity.

8324 Lull, James, ed. 1992. *Popular Music & Communication*, 2nd edition. Newbury Park, CA: Sage.

8325 Maróthy, János. 1974. *Music of the Bourgeois, Music of the Proletarian*. Budapest: Akadémiai Kiadó.

8326 Maróthy, János. 1981. A Music of Your Own. *Popular Music* 1: 15–25.

8327 Martin, Peter J. 1995. *Sounds and Society: Themes in the Sociology of Music*. Manchester: Manchester University Press.

8328 Nanry, Charles. 1972. Jazz and All That Sociology. In *American Music: From Storyville to Woodstock*, ed. Charles Nanry. New Brunswick, NJ: Transaction. 168–86.

8329 Nketia, J.H. Kwabena. 1981. The Juncture of the Social and the Musical: The Methodology of Cultural Analysis. *The World of Music* 23(2): 22–35.

8330 Peterson, Richard A. 1971. Taking Popular Music Too Seriously. *Journal of Popular Culture* 4(3): 590–94.

8331 Peterson, Richard A. 1972. *A Process Model of the Folk, Pop and Fine Art Phases of Jazz*. New Brunswick, NJ: Transaction.

8332 Peterson, Richard A. 1990. Why 1955? Explaining the Advent of Rock Music. *Popular Music* 9(1): 97–116.

8333 Peterson, Richard A. and Berger, David G. 1975. Cycles in Symbol Production: The Case of Popular Music. *American Sociological Review* 40: 158–73.

8334 Pickering, Michael and Green, Tony, eds. 1987. *Everyday Culture: Popular Song and the Vernacular Milieu*. Milton Keynes: Open University Press.

8335 Root, Robert L., Jr. 1986. A Listener's Guide to the Rhetoric of Popular Music. *Journal of Popular Culture* 20(1): 15–26.

8336 Shepherd, John. 1982. A Theoretical Model for the Sociomusicological Analysis of Popular Musics. *Popular Music* 2: 145–77.

8337 Shepherd, John. 1985. Prolegomeni allo studio critico della popular music. *Musica/Realtà* 17: 61–86.

8338 Shepherd, John. 1987. Towards a Sociology of Musical Styles. In *Lost in Music: Culture, Style and the Musical Event*, ed. Avron Levine White. London: Routledge. 56–76.

8339 Shepherd, John. 1988. *La musica come sapere sociale*. Milano: Ricordi/Unicopli.

8340 Shepherd, John. 1995. Popular Music Matters. In *Popular Music Perspectives III*, ed. Peter Wicke. Berlin: Zyankrise. 467–81.

8341 Shepherd, John, et al., eds. 1977. *Whose Music? A Sociology of Musical Languages*. London: Latimer.

8342 Statelova, Rosemary. 1990. Za sociologicheskija podhod kam masovite zhanrove sas zabaven harakter. *Bulgarsko muzikoznanie* 4: 78–93.

8343 Storb, Ilse. 1972. Beat, soziologisch gesehen. *Musik und Bildung* IV(4): 189–93.

8344 Tennstedt, Florian. 1979. *Rockmusik und Gruppenprozesse: Aufstieg und Abstieg der Petards*. München: Wilhelm Fink.

8345 Tucker, Bruce. 1989. 'Tell Tchaikovsky the News': Postmodernism, Popular Culture, and the Emergence of Rock 'n' Roll. *Black Music Research Journal* 9(2): 271–95.

8346 Valkman, Otto. 1974. Some Methodological Aspects of Preferences in Pop Music. In *New Patterns of Musical Behaviour*, ed. Irmgard Bontinck. Wien: Universal Edition. 33–43.

8347 Virden, Phil and Wishart, Trevor. 1977. Some Observations on the Social Stratification of Twentieth Century Music. In *Whose Music? A Sociology of Musical Languages*, ed. John Shepherd, et al. London: Latimer. 155–78.

8348 Vulliamy, Graham. 1977. Music and the Mass Culture Debate. In *Whose Music? A Sociology of Musical Languages*, ed. John Shepherd, et al. London: Latimer. 179–200.

8349 Willis, Paul. 1974. *Symbolism and Practice: A Theory for the Social Meaning of Pop*. Birmingham: Birmingham Centre for Contemporary Cultural Studies.

AUTHOR INDEX

Greene, Ted 5710, 5711
Greene, Victor 2003, 4258
Greenfield, Robert 3213
Greenway, John 689, 4878, 4879
Greenwood, Ben 5928
Gregory, Hugh 2955
Greig, Charlotte 969, 5161
Grein, P. 3796
Grenier, Line 3128, 3506, 7191, 8313
Grevatt, Ren 4530
Gribin, Anthony 789
Gridley, Mark C. 1192, 1295, 1566, 1596, 1597, 4435
Griese, Christof 521
Grieve, Ray 6965
Grieves, Jim 5062
Griffin, Gabriele 4342
Griffiths, David 5404, 5405
Griffus, Ken 772
Grigat, Nicoläa 3754
Grime, Kitty 1143, 5125, 8018
Grinberg, Miguel 6732
Grisales, Hernando 6908
Grissim, John 682, 724
Gritzner, Charles F. 633
Gröbchen, Walter 7534
Groce, Nancy 5601
Groia, Phil 790, 2134, 7488
Groll, Klaus-Michael 3229
Gronow, Pekka 1113, 2994, 3575, 3576, 3669, 4641, 6613, 7576–7578
Groom, Bob 329
Gross, Robert L. 2688, 5063
Grossberg, Lawrence 1976, 2210, 2287, 2313–2319, 3432, 3749, 4412, 4756–4758, 4880, 4958–4960, 5106, 5228, 5487, 7266, 7267, 8307, 8308, 8314, 8315
Grosse, Francis 2625, 7612
Grossman, Lloyd 2320
Grossman, Stefan 5712
Grossman, William J. 1144
Grundy, Stuart 3473, 5736
Grunfeld, Frederic V. 5713
Grushkin, Paul 3123, 3124
Gubernick, Lisa Rebecca 5037

Guckin, John P. 1303
Gueffier, Bernard 2625, 7612
Guernsey, Otis 1902
Guevara, Nancy 1050
Guilbault, Jocelyne 3100–3102, 3120, 3121, 3973, 3974, 4552, 4553, 5895, 6355, 8313
Guillermoprieto, Alma 2900
Gumplowicz, Philippe 1296, 7613
Gungor, Nazife 239
Guntharp, Matthew G. 5676
Günther, Helmut 4070–4074
Guralnick, Peter 297, 298, 725, 2135, 2321, 2802, 2830, 2956, 6356, 7268, 7344, 7431, 7432
Gushee, Lawrence 2039
Guterman, Jimmy 718
Guth, William 545
Guthrie, Woody 1106, 1107, 4881
Gutman, David 2678, 3826, 5893

Haag, Hubert 4073
Haapanen, Urpo 7579
Haas, Walter 2908
Haase, Ellionor 4759, 6713
Hacquard, Georges 822
Hadamowsky, Franz 1903, 7535
Hadel, Richard 6660
Hadleigh, Boze 4367
Hadley, Daniel J. 5761
Hafen, Roland 5229
Hafferkamp, Jack 7383
Hagan, Chet 621
Hagen, Earle 823
Hagen, John 546
Hager, Andrew 2803
Hager, Steven 1051
Haggard, Merle 705
Hahn, Bernd 2760
Hake, Ingrid 2597
Halberstam, Judith 1052
Hale, Antony 657
Hale, Mark 2689
Halker, Clark 1699, 3731, 4924
Hall, Bob 405–407

Hall, Charles W. 3320
Hall, Dennis 2703
Hall, Douglas Kent 2322
Hall, Fred 1629, 1630
Hall, J.H. 977
Hall, James 4887, 6146
Hall, James W. 259, 4760
Hall, Stuart 2085, 2090, 3895, 3968, 4882, 5054, 7897, 7924
Halper, Jeff 1872, 7140
Hambly, Scott 658
Hamm, Charles 1297, 1767, 1768, 2040, 2323, 2815, 3021–3023, 3507, 4436, 4761–4763, 4839, 5372, 5569, 6134–6137, 7269, 7270
Hamm, Wolfgang 3281, 7657
Hammond, Bryan 5329
Hammond, John 56
Hammond, Ray 3191, 3361
Hampton, Wayne 4764
Handy, D. Antoinette 69, 5162
Handy, W.C. 330, 7433
Haney, Wayne S. 2799, 4593
Hanly, Francis 2063, 3103, 3359
Hannan, Michael 6947, 7058
Hannover, Irmela 6532, 6533, 6551
Hannusch, Jeff 354, 2136, 7462
Hansch, Michael 891
Hansen, Chadwick 1147
Hanson, Kitty 2642, 2643
Haralambos, Michael 331, 380, 2957, 2958
Hardie, Ian 8042
Harding, James 1848
Hardy, Phil 12, 2589, 2590, 3577
Hare, Walter 1769
Harer, Ingeborg 2041
Hareven, Tamara 216, 4471
Haring, Hermann 2324, 7658, 7659
Harker, Dave 1742, 1849, 2325, 3362, 3578, 3896, 3931, 4765, 4766, 4840–

399

Meredith, John 6975, 6976
Merriam, Alan P. 1228, 1313, 6053
Metfessel, Milton 120, 5899, 6003, 8178
Metlay, Mike 3200
Meyer, Filip de 3768
Meyer, Gust de 5234, 5428, 7554a-c
Meyer, Hazel 3031
Meyer, Henry E. 3083
Meyer, Michael 4288, 7679
Meyer, Moe 4384
Meyer, Thomas 2417, 2418, 7680, 7681
Meyers, William 3807
Mezger, Werner 2912, 5128, 5237, 7682
Mezzrow, Milton 4154
Miani, Guido 390, 5554
Miceli, Sergio 850, 5429–5431, 5473, 8230–8233, 8266
Middleton, Richard 391, 1314, 1856, 2419–2423, 3032, 3033, 3908, 4439, 4477, 4845, 5073, 5235, 5432–5436, 5527, 5555, 8065, 8141, 8142, 8179–8181, 8234, 8235
Midgett, Douglas K. 4711, 6364
Miège, Bernard 3314
Mignon, Patrick 2261, 2424
Mihaiu, Virgil 6586
Milano, Dominic 3201, 3202
Milburn, George 2076
Milhaud, Darius 1547
Millard, Andre 3179, 3263, 3678, 3712
Miller, Amy 6688
Miller, Doug 2145
Miller, Fred 3808, 5909
Miller, Jeremy 6999
Miller, Jim 970, 1603, 1821, 2425, 2636, 2834, 3442
Miller, Lloyd 1579, 4890
Miller, Manfred 2371, 3370, 4194, 4970, 7946
Miller, Mark 7204–7206
Miller, Paul Eduard 1397
Miller, Ron 5528
Miller, Steve 558

Miller, Terry E. 7292
Millward, Stephen 381, 2326, 5407
Milsom, W. 6977
Milton, Donald 2856
Miner, Allyn Jayne 6255
Minganti, Franco 851, 4382, 4601, 5437, 5482, 5546, 8143, 8194, 8241, 8257, 8275, 8315
Mintz, Sidney 6339
Mischke, Jörg 8105
Mita, Munesuke 6289
Mitcalfe, Barry 7062
Mitchell, Clyde 6105
Mitchell, Elvis 1822
Mitchell, Ewen 7037
Mitchell, George 359
Mitchell, Tony 1066, 1067, 3439, 3769, 4562, 4786, 4891, 6519, 6978, 7038–7040, 7059, 7063, 7064, 7080, 7086, 7089, 7775
Mitchenson, Joe 1855
Mitsui, Torû 3, 5875, 5994, 6290–6292
Mitz, Rick 4532
Mockus, Martha 7207
Modleski, Tania 880, 8311
Mohammadi, A. 2211
Mohren, Michael 4653, 7836
Mol, Pieter Jan 7802
Moll, Dieter 311, 2426
Möllerstedt, Gunnar 7862
Moncada, Perla Valencia 4855, 6855, 6935
Monestel, Manuel 4323, 6657
Mongan, Norman 1485, 5723
Monsato Dardón, Carlos Hugo 6678, 6679
Monson, Ingrid 121, 1456, 4654, 5438, 8236
Montanaro, Bruno 5724
Montecchi, Giordano 5439, 8237
Montell, W. Lynwood 653
Montes, Jorg 2998
Moody, Bill 1315, 4655
Moody, James L. 3215
Moogk, Edward B. 3679, 7208

Mooney, H.F. 1602, 2427, 2652, 2660, 5097, 7293
Moore, Alex 4098
Moore, Allan F. 2428, 2635, 2661, 2676, 4440, 5440–5442, 5529–5531, 5556, 5577, 5588, 8182
Moore, Chauncey O. 756
Moore, Ethel 756
Moore, Jerrold Northrop 3680
Moore, John 4478, 4578, 5174, 5953
Moore, McDonald 7294
Moore, Steve 3465, 5910, 5995
Moore, Sylvia 4479, 6017, 6054
Moore, Thurston 585
Moore-Gilbert, Bart 4841, 4842
Moorhouse, Barry 5690
Morales, H. 5608
Moran, William R. 3538, 3539
Mordden, Ethan 1934, 1935
Moreau, Charles 1781
Moreira, Paul 7622
Morelli, Rita C.L. 6809
Moreno, Albrecht 6810
Moreno, Segund Luis 6915
Moreno, Yolanda 6701
Morgan, Alun 1506
Morgan, Thomas L. 88
Morgenstern, Dan 80
Mori, Akihide 6293
Morley, Bruce 7065
Morris, Gina 2734, 2735
Morris, Nancy E. 1977
Morris, Ronald L. 1316, 3945
Morrison, Craig 2807
Morrison, David 3496
Morrisseau, Miles 7170
Morse, David 1823
Morse, Margaret 3770
Morthland, John 575, 3442
Mortimer, Harry 5281
Morton, Brian 1232
Morton, David 602, 624, 4270, 4931, 6325, 6326
Mosco, Carner 4099
Mosco, Stephen 3510
Mose, Jens Allan 7561, 7562

Roseman, Marina 6439, 7495
Rosen, David M. 4902
Rosenbaum, Jill 5242
Rosenberg, Bernard 7304
Rosenberg, Bruce A. 2977
Rosenberg, Neil V. 666, 669–675, 4487, 6292, 7209
Rosenman, Joel 4324
Rosenthal, David H. 1514, 1515
Rosenthal, Ethel 6260
Rösing, Helmut 3814, 3815, 4203, 4204, 4976, 4977, 5100
Rösler, Walter 448, 509
Ross, Andrew 966, 1017, 1082, 2479, 2644, 2794, 3287, 4077, 5159, 5243, 6853
Rosselli, John 7781
Ross-Trevor, Mike 3649
Rothel, David 780
Rothenbuhler, Eric W. 3524
Rothschild, Rick 2198
Rothstein, Joseph 3203
Rothstein, Robert A. 3079, 6592
Rourke, Constance 1794, 7305
Rouselot, Philippe 1058
Roussin, Didier 5633
Rouville, Henry de 7959
Roux, Alain 2480
Rowe, David 2481, 4685
Rowe, Mike 363, 7396
Rowley, Eddie 5182, 7742
Roxon, Lillian 2611
Roy, Bruno 510, 7224, 7225
Royster, Philip M. 1083
Rubin, David S. 2482
Rubin, Martin 1943
Rubin, Paul 1493
Ruby, Jay 3873
Ruhr, Peter 5283, 7693
Ruiz, Vicki L. 4345
Ruiz Hernández, Alvaro 6902
Rumble, John 676
Rumley, Gina 2483, 5183
Rumsey, Francis 3204
Runcie, John 7496
Runciman, Sir Walter 2936

Runstein, Robert E. 3650
Rupchev, Jordan 6489, 6500
Ruppli, Michel 319, 1233, 1251–1253, 2153, 2154, 3551–3556
Rupprecht, Siegfried P. 2484, 3396
Rusch, B. 4935
Rusch, Robert D. 1516
Rüsenberg, Michael 4953
Russell, Bill 1400
Russell, Dave 1858–1860, 3914, 5284, 7987
Russell, George 5856
Russell, Henry 1994
Russell, J.F. 5285
Russell, Peggy 705
Russell, Ross 1385, 3947, 4158, 7362, 7409
Russell, Tony 340, 695, 732, 3994
Russell, William 413, 414, 781, 1401
Russo, M. 2485
Russo, Marco 5455
Russo, William 1473, 1655
Rust, Brian 1254, 1861, 3557, 3592
Rust, Frances 4111, 7988
Rust, Godfrey 3154
Rutten, Paul 3316, 3397, 4017, 4032, 4565, 7717, 7810–7812
Ryan, Jack 1826
Ryan, John 3235, 3398, 3399, 3489
Ryan, Michael 6981
Ryan, Robyn 7046, 7047
Ryback, Timothy 2486, 4667, 6470
Rycroft, David 1714, 6088, 6089, 6102, 6153–6156
Rye, Howard 1238, 1239, 5319, 5338–5341

Sabaneev, Leonid 863
Sábato, Ernesto 3001
Sachs, Curt 3113, 4112
Sackett, Robert Eben 7694
Sackett, Susan 3130
Sacre, Robert 364
Sadie, Stanley 6635, 8053
Sadler, Michael 2487

Saffioti, Tito 486, 4808, 7782
Sagi, Mária 6568
Saint, Andrew 1871
Saka, Pierre 511, 512
Sakata, Hiromi Lorraine 7117
Sakolsky, Ron 3114
Sakurai, Tetsuo 5879
Salachas, Gilbert 513
Salas, Fabio 6865
Salas, Horacio 3002
Salazar, Max 6652
Salazar Salvatierra, Rodrigo 6667–6669
Salcedo Ramos, Alberto 6880
Salewicz, Chris 3300
Sallis, James 5727
Salminen, Kimmo 3492, 3520, 5101, 7574, 7592, 7595–7597, 7865
Salmon, Russell O. 3003
Salton, R.D. 6733, 6734
Salvador-Daniel, Francisco 7110
Salzinger, Helmut 2488
Salzman, Jack 40
Sample, Duane 3080, 7306
Sampson, Henry 42, 1795, 1944
Samuels, Charles 5345
Sanabria, Izzy 2893
Sandahl, Linda 927
Sandberg, Larry 2870, 4325
Sandner, Wolfgang 1332, 2268, 2364, 2489, 3348, 5066, 5445, 8099
Sanger, Annette 6319
Sanjek, David 3402, 7308
Sanjek, Russell 3400–3402, 7307, 7308
Sankey, Ira 983
Santa-Cruz, César 4113
Santelli, Robert 4326
Santoro, Gene 1157, 1535
Santos, Joao Dos 4668
Saporita, Jay 4159
Sapoznik, Henry 1673
Sá Reg, Enylton de 6832
Sargeant, Winthrop 1474, 1475
Sarosi, Bálint 1005, 1006, 6569

AUTHOR INDEX

SUBJECT INDEX

2155, 2159, 2161, 2172,
2176, 2321, 2326, 2368,
2419, 2464, 2561, 2698,
2830, 2839, 2953, 2956–
2958, 2976, 3170, 3523,
3535, 3546, 3599, 3726,
3946, 3963, 3983, 3987,
3994, 4154, 4255, 4262,
4308, 4345, 4407, 4438,
4449, 4579, 4589, 4661,
4708, 4723, 4801, 5028,
5163, 5264, 5322, 5330,
5334, 5343, 5349, 5378,
5386, 5407, 5444, 5505,
5522, 5542, 5554, 5653,
5718, 5749, 5752, 5954,
5960, 6032, 6041, 6171,
6180, 6293, 7218, 7230,
7268, 7294, 7344, 7378,
7380, 7396, 7415, 7431,
7433, 7435, 7436, 7439,
7455, 7488, 7510, 7512,
7774, 7816, 7858, 7885,
7891, 7892, 7914, 7926,
7979, 8069, 8087, 8110,
8130, 8144, 8156, 8226
BMI 3235, 3398, 3489
Body 108, 707, 960, 1556,
4041, 4343, 4470, 4720,
5150, 6420
Bohemia 4522
Bolero 429–432, 3851,
6358, 6362, 6435
Bolivia 6751–6756
Bologna 7754, 7758
Bolton 1857
Bombay 914, 6261
Bondage 114, 208, 1048,
3831
Bongo 6876
Boogie-Woogie 306, 404,
408, 409, 412–415, 1378,
5750, 5752, 7206
Bootleggers 3447, 3942
Bop 1498, 1500, 1503,
1515, 1627, 5176
Bosnia 6479
Bossa Nova 433–438, 1593,
6764, 6765, 6804, 6805,
6810
Bourbon St. 1386, 7450
Bourgeois 1995, 3907, 3915,
5852, 7962, 8325

Brass Bands 1286, 1389,
1403, 3898, 4624, 5269–
5272, 5275–5283, 5285–
5291, 5347, 5348, 6025,
6091, 6958, 7469, 7693,
7706, 7928, 8056
Brazil 433, 437, 1593, 1874,
2898, 2901, 2903, 3845,
3856, 3902, 4037, 4249,
4385, 4476, 4484, 4625,
4656, 5614, 6012, 6023,
6756a-6758, 6760–6765,
6767, 6772, 6774–6780,
6782, 6783, 6785–6787,
6790, 6794–6802, 6804,
6805, 6807, 6808, 6810,
6812, 6814–6822, 6824,
6825, 6829–6835, 6837,
6838, 6844, 6847, 6850,
6981
Breakdance 1057, 2647,
4466, 7060, 7081
Brega 6762
Brittany 517, 7551, 7608,
7631–7634
Broadcasting 712, 947,
3234, 3491, 3493, 3501,
3506, 3530, 3597, 3713,
3788, 3813, 5101, 6098,
6928, 7075, 7191, 7573,
7595
Broadside 255, 259, 264,
277, 279, 4760, 4869,
7975
Broadway 886, 1673, 1875,
1877, 1881, 1887, 1891,
1897, 1900–1902, 1907,
1909, 1912, 1918, 1928,
1930, 1935, 1950, 1956,
2108, 3012, 4085, 4606,
7256
Bronx 2883
Buenos Aires 2979, 2993,
5099, 6736, 6742
Buffalo 2005
Bulgaria 1683, 2384, 2511,
4061, 6486, 6496–6499,
6502, 6506, 6508–6510,
6512, 6514, 7482, 7939
Burlesque 439–446, 1772,
4332
Business *see* Music Business
Buskers 5928

Cabaret 447–449, 509,
1352, 1952, 2995, 4034,
4536, 4828, 5119, 6557,
6596, 7475, 7533
Cachaca 2895
Cairo 1670, 4259, 4465,
4644, 7125–7127
Cajun 306, 450, 452, 454,
456, 457, 461, 463, 5636,
7453, 7932
Cakewalks 88
Calaloo 472, 3846
Cali 2894, 6906, 6907
California 1263, 1357, 2266,
2503, 2740, 7418
Call-and-Response 1093
Calypso 464–469, 471–482,
3844, 3846, 3854, 4355,
4449, 6444, 6446, 6452,
6454, 6455, 6457
Cambridge, MA 2871, 4327
Cambridge (UK) 7980
Canada 1241, 2776, 3327,
3357, 3506, 3569, 3679,
4018, 4454, 5927, 7167,
. 7177, 7178, 7180, 7181,
7183, 7185, 7186, 7188–
7197, 7201–7204, 7206,
7208, 7209, 7211–7213,
7215, 7216
Canboulay 3844, 6446
Cancao 6775, 6801, 6841
Cancion 1726, 1984, 2874,
3851, 4483, 4759, 4791,
4855, 4897, 5116, 6358,
6644, 6648, 6662, 6675,
6686, 6687, 6693, 6697,
6699, 6700, 6709, 6713,
6739–6741, 6838, 6855,
6869, 6897, 6899, 6901,
6902, 6935, 6937, 7828,
7839
Cantometrics 5949, 5950,
5966, 5967, 8172, 8173
Cantonese 5552
Canzone 15, 483–486, 4431,
4452, 4594, 4748, 4773,
4808, 5350, 5355, 5356,
5379, 5381, 5384, 5385,
5388, 5390, 5395, 5398,
5422, 5425, 5437, 5439,
5449, 5452, 5455, 5465,
5557, 5828, 5830, 7620,
7764, 7766, 7767, 7769,

428